Lands of Likeness

Lands of Likeness

FOR A POETICS OF CONTEMPLATION

Kevin Hart

THE GIFFORD LECTURES
2020–2023

The University of Chicago Press   Chicago and London

The University of Chicago Press, Chicago 60637
The University of Chicago Press, Ltd., London
© 2023 by The University of Chicago

Published 2023
Printed in the United States of America

32 31 30 29 28 27 26 25 24 23   1 2 3 4 5

ISBN-13: 978-0-226-82756-8 (cloth)
ISBN-13: 978-0-226-82758-2 (paper)
ISBN-13: 978-0-226-82757-5 (e-book)
DOI: https://doi.org/10.7208/chicago/9780226827575.001.0001

For a complete list of text permissions, see page 409.

Library of Congress Cataloging-in-Publication Data

Names: Hart, Kevin, 1954– author.
Title: Lands of likeness : for a poetics of contemplation : the Gifford
    lectures, 2020–2023 / Kevin Hart.
Description: Chicago : The University of Chicago Press, 2023. |
    Includes bibliographical references and index.
Identifiers: LCCN 2023006016 | ISBN 9780226827568 (cloth) |
    ISBN 9780226827582 (paperback) | ISBN 9780226827575 (ebook)
Subjects: LCSH: Contemplation—Philosophy. | Contemplation in
    literature.
Classification: LCC B105.C49 | DDC 204/.3—dc23/eng/20230427
LC record available at https://lccn.loc.gov/2023006016

for Sashanna

Everything has its mouth to manifestation.

JAKOB BOEHME

CONTENTS

NOTE ON CITATIONS
AND CONVENTIONS

Whenever possible, I have given the titles of books in English. Exceptions occur when the book has not been translated or when the book is far better known by the title in its original language. Titles of poems written in languages other than English are always given in their original language. I quote Coleridge and Hopkins from editions that show revisions and quote exactly in each case: at times their hesitations while writing can be instructive.

For the sake of clarity, I have preserved several Greek words that have become essential in the discussion of contemplation. In each case, these are explained contextually, and a full glossary with transliterations is supplied at the end of the book.

Introduction

Lord Gifford specifies in his will that the lectures given in his name are to address "'the study of Natural Theology' in the widest sense of that term."[1] Now, "natural theology" is generally pursued in two main directions.[2] The first way is to attend to natural phenomena and, on the basis of what one observes of them, to detect any evidence or trace of God found there. This construal of natural theology is ancient; it has roots in Plato's *Timaeus* (ca. 360 BCE) and in Aristides's *Apology* (ca. 124–25); it is explored by St. Thomas Aquinas (1225–74) in the first three books of the *Summa contra Gentiles* and in the second question of the *Summa theologiae*.[3] The subject flourished in the seventeenth century and the early eighteenth, with enduring contributions made by G. M. Leibniz (1646–1716) and William Paley (1743–1805), and it survived biting criticisms by David Hume (1711–76) and Immanuel Kant (1724–1804).[4] Science as well as philosophy was invested in the project. Isaac Newton says in the *Principia* (1687): "This most beautiful system of the sun, planets, and comets, could only proceed from the counsel and dominion of an intelligent and powerful Being."[5] In effect, Force becomes a new divine name. By the Romantic period, natural theology in this sense had gained ready traction, and with the Victorian era brave attempts were made to bridge what was perceived as an increasingly widening gap between the natural sciences and scriptural testimony of creation. Edward Hitchcock (1793–1864) is only one of a great many to straddle what came to seem a chasm.[6] One consequence of this experience of vertigo is the institution of the Gifford Lectures.

The second way of elaborating natural theology, which sometimes crosses the first, is to inspect the natural powers of human cognition. Can one by purely natural thought find out anything of value about the deity, including, first of all, if there is such a being? The question would have been ruled out of court by most empiricists; indeed, it would have been deemed nonsensical by the stricter school of logical positivism in the first part of the twentieth century.[7] Yet, with W. V. O. Quine's paper "Two Dogmas of Empiricism" (1951), major planks in the empiricist platform were found to be very shaky, and a new interest in metaphysics was accordingly kindled; it has been amply fueled for the past seventy years.[8] Some of those committed to analytic metaphysics, as the discipline has become known, have directed their energies toward natural theology, either as apologists or as critics. One result of this focus has been a new zeal for arguments for the existence of God that, especially after Hume and Kant, had largely been judged highly unsatisfactory. In recent decades more than due diligence has been given to the classic cases for God's existence—the ontological argument, the cosmological argument, the moral argument, the teleological argument, and the rest—along with their standard refutations, and some of these have been spruced up by modal semantics. The ingenuity and vitality of this tradition can scarcely be contested, even though today it shows signs of having entered a period of scholasticism.

The natural cognitive powers of human beings are not restricted to thinking, however, and certainly not to argumentation or, more narrowly, proof. Much contemporary analytic philosophy has unnecessarily confined what counts as philosophy by concentrating almost single-mindedly on argumentation as the proper—indeed, for some, the sole—business of the discipline. And this heavy emphasis is everywhere apparent in natural theology as practiced in philosophy (less so when practiced in theology).[9] One can see it, for example, in the avoidance of at least one natural being in the cosmos, the investigation of whom has been widely claimed to give deep insight into God. I refer to Jesus of Nazareth.[10] The difficulty for philosophers here is that even a rational, historical study of Jesus cannot be undertaken within the horizon of a logical proof for the existence of God.[11] Nonetheless, for Christians the first meaning of God is "the Father of Jesus," evidence of whom is given by the resurrection. Many other meanings precede this and succeed it, needless to say, including those that regard Jesus as one with the deity in more than one sense of *one*. The prophets and saints, too, are overlooked: one might think that their words and actions tell us something about being in relation with God.[12] Again, nothing that we say rationally about these men and women can be put in the form of an argument, let alone a logical proof, yet people have been known to find God by meeting good men and women. Not that Christians have overlooked natural theology, as it is commonly practiced. The so-called proofs, even if judged faulty or even misguided, have an enduring attraction and bolster the faith of some people. They can do so affirmatively, by adding to the available reasons for belief; more importantly, they can do so negatively, by bringing one to a barrier that the intellect must negotiate by other means, specifically by engaging love.[13]

Of course, there are other natural cognitive powers than argumentation that we use in life, if not in the seminar room, primarily thinking, meditating, and contemplating. The trio will interest us in the first chapter. Ordinarily, thinking turns on rational judgment, while meditation requires heeding images and texts. Contemplation does neither, at least not to the same extent or in the same manners. We might suppose then that natural theology can be pursued by contemplating God as he appears in the mind or the world; and, if we do so, we will find that an intense contemporary interest in validity and soundness in proofs for the existence of God suddenly widens to include experience, which has its own relation to truth and its own canons of indubitability.[14] We are turned around and find before us an immense field of reflection. Just how to engage it remains a big question. For even natural theologians admit that God manifests himself, if he does, only at the very limit of phenomenality.[15] We might think we find hints of God in the beauty or the sublimity of nature, in acts of self-sacrifice, in the faithfulness of friends and one's spouse as well as in human creativity. And here we touch again on the first way of natural theology, but our relationship to it has changed: we approach it by way of contemplation, not argument. We might also say that God gives himself in what Jesus calls *the kingdom*, a multistable phenomenon that keeps changing even as we try to think about it. It is within and without, strong and weak, here and still to come. To be sure, the kingdom has an irreducible divine dimension. But it also reaches back to the original goodness of creation, and to that extent one might think that it whispers of God in the voice of nature.

People have at many times and in many places sought to contemplate the cosmos or a natural scene or their minds and find traces of God there. If we find ourselves first thinking of the Romantic period—of Jean-Jacques Rousseau's *Profession du foi du Vicaire Savoyard* (1762), or William Wordsworth's "Nutting" (1798), or Friedrich Hölderlin's "Wie wenn am Feiertage" (1799), or Giacomo Leopardi's "L'infinito" (1819)—we have ample reason to do so. But we need not limit ourselves to that literary movement. We can go back to Hesiod's *Theogony* (ca. 700 BCE) and, more broadly, to the Greeks' abiding interest in θεωρία, contemplation of the nature of things, especially the planets and the stars.[16] Also, we can come forward to our own times and reflect on those people who identify themselves as "spiritual, not religious," some of whom seek to commune with God while enjoying nature. Along the path, we will encounter Richard of St. Victor's *On the Ark of Moses* (completed by 1162), in which we are told that, while on the way to union with the triune God, we can find the deity in nature and that we can contemplate anything at all: the humblest plant can prompt us to begin to ascend to the Trinity. Can contemplation take up any truth whatsoever, or should it be limited to God alone? The question engaged Aquinas, who answered, against Richard, in favor of the latter view. Yet, if we look back through Western Christian history, we will find that, having been loosened from God, contemplation divided itself, remaining in the church while also finding other homes where it had to adapt to new conditions and expectations.

It would be possible to look in detail at several important moments in Western history when contemplation was cued to discerning traces of God in natural beauty around us or in thrilling brushes with the sublime. The territory is familiar, however, and much solid research in Romantic studies has taken account of it, even if scant work has been done to analyze it explicitly in terms of natural theology. Not all scholarly disciplines develop at the same rate or in the same direction. Instead, I have sought to concentrate on contemplation itself, which has both natural and nonnatural tendencies even in the Western tradition, to which I shall confine myself.[17] For the most part, I bypass detailed discussion of mental prayer. Interested as I am in competing claims made for acquired vs. infused contemplation and affirmative vs. dark contemplation as well as how the beholding of God is framed in other distinctions, the concern will remain in the background here. It is not possible to ignore the religious use of the practice entirely, however, partly because this understanding of contemplation involves the transformation of θεωρία, inspection of the "first things" (τα πρώτα), into the loving suspension of the mind before God before it finds other homes, and partly because once in those new homes it does not wholly shake off its past. Plato and Aristotle agree that over time a person becomes like that which is contemplated.[18] The idea entered Christianity when St. Paul told the fledgling church in Corinth that, with unveiled face, we are all "beholding the glory of the Lord" and thereby "being changed into his likeness from one degree of glory to another" (2 Cor. 3:18 [RSV]). This notion was taken up by many of the church fathers in developing theological anthropology with reference to the *imago dei*. Augustine's *De trinitate* is exemplary here.[19] Throughout the Middle Ages and beyond, the idea was repeated and sometimes extended.[20]

To give a little more flesh to the idea of a similarity between contemplator and contemplated, I quote a passage from a sermon given on the solemnity of St. Augustine by Achard of St. Victor (ca. 1100–1171), and I choose him largely because his confrere Richard will appear from time to time in this study. Achard reminds us of the plangent moment in the *Confessions* when Augustine tells us that he found himself "in a region of unlikeness," that is, far from God.[21] We remember the serpent's words to Eve when tempting her: "You will be like God" (Gen. 3:5 [RSV]; cf. Isa. 14:14). Trying to be like God in this manner is an act of rebellion against him, for the impulse comes from the self, not from love, with the consequence that one becomes more unlike him. But trying to be like God in knowing what sin is without succumbing to it is an act of conformity to the divine will. "Three regions of unlikeness exist," Achard tells us. "The first is of nature, the second of guilt, the third of punishment." Thankfully, however: "Three regions of likeness exist: the first is of nature, the second of righteousness, the third of the blessed life."[22] One becomes increasingly like God, Achard thinks, in three rising levels: participation in creation, acceptance of justification, and enjoyment of beatification. He goes on to argue that there is a natural likeness to God in each of us, the *imago dei*, from which it follows that everything else in the fallen natural world is more or less unlike us. If, through Grace, we devote ourselves in the right spirit to reforming the *imago*, we can overcome many effects of the Fall and gain in righteousness; and, if we devote ourselves to the enjoyment of the truth, which at heart is Christ who said, "I am . . . the truth" (John 14:6 [RSV]), we can rise even higher and participate in the blessed life. Such patient devotion to the truth is what is known in Christian spiritual theology as *contemplation*.

My undergraduate reading in and around the philosophy of religion had already taught me why in the seventeenth century contemplation ventured away from Christian spirituality and accepted a more modest role for itself: the church declared it a danger, especially to female religious. In the controversy over Quietism, centered on Miguel de Molinos (1628–96), Madame Guyon (1648–1717), and Francis Fénelon (1651–1715), the church represented the new theology of mental prayer as highly dubious.[23] Mental prayer itself was not condemned, but it seemed to the ecclesial authorities that the prayer of quiet—a passive resignation to the will of God, which included nonresistance to temptation, and a teaching of pure love—compromised morality, discouraged verbal prayer, and frustrated recourse to the system of sacraments. Ignatian *meditatio* was preferable, and in many religious houses it replaced *contemplatio*. I later learned that religious contemplation was revived only in the early twentieth century, mostly in terms of the category of experience, which had been slowly developed since the seventeenth century, intensified by the notion of religious experience in Germany, and then largely presented in psychological categories—as mysticism—by Evelyn Underhill (1875–1941), William James (1842–1910), Friedrich von Hügel (1852–1925), and Rudolf Otto (1869–1937).[24] Philosophical contemplation also prospered in the first decades of the twentieth century, mainly with Edmund Husserl (1859–1938), although also, to some extent, with Ludwig Wittgenstein (1889–1951) and some of his followers, including several of my teachers.[25]

My education out of school had also taught me what happened to religious contemplation when it mostly went underground for those two hundred years and more: it sought another home. It found one in fringe Protestant groups, another by rejoining a chastened θεωρία, and in time yet another in the arts.[26] The contemplative life became contemplative lives, and likeness between contemplator and contemplated tended to drop out.[27] The Romantics recognized that religion had moved sideways: in his "Preface" to the *Lyrical Ballads* (1800) Wordsworth wrote of poetry as "emotion contemplated," and it is here that we see contemplation having passed from suspension before the deity to the poet pondering his own subjectivity.[28] It was a subjectivity not to be thematized by way of the *imago dei*, and it was a style of contemplation freed from revealed truth. More traditionally, Coleridge spent years reflecting on the higher senses of contemplation.[29] Poetry became open to contemplation not because it became philosophical but because it could not properly be assimilated to philosophy. Always oriented to the truth, to arguments and conclusions, philosophy showed itself to have little in common with poetry, which tended, rather, to ponder its statements, revise them from time to time, and circle around a topic or a set of feelings rather than reach a settled view that could be rationally defended.

We might see both aspects of natural theology in the early Romantics' sense of nature, both as external to consciousness and as consciousness directing itself into the world.[30] John Keats's idea of "negative capability" enabled him to dwell on the natural world and its human population in complete openness, while Percy Bysshe Shelley spent his years "in the contemplation of Nature," as his wife testified.[31] Thomas Carlyle (1795–1881) gave a pertinent gloss to natural theology in his coinage *natural supernaturalism* in *Sartor Resartus* (1836): the supernatural could be ascertained in the natural if one looked in the right manner. Later in the century Matthew Arnold (1822–88) underlined what had happened and what was going to happen in his highly confident essay "The Study of Poetry" (1880): "Without poetry, our science will appear incomplete; and most of what now passes with us for religion and philosophy will be replaced by poetry."[32] As is suggested by the scornful "what now passes with us for religion," mental prayer had already been drained from England by the main actors in the Reformation, and one would hardly find a vigorous philosophical counterpart in John Stuart Mill (1806–73) or Henry Sidgwick (1838–1900).[33] The quoted sentiment was later appraised from another angle by T. E. Hulme (1883–1917) in his crisp remark that Romanticism is "spilt religion," and it was thoroughly elaborated in intriguing directions by M. H. Abrams in *Natural Supernaturalism* (1971).[34]

With these things learned, I also started to see that Hulme and Abrams were far from being alone in their views and that they identified only a part of what was at issue. Robert Duncan (1919–88), who flourished in a quite different literary tradition from either, tells us that Romanticism is "the intellectual adventure of not knowing."[35] Here, Romanticism is regarded as a displaced mystical theology, one with roots in Pseudo-Dionysius the Areopagite (late fifth, early sixth century), the author of *The Cloud of Unknowing*, and Nicholas of Cusa (1401–64), among others. Abrams's student Harold Bloom (1930–2019) commends apophatic or "negative" theology as a resource for "further metaphors for the act of reading," and we need to remember that for him it is well-nigh impossible not to find Romantic elements in literature, even when it has usually been classified quite otherwise.[36] As he sees it, the tradition reaches back to Homer's *Odyssey* and forward to John Ashbery (1927–2017). Hardly any of the most memorable poetry since *Paradise Lost* (1667) leans heavily on revealed theology, although certain readers cite some verse as though it were holy writ. Martin Heidegger's scripture is Hölderlin, not Job, the Canticle, or the Psalms.[37] One might say that the study of Romanticism—or (for my purposes) the study of Romantic and post-Romantic poetry—is more than the study of how poetry and politics are entangled; it is also the study of natural religion and, therefore, a mode of natural theology.[38] It would be so "in the widest sense of that term," to return for a moment to the letter of Lord Gifford's will. As one would expect, this area has attracted literary critics and theologians, including those scholars who live the mixed life of religion and literature, far more than philosophers in the Anglo-American academy.

Before the seventeenth century, then, contemplation was a matter of seeking to enter the lands of likeness. Thereafter, in literature at least, the poet's subjectivity could at best be like what it observes in nature or could fashion likenesses from self-reflection in the creative act. The likenesses, however, would occur in the abandonment of mental simplicity, not in the quest for it. If poetry seeks the one, it usually does so by way of the many. There is an obvious sense in which poems are themselves lands of likeness. At one or another level, they operate by gestures of likeness and identity and can do so by many rhetorical means (metaphor, metonymy, simile, symbolism, synecdoche, and so on), by formal means (line, meter, rhyme, stanza), as well as by fulfilling generic and modal expectations, in which parts slide into wholes. Some poets have ventured to regard being a poet as being like God.[39] All creativity, not just that which finds expression in literature, comes with the *imago dei* but only with respect to refiguring what has already been created. Certainly, no poet starts from scratch. To want more than has been given leads to rebellion, and some poets have taken steps in that direction, either rhetorically (Blake, "To Nobodaddy") or thematically (Goethe, "Prometheus: Dramatisches Fragment") or in terms of what Jean Paulhan calls *terrorist acts* (Breton).[40] The quest for benign likeness is far more common, and it sometimes benefits from unusual insights. Even a relation between "land" and "page" has been determined. We recall being asked to think of a poem as a "field of action" or even simply as a "field."[41] Jean-Pierre Richard foregrounds this relation in the very title of his *Pages paysages* (1984). He tells us there that his essays propose readings that are based both on the "verbal essence of literary works (which constitutes them in *pages*)" and "on the forms, thematic-instinctual, through which a singular universe manifests itself (organizing them into *landscapes*)."[42] One might point to a distant analogy between the lands of likeness glimpsed in contemplative prayer and those lands of likeness we call *poems*, for both lands have votaries who claim that in devoting oneself to them one will be transformed.

The claim varies quite considerably. When I was an undergraduate, I was routinely told that reading canonical English poetry in the right manner would be a morally improving experience, and I was rather given the impression that reading too much French poetry would have a correspondingly deleterious effect on a lad of my tender years. As a teacher, I find that many of my colleagues and students say, just as routinely, that reading literature (American now as well as English and not necessarily canonical) gives one an opportunity that one should seize in order to diagnose social and political ills. One must resist the allure of those poetic lands of likeness in order to expose a great deal of unlikeness between people as borne out in inequitable material conditions. Some poets and critics will even go so far as to speak of poetry saving us—from holding unjust views about gender, race, or the working classes, from environmental degradation, and even from personal loneliness—yet we know very well that, while it can testify to dark events or be made to point to them, it cannot redeem us.[43] The Christian engaged in contemplative prayer believes that he or she is loved by God; the same person who reads a poem with care may find it beautiful, consoling, edifying (and many another thing), but knows that the love is one-sided. Nonetheless, the right poem might lead one to action all the more surely for having been contemplated. There are questions one does not ask unless one has read in a spacious manner.

In the early church, fierce thought was devoted to establishing competing schools of hermeneutics so that scripture could be read as well as possible. *Alexandria* and *Antioch* name two poles in late antiquity that engaged one another in vying for the better theory of reading. Much of this exegesis was cast as detailed commentary. When the history of slow reading is finally written, the volume on Europe will surely include long chapters on Philo Judaeus and Origen, on St. Augustine, and, in a later age, St. Bernard of Clairvaux and St. Thomas Aquinas. Not all the reading in play was commentary, however. The slow reading of scripture, *lectio divina*, came to be a major way in which professed religious could come to behold God; and reference to the *Glossa ordinaria*, a twelfth-century digest of patristic commentary, was part and parcel of this process. One was seldom left alone with scripture; rather, one joined a rich conversation about it that had been going on for centuries and that would continue long after one had left the world.

When contemplation divided itself and part of it left the church, one of the places it took up residence, doubtless at first in a spirit of deflation, was in modern criticism. Critics such as Samuel Johnson (1709–84), S. T. Coleridge (1772–1834), and T. S. Eliot (1888–1965) directed us to the contemplative mind, with respect to mortality and morals, the powers of the mind, or art. "To contemplate," Johnson tells us in the *Dictionary* (1755), means first of all "to consider with continued attention; to study; to meditate"; and this diminished and broadened sense of the word is exactly what we find in *The Rambler* (1750–52) and elsewhere. The general reflections of these critics on literature were never wholly divorced from national and political ends, although these were not the only ends in view and literature was not their sole concern. Indeed, such ends change age by age. Eliot observes with respect to Arnold: "No generation is interested in art in quite the same way as any other; each generation, like each individual, brings to the contemplation of art its own categories of appreciation, makes its own demands upon art, and has its own uses for art."[44] Eliot uses *contemplation* here, as often, in its shrunken sense to mean no more than thoughtful reflection, but at times critics have said both less and more than this. Indeed, in the Clark Lectures (1926) and the Percy Graeme Turnbull Memorial

Lectures (1933), Eliot himself had recourse to Richard of St. Victor on *contemplatio* and prized the impersonal nature of *The Ark of Moses* in guiding souls to God.[45]

The new criticism, which overlapped in time with Eliot's ascendency and aligned itself with his immense prestige, proposed a formal rhetorical analysis of poems and introduced an era of "close reading," one that found much Romantic poetry unsatisfactory. One of its principal architects, John Crowe Ransom (1888–1974), was to speak for many when in 1938 he prized the image for its worldly concreteness over the abstraction of the idea, which had been more prevalent in nineteenth-century philosophy (Coleridge and Schopenhauer, e.g.). If we look to the idea rather than the image, Ransom thought, "we lose the power of imagination, or whatever faculty it is by which we are able to contemplate things as they are in their rich and contingent materiality."[46] So contemplation is a desired end of criticism, one associated with the image, not the idea, and is tied to the world, not to anything beyond it. And slow reading is to be the means of facilitating this aesthetic beholding of the world about us. Not that such beholding need be "aesthetic" in the simple sense of recognizing and responding to natural beauty. It can lay claim to cultural sophistication. I. A. Richards, another founder of the same critical school, had written in his *Principles of Literary Criticism* (1924) in praise of poems that display "ironical contemplation." His words took root in more than one generation of readers and more deeply than his contention that "poetry is capable of saving us."[47]

If we take a step away from the new criticism (whether it be a long one or a short one is much disputed), we can then view deconstruction, some of whose practitioners wished to reclaim the Romantics both in Britain and in Europe. These critics sought in principle to read everything as slowly as Friedrich Nietzsche (1844–1900) had commended but not in the overt service of contemplation, worldly or otherworldly.[48] On the contrary, close reading would subvert many a social institution as well as any thought of literature as offering a covert theology.[49] It turned out to be possible to deconstruct everything about beholding God or nature, beginning with acts of meaning and the ontological security of the human subject. But the project could also be shown to have been partly anticipated, in some respects, by the contemplative tradition itself.[50] Indeed, Derrida also opened a path for a deconstructed subject that, rid of a self in any robust metaphysical sense, could nonetheless survey the abyss between world and language. He did not erase words from the dictionary but rather reoriented them, and his readers might therefore feel justified in thinking of his long, patient, and eddying discussions of inheritance, justice, literature, the messianic, and mortality as contemplations of the newly disarranged intellectual structures of the West that were now open to alternative figurations.[51] Christianity was subject to Derrida's critical archaeology of concepts, but at heart the faith had no deep stakes in the self (which comes into its own only in the twelfth century) or the subject (which emerges in the seventeenth century).[52] The Christian concern is the soul or, rather, the interrelations of soul, flesh, and body, and it remains a poverty that we have no thoroughgoing modern theology of the soul, let alone one that explores its relations to the flesh and the body.

Another remarkable critic deserves mention because he stands aloof from the other critical schools that dominate discussion these days. One might picture Northrop Frye (1912–91), especially the author of *The Anatomy of Criticism* (1957), perched above the whole of literature, the structures of which he takes in with panoptic command and beholds with equanimity. His actual position is more nuanced, however, and is founded on a sense of the powerful testimony that much literature provides. "The ultimate aim" of a literary education, he says, "is an ethical and participating aim." As we read that sentence, we can anticipate a qualification coming around the corner. And it does, for we are quickly assured that we often reach that moral end by following another, "an aesthetic or contemplative one."[53] This is no Quietism, to be sure, and there is much to weigh, as we shall see later, in the insouciant disjunction "aesthetic or contemplative."

The history of modern literary criticism is not my concern in this book by any stretch of the imagination. Nor is any denial of the pertinence of one part of it, what Paul Ricoeur (1913–2005) calls *the hermeneutics of suspicion*.[54] Part of any responsible reading is being vigilant about what one is told and what one is not told, and it is idle to think that novels, films, plays, and poems do not tell us things about society and that they sometimes tell us more than their authors are aware they are saying and that they occlude some things about their societies. In proposing a hermeneutic of contemplation, I do not wish to return to the old fourfold sense of scripture, also known as the *allegorical hermeneutic*.[55] Nor do I wish to expunge suspicion from readerly attention. Rather, I wish to position it as an irreducible possibility in reading, one that gains rather than loses by being placed in a broader context. Part of my concern is to pass from marginal hints in a text to contemplative currents in it that might be overlooked. Another concern is to show that classical phenomenology—that of Husserl—already has a hermeneutical moment and that it does not need a thorough overhauling in order to be turned into a hermeneutic. With respect to natural theology, static phenomenology quickly meets a limit, but, if one follows genetic and generative phenomenology, one can go a little further. They help us discern what it means for phenomena to manifest themselves at the limit of phenomenality.

I have said that, seen in the right light, the study of Romantic and post-Romantic poetry is a natural theology, whatever else it is. It is not wholly a natural theology, or all that natural theology can do, or a natural theology that is steadfast, or even always a natural theology for very long. Nor is it always a Christian natural theology. It is not concerned narrowly to establish truth but to reflect on it. Yet contemplation—especially in its life outside the church—looks to the traces of the divine in the world or in the poet's mind. Sometimes one should perhaps say *traces of the divine*, but arguing about degrees of evidence is not my brief. Having set out the modern, deflated sense of contemplation, initially by way of a difference between Richard of St. Victor and St. Thomas Aquinas, and ventured an account of religious contemplation in an exemplary post-Romantic religious poem, I examine two quite different counterexamples that are evident in modern poetry. The first is fascination, which I take to be a phased counterpart to contemplation. The phenomenon is everywhere in contemporary society with our preoccupation with screens of all sorts, but it has roots that reach back to Roman times. There is a poetry of fascination, and I would not wish it to be thought that it is of secondary value. Nor would I wish to slight what forms my second, more nuanced counterexample, consideration. There is a vital poetry of consideration, even though, beginning in the twelfth century, *consideratio* was styled as lower than *contemplatio*. Nonetheless, fascination and consideration are not contemplation, even though consideration sometimes works in concert with it. My examples are modern. Much as I love it, I felt no urgent need to return to "the poetry of meditation" of the seventeenth century, which is already well identified and has been admirably examined.

The main exhibits of my discussion, however, all concern contemplation. It is true that we can contemplate a poem when we have put down the book in which it appears, but my interest is rather in the actual reading of a poem. I do not think that all poetry is contemplative or that all of it invites this style of reading. Can one read contemplatively when going against a thick and knotted grain? It seems unlikely at best and perverse at worst. Sometimes one must read a poem several times before it can be approached contemplatively: lexical and conceptual difficulties might need to be overcome and the manner of speaking made familiar, though not suppressed, before one can proceed (as with A. R. Ammons's *Sphere*). Nor do I think that contemplative poetry is a subgenre of "religious poetry" or "devotional poetry," for various sorts of Romantic and post-Romantic poems, many of them not at all religious, can be read in that fashion. Nor do I think that contemplation is simple or singular; it is not always openly religious or theological or merely philosophical, for instance. It is one thing to set about contemplating God, quite another to reflect on one's subjectivity; the former need not draw heavily on theology, and the latter often bears little or no direct relation to philosophy. My approach is thematic; my choices are varied. I wanted to give a clear instance of religious contemplation in a modern poem, and my choice fell on G. M. Hopkins's sonnet "The Windhover" (1877), which I have known by heart since I was thirteen. I read it as a poem about two contemplative gazes, one of a blessed soul, who appears as a bird, intent on Hopkins's soul, and one of Hopkins rapt at the sight of the same soul or bird. Here, we see how a contemplative lyric can also be a brief natural theology: the divine realm manifests itself to a seminarian beholding a kestrel. This is part of what the young Hopkins meant by those strange coinages *inscape* and *instress*.

The other poems I examine at length are also post-Romantic, though chastened by modernism. They are also much longer. With Wallace Stevens's "Notes toward a Supreme Fiction" (1942) before me, I discuss the idea of aesthetic contemplation as a replacement of sorts for religious contemplation. Stevens may not be looking for traces of a supreme being in the world or his mind, but he is concerned to promote the idea of contemplating a Supreme Fiction, involving a relation of consciousness and the natural world, that compensates for the disappearance of the divine. Traces of the divine remain, nonetheless. With A. R. Ammons's not wholly successful long poem *Sphere* (1974), I concern myself with a poet who is unusual in committing himself to what Husserl calls *the naturalistic attitude*, a mental framework often adopted by natural scientists when going about their work. Perhaps the poem would have appealed to Lord Gifford. Scientist that he is in his training, Ammons involves himself from time to time in a natural theology or, perhaps better, a natural supernaturalism. And with Geoffrey Hill's powerful long poem *The Mystery of the Charity of Charles Péguy* (1983) I look at how a radical soul is presented: participation in divine love is uncovered in a dense contemplation of a Frenchman's social background and character. I also reflect on the natural theology that the poet presents in four words: "Landscape is like revelation."[56]

In developing a hermeneutic of contemplation in the opening chapters of the book, I identify several coordinates for discussing it in

poems. My sequence of thinkers devoted to modern contemplation—
Schopenhauer, Coleridge, and Husserl—converges on the last named
and yields a science of "infinite being," though not in the sense that
Lord Gifford had in mind. Phenomenology, however, offers a fresh way
to think about natural theology, and finding new paths to natural theology was certainly of interest to the founder of the lectureship. Phenomenology also proposes a new approach to contemplation; after all, it
commends a radical disengagement from the world by performing the
reduction, and religious contemplation has always sought to distance
the self from the world. Had I world enough and time, I would have
said much more about Heidegger, who in his later work says interesting things about contemplation, some of them developed from Meister Eckhart (ca. 1260–ca. 1328). But world and time are in short supply,
and, besides, I do not wish to strain my readers' indulgence.[57] The
book is sufficiently long already. My readings of the poems do not slav-
ishly follow everything that could be said, especially in formal terms;
it would quickly become tedious to illustrate each and every moment
in which the reader is able to brood on the poem before him or her.
An emergent project of "contemplative reading" in education studies
might well develop one or two motifs in its own directions.[58]

This is a book that tackles some difficult writers—Schopenhauer,
Coleridge, and Husserl, for starters—but it is also a book about leaves
and trees, birds and snails. I try to diversify what I have to say poem by
poem, by leaguing reading and theme. Thus, mystery is intimately related to contemplation in Christianity, and with adjustments the two
concepts retain a flexible relationship even when religious belief is not
a direct issue, as I try to show in my discussions of Stevens, Ammons,
and Hill. As a minor theme, the kingdom appears from time to time,
as naturalized, glimpsed, feared, or even occluded. Natural theology
does not always go directly from nature to God; sometimes it ventures
from nature to kingdom. Finally, I retain one highly important figure
from the history of contemplation, namely, the Roman *templum*, which
I find in an attenuated sense in poem after poem. Indeed, to my mind
many a modern poem is itself a *templum*, a natural place in which we
see traces of the divine or what was once taken to be divine. It is another moment in which we have reason to evoke natural theology in an
expanded sense.

CHAPTER 1

From *Templum* to Contemplation

The word *contemplation* comes to us with a divided history, not once but several times. As a placing shot, we might say that the primary division is between philosophy and religion, but in saying so we should be cautioned that this distinction is quite late and unstable. For θεωρία was widely regarded in the ancient world as central to the exercise of φιλοσοφία, which has ends we would identify today as both philosophical and religious; and these impinge on us even before we distinguish a prephilosophical commitment to religion in the activities of the θεωροί, private and public, who traveled to witness the spectacle of religious festivals.[1] And θεωρία itself was divided and became so again. First, the word was used in a broad sense ("observation") and in a narrow sense ("contemplation").[2] Not that the Greeks always noticed this difference. We see them beholding the stars and the "first things" (τα πρώτα) while also thinking about them scientifically ("theorizing"). Second, for Plato, θεωρία (in the narrow sense) was a state to be achieved by the philosopher, one that would make him resemble the gods in having sustained attention to the Forms, but it was not a condition to which one should cling single-mindedly, for one still had a moral responsibility to serve the community.[3] Yet, for Aristotle, θεωρία (in the same narrow sense) was a private reward for the philosopher or statesman who had already worked for the community and was perhaps still working for it, whether in teaching, investigating nature, examining constitutions, reflecting on political duties, or crafting legislation.[4] In the Christian tradition that broadly answers to Plato and Aristotle, one becomes blessed to the extent that one approaches the lands of likeness, that is, becomes like the divinity whose entire existence is spent in contemplation.[5]

Christianity early recognized the value of the βίος πρακτικός (active life), despite the negative evaluation of Martha in Luke 10:38–42 that had been asterisked as early as Origen (ca. 185–254).[6] The religion had the example of St. Peter always before it as well as St. Paul's commendation that members of the church have a variety of gifts (1 Cor. 12:4–31). Both helped the faithful adjust earlier Greek and Roman models of the active life: not only were the virtues to be cultivated and preaching to be done, but also works of charity were to be undertaken.[7] The religion greatly prized prayer, both petitionary and raising the mind to God, and dedication to the practice was central to what became the βίος θεωρητικός (contemplative life). A question came to the surface: how to make the brief and challenging act of raising the mind to God into a way of life, much as the Greeks had prized, without perpetual prayer excluding everything else.[8] With hindsight one could see that the βίος θεωρητικός had an exemplar not only in Martha's sister Mary but also in St. John the Baptist and St. John the Evangelist. Its devotees took comfort that the same Greek and Roman authors who identified the active life gave preference to the contemplative life, and they adapted their ideal of study in reclusion while adding extensive prayer to the eremitical or, later, coenobtic, lavritic, or sketic vocations.[9] The contemplative life changed; it became a life neither active nor passive but receptive to divine love. This way of life would begin to flourish in the third century with the desert fathers and, later, with the Benedictines who followed the *Regula Sancti Benedicti* (516), which was indebted in part to the *Regula Sancti Augustini* (ca. 400), which itself draws on Acts 2 and 4.[10] Much later, with the medieval formation of religious orders, others were to follow the rule: the Cistercians (founded 1098) and, still later, the Trappists (founded 1664).

Not that there has ever been complete agreement about this austere way of serving God. For the contemplative life finds different expressions, especially in its sense of obligation and reward. Seen in retrospect, the contemplative life in Christianity seems to be unknowingly heir to both sides of the division identified between Plato and Aristotle. In the Latin West, both sets of writings were partly lost along with Greek learning. True, many Greek manuscripts were available in Byzantine monasteries, but there was no impetus to uncover them. Only with the rise of the universities and the absorption of sources from Islam were the works of both philosophers more fully rendered into Latin. Before then, there were only limited or indirect or fuzzy indices of influence; and whatever classical heritage of contemplation remained, by way of doxographies and Boethius's translations of Aristotle, was recentered on divine truth, not just the truth that phenomena disclose.[11] So one might say, with all due caution, that those who appear to incline chiefly to the Platonic model include works of mercy in the contemplative life: the Carmelites, for example (founded in the late twelfth century but with far earlier beginnings). And those who lean more toward the Aristotelian model (usually without direct or detailed knowledge of his view of θεωρία) regard the contemplative life as itself the service that God asks of them. Nonetheless, even the strictest adherents of the contemplative life, such as the Carthusians (founded 1084), used to copy manuscripts and thereafter have written books so that the gospel might be spread.[12] In part this attention to learning as well as prayer is an acknowledgment of a variety of contemplative tasks, and in part it is a reminder that there is activity even in the contemplative life, a place for *otium* (rest) but not for *ociosus* (idleness). Besides, with Gregory the Great's *Liber regulae pastoralis* (ca. 590), we find the burgeoning of what will be called the *vita mixta* (mixed life), in which the fruits of contemplation—prayer and study—are offered to the faithful by way of preaching and other pastoral works.[13]

To be sure, Christianity likewise inherits from other Greek philosophical schools, notably the Stoics, who advocated diverse meditative exercises to help us cope with an uncertain life that certainly ends in death; but meditation, especially *consideratio*, will feature only several chapters later. My focus here is contemplation, which, admittedly, is not always easy to distinguish cleanly from meditation.[14] Its attenuated philosophical legacy is readily apparent in our ordinary linguistic acts, as when we speak of contemplating problems, situations, and places, by which we usually mean thinking about them with a view to understanding them or even merely appreciating them the better. But I will say little or nothing about those acts until much later in the book when I consider specific poems. In the third chapter, I will touch on how, in a far more specialized way, a twentieth-century philosopher, Edmund Husserl (1859–1938), regarded his practice as reflective or contemplative. In this chapter, however, I mainly restrict myself to the twelfth and thirteenth centuries and even there mostly to one small overlap between Richard of St. Victor (d. 1173) and Thomas Aquinas (1225–74).[15] I do so in order to draw attention to an account of contemplation that is somewhat broader than those that have mostly come down to us, especially Aquinas's, and to see whether recovering it at least in outline can help clarify the overall project of the book, which turns on thinking about contemplation and modern poetry. But, in order to see far into the twentieth century, we must step back to where we started. We will also be able better to see the twelfth-century renaissance from there.

*

In the early Latin West, θεωρία is translated as *contemplatio,* and it is the Western tradition that will engage me here since that is the tradition that has shaped the poetry and the ways of reading it that I wish to discuss.[16] The Latin word comes to us from Cicero: "Summa vero vis infinitatis et magna ac diligenti contemplatione dignissima est" (The mighty power of the infinite is most worthy of great and loving contemplation).[17] That Cicero introduces the word in *De natura deorum* (45 BCE) suggests that it comes bearing religious significance, and that it enters Latin by way of Cicero perhaps guarantees sufficient awareness of its philosophical birthrights.[18] The new word also brings elements of Roman religious culture with it, however, specifically the determinations of *auspicia* as pronounced by the augurs, which could not have been far from Cicero's mind when he coined the word. He was a member of the College of Augurs, after all, one of those who controlled the *ius augurale,* even though he was skeptical about the existence of the gods and therefore dubious about belief in divination. In *De divinatione,* we find arguments against *auspicia.*[19] Auguries had been important for the Republic even so, and Cicero knew very well that they needed to be preserved in a moderated way for the sake of good public order.[20]

There were two main kinds of auguries, those signaled spontaneously by the gods (*oblativa*) and those reckoned as given by the gods in answer to requests (*imperativa*). Auguries were given in many ways, although the earliest practice must surely have been *ex avibus,* by way of the flight of birds, since the word *auspicium* comes from *avis* (bird) and *spicere* (to look at).[21] In order to scan for propitious signs for a decision—with respect to a military campaign or the likelihood of abundant spring crops—recourse was made either to an established *templum* in the northern part of the Forum or to a new one that was drawn by members of the college, each with a *lituus* (shaped like a bishop's crozier but a great deal shorter) that was used to mark the four corners of a rectangle in the sky.[22] How a bird flew into a *templum* would give a trained augur the clues he needed. Not all birds could be counted as bearing signs, but the eagle was one that most certainly could, for it was known as *Jupiter's bird.*[23] The Latin word *contemplatio,* along with its English counterpart, reminds us of the word *temple,* to be sure, but it perpetually recalls the *templum* in the sky as well, the birds that flew through it, and what the activities in the sacred space might mean for the present and future.

Θεωρία and *contemplatio* bring somewhat different classical heritages in tow, then, and inevitably both are changed when they enter the densely growing world of Christianity. For one thing, θεωρία becomes intimately associated with θεός (God). Indeed, the main object of contemplation changes; it is not the Forms or the intelligible structures of reality so much as the Trinity. And this shift has a consequence since in principle the Forms can be approached by way of reason, although the Trinity cannot: by the mid-fourth century, the Christian God, always held to be mysterious, comes to be determined more exactly as incomprehensible, ineffable, and infinite.[24] Contemplation of the deity becomes seen as the fulfillment of baptism; it is an endless challenge, though sometimes a fruitful one, in this life and is promised to be a perpetual delight in the next. The contemplating subject is construed differently; the act is performed by the intellect and the will in concert. One does not only think about God; one also loves him, for he loves us in our creation, our fall, and our redemption alike, goodness, justice, and mercy being modes of divine love. And it is this love, not only philosophical enlightenment about the nature of reality, that leads one to serve the neighbor and through that person's *imago dei* to find God anew.[25] Where the practice of θεωρία was regarded as proper to the natural excellence of human beings or at least some of them, attention to Christian *contemplatio* demanded humility of the faithful. One aspect of this humility is the acknowledgment that one contemplates only as a member of the mystical body of Christ, not simply as an individual. One does not "put on Christ" by oneself. Only in the church can one be transformed.

For another important shift is the Christian emphasis on μετάνοια (change of mind) and thereafter steady moral purification of the one who seeks to behold the divine.[26] Origen tells us that the most spiritual book of the Bible, the Canticle, should be read last in a course of scriptural inquiry "that a man may come to it when his manner of life has been purified." Only when he has become "competent to proceed to dogmatic and mystical matters" may he advance to the "contemplation of the Godhead with pure and spiritual love."[27] Similarly, Gregory of Nyssa (ca. 335–ca. 94) speaks in his *Life of Moses* of the need for the one who approaches "the contemplation [θεωρία] of Being" to be purified.[28] No one just as he or she is can behold God, not even a reflection of his glory in a brightly restored and properly working *imago dei*. That restoration comes only after repentance and moral reform, study, and a strict discipline of prayer. Although the cultivation of the moral virtues is necessary, Christian contemplation requires more, namely the nurturing of the three "theological virtues" of faith, hope, and charity.[29] In *De trinitate*, Augustine (354–430) tells us: "Contemplation in fact is the reward [*merces*] of faith, a reward for which hearts are cleansed through faith, as it is written, *cleansing their hearts through faith* (Acts 15:9)."[30] It is a notable moment in a Latin tradition that was consolidated and extended by Gregory the Great in his oceanic *Moralia in Job* (completed by 595), where we learn that contemplation involves elevating the eyes to light, that it is prompted by wonder, that the attuned mind trembles when it is raised, and that even the most practiced monk is never perfect in his interior devotion.[31]

Augustine develops his theology of contemplation in an elliptical orbit of Platonism and scripture and does so in the midst of seeking to establish the correspondence of the *imago dei* and the triune life of God.[32] Over a century later, Gregory looks elsewhere than the concord of Greek philosophy and scripture, especially the New Testament, or, rather, he assumes that it has already been nicely achieved and finds *contemplatio* by way of the allegorical hermeneutic when applied to the Hebrew scriptures. He worked from the Vulgate and sometimes from the Vetus Latina, not from the original Hebrew.[33] So we need to keep in mind differences between the Hebrew, the Greek, and the Latin and to be aware that early theology of contemplation finds a ground in a typical or moral reading of the Hebrew scriptures that a literal reading of the Hebrew would not support.[34] The semantic fields of several Hebrew words overlap those of θεωρία and *contemplatio*, but none of these words has either the strong visual element or the appeal to raising the eyes that one finds in the Greek and the Latin. There is *darash* (to seek, to inquire), *bikkesh* (to seek), *machashabah* (thought), *siach* (to muse), and *hagah* (to meditate).[35] The closest, perhaps, is *hagah*, which alludes to wordless sounds, like a lion's growl or a human groan, and its association with meditation (in a non-Stoic sense) probably comes from the way in which someone brooding on a passage of scripture will mumble its words over and over.

We may well think here of *lectio divina* or sacred reading, which was commended by Benedict in his *Regula* and has roots in St. Paul's letter to the Romans.[36] It is only with Guido II's *Scala claustralium* (ca. 1150), however, that we find a formalization of the practice, which specifies a clear progression of *lectio, meditatio, oratio*, and *contemplatio*. Meditating and praying with the allegorical hermeneutic as our guide, we can pass from reading scripture to beholding Christ as the ultimate object of our reading. St. Paul offered encouragement, as we saw in the introduction, in his words about our "being changed into his likeness" (2 Cor. 3:18). To accomplish this, Guido's contemporary William of

St. Thierry (1085–1148) tells us we need to become intimate with the biblical authors, becoming more like their friends than their acquaintances.[37] Is this a natural thing, as the comparison suggests, so that our minds become fitted to scripture by familiarity? Or is it the other way around, so that scripture would be given to us to orient the mind as well as inform it? John Scotus Eriugena (fl. 850–70), for one, had argued for the latter, and, although his influence was not always certain, the position he advocated became widely accepted.[38] In his view, thanks to divine Grace our immersion in scripture allows us to regain the ability to behold God that we lost at the Fall, and presumably it also stimulates our desire to do so.[39]

Accordingly, when Christians read or say *contemplation*, we are convoking and changing Greek religious and philosophical practices, along with Roman religious practices, while conjointly appropriating the Hebrew scriptures in ways that Judaism would reject. A word that today suggests tranquility, *contemplation* contains a history that is not free of the treacheries of translation and, within that, of hermeneutical torsion. Whether or not it is conducted within a religious order aligned with it (Benedictines, Carmelites, Carthusians, Cistercians, etc.), the contemplative life is not always as peaceful as we might be led to believe; it is a struggle, marked at times by the upsurge of psychic darkness, as well as a Graced achievement.[40] That last adjective indicates another major adjustment to the classical construal of θεωρία or *contemplatio*: it is not something that we human beings can practice just by ourselves, relying on our own moral probity. An experienced spiritual director is required, something not mentioned in many medieval treatises on the subject because the need was presupposed in religious orders.[41] Certainly, spiritual direction was not taken lightly, especially beginning in the fifteenth century, as a study of the manuals issued to directors bears eloquent testimony. To contemplate is not to escape temptation but to become vulnerable to it in more subtle ways.[42] More importantly, one must be transformed by divine love, often by way of reading scripture, in order to gaze on that love: a gaze that cannot limit its object but that can only behold the divine. It is an early tradition that testifies that Mary, the mother of Jesus, was herself a devout reader of the scriptures, a practice that enabled her to respond appropriately to the angel when he came to her.[43]

*

One of the most impressive attempts to overcome the divisions in θεωρία or *contemplatio* is a treatise by Richard of St. Victor, *On the Ark of Moses* (completed by 1162), which is also known as *Benjamin major* and *De gratia contemplationis*.[44] In formal terms, it is a tropological exegesis of Exod. 25:8–40, the instructions the Lord gives to Moses how to build the Ark of the Covenant. It has no autobiographical dimension. Thematically, it explores contemplation, both natural and, as people will come to say in the Counter-Reformation, infused. That Richard takes the ancient philosophers overly to restrict themselves to natural phenomena and to ignore the divine reality behind them is evident to any reader.[45] His interest in nature is in the first creation as a way of seeking our re-creation in Christ. If we take *philosophy* more broadly, as φιλοσοφία (the endless task of understanding what is, how we know it, and how we should act in accordance with it), we can see that his vision of contemplation integrates what would otherwise be the philosophical and the religious by way of specific approaches to phenomena and the deity and the manners in which those approaches are made.

Richard most likely came to the Abbey of St. Victor, on the left bank of the Seine, during the abbacy of Gilduin (d. 1155), and by 1162 he was prior of the community of canons regular there.[46] Like Hugh of St. Victor (d. 1141) before him, he distinguishes thinking, meditating, and contemplating.[47] He does so with impressive vivacity:

> Thinking wanders through whatever by-ways, with a slow pace, without regard for arrival, in every direction, hither and thither. Meditation presses forward to what it is heading for, often through arduous hardships, with great diligence of mind. Contemplation moves around with astonishing mobility in a free flight wherever its impulse carries it. [*Contemplatio libero volatu quocunque eam fert impetus mira agilitate circumfertur.*][48]

This is not a hierarchy of objects of cognition but three ways (*tria in modo*) of plumbing the nature of anything at all. We can regard the one object, whatever it may be, in any of three gazes. But we are not utterly free in our choice. If we think with attention, we will find ourselves nudged to meditation and then contemplation. And we will further find that we cannot remain for long in contemplation; it is not easy to hold still, and after a while one will slip back to one or another mode of cognition. But what impresses Richard is the different sorts of cognition that we have at our disposal. "And so one should know," he writes, "that we regard one and the same matter in one way by thinking, we explore it in another way by meditation, and in another way we marvel [*miramur*] at it by contemplation."[49]

The differences between these three mental attitudes—regarding, examining, and marveling—are specified by Richard in prose that is at once terse and lyrical, which is a characteristic of his Latin style at its best:

Thinking creeps along, meditation marches forward and, at the most, runs. Contemplation however flies around all things and when it wishes it balances itself in the highest things. [*Cogitatio serpit, meditatio incedit et ut multum currit. Contemplatio autem omnia circumvolat, et cum voluerit se in summis librat.*] Thinking is without labor and without fruit. In meditation there is both labor and fruit. Contemplation persists without labor but with fruit. In thinking there is wandering, in meditation investigation, in contemplation wonder [*admiratio*]. Thinking is on the basis of imagination, meditation on the basis of reason, contemplation on the basis of insight.[50]

The motif of freedom with respect to contemplation is long-standing and irreducible. For Iamblichus (245–325), who early on emphasizes it, the man given to θεωρία is "the most free." Although the Syrian philosopher is writing about Pythagoras (ca. 570–495 BCE), he has Plato (ca. 429–347 BCE) in mind, and he plainly wishes to give Plato's ideas as long and as rich a heritage as possible so as to bolster their authority.[51] For his part, Richard takes contemplation to be a Grace that God freely bestows; it allows one to delve more deeply and without restraint into being than thinking or even meditating does.[52] It is "the free [*libera*] perspicacity of the mind into the sights of wisdom [*sapientiae spectacular*], hovering in wonder."[53]

In *On the Ark of Moses*, Richard follows Boethius (ca. 477–524), that linchpin of the classical and medieval worlds, in articulating his theology in a threefold fashion.[54] Knowledge, for Boethius, is not simply subjective, but the manner in which something is known depends on the faculties used by the one who seeks to know. Similarly, for Richard, we cognize by way of imagination, reason, and understanding, where *imagination* names the ability to perceive something through its image so that, in turn, it can be rendered universal by reason. This schema enables Richard to identify six levels of contemplation, each of which has subdivisions.[55] It can take place (1) in the imagination and according to it (with respect to corporeal things), (2) in the imagination as monitored by reason (with respect to the ordering of corporeal things), (3) in reason as approached by the imagination (with respect to reflecting on the passage from the visible to the invisible), (4) in reason as regulated by reason (with respect to invisible things that are beyond the reach of the imagination), (5) above reason but not contrary to it (with respect to turning on what divine illumination tells us and what makes sense to us), and, finally, (6) above reason and contrary to it (with respect to the doctrine of the Trinity). The mental triad of imagination, reason, and understanding is therefore arranged in groups of two in an ascending order of being, passing from the sensual (nos. 1–2) to the invisible (nos. 3–4) to the transcendent (nos. 5–6).

The import of Richard's schema can be grasped without leaning unreflectively on the metaphor of ascent, which came far more readily to him than it does to us.[56] We do not usually think of climbing Jacob's Ladder (Gen. 28:11–19) in Platonic fashion from the sensual world to the intelligible world, where true being abides. Nor do we usually think of our curriculum of study leading us by magisterial predesign to the sublime heights of the Forms or the love of God, and we tend to figure a vision of the One quite differently than we do the movement of the soul from *extra se* to *intra se* (as it was for Plotinus) and, from there, to *supra se* (as it was for Augustine).[57] Nonetheless, Christians still often think by way of ascent and rather more broadly than is countenanced even in the medieval notion of semantic ascent.[58] For *ascent* can also bespeak what happens when we proceed from regarding the world as nature to coming to reflect on it as creation, that is, from the world as given to us through the lenses of natural science to the world as given to us in terms of divine power. In this way, we can pass from lower to higher categorial kinds until we are summoned to attend to that which has no kind at all, the absolutely singular deity.[59]

When we look at a leaf—for example, "one that was yellow, slightly green, wilted around the edges"—we may, like Dostoevsky's Kirillov (whom I am quoting), regard it as "good."[60] We may take pleasure in its greenness, the patterning of its veins, its glossiness, its shape; we may feel its fine texture or regret any places where it is malformed, withered, or diseased. We may appreciate the abundance of leaves in spring, summer, and fall and grieve their loss in winter. Throughout, we are making images of the leaf and considering only these. In doing so, however, we may almost unnoticeably pass to the second level that calls for attention, the order in which sensible objects may be found. We may mull over the arrangement of the leaves in the tree, the relation of branches and the trunk, the distribution of seeds, and so on. Order, as Augustine had stressed, is the beginning of ascent, and modern science teaches us that rising levels of categorial ascent lead to increasingly complex biological organization.[61]

To rise to the next level—reason according to the imagination—would be to reach from the visible to the invisible, to grasp the εἶδος, the invariant structure, of the tree, including its pattern of parts and whole, and in doing so, Richard thinks, we begin to live the spiritual life. In going further, one would leave the guidance of sensuous images and grasp truths that have no physical image at all. For Richard, committed to an Augustinian theological epistemology, this requires divine Grace as well as human effort. Aquinas rethought this theory of knowledge so as to grant natural reason a legitimate space of its own. And, for those of us who come after him (especially after the scientific advances of the seventeenth century), this second stage of Richard's would call for reflection on the chemical and physical structure of the tree. More particularly, today it would involve study of the tree's morphology, which would depend on mathematical models to describe symmetry around the central axis. It would summon the calculus of variations to establish leaf density. And it would appeal to the Fibonacci sequence to grasp the distribution of seeds and the arrangement of leaves.[62]

Such would be the limit that natural science currently reaches, and, were we to pass to the fifth object of contemplation, we would begin to regard the tree as combining created elements as arranged in the periodical table. We would rise from what Augustine calls *evening knowledge*, which was given to the angels first of all, the knowledge (as we would say today) of the mathematical, physical, and chemical structures of what had been created, to *morning knowledge*, which was granted to them only afterward and allowed them to taste God's deep love for all that he had created.[63] For Aquinas, morning knowledge is above reason but not always contrary to it: we can use the natural light of reason to establish that there is a creator God and even to know something of his love.[64] What we cannot do is comprehend the triune nature of this God, the ground and abyss of his love; we cannot fathom what it means for the Father to love the world into being in and through trinitarian action. To hover before triune love, participating in it, would be to have attained the highest level of contemplation, a state we cannot expect to prolong in this life, for it exceeds our capacities, even if they have been augmented by Grace; but we may hope to enjoy it more fully in eternity.

According to Richard, everything in reality, whether created or uncreated, offers itself to human contemplation as well as to meditation and thought. There is nothing so small or so banal that it does not respond to a free attentive gaze that has been educated in the faith; if followed, it will direct us to spiritual levels of being.[65] Even a single leaf, to the extent that it *is*, can dispose us to consider it with wonder, whether because it is intelligible or just because it is at all. More striking than this, however, there are diverse ways of contemplating reality that can comport with any cognitive act, regardless of level.[66] For

Richard, there are three modes in which contemplation occurs. The first is *dilatio mentis*, the enlarging of the mind, which takes place by pursuing exercises of attention. I can expand my mind simply by examining a leaf when I pause on a mountain trail. *Sublevatio mentis*, the raising of the mind, is a way of gazing in which one's knowledge is increased, whether by adding to what one already knows, by adding to what any individual can know, or by adding to what humanity can possibly know. In each case, and notably the third, the charism of prophecy, I must receive divine Grace in order to raise my mind to attain such knowledge; it is directly experiential, not discursive. Finally, with special Grace, I may approach God by way of *excessus mentis*, the overflowing of the mind, or ecstasy.

One of the aims of *On the Ark of Moses* is, by way of commentary on the cherubim at the top of the Ark, to cultivate angelic wisdom in the attentive soul.[67] To put it more mildly, if we follow Richard's teaching, we will be stretched beyond our usual human limits; we will transcend our thinking, even our meditating, and our contemplation will finally enable us to glide before the divine.[68] Once again, if only for a moment, we will become human in the manner that God intended us to be. None of this is to suggest, however, that the person engaged in contemplation can do nothing else in life or that he or she thereby becomes fit to do nothing else. Contemplation, for Richard, is part and parcel of the mixed life, a life encompassing the gifts of Leah and Rachel, Martha and Mary.[69] What is striking in Richard is less the levels of ascent or the three modes that he describes than the three attitudes one can adopt with respect to anything. We can behold created things as well as the uncreated God, although ecstasy comes only through burning desire for and wonder at the divine.[70]

None of what I have outlined is very much like the idea of spiritual contemplation that we moderns generally inherit in the Christian West, and one main reason why is that a highly effective theology of contemplation tends to block it and seeks to overcome it. Aquinas insists in the *Summa theologiae* (abandoned 1274) that the contemplative life consists only in beholding God, not also in the consideration of any truth whatsoever. The angelic doctor's authority is formidable in the nineteenth- and twentieth-century Catholic world and beyond and never more so than in the period beginning with the encyclical *Aeterni patris* (1879) and continuing up to *Fides et ratio* (1998) and thereafter. There are ample grounds for his high theological standing, not the least of which is his careful defense of moderate realism. In addition, there are good reasons to follow his account of Christian contemplation, in the various senses with which he engages it (philosophical, theological, eschatological, prayerful); it is exacting, forceful, and subtle.[71] Nevertheless, there may be other incentives, just as appealing within their own limits, for us to begin with Richard's theory of contemplation when associating the practice with the arts, including modern poetry. Let us first look at what Aquinas has to say about Richard's schema.

*

Aquinas chiefly considers Richard's views of the contemplative life in *Summa theologiae* 2a2ae q. 180 art. 4. In his usual calm and thorough manner, he begins with objections to the position he will eventually clarify and defend, namely, that the contemplative life consists only in a simple, intellective beholding of God that is underwritten by love for God and neighbor. The four objections propose reasons why this life should also embrace "the consideration of any truth whatsoever [*etiam in consideratione cujuscumque veritatis*]." The first objection reminds us that Ps. 139:14 speaks of how wonderful God's works are and, therefore, that these works are worthy of our attention. The second objection quotes St. Bernard of Clairvaux's *De consideratione* (completed by 1153) to the effect that contemplation admits of three degrees, only one of which is divine truth: the others engage this truth by way of its effects in the world. The third notes that, in *On the Ark of Moses*, Richard distinguishes six types of contemplation, as already summarized, only the last of which approaches the divine truth as it is in itself. And the fourth objection, not relying on any text, points out that beholding any truth aids the perfection of the human mind. I will attend only to the third objection and Aquinas's response to it.[72]

Aquinas swivels away from all four objections by way of the *sed contra*. The pivot is a statement of Gregory the Great's in the *Moralia in Job*: "In contemplation indeed it is the beginning or God that is sought [*quod in contemplatione principium, quod Deus est, quaeritur*]."[73] One reason why Aquinas gravitates to this remark rather than to another goes back to a settled view he had proffered in the early *Scriptum super Sententiis* (1252–56) and repeated in *De veritate* (1256–59). The judgment is that, as *principium*, God can be grasped only by simple intuition. Coordinate with it is the judgment that only if one properly participates in the divine being can one be granted mental certitude about God through sanctifying Grace.[74] Aquinas is not proposing that we can intuit God's existence by dint of this existence being the same as the principle by which he exists; he gives a brief theological semantics of the word *God* at the start of the *Summa theologiae*, which takes quite other paths, and he places no weight on the ontological argument

devised by St. Anselm.[75] Rather, his point is that we have a vague, in-
choate sense of divine being as fundamental that, in and through one's
Christian formation and with the help of Grace, can become increasingly explicit. That said, there is no doubt that, had Aquinas thought of
contemplation as including more than restful attention to divine truth,
he could have found other points in Gregory to give tacit support to
his view. For example, we read in the *Moralia*: "The aim of contemplation should be such that it passes from the consideration of a few to
the many and from the many to all things, inasmuch as it is led to move
gradually, and by embracing all that is transitory it determines them
and, itself nearly incomprehensible, goes on growing."[76]

Yet Gregory, as quoted in the *sed contra*, allows Aquinas neatly to
divide what in his view is primary from what is secondary in contemplation.[77] Richard is not misguided, Aquinas thinks, when he finds
suitable objects of contemplation in nature and the intellect, for these
identify stages of an ascent that, when achieved, perfects the intellect.
The contemplation of creatures has value, but it is imperfect.[78] In the
third article of q. 180 he freely admits that contemplation "has several
activities by which it arrives" at its "final activity" and that the proper
development of the moral virtues disposes us to the contemplative
life.[79] Nor does he disregard the beauty of the created order, although
he favors the active use of the mind over its passive reception of form
in appreciating beauty since it is that which directs one to God.[80] What
Aquinas takes to be the secondary nature of much that attracts Richard
in *On the Ark of Moses* accounts for the celerity with which he passes
through the six stages as enumerated in 2a2ae q. 180 art. 4 obj. 3.

For Aquinas moves very quickly indeed when responding to the
third objection. This Richardine argument concludes: "Therefore the
contemplation of truth concerns not only divine truth, but also that
which is considered in creatures [*in creaturis consideratur*]."[81] The tacit
distinction drawn between contemplation and consideration is well
worth noting, for *consideratio* is, as we shall see more fully in chapter 5,
a lower form of spiritual exercise than contemplation, one that turns
on seeking the truth, not on possessing it surely and enjoying full assurance of it. Aquinas adheres to St. Bernard's sense of the difference
between the two mental attitudes and even goes a step further, aligning *consideratio* with *ratio* (reason) and *contemplatio* with *intellectus*
(understanding). Long before this moment, both in the *prima secundae* and toward the start of the *secunda secundae*, he has prepared us
to take *intellectus* more deeply than we would otherwise be inclined to
do. For all those living in a state of habitual Grace the intellectual virtues of understanding and wisdom are aided by the Holy Spirit's gifts

of understanding and wisdom.[82] On receiving them, one's intellect is thereby disposed to read (*legi*) the truth within (*intus*) the essence of something, that is, to discern the spiritual end of an activity, and in doing so one is transformed and becomes more Christlike.[83] *Contemplatio* will require these supernatural gifts of understanding and wisdom while making apt use of the other gifts. Accordingly, Aquinas speaks to the third objection as follows:

> These six types designate the steps by which one ascends to the contemplation of God through created things. The first step is the consideration of things of sense [*Nam in primo gradu ponitur perceptio ipsorum sensibilium*]; the second is the transition from sensible to intelligible things; the third is the evaluation of the things of sense through those of mind; the fourth is the consideration [*consideratio*] in their own right of intelligible things which have been reached through the sensible; the fifth is the contemplation [*contemplatio*] of intelligible realities which cannot be reached through the things of sense but can be understood by reason; the sixth is the consideration [*consideratio*] of intelligible things which the intellect can neither discover nor exhaust; this is the sublime contemplation of divine truth wherein contemplation is finally perfected.[84]

For Aquinas, Richard's six levels are not all stages of contemplation; rather, they are mostly ways by which one reaches *contemplatio* proper. Often, he thinks, Richard engages merely in *consideratio*.[85] He passes into *contemplatio* when the intellect settles on intelligible realities, which can be known for sure, but he returns to *consideratio* when pondering things for which reason searches but that the intellect does not yet know. *Contemplatio* is not to be found "in any [*qualibet*] contemplation of truth," he adds.[86] That is, we are not to look for it in acts that merely "enrich the intellect by their order to divine truth." Instead, it abides solely in the simple intuition of divine truth, an intuition in which we rest and behold God.[87]

One reason why Aquinas is able to proceed so rapidly in his treatment of Richard is that he has formed his ideas of speculative contemplation in theology and philosophy as early as the *Scriptum super Sententiis* and has already reflected a little on his predecessor in *Summa theologiae* 2a2ae q. 180 art. 3: "whether there are various activities [*diversi actus*] in the contemplative life." The first objection in this previous article points to Richard's distinction between thinking, meditating, and contemplating and claims that all three belong to the contemplative life. Responding to this argument, Aquinas notes his agreement with Richard's definition of *contemplation* (actually, Richard is citing Hugh of St. Victor)—"the penetrating and free view [*contuitus*] of the mind extended everywhere in perceiving things"—although he may have a more technical sense of the words in mind.[88] For he restricts the contemplative life to attaining what he calls a "simple gaze upon a truth [*simplicem intuitum veritatis*]": one grasps a simple intuition when looking past images (even of the Trinity) into the truth behind them.[89] All that leads up to this moment, including all acts of thinking and meditating, disposes one to the contemplative life but does not constitute its essence. On reading this account, one might reflect that a simple gaze on the divine is a privileged event in the contemplative life, perhaps attained several or even many times by a devout monk or nun, but is not the whole of the life to which he or she is committed by solemn vows. That life might well be filled with many another activity, including attending the liturgy, studying, performing assigned work in the monastery and its garden, and other spiritual exercises.

As is sometimes the case, in order fully to grasp the Aquinas of the *Summa theologiae* one must step back and listen to the younger author of the *Scriptum super Sententiis*. If we do so with this issue in mind, we will be told that human life is to be understood in a twofold manner:

> Therefore there will be two human lives: one that consists in the activity that belongs to the intellect in itself—and this is called *contemplative*—and the other that consists in the activity of the intellect and reason insofar as it orders, rules, and commands the lower part—and this is called the *active life*. [*erit duplex vita humana: una quae consistit in operatione quae est intellectus secundum seipsum, et haec dicitur contemplativa; alia quae consistit in operatione intellectus et rationis secundum quod ordinat et regit et imperat inferioribus partibus, et haec dicitur activa vita.*][90]

So contemplation is an affair of the speculative intellect, but it must be prompted by an act of love for God (*caritas*), for only such love can bind together a human being and God. Without divine love, the Holy Spirit will not give the *auxilia* of understanding and wisdom or any other of its gifts, and, without the gifts of understanding and wisdom, God can never be grasped in the intellect.[91] The speculative intellect is the most noble part of the human being, as St. Augustine had steadily maintained (influenced here by Plotinus), for the higher part of *homo interior* is that which most closely resembles God; it seeks not to perform acts in the world but to gaze on divine reality.[92] Aquinas will deepen this position by reference to the Pseudo-Dionysius: the intellect brings us closer to angelic cognition than reason ever can.[93] Richard would not disagree with the main point since, as we have seen, for him the contemplative monk or nun must forge angelic wisdom.

Earlier in the same passage of the *Scriptum super Sententiis*, Aquinas specifies how we are to take the word *life*. Hewing closely to Aristotle in book 9 of the *Nicomachean Ethics*, he says that a man's life "is said to consist in that toward which he exerts the highest care and devotion."[94] This is why he can speak in the *Summa theologiae* of the contemplative life being the attainment of immediate intuition of divine truth. It is an answer to a long-standing question posed much earlier in this chapter about how to make a momentary act into a way of life. However, as he goes on to show, by way of Gregory the Great, the contemplative life is not wholly absorbed by the operations of the speculative intellect; it already tastes the bliss that is to come, and so a nontheoretical sense is intimately involved when one beholds God.[95] Just as the intellect transcends mere reason because it has glimpsed truth, so too the intellect is itself transcended when it is conformed solely to the Lord. This time, however, divine transcendence humbles the one who hovers before God: one cannot maintain a pure theoretical gaze on the triune God in this life. All this might well dispose us to think that, as far as Aquinas is concerned, only those specially chosen by God to serve in certain religious orders are fit to practice contemplation. However, in his reflections on the active life, he notes that all Christians in a state of Grace must participate in contemplation at the level to which we are called. The Psalmist's injunction "Be still, and know that I am God" (Ps. 46:10 [RSV]) has a universal application and a temporal designation, for it relates to the Third Commandment: "Remember the sabbath day, to keep it holy" (Exod. 20:8 [RSV]).[96] Every Christian can and should contemplate God at Sunday Mass and, in his or her own way, throughout the day of rest.

Almost everything that Richard calls *contemplation* in his six levels involves a discursive process, passing from imagination to reason to understanding. Aquinas, however, restricts contemplation to a given end, the fulfilling of the understanding as enriched by the Holy Spirit; it is there and only there that a simple apprehension of the divine can occur. (It is a seeing of the whole but not a whole seeing of the whole.)[97] Because it is not a *principium*, a leaf (or anything created) cannot have its characteristics resolved into an immediate intuition and thereby yield the certitude that Aquinas associates with *contemplatio*. As early as the *Scriptum super Sententiis*, he draws a distinction to make his point clear: Richard restricts himself for the most part to *speculatio*, finding God in creatures, and opens onto *contemplatio*, finding God in himself, only at the end of his intellectual journey.[98] Could it be that Aquinas thinks that only then one can discern the three modes of contemplation? He makes no mention of them in his treatise on action and contemplation. Not that in the *Summa theologiae* he neglects to distinguish the expansion of the mind in passing from *ratio* to *intellectus* (all the more so, in receiving the gifts of the Holy Spirit, or the charism of prophecy, or ecstasy). By the time he reaches the stage in the *Summa* when he reflects on contemplation, he has already given his views on degrees of prophecy and ecstasy in 2a2ae qq. 174–175.[99] Ecstasy presumes "a certain violence," he admits, for the soul of the person contemplating God is carried beyond nature.[100] Rapture adds something to ecstasy since it increases the violence experienced.[101] And, following Augustine, he maintains that St. Paul actually saw the divine essence.[102]

The precision, range, and grandeur of Aquinas's theology of contemplation is evident from even a brief encounter with it. But it does not wholly occlude Richard's theology of contemplation or others that are contemporary with it or have come after it, for a sense of the value of contemplating God in creation remains, as even Aquinas would admit. It is hard to think of Richard affirming "imperfect contemplation" when his arc of thought passes from sensible particulars to the Trinity. Clearly, Aquinas's theology of simple intuitive insight would be of little help in making sense of "contemplation and poetry" since for him only God is the proper object of contemplation and the act is an immediate and uncomplicated intuition, whereas poems are, even if highly charged with metaphor, discursive. When we understand a poem, we do so in a complex act, one that in practice always anticipates a further stage of reflection. For poems do not give themselves to us in the ways that God does. We love them; they do not love us. Yet there are things to draw from Aquinas, not least of all the thought that the reading of poetry might be part of our imperfect, natural happiness on earth, the philosophical quest for understanding. This reading might not always involve love on the part of a reader—one cannot love all poems even if one loves some deeply—only a knowledge of one or another set of principles of literary criticism, and in that way it bears a resemblance to the theological contemplation of God, which presumes assent to the articles of faith but does not always embody true love of God. Part of the appeal of Richard's schema is that it keeps two of the things that nourish poetry—sensuous nature, including human nature, as well as human thinking—in play. It does not countenance the sensuous world as an inevitable distraction from spiritual maturity.[103] We need to take a step away from Aquinas, if only to see what we need

from him and from others in order to elaborate a theory that might
serve our purposes.

*

In the history of Christianity there have been copious guides to the
spiritual life, many of them written for novices by others who are experienced in the practice, and all of them drawing with a greater or
lesser sense of acknowledgment from pre-Christian sources.[104] A relatively early and impressive one is the treatise on the eight stages of contemplation by St. Peter of Damaskos (d. ca. 750).[105] Among the most
memorable in the Middle Ages, there is Richard of St. Victor's *On the
Ark of Moses* (completed by 1162), which, as we have seen, has six levels and three modes. There are many others: Giles of Assisi in his *Dicta*
(completed by 1226) proposes seven levels; St. Bonaventure in *De triplici via* (completed by 1260) outlines three groups of seven steps in the
quest for wisdom; Jan van Leeuwen's treatise *What Pertains to a Person
Poor in Spirit* (completed before 1378) identifies four rungs of spiritual
elevation; Walter Hilton's *Scala perfectionis* (printed in 1494) has just
three stages of contemplation (reason, affection, and cognition com-
bined with affection); Denis the Carthusian (ca. 1402–71) agrees with
Walter about the number of grades but differs as to how best to describe them; St. Teresa of Ávila's *Interior Castle* (printed in 1588) identifies nine grades of prayer, including modes of active and passive contemplation, that take place in seven inner mansions through which the
soul can pass on its pilgrimage to Christ; and St. John of the Cross's
The Dark Night (1584–85) evokes the secret ladder of contemplation
by which one climbs in darkness to God in ten steps.[106] Inevitably, the
taxonomies seldom overlap; and their emphases differ significantly as
well.[107] Some are seen by way of ascent, whether of a ladder or a mountain, while others favor metaphors of marriage, drawn directly or indirectly from the Canticle. Aquinas's theology of contemplation is
broadly intellective, while Angela of Foligno (1248–1309), Jean Gerson
(1363–1429), and Richard Methley (1450–1527), among others, emphasize the affective dimension of prayer.[108] Some guides to the contemplative life stress, to different extents and in distinct ways, both the
intellect and the will. Yet, for St. Teresa, as one's relation with Christ
deepens, so too the will along with the intellect is illumined. Being
the seat of love, which joins the soul to Christ, the will becomes dominant, and eventually all the faculties, including those St. Teresa finds
the most worrisome (imagination and memory), are filled with divine
light.[109]

One big thing on which several of these authors agree—especially those writing in the thirteenth century and thereafter—is that there is a qualitative difference between discursive and nondiscursive prayer. By and large, everything from vocal prayer to meditation involves language, spoken or not, and hence the mediations that language and concepts bring in tow, and great concern is shown about advancing from discursive to nondiscursive prayer. When the passage occurs and how it is to be negotiated are delicate points for a spiritual director. Some souls advance to contemplation and fall back into meditation for a spell; others find that, after tasting God in mental prayer, they cannot bring themselves to meditate without experiencing an almost unbearable dryness of spirit.[110] St. Teresa locates the change at the end of purgation, after one is well versed in vocal, meditative, affective, and recollective prayer. Then, first with infused contemplation and subsequently with the prayer of quiet, one enjoys spiritual illumination. Thereafter, one enters the highest stage of the Christian life, that of union, in which through prayer one is led to a spiritual betrothal with Christ and, finally, to spiritual marriage with him.

The longer the perspective one adopts in the history of Christian spirituality, the more Richard of St. Victor's *On the Ark of Moses* seems to stand alone in at least one respect. For here everything on the path to God can be contemplated, God as he manifests himself in representations, reason, and the understanding, and not only God as he is in himself, above, beyond, and contrary to reason. When Aquinas objects that Richard is mostly addressing *consideratio* or *speculatio*, not *contemplatio*, it is because the angelic doctor has already decided that contemplation is nondiscursive. This stipulation is appropriate if contemplation is to be directed only to the eternal, simple deity whom one begins to acknowledge vaguely and inchoately as the principle of being. For one cannot behold God as one might survey a mountain or monitor a gradual seismic shift. God offers himself to discursive thought, Aquinas might say, only by way of the historical manifestations of the economic Trinity, such as we find in the scriptures, and as the scriptures are a legitimate sphere of meditation. For Aquinas, as for many others, only God can truly be contemplated because only he, love itself, deserves our complete attention and because he, alone of all beings, cannot exhaust our regard.[111] Looked at in one way, God is absolutely singular and thus escapes all human concepts: we can gaze and gaze on him but can only wait for him to communicate with us or, better, hear the communication. The absolute nature of his singularity is what constitutes his mode of hiddenness or his mystery. Looked at in another way, he is Love, Truth, Justice, Mercy, all modes of divine love, each of which we tacitly understand and each of which endlessly calls forth our reflections. This happens up to and including the moment when mystery imposes itself again, which is when we reflect that all these different properties, often hidden in our experience of life, are one in the deity. We can never fathom the depth of God's love, and only he can raise our faculties above their usual operations and allow a soul a taste of eternal delight.

I do not propose to argue about the proper object of Christian contemplation in the register of spirituality or theology. My concern here is restricted to the possibilities that arise from allowing contemplation to associate with poetry, possibilities that center on regarding some poetry as contemplative and reading poetry in a manner that intuitively seems to be *contemplative*, even if I sometimes use the adjective in a way that many theologians would not. I will say very little about contemplation as it relates to composition, for it varies greatly from poet to poet and sometimes refers to the material for poetry and not poems. Yet Robert Frost's caveat needs to be acknowledged: "[A poem] is never a thought to begin with. . . . It finds its thought or makes its thought."[112] That said, the intuitions I just mentioned about contemplation and poetry can readily be distinguished from those explored in critical work on the poetry of meditation, especially as composed in the sixteenth and seventeenth centuries—John Donne, George Herbert, St. Robert Southwell, and Thomas Traherne, among others—for that poetry follows identifiable movements of Christian meditation, some of which were foregrounded by St. Ignatius Loyola (1491–1541) and his followers and penetrated even some Puritan circles.[113] This genre of poetry adapts meditative techniques based on the use of the imagination such as composition of place, composition of similitudes, examination of points, colloquies, and so on, to its own ends, which are thereafter literary as well as religious.

Readers of some modern poets, including writers and readers who are not at all religious (but who might regard themselves as spiritual), will testify to contemplative currents that run through the work and offer themselves to be read accordingly. Always, these poems will reset the coordinates for contemplation that are respected by its religious practitioners, including Richard. For no poem—not even one that is compounded mainly of intense metaphors—is anything other than discursive. More, there are no purely contemplative modern poems, only borderline cases. Much Romantic and post-Romantic poetry is concerned with self-address, mulling over one's subjectivity, rather than seeking likeness to God by way of the *imago dei* or attempting selfless suspension before the deity. But such concern is usually a sublime phase in a poem, not the whole thing. At least in the West, no very modern poem reaches the heights of contemplation for long. (One would have to go back to the sixteenth century, to St. John of the Cross's "Una noche oscura," for an example of one that does.) But there are many borders, and sometimes they shift, even as we look at them. Besides, there are few strong contemplative poems, even impure ones, of recent times that are explicitly Christian. T. S. Eliot's *Four Quartets* (1943) may well be a lone exception, and it needs to be remembered that it is not exclusively Christian: it engages a theology of religions, especially in its third part.

As an example of modern contemplative poems—one among many that are possible—I offer a passage from Gustave Roud's *Air de la solitude* (1945), which is written in lyrical prose of a kind familiar to readers of Rousseau's *Les rêveries du promeneur solitaire* (left incomplete in 1778) and developed in different ways by Charles Baudelaire (1821–67), Arthur Rimbaud (1854–91), and Marcel Proust (1871–1922) and, in more contemporary writing, Yves Bonnefoy (1923–2016) and Philippe Jaccottet (1925–2021). The passage may well sound unfamiliar and even strange to anglophone readers; but the French literary tradition offers sharper examples of what I have in mind than the American and English traditions. I quote only several sentences taken from over four pages in the original French, which I will fill in a little when commenting on it:

> Rien n'offusque le pan de paysage que je contemple et je puis ceindre et secourer les sacs pleins. . . . Et je n'ai qu'à tourner les yeux verse le morceau de paysage qui m'est donné par rejoinder une sorte d'absolu. . . . La lumière n'augmente ni ne decline. Un jour égal baigne toutes choses; l'herbe à mon seuil verte de son *vrai* veret de toujours. . . . [J]'ai *vu* l'immense paysage jusqu'aux montagnes changer brusquement d'apparence, devinir, d'une minute à l'autre, pareil à un visage fermé.

> (Nothing obscures the stretch of landscape that I contemplate and I can tie and secure the full bags. . . . And I have only to turn my eyes toward the little bit of landscape given to me to return to a sort of absolute. . . . The light neither increases nor decreases. An equal day bathes all things; the grass at my threshold green with its *true* everlasting green. . . . I *saw* the immense landscape, even the mountains, suddenly change in appearance, becoming, from one minute to the next, like a closed face.)[114]

Here a speaker (call him Roud) contemplates, as he says, a Swiss land-scape at harvest time, most likely one near Carrouge in the Vaud, where he spent his entire life, and he does so *par derrière*.[115] He is filling sacks of hay in a bagging room, and from a window he can make out some of the countryside. He says that without having to fill one bag after an-other he would "live here outside time [*je vivrais ici hors du temps*]," and indeed the landscape he sees allows him "to return to a sort of ab-solute." His gaze is in the aesthetic attitude as he indicates when telling us that the time of day with its "grey weather [*temps gris*]" reminds him of painters who take objects from their proper moment in time and "set them in their eternity [*les réinstaller dans leur éternité*]"; the very grass directly outside the bagging room manifests not just green but "*true* everlasting green"; the water in the stream shows "its eternal dis-order [*son désordre éternel*]"; and the wagtails, alders, and ash trees are all "eternal." So too Fernand, a young peasant who falls within Roud's eroticized gaze, becomes "this young eternal peasant [*ce jeune paysan éternel*]."[116]

We may think as we read Roud that he is about to testify to behold-ing the landscape, gaining an insight about it of a spiritual sort. Anyone who has read Wordsworth's "Ode: Intimations of Immortality from Recollections in Early Childhood" (1804) or Emerson's essay "Nature" (1846) or Rimbaud's *Illuminations* (1886) will recognize the basic ges-ture and some of the ways it can be made. Instead, all that Roud sees becomes fulfillment, "our deep hunger for poetry finally satisfied [*notre profonde faim de poésie enfin soit apaisée*]." The contemplation leads not to God, not even to the divine in and through nature, but to poetry, an alternative Λόγος. No sooner does Roud say those words, however, than the satisfaction vanishes: "A sudden return of memory takes me by the throat and everything collapses into anguish [*Un brusque retour de mémoire me serre à la gorge et tout s'effondre dans l'angoisse*]." He re-members the Second World War that is furiously going on elsewhere in Europe. Only once that collapse has happened and once he sees Fer-nand return as a soldier on leave does he hear a bell ring in a village "outside any hour [*dehors de toute heure*]." And then he sees the land-scape become a face, one that knows what it sees but cannot or does not wish to communicate anything whatsoever to human beings.

Roud's interrupted contemplation inherits elements from the re-ligious tradition I have been outlining while silently adapting what is given to it. The imagination, understood as perceiving something through its image, becomes the Romantic imagination, productive and not merely reproductive; reason remains, but its universalizing powers are tightly held in check or even subverted; and the understanding is by turns satisfied in unforeseen ways (it can continue) or frustrated by digression or disunity. Inevitably, Roud brackets or declines much of what is offered to him from the tradition: prayer, stillness before God, and divine aid by way of augmenting the virtues—intellectual, moral, and theological—as well as having God as the focus of contemplation. His interest is more modest, the landscape (and a handsome peasant in it). He shifts his main mode of attention from the religious to the aesthetic, from the *imago* to subjectivity, while continuing to use a religious (or at least metaphysical) vocabulary. Accordingly, the illumination of his faculties, while vivid, can be at best temporary. Also, he adds something that would not have appealed to any of the writers I have mentioned: a registration of anxiety and a taste for discontinuity, whether by a shift of focus or a slide into another mode of attention. For Roud, the understanding remains in play as it looks over its world, even though it finds only a closed face, one that offers no comfort or even much intelligibility. Whatever this face is, it is not that of the Christian God.

Other poets, contemporary with Roud or coming after him, will contemplate but not find any satisfaction, however temporary or negative, by way of understanding. At least there will seldom be any stretching to the sublime or a crystallization by way of epiphany. What they seek often falls between acts of discernment or seems tantalizingly out of reach. W. H. Auden's "Caliban to the Audience" (1944) would be one instance, but, for all its stark differences in tone and rhetorical manner from Roud's *Air de la solitude*, Auden's rather arch Jamesian poem in prose is too close in time to it to give an impression of the scope of contemplative poetry over the last century.[117] Better to touch on one of its most impressive descendants, John Ashbery's *Three Poems* (1972). No doubt Ashbery's prose already differs from that of the Swiss poet in that it is neither lyrical nor overtly Romantic. Nor does it inherit much from *les petites poèmes en prose* as exemplified by Baudelaire, Stéphane Mallarmé, Pierre Reverdy, and Francis Ponge; its rhetorical stance is not deliberately poetic.[118] Instead, *Three Poems* is variously American in its diction, ranging from the demotic to the Jamesian.[119] Yet it too interlaces soliloquy and reflection while adding other, less likely discursive acts such as the lecture and the sermon. A reader will rightly regard the book as contemplative, albeit in an utterly disorienting way, for like the contemplative gaze as Richard figures it the speaker's attention flies here and there.

There is more at issue than digression, however. As Ashbery says: "Lesser artists correct nature in a misguided attempt at heightened realism, forgetting that the real is not only what one sees but also a re-sult of how one sees it—inattentively, inaccurately, perhaps, but never-theless that is how it is coming through to us." One can overcome this misguided attempt at improving nature, Ashbery thinks, and "let things, finally, be."[120] The poetry is contemplative in the unusual way that apparent disorientation is in fact a letting be. If attentive, a reader will recognize traces of a love story in *Three Poems* becoming appar-ent from time to time, a story that moves from the sensual to the spiri-tual. As "The System," the central piece of *Three Poems*, shows, Ashbery is drawn—like Richard but in a more limited way—to taxonomies of the spiritual life. One can think, he says, of lives centered on career that "will 'peak' after a while and then go back to being ordinary lives," and one can think of life as ritual "in which no looking back is possible." A backward look would not be desirable, we are told, because "the im-mediate object of contemplation" would unbalance the present. In ad-dition to these "twin notions of growth" there are two kinds of happi-ness, "frontal" and "latent."[121]

As Ashbery acknowledges, frontal happiness is something the Christian authors under discussion have very much before them as the aim of contemplation; it is the "kind of bloom or grace" that "souls 'in glory' feel . . . permanently," but "very few among us will ever achieve . . . this inundation which shall last an eternity." Ashbery none-theless gives it its due, albeit in a mundane way. We may enjoy "a singu-lar isolated moment," to be sure, but once it is over it slips "so far into the past that it seems a mere spark." Unsurprisingly, he finds a certain attraction in latent or dormant happiness. As he says, it is "harder to understand" than its counterpart, for it usually evades the present:

> We all know those periods of balmy weather in early spring, some-times even before spring has officially begun, days or even a few hours when the air seems suffused with an unearthly tenderness, as though love were about to start, now, at this moment, on an endless journey put off since the beginning of time. Just to walk a few steps in this romantic atmosphere is to experience a magical but quies-cent bliss, as though the torch of life were about to be placed in one's hands: after having anticipated it for so long, what is one now to do? And so the happiness withholds itself, perhaps even indefinitely; it realizes that the vessel has not yet been fully prepared to receive it; it is afraid it will destroy the order of things by precipitating itself too soon. But this in turn quickens the dismay of the vessel or recip-ient; it, or we, have been waiting all our lives for this sign of fulfill-ment, now to be abruptly snatched away so soon as barely perceived.

And a kind of panic develops, which for many becomes a permanent
state of being, with all the appearances of a calm, purposeful, reflective life. These people are awaiting the sign of their felicity without
hope; its nearness is there, tingeing the air around them, in suspension, in escrow as it were, but they cannot get at it.[122]

The sense of an "unearthly tenderness" and the prospect of an "endless
journey" are well-known motifs of medieval mystical theology. Here,
however, Ashbery is closer to Traherne than to the monastic and scholastic treatises that have interested us in this chapter.[123] Notice that the
anticipation of the soul's mortal journey to fulfillment in love remains
empty, merely indicating a state of unpreparedness. There is to be no
satisfaction in life for such people, even though they may well appear
to be calm and reflective. And, lest we begin to look back with a mixture of indulgence and regret on those who have sought frontal happiness, Ashbery in passing views them from the dark side of the spectrum and sharply calls them "spiritual bigots."[124]

Already, then, Ashbery's reader will have started to come to terms
with the ways in which the poet resets categories that are commonplace to us. In his case at least, the system *is* breaking down, as we are
told in the opening line of the poem. Even something as ordinary as the
threefold distinction between thinking, meditating, and contemplating
comes under pressure in *Three Poems*. Ashbery's prose does not distinguish the three but rather wanders (across a landscape of judgments,
perceptions, syntheses, and so on), dwells on rough spots of thought
or feeling, and glides quickly at a height, passing from one mode to another without regard to hierarchy or order. Nor does it move from one
experience to another, rising from love of creation or human beings
to anything celestial, at least not for long, but mostly reflects on how
we experience our experiences. Images are incidental, as are tableaux.
For Ashbery, this reflection on experience does not result in a poetry
of intense psychological interest, for little or nothing is represented of
his ego's particular responses to the world about him and the people
it contains. Rather, his stance is more distant; he disentangles how he
regards an object or a person from how that object or person is manifest in the world. It would not be quite right to consider him disinterested, let alone uninterested, since he cares for many people, few of
whom are ever named in and around the poetry, and since, as a writer,
he is deeply invested in the how of his gaze on them. Nonetheless, he
has freed himself from the bewitchment of individual psychological
states and their allure for the writing of poetry. His poetry will be contemplative in part because it reflects in and through the freedom of an

ego that is deeper than the psychological ego: what Kant and Husserl name the *transcendental ego*.[125] It will also be contemplative in part because it articulates what Angus Fletcher refers to as an "understructure of thought," something we guess at or brood on that is not explicitly addressed in the poem.[126]

Roud and Ashbery give us preliminary reasons why we might associate contemplation and poetry in a century in which religious contemplation has largely faded from literary interest. In reflecting on Gerard Manley Hopkins, in chapter 4, I come as close as I can in modern times to a poet writing in English who took religious contemplation with absolute seriousness in his verse as in his life. His example is more instructive for my purposes than that of T. S. Eliot, whose *Four Quartets* I have in any case discussed elsewhere.[127] Later, I turn my attention to other figurations of contemplation in poetry. But none of this can happen until I outline the hermeneutic of contemplation in the following two chapters.

CHAPTER 2

The Sabbath of the Idea

When contemplation passed through the increasingly dense and intense world of early Christianity, it was changed from the inherited Greek and Roman notions of it.[1] We find it shifting from being an index of freedom on the part of a person seeking reclusion from the turmoil of civic life and, hence, from being a putative natural excellence achieved by that person to being a sign of humble devotion to Christ, the true philosopher.[2] And we find it assuming an intersubjective element: if the shared audition at Ostia of Augustine and Monica is an unusual element of contemplation in late antiquity, the shaping of how one gains intimacy with God by way of an evolving tradition is not.[3] In its passage through the first centuries, Christian contemplation partly detached itself from a philosophical project closely associated with it, of wisdom being fulfilled in steadily beholding what there is, in other words, of θεωρία becoming *theory*. It is a project that would later intersect with scholastic theology and its extensions and find its consummation in modern science and technology.

The main changes I have in mind in early Christianity turn on a loving God being the sole proper object of contemplation for Christians. Tightly coiled within the word *proper* are three views about God and the soul. (*a*) God is hidden and hence mysterious (thereby requiring attention of a special sort); (*b*) God is simply and therefore infinitely good (and therefore worthy of endless regard); and (*c*) human beings bear the *imago dei* (and thus are oriented to its original). This last is not merely an epistemic correlation, however, for Christianity affirms that the relation of divine and human in contemplation is motivated in all ways and at all times by love (ἀγάπη or *caritas*) on each side of the relationship but very unevenly and always in favor of the Creator and Redeemer. In beholding God, through one or another spiritual exercise and with the Grace appropriate to it, one can begin the difficult task of transforming one's first, fallen nature into a second nature. One begins with κένωσις (self-emptying) and proceeds to ἐπέκτασις (striving), an endless movement that, as St. Gregory of Nyssa contends, will not cease in heaven.[4] To raise the mind to God is to take one's first steps into the lands of likeness in the hope that one will increasingly become more like Christ, himself the very image of the Father.

Yet contemplation was not to remain exclusively religious, although attenuated religious assumptions often cling to it in one way or another and to differing degrees. We have seen that in the twelfth century Richard of St. Victor tacitly loosened contemplation's attachment to God. He proposed that anything, even a leaf, can be contemplated and that attention to sensuous particulars (*speculatio*) will provoke an ascent on the part of the soul from the visible to the invisible, an ascent that ends only in loving suspension before the Trinity (*contemplatio*). And, if we look ahead past the seventeenth century, when philosophy and theology started to part ways, we will find that from the eighteenth century through to the twentieth some philosophers urge their readers to take nature as the object of contemplation without any Christian ascent being involved. It is the beautiful and the sublime that attract our attention, we are told, and so contemplation finds itself relocated in aesthetic experience. Not that it remains only there, as we shall see, but in modernity it settles outside Christian spirituality more surely than it develops within it. One might say that there comes to be a secular counterpart to contemplation, if only because with the Enlightenment the deity is seldom called to play a vital role in beholding an idea, a problem, a landscape, another human being, an artwork, or anything at all. Divisions between the secular and the sacred are, however, rarely as clear-cut as some of the more passionate votaries of the secular would like to believe. The latter comes to haunt the former, sometimes in surprising ways, whether at its margins or at its center.[5] When a Western nation-state affirms itself as secular or *laïque* by way of distinctions between church and state, more often than not it mobilizes secularized versions of theological notions.[6] When we are encouraged to prize the arts, the commendation is given with confidence that they will help us transcend our situations and give us something like the consolation that religion used to provide.[7] And, when the North American medical world promotes "mindfulness" as a way to improve one's health, it does so by drawing—often in an untutored way—from Buddhism. Yet it also draws unknowingly from Christian spiritual exercises that once promoted salvation (σωτηρία, "health," "delivery," etc.).

In this chapter and the next, I propose to outline accounts of contemplation by three major modern writers, each of whom figures it largely outside the confines of Christian spirituality. And I wish to do so in order to give credence to the notion of a hermeneutic of contemplation, that is, in order to find a mode of contemplation that justifies the claims that some poetry is contemplative and that that poetry calls to be read in a similar manner. The thesis is modest: one might argue alongside Benedetto Croce (1866–1952) that all poetry is contemplative and that it invites its readers to approach it in that manner.[8] Not that Croce thought in such terms, but this stronger thesis gains support from the idea that poetry is marked by an excess of thought with respect to meaning and reference, but this excess is not always apparent in the same ways. Only some poems manifest it to such an extent that a reader follows its leads in thinking around and beyond its speech acts, including those that are animated by metaphor. To be sure, all writing responds to immanent reading, and all poetry solicits it to a greater or lesser extent, but a poem or a reading suggests being called *contemplative* when there is a movement from the realm of the immanent to circling or gliding around something held to be above, beneath, or beyond it. For some poems, this "something" will be called *God* or *the sacred*, while, for others, it will be *the void* or *the abyss*, and in recent decades we have become familiar with several remarkable readers— Maurice Blanchot and Jacques Derrida come especially to mind—who prize literature, not just poetry, for pointing us more surely to the abyss than to the sacred.[9] One can contemplate the abyss just as one can behold the divine, as Milton's Satan was one of the first to show us. My concerns in this book are otherwise, however.

Hermeneutic, for my purposes, refers not to a method of interpretation, by which a textual surface X comes to mean Y, which abides at a height or depth judged (for whatever purpose) to be fitting, but specifically to the quest for understanding.[10] This quest has always and already commenced, and it never ends since it is an irreducible dimension of being human and broader than the desire for knowledge. One always desires to proceed intellectually with confidence or, with certain persons, to develop the emerging relationship. Of course, this pursuit can be religious (most often in the mode of St. Anselm's *fides quaerens intellectum* [faith seeking understanding]); it is so, for instance, in the poetry of G. M. Hopkins, a little of which will occupy us in chapter 4. But it need not be. The two claims just raised— that some poetry is contemplative and that some poetry can be read contemplatively—are distinct. For a writer may seek to apprehend a complex or even mysterious state of affairs and do so in and through the writing of a poem. Indeed, the state of affairs may appear only in and through the writing of the poem. Nonetheless, this understanding might not be fully conscious to the poet, and, even if the experience of writing the poem satisfies the poet at the level of what is said and how it is said, the poem itself cannot be said otherwise in prose, not even in a wealth of prose. Often enough, it prompts not explanation or interpretation so much as another poem by the original poet or another, one that finds its origin in something that came to light or was concealed in the earlier poem and that does not directly address the earlier work. All poems have modes of hiddenness—thoughts or perspectives not fully disclosed even by the most fecund metaphors or the most disarming declarations—which is one reason why even some atheists are moved to talk of *mystery* in poetry.[11]

No understanding of anything mysterious or even difficult that has been achieved by a poet is directly transferable to a reader, even if the completed poem seems lucid. That reader must seek, firsthand, to grasp the poem put before him or her in as many of its profiles as can be identified, even if these turn out to be superfluous to any immediate application. Even when teaching, one cannot hope to transfer one's testimony of the value of any poem, including those I will be discussing in later chapters. One can communicate knowledge of poetics and noetics, yet, especially at the beginning of a semester, one can only guide students through a poem in order that each might fathom it in his or her own manner, sometimes prizing profiles that the professor might not figure at all prominently. Teaching is required, however, to dispel illusions of understanding that come from restricting the poem's horizons. A poem will enter the mental landscape of each person, opening pathways from one work to another, and there it will grow or diminish, depending on how often and how richly it is pondered by itself or in relation to other works, poetic or not. Not all poems have infinite horizons for all readers; we all have works that we appreciate but that do not engage us deeply or in perpetuity. All poems *think* in various degrees; only some of them think beyond highly particular ends, and only a few of those set us meditating for years on what has been given to us in monologue or dialogue, argument or association, description or narration, dialectic or insight, and only a few of these might have us suspend ourselves before them, endlessly pondering their acts of making present and absent, their challenges, delights, and solaces, seeking a whole that always seems to be beyond our capacities at the moment.

What occurs once a poem has started to be understood partly escapes the classroom and even the dissertation, where a heavy emphasis has been placed in recent decades on using literature to diagnose social maladies.[12] Poems do far more than this, however. They can comfort us and gladden us, they can give us wider horizons or more pressing ones, and they can preserve fragile phenomena, the being of which, whether in culture, history or nature, is all too easily overlooked.[13] They can lead us into unvisited corners of ourselves; they can prepare us for falling in love, indicate how love might perplex us, and advise how to conduct ourselves when love fades and even when death approaches. Indeed, they can display facets of being human, in all its spheres of thought and action, some of which we might otherwise reduce, bypass, or ignore. Doubtless they can also blind us to events that we should notice; they can mystify social structures; and they can hasten us to think or act too quickly or to idealize too lavishly. To register these things and then act justly with respect to them presumes capacious understanding. Deep understanding does not mean bland acceptance of all things, and it excuses nothing; it signals an awareness of how certain facets of a poem light up in particular situations, and it points to the need for a responsible attitude to what is thereby illumined in the world.

Poems are not all depth or height; they have surfaces, sometimes glittering and sometimes resonant, that can beguile us and give us pleasure. If a poem leads us to reflect, it does so often through idiom and tone, rhythm and rhyme, surface phenomena that simply will not go away. We feel them on the tongue, and we return to them to experience the feeling of them time and again. No one who has fallen in love with a poem could truly say that it is a purely cognitive event. It is an experience with experiences, the poet's and one's own. Appeals to our senses motivate us to understand what we are feeling and thinking, and understanding summons, educates, and directs affect, which in turn enhances understanding and makes us relish idiom and tone, tropes and schemes, rhythm and rhyme, even more. Poetry enters our flesh—our direct awareness of our bodies—as well as our minds.[14] We experience people we love through cherished metaphors, idioms, and tonalities, and this includes when we touch them with our fingertips, hands, and lips. It is seldom to our benefit if poetry makes us merely intellectually sophisticated. Woe betides the person who kisses ironically. But, in order for anything positive to happen from poetry, one must learn to read well, being aware of seductions and feints as well as bounty. When it is practiced with any seriousness, contemplation is most often in excess of any given action consequent on it, and it is always needed for there to be any informed action, regardless of whether it meets its desired end.

Such an understanding, whether achieved inside or outside the classroom, will not turn on resolving a poem into so many speech acts,

for poems of any vitality concatenate various rhetorical procedures —
affective, cognitive, visual, and tonal — that interact with one another in different ways and never quite settle down. They can quietly
or fiercely alert us to gaps between presences and representations that
lead us to ponder what might span them or be swallowed by them. Not
that the situation is simply semantic. For our reading of poems pivots
on inhabiting one or more attitudes, in Husserl's sense of the word *attitude*, which I shall explicate in the next chapter. *How* a poem presents
itself to a reader — the precise nature of its manifold — shapes how we
will receive it; and *how* one seeks to engage a poem determines what
one registers of it at any given time. This how traverses the reader's or
the writer's appeals to what is apparently outside the poem ("context"
of one sort or another) and apparently within the poem ("textuality"
as construed by this school or that). Poet and reader will usually agree
withal that a poem is better understood only after many readings, silent or voiced, private or public. When Wallace Stevens wrote that a
poem "must resist the intelligence / Almost successfully," he was not
simply being mischievous; he was also alerting us to a continuing relation of contemplating any memorable poem, and he rightly included
his own works in that remark.[15] He knew very well that intelligence is
not merely cleverness but primarily the operation of the understanding
(*intellectus*). Short poems, such as "The Snow Man" and "The Course
of a Particular," pierce us even on a first reading, and we can never bring
reflection on them to a complete standstill. They are lenses through
which light comes, whether chilling or warming. Longer poems such as
"Notes toward a Supreme Fiction" (1942) and "An Ordinary Evening in
New Haven" (1950) are sufficiently extended as well as thickly thought
to frustrate any mental attempt to integrate all their parts into a satisfy-
ing whole. We go back and forth with them, always resisting making a
totality if we read well, whether it be one of our own devising or that of
another, and always seeking a whole.

To give some sense of the hermeneutic of contemplation, I would
like to draw attention to three of its most thoughtful modern advocates: Arthur Schopenhauer (1788–1860) and Samuel Taylor Coleridge
(1772–1834) in this chapter and Edmund Husserl (1859–1938) in the
next. They will not help us specify narrowly how a poet writes by way
of adopting a contemplative attitude. No one can since contemplation
cannot be transferred, no more in poetry than in prayer or even in relatively challenging acts of apprehension or comprehension. But sometimes we can intuit a writer's train of thought, recognizing that we are
not being asked to follow one proposition after another, that we are not
merely being pressed to assent to everything said, and that the author

is writing in a state of openness to what comes. We notice one or another manner of proceeding so that the poem attends to an idea or a set of ideas and, in attending, circles, eddies, glides, pauses, backtracks, loops, spirals, and leaps and has us do so as well. The three thinkers might well be able to aid us in establishing a level at which we can seek to understand a range of poems when we read them and give us some coordinates for discussing them.

*

I begin slightly out of historical sequence with Schopenhauer because he argues the most clearly and concisely for the centrality of contemplation in aesthetic experience. Thoroughly Kantian in conviction, he nonetheless strives for simplicity in his version of transcendental idealism.[16] He retains from *The Critique of Pure Reason* (1781, 1787) the notion of space and time as the forms of outer and inner intuition yet resolves them, along with the twelve categories of the understanding, to causality; and causality in its various modes is comprehended by the one principle, that of sufficient reason.[17] As his early *The Fourfold Root of the Principle of Sufficient Reason* (1813; 1847) maintains, any phenomenon can be explained by reference to one of four core domains: the physical, the logical, the mathematical, and the moral.[18] All things in the phenomenal realm present themselves to human beings as distinct items that can be known; and, like Kant, Schopenhauer also affirms a noumenal realm. For Kant, that realm is unknowable in principle; for Schopenhauer, it is *almost* wholly beyond our ken since we have a limited sense of it that we gain by reflecting on ourselves. One's body (*Körper*), Schopenhauer says, is certainly a representation, like everything in the world of experience. However, it is distinct from any other representation, for "we have immediate cognition of the thing in itself when it appears to us as our own body."[19]

When we know our body from within, as *Leib* rather than *Körper*, we recognize that this living body is directly acknowledged through acts of the will; they escape the outer intuition of space but not the inner intuition of time for the acts are successive; and because they come from within ourselves causality plays far less of a role than when the body (*Körper*) moves or is moved in the world about it.[20] We are entitled to surmise, Schopenhauer thinks, that the noumenal self is nothing other than an objectification of the will, and for all we know the whole noumenal realm might well be will.[21] Schopenhauer therefore differs markedly from Kant in two major ways. First, the will, for him, is a fundamental, not wholly cognizable, general force, anterior to and independent of human cognition (i.e., the power to represent); it is not an index of individual autonomy, something that can be harnessed by the moral law into a "holy will." In this, he is closer to Friedrich Wilhelm Joseph von Schelling than to Kant—or, more pointedly, one might say that he is closer to Jakob Böhme.[22] Second, where Kant takes the three practical postulates (Freedom, Immortality, and God) to indicate something, albeit little, about the noumenal realm, for Schopenhauer all these things are denied. The will as such is free, although each human being is increasingly bound by past actions that he or she has willed. The individual soul is mortal. And there is no sound reason to believe in God.[23]

It can be no surprise, then, that for Schopenhauer human life is largely taken up with desiring and striving to fulfill desires that often elude us or show themselves to be frustrating whether or not we attain them. Worse, no religious consolations are available, at least none that Christianity can plausibly offer. It is a bleak view of life, one in which a prephilosophical disposition toward melancholy has achieved both elegance and rigor.[24] In this philosophy, there is not the slightest reason to follow St. Gregory of Nyssa in the twin practice of κένωσις and ἐπέκτασις. There is κένωσις of a sort but no ἐπέκτασις, only reprieve. Usually, Schopenhauer says, we are concerned with the "Where, When, Why and Wherefore of things," that is, with following the principle of sufficient reason. But another possibility is always before us:

> If, instead of all this, we devote the entire power of our mind to intuition and immerse ourselves in this entirely, letting the whole of consciousness be filled with peaceful contemplation [*die ruhige Kontemplation*] of the natural object that is directly present, a landscape, a tree, a cliff, a building, or whatever it might be, and, according to a suggestive figure of speech, we *lose* ourselves in this object completely, i.e. we forget our individuality, our will, and continue to exist only as pure subject. . . . [W]hat we thus cognize is no longer the individual thing as such, but rather the Idea [*Idee*], the eternal form. . . . [T]he individual has lost himself in this very intuition: rather, he is *pure* [*reines*], will-less, painless, timeless *subject of contemplation* [*Subjekt der Erkenntniß*].[25]

Emptying the self does not thereby allow the divine to approach one; and in any case there could be no fulfillment in an endless experience of divine goodness. We would become bored by such intensity, just as Origen imagined.[26] Religious contemplation is out of the question then, or so it seems, for what is given to hold the mind so peacefully is not a natural object but "the eternal form," and, in beholding it, one momentarily becomes pure and timeless: our understanding overcomes its inherent imperfection.[27] It is, if you wish, a very small natural theology. Consciousness is arrested before the Idea (*Idee*), but, since the Idea cannot love, there can be no movement of ἐπέκτασις or anything like it that draws the subject to itself. Striving must be restricted to the phenomenal world, and as Schopenhauer tells us again and again it is no good thing.

Incessant striving can be stilled when faced with beauty or the sublime, however. For the self dissolves for a time into what it beholds. Kant says that one must be disinterested when contemplating anything beautiful. The pleasure we take in judgments of taste "is simply contemplative [*kontemplativ*], i.e., it is a judgment which is indifferent as to the existence of an object, and only decides how its character stands with the feeling of pleasure and displeasure."[28] Love, note, drops out of contemplation. Schopenhauer follows Kant with respect to the former but does not expatiate on the latter; it is only rarely that he mentions disinterest.[29] This is because his primary concern is not with the status of judgments about the beautiful or the sublime but with something more basic, the aesthetic experience itself. As the passage just quoted makes plain, the loss of everything individual about the reader of a poem, the listener of music, or the viewer of a painting is essential when contemplating the beautiful or the sublime. And this includes everything to do with space, time, cause, and effect. In aesthetic experience we do not look *through* a phenomenon to find its ground; we look *at* it and are blessedly released from the quest for grounds. Understanding, here, excludes explanation taken to involve the capturing of reasons, including those that feature in methodologies.[30]

Such is aesthetic experience, as Schopenhauer conceives it, and it is one of the main ways in which contemplation figures in his philosophy.[31] It is crucial for him that our regard be absorbed by an Idea (*Idee*), not by a particular or a group of particulars, for the Ideas are eternal, as he says, and we might observe that the remission that they offer us from desire and frustration has a quasi-religious quality to it. Subject and object become one.[32] In his own way, Schopenhauer has the observer take a step into the lands of likeness: we become for a short while what we behold. The experience is more general than the philosopher's account of it. T. S. Eliot, no follower of pessimistic aesthetics (but, like Schopenhauer, touched by an early encounter with Indian religions), testifies to hearing music "so deeply / That it is not heard at all, but you are the music / While the music lasts."[33] The reprieve from the perpetual cycle of desire and pain is only a *quasi-religious* quality, however. For the Ideas do not give us reality as such since that would presume that they converge with the noumenal realm and Schopenhauer does not think that this is the case. When he writes of an Idea, he takes himself to be far closer to Plato than to Kant: εἶδος or ἰδέα, not *Idee von reiner Vernunft* or *ästhetische Idee*.[34] In fact, Plato's Ideas or Forms are for the German thinker nothing other than the levels of the objectification of the will, from stones to humans, and thus are rather more than immanent forms.[35] Kant was mistaken to regard them transcendentally, as pure concepts of reason, quite beyond experience, in an effort to distinguish them from the concepts of the understanding.[36] Perhaps so; but the reader will be puzzled by Schopenhauer's claim in turn. How the will objectifies itself and how it does so by way of levels that render the Ideas individual even though they are outside space and time remains obscure; maybe it has something to do with the largely inscrutable noumenal reality, but this would require more insight into that realm than Schopenhauer thinks is available.[37] That said, the insistence on *levels* of the will points to the philosopher's conviction that the eternal Ideas are variously situated ontologically between phenomenal particulars and the noumenal realm; they cannot be sensuously perceived or even intuited since they are not spatial, but they can nonetheless be contemplated.[38]

Contemplation, for Schopenhauer, is therefore cognitive, both in its remission from pain and in the sense of intellectual satisfaction it gives, and this thought might lead us loosely to range his view with Aquinas's in the field of religious contemplation. Before doing so, we should pause and see exactly what he says. Here is Schopenhauer expatiating a little more fully on what is involved in contemplating a Platonic Idea:

> Thus, when I regard (for instance) a tree aesthetically, i.e. with artist's eyes, and thus do not have a cognition of it but of its Idea, then suddenly it does not matter [*es sofort ohne Bedeutung ist*] whether it is this tree or some ancestor of this tree that blossomed thousands of years ago, or similarly whether the viewer is this or some other individual living in some place and at some time; the individual thing and the cognizing individual are suppressed along with the principle of sufficient reason, and nothing is left except the Idea and the pure subject of cognition, which together constitute the adequate objecthood of the will on this level. And the Idea is exempt from space as well as time, since the genuine Idea is not this spatial figure before my eyes but rather the expression, the pure meaning of

this figure [*die reine Bedeutung derselben*], its innermost essence that opens itself up and speaks to me [*das sich mir aufschließt und mich anspricht*], and this can remain the same through vast differences in the spatial relations of the figure.[39]

Schopenhauer has fully released contemplation from its traditional role in Christianity, sole attachment to God—indeed from what he takes to be the Western religious gaze—and has reattached it to the beautiful and the sublime. He is not concerned with the divine manifesting itself in creation or with natural beauty shaping our sense of the deity, only with how the tree is given to me wholly in perception. "The world is my representation," as the bold opening sentence of *The World as Will and Representation* (1818; 1844) declares.[40] But perception, for him, involves more than passively receiving hyletic data. One can contemplate a great many things in nature—there are a few exceptions—and, in doing so, we are raised from thinking about representations (and desiring them) to beholding Ideas, which subsist at different levels.[41] To that slight extent, we might be reminded of Richard of St. Victor (and of the natural theology in the first stages of the spiritual life evoked in *The Ark of Moses*). In twelfth-century terms, the most that can be hoped for in contemplation as Schopenhauer conceives it would be *dilatio mentis* or perhaps *sublevatio mentis*, as happens when the essence encountered "opens itself up and speaks to me." The language is almost visionary, but it is only a metaphor. For Schopenhauer, *excessus mentis* would be no more than a reverie.

A good deal turns in this passage on the adoption of an aesthetic stance, understood as looking with an "artist's eyes." For Schopenhauer, an artist is a genius; he or she has more cognitive power than others either continuously or at privileged moments: "[One can] lose oneself in intuition and . . . temporarily . . . put one's interests, willing and purposes entirely out of mind . . . and this not just momentarily, but for as long and with as much clarity of mind as is necessary to repeat what has been grasped in the form of a well-considered art." One enjoys, as he says, "the Sabbath of the penal servitude of willing."[42] The artist is conceived here in terms of what Schopenhauer's milieu regarded as *Weimer Klassik*; even so, it seems unclear why art would benefit from detaching an Idea so completely from the sensuous particulars by which it displays itself and why this activity is restricted solely to the artist. Could it not be that what is artistically valuable is precisely the relation of Idea and particular and that the genius of the artist consists in seeing and expressing it? Indeed, should not the how play a part in what the artist sees, not necessarily by way of how something works but by way of how it appears? Schopenhauer admits that to a certain extent everyone must be able to see Ideas in things.[43] The child glancing at a tree on the way to school, the arborist who comes to check that the same tree will stand another year: each sees in passing that the tree is beautiful as well as bearing a colorful swing or being infested by wood-boring insects. Otherwise, there could be no general appreciation of beauty, and it would not make any sense to speak of someone looking at something "with artist's eyes."[44] Presumably, also, such a mundane seeing would be a highly attenuated gaze compared with that of a genuine artist.

It is the artist, one might think, who would be attracted by this or that tree as well as by specific challenges in painting it at varying times of the day with different intensities of light and shade. For Schopenhauer, however, the artist sees the Platonic idea and wishes to embody it in a work, while the rest of us tend to see something particular.[45] So Schopenhauer retains something of Plato's metaphysics while rejecting his aesthetics, in which art merely produces copies of copies of reality.[46] Montaigne tells us: "Each man bears the entire form of man's estate [*Chaque homme porte la forme entière, de l'humaine condition*]." By this he means that one can find the material for a moral philosophy in a poor person or a wealthy one. He has no interest in ontology. In the same essay he also tells us: "I do not portray being: I portray passing."[47] But Schopenhauer goes further and observes that in viewing an individual human an artist discerns the Idea of mankind in itself.[48] Perhaps some artworks present an Idea of the species *Homo sapiens sapiens* in terms of the artist's general culture and, to some extent, beyond it: Michelangelo's *David* (1504) might be an example, although even here it would be challenging to claim that humankind is wholly and essentially present in the statue. *David* is of a white male figure, for one thing. Schopenhauer admits that particular Ideas might be involved in the perception of the human species while insisting that an artist will nonetheless show the general Idea of being human.

The question that remains is what counts as "the accidental form of appearance of the Idea"; we might agree to customs and fashions as accidental but not to gender and race, for instance.[49] One might say in response that Schopenhauer is speaking only of a biological species, not of being human as a cultural or spiritual state. For new figures of what it means to be human appear from time to time—Sir John Falstaff, Clarissa Harlowe, Ralph Nickleby, Catherine Ernshaw, Leopold Bloom, Murphy, etc.—and give us a fuller idea of what it is or can be to be human.

Certain allegorical poems will give us the Idea of a particular type

of person and nothing more. When the speaker in a sonnet by Thomas
Hood (1799–1845) calls his wife "Delight" and his son "Frolic," we
grasp only the Ideas of them (here, allegorical aspects of a relationship or a character), and it would be foolish to complain about not having been supplied with appropriate details.[50] For that, we would need
to read a completely different poem. In a contrary way, and operating
boldly with an original poetics, G. M. Hopkins (1844–89) presents the
sensuous details of an English spring:

> When weeds, in wheels, shoot long and lovely and lush;
> Thrush's eggs look little low heavens, and thrush
> Through the echoing timber does so rinse and wring
> The ear, it strikes like lightnings to hear him sing.[51]

If there is a Platonic Idea here ("Spring"), it is largely exhausted
by the sensuous details of what is depicted, and we respond strongly
to the hyletic data even before we come to the more theological reflections in the sestet of the lyric.

A large question remains that invites a short digression: Is an aesthetic regard the only one that can be at issue in Schopenhauer's example of the tree? One can imagine a religious genius—a monk, say—
more or less contemporary with the philosopher looking at a tree in a
similar manner but not only with an artist's eye. We might admit that
his subjectivity would have been temporarily emptied of everyday concerns by his experience of the tree's beauty. For him, the "pure meaning" of the Idea would not be rigidly contained by the Idea; it would
overflow and extend to the deity. If we can imagine a monk having
been impressed by Kant's critical philosophy, as happened with some
eighteenth-century German Benedictines, he might well go a little
past the will and take love to give the clue to his noumenal self, and
he would be disposed to muse, without theoretical confirmation, that
noumenal reality as a whole is love.[52] Of course, Schopenhauer would
not accept this way of thinking. Yet he clearly affirms ἀγάπη or *caritas*,
not because he thinks it has redemptive value, but because for him it
is one with compassion, which he takes to be a positive value.[53] In his
view a monk might well deny the will to life—which would save him
from an endless, painful cycle of desire and frustration—by adopting
an ascetic existence. Schopenhauer keeps the door slightly ajar to the
sort of mysticism elaborated by Meister Eckhart (ca. 1260–ca. 1328)
and the Quietism of Francis Fénelon (1651–1715) and Madame de
Guyon (1648–1717).[54] In one sense, he has no choice but to do so,
despite his pessimism, since his own Kantian principles, however

adjusted, do not allow him to speak exhaustively about the noumenal realm. In its own way, this realm is as mysterious as the Christian deity. The deity is hidden for the most part and is taken by many believers to reveal himself directly not only in Jesus of Nazareth but also in the transports of mystics. Nonetheless, Schopenhauer thought, no mystic can convince us of his or her experience.[55] It comes down to testimony, not argument.

To return to the delicate issue of borrowing the "artist's eyes," one might object that an artist will never truly experience a complete suppression of the will, at least not for as long as Schopenhauer imagines. Let us say that an artist gazes at a beautiful tree and beholds its Platonic Idea. But he or she is an *artist* and therefore concerned to produce works of art. A painting of the tree or a poem about it might begin to form in his or her mind, and, if that happens, the artist will recoil to the realm governed by the principle of sufficient reason. This will happen in different ways. William Blake (1757–1827), for example, starts to ponder "A Poison Tree"; Robert Frost (1874–1963) begins to imagine what will become "Birches"; Eugenio Montale (1896–1981) embarks on apprehending a poem he has long itched to compose, "I lemoni." Any of these poets prepares, on viewing the tree, to bring his habits and the rules of his art into play, even if the poem just named does not get written for years. The reprieve from the constant pressure of the will does not last long, and the pleasure of imagining a new work to come supervenes.[56] Like everyone else, poets are caught in an endless cycle of desire, even if the poems they write release them and us from it for a time.

One final question before leaving the passage about the tree. What is the relation between seeing a Platonic Idea and actually composing an artwork? To be sure, the will intervenes between seeing the Idea and executing the work.[57] Schopenhauer therefore observes: "Poetry wants [*will*] to acquaint us with the (Platonic) Ideas of essences by means of particulars and examples."[58] The verb *wants* should be stressed since the philosopher goes on to acknowledge that "meter and rhyme" are responsible for about half of what the poet wishes to say. And one might presume that this part is not separable from the whole. Certainly, drafts of poems indicate how unusual it would be for a poet directly to seize a poem in and through its Platonic Idea; a poem mostly comes into being by a complex dialectic of a consciousness and the work as it is being formed on the page.[59] This is all the more relevant in that many poems, including those that are the main exhibits of this book, would appear to deal with several Ideas at once if one is to employ this Platonic language in the first place. Contemplation plays a role, but composition also involves action, an ability to respond to chance as well as to emergent design, chance that may well direct the writer in an unforeseen direction. The poet lives a mixed life, even as poet.

Schopenhauer is not open to the importance of this claim, despite his acknowledgment of the far-reaching roles that meter and rhyme have to play in composition. When he comes to situate poetry in his ascending series of modes of art, from architecture to tragic poetry, his admiration is captivated by the poet's ability to intuit Ideas, even of merely possible phenomena, and to deal adequately with the abstract concepts to which all thought is bound.[60] In poetry, he writes, "no concept can persist in its abstract generality; instead an intuitive representative appears before the imagination and the poet's words continually modify this in keeping with his intentions." Modification is restricted to dealing with concepts, not Ideas; for the latter can be directly intuited and distilled into the work, thereby becoming "concrete and individual, the intuitive representation," and the mark of poetic excellence is consistently to obtain "the precipitate one has in mind."[61] This allows a reader to conceive the Idea and, like the poet, to contemplate it. The Idea governs both the artist and the one who responds to the art produced. It seems more reasonable to say that the relation of Idea and particulars is critical in the creation and appreciation of art.

In the Enlightenment it is Kant who disengages contemplation and God and situates the former in the realm of judgments of taste.[62] (In that realm contemplation does not even require the existence of the object; it certainly does not assume faith animated by love.) Influenced by him or not, artists did the same: Caspar David Friedrich's canvas *Two Men Contemplating the Moon* (1819–20) is an example, even though it is susceptible to a Christian interpretation. That said, it is Schopenhauer whom we must credit as extending Kant's insights so that contemplation becomes secure in the field of aesthetics, even though the aesthetic gaze, as he figures it, is shot through with religious or quasi-religious motifs. He acknowledges that the understanding is imperfect: we cannot hope to grasp an artwork in one sitting or perhaps even many. His notion that contemplation is a looking at and not a looking through also remains valuable when conceiving a hermeneutic. Less appealing at the level of his philosophical architectonic is his importation of Platonic Ideas, which are unrelated to his voluntarist development of the critical philosophy, especially in the way he thinks about the relation of Idea and artwork. Also unconvincing is his insistence that contemplation of beauty and the sublime is purely cognitive, as abeyance from frustration and as intellectual satisfaction, without affective and sensual elements. Let us see whether another post-Kantian, another Platonist, though one who did not know Schopenhauer at all, gives us the means to correct and enrich this account of contemplation. Let us begin to read Samuel Taylor Coleridge.

*

Sometime in the mid-1820s, Coleridge was reading and annotating the later volumes of Wilhelm Gottlieb Tennemann's ten-volume *Geschichte der Philosophie* (1798–1817), a work that concluded just before Schopenhauer's *The World as Will and Representation* (1818) appeared to little notice.

Coleridge had started reading Tennemann in 1818. Among other things, he found himself unsatisfied by the historian's treatment of what both agreed to call *Mystic Philosophy*, protesting in particular against the obscurity introduced by the word *Gefühl* (feeling) in the discussion of Jean Gerson (1363–1429). Tennemann objects in Gerson to "das Gaukelspiel der Phantasie und die Macht lebhafter nicht aufgeklärter Gefühle in die gröbsten Irrthümer führe" (the tricks of fancy and the force of lively but unclear feelings). For Coleridge, those committed to mystical philosophy are oriented to proper use of what he calls *Reason*, and in his view Tennemann writes as though medieval contemplatives are merely reacting to an overly chilly scholasticism.[63] No doubt, Gerson was responding to that tendency in his affirmation of affective repentant theology as an antidote to the burgeoning cult of cleverness at the University of Paris during his term there as chancellor. Be that as it may, this is not the whole of Gerson: he was firmly influenced by the Pseudo-Dionysius and the Victorines, after all. In writing as he does about Gerson, Tennemann promotes a "Misty Schism" from the "Church of Common Sense," as Coleridge wittily puts it.[64] True "Mystical Philosophy," Coleridge maintains, can be found in the twelfth-century Victorines, Hugh and Richard, and in fourteenth-century divines such as Johannes Tauler (1300–1361) and Gerson.[65] He goes on to describe what he takes "true Mystic Philosophy" to be, and I will return to it in a moment, but before I do I would like to look back about fifteen years to his earlier reflection on the same topic. It will help orient us.

For Coleridge had not fundamentally changed his mind about contemplation since reading Ralph Cudworth's *True Intellectual History* (1678) in the last years of the eighteenth century. It was metaphysical contemplation that attracted him and, indeed, Cudworth's construal of natural theology.[66] This orientation can be seen in the volume he and

Robert Southey (1774–1843) anonymously published, *Omniana; or, Horae Otiosiores* (1812). One of the entries in that compendium is entitled "Meditation, and Contemplation." The two authors quote Louis Richeome (1544–1625), whose *Le pèlerin de Lorete* (1604), as translated into English by Edward Worsley in 1629, was to be prized by recusant Catholics in England. In the second chapter of his second section, devoted to prayer, Richeome distinguishes meditation and contemplation and in particular stresses the role of understanding in prayer, both verbal and mental, which is more apparent in the passage immediately before the one that the two poets quote:

> Contemplation is a regard of the eyes of the Soul fastened attentively upon some object, as if after meditated of the creation, she should set the eye of her understanding fast and fixed [*voeüe fixe*] upon the greatness of God, upon the beauty of the Heavens; or having discoursed on the passion of our Saviour, she beholdeth him present [*le voit present*], and seeth him crucified, and without any other discourse, persevereth constantly in this spectacle. Then the Soul doth contemplate upon her meditation; so that contemplation is more than meditation, and as it were the end thereof, and it groweth and springeth upon it many times, as the branch doth upon the body of the tree, or the flower upon the branch. For the understanding [*l'esprit*] having attentively and with many reasons to and fro meditated the mystery, and gathered divers lights together, doth frame unto herself a clear knowledge, whereof, without further discourse one way or other, she enjoyeth (as I may say) a vision, which approacheth to the knowledge of Angels.[67]

The teaching is entirely traditional, with *contemplatio* consequent on *meditatio*, as in *lectio divina*, but set in a whole that appeals to the religiosity of the Counter-Reformation. Neither the Jesuit's florid Mariology nor his attention to fringe devotions would have gained the sympathy of either English poet. Notice, however, that there is no mention of feeling, as was to become prominent in Germany about two centuries later with the rise of *Gefühlstheologie* with and after Friedrich Schleiermacher (1768–1834).

Coleridge and Southey pass over several lines of Richeome's text without marking an ellipsis and then quote him on differences between meditation and contemplation:

> Hereof we learn the difference betwixt these two actions; for meditation is less clear, less sweet, and more painful than Contemplation:

it is as the reading of a book, which must be done sentence after sentence; but contemplation is like casting the eyes upon a picture discerning all at once. Meditation is like eating: Contemplation is like drinking, a work more sweet, cooling, and more delicate, less labour, and more pleasure than eating is. For he that meditateth taketh an antecedent, doth behold, weigh, and consider it, as it were chewing the meat with some pain; and afterward doth gather conclusions one after another, as it were swallowing down of morsels, and taketh his pleasure by pieces; but he that contemplateth receiveth his object without pain, swiftly and as it were altogether, as if he took a draught of some delicate wine. Such is Meditation, and such is Contemplation.[68]

Again, the distinction is elaborated in terms that were familiar in Counter-Reformation Catholicism, and it should be noted that this time we see *consideratio* folded into *meditatio*. Reflecting on this division between contemplation and meditation, the two Romantic authors observe:

Philosophical as this is, the consequences which must result from applying it to acts of devotion are apparent, and of this is no doubt the Jesuit and the other teachers of this doctrine were well aware. Let but an enthusiast be once taught to keep the understanding passive, and the imagination awake, and dreams, apparitions, rapts, ecstasies, with all the other symptoms of hagiomania, will follow in the natural course of the disease.[69]

Contemplation is valuable, then, when it takes place in the understanding, not the imagination. Richoeme's discussion of prayer—directly before his delineation of meditation and contemplation—stresses prayer as able to illuminate the understanding—he repeats *understanding* several times—and is best taken as a baroque rephrasing of St. Anselm's *fides quaerens intellectum*.[70]

Not noticing this traditional linking of faith and understanding, the two poets observe that contemplation can become a danger when the faculty is allowed to fall passive (as in the example of drinking rather than eating). Now, passive or infused contemplation is an emphasis of Counter-Reformation theology of prayer. For St. John of the Cross (1542–91), for instance, it is required for the deepening of one's intimacy with God.[71] For St. Teresa of Ávila (1515–82), it comes to those whom God draws most surely to himself.[72] Coleridge took up reading Teresa's *Works* in 1810 but did not persevere with them. He laments:

"This poor afflicted spotless Innocent could be so pierced thro' with fanatic preconceptions."[73] The peril that an "enthusiast" faces, as Coleridge and Southey see it in 1812, is that the imagination can take over from an understanding that has been rendered passive and the enthusiast can become prey to religious delusions.[74] There is a dark side to Coleridge's later aphorism, "Things take the signature of Thought."[75]

True mystical philosophy, for the older Coleridge, can be found in Hugh and others associated with the Abbey of St. Victor. The vocabulary of Augustinus Secundus, as his contemporaries called Hugh, converges with Coleridge's own if one allows for some translation. "He uses *Ratio* for the Understanding," Coleridge says, "Intellectus for the Reason as the Source of the Principles by which the Understanding is enlightened and <thus> becomes <a> Logos, or 'Discourse of Reason'; while a yet higher Power, which he elsewhere calls *Contemplatio*, he entitles *Intelligentia*, or the Ideal Power, by which the purified Soul is enabled to contemplate God and Supersensual Realities."[76] We see here a crucial change of vocabulary for Coleridge, one that he puts in place only after the *Omniana* but to which he adheres throughout the rest of his writing life. Reason is the source of principles, and the understanding is merely a faculty of rules; indeed, Reason is what Plato means by ἰδέα.[77] As Coleridge says in *Aids to Reflection* (1825), one's "main chance" of "*reflecting* on religious subjects *aright*" and "attaining to the *contemplation* of spiritual truths *at all*" turns on grasping the nature of the difference between the understanding and reason.[78] And part of this difference is that the reason is close to sense in one key respect: both work directly, one with regard to the intelligible, the other with regard to the phenomenal. This is why passive contemplation is so worrying to Coleridge. In the terms of his new vocabulary, Reason must be active in order to detect the differences between its direct apprehensions of the intelligible realm and those of the senses of the physical realm. Passive contemplation can easily be seduced and turned to fanaticism.

Tennemann cannot grasp Hugh's profundity, Coleridge thinks, because he reads him through somewhat distorted Kantian lenses, following the strict letter of Kantianism rather than the lively spirit of Kant. This is in evidence in his reading of ancient philosophy. The result is that *Geschichte der Philosophie* is more the work of a dogmatist than that of a historian, animated less by the desire for an accurate portrayal of Neo-Platonism than by covert criticism of Schelling's *Naturphilosophie*.[79] Even if those lenses were ground correctly and *mystical philosophy* were read strictly "according to Principles of Kantianism,"[80] as Tennemann avowed it would be at the outset of his venture, the account of mysticism would not likely be sympathetic, and Coleridge would not have reacted well to it. With reference to Kant, he believed that transcendental reflection, as developed in the *Critique of Pure Reason* (1781; 1787), was adequate to deal with Kant's fears about *Schwärmerei* and *Illuminatismus* in his *Religion within the Limits of Reason Alone* (1793). Besides, he was strongly committed to the genius of Jakob Böhme, to whom he consecrated a long commentary in the margins of the theosophist's *Works*.[81]

A few pages further on, Coleridge offers what he takes to be a better way of thinking of "true Mystical Philosophy." It is divided into three stages. The first is perfectly familiar:

> First, the introductory and purifying, which Gerson rightly describes as consisting of *abnegation,* or a watchful repelling and setting aside the intrusive images of Sense, and the Conceptions of the Understanding, both these generalized from the Data of the Senses or formed by reflection on its (the Understanding's) own processes.

The second stage is more interesting. As already noticed in the remark about Hugh's sense of contemplation, and as with Schopenhauer, the emphasis is on Ideas, to which I shall turn in a moment:

> Secondly, the contemplation of the Ideas, or Spiritual Verities, that present themselves, like the Stars, in the silent Night of the Senses and the absence of the animal Glare.—That these Ideas have a true Objectivity is, as Gerson seems to have seen, implied in the Soul's *Self*-knowledge.

And the third phase, neither a ground nor a source of evidence, concerns the aim of contemplation, which is not to be realized in this life:

> To these solemn Sabbaths of Contemplation we must add the Workdays of Meditation on the interpretation of theory Facts of Nature and History by the Ideas; and on the fittest organs of Communication by the symbolic use of the Understanding which is the function of the *Imagination*.[82]

Tennemann had paid no attention to symbols in the religious life; but in their rightful place they are important, for they participate in the reality they announce.[83] Writing of Hugh, Coleridge notes,

I would not say, We learn to know God *by* the symbol; but we know
God *in* the Symbol. By the Symbol the Idea of God is rendered *cogi-*
table; but by the Idea the Symbol is rendered intelligible.

He adds just a little later: "Gerson's & [Richard of] St Victore's [*sic*]
Contemplation is in my System." It is a metaphoric Sabbath, and it
goes by the name of "Positive Reason."[84]

*

In May 1825, about the same time that Coleridge saw a parallel between
his thinking and that of the Victorines and Gerson, he makes a note
that helps us fathom what he has in mind. "Reason," for him, is "the
source of Ideas, ~~and~~ which Ideas in their conversion to the responsible *Will* become *Ultimate* ends—."[85] If we think of Schopenhauer
when we hear the word *will*, we should try not to be misled; but, if
we hear the word *Ideas*, we will find a commonality between the German and the Englishman. Both are Platonists. Ideas for Coleridge, as
for Schopenhauer, are not regulative, as they are for Kant, but constitutive, as they are for Plato.[86] Indeed, Ideas are irreducible to the
human mind, and, as with a Middle Platonist such as Philo Judaeus
(b. 25), they abide in God as divine ideas. Coleridge goes a step further in a later notebook: "Reason *is* the Verbum Vivens, ens realissi-
mum, τὸ ὄντως ὤν—the Light, that lighteth every man—from whom
proceedeth the Spirit of Truth, Lumen a Luce lucificâ."[87] The sentence
looks both to philosophy and to scripture. Reason is, as Plato says in
the Greek expression quoted, "the beingly being" or "the really real."
It is also the Johannine Logos. If we look ahead to the *Opus Maximum*
(dictated in 1819–25), we find another gloss on *Ideas* that extends the
biblical view: "The Ideas are necessarily immutable, inasmuch as they
are One with the (co-) Eternal Act, by which the absolute Will self-
realized begets its ~~i~~Idea as the other Self."[88] This emphasis on the primacy of the will might make us momentarily recall Schopenhauer once
again, but Coleridge's thought is trinitarian even if the divine persons
are not appropriated according to the usual biblical divine names or do
not follow the schema made familiar by Augustine: the Father is Will,
the Son is Reason, and the Holy Spirit presumably is Love.[89]

I can now return to the beautiful expression "Sabbaths of Contemplation," which echoes Schopenhauer's view of aesthetic experience.
It is not the only time Coleridge writes in these terms. In *The Friend*
(1809), he had pointed to "those brief Sabbaths of the soul, when the
activity and discursiveness of the Thoughts are suspended, and the

mind quietly eddies round, instead of flowing onward."[90] And, commenting on Manuel Lacunza's *The Coming of the Messiah* (1811), he evokes "the Idea of the True—a Jubilee Sabbath!"[91] What is contemplated, for Coleridge as for Schopenhauer (each in his own way), is the Idea, and we therefore have cause to speak of the Sabbath of the Idea, our rest in eternal archetypes. For Schopenhauer, it is a reprieve from the endless circuit of desire and frustration that is life in the world of representations. And, for Coleridge, it is that "which successively we may be evermore realizing but totally can never have realized," which resembles what St. Gregory of Nyssa calls ἐπέκτασις.[92] Just as for Schopenhauer the observer momentarily becomes one with the object of beauty, so for Coleridge the one who contemplates a Platonic Idea sees it as giving ultimate value to himself or herself and thus begins to realize it in himself or herself. It is not a reprieve but a transformation: one enters the lands of likeness. Also, however, commitment to the eternal Idea as it is embodied in oneself prompts one to action in the here and now. One begins to stretch into the kingdom.

Following Schelling, Coleridge distinguishes the primary imagination from the secondary imagination. It may be that the primary imagination is necessary to a poet, for without it no one would ever compose an oeuvre or be answerable to what Wallace Stevens calls a *Supreme Fiction*. Yet it is the secondary imagination that is mostly manifest to readers of poetry. One might doubt claims that a poet enjoys a pure moment of contemplation before beginning his or her poem: whether quick or slow, the act of composition seems to involve more than a degree of back-and-forth with what comes into being before one's eyes; it is a balance of beholding and acting, responding to feelings and ideas (not just Ideas) and to chance opportunities that suddenly appear by virtue of alliteration, assonance, consonance, enjambment, rhyme, meter, and so on. And we moderns will surely doubt whether there are Ideas in Plato's sense of them or even in the Middle Platonic or Neoplatonic sense of them as lodged in the divine mind.[93] Some poems bid contemplative readings, responses to eddies of meaning, the gliding of lines, suspensions, the balancing or unbalancing of parts and wholes, as well as much more. The reader may accept the call for a while or for the entire reading. He or she might even intuit something hidden or mysterious. Equally, he or she may decline or limit the call in favor of practicing a hermeneutic of suspicion. The latter possibility can never be erased in any reading experience. There are times in reading when we remember Henry James's Millicent Henning, when we itch to repeat what she says to Hyacinth Robinson: "I don't understand everything you say, but I understand everything you hide."[94]

Neither poet nor reader is usually a mystic, however, not someone engaged in positive Reason, not one of those "Fewest among the Few" for whom the Ideas are pure Light.[95] But he or she can be open to the manifestation of phenomena, including those in which being is easily overlooked. One of Coleridge's recent interpreters is entirely correct in admitting that, in everyday life, contemplation for the Sage of Highgate "pertains to noesis, the directedness towards ideas and their subsequent intuition."[96] Indeed, this noesis takes place within discourse and, in poetry, within the openness to feeling and thinking that occurs by way of figure and form. I would say that it occurs by way of looking into a *templum*, not a rectangle in the sky through which the gods might reveal the future by the flight of birds but a poem on a page before one through which pass ideas and feelings, some that are readily identified, and others that call for further meditation, before which we hold ourselves, anticipating something that will make us not more than human but perhaps a more reflective human. If this is not the Sabbath of the Idea, it is at least a Sabbath of contemplation aimed at things and charged with emotion. This noesis is announced in Coleridge but is explored in its full concrete realization by Edmund Husserl, to whom we now turn.

CHAPTER 3

Hermeneutic of Contemplation

The first philosopher whom Edmund Husserl read was Schopenhauer.[1] Later, as a *Privatdozent* at the University of Halle, he taught *The World as Will and Representation* in his 1892–93 seminar, and four years afterward he focused again in the classroom on the same thinker. His own writing at this time was centered on mathematics and logic and would lead to the publication of his first major work, the *Logical Investigations* (1900–1901). There, he refers to Schopenhauer just twice. The first time it is to illustrate that normative interest in real objects does not have to converge with practical disciplines. Schopenhauer rejects "all practical moralizing" by virtue of his commitment to "inborn character" yet develops an ethics along normative lines.[2] The second time the philosopher is mentioned it is to make the point that, even if one "would refuse to say with Schopenhauer that 'the world is my idea,' one would most likely be accustomed to speak as if apparent things were compounded out of sense-contents."[3] But the properties of something are manifest as analogues of sensations, Husserl stresses; they appear in consciousness solely as representations. All manner of experiences, inner and outer alike, can be reflected on, and Husserl broadly calls those experiences lodged in the ego *phenomena*. From here he goes on to offer an early description of his lifetime project: "*Phenomenology* is accordingly the theory of experiences in general, inclusive of all matters, whether real [*reellen*] or intentional, given in experiences, and evidently discoverable in them."[4] The empiricist theory of mental impressions or representations that resemble their real objects is thereby put out of play. The important question that arises now is how one might discover these real or intentional matters.

By way of answer, there follows an early account of "pure phenomenology," one that gives a bit more detail than we heard earlier in the rousing cry: "Back to the 'things themselves.'"[5] There, we were pointed away from preformed philosophical problems into which phenomena had been squeezed and invited "to render self-evident in fully-fledged intuitions," simple or categorial, what is given in words. Here, we are told more how this is to occur. The first part of the description is phrased negatively:

> Pure phenomenology is accordingly the theory of the essences of "pure phenomena," the phenomena of a "pure consciousness" or of a "pure ego": it does not build on the ground, given by transcendent apperception, of physical and animal, and so of psycho-physical nature, it makes no empirical assertions, it profounds no judgements which relate to object transcending consciousness: it establishes no truths concerning natural realities, whether physical or psychic— no psychological truths, therefore, in the historical sense—and borrows no such truths as assumed premises.

Phenomenology completely excludes psychology as a natural science from the analysis of logical operations. For logical procedures do not rest on psychological states. Yet Husserl has no impetus thereby to reject transcendental or phenomenological psychology, as begins to become clear in the second, affirmative part of the account:

> It rather takes all apperceptions and judgmental assertions which point beyond what is given in adequate, purely immanent intuition, which point beyond the pure stream of consciousness, and treats them purely as the experiences they are in themselves: it subjects them to a purely immanent, purely descriptive examination into essence.[6]

One might well see here Husserl continuing the tradition of transcendental idealism inaugurated by Kant (who coined the word *apperception*, which for Husserl is the apprehension of more than is directly perceived) and explored in his own way by Schopenhauer, among others. It is far from being the whole story about Husserl, however, for he does not inherit from Kant the overarching conception of philosophy as critique. His metaphilosophy is quite different and, if anything, resonates distantly with Schopenhauer's aesthetics. Nor does Husserl straightforwardly identify his project with idealism in any of its historical forms, even though his language at times makes it seem that he does. Let us follow these thoughts.

There is a twofold affinity between Husserl and Schopenhauer.

The first consists in the Platonism that they apparently share. As we have seen, Schopenhauer is committed to the Platonic εἶδος or ἰδέα, which he rethinks along voluntarist lines, and the phenomenologist resembles him to the extent that, especially from the period beginning with the first volume of *Ideas* (1913), he wishes to preserve the sense of εἶδος as a universal form of things, in other words, as an essence.[7] Husserl adopts the Greek word but uses it in his own way; for him, εἶδος names the laws we can discern in a phenomenon's particular way of appearing, its "region of being." It is distinct from *Wesen*, as used by the German Idealists to denote either an individualizing property or something's "whatness." (Also, it should be pointed out that he uses the word εἶδος in preference to ἰδέα, in order to distinguish it from Kant's *Idee von reiner Vernunft*.)[8] No doubt Husserl grants a far greater extension to essences than we find in Plato: everything has an εἶδος, no matter how broad its scope and whether or not it exists.[9] For intentionality, the directedness of our mental states, can be fulfilled or empty; it can gain self-evidence in the presence of its object, or it can have little or none of the same. There is a further difference with Plato, one that was not widely recognized at the time the *Logical Investigations* appeared.[10] Husserl rejects the Greek philosopher's realism as regards universals. Following Herman Lotze (1817–81), he takes the Platonic ideas to be ideal unities, not realizations of universals that are external to thought and independent of it.[11] Finally, where Schopenhauer conceived the Ideas to be levels of objectification of the will, ranging from the inanimate to the human, Husserl proposes a hierarchy of essences that stretches from the specific to the general, from the material to the mental, from the inexact to the exact: the notion of region of being that I have already mentioned and to which I shall return.

The second affinity between the two German thinkers is that Husserl's metaphilosophy recalls aspects of Schopenhauer's aesthetics. As we have seen, Schopenhauer advocates (with caveats) a contemplative stance toward the beautiful and the sublime. One gazes at a tree and loses oneself momentarily in the aesthetic experience, and this gives one a reprieve from the endless cycle of desire and frustration; it also grants one a brief period of intellectual pleasure. In the main, one might say that Husserl conceives philosophy by way of contemplation or reflection (*Besinnung, Reflexion*).[12] Three reservations should be registered right away. First, the contemplation at issue here is entirely neutral, there being no question of love, emotion, or ascription of value, on either side, though modalizations from assumption to questioning to affirmation (or some quite other sequence) will doubtless occur.[13] Second, the contemplation is immanent, not transcendent, willed and not Graced.[14] Third, a contemplation of a tree for Husserl not only would involve the one perception of it in which one might lose oneself but also would retain earlier perceptions of it. Philosophical contemplation is nuanced, then, by consciousness of my intentional acts. One finds oneself as much as one loses oneself.[15]

In speaking of metaphilosophy, one must always tread with care. In the most straightforward sense, metaphilosophy is no more than the philosophy of philosophy, the discipline examining itself as a field of interest much as it does art or history or science. Even if it is figured as "above" or, preferably, "beyond" philosophy as usually practiced—a meditation on the area's assumptions, methods, and aims—it will still be judged as philosophical through and through. The same is true if one takes it to be a final philosophy and, hence, an examination of everything assumed and achieved in all branches of learning. Only if one takes *beyond* to signal a point of observation that philosophy itself cannot reach is metaphilosophy something else: a dialectic, an encyclopedia, a history, a religion, and so on.[16] Husserl adopts a third position, thinking of philosophy as a sort of θεωρία that can be undertaken only from the very bounds of the world. Nonetheless, it is highly doubtful whether strong philosophers, including Husserl, restrict themselves to any one metaphilosophical position, whether that be a putative answer to the question, What is philosophy? or a rationale for doing philosophy or an explanation of how it might be accomplished.[17] Nor is metaphilosophy always pursued evenly; one might attempt to reflect on the nature, tasks, and methods of one's epistemology but not of one's metaphysics, for instance, although, if one so acts, one will surely also have an implicit meta-metaphysics partly in place.

Like many others before him, including Kant and Fichte, Husserl conceives philosophy to have a variety of tasks, both technical and popular, including the laying down of foundations for rigorous science and the renewal of European thought after the First World War.[18] While Kant was a precursor in some respects, especially in his stress on intuition as what gives us knowledge, Husserl does not continue the hunt for unshakable conditions for epistemic judgments and for the trimming of metaphysics accordingly.[19] Indeed, Kant becomes fully readable, Husserl thinks, only through the lens of phenomenology.[20] Nor does he figure philosophy as analysis, even though he has a very keen eye for distinctions. In no way does he see philosophy as a struggle (Lev Shestov), a pragmatics (C. S. Peirce), a worldview (Wilhelm Dilthey), a therapy (the later Wittgenstein), a science (Quine), a means of social emancipation (Theodor Adorno), or an endorsement of irreducible pluralism (Richard McKeon). Although he attends to the sedimentation of experiences and launches a "regressive inquiry" (*Rückfrage*) into them, he would not have endorsed either *Destruktion* (Heidegger) or deconstruction (Derrida) as the aim of philosophy. Phenomenology, for him, is a descriptive enterprise, that is, a philosophy without construction or deduction. He had no time for speculative excess in metaphysics and would have found Schopenhauer's doctrine of the noumenal realm as likely coordinate with the will as regrettable. But he had a metaphysics of his own to pursue.[21]

Philosophy, for Husserl, is reflective in the sense that consciousness can always take itself as an object. The formulation is susceptible to two interpretations, and it is only in following the second of these that we begin to grasp what philosophy is for Husserl.[22] The first way of understanding reflection occurs when one is living naively within the "general thesis," namely, that the world around one is constituted exactly as it appears without reference to consciousness. Quietly supporting this thesis is a particular mind-set, the "natural attitude" (*natürliche Einstellung*), in which we respond to the world as completely pregiven and, as Schopenhauer would say, answerable to the principle of sufficient reason.[23] Within the natural framework one can undoubtedly reflect on one's experiences; one does so with what Kant calls the "I that intuits itself."[24] We can inspect this ego, as we all do from time to time, by ourselves or with the help of others and try to become clearer about our motivations and desires, our emotional investments and overinvestments in other people, our compulsions, and our psychological defenses. We will do so only with reference to temporal profiles since consciousness has no spatial ones, which is one reason why we go to it when in search of certitude, as Husserl so often is. It is this ego in which a therapist or an analyst is interested, as are, in quite distinct ways, one's confessor and one's family and friends. One might engage in criticism in this reflective state, even philosophical criticism, but for Husserl the philosopher should always have another object in view.

For Husserl, philosophy begins with questioning the general thesis and thereby troubling one's blithe acceptance of the natural attitude. Such questioning does not commence in the normal course of events, however; one needs to be prompted to start it. Husserl calls this spur ἐποχή, the Greek word for "suspension of judgment," and it can assume many forms, which are not restricted to those that appeal to Husserl's own ways of thinking as a mathematician and a logician. Put concisely, it stimulates a change from seeing the world as pregiven to regarding it as given.[25] In order for this to happen, the world as posited by the general thesis must be set in brackets or suspended altogether, Husserl says. This is dissimilar from abstaining from judgment about something *in* the world. For when one suspends the world—all one's acts, all one's experiences, including other people, animals, and their acts—one performs *reduction*. Husserl takes the word in its full Latin sense to mean "leading back," by which he wishes to convey reverting to the very margin of the world one has been naively inhabiting.[26] It is not a matter of leaping over one's shadow, or of "unhumanizing" oneself, only a question of excluding oneself as a participant in worldly acts and becoming a neutral observer of those same acts.[27] One begins to grasp that how one directs oneself at something is correlated with how the phenomenon manifests itself. In terms established in the previous chapter, one engages in κένωσις of a sort in order to benefit from ἐπέκτασις of a philosophical kind.

Reduction can occur in all sorts of ways, have disparate strengths, point in various directions, and pose distinct problems for the person attempting it. Husserl himself explored several paths of reduction, most notably the Cartesian and the ontological, although he became dissatisfied with the celerity of the former: it never quite delineated consciousness as a field of activity.[28] In conversation with Dorion Cairns and Eugen Fink in November 1931, he observed that a conversion of the gaze can happen simply by noting that the world, which we are told exists in itself, always appears to one as experiences that apply to one's own subjectivity.[29] It is a concise formulation of what prompts the ontological path of reduction, one that is regressive in that the passage one undertakes is from transcendent being to phenomenon or, more precisely, from noema to noesis. The same path can be broached by shifting from asking our habitual questions that are sponsored by the principle of sufficient reason, the "Where, When, Why and Wherefore of things," as Schopenhauer puts it. Instead, one would ask, How? in the spirit of not, How does it work? but, How does it appear? The major point at issue is that, when led back to a position from which one can question the general thesis, one becomes what Husserl will eventually call a "disinterested spectator" (*uninteressierte Zuschauer*).[30] Where Kant thought that one must be disinterested in order to make an aesthetic judgment about a natural scene or an artwork, Husserl maintains that one must cultivate that state so as to contemplate the world and its people, regardless of beauty or sublimity.

Phenomenology, then, is not a part of the natural course of life. Phenomena disclose themselves only when one is no longer captive to the natural attitude.[31] And one does not begin phenomenology merely by changing mental frameworks, for there are quite a few of them, some nearer to the outlook of phenomenological openness and others further from it. If one engages in mathematics, chemistry, or physics, for example, one quickly and seamlessly adopts the "theoretical attitude." If one takes a class in robotics or prosthetic technology, one will find oneself taking on the "naturalistic attitude," which overlays the natural mind-set and makes it all the more rigid, perhaps inviting one to adopt "the view from nowhere."[32] If one takes an interest in the beauty of a tree outside the window, one will pass to the "aesthetic attitude." The affective, axiological, practical, and willing outlooks speak for themselves.[33] And, if one begins to think religiously, Husserl surmises, one will slip into the "religious-mythical attitude." When reading the adjective *mythical* here, we should not think of how Rudolf Bultmann (1884–1976) was to use the word in the early 1940s and thereafter. For Bultmann, myth is incompatible with the scientific worldview we all unquestioningly follow, with narrower or broader borders. More importantly, it occludes the κήρυγμα or proclamation of the gospel and hence must be identified and sheared away to let the proclamation be heard. Husserl uses *myth* in a more affirmative manner in order to pick out those narratives that account for the communities and traditions in which we live: their origins and what develops from them.[34] It is one of the signs of Husserl's interest in generative phenomenology.[35]

Each of these attitudes must be willed, at least tacitly, although ingrained habit often occludes the resolve that must initiate and sustain them. One might also notice oneself effortlessly sliding into the personalistic mentality, as in one's usual relations with other people, which Husserl will figure in his late work as part of the *Lebenswelt* or "life world." For example, I shake hands with a friend I meet downtown and chat about the weather. Even were I to be an eliminative materialist, I would respond to this person not as another cognitive unit but as a friend. And, if I were an empiricist, I would not concern myself with whether folk psychology is mistaken in its commonsensical relation to mental acts for the period in which we converse. I respond to my friend only as another person, and for a while the natural framework has less of a hold over me. It is possible to change outlooks often in certain circumstances and do so without preparation or awareness.[36] If I am reading a poem I love, I am momentarily caught up in it, but, if I put down the book and reflect on what I have been reading, I immediately pass from one stance to another: I am no longer living in the enjoyment of the poem, in the affective mind-set, but in the theoretical framework, even though I may still be experiencing pleasure from what I have read (and indeed compounding the pleasure).[37] In quite other circumstances one might require mental exercises, including prayer, to make one or another shift. Of particular interest to Husserl is what he calls the *phenomenological attitude*, which one reaches by reduction, in the process undergoing what Fink memorably describes as "the awful tremor" of realizing that what was once taken as absolute is only one way of inhabiting the world and perhaps not the best one in all circumstances.[38]

Only if one gains this particular frame of mind can one discern the correlations between consciousness and the world. Unlike with the other frameworks, achieving the phenomenological slant involves a total change of mind-set, as Husserl observed from the first volume of *Ideas* until his last writings.[39] Like Christian μετάνοια (change of mind), it also presumes a firm resolve to remain in it unless one is content to be a philosopher only for an hour, though doubtless there are backsliders in phenomenology as well as in Christianity.[40] One can begin to contemplate how the world is given in a flow of representations that appear not in the empirical ego but in another aspect of the ego, which Husserl (following Kant but giving the word a new twist) calls *transcendental*. Kant wrenches *transcendental* from its medieval context so that for him it denotes the subjective conditions of experience. Husserl uses it to specify the universal structures of experience, which are discovered only in and through the reduction. Other main differences between the two philosophers here are that, for Husserl, the ego is not atemporal and the key philosophical question is not how things (and indeed the world) are known but how they are given. "The point is not to secure objectivity but to understand it," as Husserl says in *The Crisis of European Sciences*.[41] In other words, for Husserl, the ego is temporal, and its experiences are to be described by way of static, genetic, and generative analyses.

To attain the phenomenological attitude is an achievement, as Husserl sees it; it opens up an entirely new field of being, the sphere of "transcendental experience."[42] It is easy to be mystified by this expression, especially if one approaches it from having just read Kant. To him, it would have been a contradiction in terms; we cannot experience the transcendental at all. Husserl himself can be overly fussy in his many delineations of the procedure, all undertaken, it must be said, in the interest of achieving high levels of clarity and rigor. And he can be overly dramatic in his presentation of the reduction. Even one of his most devoted students, Roman Ingarden (1893–1970), thought that phenomenological reduction leads only to a "fairy world."[43] Another of Husserl's students, Eugen Fink (1905–75), contended that the phenomenological reduction entangles one in circular reasoning since it presumes what it seeks to find.[44] Husserl's language can often be ambiguous or even misleading. For example, one must be careful not to think that in reduction one is passing from one ego to another, from the empirical *I* to its hidden transcendental counterpart. There are not two egos in the sense of two distinct entities; the transcendental ego is the set of conditions for disinterested examination of phenomena, and it is from these conditions that one sees that the natural attitude comes not from any misuse or restriction of the empirical ego but from the transcendental ego; it produces what it will transform.[45]

What is revealed in reduction, then, is not another world but the intelligible structures of apprehending the one in which we live — in all its natural, social, and cultural aspects — which includes the structures of things that we imagine. Reduction does not in any way disregard or diminish the accomplishments of anyone who works even unreflectively in the natural posture. It is no procedure for validating an earlier version of idealism, whether epistemic or metaphysical, subjective or absolute, which is not to say that it has no relations whatsoever with idealism. Rather, it allows us to contemplate the activities of the ego, which includes how certain human activities at an angle to everyday life in the natural attitude — doing philosophy or science, writing and reading poems — light up life as we actually live it. And once one has made the reduction one cannot fully return to a state of naïveté with respect to the apparent naturalness of fit between mind and world.[46] One thinks of Wordsworth's thought in the "Preface" to *The Recluse* (eventually appended to *The Excursion*): "how exquisitely, too— / ... / The external World is fitted to the Mind."[47] And then one thinks of Blake's truculent riposte: "You shall not bring me down to believe such fitting & fitted I know better & please your Lordship."[48] Or we might think of Plato's prisoner who escaped from the cave, how he can only imagine his former captivity.[49] But Husserl's point is that, after reduction, one lives with a new question: How does something appear? not What is this being?[50]

Husserl explains the intelligible structures by way of noetics, the study of thinking, which for him includes the examination of the relation of noesis (intellectual apprehension) and noema (what is thought). Just as Schopenhauer took a tree as his example for aesthetic experience, which is the contemplation of the Idea, so Husserl also chooses a tree, not once but twice, to illustrate the noema.[51] The first passage reads as follows:

> *The tree simply*, the thing in nature, is nothing less than this *perceived-tree as such* that belongs, as the sense of the perception, to the perception and does so inseparably. The tree itself can burn up, dissolve into its chemical elements, and so forth. The sense, however, — the sense of *this* perception, something necessarily inherent to its

essence—cannot burn up; it has no chemical elements, no forces, no real properties.

The noema is not an essence, then, but a correlate of consciousness. The second passage occurs only a few pages later:

> In one, unified consciousness we observe this tree here, first standing still where it is, then appearing to be moved by the wind. All the while, it affords itself in quite different manners of appearance as we change our spatial position toward it, stepping toward the window or merely altering the position of our head or eyes, first relaxing our focus, then sharpening its turn, and so forth, while continuing to observe it. In this way, the unity of *one* perception can contain in itself a great variety of modifications. As observers in the natural attitude, we ascribe this manifold one time to the actual object as changes *in it*, another time to a real and actual relation to our real, psychophysical subjectivity, and ultimately to this subjectivity itself. What matters now, however, is describing what remains of this as a phenomenological residuum, if we reduce it to "pure immanence," *and what should count thereby as a really obtaining, integral part of the pure experience,* and what should not. And that means making perfectly clear here that, on the one hand, the "perceived-tree as such" or the full noema (that remains untouched by the suspension of the actuality of the tree itself and the entire world) is part of the essence of the perceptual experience in itself but that, on the other hand, this *noema* with its "tree" in quotation marks *is not contained in the perception as really inhering in it any more than the actual tree is* [*ebenfowenig in der Wahrnehmung reell enthalten ift, wie der Baum der Wirklichkeit*].[52]

Of the many tangled threads in this text, I draw out just two.[53] First, the philosopher—the one who lives within phenomenological reduction—can contemplate the noetic-noematic correlation, namely, how our thinking relates to what is thought. Second, the one gazing on the tree does not lose himself or herself in a Platonic Idea but apprehends the noema—that is, the tree—exactly as perceived (or, if the example were varied, as imagined or remembered and so on). The noematic structure of the tree is in one's subjectivity but as *irreal*, within the noetic act but not an inherent ingredient of it.

This intelligibility—this correlation between our intentional acts and phenomena that disclose themselves—can be found in distinct ways. I have already mentioned one. Another is by way of the theoretical perspective, for to have adopted this mental framework is already to have departed slightly from the natural attitude. Advanced math and theoretical physics often lead one a fair way from common sense, and, even when starting to read philosophy or theology, one sees the world as a little stranger than it was before. One can insouciantly slide from the theoretical attitude to the phenomenological attitude. Put otherwise, it is possible to shift from θεωρία as a scholarly mind-set to seeing phenomena, which calls forth contemplation long before it settles into theory. With the conversion of the gaze there comes θαύμα, wonder.

*

I will say something in a moment of another way in which one can approach the phenomenological attitude. Before that could have much value, however, we need to be clear whether the statement of this mind-set adheres in any rigorous way to idealism. For Husserl calls his project *transcendental-phenomenological idealism*, and the description has encouraged many of his readers to set it in the lineage of Kant and Fichte, in particular.[54] The debate has clouded what is most important in Husserl—how phenomena appear—by investing too heavily in the priority of the real or the ideal. My sense, rather, is that, even before the first book of *Ideas* (1913), phenomenology is somewhat more hermeneutical than has been acknowledged and that it does not need to be transformed into a hermeneutic by contesting its idealism, as Martin Heidegger, Hans-Georg Gadamer, and Paul Ricoeur assure us it does, in order to do its job properly.[55] No doubt idealist philosophies themselves have hermeneutical moments, but my concern is not to defend an idealist hermeneutic. Nor do I wish to contend that Husserl is as thoroughgoing in his thinking of the subject as hermeneutical as Heidegger is in his treatment of *Dasein*'s ontological structure.[56] My point is that classical phenomenology provides us with sufficient means to clarify and complement the hermeneutic of contemplation that we have already started to trace in Schopenhauer and Coleridge. What Heidegger, Gadamer, and Ricoeur do in their own projects is immensely valuable but beyond my purview here.

For his part, Husserl already affirms the irreducibility of the "'as what' of interpretation" (*des "als was" der Auffassung*) in the *Logical Investigations*, which is considerably before any charges of idealism were directed against his enterprise.[57] Interpretation, whether *Auffassung* or *Deutung*, has only a little room in which to move here, for instance, in grasping the manner in which intentionality animates sensations.

This is a long way from saying that X (sensations) can be rendered as Y (objectivity), and throughout *interpretation* ultimately refers for Husserl to understanding. His interest is in ontology, not method or technique, despite his overgrooming of procedures in the *Nachlass*.[58] His commitment to doing phenomenology without presuppositions (*Voraussetzunglosigkeit*) is confined to not accepting any assumptions from elsewhere, especially empirical psychology; only what is directly given in intuition will count.[59] The degree to which this action is mediated by one or another natural language will enter the discussion in a moment. For now, suffice it to say that, for the later Husserl, there are at least three moments that engage interpretation, more broadly understood than animation of sensation. First, one's cognitive acts are always rooted in secondary passivity—we are always and already part of a community or a tradition that shapes us—even though one can in principle neutralize many of its effects in pursuing ἐποχή and reduction. Second, when one apprehends a phenomenon, one does so by directly taking the subject and its predicates together: Husserl always points us to articulated wholes and elaborates an account of this process with his formal ontology. Third, all perceptions involve apperception, that is, reference to more than one is directly perceiving at any one time.

To these three quite formal hermeneutical moments can be added one or two others from elsewhere in Husserl's philosophy. To begin with, one should note that in each perception there are retentions and protentions of what is intuited, and these point us to acts of memory, on the one hand, and acts of anticipation, on the other. Remembering is always a part of understanding, as is anticipation, which we experience as an excess that comes with any intentional act. Imagining is freer than either, and it richly contributes to understanding of phenomena, simple or categorial, as any strong poem shows. Second, it worth thinking of material ontologies, which indicate how being is given in any one region. To extend Husserl slightly: in math beings appear weak in intuition; in figural art they appear by way of resemblance; in literature they appear without their being; and so on.[60] We can almost see a parallel between the levels of contemplation that absorbed Richard of St. Victor and the regional ontologies delineated by Husserl. Richard's levels elicit the moral and spiritual ascent to God; Husserl's ontologies, with different modalities of reason, encourage human self-responsibility. Richard's levels rise all the way to God as triune, while Husserl's ontologies go no higher than the highest generic unities of nature, consciousness, and culture. Both writers are concerned with answering the how question, although only Husserl poses it with transcendental awareness.

To a limited extent, we can think of some of the attitudes as very broad construals of the pregiven world that are finally answerable to the transcendental ego. Husserl is plain to the point of being inordinate when he says that the natural framework is a *mis*interpretation of the world.[61] Accordingly, the phenomenological stance is an overcoming of a misinterpretation, not a reinterpretation. Yet certain of the attitudes give those who inhabit them a particular frame of mind when dealing with worldly tasks. These postures are adopted to meet certain ends, and accordingly they must be individually elected. In some circumstances a person changes readily from one to the other, but these postures all apply to the one world in which we all live. (They are not like worldviews, then, and do not imply incommensurability or relativism.)[62] At times, one attitude overlays another. As we shall see in later chapters, A. R. Ammons writes much of *Sphere* (1974) with an aesthetic attitude set over a scientific attitude, which itself presumes a naturalistic attitude. And he adopts the personalistic outlook from time to time. Achieving the phenomenological position is not a matter of gaining of an interpretation of the world, however. For, if one releases oneself from the pregiven world so that, with patience, one can see phenomena exactly as they are given, one also detaches oneself from interpretation.[63] One might almost say that interpretation is lost in order that there may be understanding: the ability to continue with some assurance along the path one has started. In the phenomenological attitude, one is also disengaged from one's own hermeneutical investments in life, although of course they remain to be acted on or adjusted.

Is phenomenology committed to one or another version of idealism? To begin with, Husserl does not deny the existence of nature, and we have already seen that he distances himself from Platonic realism on the topic of universals.[64] Nor does he dispute the reality of things beyond current human experience or affirm that objects are mind dependent or even that our knowledge of them is shaped by mental acts. Rather, his claim is that some mental acts manifest the intellectual structure of phenomena. When he says, "Experience is the force which guarantees the existence of the world [*die Kraft, welche die Existenz der Welt verbürgt*]," he is responding to the old problem, unsettling for some philosophers, that we have no convincing *argument* for the existence of the world.[65] To be sure, he sides with Descartes in thinking that the ego can be known with certainty, although for him it is the ego in its transcendental mode that can be found. This is an ego in which, as he came to see, there is an irreducible intersubjective component, one that can be partly explicated through genetic and generative phenomenologies and that decenters the gaze.[66] Does this commit him to a foundationalism, one that is rooted in the gaze of the individual subject? Does the emphasis on transcendental subjectivity inevitably lead to monism, with intentional consciousness supplying a ground for all being?

Reading Husserl, one is sometimes inclined to answer both questions affirmatively. When he proposes *"nullifying the world of things"* in the first book of *Ideas*, it seems as though he is thereby securing the living presence of a sole transcendental subject, one in which intersubjective life has been occluded or sequestered.[67] A closer examination will show that it is no more than a hyperbole used to dramatic effect to illustrate the suspension of the general thesis. It is a thought experiment, not a dogmatic claim, and certainly not a restatement of a dualism between subject and object, a position that Husserl rejects in no uncertain terms. However, if consciousness is not the cause of reality, it is nonetheless true that sense relies absolutely on consciousness; and nothing is said about consciousness relying on anything else, even though Husserl acknowledges the transcendence of the world with respect to it.[68] Appeals to the body—both *Körper* (physical body) and *Leib* (lived body)—are made, attention is given to the body's role in the constitution of higher objectivities, and the lived body is held to be intertwined with consciousness as mediated by natural language.[69] But no reciprocal constitution of mind and body is proposed.[70] The absence of any thorough explanation of the relation of worldly transcendence and transcendental consciousness is what generates a constant charge of idealism in Husserl.

One might then look, with reason, to Husserl's prizing of ideal meanings, full intuitions, and the power of the gaze to see into phenomena. Thinking back to the passage from the *Logical Investigations* that I quoted at the start of this chapter, one cannot but be struck by the emphasis on purity ("pure phenomena," "pure consciousness," "pure ego," "purely as the experiences they are in themselves," "purely descriptive"). Does this emphasis prize the ideal over the empirical? In one way it does: *ideal* for Husserl means "a condition of possibility of objective knowledge in general," one that is not interpreted "in psychologistic fashion."[71] But this is not thereby to subscribe to idealism, and the import of the emphasis in the passage I have quoted is twofold. In some instances, *pure* means no more than "formal" (in the sense of not material), as in *pure phenomena* and *pure consciousness*.[72] In other instances, *pure* means that only intuitions are to be accepted, not anything that is theory laden: for example, "purely as the experiences they are in themselves." From the beginning of his mature work, Husserl clearly distinguishes between object (*Gegenstand*) and meaning (*Bedeutung*), and he takes meaning to correspond to an act of meaning, one with an intersubjective moment.[73] Only intentional existence matters for the human subject, and whether an object really exists or exists as it is received is beside the point in phenomenological analysis. Meaning, then, does not hinge at all on intuition (or even, at a fundamental level, on language), even though Husserl spends a good deal of time attending to signitive (and significative) acts that point to their objects.

There can be no doubt that Husserl grants priority to those mental acts, such as perceptions and memories, in which something is held to exist.[74] The range of such objectifying acts is therefore quite broad, but there are other acts I perform in which I do not perceive or recall any object, and Husserl also classes these as objectifying acts. I might read of someone (the blessed soul Hopkins "sees" flying above him, Stevens's plantation owner, Ammons's friend George, or Hill's "Clio," all of whom we shall encounter in later chapters), and I do not posit existence for any of them. I will have an intentional relation with each of these characters, however, if I read the poems in which they appear. Thus, I might find myself respecting—even honoring—the plantation owner by virtue of what Stevens tells me about how he has lived, and I might take pleasure in reading and rereading the lines about the home he made for himself on the imaginary island in the Caribbean. On reading about Clio mercilessly conducting history (taken in large part as the history of conflict), I might feel only a chill, a passing sensation that is merely lived through. The former nonposited act is based on a judgment I make; the latter feeling I have is only founded on a previous act. No doubt there is a Husserl who looks to ideality; it is the philosopher for whom consciousness depends on nothing else and for whom indicative signs (*Anzeichen*), which merely indicate associatively, need to be purified by philosophical means, reduced, as much as possible, to expression (*Ausdruck*), which is oriented to univocal meaning.[75] But there is also a Husserl who opens a way to contemplate being, including the characters and situations we imagine or read about in poems, and it is the second one who interests me here.[76]

*

Few philosophers have devoted as much attention to the imagination as Husserl has done, and few have appreciated it as much as he does.[77] If Kant holds dear the faculty of the productive imagination in the first version of the *Critique of Pure Reason*, Husserl goes a step further

when he makes the transcendental turn, observing (while flourishing the paradox) that *"'fiction' makes up the vital element of phenomenology, as it does of all eidetic sciences."*[78] Without imaginative variation,
one would not be able to see essences. (The thought is less arcane than
it might seem. When arranging fruit on a stand, for instance, I set too
few apples there first, then too many; only by varying the placing and
the number of the pieces of fruit can I see the εἶδος of the situation,
that the stand will hold only five articles of fruit no matter what they
are or how I position them.) Perception and imagination are nonetheless distinct sorts of rapports with the world. Not that they differ in all
ways, for Husserl points out that one can gain a fulfilled intuition by
the imagination and not only by perception: the difference is that the
former will have meaning but no reference.[79] Like Kant, however, Husserl has little to say about poetry and poems.

An exception occurs in a letter Husserl wrote to the poet Hugo
von Hofmannsthal (1874–1929), who had visited his distant relation
Malvine Husserl (née Steinschneider), the philosopher's wife, in Göt-
tingen in December 1906. Hofmannsthal presented the couple with an
advance copy of his *Kleine Dramen* (1907), which was more than dutifully read. The philosopher wrote an admiring letter to the author on
January 12, 1907. The date is significant, for it was about then he was
preparing to lecture for the first time on the reduction, and it is this
philosophical concern, not literary appreciation, that animates most of
his letter, from which I quote only a short passage:

> The *artist*, who "observes" the world in order to gain "knowledge"
> of nature and man for his own purposes, relates to it in a similar way
> as the phenomenologist. Thus: not as an observing natural scientist
> and psychologist, not as a practical observer of man, as if it were an
> issue of knowledge of man and nature. When he observes the world,
> it becomes a phenomenon for him, its existence is indifferent, just
> as it is to the philosopher (in the critique of reason). The difference
> is that the artist, unlike the philosopher, does not attempt to found
> the "meaning" of the world-phenomenon and grasp it in concepts,
> but appropriates it intuitively, in order to gather, out of its plenitude,
> materials for the creation of aesthetic forms.[80]

The poet proceeds phenomenologically to the extent that he or she
grasps phenomena, regardless of whether or not they actually exist.
Yet the philosopher is concerned also to ground the meaning of the
world as phenomenon, and this can properly be done only in a philosophy that does not itself rely on imported presuppositions.[81] Since

phenomenology takes only what is given, without recourse to previously elaborated theories, it aims to be a self-founding discipline, which is not the same thing as the laying down of incontrovertible first principles. Whatever interpretations occur in the grasping of phenomena do not stem from outside the gaze but leak into it from secondary passivity that has not been neutralized. Some philosophers might wish to live glassily in a perpetual noon, but for better or worse we live in a world in which shadows fall across us.

That Husserl did not fundamentally change his view of the aesthetic gaze after 1907 is clear from a conversation that Cairns reports having with him and Fink on December 23, 1931:

> Husserl spoke of the aesthetic contemplation of a landscape as involving a neutralization of the normal doxic or thetic comprehension of the landscape. It is not the phantom of the landscape but the "natural" objective landscape-aspect which is the aesthetic object. But the natural landscape is considered beautiful as phenomenon, not as existent object. In passing he noted that the appreciation of goodness was not so based on a neutral phenomenon-perception. When one says, "What a fruitful landscape!" one is expressing a value-appreciation which involves the positing or the quasi-positing (?) of the existence of the landscape.

When I gaze at a landscape in the aesthetic attitude, I do not see just its perceptual characteristics separated from its causal matrix (i.e., I do not see what Husserl calls a *phantom*). I see the natural landscape as a correlative to my intentional consciousness, but what is beautiful is the interpreted phenomenon, not the landscape as such. For landscapes are neither beautiful nor ugly in themselves; it is the intentional relationship with something that confers aesthetic value. So values are formed by correlation. To this we might add that the generative community — the tradition or traditions to which one belongs — contributes passively to this value. There was a time when the Alps were not sublime, as we well know. Unlike Kant, however, Husserl considers a common layer in aesthetic appreciation, one in which the utility or potential utility of what is viewed is acknowledged. To exclaim, "What a fruitful landscape!" can be said while nonetheless accepting that it is beautiful. Once again, one is not entirely lost in aesthetic experience, as Schopenhauer thinks. A problem therefore emerges:

> The aesthetic contemplation is an act executed while the contemplator is executing an unneutralized perception of the world in general.

He is aware of himself as standing in a certain place in the world, and this awareness is non-neutralized. But the landscape which he contemplates aesthetically is a continuation of his non-neutralized immediate environment and as such is itself non-neutralized. Thus we have, if we accept the above-given theory, one and the same landscape as at the same time neutralized and non-neutralized.[82]

Husserl's theory of art must expand to include a paradox, one that acknowledges appraisals of value that are made alongside disinterested aesthetic experience.

There is reason to doubt that phenomenology can be wholly self-founding, as Husserl wished it to be: secondary passivity emerges as soon as one admits intersubjective life, and, unless it considers such generative life, near or far, phenomenology would not be able to do justice to the richness of the world; it would retreat to solipsism, a position Husserl regarded as nonsense.[83] Once I have acquired natural language, even when I contemplate a phenomenon in complete silence and still my thoughts as much as possible, nonetheless I reflect on it in categories that have come to me from conversation and study. A language of pure expression might be the dream of a logician but not of anyone else. A poet's phenomenology is nonfoundational, for Husserl, and to explore it is not thereby to dismiss the philosopher altogether but to recognize claims on us other than those of absolute consciousness or the wrangles of realism and idealism.[84] One of those claims comes from something in a regional ontology, empirical writing, which gives us a clue to a quasi-transcendental structure that invites an endless and sometimes exuberant play of text and context.[85] There is no pressing need, however, to prize one region of being over all others, including those within nature and consciousness as well as culture, as a response to realizing that language mediates our intuitions. If I stand in the woods, the trees give their being to me sensuously; they also give it to me genetically, should I be attentive to them in the right way. If I remember walking in the woods, the trees give their being to me in memory, perhaps by way of recollections of following trails in different states or countries. However, if I recite to myself "Stopping by Woods on a Snowy Evening," Robert Frost's trees give themselves to me in language, as being without any of a tree's natural being: no oils to smell, no texture to touch.[86] I imaginatively add to what is given to me in the poem by reference to my prepredicative experience of the world. And, if I recall thinking of that poem as part of my memory of a walk in the woods last year while I am currently standing in the woods, I will be given woods in a richer manifold. Different situations call for distinct acts of understanding.

One does not need to have recourse to literary language to do justice to the thesis that language mediates our relations with the world. One does not even need to depart from Husserl. Although he seldom treats language as a theme, he was nonetheless alert to the power of language in reflections relating to his *Cartesian Meditations* that he made in the summer of 1931.[87] Considering the "home world" (*Heimwelt*), the place where those to whom I am near are born, live, and pass away and that for me embodies normality, he observes:

> *The home world of man,* which is the basis for the structure of the objective world for <him> or can become so for him in ever more meaningful forms with higher development, *is essentially determined by language.* [Die Heimwelt des Menschen, *die das Grundstück für Struktur der objektiven Welt für <ihn> is oder für ihn in höherer Entwicklung in immer bedeutasmen Formen warden kann,* ist grundwesentlich von der Sprache her bestimmt.][88]

One's intersubjective life is essentially related to a shared language that precedes one's birth and in which one participates for one's lifetime. This is not a philosophically purified language, in which expression has been prized over indication; it presumably includes, for anyone who has lived a long time in Freiburg im Breisgau, the High Alemannic dialect as well as its characteristic accents (in French as well as German), its speech rhythms, its idioms and slang, its expletives and exclamations, its tonalities, lexical stress, curious phrasings, and so on. Although "higher development" is significant, there is also much to be said for the earthiness of daily language that binds one to a place. Many manifestations of *home* come more from the sound of words than can appear as propositional content. The intersubjective reduction for which Husserl searched for many years perhaps leads us back to our lived body.[89]

Natural language relates to one's home world even when its sentences and paragraphs are only partly constituted, not displaying anything like the full possibilities of expressiveness (not *expression* in Husserl's narrower sense) that are possible at any one time for the person writing (and therefore constitut*ing*). Journalistic prose heard on the radio or read in a local newspaper discloses one's territory (or territories if one listens to news from elsewhere, perhaps in another language). Even Administrative English, with its toneless policy speak, concealed stipulated definitions of words, and deployment of double-speak, minimally announces one's institutional home in a college or university. (It might also whisper, "This is not your true home.") Quite different is poetry, especially when written in a more thoroughly constituted language, one that manifests itself to the reader as well as revealing phenomena in that same language; it manifests a community or communities, tradition or traditions, even if what is revealed is distant, is imagined, or belongs to another. If I read a poem by G. M. Hopkins (1844–89), I will hear *home* in several registers, partly because I was born near where he lived as a child and young man, and partly because we are both Catholic and therefore share a vision of life and death. If I read a poem by John Ashbery (1927–2017), I will also hear *home*, though in a less full way since I have lived in the United States for well over twenty years and am familiar with the poet's conversation and voice. If I read a poem by Yves Bonnefoy (1923–2016), I also hear *home*, but in a far more attenuated way: French is not my maternal language, and even French poems that move me and that I have known by heart for forty years are a little distant from those I can truly inhabit. I will not always have affirmative experiences, however. Alfred Lord Tennyson's *The Idylls of the King* (1859), with its fantasy of Arthur founding an authentic British kingdom in the late fifth century, proposes a sense of community I find belated and implausible; and I read it, if I must, with a weary sense of being led astray from the norms I expect to find. And there are always poems that will strike me as alien for one or another reason; some of them will shed their sense of difference over the years, while with others I must acknowledge the boundaries of my empathy or insist on my aesthetic values.

Language in poetry can be constituted, both actively and passively, to a greater or lesser extent and in a vast variety of ways. It is not a matter of appealing to an enshrined literary or poetic vocabulary, theme, or rhetorical stance. Rather, it is a question of language, articulated with respect to shape and sound, providing a range of possibilities of expression. Literary criticism has proved itself highly adept at isolating many of these possibilities, sometimes formally (by way of grammar, prosody, and rhetoric), and at other times historically or socially (by way of representations or relations). Put highly schematically, familiar groups include *allegoria, ductio,* and *inventio* (medieval criticism), apostrophe, periphrasis, and metabasis (neoclassical criticism), anaphora, antimetabole, and metaphor (Romantic criticism), ambiguity, irony, and paradox (New Criticism), aporia, discontinuity and mise en abyme (deconstructive criticism), and cultural production, social marginalization, and self-fashioning (New Historicism). Each group could be expanded, with formal possibilities being augmented by historical or social ones (and vice versa), and other sorts of groups (e.g., genres and modes) that would cut across the divisions just described could be given. Like other disciplines, phenomenology also contributes its own insights, some of which I have already introduced (e.g., attitudes, intentionality, regional ontologies). At any given time in history, literary criticism will look to one or another discipline while overlooking others. It wanders in the space between epistemic and ethical judgments.[90]

In the main, the more highly constituted the language, the more that is offered to contemplation—and not just neutrally. The materiality of language cannot be effectively reduced. If I read Stevens's "The Snow Man," I do not get far before I am prompted to pass from the world as being to the world as phenomenon.[91] To begin with, I am asked to consider not a snowman but a man made of snow: the natural attitude has been peeled away at a corner, as it were, by a simple space between two words. A snowman has a thetic characteristic, but a snow man does not. Something similar happens with Ammons's "Visit," though it might take a moment or two longer.[92] By the time I am pondering a man who attracts reflections and silences, however, I have departed from the natural position. The truth to which Ammons alerts us about the man cannot readily be accommodated in its terms. And, if I read Hill's "Annunciations" and reflect that the Word is back with a tanned look, the world is no longer quite how it is usually presented to me, neither the world of events and words nor the world of Christianity in which Jesus is the Word.[93] Even a poet such as Philip Larkin who hews tightly to the natural outlook, writing in the "plain style," lightly disturbs the general thesis: "Mr. Bleaney" (1955) stages in a tableau two layers of reflection on how consciousness relates to the dreary world of postwar England.[94] The poem is a report of Larkin's consciousness taking in the stratum of Mr. Bleaney's consciousness (as interpreted by his prospective landlady) and evaluating the projections of *world* with which it correlates. As Derrida says, the reduction "is perhaps the very condition (I do not say natural condition) of literature."[95] What he does not say is that reduction occurs in a great many ways, even more, perhaps, than Husserl countenanced.

Even Husserl, connoisseur of logically refined language, engages in reduction when he reads Hugo von Hofmannsthal's dramas. As he admits, the poet does not go as far as the philosopher: description satisfies the poet, as it were, and he or she has no desire to furnish complete phenomenological description. Or the description becomes more and more complete by the operations of *tout dire*, which will interest us in chapter 10. The transcendental never quite closes around a poem, not

least of all because what often attracts us in a poem is a voice, the utterance of another person, and the alterity of this voice resists reduction.
One is confronted with an enigma that will not reveal itself fully in an
essence.[96] What Husserl does not tell us, however, is that the reader of
poetry will always be faced with two levels at which to engage what is
before him or her. At the level of proposition, one is invited to contemplate a truth that is presented as registration, report, or opinion. At the
level of sentence, one is led to ponder the speaker's words, whatever
they may be and however they are articulated by syntax and with respect to genre and mode. And it often happens that there is a tension
between proposition and sentence: for the one sentence might contain
several propositions or there may be just the one proposition spread
over an entire stanza or poem.[97] Reading will therefore require passing
back and forth from one level to another, and highly constituted poems
will keep manifesting meanings beyond any single reading. Rereading
a poem over several years will reveal different layers of judgment about
it, including memories of each reading and past anticipations that may
or may not have come to fruition, each of which can become the subject of reflection, teaching me something about myself and those from
whom I have learned as well as the poem.

*

Schopenhauer, Coleridge, and Husserl all center their writing on the
word *idea*, although each has his own sense of it. In a way, each proposes the idea as the Sabbath of contemplation. For Schopenhauer,
one is freed momentarily from the cycle of desire and frustration;
for Coleridge, one is raised to the level where one can think of God;
and, for Husserl, one can begin to understand the essences of things.
All three follow a philosophical sense of *contemplation*, although only
Husserl makes explicit remarks to that effect. For him, God transcends
phenomenological inquiry.[98] He rightly assumes that the divine transcendence exceeds that of mundane things and makes the interesting
suggestion that, if God appears, it could be only in "the absolute stream
of consciousness."[99] Contemplation, then, must be of this world only.
Yet Husserl perhaps is a little too quick to remove God from the picture. One does not have to engage a supernatural attitude in order to
contemplate the deity. Although absolutely singular in having his existence and essence coincide perfectly, God also has attributes, including
Goodness, Justice, Power, Wisdom, and Truth, all of which are modes
of divine love and open to contemplation without ever being able
to be exhausted. From a Christian perspective, even an atheist who

contemplates any one of these rises unknowingly closer to God. When one engages in *lectio divina*, one passes, as we have seen, from *lectio* to *meditatio* to *oratio* and, from there, to *contemplatio*, and that final temporary suspension before God has been enabled by each of the preceding three levels. Contemplation of God can occur in and through nature and in and through the kingdom, elements that are not rendered as themes in the religious-mythical attitude.

A hermeneutic of contemplation can be philosophical or theological, depending on the one who beholds and what is beheld. If we look back to include Schopenhauer, Coleridge, and Husserl (and beyond them to Richard of St. Victor, among others), we can see several principles of the hermeneutic. The first is that, with caveats already noted, anything and everything can be contemplated, regardless of whether it even exists. An essence can be beheld in an act of understanding that might or might not be finite. Certainly, the understanding itself is imperfect. The second is that, as refined over these two past chapters, contemplation commends us to look *at* something, not *through* it to find its ground. In doing so, one may well "lose oneself," as Schopenhauer testifies; but, as Husserl points out, we will also find ourselves by way of becoming conscious of our intentional acts. There are various stances one can adopt, in varying degrees of volition, in order to contemplate in particular ways. One can expect to find, from time to time, the aesthetic, affective, axiological, naturalistic, theoretical, and phenomenological attitudes adopted in poems just as they are in life. When reading a poem, which is the focus of this book, one can accept an invitation to ponder the relation of parts and whole, the twofold stretching of anticipation and recollection, the play of text and context, the levels of proposition and sentence, and disparities between history and fiction. One can behold what is brought about in a correlation of consciousness and sense, and one can trace the modalizations of a poet as he or she writes a poem of some length (as well as one's own modalizations while reading it). And by genetic analysis one can uncover conventions and traditions in the noema of a text, traditions that are also apparent in generative analysis. Of course, one can also behold gaps in argument, perception, or evaluation; and at any point this can introduce suspicion, which I shall consider in chapter 5. Although any phenomenon, any poem, can be contemplated, it is more usual for only some poems to call one to respond in this manner. In the modern hermeneutic of contemplation, no poem loves us, although we might come to love it (but not if we remain good Kantians). Not all poems grant *dilatio mentis*. Some poems cultivate mystery, rightly or wrongly, and, if we find the latter to be the case, we surely will respond suspiciously. A mystification is not a mystery. Finally, contemplation is not always passive, at least not while one is reading a rich work, for, just as a work thinks, so too one thinks while reading. Nor does it exclude action. The quest for understanding, whether animated by faith or by reason, yields a deeper appreciation of what it is to be human, whether that be in the theaters of aesthetics, history, religion, science, or society.

CHAPTER 4

Contemplation
with Kestrel

In a vivid passage of *The Ark of Moses* in which he advances the claim that contemplation operates in many ways, Richard of St. Victor compares the soul's gaze on God to the movements of birds as they wheel in the sky. They rise and dip, moving from side to side, sometimes holding themselves for a long time in the air by rapidly vibrating their wings:

> You may see some now raise themselves to the heights, then again plunge deep down, and repeat the same manner of ascending and descending many times. You may see others now turn to the right, then again to the left and bend now in this direction, then again in another, they make little or almost no progress and again and again repeat with much perseverance the same alternations of their toing and froing. You may see others again that stretch themselves with the same swiftness and often do this same thing and continue and prolong the same charge forward and backwards in long and frequent repetition. One can see others, how they turn in a circle, and how suddenly or how often they repeat the same or similar circuits how a bit wider, now a bit narrower, always returning to the same point. One can see others, their wings quivering and often beating, how they hover for a long time in one and the same place and by their rapid movements they keep themselves as it were fixed and immobile [*et mobile se agitation loco quasi immobiliter figunt*], they do not at all retire long and strongly attached, as if by steadfastly accomplishing their work they precisely seem to cry out and say: *It is good for us to be here.*[1]

It is an arresting description and a beautiful one. And it is easy enough to imagine that Richard enjoyed watching birds whirling about in the sky. But three things strike the reader. The first is that we are not told what sorts of birds they are: they might be crows, falcons, red kites, starlings, or many another bird, but their particularity is less important to Richard than their movements. The second is that no mention is made of what the birds are presumably doing, namely, searching for small birds, mice, and insects: clearly, a metaphor is firmly in place, one that excludes as well as includes. The third is that it is a completely untraditional picture of contemplation.

In the Latin tradition, contemplation has several grounds, including Augustine's *De trinitate*, Gregory the Great's *Moralia in Job* (578–95), and the fourth chapter of *The Divine Names* of the Pseudo-Dionysius, composed no earlier than the late fifth century and translated into Latin as *De divinis nominibus* twice in the ninth century.[2] In *The Divine Names*, we are told that there are only three movements of the soul toward God: circular, straight, and spiral. The reasons are well worth a brief inspection:

> The soul too has movement. First it moves in a circle, that is, it turns within itself and away from what is outside and there is an inner concentration of its intellectual powers. A sort of fixed revolution causes it to return from the multiplicity of externals, to gather in upon itself and then, in this undispersed condition, to join those who are themselves in a powerful union. From there the revolution brings the soul to the Beautiful and the Good, which is beyond all things [ὑπὲρ πάντα τὰ ὄντα], is one and the same, and has neither beginning nor end. But whenever the soul receives, in accordance with its capacities, the enlightenment of divine knowledge and does so not by way of the mind nor in some mode arising out of its identity, but rather through discursive reasoning, in mixed and changeable activities, then it moves in a spiral fashion. And its movement is in a straight line when, instead of circling in upon its own intelligent unity (for this is the circular), it proceeds to the things around it, and is uplifted from external things, as from certain variegated and pluralized symbols, to the simple and united contemplations.[3]

This is Christian Platonism of a particularly ripe sort. Debate continues over the extent to which the adjective (*Christian*) permeates the noun (*Platonism*) and the force with which it does so. Certainly in this passage we can readily see an emphasis on how, having come from the One and become mired in the Many, the soul concentrates and simplifies itself as it seeks to return to the One, which, for the Pseudo-Dionysius, is above or beyond being (ὑπὲρ πάντα τὰ ὄντα) and therefore calls for apophasis. This apophatic or negative theology, as it is sometimes called, recognizes, as Hopkins himself does, that God is mysterious, abiding in one or another manner of hiddenness: "No answering voice comes from the skies."[4] Apophatic theology encourages the soul to conceive the deity spiritually, at first by the power of reason, then by allowing itself to be intuitively drawn in pure love to the triune God. The movement is vertical, and the influence of Proclus (412–85) can be felt, both as regards the relation of cause and effect, and with respect to hierarchical ordering of being from lower to higher orders: "Every thing caused, abides in, proceeds from, and returns, or is converted to, its cause."[5] So reads proposition 35 of the *Elements of Theology*.

Proclus's theology is metaphysics, the study of first principles, which for him is of God as *principium*. This is how Aquinas will phrase matters when he appeals to Gregory the Great in *Summa theologiae* 2a2ae q. 180 art. 4, as we saw in chapter 1. And, if the Pseudo-Dionysius's authority was sustained and empowered in its influence, it is partly because of the prestige of the School of St. Victor and of Aquinas, especially of the latter's *Summa theologiae*. Hugh of St. Victor produced a commentary on *The Celestial Hierarchy*, which allowed him to systematize elements of Augustine along with the spirituality of the Pseudo-Dionysius, especially about modes of sight, and this general influence was widespread throughout the abbey, perhaps most markedly in Gilbert de la Porrée (ca. 1085–1154) and Thomas Gallus (ca. 1200–1246).[6] Aquinas, himself absorbed by angelology, supported the Pseudo-Dionysius's delineation of just three movements of the soul in contemplation in *Summa theologiae* 2a2ae q. 180 art. 6, where he rejects Richard's "many different kinds of movement, based on a comparison with the birds of the air." In the *sed contra*, he recurs to "the authority of Dionysius," which derives from the latter's supposed status as the disciple of St. Paul and member of the Areopagus or Athenian judicial council. An appeal is further made in the *responsio* to Aristotle's views on the motion of bodies. The philosopher distinguishes three sorts of motion—change of quantity, change of quality, and change of place—and it is the last, he thinks, that is primary.[7] There is always motion, in a general sense, he says, and local movement, from place to place, tells us best what it is. Aquinas turns to Aristotle here because, for him, "the highest intellectual operations," such as contemplation, "are described by a comparison" with the sorts of motion (*ST*, 2a2ae q. 180 art. 6 resp.). His view converges with that of the Pseudo-Dionysius. Contemplation, like local movement, is therefore circular, straight, or spiral.

Everything Richard says in his description of the birds' flights, Aquinas contends, is "contained under the straight and spiral movements, for they all refer to the discursus of reason" (*ST*, 2a2ae q. 180 art. 6 ad 3); that is, it all falls within the scope of Aristotle's philosophical reflections. We have met in chapter 1 a similar reservation about Richard remaining at the level of *consideratio* rather than rising to *contemplatio*.[8] All that Richard says about the movements up and down, back and forth, and so on can be resolved in the following way:

> For if it is a movement from genus to species or from the whole to a part, it will be, as he explains, an upward or downward movement. If it is a movement from one opposite to another, it will be a movement to the right or left. If it is a movement from causes to effects, it will be a forward and backward movement. If it concerns a thing's surroundings, whether immediate or remote, it will be a circle.[9]

At issue is more than the superior economy of the Pseudo-Dionysius's theology of contemplation, let alone the prizing of dry theologizing over lyrical observation, for, as Aquinas notes in an objection about differences between human and angelic contemplation, there is a vertical hierarchy that is firmly in place: God, angels, humans, other creatures. Angels move in a straight line with respect to creation, we are told, because "superior angels enlighten lower angels through intermediate angels."[10] In practicing the virtues and receiving Grace and thus becoming able to behold God as *principium*, we move up that hierarchy, if only a little way in this life.

Now, Richard is also committed to a hierarchy of being, and we remember his stress on acquiring angelic wisdom in *The Ark of Moses*, but he is additionally heedful of nuances in individual human spiritual ascent, which he acknowledges in the details of rising and plunging, the movements to right and left, the hovering (while having to forge ahead in order even to stay where one is), speeding back and forth, and so on.[11] He prizes circular movement as well as vertical and spiral movements, as Aquinas acknowledges. For us, Richard says, "our enchanted reflection [*considerationis*] rests as if it were immobile in one and the same place, when the attention of the contemplative [*contemplantis*] readily dwells on the observation and wonder of the being or characteristic property of something, whatever it may be."[12] Notice that Richard speaks of *consideratio* and *contemplatio* almost in the one breath and that he stresses "the being or characteristic property of something, whatever it may be [*qualiscunque rei esse*]." One can behold anything at all in nature and can do so in order to "wonder" at its being, that is, not with an eye on passing from it as quickly as possible to the transcendent deity.

It is perhaps inevitable that the metaphor of contemplation as ascent to God leads one to associate the practice with birds and thus to imagine a Christian *templum*. It is one that gives auguries not about crop yields or the success of military campaigns but about how Christ appears in and through the relations of faith, hope, and love: as Creator, Judge, Savior, and so on. We can see one association of this metaphor in the *Commedia* where Dante calls the first angel that he sees in Purgatory *l'uccel divino* (the divine bird).[13] How pervasive the association of contemplation and birds is can be seen simply by reading St. Bernard of Clairvaux. He is not known for having had a deep appreciation of the natural world, yet he had no hesitation in figuring *consideratio* as bird flight. *Consideratio* is strengthened by virtue or by Grace, or it flees any scene of temptation. "In the first instance," Bernard says, "consideration is more powerful, in the second more free, in the third more pure: indeed, that flight is made with wings of purity and ardor." The original Latin is brisker: "In primo potentior, in secondo liberior, in tertio purior. Puritatis siquidem, & alacritatis pariter alis, sit ille volatus."[14] For all its spiritual depth, however, *consideratio* does not always end in the heights of *contemplatio*, which requires certainty, not seeking, as we shall see more fully in chapter 5.[15]

Natural images of contemplation are commonplace in the early church, even when the practice does not aim at anything natural. Tertullian (155–220) concludes *On Prayer* by reminding us: "The birds now arising are lifting themselves up to heaven and instead of hands are spreading out the cross of their wings, while saying something which may be supposed to be a prayer [*dicent aliquid quod oratio*]."[16] Their cries may sound like petition; they may sound like ecstasy. Either way, the image is memorable, especially the sight of the wings as a cross. Somewhat to the side of the tradition, Evagrius Ponticus (345–99) thinks of the bee, which often flies as high as, if not higher than, many birds. "A clever monk," he says, "imitates the bee; he plunders the flowers outside while inside he produces the honeycomb."[17] Sometimes the bee must fly high and far to reach the right flowers. The Pseudo-Dionysius remains with birds, and he does so in terms that any Roman would recognize and Aquinas would approve. He observes: "The eagle tells . . . of the contemplation which is freely, directly, and unswervingly turned in stout elevations of the optical powers toward those generously abundant rays of the divine substance."[18] The most robust images of the eagle, however, occur in Gregory the Great's *Moralia in Job*. The thinking there is taken by the latter half of Job 9:26: "Like an eagle hovering over its prey [*sicut aquila volans ad escam*]" (Vulg.). Gregory observes:

> It is the eagle's usual practice to eye the sun with unwavering stare, but when the need of food becomes insistent, he bends the stare of his eyes, with which he had glared at the rays of the sun, toward the focus of carrion; although he flies in heaven, yet for the sake of eating flesh he seeks the earth. In exactly the same way the ancient fathers, as far as human weakness permitted them, contemplated the light of the Creator with minds awake [*Creatoris lucem erecta mente contemplate sunt*]. Yet they foreknew that he would take flesh at the end of the world, so they bent their gaze to the earth as though turning away from the rays of the sun. As though they came from the highest to the lowest, they knew him as God above all things and as man within all things. From afar they saw him who would suffer and die for the human race, by which death they knew that they themselves would be refreshed and re-created for life. Just like the eagle, after contemplating the rays of the sun [*post contemplatos solis radios in cadauere escam quaerunt*], they sought food in a dead body.[19]

Gregory's words have deep roots in the world of the Roman *templum*, with the eagle, Jupiter's bird, giving the *auspicia*, yet those same words are profoundly Christian. As the eagle looks for dead flesh to nourish it, so too the prophets contemplated the coming of Christ, true God and true man, who would be crucified for the salvation of all and whose flesh and blood would be offered by a priest to God the Father on the altar.

It must be said that the hermeneutic that enables Gregory to interpret Job 9:26b in this manner needs a firm guiding hand, for, as he readily admits, the word *bird* can be taken in conflicting ways. "He even hides from the birds of the air [*abscondita est ab oculis omnium viventium volucres quoque caeli latet*]" (Job 28:21): the verse leads Gregory to associate birds with demons.[20] A reassuring look at the New Testament, however—specifically the parable of the mustard seed—allows him to see that "the birds of the sky nested" in the branches of the tree that sprung up from the tiny seed (Luke 13:8–19).[21] Hence *bird* also suggests contemplation. No doubt, in the exegesis of Job 9:26 the eagle is associated with contemplation, which he shifts from the sun to his prospective nourishment; and the prophets do the same thing, Gregory thinks, and each time they behold God in the posture of active anticipation ("mind awake").

The eagle is not the only bird associated with contemplation in the

Middle Ages. Much later, Hugh of Fouilloy (d. ca. 1172), an Augustin-ian friar, writes so much about the dove (*columba*) in the first eleven chapters of the *Aviarium* that the entire work was better known in the Middle Ages as the *De columba deargentata* or even as *De tribus colum-bis*. The dove is an *exemplum* for the choir monk, for it "flies in flocks, because it loves the community." Hugh continues:

> It does not live by predation, because it does not take from its neigh-bor. It collects the finer grains, that is, moral teachings. It does not feed on corpses, that is, carnal desires. It nests in the crevices of a rock, because it places hope in the Passion of Christ. <The dove> lives near flowing water, so that when it sees the shadows of the hawk it can more swiftly avoid its approach, because it studies Scrip-ture in order to avoid the deceit of the approaching Devil. It raises twin chicks, that is, the love of God and the love of neighbor. Who-ever, therefore, has these traits, let him put on the wings of contem-plation by which he may fly to heaven. [*Geminos nutrit pullos, id est, amorem Dei et amorem promixi. Qui has igitur naturas habet assumat sibi cointemplationis alas quibus ad caelum volet.*][22]

For Hugh as well as other authors of medieval bestiaries, right up to Renaissance volucraries, the dove was commonly paired with the hawk as cloistered monk with lay brother (*converso*).[23] The avian twosome goes back at least as far as Pliny the Elder (23–79).[24] The dove is often represented facing a tamed hawk, both standing on the one perch, that is, following the same monastic rule.

In its wild state, the hawk is allegorized unfavorably, as Satan, who comes from the cold north, set on attacking the Christian soul. The dove outwits the Tempter, however, for it "lives by flowing water, so that when it sees the shadow of the hawk [*accipitris umbra*] it can more swiftly avoid its approach, because it studies Scripture in order to avoid the deceit of the approaching Devil."[25] The same hawk can nonetheless overcome its association with the Evil One by seeking religious seclu-sion and being remade by the Holy Spirit. An allusion is made to Job 38:26: "Is it by your wisdom that the hawk soars, and spreads his wings toward the south?" (RSV). More than a passing reference is made to Gregory the Great's commentary on Job, for the whole discussion of hawks in the *Avarium* is taken from his *Moralia in Job*. There we read that a wild hawk will beat its wings in a warm south wind in order to loosen them and to encourage new growth.[26] The south, for Hugh, is the monastery or *claustrum*: "Safe and warm places are needed for tame hawks, where they might more easily grow feathers. Safe places

are enclosures [*claustra*] in which, when a wild hawk is placed there it
is kept confined in order to be made tame."[27]

*

I would like to place a poem by Gerard Manley Hopkins (1844–89)
in the space opened by the patristic and medieval traditions I have
just outlined and take into account their classical inheritances when
it seems right to do so. How inward Hopkins was with this tradition is
hard to specify at all narrowly. His training as a Jesuit was centered on
the writings of Francisco Suárez (1548–1617), an early modern scholastic, and the readings he heard while in refectory were drawn from the
Rules of the Society and spiritual texts in favor at the time (by Claude
Colombière and Frederick Faber, e.g.), rather than the fathers, any of
the Schoolmen, or the great Catholic contemplatives.[28] The history of
dogma was not a prime study in the English Jesuit theologate in the
Victorian era.[29] Nor was spiritual theology in its higher reaches, including contemplation: the Society of Jesus has always been oriented
to meditation. Nevertheless, Hopkins must have absorbed some of the
tradition, for he refers, especially in his devotional writings and sermons, to Athanasius, Augustine, Cassian, Clement of Alexandria, and
Chrysostom, among the writers of the early church, and Anselm of
Canterbury, Aquinas, Bonaventure, Lombard, and Scotus, among the
medieval writers.[30] Hopkins may well have known Newman's piece on
mental prayer, and he certainly thought long and hard about the relation of contemplation and love while on retreat.[31]

More narrowly, medieval metaphors for divine contemplation
were familiar to Victorian Catholics. As early as October 1865, Hopkins writes, "Let me be to Thee as the circling bird," although the lyric
converges on music rather than flight.[32] Also, after a period of characteristic Protestant recoil from ascetic practices, nicely embodied in
Tennyson's satiric "St. Simeon Stylites" (1842), a certain Victorian me-
dievalism becomes apparent in other early lyrics.[33] (And no student of
Greats at Oxford, even though it focused on philosophy, could avoid
learning a little about augurs.)[34] Of course, Hopkins refashions what
he has absorbed to his own ends, beginning with his choice of a falcon
rather than a hawk or an eagle, and continuing with his indifference
over the number and manner of movements of the soul with respect to
God.[35] The falcon appears far less often in bestiaries than do hawks or
eagles, mostly because it is not a biblical bird.[36] Nonetheless, throughout the medieval ages it was greatly prized as an emblem of nobility,
which well serves Hopkins's purposes in the poem.

The bird appears in Hopkins's sonnet "The Windhover," composed at St. Beuno's on May 30, 1877:

I caught this morning morning's minion, king-
 dom of daylight's dauphin, dapple-dawn-drawn Falcon, in his riding
 Of the rolling level underneath him steady air, and striding
High there, how he rung upon the rein of a wimpling wing
In his ecstasy! then off, off forth on swing,
 As a skate's heel sweeps smooth on a bow-bend: the hurl and gliding
 Rebuffed the big wind. My heart in hiding
Stirred for a bird,—the achieve of, the mastery of the thing!

Brute beauty and valour and act, oh, air, pride, plume, here
 Buckle! AND the fire that breaks from thee then, a billion
Times told lovelier, more dangerous, O my chevalier!

 No wonder of it: shéer plód makes plough down sillion
Shine, and blue-bleak embers, ah my dear,
 Fall, gall themselves, and gash gold-vermillion.[37]

The lyric has been the subject of a great many analyses, although, to be sure, it has not benefited from the sort of slow reading—or perhaps *tortoise-like reading* would be better—one finds Gregory attempting in his commentary on Job. It would be interesting to see how long a discussion the poem would justify, especially a reading that took the poem's genesis into account.[38]

My task is far more modest, for I wish merely to identify the motif of contemplation in the poem and to follow it for a while, being attentive to what might come from it.[39] The motif is divided, for contemplation is an act invisibly practiced in the poem as well as in the highly visual language of the sonnet. Hopkins himself writes (in 1873 or 1874): "Poetry is speech framed for contemplation of the mind by the way of hearing or . . . speech framed to be heard for its ^own^ sake and interest even over and above its interest of meaning."[40] No specific theological meaning is to be supposed here, but it is plain that for Hopkins both the intellectual and the material dimensions of language are in play in any contemplation of poetry or in poetry as contemplation. As he writes elsewhere: "[In contemplation] the mind is absorbed (as far as that may be), taken up by, dwells upon, enjoys, a single thought. . . . [I]t includes pleasures, supposed they, however turbid, do not require a transition to another term of another kind, for contemplation in its absoluteness is impossible unless in a trance."[41]

W. B. Yeats (1865–1939) says something related to this remark in an essay of 1900, although we need to keep in mind, here and throughout, that his metrical practice is markedly different from Hopkins's: "The purpose of rhythm, it has always seemed to me, is to prolong the moment of contemplation, the moment when we are both asleep and awake, which is the one moment of creation, by hushing us with an alluring monotony, while it holds us waking by variety, to keep us in that state of perhaps real trance, in which the mind liberated from the pressure of the will is unfolded in symbols."[42] Hopkins does not incline to monotony in his prosody, far from it; even so, one can be entranced by his sprung rhythms, his wordplay, and the music of his lines. The material dimension of language—its rhythm and its vocal play—can be as important to contemplation when reading poetry as its expressive dimension, which bears the meaning of the poem even when not presented by way of symbols.

Yet Hopkins has more than this in mind. He draws our care to poetry's ability "to carry the inscape of speech for the inscape's sake," which is something that will interest us as we go along, including what this odd word *inscape* and its cousin *instress* mean with respect to the poem.[43] Also, not said here by either poet, the indicative dimension of language, its capacity to motivate empirical associations, whether natural or conventional, can play a role in the ever-widening circle of what one beholds as object and how one does so.[44] If elements of a contemplative hermeneutic begin to emerge as I read the poem, they will differ from those elected by Gregory in responding to Job in part for reasons that Hopkins and Yeats have both suggested. But my first concern is reading the poem itself, which, as already noted, I take to involve contemplation as an affective act, not only as cognitive and linguistic, and in order to do so I must begin with what might seem to be a painfully slow approach to it in order to grasp the meanings of *inscape* and *instress*, Hopkins's coinages that orient his sense of contemplation.

*

Hopkins catches sight of a kestrel, a smaller sort of hawk common in Britain, perhaps alerted by its piercing call—its scientific name is *falco tinnunculus* from *tinnulus*, "shrill"—when taking prey back to the nest: voles, mice, larks, shrews, lapwings, thrushes, even slugs.[45] It is seen hunting again, silently hovering over the valley in the morning, and Hopkins allows his eyes to linger on it as it revolves in the air. As the title makes plain, he prizes the bird under one of its older regional names, *windhover*, which fits neatly into the Latin contemplative tradition in a way that its more archaic names and its modern name do not.[46] That such a tradition might be summoned is signaled in the liminal space between the title and the first line. There we read *"To Christ our Lord,"* and, while doing so, we note that the words are introduced by a colon in the title itself, which is an unusual practice for dedications in poems.[47] The colon inflects how we are to read the four words in italics. No doubt here the preposition *to* means "dedicated to." There is reason also to think of it signaling an approach to Christ: a direction that can and perhaps should be followed by Hopkins and that, in its own way, the poem beneath will describe, explain, or enact. Title and dedication, taken together, thus denote that the bird points to the second person of the Trinity. The kestrel would therefore exemplify one or more profiles of how one must be in order to be Christ's minion; it is an imaginative epiphany, not of the Son, but of a soul in bliss, which Hopkins aspires to be through his conversion to Catholicism and, indeed, his vocation as a Jesuit. Again, I recall, "Let me be to Thee as the circling bird," and add its traditional biblical support: "How can you say to me [*nephesh*: soul, life; ψυχῇ μου; *animae meae*], 'Flee like a bird to the mountains'" (Ps. 11:1 [RSV]). For Augustine, the question answers itself: the mountains are an image of Christ.[48]

"I caught" the poem begins, and any devoted reader of Hopkins will recall his memorable entry in his journal for February 24, 1873:

All the world is full of inscape: // and chance left ~~to~~ free to act falls into an order as well as purpose \\ looking out of my window *I caught it* in the random clods and broken heaps of snow made by the cast of a broom.[49]

And, just as likely, one will further remember the following entry from a year later, made for September 10, 1874:

The woods, thick and silvered by sunlight and shade, by the flat smooth banking of the tree-tops expressing the slope of the hill, came down to the green bed of the valley. Below at a little timber bridge I looked at some delicate flying shafted ashes—there was one especially of *single sonnet-like inscape*—between which the sun sent straight bright slenderish panes of silver sun~~light~~ beams down the slant towards the eye and standing above an unkept field ~~of~~ stagged with patchy yellow heads of ragwort.[50]

"I caught it," Hopkins tells his journal. He grasps what he calls *inscape*, which we might lightly gloss in preliminary fashion as a sort of εἶδος, a

distinctive inner pattern, divinely made, that something or a situation
or even a line of poetry shows to a diligent viewer. Two years earlier,
in his journal for July 19, 1872, he says: "At this time I had first begun to
get hold of the copy of Scotus on the *Sentences* in the Baddely Library
~~was~~ and was flush with a new stroke of enthusiasm. It may come to
nothing or it may be a mercy from God. But just then I took in any inscape of the sky or sea I thought of Scotus."[51]

These two sentences have led many readers to associate or even
identify inscape and *haecceitas* (this-ness), but, if one reads Scotus's revision of his Oxford lectures, the *Scriptum Oxoniense super Sententiis*
(1300), no easy thing, one finds few references to it and nothing at all
anywhere near the start of the commentary.[52] One finds, rather, talk of
a *formalitas* or *realitas* (or *intentio* or *ratio realis*).[53] Nevertheless, Hopkins does not give us any reason to think that he made such a study of
Scotus so that he became familiar with the whole commentary. (Besides, an interest in singularity is not confined to Scotus: think of John
Buridan [d. 1358] in his commentary on Aristotle's *De anima*, e.g.)[54]
Now, *haecceitas* marks the singularity of any human being; it is utterly
unable to be perceived by us. Only God "sees" what is radically unique
in anyone, his or her *haec*. Perhaps human beings will enjoy such perception in heaven, but certainly not before. On the other hand, *formalitas* or *realitas*, an intelligible feature of something, can be discerned if
one is sufficiently patient and alert.[55] As the alternative word suggests,
these forms are real, existing outside the consciousness of an observer,
in things that are being perceived, and they are unable to be separated
from that of which they are properties. Yet they are able to produce
quite different concepts of whatever it is to which they belong. Such
concepts do not tell us about the whole of what is intelligible in a phenomenon. Nor need they ever be formed. But the possibility of their
being formed is objective and cannot be annulled. More finely, a *formalitas* or *realitas* is identical with the essence of the thing in question but
is formally distinct from it.

In fragment 8 of his poem *On Nature* (Περὶ φύσεως), Parmenides
(b. 515 BCE) noted that Being has various properties ("ungener-
ated and imperishable, whole, unique, immovable, and complete").[56]
He was the first to do so. Only in the thirteenth century, however—
perhaps as early as Roland of Cremona (1178–1259)—was a distinction
drawn between Being and the transcendentals, namely, whatever by
virtue of its generality cannot be contained in any genus as detailed in
Aristotle's *Categories*. The transcendentals are transcategorical. We can
see the point of the formal distinction when we reflect on the relation
of *ens* with *res, unum, bonum, aliquid, verum,* and other appeals to the

transcendental such as is determined in logic (transgeneric terms, e.g.) and in other parts of philosophy (*pulchrum* in aesthetics, e.g.).[57] Each of these properties is ontologically one with Being, yet each is formally distinct from it. This sort of distinction was primarily used—notably by Scotus—to clarify the relations of the divine persons to the divine essence and various predications of perfection made of the deity, answerable to his infinity (e.g., truth, goodness, justice, holiness). Furthermore, the study of the transcendentals was itself conceived as θεωρία or *naturalis contemplatione*.[58] But the transcendentals are not limited to trinitarian theology. When I view a leaf, say, as Hopkins does in his journal, I can see it as one, as good, as beautiful, and so on.[59] These distinctions are not simply logical; they are grounded in reality outside my consciousness (for other people can see them in the same ways). Nor are the distinctions real since I cannot actually separate the unity of the leaf from its Being, its goodness from its Being, and so on. There are distinct formalities (*formalitates*) in play.

My shift of attitude from the one formality to another can occur in an instant; but it is not merely subjective, nor does it change the leaf in any way. It is entirely consistent with realism. The leaf itself allows me to see it in conceptually distinct ways. In the same manner, I am entitled to see the leaf as having both universal and particular characteristics: it is a leaf, sharing the features of all other leaves, but it is this leaf in particular with a curved edge and a small white blotch on its midrib. It has a particular "pitch." Hopkins seems to have extended his understanding of inscape by acquainting himself with Scotus, and he doubtless went further than the thirteenth-century doctrine of the transcendentals or the older distinction between the particular and the universal. Attracted to bluebells in May 1870, he writes about one he had observed: "I do not think I have even seen anything more beautiful than the bluebell I have been looking at. I know the beauty of our Lord by it." Then he continues: "~~The~~ ^Its^ <inscape> is <mixed of> strength and grace, like an ash <tree>."[60] The specific mixture of properties, held together as one, is what absorbs him. To be so taken with a particular phenomenon or situation he needs a certain mood to come over him so that the instress can be spotted. It is not just that "these things were here, and but the beholder / Wanting," as he writes in "Hurrahing in Harvest" (1877),[61] for the beholder must not only be in place but also be motivated to see what is there in order to hold it tightly. Scotus says nothing at all about moods in shifting from one formal feature to another. There is no need to wrap Hopkins wholly in Scotus, or vice versa.

Hopkins uses both of his coinages, *inscape* and *instress*, in 1868, in notes made as an undergraduate on Parmenides's *On Nature*. He begins

by paraphrasing the philosopher's central contention that "Being is and
ɴNot-Being is not" in his own idiom: "ʜe means that all things are upheld by instress and are meaningless without it."[62] It is the first time he
uses the word *instress* on any page that has come down to us. On a first
pass, it seems to name a force that maintains things in Being, although
it is not specified here whether this force is absolute, objective, or subjective. The word *inscape* follows shortly after. Then, seeking to characterize the philosophy at the root of the poem, he first intends to write
"An undetermined idealism . . . runs through the fragments," but he
crosses out *idealism* and writes instead, "An undetermined . . . Pantheist idealism runs through the fragments," adding: "which makes it hard
to translate them satisfactorily in a subjective or in a wholly outward
sense."[63] The qualification is intriguing, for in modern terms it turns a
philosophical position into a religious one. For Hopkins, a pantheist
would maintain that natural phenomena exist by virtue of a particular
force one could consider divine. Similarly, one might think, a Christian
would hold that those same phenomena exist because of God's power
to maintain them in Being. The problem translating Parmenides is, as
stated, less with the Greek language—the use of the middle voice, for
example—than with what *On Nature* says in this particular case: for
Being to reveal itself, there must be both a genitive and an accusative,
a manifestation *of* and a manifestation *to*. The same would be true if
one is speaking of God, taken as infinite Being, although the modes of
manifestation and reception might very well be different from those
that a Pantheist experiences.

After these brief introductory remarks on the Greek poem, there
comes a memorable sentence with a beautiful, if odd, characterization
of Hopkins's insight into Parmenides: "His feeling for instress, for the
flush and foredrawn, and for inscape/ is most striking and from this
one can understand Plato's reverence for him as the great father of Realism." Natural phenomena are upheld, maintained in Being, by a capacity Hopkins describes as "the flush and the foredrawn," but, as he
adds a little later, this is seen only when one is in a certain mood.[64] Before reflecting on this complex claim, it is worth noting that Hopkins
figures Parmenides as an idealist and as a realist. There is no contradiction, for Platonic realism is the view that universals or abstract objects
(numbers, concepts, and, for a Christian, God) exist irrespective of our
beliefs or engagements with them. One might allow all material objects
in the cosmos to fade into nothingness, and no abstract object will be
affected. But what attracts Hopkins to Parmenides is less the philosopher's view of changeless objects than his insight into permanent spiritual reality (Being) in the phenomena of nature.

It is worth tarrying with "the flush and the foredrawn" for a minute or two, beginning with *foredrawn*, and taking the risk of rephasing
it in a soberer language, one with roots in philosophical Greek. When
observed in a certain frame of mind, a phenomenon seems to draw itself forward into one's sphere of regard so that its medley of unity and
distinctiveness can be noticed, Hopkins suggests.[65] That is, one receives an intuition that can be gained only when one is in an appropriate mood, one that makes one receptive to recognizing a peculiar
strain of unity and diversity in a phenomenon. What this mood might
be we are not told; it may well be tranquility, or it may be one or more
moods in a spectrum, from thankfulness or joy, at the one end, to anxiety or deep boredom, at the other. We may recall Heidegger criticiz-
ing Husserl's affirmation of the need of tranquility when doing philosophy and telling us that only particular dark moods that come over us
disclose Being to us; and in response we may ask the thinker why the
fundamental attunements he discusses—*Angst* (dread) and *Langeweile* (deep boredom)—happen to be on the gloomy side of the psychological (or, for Heidegger, ontological) spectrum.[66] Can we not see
something—a falcon for instance—more richly when in an affirmative
mood than when in a black one? Does not such an event sometimes
shift one's mood from the darker to the brighter?

Hopkins was well aware that natural phenomena do not simply
manifest themselves as inscape at any time. We must approach them
with the right degree of heightened awareness, but even this can lead
to problems. In March 1871, he tells his journal: "What you look hard
at seems to look hard ~~and~~ at you, hence the true and the false instress
of nature."[67] One must prepare for one's perception (and thought) of
natural things, be aware, if you wish, of the *realitates* and formal distinctions, and not allow oneself to slip into a state of fascination with
the phenomenon that would only blankly captivate one and not allow
the discernment of the inscape and the instress upholding it. Hopkins
admonishes himself: "Unless you refresh the mind from time to time,
you cannot always remember or believe how deep the inscape of things
~~goes~~ is."[68] Retreats, prayer, exercises of attention, and country walks
are all in play here. Among other things, this refreshment would for
Hopkins be the difference between saying to oneself "mere nature" or
"Creation" in response to what is seen, but it would be a mistake to
think that inscape is always pious, that it is always the same for each
and every observer or even for the same observer at different times.
What is discovered changes, as does the proportion of what one de-
tects in what one sees.

Only Being, which is changeless and permanent, can manifest itself

in inscape. And only Being comports with λόγος. As an undergraduate, Hopkins reads lines 7 and 8 of fragment 2 of the poem: "οὔτε γὰρ
ἂν γνοίης τό γε μὴ ἐόν—οὐ γὰρ ἀνυστόν— / οὔτε φράσαις." He translates: "Thou couldst never either know or say / a ~~thing that~~ what was
not, there wd. be no coming at it." (Leonardo Tarán renders the lines:
"For you could not know that which does not exist (because it is impossible) nor could you express it.")[69] Language could not even begin
to describe Non-Being, Hopkins thinks; the copula would not function. As soon as one says "It is . . ." about Non-Being, one has made an
obvious mistake and must start over. But where? The question has no
viable answer. Now, Being does not arise from Not-Being; it is absolute
and has no genesis whatsoever, Parmenides says. Even when absent to
consciousness, it still is and (as remembered) is present to consciousness, which calls forth the remark: "It is the unextended, foredrawn."[70]
The negative of the *foredrawn* comes up when Hopkins reads lines
46–47 of fragment 8 of Parmenides's poem—"οὔτε γὰρ οὐκ ἐὸν ἔστι,
τό κεν παύοι μιν ἱκνεῖσθαι / εἰς ὁμόν"—which he translates as "nor is
there, Not-Being which could check it from reaching the same point."
(Tarán's version runs: "neither is there non-Being to prevent it from
reaching its like.")[71] Parmenides has been explicating what the goddess has told him of Being, that it does not derive from anything and
does not pass away. It is perfect, but Non-Being has no reality whatsoever and therefore cannot interrupt the continuity of Being. Hopkins
glosses the line and a bit as follows: "Not-being is here seen as want of
oneness, all that is unforedrawn, waste space which offers either nothing to the eye to foredraw or many things foredrawing away from one
another."[72] Something *is* only if it is unified; its inscape can be grasped
by consciousness only because it manifests itself, Being, and does so in
truth. It is the coming forward of a phenomenon when engaged by a
vigilant look that prompts Hopkins to recall: "Plato's reverence for him
[Parmenides] as the great father of Realism."[73]

The verb *flush*, which Hopkins uses also in reference to Scotus, is
perhaps even more evocative than *foredrawn* for two reasons: its association with speed directs us to the phenomenality of the phenomenon, its power to manifest itself from a particular region of being, and
the word's semantic field is extensive. The *Oxford English Dictionary* informs us of meanings that teem in the passage I have quoted. Consider
the verbal form of *flush*: "to fly up quickly and suddenly, to start up and
fly away"; "to flutter (the wings)"; "to reveal; to bring into the open;
to drive"; "to rush like birds on the wing"; "expressing sudden movement, *esp.* of a liquid"; "to cleanse (a drain, etc.); to drive away (an ob-
stacle) by means of a rush of water"; "to emit light or sparks suddenly";

"to come with a rush, producing a heightened color"; "to inflame with pride or passion; to animate." Some entries under the nominal form of the word are additionally worth noticing because Hopkins uses *flush* as an active verbal noun. A flush is "a sudden plentiful increase or abundance in anything"; "a sudden shooting up; a fresh growth of grass, leaves, or flowers"; "glow, freshness, vigor." Without being fussy about particular meanings here, we might say that Hopkins alerts us to the ways in which a phenomenon discloses its instress and the effect that these have on us. It comes quickly (we see it in a glance, not in a disciplined gaze), and it fills us momentarily, perhaps cleansing and/or heightening our sense of reality. ("I saw the inscape though freshly, as if my eye were still growing," as Hopkins tells his journal in December 1872 about some grass that he had seen.)[74] This is true instress, producing an alert look's response to what is real, and part of this reality is the inscape, the distinctive pattern of a thing or a situation that for Hopkins bespeaks divine beauty.

What the young Hopkins values in Parmenides is his emphasis on ἔστι, which he renders as "<u>it is</u>" or "<u>there is</u>," but it is suggestive that this disclosure occurs only in particular moods. When that has happened, he writes: "He has felt the depth of an instress or how fast the inscape holds a thing that nothing is so pregnant and straightforward to the truth as simple <u>yes</u> and <u>is</u>."[75] By the time Hopkins is writing his mature poetry, his sense of inscape is given in terms that are as much artistic as they are philosophical. As he says in February 1879, in a letter to Robert Bridges (1844–1930): "Design, pattern or what I am in the habit of calling 'inscape' is what I above all aim at in poetry."[76] He does so both in what writing poetry allows him to see and in how the writing itself forms patterns and designs. It is tempting to refer back to Schopenhauer, Coleridge, and Husserl. Yet a passage from John Ruskin (1819–1900), whose work Hopkins had known since he was a teenager and certainly admired, is as expressive in its own way as anything in Parmenides or Scotus:

> There must be observance of the ruling organic law. This is the first distinction between good artists and bad artists. Your common sketcher or bad painter puts his leaves on the trees as if they were moss tied to sticks; he cannot see the lines of action or growth; he scatters the shapeless clouds over his sky, not perceiving the sweeps of associated curves which the real clouds are following as they fly; and he breaks his mountain side into rugged fragments, wholly unconscious of the lines of couch in which they repose. On the contrary it is the main delight of the great draughtsman, to trace these

laws of government; and his tendency to error is always in the exaggeration of their authority rather than in its denial.[77]

More than respect for "the ruling organic law" is needed, for the very next paragraph tells us: "We have to show the individual character and liberty of the separate leaves, clouds, or rocks."[78] One difference between a great draughtsman and God, Hopkins might add, is that the former often repeats himself or herself, while the latter never does: each and every frozen puddle, branch of leaves, flower, air scape, or snow scape is singular, never to appear exactly so again. Not only is God infinite Being, but also he is above and beyond all genus, absolutely singular, so, when he leaves traces of himself in Creation, each one will be relatively singular.

I have been explicating Hopkins's journal entry for February 24, 1873, and much that I have said applies equally to the journal entry of the following year that I have quoted earlier. The first thing to notice with this second passage, however, is that on September 10, 1874, Hopkins was in coal-mining country in South Wales. On the day concerned, the evening of which would mark the beginning of a retreat at St. Beuno's College, he was engrossed with a pilgrimage site rather than the social and economic problems of coal miners. He was visiting Ffynnon-Fair, also known as St. Mary's Well, in Penrhys, Rhondda. The well is near a ruined chapel and is renowned for the curative property of its waters; pilgrims have long visited it, even after its desecration had been accomplished in 1538 by Thomas Cromwell, chief minister to Henry VIII. Hopkins drank water from the sacred spring, the basin of which was, he thought, shaped like the pool of Bethesda, where Jesus had healed a man who had been an invalid for thirty-eight years (John 5:2). If anywhere, one might suppose it would have been here that he would be inclined to sense the presence of God. Instead, it is later, when he is visiting Cefn Rocks, that he spots one in a group of "delicate flying shafted ashes" that attracts him with its "sonnet-like inscape." The epiphany may well be spiritual—a distinctive pattern that God has given to the ash tree and that Hopkins catches in passing—but it is also aesthetic, which leads one to doubt any strict, continuous distinction between the two when reading him. Divine goodness and divine beauty are convertible, after all. One might write a sonnet and, in doing so, capture something of the inscape of a phenomenon in its language and, in particular, in an idiom ("inscape of speech"). This could not happen simply because of the structure of a Petrarchan sonnet, eight lines of an octave, followed by a *volta* that introduces six lines of a sestet. That pattern is entirely general. But perhaps it could happen if the sonnet were written with intense attention to the concretion of formal, figural, and thematic elements. Its idiom would not be absolutely singular, but it would be as close to being so as language allows.[79] With these things in mind, let us finally return to "The Windhover," Hopkins's greatest sonnet, written three years after the visit to St. Mary's Well.

*

"I caught." The octave is cast as recent recollection, Hopkins's catching sight of a kestrel and registering its pattern in the air. Its appearance and performance are wholly unexpected, and, just months before his ordination, the young Jesuit looks up in wonder and seizes the bird, both with his senses and with his mind, at this stage presumably without any awareness of how deeply he will become affected by what he has seen or the direction this affect will take. Suddenness or surprise can prompt reduction. All the drama of the rapid glimpse and what comes from it can be registered more surely by reminding oneself of Tennyson's fragment "The Eagle" (1846? 1851):

> He clasps the crag with crooked hands;
> Close to the sun in lonely lands,
> Ring'd with the azure world, he stands.
>
> The wrinkled sea beneath him crawls;
> He watches from his mountain walls,
> And like a thunderbolt he falls.[80]

The eagle is not glimpsed here; it is encompassed by a look undertaken in the natural attitude. Although the fragment is short, visual, and dramatic, it does not promote a poetics of the moment, as one finds in Hopkins, by way of Pater, and as the Imagists were to develop as part of their program in the early twentieth century.[81] The bird is not made to bear any theme of transcendence or contemplation. No *templum* is imagined. Instead, Tennyson steadily looks with admiration at the bird's sovereignty without explicitly introducing himself into the scene. The fragment's drama converges on the last line and especially on its final word. The eagle falls from the crag, moving quickly and powerfully, and we know that it is very likely to be riveted on prey.

With "The Windhover," however, the bird is first given in the speaker's glance, which is then stretched into an admiring look of captivation.[82] That glance is gorgeously drawn out by sprung rhythm for six and a half lines: the second line of the octave, for instance, runs to sixteen syllables, and the syntactic unit of which it is a part crosses three lines, while the following syntactic unit also encompasses three lines with its full line being a flow of fifteen syllables. Hopkins's eyes have swiftly been pulled upward, as "I caught" suggests, and the poet speaks as a witness, not as a spectator. The notes struck by the -ing rhymes, both strong and weak, that govern the entire octave in a singular manner pitch it high and then low. From the beginning, we are held aloft in the recounting of the event and, like the poet, attuned to the kestrel's ways of flight. There are four of them, designated by *riding, striding,* and *hurling and gliding,* which are more energetic than Aquinas's depictions of the soul's movements, and it will be seen that only the last one inclines to the passivity associated, rightly or wrongly, with contemplation. The first two are equestrian metaphors: a motif that will be picked up in the compacted insight of the "rein of a wimpling wing" and in the figure of the chevalier. The third is an active verbal noun (*the hurl*). Taken together, the implication of the four modes is clear; in order to enjoy gliding, one must first be active. A kestrel lives a mixed life, like a Jesuit.

If the poem's octave makes us think of a *templum,* we should recognize that there has been no anticipation of anything auspicious: the bird's coming into view precedes the poet's awareness of it, and Hopkins takes himself to be called to respond. Further, we should recall that we would be witnessing a Christian version of what the ancient Romans would have called an *oblativa,* although it will be of an entirely different character from anything that they divined *ex avibus.* More, the *templum* is reversed: it is the bird who looks down on Hopkins and seeks something of him. Even when perceiving the raptor, Hopkins's gaze is extended beyond the realm of the visible to the invisible: he aspires to greater intimacy with Christ in and through the abrupt appearing of the bird. The morning light is compared with the Dauphiné Viennois, ruled by the French king's son from the eleventh century to the fifteenth. (The Dauphiné was a wild area of southeastern France, a territory that roughly covered the same terrain as the *départements* of Isère, Drôme, and Hautes-Alpes do now.) The very word *minion* enters English from Middle French (*mignon*) at the very end of that period. The French context is almost everything here, for *minion* must be taken in its fifteenth- and sixteenth-century sense in French—"favorite," "darling"—and not in the sense it came to assume in English in the mid-seventeenth century, "a subordinate."[83] Christ is the Lord, the King (the Sun), whose light-drenched morning is his kingdom ("king- / dom of daylight's dauphin"), and the Falcon, belonging to the kingdom, is illuminated by the light that streams from him.[84]

Hopkins's glance is not just a glance for long; it becomes thoughtful, taking in the movement of the bird, and beginning to articulate a
complex whole, both natural and supernatural. As this glance prolongs
itself into consideration (looking above, around, and down) or even
rises to contemplation, so it takes in the kestrel in its act of ecstatic joy.
As with Richard's birds, it circles in the air, apparently without effort,
although the word *wimpling* finely indicates that its wings are rippling
in folds (like a French nun's cornette in the breeze) as the feathers keep
rising and falling in order for the bird to remain in stasis with the wind.
So we have two gazes, one more fully achieved as contemplative than
the other.[85] For the kestrel has complete mastery of his environment,
he is immanent within it while also transcending it, and he enjoys his
free awareness of the world around him and beneath him. Meanwhile,
Hopkins considers or even contemplates the *excessus mentis* of the kestrel, its instant of unsayable bliss at the peak of its absorption in the sun
before it moves at tremendous speed in quest of its prey. It passes from
contemplation to action, and Hopkins sees both.

We are not explicitly told that the bird turns its eyes on Hopkins,
but the young Jesuit hides from it since it is a favorite of Christ's, perhaps feeling its eyes on him like those of a living icon or at least inter-
nalizing the judgment of his community and its founder. If we think
here of Nicholas of Cusa (1401–64), who says to Christ, "Your seeing, Lord, is your loving [*Domine, videre tuum est amore*]," we must also
take in the full weight of love as ἀγάπη, recognizing that it comes from
supreme sacrifice and calls for sacrifice in return.[86] Here, in the final
lines of the octave, there is less *dilatio mentis* or *sublevatio mentis* than
the temptation of *occultatio mentis*. At the same time, so elated is Hopkins's description of the kestrel that the unwary reader could almost
forget the framing dedication for a moment. We see a natural bird, yet
we witness a bird that in its freedom and mastery points us to Christ,
to the possible intimacy that a soul can have with its King. It is a brief
natural theology, one that is utterly dynamic and thereby completely
different from what Hopkins had been taught of the static natural theology in the manuals of the day.[87] The description of the bird's sudden swing out of its period of hovering orients us to the kestrel, while
the allusions to the kingdom, to the nun's wimple, to ecstasy, and to the
King all keep "*To Christ our Lord*" in mind, both as dedication and as
orientation. But in what ways?

Not as allegory, even though *Falcon* is granted an initial capital letter. The majuscule, along with the French resonance of *falcon* (*faucoun*,
ME, from *falcun*, OF) rather than *kestrel*, gives the bird a dignity appropriate to the blessed soul it begins to evoke who points Hopkins to

the Son. Rather than allegorizing, Hopkins proceeds in a manner that phenomenologists would recognize as concretion. The kestrel is not a token of a general type; instead, it is charged with meaning because it appears in a particular situation, which makes the sky a *templum* of a Christian kind. This meaning, as we have seen, has not been anticipated, actively or passively, and Hopkins takes pains to specify it, differently, in the octave and the sestet. In the octave, the focus is on the how of the bird, its riding of the air, its striding in the heights, and the posture of its ecstasy. And, in the sestet, our attention is claimed by reflection on the beauty and danger of the bird. Before we reach the sestet, however, we will have realized that the poet's intentional rapport with the bird is not only with a bird; it is also with something rendered just as concrete as the bird, though in another manner.

That this intentional consciousness reaches beyond the phenomenon, passing from the visible to the invisible, is something we might expect, whether we be readers mainly of Husserl or Richard. Intentionality always exceeds its intentional object, the philosopher tells us, while the theologian points to how contemplation has an almost irresistible movement from the visible to the invisible.[88] If we abide with Husserl, we will say that we have a categorial intuition with two rays twined together, as it were, in the octave of the poem, perception and belief, the one pointing us to a bird in flight and the other to a blessed soul thrilling in its intimacy with the divine. The lyric is not one solely of perception; it is one of thinking, for the bird and the saint are articulated as a whole: a new style of natural theology.[89] Put differently, we pass very quickly, by way of a reduction prompted by surprise, from the natural attitude in which a bird is caught at the edge of vision to the phenomenological attitude in which how it is seen—as free, as masterful, as able to achieve what it is created to do—is paramount, in an abundant interaction of theme, figure, and form (all of which converge on idiom or "inscape of speech"). Part of that interaction is the ancient idea—pagan, Jewish, and Christian—that the soul can fly like a bird. (Prudentius [348–413], e.g., sees the soul flying from the mouth of the martyr Eulalia at the height of her passion.)[90] No surprise, then, that the poem also adopts the basilaic attitude in which we shift from being oriented to the world, which retains an evident pull on the young Jesuit, to entering the kingdom.[91] For it is only in and through faith in the kingdom and the exercise of hope and love there that one has hope of finding the beloved King.

How does one enter the kingdom? If it were really like the Dauphiné Viennois, there would be no need even to pose the question. But, as the Jesus of the synoptic Gospels depicts it, the kingdom is a multistable phenomenon, at once here and to come, internal and external, strong and weak. One enters the kingdom by faith, it will be said, which is true enough, as would be the answer that one enters by baptism; but the sort of faith that is required—what Augustine and Aquinas both call *credere in deum*, believing oneself into God—presumes a stirring of love in order to make an act of faith that is not narrowly intellectual but fully embodied.[92] One believes with one's whole being—as a thinking, acting, praying person nourished by sacrament, food, and deed—not just with one's mind, and the life of faith stretches one backward to Creation as well as forward to life with the saints in glory. One's mode of being is changed, from the natural to the Graced. That Hopkins takes himself not to be fully in the kingdom is freely admitted: "My heart in hiding / Stirred for a bird,—the achieve of, the mastery of the thing!" The price of achievement and mastery is, for him, obedience to and in the Society of Jesus, giving himself in solemn vows without reserve to Christ by way of the society.

Consideration or contemplation can lead one to transcend oneself, to experience *dilatio mentis* or more, and it can overflow from the self to the kingdom. Also, it can, almost at the same time, make one pull back in fear out of self-distrust or because of moral impurity.[93] Worldly attachment is a *pondus*, as Augustine said; it counteracts the attraction of divine love.[94] The world drags Hopkins back from the kingdom just at the moment that the bird displays its natural prowess, "the achieve of, the mastery of the thing!" In addition, it is the instant when the kestrel, rebuffing the wind, appears cruciform.[95] To enter the kingdom of God one must be purified of sin and accept the "incomprehensible certainty" of the mystery of the cross; nothing must be hidden in a supposedly private space.[96] That Hopkins's heart hides from Christ suggests clearly enough that any ascent to God meets resistance. (We think of Richard saying that the birds *"by their rapid movement* they keep themselves as it were fixed and immobile" [emphasis added].) Does his heart hide, whether because of its impurity or because of anxiety about the exigency of the cross? Either way, Hopkins not only catches the kestrel in the morning but also catches himself.

When Hopkins says that he has a heart in hiding, he suggests that his heart is actively hiding, that it has been caught by the falcon in the very act of hiding from its gaze and from its talons. (We may well recall with a chill Richard Lovelace's fine image "The *Falcon* charges at first view / With her brigade of Talons.")[97] We do not see the kestrel's stoop in the poem, only Hopkins's response to it: hiding from a predator of souls. His heart, the seat of volition, is still partly attached to worldly values; it conceals itself from the bird while nonetheless unable to stop looking at it, doubtless with some guilt, wanting the achievement and mastery that he intellectually recognizes as fully embodied there but not being entirely prepared as yet to give himself wholly to Christ so that he might gain them. A further act of volition must be made: the bird (or soul in bliss) prompts Hopkins to remember that he is soon to make his solemn vows as a Jesuit. Yet the will can rapidly reach out, as the sestet of the poem tells us. More generally, as Gregory the Great and Aquinas both see, contemplation is not a state of steady tranquility; it is furthermore a response to being wounded by an overwhelming rush of divine glory.[98] One must strive to reach a state of beholding God and must strive in order to stay there. There must be both "hurl and gliding."

The heart will not risk itself without knowledge of what it will invest itself in. This self-protection is traditional and commonsensical; we remember the adage of the Schoolmen: *nihil amatum nisi prius cognitum* (We can love something only if we first know it).[99] Not all knowledge that leads to love is as coolly intellectual and firmly clarified as *cognitum* suggests; we can love someone with whom we are familiar and whom we wish to know much better. For we can likewise say, *nihil vere cognitum nisi prius amatum*, which we might render in English as: "Unless we love first, we do not truly know."[100] It is this reversal of scholastic theology that Hopkins implicitly risks at the start of the sestet when, shifting from the recent past to the present, he exclaims, "O *my* chevalier!" (emphasis added), the kestrel riding on the air and a blessed soul figured as a mounted knight: "Brute beauty and valour and act, oh, air, pride, plume, here / Buckle!" Such diverse elements, from distinct regions of being (elemental being, animal being, empirical features, moral values, actions [including the force suggested by *brute*], cultural signs, human being), are suddenly united in the one place, in the Vale of Clwyd, and beheld by Hopkins. Everything comes together in a glimpse of inscape, an affective sense that is momentarily attuned to an objective pattern, and the speaker is elevated in a moment of *sublevatio mentis*.[101] The Jesuit who had not met the bird's or the soul's look now meets it and in doing so knows him in and through love. Yet both gazes, poet's and bird's, are fundamentally directed to Christ. No gaze is unmediated, and this one is elevated in its mediation.

Hopkins has not actively anticipated this display of intimacy with Christ, and probably his passive anticipation has not presumed such an encounter either. Surprise and speed precipitate an expression of intense love of Christ. We may well recall the trope of Christ as mounted knight late in the *Moralia in Job* (no later than 595) and in the *Ancrene Riwle* (ca. 1215–21): "He entered the lists, and for love of his love had his shield pierced on every side in the fight, like a brave knight."[102] Later, in the early sixteenth century, there is the "Corpus Christi" carol with its moving evocation of Christ as a dying knight. Perhaps most point-edly, however, the figure of Christ as knight is given by the Franciscan friar William Herebert (ca. 1270–1333) in a memorable poem, a Christian paraphrase of Isa. 63:1–7, "Quis est iste qui uenit de Edom?" The paraphrase is cast as a dialogue between the angels, who see a doughty knight returning from battle, and Christ, who is that very knight:

Questio angelorum:
What ys he, þys lordling, þat cometh vrom þe vyht,
Wyth blodrede wede so grysliche ydyht,
So vayre ycoyntised, so semlich in syht,
So styflyche ȝóngeþ, so douhti a knyht?

Responsio Christi:
Ich hyt am, Ich hyt am, þat ne speke bote ryht,
Chaunpyoun to hélen monkunde in vyht.

Questio angelorum:
Why, þœnne, ys þy shroud red wyth blod al ymeind,
Ase troddares in wrynge wyth most al byspreynd?

Responsio Christi:
Þe wrynge ich habbe ytrodded, al mysulf on,
And of al monkunde ne was non oþer won.

Ich hœ´m habbe ytrodded in wréþe and in gróme,
And al my wéde ys byspreynd wyth hœre blod ysome,
And al my robe yuúled to hœre gréte shome.

Þe day of þ'ylke wréche leueth in my þouht;
Þe ȝér of medes ȝeldyng ne uorȝet ich nouht.

Ich loked al aboute som helpynge mon,
Ich souhte al þe route bote help nas þer non.
Hyt was myn oune strengþe þat þys bóte wrouhte,
Myn owe douhtynesse þat help þer me brouhte.
Ich habbe ytrodded þe volk in wréthe and in grome,
Adreynt al wyth shennesse, ydrawe doun wyth shome.

Ista sunt uerba Iudeorum penitenciam agencium:
On Godes mylsfolnesse ich wole byþenche me,
And heryen hym in alle þyng þat he ȝeldeth me.[103]

Yet the knight that appears in "The Windhover" is not the Christ of medieval devotion but the Christian as knight, bound in honor to serve a high ideal, that one finds later in St. Ignatius Loyola (1491–1556). One need not specifically identify Loyola as the chevalier, although it is tempting to do so ("O *my* chevalier!" cries the young Jesuit). Loyola is his patron, and Hopkins is soon to take solemn vows. The bird is seen as a noble soldier committed in love to serve his Lord. One remembers that, while convalescing from an injury sustained at the Battle of Pamplona (1521), Loyola read the Cisterican Gaulberto Fabricio de Vagad's preface to Jacobus de Voragine's *Flos sanctorum* (1511), in which the saints are represented as *los cavalleros de Dio* (the knights of God).[104] The metaphor is hardly original, and Ignatius might have encountered it elsewhere.[105] But it took him by surprise in de Vagad's preface, and he responded to it with force.

If we refocus on the tenor of Hopkins's metaphor, the kestrel, we see that the bird exhibits animal beauty, spirit, and pride in its act of rapid descent through the air for prey, a descent enabled by its contour feathers (a sense of *plume* in circulation since the early nineteenth century). In the one place and time all these things come together. Indeed, Hopkins affirms the bird's act: the line is an imperative as well as an exclamation. It is part of what St. Paul considered being conformed to the image of Christ (Rom. 8:29), and we are left in no doubt that this compliance has a military association. We are to buckle on the armor of God (Eph. 6:11), as any Jesuit knows. In that one act, the tremendously fast stoop, the natural and the spiritual momentarily fuse: the kestrel illuminates something of what a blessed soul enjoys. In addition to this, in that one act the limits of that fusion are recognized. No kestrel, no bird of any sort, can support the glory of the divine or even a soul in bliss.[106] The poem urges a structure of double revelation in that being in the kingdom of heaven is like the bird's joy but also quite unlike it. As in all parabolic utterance, the poem is thrown quickly past what it proposes to illumine, Christ manifesting himself in his kingdom by way of an epiphany of a blessed soul, and only one or two facets of the reality can be captured.

"Oh" Hopkins interjects into his list of elements that are unified by the kestrel's swoop on its prey. He is delighted by all that comes together there. If his heart had been hiding from what surprised it, if his heart in hiding had been unwilling to affirm what his eyes had been seeing, now it is engaged with what Parmenides calls ἔστι or "it is." In three lines we pass from *oh* to *O*, from an interjection to a vocative exclamation. A dedicated chevalier, claimed by the votary Hopkins as *his* knight, is apostrophized in the midst of his magnificent act, and again we recall the French context (and remember that the word *chevalier* comes from Middle French of the same period as *mignon* and *dauphin*). Something else is worth noticing. Three months after composing "The Windhover" (May 30, 1877), and just three weeks before being ordained, Hopkins was to write "Hurrahing in Harvest," which, in its octave, declares, "I walk, I lift up, I lift up heart, eyes," and two lines later addresses "éyes, heárt," as to who has actually been "seen," namely, Christ.[107] Spiritual insight occurs only if perception is preceded and supported by love, yet, once that insight has been attained, the eyes, as the means of understanding what has been seen, are addressed first.[108] So here, in the sestet of "The Windhover," the involvement of the heart is presumed in attaining insight into a momentary spiritual and natural fusion that is upheld only by instress, and then, in what follows, the eyes are privileged: "AND the fire that breaks from thee then, a billion / Times told lovelier, more dangerous, O my chevalier!" Hopkins sees the chestnut brown plumage of the kestrel become radiant as it dives with the sun climbing behind it, and besides he "sees" the light that comes from Christ illuminating and exceeding the blessed soul. Both have higher degrees of being than any earthly phenomenon. So we pass from *oculus carnis* to *oculus contemplationis*. That Christ's Tabor light is dazzling, far more so than created light, is well-known in commentaries on the Transfiguration; but so is the awareness that to follow him is to accept the possibility of martyrdom.[109]

The poem that began with unexpected wonder seeks closure by denying that the event just witnessed is indeed surprising. The reason for this deflation, itself quite unexpected, turns on the Jesuit's commitment to a life that is active as well as contemplative, the mixed life that actually aids the chevalier and the one he serves. Here, in the final tercet of the sonnet, Hopkins reflects on the present and the past, and the evidence he adduces is recollected. He lowers his eyes to take in two familiar things, plowing and a home fire; but, although the gaze is cast down, it does not shift its attitude. It registers what it sees with phenomenological concreteness, and it also remains oriented to the kingdom rather than to the world. The things and events of our workaday life can be contemplated, as Gregory and Richard agree, for they participate in divine Grace, even if they are not as spectacular as the flight and abrupt decent of the kestrel. If we reach back to the *templum* at the heart of contemplation, we can see that auspices of a sort have been given: the realm of the divine manifests itself in everyday occurrences, giving believers hope for our hard lives, even if we share our lives with God. There is not just the one occasion of inscape in the poem, of various regions of being buckled together; there are three. For, even when our eyes are lowered, we can see the "shine" of the earth and the "gold-vermillion" of the dying fire. Let us see how this is achieved.

"No wonder of it: shéer plód makes plough down sillion / Shine." Once again, we have an English word (*sillion*), here regional, that comes from the French (*sillon*). The brightness of lumps of soil turned over by the steady handling of a plow is caused by them being cut by the blade; it is not the radiant plumage of the kestrel in its arresting dive, and it cannot support the contemplation of the glorified Christ streaming behind the epiphanic bird, but it is to be valued, nonetheless, for its illumination and consolation. If the display of the kestrel is utterly unexpected and gratuitous, the shining of the soil comes from hard work: the effort of managing the plow "*makes* plough down sillion / Shine" (emphasis added). We are reminded of Jesus's words to a man he encounters on the road: "No one who puts his hand to the plow and looks back is fit for the kingdom of God" (Luke 9:62 [RSV]). Only if one looks ahead, when plowing the next furrow, does one see the sillion shine by virtue of one's labor; only then does one see nature perfected by Grace. For Grace does not appear in the present: the sign of it is manifest elsewhere in time. Once again, we have a new inflection of natural theology. We might say, with Gregory and Richard, that we are invited to mull over what is around us in life as much as the principle (and principal) of life itself. One of those things, for some people, is the writing of poetry, and while we, Romantics or post-Romantics, may consider the act of composition sometimes kin to *dilatio mentis* or *sublevatio mentis* or even, if one credits Plato and certain orphic poets, *excessus mentis*, we will also remember that the word *verse* comes from the Latin *versus*, meaning "a turn of the plow."[110] The poet, like the Jesuit, Hopkins thinks, lives a mixed life, though more often it is more like a plowman's than a kestrel's, at least until one recalls that a kestrel does not get its prey on each and every stoop.

Similarly, when "blue-bleak embers" in a fire seem about to be extinguished yet collapse on those beneath them, they break one another apart and flare with the last of the fire, which, when viewed, appears profoundly rich, "gold-vermillion." It is not the fire that magnificently breaks from the kestrel, but the image is nonetheless striking, and both fires have the beauty and power of the divine. Perhaps as well it evokes the blood of the martyrs who have accepted the cross. Certainly, the fall of the embers reminds us of the stoop of the kestrel, albeit greatly diminished. At any rate, physical and spiritual exhaustion can lead to illumination, Hopkins says. The sonnet concludes with one more instant of inscape, one more manifestation of Being, one more moment of *dilatio mentis* (or even something higher). It is introduced by the

third exclamation of the poem and the most tender of them: Hopkins
has sighed "oh" and has raised himself in admiration and awe to sing
"O," but now, more intimately, he says to the chevalier or perhaps to
Christ himself "ah my dear." The allusion is to George Herbert's "Love"
(III), the final lyric of *The Temple* (1633), where the sinful soul, being
welcomed into heaven, says, with a heart in hiding, "Ah my dear, /
I cannot look on thee," only to be invited nonetheless to the eucharistic
feast because Christ himself is the one "who bore the blame."[111] (The
allusion nicely answers the penitential foreboding of having a heart in
hiding.) I emphasize that in reading Hopkins's line one needs to remember how Herbert continues the stanza: "I cannot look on thee."
Christ is the dangerous fire streaming from the kestrel. (We recall Luke
12:49: "I came to cast fire upon the earth" [RSV].) Yet he is also a close
companion in scholarly and pastoral drudgery. It is no wonder that the
extraordinary breaks into the ordinary because that is how Christ, true
God and true man, manifests himself, if we will only allow ourselves
to be trained to see such things. If the unanticipated spectacle of the
dappled kestrel at first points to Christ, indeed, shows Hopkins how
to become intimate with him (by giving himself fully to the Society
of Jesus), so too do other things that we might almost expect. The entire sonnet points to Christ, to different ways of reaching him, as well
as being dedicated to him as his finest piece of work to date.[112] Finally,
Hopkins might say, quoting Herbert's "The 23rd Psalm," that it serves
to "bring my minde in frame," which is one of the ends of contemplation.[113]

*

If I am right, my reading of Hopkins's poem shares little or nothing
with allegoresis, which relies on one or another trope of ascent, or with
the hermeneutics of suspicion, which, as we shall see in the following chapter, reverses it and promotes various tropes of descent, usually for social or political ends. Nor, although it is deeply informed
by Christian faith, does it have anything in common with what Paul
Ricoeur identifies as the opposite pole to suspicion, namely, an untutored trust that meaning can be skimmed from a textual surface.[114]
I venture another way of reading, a hermeneutic of contemplation,
which, as we have seen, learns from Gregory and Richard, among others of the fathers, but which reads them through the invisible presence
of Coleridge, who himself valued Richard, through the equally invisible presence of Schopenhauer, and through the exacting presence of
Husserl, who sums up and exceeds the nineteenth-century attention

to contemplation.[115] The fathers are adjusted by reference to Schopen-hauer, Coleridge, and Husserl: ascent is replaced by modes of manifes-tation. And Husserl is himself modified by reference to Richard in par-ticular; the regions of being are expanded so as to allow the divine to manifest itself in all the regional ontologies, including those of faith, hope, and love.

What makes the reading hermeneutical is a patient care as to how part fits with part in order to make a whole, one that always, despite one's best efforts, points to a further whole that appears in anticipa-tion. For no whole makes of itself a totality: the one is open, whether oriented by a horizon of unity or one of disunity, while the other is closed. Always, the attraction to the language "even over and above its interest in meaning," as Hopkins says, keeps the poem from doubling over on itself. And what makes this hermeneutic contemplative is that in principle it attends to all the regions of being—natural, cultural, and spiritual—and their various ways of manifestation, including divine revelation, in the poem itself, along with everything that is empirically associated with what is said there. The hermeneutic is resolutely antire-ductionist. The beholding does not occur out of time, as if such a thing were ever possible; rather, it is conducted by the rhythm of the poem, its abrupt movements, its stretching of a glimpse into a gaze, and by the rhymes, which keep one attuned to the *templum* by their pitch as much as by what they say. Inevitably, then, this hermeneutic expands the realm of attitudes and intentional rapports. Husserl conceived the phenomenological attitude (not just the theoretical attitude) by way of θεωρία, which he regarded as a manner of detachment from participa-tion in the world. We tranquilly regard our intentional investments in the world—our doubts, affirmations, anxieties, and perceptions—in order to take note of how they are constituted, but we do not act on them. This conception of philosophy was vigorously contested by Hei-degger, who relentlessly found the attitudes that interested him on the darker side of the spectrum: *Angst, Langeweile,* and so on.[116] Christi-anity, however, also looks to the brighter end of the same spectrum of attitudes—admiration, gratitude, joy, and wonder, for example—and is open to what discloses itself there. If "The Windhover" invites us, in wonder, to see inscape in the flight of a kestrel, it asks us as well to rec-ognize that other inscapes can be viewed in deflated moods as well.

On my reading, "The Windhover" captures a momentary crossing of two contemplative gazes, one *excessus mentis* and one *dilatio mentis* (or even *sublevatio mentis*). So intense is the blessed soul's gaze that the speaker is frightened by it, but the two gazes find unity in that both are directed ultimately to Christ. The poem itself concerns two religious minds, each pressing into the mystery of God, and it is perfectly possible for someone to read the sonnet in the same way, as an extended form of *lectio divina*, and to do so with feeling.[117] My reading, however, has been contemplative in another manner. I have not adopted a motif of ascent. Rather, I have sought to see the poem as a brief natural theology, of the kestrel as articulated with a soul in bliss, and in doing so I have tried to heed the question How? in all its inflections, which, in the sonnet under inspection, prizes gliding, hovering, and flowing. Inevitably, the poem calls for more. The reading construes reduction as a shift to the anterior, less the world about us into which we come than the kingdom that calls us away from worldly values.[118] We are summoned to contemplate the bliss of that kingdom and the difficulty of entering it by a "single sonnet-like inscape."

CHAPTER 5

Fascination

The person given to θεωρία is "the most free," Iamblichus said; and we have seen that the entire Western tradition, Christian as well as pagan, maintains that this is so with regard to contemplation but that Christianity gives it a unique twist. The person engaged in mental prayer or in *lectio divina* freely desires God and seeks to transform that desire into divine love, knowing all the time that God has always and already freely turned toward one in love. Only in mutual love is there true freedom: such is one of the refrains of Christian thought, liturgy, and spirituality. Similarly, a contemplative hermeneutic allows one to press into the mystery of God if one regards it as a mode of prayer or, if not, lets one freely pass from one region of being to another, from one empirical association to another, to reflect on the correlation of noesis and noema and so on, regardless of whether the text in question has a horizon of unity or one of disunity. There can be no forced contemplation with respect to either subject or object. It is love, natural or infused, that prompts one to understand something, and in beginning to understand one loves what one wishes to understand all the more.

Yet, as we know, there are times when an object seems to compel our attention and does not readily release us, even when we sense that it does no good at all to continue attending to it. (At times it might not even be a concrete object, able to be perceived by one or another sense; it might be elusive yet have one or more properties, as we shall see.) There are many varieties of this state, and I will mention several of them later, but the principal one is the phenomenon of fascination. It affects us in several ways and to varying extents. Traditionally, it is associated with desire, envy, and fear. In the terms of this common view, fascination can come on us quite suddenly. We find ourselves rendered passive, unable to respond to a situation, one that may well endanger us, as happens when Odysseus encounters the Sirens in book 12 of the *Odyssey*. The same thing occurs even if the danger is merely social disapproval (as when one cannot take one's eyes away from a singularly beautiful person in the same room). For the beautiful can also fascinate us—and in more than one way. Think of Walter Pater's Gaston when he encounters Montaigne: "To Gaston there was a kind of fascination, an actually aesthetic beauty, in the spectacle of that keen-edged understanding, dividing evidence so finely, like some exquisite steel instrument, with impeccable sufficiency, always leaving loyally the last word to the central intellectual faculty, in an entire disinterestedness."[1] Fascination can come on one slowly, becoming a darkly ingrained habit, as when we find ourselves, day after day, gazing at a cell phone, passing from app to app even though we have already checked each one. The activity no longer has any meaning and does not lead anywhere. One can become fascinated by a past event, in one's life or in history, that cannot be changed; and something similar can happen with anticipation. One can be entranced by an event that is supposed to occur, as with an expected promotion at work, a travel opportunity, or a forecast the end of the world.

At times fascination can lead to productive work, as when one becomes enchanted by an idea or a situation that, in time, opens onto a new vein of thought or writing. A shift of gears takes place. Fascination has been a spur, not an impediment, and it persists, although at a less intense level. The same holds for some romantic relationships; perhaps romance is linked to fascination at a deep level, at least at the beginning of romantic liaisons, although it must leave this phase behind for love to develop. At other times, it can lead nowhere. For example, one can find that one has become captivated by another person, known personally or solely through the media. No affinity is or can be pursued, yet there is an empty passion for the image of the person or an enthrallment borne out of envy. Still worse situations can occur to us: we can binge watch movies or reruns of football games and experience, along with what is shown on the screen, a vague sense of pointlessness and endlessness that tires the intellect and the will alike. One is caught in the inertness of the temporal phenomenon of the overlong. Finally, we can become morbidly attracted to something or someone unpleasant, even frightening, and nonetheless feel a compulsion to approach or gawk. This happens to individuals who become dependent on certain forms of fantasy, political conspiracies, the fantastic, or violent movies or who come to think that they are being persecuted.

These examples show how we can become fascinated in the natural attitude, including being prey to pathological distortions that take

place within it. Yet, if we can shift our mental frame and adopt the theoretical attitude, we can quickly become transfixed there as well. How
easy it is to dwell on a challenging math problem without lifting one's
eyes from the page, even when one gets stuck on a detail. One starts
again from the beginning, gets to the point where one stalls, and remains there, with one's mind idling. Or in the aesthetic attitude one
can become so absorbed in writing a poem that hits a snag that cannot be overcome that the words one tries turn to glue in one's hands,
or one can focus on making something in the shed and find that one
is thrown off for hours by a difficulty of construction that hovers before one's eyes, that (it seems) can never be resolved, and that does
not allow one to do anything else. And, if we pass into the religious-
mythical attitude, there too we can be fascinated: we can be captivated
by an idol, these days most likely secular, or, less disturbingly, we can
find ourselves too dry to pray and unable to think of God at all richly.
He appears as Judge, say, and we find ourselves frozen before the image,
unable to recall God as Creator and Savior. Only in the phenomenological attitude, when it has been consistently achieved, does wonder
entirely replace fascination; at other times the words share elements
of the same meaning. Yet sometimes the contemplation proper to that
mind-set is arrested; one can become stuck on something that prevents
one from incorporating it into a whole and then slide from contemplation to fascination. There are times when the intensity that characterizes bewitchment fades away; we rouse ourselves and go back to what
we were doing. And there are other times when one must wrench oneself away by an act of will or by having someone or something nearby
dislodge us from the compulsion.

If we reflect on the situation with which we find ourselves fascinated, we will say that we are not actually constrained to keep looking
at it. It may be that the intensity of my interest in a math problem keeps
me fixed before it even if doing so frustrates me. In principle, I can stop
at any time, and, once I have solved it, I will no longer be captivated by
it, although I might admire its aesthetic structure. It may be that my
emotional investment in another person I see every day (or never actually see except on a television screen or in memory) keeps one or
more images of that person always close to mind. Yet I can recognize
that I have been enchanted and, with self-discipline, wean myself from
fruitless emotional investments. Such reflection leads us to see that,
for all the feeling of oneself as a subject being bound to an object, the
last knot of fascination is that of detachment. The person who is bewitched by violent movies or video games is viewing the knife fights

and car chases at a safe distance, not engaging in them, although it is distinctly possible for people to establish patterns of stimulus and re-action that encourage them to pass from fascination to action. And the person who is tantalized by his or her memories of an event or an indi-vidual is also regarding that event or person from a psychological dis-tance. Detachment is not freedom, however, and only in highly circum-scribed theological contexts can it be regarded as higher than agapeic love.[2] Besides, in a state of fascination we do not usually find ourselves able to reflect at all; the mind spins rather than hovers.

Whatever the case (and it might vary quite considerably, depend-ing on the object that compels us and the strength of the attraction we feel), this general relation I have been describing calls for analysis since it seems to be a negative counterpart to contemplation, one that can easily be confused with it, especially, what we call *passive contempla-tion*. Doubtless, it has distinct filaments. In the thirteenth century, a number of these were classified under the general title *vices of the gaze*. Such is how Vincent of Beauvais (d. 1264) evokes them in his manual *Speculum morale*, and in doing so he is merely gathering the accumu-lated wisdom of the church.[3] For Vincent and the tradition that formed his way of thinking, evil thoughts and the practices that often follow them enter us through the eyes and take possession of the soul. In-deed, the eyes of others are perfectly capable of endangering us, espe-cially by way of envious looks. In ancient Roman times, eminent per-sons would walk or ride with a deformed slave in order to deflect the eyes of the envious or would wear an amulet, a *fascinans*, that would do the same thing.[4] Victorious generals enjoying a triumph were careful to have an image of the god Fascinus, most likely in the form of a phallus, placed underneath their four-horse chariot that, even though hidden, would repel malicious looks from the crowd.[5] The "evil eye," *malus ocu-lus*, was a deeply held fear, and the superstition remains so in parts of the world today. Only slowly has it been countered by a new sense of fascination—of being spellbound by something or someone—that started to be recognized in the early seventeenth century. But this sense is not to be my main concern.

The thread I wish to examine has been drawn by modern philoso-phers since Immanuel Kant and has been apparent, though mostly un-named as a theme, in phenomenology since Husserl. I refer to *fasci-nation*, not in its folk meaning ("sorcery") or in its current colloquial meaning ("to attract and 'hold spellbound' by delightful qualities; to charm, enchant" [OED]), but in its late eighteenth-century philosoph-ical sense, as ventured by Kant, to which I shall turn in a little while.

To be sure, there are other phased counterparts to contemplation—brooding, curiosity, fantasy, and prying, among them—and later in this book aesthetic contemplation, which sometimes avails itself of fantasy, will interest us, just as it did in chapter 2.[6] Here, however, my focus is on fascination. It shares some traits with other mental states, both natural (allurement, awe, bedazzlement, captivation, obsession, preoccupation, reverie, shock, and vertigo, e.g.) and induced (by alcohol, hypnosis, marijuana, trance, among other things), but I will not be addressing its similarities and differences with these states.[7]

Psychoanalytic literature, clinical as well as theoretical, on all these mental states and their treatments abounds, and, although some of it will worry at what I have to say, I will not engage directly or consistently with it.[8] Nor will I be concerned with different ways of distinguishing fascination. One might say, for instance, that it contrasts with distraction or boredom or with simple repugnance, and there is truth enough in these remarks for intriguing developments from them to take place. But here I am interested primarily in the doublet of contemplation and fascination. Assuredly, the phenomenon of being fascinated by certain intentional objects (and, strictly, with that which has no concrete objecthood) has been distinctively proposed by philosophers of our times, from Heidegger to Derrida and from Derrida to Claude Romano, who draw on phenomenology but set themselves either against or to the side of the adventures and consolations of religion.[9] Only Romano has explicitly examined it in any detail. To look into the depths of the tradition is not simply a matter of posing the question in a richer context. It is also to see more clearly what happens in the modern competition for primacy between transcendence and the transcendental.

We have encountered this distinction before, and already we know that it takes various forms. Contemplation has long been associated with divine transcendence, with that which is above or beyond any genus; accordingly, in the twelfth and thirteenth centuries, this supreme transcendence was addressed by way of the doctrine of the transcendentals. God is to be approached by way of being, unity, goodness, truth, and so on. We can properly grasp the divine persons in their relation to the divine essence only by way of real distinctions. Also, we can understand the pure perfections we ascribe to the deity only by following the doctrine of the transcendentals. The proper study of the transcendentals therefore introduces us to the practice of contemplation itself. Now, this metaphysical theology has usually been shadowed by one or another version of the allegorical hermeneutic, which is based on the figure of ascent in the intellectual or spiritual life. Yet, with a felt breakdown of confidence in being able to speak convincingly of divine transcendence as the Schoolmen did, there begins the rise of both the hermeneutics of faith and the hermeneutics of suspicion.[10] The former starts to appeal to those Christians invested in Luther's Reformation for whom the Word of God is given primarily or even exclusively in scripture (and not in natural theology, regarded as a part of metaphysics), and for whom scripture is more likely to be understood by way of types, and not by reference to allegory. It is a matter of restoring or recollecting meaning. The latter is to be located among those skeptical of the dogmatic claims of Christianity. Some of these people have been agnostics or atheists; others have been on the liberal wing of the religion, attempting to disclose a faith unencumbered by doctrinal accretion derived, in part, from Greek philosophy or unduly influenced by fringe devotions.[11] In each case, suspicion of what is on the surface leads to a diagnosis of illusion, and consciousness must be expanded in order to find the truth. Expansion tends to occur by deciphering surface codes by an appeal to something anterior to them or hidden in them that must be made manifest.[12]

Suspicion is a specular version of allegoresis. Karl Marx (1818–83), Friedrich Nietzsche (1844–1900), and Sigmund Freud (1856–1939), the three "masters of suspicion," favor one or more figures of descent. We pass from a textual surface, which we are enjoined not to trust, until we find a satisfactory level far beneath that will manifest a hidden truth that affects the surface conditions. For Marx, capitalist society hides the social importance of controlling the mode of production from the working class, from whom it derives the power that it uses to subjugate them. For Nietzsche, Christian morality has occluded the significance of the will to power and reduced the force of life itself. For Freud, the superego has repressed the urgent strivings of the id, detaching them from their original objects of desire, and rerouting them into other areas of the psyche, where, if not safely released, they can bring about neurosis. In each case, a combination of careful reading, which often goes against the grain of the text or fastens on an apparently marginal concern, and elements of quest romance enables us to view structures that, exercised by one or another source of power, have been responsible for diminishing our lives and will continue to do so unless they are radically addressed and changed. We are not enjoined to contemplate the structures we find in the depths, and we need to take precautions not to be overly fascinated by what we find there, for we need to free ourselves from their spell. Action, not contemplation, is called for, whether it be taking to the streets, revaluing values, or driving to an appointment with one's analyst.

We might see a ground for the hermeneutic of suspicion being put in place earlier than Marx, by someone with quite other interests: Kant. It is Kant who changes the meaning of the word *transcendental* so that it denotes not an object of knowledge but a mode of our knowledge that is held to be possible a priori.[13] We cannot have empirical access to the transcendental employment of categories, but we can correctly deduce that these categories are real and even tabulate what they are.[14] Where the Schoolmen took the transcendentals to be the very subject of metaphysics (or at least an important part of it), Kant reworks the notion so that it limits metaphysics to a small area. A critique of pure reason is needed to expose the folly of thinking certain things—God, the Soul, and Freedom—on the basis of pure reason and to uncover the grounds of any metaphysics that might be proposed in the future.[15] Metaphysics becomes confined to the realm of possibility, not actuality. To this end, Kant shows that reason errs when it applies concepts to objects that are supposedly outside or beyond space and time, and we must restrict our intellectual activities to those items that appear within the sensible forms of space and time. Natural theology is dismissed in favor of reflective faith, and God discloses himself to us only in moral action, not in mystical intuitions, prayer, sacraments, revealed theology, or dogmatic interpretation of the scriptures.[16]

An appeal to a descent—one that deduces the structure of the human mind—overcomes illusions, just as Marx, Nietzsche, and Freud were to do later in their own ways. Critique need not necessarily be in the service of suspicion, as in modern times, but the hermeneutic of suspicion always uses one or another style of critique. Always looking down into the depths, secular critique rejects contemplation: its watchword is *mystification*, but it allows no room for a genuine mystery. Its concerns are invariably social, sometimes understood quite narrowly, and no hermeneutic of suspicion, deployed by itself, has ever uncovered impulses of delight, generosity, love, thankfulness, or wonder. Of course, this hermeneutic must also finally reject fascination, but it is often courted by it. The suspicious reader looks at what hides from us in the darkness beneath texts, what is truly monstrous: hysteria, illusion, neurosis, oppression, weakness. Only if we resist such temptation can we bring about a revolution, revalue values, and live a life (as Freud glumly put it) of common human unhappiness.[17] The operation has been essential at times and remains useful, but it does not tell us how to live once the monsters have been exposed and defeated. Contemplation, however, seeks to give an answer, one that retains the surface of the text rather than annulling it, one that decenters the ego that thrives on suspicion.

*

Husserl did not inherit the idea of philosophy as critique; rather, as we have seen in chapter 3, he recovered, in his own way, a mode of reflection or contemplation that he took to be essential to the activities of the philosopher, and this recovery occurred by way of ἐποχή and reduction. Intriguingly, when he came to dispute the doctrine of reduction in Husserl, Heidegger seized on the very tranquility that he saw at the heart of the converted gaze, which is at one with wonder and which Husserl thought could be a permanent achievement of the philosopher. Not so, Heidegger objects; tranquility is a *Stimmung*, one of many, and not the one most needed to philosophize, at least not if the aim of philosophizing is to attune oneself to being. *Stimmung* has a wider range than the English word *mood*, taken as a psychic feeling, for Heidegger, and he prefers the coinage *Befindlichkeit*, which combines the senses of being in a situation and finding oneself having to deal with it. It is not a transcendentally purified state.

For Heidegger, moods come over one and disclose *Dasein* in its thrownness (*Geworfenheit*), and he mostly attends to those moods found at the darker end of the spectrum, fundamental attunements such as dread (*Angst*) and deep boredom (*Langeweile*) and, less basic, states such as fright (*Erschrecken*), which is a component of foreboding (*Ahnung*).[18] Presumably, positive moods such as elation, joy, and gratitude, all of which we associate with the heights of contemplation, do not manifest being human to ourselves. Certainly, Heidegger does not think that tranquility is appropriate for philosophizing. But he makes no remark about religious contemplation. In any case, when a dark mood overcomes one, when philosophy is refigured as a *Kampf* (struggle) in concrete factical life rather than reflection in the phenomenological attitude, there can be no room for contemplation in phenomenology.[19] Contemplative reflection becomes one *Stimmung* among others and is to be excluded (*auszuschalten*). Given that Husserl characterizes ἐποχή in just this way, this is nothing short of ironic.[20] There can presumably be interest, which responds to a "heightening of intensity" (*Intensitätssteigerung*) in one's intentional rapport with something unusual; but, when reading Husserl, Heidegger does not separate tranquility and interest.[21]

Instead, Heidegger notices a phased counterpart to tranquility that I will call *fascination*. (For ease of discussion, I will keep to the English

rather than pass each time to one or another German word; we will
have enough lexical difference to keep in mind by way of reminding
ourselves of the Greek and the Latin.) His acknowledgment of this
phenomenon marks a decisive break with the sort of protophenom-
enology one can uncover (with one eye looking ahead and squinting
more than a little to Husserl) in Richard of St. Victor. To be sure, *fascinatio* was well known in the twelfth century by anyone with even
a rudimentary classical education, let alone knowledge of the fathers.
I have already mentioned Vincent of Beauvais and alluded to Roman
practices. Basil of Caesarea (330–79), for one, had spoken long before
of βάσκανος (bewitchment) in his often-cited homily on envy that continues and redirects Greek reflection on the emotion: it is the condition in which one is infected by what became known in the Latin West
as the *malus oculus*, the evil eye previously mentioned in passing.[22]

Taken up by Evagrius Ponticus (345–99) in his discussion of λύπη
(grief, especially as caused by nostalgia) as one of the eight negative
thoughts, we find *invidia* (*in* + *videre*: "look on" with a sense of looking
too closely) or envy becoming a distinct mortal sin in the view of Gregory the Great and, thereafter, a familiar theme in homilies on the seven
deadly sins.[23] Aquinas himself continues the idea of the eye being active in the context of corporeal matter's being changed by a being composed of form and matter or by God himself (and not by the imagination, as Ibn Sina thought in his comments on Aristotle's *De anima*).[24]
He extends the tradition of eyes infecting the air. Yet the sense of fascination in play in later phenomenology does not come from the fathers, or the Greeks before them, or Aquinas, or even Renaissance figures such as Marsilio Ficino (1433–99) and Francis Bacon (1561–1626),
although certain associations, going back to βάσκανος, still cling to the
relation in some contexts.[25]

We must look to Kant to find this modern sense of fascination,
which he details, almost in passing, in his *Anthropology from a Pragmatic Point of View* (1785). "Fascination [*Bezauberung (fascinatio)*],"
he says there, is "a false sense impression that, as we say, is not natural."[26] Unlike contemplation, which has a fixed focus, "in one and the
same place," as Richard says, the object that holds us changes, it seems,
when one examines it more closely: multistable phenomena, such as
Jastrow's duck-rabbit or the Schröder staircase, along with illusions,
such as those in M. C. Escher's graphic works, supply different sorts of
examples, but the reflection of Narcissus, which remains the same as
the one who gazes at it, also gives us a potent example.[27] We recall with
the force of inevitability Ovid's beautiful story in book 3 of the *Metamorphoses* of Narcissus gazing at his reflection in a pool so pure that

no bird has ever ruffled its surface. Tiresias has already foretold that he will live a long life only if he does not know himself, and, when he sees his reflection, the seer's words begin to come true:

quid videat, nescit; sed quod videt, uritur illo,
atque oculos idem, qui decipit, incitat error.

(What he sees, he does not grasp but burns for it,
and the same error attracts and deceives his eyes.)

And a few lines later:

Non illum Cereris, non illum cura quietis
abstrahere inde potest, sed opaca fusus in herba
spectat inexpleto mendacem lumine formam
perque oculos perit ipse suos.

(No care for bread or rest can make him leave,
but stretched on the shadowy grass he gazes at
that false image with eyes that cannot be satisfied
and perishes because of his own eyes.)[28]

Narcissus is fascinated by his own image to the point of being seduced by it but with no positive outcome being possible, and his particular experience of this state of mind shows several things about it. Despite appearances, the gaze is fundamentally empty; there is an absorption to the point of fatal obsession with what arrests one, and there is an erasure of crucial differences between subject and object.

With Ovid's lines in mind, we return to Kant's idea of fascination as giving us a sense impression that is false and unnatural. Objects that hold us spellbound have a special epistemic status. False sense impressions are joined by an awareness of irresistible attraction and a quality of feeling (passion), and the combination prevents an appropriate epistemic judgment from being made. The state in which a fascinated person finds himself or herself is "like a bird that flutters against a mirror in which he sees his reflection [*Wie ein Vogel der gegen den Spiegel, in dem er sich selbst ficht, flatter*]," Kant says, "and at one moment takes it for a real bird, at another, not."[29] So there is no steady gaze on a kestrel, such as Hopkins enjoyed in the Clwyd Valley and celebrated in "The Windhover," but sheer frustration and a dead end as regards coming to a sound judgment about what one sees. Kant's understanding of fascination slowly becomes changed over the centuries, without anything being explicitly remarked, into an intentional relation one can have with some phenomena, to be sure, but also with anterior states that never quite manifest themselves. Like contemplation, fascination comes with increased attention, although it results less in wonder than in petrifaction; unlike contemplation, it stems wholly from the subject who becomes committed to a state of endless reflection, an involuntary absorption with something hovering before him or her. It is quite the opposite of freedom.

The influence of Kant's rethinking of fascination can be felt in even the most cursory reading of major writers who have lived in his wake, which itself becomes the very space of phenomenological investigation.[30] A first case in point, which suggests itself by virtue of the Kantianism of the author, occurs in a work of Rudolf Otto's of enduring theological interest, *The Holy* (1917), which popularized the expression *mysterium tremendum et fascinans*.[31] Otto points out that, for all its horror and dread, the "daemonic-divine object" is also something "that allures us with a potent charm" and the one who stands or kneels before it has an impulse "to make it somehow his own." He distinguishes the mysterious and the fascinating only to find a trait common to both:

> We saw that in the case of the element of the mysterious the "wholly other" led on to the supernatural and transcendent and that above these appeared the "beyond" (ἐπέκεινα) of mysticism, through the non-rational side of religion being raised to its highest power and stressed to excess. It is the same in the case of the element of "fascination"; here, too, is possible a translation into mysticism [*so wiederholt sich auch beim Momente des fascinans die Möglichkeit des Überganges in Mystik*]. At its highest point of stress the fascinating becomes the "overabounding" [*Höchstspannung*], "exuberant" [*Überschwänglich*], the mystical "moment" which exactly corresponds upon this line to the ἐπέκεινα upon the other line of approach, and which is to be understood accordingly.[32]

There is little doubt that fascination belongs to biblical experience and all the more to mysticism, though not always in the sense that Otto has in mind. He adduces Mark 10:32: "And they were on the road, going up to Jerusalem, and Jesus was walking ahead of them; and they were amazed [ἐθαμβοῦντο], and those who followed were afraid."[33] Here, amazement is taken to be stupor or fascination. One might also recall Paul's words to the Galatians: "O foolish Galatians! Who has bewitched you [ἐβάσκανεν], before whose eyes Jesus Christ was publicly proclaimed as crucified?" (Gal. 3:1 [RSV]). In a different vein, we might also recall Moses's stunned encounter with the burning bush (Exod. 3:2–3) or Isaiah's sublime vision of the seraphim, followed by hearing the Lord's commandment (Isa. 6:1–13), or the disciples' stupefaction at the transfiguration of Jesus on Mt. Tabor (Matt. 17:6–7 as well as the other synoptics). All the same, we must be careful to recognize that Otto was one of several who helped establish the late nineteenth- and early twentieth-century discursive formation of mysticism, which, among other things, tends to present contemplation in psychological categories.[34] We must tread with care.

It comes as no surprise that Otto links fascination (*das Fascinans*) to religious longing and to solemnity. The latter occurs as an encounter between the human and the divine intensifies, which leads the subject to overflow all reasonable bounds of experience and become ineluctably drawn to features in the divine that exceed morality and rationality.[35] I might be horrified by the effulgence of the sacred; I might be disgusted by it, especially if I encounter it in a religious practice that I regard as frenzied or manic (snake handing and *toque de santo*, e.g.). I will certainly be overwhelmed by it. Otto points out that, since the radical transcendence of the divine is of the ontological order, not the moral order, an element of ambiguity will be irreducible. It is a curious claim. Strictly, there cannot be an ambiguity of being and value, but divine being can be ascribed a value by a votary or a cult. "There will, then, in fact be two values to distinguish in the numen," Otto says, "its 'fascination' (*fascinans*) will be that element in it whereby it is of *subjective* value (= beatitude) to man; but it is 'august' (*augustum*) in so far as it is recognized as possessing in itself *objective* value that claims our homage."[36] To this the church will respond by saying that the *mysterium tremendum et fascinans* will have been divine if the encounter with it leads to good works and not moral sterility. But even to speak of *the church* in this way is to assume a minimally developed Christianity, and it is when Otto finally turns to this stage of ecclesial life that we find him considering contemplation.

When the deeply Protestant Otto turns to contemplation, we would not expect him to encounter Richard of St. Victor or Aquinas or evoke the ontological structures of reality that are to be contemplated. Even so, we might be a little surprised that he does so by way of Schleiermacher. He settles on the great preacher's doctrine of divination, the thinking and recognition of the holy in its appearances:

What Schleiermacher is feeling after is really the faculty or capacity of deeply absorbed *contemplation* [K o n t e m p l a t i o n], when confronted by the vast, living totality and reality of things as it is

in nature and history. Wherever a mind is exposed in a spirit of absorbed submission to impressions of "the universe," it becomes
capable—so he lays it down—of experiencing "intuitions" and
"feelings" (*Anschauungen* and *Gefüle*) of something that is, as it
were, a sheer overplus, in addition to empirical reality.

Contemplation is to be distinguished from fascination, then, but in a
manner that Richard and Aquinas would not have recognized. The terrifying experience of the *fascinans* properly belongs to an early stage of
religious sensibility, and, as a religion develops, so its rational elements
by way of liturgy and doctrine serve to "schematize" what entrances
earlier human beings. This happens "by means of the ideas of goodness, mercy, love, and, so schematized, becomes all that we mean by
Grace."[37] Only once the intoxicating relation with the divine has been
sobered up by recourse to reason can there be the calm and freedom
required to contemplate the cosmos. *Fascinans* and *augustum* no longer present themselves as an irresolvable ambiguity and no longer even
compete once they have been rethought by way of value; the subjective
and the objective attain harmony.

When we examine the judgments "that spring from pure contemplative feeling [*reiner Kontemplation*]," we find (in good Kantian fashion) that they "also resemble judgements of aesthetic taste in claiming,
like them, objective validity, universality, and necessity." Fascination
stymies judgment, either by overwhelming us or by puzzling us, and
only when it has been diluted can judgments properly be formed. Just
as judgments of taste cohere in a society as the individual tastes of its
citizens mature, so, too, Otto thinks, do judgments arising from the
practice of contemplation become able to be taught:

> Where, on the basis of a real talent in this direction, "contemplation"
> [*Kontemplation*] grows by careful exercise in depth and inwardness,
> there what one man feels *can* be "expounded" and "brought to con-
> sciousness" in another: one man can both educate himself to a gen-
> uine and true manner of feeling and be the means of bringing oth-
> ers to the same point; and that is what corresponds to the domain of
> "contemplation" to the part played by argument and persuasion in
> that of logical conviction.[38]

Not everyone possesses the ability to discern the holy, despite what
Schleiermacher thought about the universality of religious experience,
but, in a religion that has reached maturity (i.e., Christianity in the Enlightenment), anyone can learn to divine it from others.

Having isolated one defect in Schleiermacher's theology, Otto proceeds to identify another: the great Romantic theologian does not
specify Christ as the object of contemplation.[39] Even in the *Glaubens-
lehre* (1830), the emphasis is on the kingdom of God, not Christ as the
one who proclaims and inaugurates it. But, unless one can discern the
holiness in Jesus of Nazareth that led his contemporaries to hail him as
the Christ and suffer for believing in him, one cannot satisfactorily explain the extraordinary rise of Christianity, and, in any case, one develops a lopsided theology. To this one might add that Kant's new sense of
fascination applies at least as richly to Jesus as does the older sense in
which his preaching and his miracles were indices of him being a holy
man, perhaps more charismatic or more powerful than others who appeared after him—Simon bar Kokhba (d. ca. 135), for instance—but
in essence no different from them. Instead, one might say that Jesus
enthralled his disciples even though there was no sense impression
that favored him. He irresistibly attracted them and called forth a religious passion in them and in many other people who heard him, yet
they could not make appropriate judgments about him while he lived.
He was himself a parable. Only with the resurrection, which retrospectively casts a light on his ministry and its significance, could they begin
fully to grasp what it means to say that Jesus is the Christ. Resurrection
is a hermeneutic as well as a doctrine.

*

Returning to philosophy, we find another principal heir to Kant and a
contemporary of Otto's in Heidegger. In no way does Heidegger seek
to resolve the ambiguity of fascination, as Otto does; rather, he sets
in motion the spinning of that ambiguity that will dazzle those who
come after him. Consider *Being and Time* (1927) where the experience
of primordial difference leads to fascination, considered ontologically
and not only psychologically, and, to begin with, where the idle talk or
chatter (*Gerede*) that dazes one is linked to ambiguity:

> Dasein fails to hear itself, and listens away to the "they"; and this
> listening-away gets broken by the call if that call, in accordance with
> its character as such, arouses another kind of hearing, which, in rela-
> tionship to the hearing that is lost, has a character in every way op-
> posite. If in this lost hearing, one has been fascinated [*benommen*] by
> the "hubbhub" of the manifold ambiguity which idle talk possesses
> in its everyday "newness," then the call must do its calling without
> any hubbub and unambiguously, leaving no foothold in curiosity.[40]

Idle talk absorbs us in "average everydayness" and seems to give us a comforting world in intersubjective relations, yet at the same time it uproots us from the tradition of thinking and feeling by means of which we are called by conscience to live; it seems to tell us something yet indicates nothing of lasting value; it seems to be brand new yet is always going out of date at a breathtaking speed.[41] Today, the brevity of news cycles makes even alarming items of national and international politics flare up into significance and then die down just as quickly. We have become inured to politicians speaking of recent events for which they are responsible and that they would rather forget as "ancient history" while journalists who feel the momentum of the news cycle just as keenly are eager to move on to new topics, almost always on the dark side of the spectrum.

Several pages later in *Being and Time*, fascination in the sense of being dazed reappears, this time to do with *Angst*, and once again in the context of an ambiguity:

> The temporality of anxiety is peculiar; for anxiety is grounded primordially in having been, and only out of this do the future and the Present temporalize themselves; in this peculiar temporality is demonstrated the possibility of that power which is distinctive for the mood of anxiety. In this, Dasein is taken all the way back [*zurückgenommen*] to its naked uncanniness, and becomes fascinated [*benommen*] by it. This fascination, however, not only *takes* Dasein back from its "*worldly*" possibilities, but at the same time gives it the possibility of an *authentic* potentiality-for-Being.[42]

The fascination that comes with dread—specifically of my death— takes me back from the possibilities of being in the world that I constantly project; at the same time, it allows me to grasp an authentic way of being in the world and thus accords me the possibility of an authentic future. I can learn to see that *Dasein* is always mine, that I need not lose it by being absorbed in my dealings with the world, that future choices can be mine, and that I can eventually embrace my own nothingness in death.

Fascination is a phenomenon in which some of the reactions it produces do not always appear in the subject (or *Dasein*). Heidegger does not foreground anything about an altered state, a dilation of time, or a feeling of stagnation or even disgust when he considers the spell that gossip or the news can cast over us. Yet these things are precisely what impose themselves on Jean-Paul Sartre in his early novel *Nausea* (1938) when his protagonist, Antoine Roquentin, goes into a municipal park.

The event has nothing whatsoever to do with hearing idle talk; it is simply about regarding the roots of a chestnut tree. It is a "revelation" (*illumination*), the details of which have become very well-known to modern readers: "The root, the park gates, the bench, the sparse grass on the lawn, all that had vanished; the diversity of things, their individuality, was only an appearance, a veneer. This veneer had melted, leaving soft, monstrous masses, in disorder—naked, with a frightening, obscene nakedness."[43] It is this event that plunges Roquentin into a sense of his superfluity in the world, a world that he has no alternative but to describe as absurd since it supplies no ground that accommodates and nurtures him. Coming out of his reverie, he asks himself: "How long did that spell last? [*Combien de temps dura cette fascination?*]"[44] To use a slightly later view of Sartre's, in observing the chestnut tree, Roquentin has seen an object cutting its figure against emptiness.[45] His consciousness has thereby been altered; time has stretched. The reverie he has experienced is plainly marked in his oxymoronic description of what he has beheld, "a horrible ecstasy [*un extase horrible*]."[46] He has known fascination by way of ambiguity or, if you wish, ambivalence.

Ponder too Maurice Blanchot at the start of *The Space of Literature* (1955) where fascination is more distinctly rendered as a theme. "If our childhood fascinates us," he writes, "this happens because childhood is the moment of fascination, is itself fascinated." He continues:

> And this golden age seems bathed in a light which is splendid because unrevealed. But it is only that this light is foreign to revelation, has nothing to reveal, is pure reflection, a ray which is still only the gleam of an image. Perhaps the force of the maternal figure receives its intensity from the very force of fascination, and one might say then, that if the mother exerts this fascinating attraction it is because, appearing when the child lives altogether in fascination's gaze, she concentrates in herself all the powers of enchantment. It is because the child is fascinated that the mother is fascinating, and that is also why all the impressions of early childhood have a kind of fixity which comes from fascination.

In fascination, he says, "the gaze gets taken in, absorbed by an immobile movement and a depthless deep. What is given us by this contact at a distance is the image, and fascination is passion for the image [*la fascination est la passion de l'image*]."[47] The difference between Sartre's view of fascination (centered on an object) and Blanchot's (related to image) is patent, and it should be noted that in his own way Blanchot retains the active element of the evil eye (but without it being evil), for fascination, as he says, not only takes in the gaze but also "seizes sight [*saisit la vue*]."[48] It does so without inauthenticity becoming a problem.

Image, for Blanchot, is not an image in the sense employed by the Imagists at the start of the last century, namely, (to cite Ezra Pound) as "that which presents an intellectual and emotional complex in an instant of time."[49] Blanchot is not concerned to prize the concrete, visual image in a poem, to see the faces of passengers in a Paris métro station as "Petals on a wet, black bough," for instance; rather, he alerts us to a situation that is neither real nor unreal.[50] It is found in literature, of course, but also in everyday life. He continues:

> What fascinates us robs us of our power to give sense. It abandons its "sensory" nature, abandons the world, draws back from the world, and draws us along. It no longer reveals itself to us, and yet it affirms itself in a presence foreign to the temporal present and to presence in space. Separation, which was the possibility of seeing, coagulates at the very center of the gaze into impossibility. The look thus finds, in what makes it possible, the power that neutralizes it, neither suspending nor arresting it, but on the contrary preventing it from ever finishing, cutting it off from any beginning, making of it a neutral, directionless gleam which will not go out, yet does not clarify—the gaze turned back upon itself and closed in a circle. Here we have an immediate expression of that reversal which is the essence of solitude. Fascination is solitude's gaze. It is the gaze of the incessant and interminable. In it blindness is vision still, vision which is no longer the possibility of seeing, but the impossibility of not seeing, the impossibility which becomes visible and perseveres—always and always—in a vision that never comes to an end: a dead gaze, a gaze become the ghost of an eternal vision.

A little later, he adds: "To write is to let fascination rule language [*disposer le langage sous la fascination*]."[51] Writing, then, has no part of freedom; it is being in the grip of that from which one cannot turn away: the gaze of the words, as they begin to form on the page or the screen. The gaze that looks back as I write is not me; it is my consciousness without me, a specter, an encounter with my present consciousness as it will be, preserved on a page, when I am dead.[52] My dead self will have nowhere to go other than back and forth in what I have written. It is a dark gloss on what Husserl calls *the transcendental life that survives empirical death*.[53]

By the end of *The Space of Literature*, Blanchot will have concluded that this fascination springs from a "radical reversal," an unstoppable shuttling back and forth of death as possibility and impossibility.[54] The former notion comes from Heidegger; the latter Levinas. And we may take them to be two faces of death.[55] On the one hand, *Dasein* grasps his or her last possibility in life, the possibility of impossibility; and, on the other hand, we experience death as fear of violence in which passivity is a condition, not a choice: there, death confronts us as the impossibility of possibility. With the one, I must face my own nothingness; with the other, my possibilities in life flake away. For Blanchot, the space of enchantment is opened and maintained by this irresolvable ambiguity before which the writer sits, pen in hand or fingers on a keyboard. Later, he will expand this scenario. We encounter all events as images, he says. At first, they interest us, then we are merely curious about them, and, finally, we behold them with an "empty but fascinated look."[56] We cannot prevent phenomena from becoming images: as soon as a phenomenon appears, the condition for becoming an image is already in place. When we face an image, Blanchot thinks, we are finally rendered passive in our encounters with it. Yet, where some people respond to this situation by insisting on the need to be more attentive, to do all that we can to regain the freshness of direct experience, Blanchot explores the implications of succumbing to the staleness of fascination and proposes the category of the experience of nonexperience. It is in admitting to the unworking of experience, he tells us, that we become attuned to those experiences—of *désoeuvrement, le désastre, le dehors*—which are never actually present to consciousness and point us ineluctably into the heart of atheism.[57]

Before leaving Blanchot, let us recall Jacques Derrida reflecting in *Parages* (1986) on Blanchot's narratives and noting how they gather around the motif of fascination. "*Come* would be the word of this fascination, of this attraction without attraction, of this identification without identity," he says. And his miming of Blanchot's characteristic syntax, *X* without *X*, is suggestive of fascination itself: I am attracted to someone or something I do not find attractive, and I identify with the person or object in the moment of losing my sense of self-identity.[58] (We might recall Swann's fascination with Odette in *Du côté de chez Swann* [1913].) In one of his last seminars, published as *The Death Penalty* (1999–2000), Derrida speaks of the spectacle of public executions exerting a fascination on those who assemble to view them, attracting and repulsing them at the same time.[59] Earlier, in *Dissemination* (1972), he continues to pull the delicate thread of ambiguity that dangles from Kant's text, this time noticing its play in φάρμακον, one of the many instances of that general quasi-transcendental structure he calls *la dif-férance*:

> This *pharmakon*, this "medicine," this philter, which acts as both
> remedy and poison, already introduces itself into the body of the
> discourse with all its ambivalence. This charm, this spellbind-
> ing virtue, this power of fascination [*Ce charme, cette vertu de fas-*
> *cination, cette puissance d'envoûtement*], can be—alternately or
> simultaneously—beneficent or maleficent.[60]

It is worth noting that, for Blanchot and Derrida at least, some of what
often fascinates us appears (the mother's face, the criminal about to be
executed), while other things that fascinate us—*le désastre, le dehors,
la différance*—cannot appear as such.[61] In their work, entrancement
is frequently leagued with what is anterior to phenomena, which, for
Blanchot, is what remains of the sacred and, for Derrida, is the quasi-
transcendental condition that prevents any identity from freezing into
self-identity.[62] If contemplation is tied to a thematic of presence, fascination is not, for it turns on an unstable ambiguity, here that of remedy
and poison, not a fixed point.

This ambiguity is further examined by Claude Romano in *Event and
World* (1998) in several rich pages on the relation of trauma and fascination.[63] The topic is not only of intrinsic interest but also salient
for Romano in his elaboration of the post-Heideggerian figure of *l'advenant*, the human being considered along the axis of starting *from*
something and being answerable (or not) *to* what happens to him or
her.[64] So trauma serves for Romano as a counterexample to the sort of
change that essentially marks *l'advenant*. A trauma is an event that we
cannot appropriate as our own or, at least, we might say, by way of re-
finement, that we cannot wholly appropriate. For all its enforced intimacy, a trauma remains outside us and paralyzes us. This can happen
in many ways, both before and after a brush with death.[65] Doubtless,
it occurs when circumstances force us to shift from thinking of death
as a general human possibility to thinking of it as something that im-
pinges on me here and now. When I face my impending death, I am
not merely afraid of it; I am terrified by it. The Office for the Dead has
told us this for centuries—*Timor mortis conturbat me*—not so much in
the nouns but in the verb.[66] We are *confounded* by the fear of imminent
death: baffled, confused, paralyzed. We find ourselves faced with diminishing possibilities and standing before the possibility of nothingness or, for believers, divine judgment, which may be worse.

If Romano begins to sound more than a little Heideggerian here, it is no accident. Heidegger has many readers who become apparent as his heirs when they philosophize about death, even if they depart from him when they philosophize about other matters.[67] Romano says: "My selfhood collapses [in the trauma of facing death], unable to respond to what happens to me; I am entirely delivered over to the anonymous empire of death, to the impersonal 'one dies,' which is its most proper sense. Here, death is no longer something I can avoid, but is what surrounds and envelops me, taking all power away from me, not only over it, but first of all over myself."[68] This situation gives rise to fascination. This loss of self is quite distinct from the *mors mystica* of rapture and from that which aesthetic contemplation calls forth, which Schopenhauer has examined with care.[69] In contemplation, our personality is set aside as much as is possible, and we encounter the object of contemplation in a subjectivity as pure as it will ever be; we see less the thing or the event than its εἶδος. Yet, in fascination, our entire sense of self is threatened, and we are incapable of identifying the threat in its idea. We can pass from fascination to contemplation, Schopenhauer suggests, only if we acknowledge the power of what is before us and wrench ourselves away from it by a supreme act of will. Notice that I can contemplate someone else's demise and that I can contemplate death in the abstract, but it seems that, when I am brought up sharply before my own death, in the doctor's office or when I hear someone break into my house in the middle of the night, I become fixated by the event. Indeed, one can be enthralled by it before it happens or even if it never actually happens at the time. Phantasy and fascination sometimes go hand in hand.

Romano's observations recapitulate and clarify the philosophical trajectory I have been tracking since quoting Kant while at the same time extending at least one aspect of it into psychology:

For there is no terror without fascination, without the captivation by the terrifying, which belongs to terror as such. But what does "fascination" mean here? It is, as we will see, an attitude that is in some way double [*une attitude en quelque sorte double*], whose two "faces" are nevertheless like the obverse and reverse of a single phenomenon: on the one hand, the impossibility of understanding and "recognizing" oneself in what happens to us, an impossibility that belongs necessarily to all traumatism; on the other hand, a seizure by the event, which can no longer appear except with its "objective" face, as pure chance or fate utterly deprived of sense, holding us more in its grasp the less we can recognize ourselves in it. Here, events are no longer that from which I can understand myself in my singularity. Rather, precisely to the extent that I am no longer capable of appropriating their meaning, they are that which reflects my image to me as a hallucinated double, and that of which the occurrence stupefies me, grips me, and leaves me thunderstruck. Thus, *the less* I am able to understand myself from what happens to me—because of traumatism's excess beyond any possible appropriation—*the more* it holds me in its grasp, in the mode of fascination.[70]

These lines nicely capture the nature of the ambiguity, as it presents itself in trauma, that generates and maintains fascination. An event comes on me out of the blue, without any apparent reason or justification that it should come to *me*; it offers me no mirror, only a blankness in which I cannot see myself, let alone recognize myself, yet, even though it does not grant me a clear picture of myself, only at best a hallucination of myself, it will not let me go. The grip of my hallucinated gaze is not steady, however. For, the less I can find myself—unique, irreplaceable—in a traumatic event, the more I am traumatized and utterly beheld by what terrifies me.

*

In order to probe fascination a little more and to do so as concretely as possible, I turn to Coleridge's long poem "The Rime of the Ancient Mariner" (1798). It was reprinted, with changes, in the second edition of the *Lyrical Ballads* (1800), which Coleridge coauthored with Wordsworth, and to which a gloss was added in 1815–16 for a collection of Coleridge's verse. The poem is widely taken as an early and lively flourishing of British Romanticism. Its orthography, ballad form, along with the Christianizing gloss, and its attention to sublime prospects in the distant seas and the evocation of a spirit world give it the air of an earlier age.[71] Its deliberately antiquated aura is important for the scene of bewitchment it depicts and for the gripping tale that is told. Admirer of Kant that he was, Coleridge here does not take up the philosopher's new sense of fascination, which he did not know about at the time, even if a modern reader might find it there.[72] He depicts an older world in which spirits and sorcery are taken for granted, from which Kant would shrink with distaste, and he concerns himself with the enchantment of a story.

Kant would have had some sympathy for the man Coleridge takes to orient us to his long poem, however. For the theologian Thomas Burnet (ca. 1635–1715) was, after John Dennis (1658–1734) and Joseph Addison (1672–1719), one of the first British people to speak of wild mountains as sublime and to experience what Kant was to call *negative pleasure*.[73] More, he would have approved Burnet's skepticism about undue speculation about spirits. Nonetheless, he would have turned away from belief in invisible beings to be found in all parts of the world. The epigraph to "The Rime of the Ancient Mariner," added in 1817, is a curious condensation of a long passage in Burnet's *Archaeologiae philosophicae sive: Doctrina antiqua de rerum originibus* (1692) that looks askance on the religious ontology of the kabbalah:

> Facile credo, plures esse Naturas invisibiles quam visibles in rerum universitate. Sed horum omnium familiam quis nobis enarrabit? et gradus et cognnationes et discrimina et singulorum munera? Quid agunt? quae loca habitant? Harum rerum notitiam semper ambivit ingenium humanum, nunquam attigit. Juvat, interea, non duffiteor, quandoque in animo, tanquam in tabula, majoris et meliorism mundi imaginem, contemplari: ne mens assuefacta hodiernae vitae minutilis se contrahat nimis, et tota subsidat in pusillas cogitations. Sed veritati interea invigilandum est, modusque servandus, ut certa ab incertis, diem a nocte, distinguamus.

> (I can easily believe, that there are more Invisible than Visible Beings in the Universe. . . . But who will declare to us the Family of all these, and acquaint us with the Agreements, Differences, and peculiar Talents which are to be found among them? It is true, Human Wit has, always desired a Knowledge of these Things, though it has never yet attained it. . . . *I will own that it is very profitable, sometimes to contemplate in the Mind, as in a Draught, the Image of the greater and better World; lest the Soul being accustomed to the Trifles of this present Life, should contract itself too much and altogether rest in mean Cogitations;* but, in the mean Time, we must take Care to keep to the Truth, and observe Moderation, that we may distinguish certain from uncertain Things, and Day from Night.)[74]

By leaving out Burnet's theological worries about the speculative excesses of kabbalah and St. Paul's reticence about speaking of the angelic hierarchies, Coleridge gives us a Burnet who justifies the use of the Polar Spirit and its attendant demons in the poem.[75] Also, perhaps, the epigraph gives an apology for the spiritual scope of the poem. "The Rime of the Ancient Mariner" will be an aid to contemplating "the greater and better world" if by that one understands a world that is charged with mystery, not one marked by arbitrary events.

No sooner has the ballad commenced than we witness a scene of attenuated bewitchment, not a gaze that utterly debilitates the one who receives it, but one that holds him captive for the duration:

> It is an ancient Mariner,
> And he stoppeth one of three.
> "By thy long grey beard and glittering eye,
> Now wherefore stopp'st thou me?" (lines 1–4)[76]

About to enter a wedding feast, the framing narrator is halted by the old mariner, who "holds him with his skinny hand" and, more unnervingly, "holds him with his glittering eye." (The first version of the poem is more explicit about the nature of the gaze. The wedding guest says in pt. 5: "For that, which *comes out of thine eye*, doth make / My body and soul to be still.")[77] Stopped by the mariner while his two friends file past to join the feast, the narrator alone is chosen to hear a strange tale for a reason that is given only right at the end of the ballad. At the start of the poem, the choice seems entirely unmotivated. The mariner is required as penance to travel from land to land and knows "the man that must hear" his story the very moment that he sees his face (lines 588–90), the most exposed and vulnerable part of him.

This restless narrating of his story is the burden of the mariner's ongoing penance for a strange crime that is the spiritual center of the poem. From that moment on, his life is consumed, first, by the events that the tale relates and, second, by the perpetual retelling of his tale. Only the homiletic final words of the poem—"He prayeth best, who loveth best / All things both great and small!" (lines 614–15)—indicate anything of his life outside the story. Equally striking as the sudden appearance of the mariner out of nowhere is the effect that he has on the wedding guest. Caught in the mariner's gaze, he can only stand still. Instead of pushing the old man aside, he regresses and "listens like a three years' child" (line 15).[78] Even when he hears "the loud bassoon" within the hall, which announces the arrival of the bride, and is roused to his duty and pleasure as a guest, "he cannot choose but hear" the mariner (lines 32, 18). He is held by the old man's gaze and voice, for the story has barely started: all he has heard so far is that a ship left dock, that dawn rose, and that the ship sailed south so that the sun became higher and higher in the sky. Thus far, the story is less than compelling. Later, when the narrative is well under way, the wedding guest will recoil from the mariner only when he suspects that he might be a damned spirit or associated with hellish fiends. The story itself draws him in, further and further; we hear no more about wishing to enter the wedding feast.

The mariner's tale converges on a peculiar event the significance of which is hard to establish, especially without the gloss. As the ship approaches the South Pole, an albatross unexpectedly crosses the sky and disperses the snow fog that has beset the crew, presumably making their navigation of the icy seas extremely dangerous. Two quite distinct movements are in play here, one attenuated and looking back to Roman times, one very new, arising in eighteenth-century Germany:

1.   The bird is hailed as an omen, and here we may see a vestige of a bird flying through what, in retrospect, is taken to have been a *templum* and giving good auspices to the sailors. The old mariner reflects: "And an it were a Christian soul, / We hail'd it in God's name" (lines 65–66). And the "And an" will weigh heavily on him and the crew as events unfurl. For the sailors, the appearance of the bird is undeniably auspicious, for "The Ice did split with a Thunder-fit; / The helmsman steer'd us through!" (lines 69–70). More, "a good south wind" (line 71) speeds the ship along, and the albatross remains with the ship as it heads northeast, playing with the crew and eating the scraps of food that they leave for him (the first version says the offering is "biscuit-worms") (line 67).[79] Soon, however, the weather becomes misty again and remains so for nine nights; and it is then that the mariner takes matters into his own hands. He doubts the *templum* and the auspices that it gives and acts precipitously: "With my cross-bow / I shot the Albatross" (lines 81–82). The crime committed is, whatever else it is, finally against the motivation of the supernatural order, indeed, against the practices of auspices.[80]

2.   The bird that crosses the path of the ship gives a false impression of being motivated to help the crew; its appearance and the dispersal of the snow fog, along with the coming of the south wind, is pure coincidence. The "As if" is entirely delusive on the part of the sailors, yet it gives rise to an irresistible attraction to the bird over the coming days on the part of the entire crew. They cathect onto the bird, with a religious or quasi-religious passion that has no basis in reality, and in the end find themselves quite incapable of making a sound epistemic judgment about it. Is it associated with the divine (clearing the snow fog), or with the merely natural, or with the demonic (bringing about more snow fog)? Here, the albatross would have nothing to do with divine auspices; rather, it would be fascinating, either in the old sense of sorcery or in the modern Kantian sense of the word that Coleridge did not know at the time but that is likely to be familiar to the modern reader. Even if one has not read Kant's *Anthropology*, one is likely to have internalized the sense of *fascination* ventured there. It is a part of our philosophical culture.

This ambiguity between the motivated and the unmotivated albatross (and the killing of it) will stay with us as we continue to read
Coleridge's poem; it is a structural element that makes the ballad fascinating. The bird is a powerful part of this entrancement, as Mary Shelley, Baudelaire, and Melville were quick to testify.[81]

Now the ship heads north, toward the equator, but without any
"sweet bird" following it (line 88). The crew roundly condemn the
mariner and then, reflecting that the albatross perhaps was responsible
for the snow fog, agree that it was right that the bird had been killed.
They thereby become complicit in the act. Only later, when "a blessed
troop of angelic spirits" (marginal gloss accompanying lines 359–62)
appears, is there another mention of birds, and we are invited to believe that the sounds are actually those of the angels as they enter the
bodies of the dead who will be saved:

> I heard the sky-lark sing;
> Sometimes all little birds that are,
> How they seemed to fill the sea and air
> With their sweet jargoning! (lines 359–62)

No good auspices are brought by this birdsong, however, for the Spirit
of the South Pole that has followed the sailors through the Pacific
Ocean has agreed to leave the ship it has been tormenting only at the
price of more vengeance being wreaked on the one who slayed the albatross. More vengeance: the mariner and crew have already suffered
for condoning the killing of the Spirit's beloved bird. One of the invisible spirits of the air tells another (and perhaps us as well):

> The spirit who bideth by himself
> In the land of mist and snow,
> He loved the bird that loved the man
> Who shot him with his bow. (lines 402–5)

So the albatross had a special love for the old mariner who killed it,
though why is quite unclear. The act of destruction not only ends an
innocent life but also has no sense. The result is trauma for the ancient
mariner. He is now condemned to be alone and increasingly alienated
from all that is around him.

Becalmed in the hot Pacific Ocean, the ship can make no headway,
and the crew begins to dehydrate, perhaps making them prey to hal-
lucinations. They blame the mariner once again and hang the dead

albatross from his neck where a cross should rightly be. But the mariner, who must bite his arm and drink his own blood so that he can
speak, is not mistaken in what he sees, and he yells out that a ship is
in the offing. A skeletal ship approaches them out of the blue with
two figures on board who turn out to be Death and Life-in-Death. As
they draw close, it turns out that they are casting dice in order to see
whom they will claim of those on the beleaguered vessel. Again, we
have a scene of arbitrariness. Death claims the lives of two hundred
sailors, complicit in the crime, but Life-in-Death wins the choice soul
of the mariner. Who is this strange figure, this near double of Death?
Coleridge devotes a stanza to describing her:

> *Her* lips were red, *her* looks were free,
> Her locks were yellow as gold:
> Her skin was white as leprosy,
> The Night-mare LIFE-IN-DEATH was she,
> Who thicks man's blood with cold. (lines 190–95)

To be seen and claimed by this terrifying woman is to be beholden to
her. Thereafter, the mariner can be nothing; his condition is worse than
that of the dead men who lay about him, one index of which is that he
is unable to pray. (In the first version of the poem we are told: "And she
is far liker Death than he," a remarkable line, which means that Life-in-
Death is more like how we conceive death than death itself.)

Now alone on the ship, the mariner must live death as impossibility and must bear his fellow crew members' final curse, having brought
them to such an end: "The look with which they looked on me / Had
never passed away" (lines 255–56). Earlier, he had noted creatures on
the ocean that revolted him: "Yea, slimy things did crawl with legs /
Upon the slimy sea" (lines 124–24). Only when he sees them in the
moonlight, as water snakes, and blesses them without being aware that
he is doing so does he gain some reprieve: the dead albatross falls from
his neck (lines 290–91). We might take this event to be unmotivated.
Or we might take it to be motivated in a special way. It is the result
not of petitionary prayer but of a silent raising of the mind to God,
prompted not by care for the self but by observing the creatures and
appreciating their beauty. "O happy living things! no tongue / Their
beauty might declare: / A spring of love gushed from my heart" (lines
282–84). If we take the latter path, the poem stages a clear opposition
between contemplation and fascination.

The mariner has more penance to do. He wakes from a slumber

while the ship has been moved by the Polar Spirit's fellow spirits, and
once again he becomes spellbound. He sees the dead crew at their
work and, once again, is terrified:

> All stood together on the deck,
> For a charnel-dungeon fitter:
> All fixed on me their stony eyes,
> That in the Moon did glitter.
>
> The pang, the curse, with which they died,
> Had never passed away:
> I could not draw my eyes from theirs,
> Nor turn them up to pray. (lines 434–41)

Only the return to his home releases the mariner from the spell of fascination, the life in death to which he has been subject. He comes to a
settled Christian view, as we have seen: "He prayeth well, who loveth
well" (line 612). But he does not wholly escape the spell. Immediately
on landing in his native land, he confesses his sin to a local hermit, at
which point the mariner is freed from his sin. His penance is to travel
from land to land telling his story whenever an inner impulse demands
it of him. His story is enchanting, as we have seen, and he is as absorbed by it as the wedding guest is. Freed from the power of the Polar
Spirit, the mariner's penance is nonetheless to live within the narrative,
as a cautionary tale of sin, never coming to a final conclusion until he
dies, and, even then, his story will survive him in precisely the poem
we have been reading.

The mariner has never quite escaped life-in-death. Nor does he
know for sure whether the appearance of the albatross was a good
omen or a false impression. His knowledge is restricted to what came
after, the senselessness of his crime and the endlessness of its consequences. With the exception of the holy hermit, no one who hears the
story ever fully escapes life-in-death thereafter. Even the following day,
the wedding guest feels "stunned" (line 622) by what he has heard. He
is "of sense forlorn" (line 623), remaining not in the home world of
friends, family, and work but in the alien horizon of the sinister narrative he has been made to hear and cannot stop hearing in his head.
If the wedding guest is a sadder and wiser man on hearing the story,
it is not because he has learned more about himself or strange events
on the high seas or the ways of the world. It is because of the trauma
of being wounded by the story in the first place, a story that entrances

him long after the ancient mariner has departed looking for another person to buttonhole, among whom must be numbered you and me.

*

I turn now to another poem, one about as far from Coleridge's ballad as is possible, in order to see whether fascination can be held in a pincer movement and thereby reveal more of itself. After reading "The Rime of the Ancient Mariner" and turning to Philip Larkin (1922–85), one might expect to encounter "Next, Please" (1951) with its own dark ship, much like the one that carries Death and Death-in-Life:

> Only one ship is seeking us — a black-
> Sailed unfamiliar, towing at her back
> A huge and birdless silence. In her wake
> No waters breed or break.[82]

"And no birds sing," Keats says in "La Belle Dame sans Merci," itself a poem of fascination.[83] Yet in his mature work Larkin is anti-Romantic in spirit. There are no fairy children in any of his poems or any endorsements of the medieval tradition. The closest one gets to medieval mores in Larkin, one might think, is "An Arundel Tomb" (1956), which refers to effigies in Chichester Cathedral of a husband and wife with their hands joined. But there is another exception, his late lyric "Aubade" (1977), which in its title ironically cites one genre of the medieval tradition. Nonetheless, it is decidedly secular in orientation and far from any practice of contemplation.[84]

"Aubade" has fascinated readers since it first appeared in the *Times Literary Supplement* in December 1977, and it lends itself to the discussion of *Angst* and trauma as examined by Heidegger and Romano even as it revolves in a state of English melancholy rather than German profundity or French brilliance:

> I work all day, and get half-drunk at night.
> Waking at four to soundless dark, I stare.
> In time the curtain-edges will grow light.
> Till then I see what's really always there:
> Unresting death, a whole day nearer now,
> Making all thought impossible but how
> And where and when I shall myself die.
> Arid interrogation: yet the dread

Of dying, and being dead,
Flashes afresh to hold and horrify.

The mind blanks at the glare. Not in remorse
—The good not done, the love not given, time
Torn off, unused—nor wretchedly because
An only life can take so long to climb
Clear of its wrong beginnings, and may never;
But at the total emptiness for ever,
The sure extinction that we travel to
And shall be lost in always. Not to be here,
Not to be anywhere,
And soon; nothing more terrible, nothing more true.

This is a special way of being afraid
No trick dispels. Religion used to try,
That vast, moth-eaten musical brocade
Created to pretend we never die,
And specious stuff that says *No rational being*
Can fear a thing it will not feel, not sensing
That this is what we fear—no sight, no sound,
No touch or taste or smell, nothing to think with,
Nothing to link with,
The anesthetic from which none come round.

And so it stays just on the edge of vision,
A small, unfocused blur, a standing chill
That slows each impulse down to indecision.
Most things may never happen: this one will,
And realization of it rages out
In furnace-fear when we are caught without
People or drink. Courage is no good:
It means not scaring others. Being brave
Lets no one off the grave.
Death is no different whined at than withstood.

Slowly light strengthens, and the room takes shape.
It stands plain as a wardrobe, what we know,
Have always known, know that we can't escape,
Yet can't accept. One side will have to go.
Meanwhile telephones crouch, getting ready to ring
In locked-up offices, and all the uncaring

Intricate rented world begins to rouse.
The sky is white as clay, with no sun.
Work has to be done.
Postmen like doctors go from house to house.[85]

I would like to pause for a moment to mark how this dismaying poem is at variance with the entire tradition of contemplation that I have been trying to delineate and understand in the earlier chapters of this book.

The difference I have in mind is not signaled by death since the contemplative tradition that comes from Socrates figures θεωρία and φιλοσοφία as curing or freeing the soul by death.[86] Indeed, Larkin does not side with philosophy over against religion in his response to his eventual demise; if religion offers no viable consolation, neither does philosophy. All that Socrates, Epicurus, Seneca, and Spinoza, among others, have said about the irrationality of fearing death is dismissed, although, to be sure, each of them would respond by saying that Larkin has not properly prepared himself for his exit from life.[87] (It is evident that Larkin does not accept Heidegger's sense of philosophy as coming with a *Stimmung* that attunes one to human being.) Nor is Larkin's difference from the contemplative tradition characterized by anything other than ocular metaphors, which are as present here as anywhere in that tradition, although positioned in their own ways. "I stare," Larkin says, and death itself "stays just on the edge of vision, / A small, unfocused blur." No one can see his or her own death, know the day on which one will die, and only in dire circumstances can we say, with Marguerite Yourcenar's Hadrian: "I begin to discern the profile of my death."[88] What Larkin does see, however, is the *fact* of his death in all its banality; it "stands plain as a wardrobe," a wardrobe being the piece of bedroom furniture most like a coffin.

If we look back in the tradition of English poetry, we will of course find many another poem that meditates on death, and it is worthwhile to reach back and touch one of these in order to see how "Aubade" differs so markedly from the tradition. It does so as decidedly as it contrasts with the love tradition (Donne's "The Sunne Rising," e.g.). There are many poems from which to choose, not least of all Shelley's "On Death" (ca. 1813), but William Dunbar's "Lament for the Makars" (ca. 1505) serves my purposes more economically. I will give only the opening stanzas:

I that in heill wes, and gladnes
Am trublit now with gret seiknes

And feblit with infermité:
Timor mortis conturbat me.

Our plesance heir is all vane glory,
This fals warld is bot transitory,
The flesh is brukle the Fend is sle:
Timor mortis conturbat me.

The strait of man dois change and vary,
Now sound, now seik, now blith, now sary,
Now dansand mery, now like to dee:
Timor mortis conturbat me.[89]

As the poem continues, Dunbar laments the great poets who have died before him—Chaucer, Giower, Henrisoun, and others—and recognizes that he will follow them into the darkness before long. What we have here—and in other poems that use the same refrain (e.g., "Alas, my hart will brek in three")[90]—is a meditation on death that is structured by reference to topics well known to all. The *timor mortis* motif was traditional in poets before Dunbar and had been channeled into penitential carols, but there is no sign of such liturgical use here.[91] Nor does one find the image of a bird announcing the *timor mortis* motif, as is done in an anonymous late medieval carol.[92] One is invited to take on the *I* when reading the poem because one knows full well that death comes to all and that the Office of the Dead or something similar will one day be said over one's grave. How does Larkin's "Aubade" differ from Dunbar's "Lament"?

To begin with, in "Aubade" Larkin is concerned with the loss not of others but only of himself in time to come. The first-person singular pronoun occurs four times in the first stanza, and only in the final stanza does it turn into a first-person plural pronoun. He is not contemplating death or even brooding on the empirical fact of death; instead, he is existentially fascinated with both.[93] "The dread / Of dying, and being dead, / Flashes afresh to *hold* and horrify" (emphasis added): he is held in a state of fascination, just like the wedding guest in Coleridge's poem. His enthrallment is not with something steady, even passive, or perhaps nonexistent but with death conceived from the start as active ("Unresting death"), coming closer a day at a time. A false sense impression becomes leagued with passion. We feel death's approach throughout the entire poem, somewhat stealthier than Donne grimly imagined it in the first of his "Divine Meditations" (1633): "I run to death, and death meets me as fast."[94] Yet death does not appear as such; it is never more than a blur, quite "unfocused." It cannot be adjusted to form a point of convergence, and it "slows each impulse down to indecision," which is a clear consequence of fascination. There is no meditation on or contemplation of death in general and oneself as answerable to that general situation; rather, he finds himself inexorably in a situation in which there is no exit. Nor is any comfort derived from the *non omnis moriar* theme that we find in Horace, Ovid, and others.[95]

Larkin is not even ill, let alone fatally ill, so far as we know in the poem, and plainly there is no confession of being "half in love with easeful Death."[96] Instead, as he ages, he feels possibilities falling away from him, leaving only the possibility of impossibility: "the total emptiness for ever, / The sure extinction that we travel to / And shall be lost in always." Contemplation is at heart free, as we have seen, but fascination is a phased negative counterpart to it: an attraction that takes place with yet despite desire, from which one cannot readily free oneself and that bears no fruit. Whereas appropriate training in contemplation can perhaps help one cope with the hardness of living and dying, Larkin realizes that, outside the grim comforts of the *ars moriendi*, in which God and Judgment are always presumed, death can only transfix and that there is nothing one can do to overcome it: "Being brave / Lets no one off the grave."[97] We can mature in and through contemplation, but we cannot do so with fascination; if anything, we regress.

I return to dread as it is manifested in this poem. The thought of death, Larkin says, makes "all thought impossible," the exact opposite of *dilatio mentis*. "The mind blanks at the glare" not of death but of the dread of one's impending annihilation, and the "standing chill" of one's imminent demise "slows each impulse down to indecision." One is submerged in a state of altered awareness where one experiences a stretching of time, and we may well think that Larkin is experiencing life-in-death, albeit in a less Romantic manner than the ancient mariner did. In this state, death is first apprehended by way of terror ("nothing more terrible") and then fear ("fear," "furnace-fear," "afraid"). The combination changes home world into alien world: "telephones crouch, getting ready to ring / In locked up offices, and all the uncaring / Intricate rented world begins to rouse." This fusion of technological, social, and bestial metaphors near the end of the poem is compelling and indicative of the alienation the speaker feels from the world that he has known. Nothing is "more true" than that we will die, as Dunbar has reminded us, as if we needed any reminding. Yet the commonplace shifts its weight somewhat when we hear it in "Aubade." We recognize that, while Christians hold that God is Truth, Larkin reverses the claim and invests absolute truth in death, and we also sense, with a shudder, that "true" seems to gulp "terrible" whole. We might say that "Aubade" is a dark counterpoint to the morning knowledge to which Christian contemplation is attuned: Larkin tries to gaze at death, which, like God (but for quite other reasons), cannot be brought into focus. Whereas God is above or beyond consciousness and thus cannot be experienced in any usual sense, death is the extinction of consciousness and therefore cannot be experienced at all. The mind circles and circles around death, just as it does around God: the one turning around a "notional assent," as Newman would say, and the other around an object of faith.[98] In "Aubade," nothing is "understood," for it has already been tacitly foreknown in the mode of fate. We get no special light cast on our images of death; it absorbs all light, giving nothing back: a blank mystery or the mystery of total blankness.

It is striking how firmly Larkin stresses at the end of the poem our knowledge of death. He evokes "what we *know,* / Have always *known,* *know* that we can't escape, / Yet can't accept" (emphasis added). True enough, we all know that, as finite, complex beings, we are bound to die. But Larkin does not have obvious recourse to the version of Moore's paradox that is common when thoughtful people talk of death. Jacques Madaule puts it concisely: "Je sais que je mourrai, mais je ne le crois pas" (I know that I will die, but I do not believe it).[99] For Larkin, this would be a prime example of "specious stuff" if put in such direct terms, yet it is not philosophical evasion masked as cleverness, as Larkin thinks he finds in Spinoza, but ordinary human psychology to which Madaule points. If death possessed us in the attitude of belief (in the strong sense of *credere in mortem*) as well as knowledge, we would be unable to love and work. Larkin appears to forbid himself belief in favor of knowledge, not only with regard to religion, but also with respect to death (where natural belief suffices). It is one of the severe curtailments that characterize the poem from beginning to end and give it such force.

Yet Larkin modifies his claim, apparently just a little, when he admits that, even though we know we cannot escape death, we "can't accept" that knowledge. Is this lack of acceptance a matter of not consenting to our demise? Or not believing that it is a correct description of a state of affairs? Presumably the former; but the questions are dislodged by an allusion to some of the last words that Oscar Wilde is supposed to have said that follows the lines I have quoted. "One or the other of us has to go," the Irish wit is believed to have quipped to Claire de Pratz when he was mortally ill, referring to the dreadful wallpaper in his room in L'Hôtel d'Alsace, in the tenth arrondissement of Paris.[100]

Nonetheless, the questions are too insistent to be joked away. The image of the telephones about to ring makes us think of a call that we must accept even if we think that it might bring harrowing news. We look again at the image of the telephones crouching and know that soon they will spring, like lions or tigers, and we recall the description "Unresting death." If we think that religion has been dismissed in favor of secular life that is wholly preferable, we would be mistaken. The devastating threefold rejection of religion as "vast, moth-eaten musical" is paralleled right at the end with an equally bleak vision of a post-religious world as "uncaring / Intricate rented." Almost at the very end of the poem we hear: "The sky is white as clay, with no sun." The *templum* is utterly blank; no bird flies through it. We reflect also that it is white "as clay," the very material from which human beings were said to have been created and to which we return.

This minor note at the end of the poem is perhaps more significant than most readers of "Aubade" have realized. Whereas the European philosophical tradition, from Kant to Romano, correctly diagnoses fascination by way of ambiguity, none of its representatives show how one might break out of it. Larkin tells us that, if one cannot overcome the spell of death, one can at least distract oneself from it through the banality of work. In "Toads," he memorably captures work in the metaphor of a toad that squats on one's life; yet later, in "Toads Revisited," he writes: "Give me your arm, old toad; / Help me down Cemetery Road."[101] It is striking that, if we return to Hopkins's "The Windhover," we find in the sestet, after the contemplation of the hawk's ecstasy (and the fear of being fully brought into the life of the kingdom), that Hopkins also settles on the figure of work. Plowing one's narrow furrow of land can at least make the clods of earth shine. There is hope here, for Hopkins lives the mixed life of a Jesuit: one gains access, of a limited kind, to the divine light in pursuing one's vocation. Larkin can claim only a greatly diminished hold on life in ordinary work, which at least distracts one from the terror of death. Yet it delivers one from fascination for a while.

*

Contemplation falls on the side of *transascendance*, if I may borrow Jean Wahl's word in *Human Existence and Transcendence* (1944), and fascination may usually be found on the other side, that is, *transdescendance*.[102] For Wahl, *transascendance* is precisely what eliminates immanence. Otherwise, he thinks, each step of transcendence merely establishes a higher plane of immanence, and this is what we find in the

phases of contemplation according to Richard until we rest in the triune God. Things are a little more complicated with *transdescendance*,
for it encompasses both phenomena and what is taken to be anterior to
them. Wahl directs us to D. H. Lawrence in *The Plumed Serpent* (1926),
who pointed surely to the *transdescendant* in his account of the sacred
in Mexico. Most likely, he was thinking of Ramón's observation to
Kate: "They say the word *Mexico* means *Below this!*"[103] Also, however,
he most likely would have had in mind Kate's encounter with the men
of Quetzalcoatl: "She was attracted, almost fascinated by the strange
nuclear power of the men in the circle," men who say, "When the snake
of your body lifts its head, beware! It is I, Quetzalcoatl, rearing up in
you, rearing up and reaching beyond the bright day, to the sun of darkness beyond, where is your home at last." Are they just men, or are
they truly possessed by a god? When asked why she danced with the
circle of men, Kate answers, "I was fascinated," only to be told: "No,
you must not be fascinated. No! No! It is not good."[104] What is said of
fascination in the colloquial sense is heard in the folk sense. Clearly, all
these events involve phenomena even if they appear in more than one
way.[105]

Yet post-Kantian philosophical modernity, unlike popular Mexican
religion, is concerned also with what precedes phenomena, whether in
a transcendental, or a quasi-transcendental manner, or another way entirely. We can see this clearly when we put Larkin's terse simplification
of religion in a broader context. He says of religion—which is already,
in his mind, a thing of the past—that it used to be a "trick" to overcome or at least contain our fear of death. In the first stanza he can
think only "how / And where and when [he] shall . . . die." The question Why?—the religious question about death par excellence—is not
countenanced. Indeed, religion is diminished by characterizing it in a
fine, slicing line we have already heard: "That vast, moth-eaten musical brocade." And the very next line twists the blade: "*Created* to pretend we never die" (emphasis added). Not only has religion, for Larkin, been a discourse on creation, but it is also itself created ex nihilo,
with no evidence whatsoever for its claims, and not even brought into
being with a worthwhile aim in view. It was created merely to *pretend*
"we never die." It is little more than a child's game of pretend.

Of course, we may demur over some of what Larkin writes. First of
all, far from teaching that we never die, religion has resolutely taught
that we certainly die and that we need to keep that thought in the front
of our minds. It is because we die that we need to live well now, for
after death comes divine judgment. No doubt, Christianity promises
hope to believers, but no one may hope not to die before attaining

bliss. Second, the pathos that comes from being told that we shall "be lost" in "total emptiness" is at variance with what he urges: for in his view there will be no *we*, no *I*, to be lost anywhere. Such talk makes sense only in anticipation of death, not in death itself. A Husserlian of strict observance would also say that the very poem we are reading belies what it says, for "Larkin" is not lost in total emptiness but survives in his transcendental life, in the dissemination of his poem, and its will to survive is lightly marked in the sheer craft of the stanzas, the meter, the rhyme, the careful modulations of tone, and so on.[106] And, as we have noted, Blanchot develops Husserl's claim in a dark direction, worthy of Edgar Allen Poe: Larkin would be lost in the perpetual recitation of his own poetry, his consciousness at the time of writing unmoored from his *I*. It is always possible to turn a contemplative reading of a poem into one informed by the hermeneutic of suspicion, and vice versa. The hermeneutic of contemplation never rejects suspicion; it incorporates its possibility into a larger whole that is always able to become yet larger.

For example, it would be possible to read "Aubade" in a post-Freudian manner, and it is worthwhile to see what procedures drawn from psychoanalysis would lead us to see in the poem. As I have mentioned, there is a wealth of clinical and theoretical material on fascination, both explicit and implicit, and some of it is highly suggestive with regard to the poem. Melanie Klein (1882–1960), for instance, might attract a reader with her observation that "anxiety arises from the operation of the death instinct within the organism, is felt as fear of annihilation (death) and takes the form of fear of persecution."[107] That the grown man Philip Larkin seems to feel persecuted by death seems clear: it appears to stalk him, getting closer and closer each day of his life, and it prompts him to fantasize where and when he will die. Guided by psychoanalytic practice, a reader might well be skeptical of Larkin's demurral that his fear is *not* a consequence of remorse—"The good not done, the love not given, time / Torn off unused"—or that it does not originate, obscurely, in early childhood ("An only life can take so long to climb / Clear of its wrong beginnings, and may never"). For one thing, we might ponder his sharp exclusions and sense of guilt "when we are *caught* without / People or drink" (emphasis added), which gives a sense of how people have been instrumentalized by the speaker. His fear of annihilation may well come from a projection of the unwanted parts of himself (his lack of goodness and love, his wasting of time, an unhappy childhood) that are grouped together and identified with death as exterior to him and seeking him day by day. What he finds to be distasteful about himself might be projected out into the forms of "religion" and "philosophy" that are sharply criticized in the lyric, not to mention the "uncaring world." Larkin's enchantment with death—especially with the fear of it—is needed to defend his fragile sense of self, and to that end he takes into himself all that he can plausibly see as good: alcohol, mail, people, and work. It is work, with which the poem begins and ends, that most surely buttresses his precarious hold on reality. What takes away so much of his life is what keeps him going.

Doubtless such a reading could be extended, and someone with clinical experience might well see a good deal more in the poem, including many things I have not noticed in my own reflections on it, by using object relations or another psychoanalytic theory. It is easy to imagine a reader trained in psychoanalysis being caught by the word *rages* and seeing there a clue for interpretation: the speaker's rage at all that is bad or unworthy in his life is precisely what expels those things and turns them into the figure of death persecuting him and the unhelpful words of consolation offered by religion and philosophy. The theory that is presumed is exactly what would justify the movement from "rages out / In furnace-fear" to "rage," and that would perhaps call one to witness a horror of cremation. It may be that to the psychoanalysis of fascination as a pathology one could add insights into the nature of trauma. In the end, however, such a reading projects a horizon that, in its elected terms, cannot be surpassed and that encloses the poem within it, and the constant threat is that the poem is quietly turned into a totality and/or made to serve a pregiven end.

One can be fascinated by "The Rime of the Ancient Mariner" and "Aubade," and one can contemplate each of them. To be in thrall to either poem is less to share its horror of death than to be seduced by the vision of life-in-death that each offers us. One can commune with the spirits of Coleridge and Larkin condemned to flitter through their own words, which is how Blanchot sees things. Or one can never quite free oneself from the world of either poem; it keeps returning, like a ghost, haunting one's life. Or one's enthrallment with either poem can be kept in bounds by restricting it to a thoroughly demystified world in which literature can scarcely be of any help in living life more richly. But there are other possibilities. To read either poem slowly is to attend to the many regions of being that gather there—given by way of anticipation, cognition, fantasy, recollection, and so on—and follow them until a whole appears. But one knows, in part from one continuing experience of reading the poem, that in principle the whole can always be extended. One's judgment about either poem can be revised. New profiles of each composition can come into view by reading other poems by Larkin, by reading biographies of him, by reading more about early Romanticism or the aubade tradition, and by reading in a generous spirit what other readers have made of the poems or what they tell us about the act of reading.

*

When Richard of St. Victor was alive, troubadours in France, such as Giraut de Bornelh (ca. 1138–1215), would sing lyrics called *aubades*, poems in which the lover who has had to leave before dawn praises his beloved. The love spoken of here is courtly, going back to Ovid, whose carnal poetry it transforms to some extent; it bears no relation to the love spoken of by the monastic writers, right up to Giraut's contemporaries St. Bernard of Clairvaux and William of St. Thierry.[108] For Richard, the coming day would be taken up with contemplation of the visible, the invisible, and the transcendent in all their modes of appearing, although, to be sure, it would be challenged by the fascination of sin, and the day would always be woven with pastoral work and liturgy. He would have found "The Rime of the Ancient Mariner" a strange tale, but it would have remained at the edge of a world that was vaguely familiar to him. On the other hand, were we to ask ourselves what life would look like without all that contemplation, in Richard's sense, can offer us, we could do no better than read Larkin's "Aubade" and, in its fierce diminishments, prompted by dread, by foreboding, and by fright, see there a triumph of fascination over contemplation. Even before a critic informed by Marx, Nietzsche, and Freud approaches it, the poem is already a thoroughgoing product of a hermeneutic of suspicion and, as such, one profile of our modernity.

CHAPTER 6

Consideration

When Dante meets St. Thomas Aquinas in the heaven of the sun, the great theologian indicates to the pilgrim the souls of Isidore, Bede, and Richard of St. Victor, and with regard to the last of the three he observes: "e di Riccardo, / che a considerer fu più che viro" (and Richard, / who in consideration was more than man).[1] The differences over the nature and practice of contemplation between Aquinas and Richard, as discussed in the opening chapter, are not remarked. It is only several cantos later, when he is in the heaven of Saturn, that Dante encounters by way of St. Benedict the souls of the contemplatives: "Questi altri fuochi tutti contemplanti / uomino fuoro, accesi di quel caldo / che fa nascere I fiori e' frutti santi" (These other flames were all contemplatives / men lit by that heat / from which arise holy flowers and fruits).[2] Two representatives of this higher spiritual life are named, one from the Eastern church (Macarius), the other from the Western church (Romualdus). We see here, as clearly as anywhere in medieval thought, that *consideratio* is a lower spiritual practice than *contemplatio*, although, if we examine religious writings of the twelfth century and before, we will find the two words being used almost interchangeably, just as *contemplation* and *meditation* (along with *consideration*) often were in late sixteenth- and early seventeenth-century England.[3] For Dante and his world, the two practices both involve broaching the mystery of divine love, although only the latter involves being swept to the heights of ecstasy. Both come from the classical world, from Cicero in particular, and are used extensively in the Middle Ages. And both are reset in poetry of the modern world. Sometimes we find verse that is contemplative, in one or another sense or intensity, and at other times we find verse that distinguishes itself from contemplative poetry by drawing more attention to itself as consideration.

In *De finibus* we find Cicero writing "consideratio cognitioque rerum caelestium" (the consideration and study of the heavenly bodies), in *Brutus* we come across, "quam nihil non consideratum exibat ex ore!" (how nothing unconsidered came from his mouth!), and in the *Tusculanae disputationes* we read "eos casus . . . mecum ipse considerans" (when I consider within myself . . . the misfortunes).[4] *Consideratio*, for Cicero, then, denotes a person's mental reflection, careful thought, or attentive inspection of a situation or topic.[5] The practice becomes equivocal with respect to academic disciplines by the sixth century. Boethius (ca. 477–524) tells us in his commentary on Aristotle's *On Interpretation* that *consideratio* is properly linked to rhetoric and poetics, yet in his commentary on Porphyry's *Isagoge* he aligns the same word with philosophy.[6] It is possible that St. Bernard of Clairvaux, the main theorist of *consideratio*, was heir to both understandings of the word from Boethius, perhaps by way of William of Champeaux (1070–1121), and that he placed his stamp on the latter choice.

In any case, if we read *On Consideration*, St. Bernard's five books of advice to Pope Eugenius III (completed by 1153), we find a fuller, rounder, more systematic account of consideration than was previously available, one that surely influenced Dante. St. Bernard's account is firmly tied to religion and is structured by Augustine's fourfold distinction in *De doctrina christiana* among what is above us, what we are ourselves, what is on a level with us, and what is beneath us.[7] All these things, visible and invisible alike, are to be pondered so as to find the truth about them, which is no easy thing, and in doing so we can foresee difficulties in life and sustain ourselves against adversity. One begins by seeking to know oneself; it is the first step to humility. *Nosce teipsum* (γνῶθι σεαυτόν): the directive goes back to the Delphic oracle chiefly by way of Ephraim the Syrian, Augustine, Basil of Caesarea, Cicero, and Plato.[8] St. Bernard divides it nicely into what one is by nature (a mortal), who one is (one's position in church or society), and what sort of person one is (one's character).[9] Knowing oneself and reflecting on one's responsibilities to those above us, those who are on a level with us, and those for whom we are ourselves responsible can be only a salutary exercise for all of us, both in the twelfth century and today. But what is the nature of this quest for St. Bernard?

Toward the start of his second book of papal advice, St. Bernard compares *consideratio* and *contemplatio*. They are not wholly different, he concedes, but their starting points are distinct:

First of all, consider what it is I call consideration. For I do not want it to be understood as entirely synonymous with contemplation, because the latter concerns more what is known about something while consideration pertains more to the investigation of what is unknown. Consequently, contemplation can be defined as the true and sure intuition of the mind concerning something, or the apprehension of truth without doubt [*verus certusque intuitus animi de quacunque re; siue apprehensio veri non dubia*]. Consideration, on the other hand, can be defined as thought searching for truth, or the searching of a mind to discover truth [*intensa ad investigandum cogitatio: vel intensio animi vestigantis verum*]. Nevertheless, both terms are customarily used interchangeably.[10]

Consideration comes only with piety; it leads us to humility and in doing so encourages us to ascend to God.[11] There are three levels to it. One can use the senses in an orderly way with a view toward winning divine favor, and one can use philosophy in order to reflect on our state. Both lead us, each in its own way, to meditate on how we are like and unlike the deity, conceived as αγάπη or *caritas* (1 John 4:8), in how we love and thereby prompt us to burn for *amor purus*. We are then oriented to the third and highest level. For consideration can collect its energies within itself (*se in se colligens*) and have us pass from seeking to finding what we have sought. In doing so, it orders itself to the sure presence of God so that, if the one practicing it is virtuous and also receives Grace, it unfurls into divine contemplation.[12] If one reaches this final stage, one is not so much in flight, like the birds, as swept up by God himself. We fly through the heavens with wings of purity and ardor. In St. Bernard's Latin: "Puritatis siquidem et alacritatis pariter alis fit ille volatus."[13] In such a free and exalted state, we contemplate the promises of what we may expect, or the blessings that we remember, or the divine judgment that awaits us, or, at the pinnacle of ecstasy, we lovingly admire the divine majesty.[14]

In *The Ark of Moses*, Richard of St. Victor likens the movements of the birds of the air to souls in contemplative bliss, and we have seen that it was an unusual way of thinking about contemplation, one that Aquinas contested in the *Summa theologiae*. In St. Bernard's terms, Richard's birds enjoy "the true and sure intuition of the mind concerning something, or the apprehension of truth without doubt."[15] They glide and hover before a truth that is grounded in divine revelation, and they have been led there by *consideratio* that opens onto *contemplatio*. I will approach what I take to be a modern, lower mode of consideration by way of what at first glance might seem to be a similar passage, then touch on some issues to do with consideration and contemplation as they occur, almost out of sight but nonetheless in an exemplary fashion, in and around the modern author whose work will concern us first, Elizabeth Bishop (1911–79).

*

I begin with a passage by Bishop that bears comparison at one or two points with Richard of St. Victor's depiction of the birds of the air as a figure for contemplation of God, although I am chiefly interested in it here for how it differs from Richard's lyrical description of the birds as described in chapter 4. I have in mind the framing device of Bishop's early essay on time in the modern novel, "Time's Andromedas" (1933):

> As I waited I heard a multitude of small sounds. . . .
> Of course it was the birds going South. They were very high up, a fairly large sort of bird, I couldn't tell what . . . and at first their wings seemed all to be beating perfectly together. But by watching one bird, then another, I saw that some flew a little slower than others, some were trying to get ahead and some flew at an individual rubato; each seemed a variation, and yet altogether my eyes were deceived into thinking them perfectly precise and regular. I watched closely the spaces between the birds. It was as if there were an invisible thread joining all the outside birds and within this fragile network they possessed the sky; it was down among them, of a paler color, moving with them. The interspaces moved in pulsation too, catching up and continuing the motion of the wings in wakes, carrying it on, as the rest in music does—not a blankness but a space as musical as all the sound.[16]

Like Richard, Bishop observes unnamed birds flying at varying rates; but she sees them crossing the sky above her, not simply circling and swooping overhead. She appreciates the precision and regularity of their formation, although she realizes that both are deceptive. The "as if" is significant when she turns to consider the category of the invisible ("as if there were an invisible thread"). Music is used as a figure to understand the flight of the birds as well as the illusion that the sky also is moving. The references to "rhythmic irregularity" and "rubato" draw attention to a lack of harmony in the skies, and there is no piety informing her attitude.

Let us see how Bishop continues, paying attention to how she reasons about what she sees. She does not merely perceive what is above her; she takes in the syntax, as it were, of what is seen, notices an articulated whole, and thus passes from perception to thinking:

It came to me that the flying birds were setting up, far over my head, a sort of time-pattern, or rather patterns, all closely related, all minutely varied, and yet all together forming the *migration*, which probably in the date of its flight and its actual flying time was as mathematically regular as the planets. There was the individual rate of each bird, its rate in relation to all the other birds, the speed of the various groups, and then that mysterious swath they made through the sky, leaving it somehow emptied and stilled, slowly assuming its usual coloring and far-away look.[17]

As Bishop looks again and again at the sky, she passes from part to whole, noting a fractal, until she grasps what is happening, not what the birds are doing, which she sees right from the start ("going South"), but how they are doing it. The intricate temporality of the phenomenon is what interests her ("a sort of time-pattern, or rather patterns, all closely related, all minutely varied"). If there is something left unexplained by her thoughtful gazes into the sky ("that mysterious swath"), it is not because she establishes a *templum*, or finds a pregiven sacred space, or ponders a mode of divine hiddenness, but because at present she cannot rationally account for it. The invisible enters her thought only by way of mathematics. The migration is entirely natural. If we are tempted to speak here of Bishop contemplating the birds, we must do so by minimizing St. Bernard's distinction between *contemplatio* and *consideratio* and deflating our expectations of both. For Bishop does not have a true and sure intuition of what is happening when she is prompted to look into the sky or even when she finds herself looking again and again. The birds know what they are about, but that is not the primary focus of the passage. The observer is searching to discover the truth of the event, and she does so when she hits on how it occurs. Her moment of insight has nothing to do with ascent unless, of course, one regards passing from the sensuous world to the how character of the event in that manner.

Toward the end of "Time's Andromedas" Bishop reflects on Gertrude Stein's novel *The Making of Americans: Being the History of a Family's Progress* (1925). She touches on contemplation there, and it is worth pausing in order to hear what she says about it. "Whenever we stop in the midst of doing something to contemplate and inform ourselves what it is we are doing," she writes, "we announce it with the help of an i-n-g word." Contemplation, here, is not religious in the slightest but mulling over a situation. Bishop has in mind a group of verbs that Stein lists in her novel: "living, working, loving, dressing, dreaming, waking, cleaning. . . ." She reflects: "That very ending has a peculiar ringing effect, carrying the word on from the actual sense of the verb into the realm of present time, into action."[18] In terms of *-ing* terminations, one might well recall the octave of Hopkins's "The Windhover," a poem that Bishop knew well and, in the following year, 1934, mentions in an essay, esteeming it for its "timing and tuning of sense and syllable." Not all her admiration for the poem is taken up with technique, however, for one of the things she values in general about Hopkins's verse is its "depiction of 'a mind thinking.'"[19]

This three-word quotation is taken from a scholarly paper by Morris W. Croll (1872–1947), who at the time was teaching seventeenth-century prose at Princeton University. In "The Baroque Style in Prose" (1929), Croll examines an early seventeenth-century revolt against the classical—actually, Ciceronian—style that had been widely adopted in the vernacular languages of the high Renaissance. This anti-Ciceronian reversal generates in its new diction, use of figures, and phrasing of sentences a more self-conscious tradition in English and French prose, one oriented to experiencing the world and ideas about it. We find it chiefly in Montaigne, Browne, Burton, and Pascal. For these authors prize what seems to be a naturally unfolding expressiveness in their periods, Croll believes, in preference to setting down a resolved formal beauty, one that has been mentally reached and then put into balanced prose. In his *Short View of the Long Life and Raigne of Henry III* (1627), Sir Robert Cotton supplies Croll with a characteristic instance of a baroque sentence: "Men must beware of running down steep hills, with weighty bodies; they once in motion, *suo feruntur pondere*; steps are not then voluntary."[20] Croll comments: "He has deliberately avoided the process of mental revision, in order to express his idea when it's nearer to the point of origin in his mind."[21] The thought comes in three phases without syntactic connections: a warning, a commonplace about natural forces (being propelled by one's own weight when running downhill), and a consequence if one ignores the warning.

With this example in mind, I quote what Bishop quotes from Croll's "The Baroque Prose Style" in full:

> Their purpose was to portray, not a thought, but a mind thinking. . . . They knew that an idea separated from the act of experiencing it is not the same idea that we experienced. The ardor of its conception in the mind is a necessary part of its truth; and unless it can be conveyed to another mind in something of the form of its occurrence, either it has changed into some other idea or it has ceased to be an idea, to have any evidence whatever except a verbal one. . . . They . . .

deliberately chose as the moment of expression that in which the idea first clearly objectifies itself in the mind, in which, therefore each of its parts still preserves its own peculiar emphasis and an independent vigor of its own—in brief, the moment in which truth is still *imagined*.[22]

"A mind thinking," here, points us not to *contemplatio*, at least not as St. Bernard would construe it, but rather to "emergent devices of construction," as Croll nicely puts it. It is the investigation of a truth that is not yet firmly known, a truth pursued and registered freshly as one meets it in a mind in motion, not revolving around something that it already knows.

In a phenomenological register, we might say that Croll identifies at the level of prose style that "a mind thinking" is more than abstraction, drawing universals from particulars or reaching a reliable conclusion by way of sound assumptions and valid reasoning; it is also the mental activity of categorial intuition, in which a structured phenomenon is comprehended by distinct intentional acts.[23] A baroque sentence is a culturally shaped way in which a compound phenomenon—for Wootton, a heavyset man running down a hill—is made present to writer and reader (though not in quite the same way). We do not simply have something given to consciousness holus-bolus; rather, the thing both as a whole and with the warning not to run downhill when one is overweight is asterisked as a comic theme for our judgment. This is more than drawing attention to one or another facet of a phenomenon, for it is the receiving of it in the temporal manner of a lived experience, almost as three distinct frames. As the phenomenon is given, so too the individual subjectivity of the author appears; how his or her consciousness works is revealed in the way he or she constructs a sentence and, in doing so, apprehends the world and offers a truth about it.

Bishop uses Croll in support of her own view of Hopkins's way of composing verse, which, like others before her, she believes to be more akin to the metaphysical poets of the seventeenth century than to his Victorian contemporaries (Matthew Arnold, Dante Gabriel Rossetti, and George Meredith, among others). It is significant that the metaphysical poets were revived at about the same time that Hopkins's verse became generally available in Robert Bridges's edition of it (1918). Herbert Grierson's anthology *Metaphysical Lyrics and Poems of the Seventeenth Century* (1921) and Eliot's signal essay "The Metaphysical Poets" (1921) were both influential in this regard.[24] Also, however, Bishop thinks that Hopkins's style is illuminated by the anti-Ciceronian prose writers of the seventeenth century:

Hopkins, I believe, has chosen to stop his poems, set them to paper, at the point in their development where they are still incomplete, still close to the first kernel of truth or apprehension which gave rise to them. . . . The manner of timing so as to catch and preserve the moment of an idea, the point being to crystallize it early enough so that it still has movement—it is essentially the baroque manner of approach.[25]

Every reader of Hopkins will admit the trenchancy and value of the observation: one senses Hopkins writing with an openness to his subject. Sometimes it is an openness in finding truth, sometimes an openness when responding to a found truth. But a little deliberation is likely to bring about a modification of the claim. Bishop's insight would have more authority if "The Windhover" were simply a descriptive poem about a kestrel in flight, for in the octave, in particular, its sensual registration is acute and overt, with one image of the bird's movements quickly following after the one before it. But it is also a poem in which a new mode of formal beauty is brought to a high and original gloss: recall the exquisite skill with which Hopkins handles the strong and weak -*ing* rhymes and the sprung rhythm in the octave of the sonnet. Even more to the point, as we saw in chapter 4, "The Windhover" is about a blessed soul in ecstasy who appears as a kestrel; it leagues the invisible and the visible, and this understanding of the poem requires us to distinguish what Hopkins took to be true without doubt (the reality of blessed souls in ecstasy) and the means by which he apprehends one of these souls (as a kestrel flying above him). The bird is a categorial object for Hopkins, as explored in chapter 4, and his poem about it embodies two distinct intentional acts: a contemplation of a blessed soul (which, in turn, contemplates the young Jesuit and eyes his "heart in hiding") and an act of composition during which Hopkins is searching for the truth of the blessed soul as kestrel, that is, how to depict it. It is a little natural theology.

Bishop's remarks about Hopkins are really about her own practice as a poet or at least her early ambitions as a verse stylist, ambitions that came to be richly fulfilled. No one has grasped her way of proceeding as a poet better (or done so earlier) than Marianne Moore (1887–1972) when introducing three of her protégé's early poems in the anthology *Trial Balances* (1935):

Some authors do not muse within themselves; they "think"—like the vegetable-shredder which cuts into the life of a thing. Miss Bishop is not one of these frettingly intensive machines. Yet the rational considering quality in her work is its strength — assisted by unwordiness, uncontorted intentionalness, the flicker of impudence, the natural unforced ending.[26]

Readers of Bishop's mature poems will immediately recognize "the rational considering quality in her work" as one of its strengths. (Another would be its ability to describe as though there were no observer present with the usual human perceptual filters.)[27] Think of a fairly late poem, "Under the Window: Ouro Preto." The street scene Bishop sees seems to compose itself before our very eyes: we can see constituting become constitution. We sense a mind searching for the truth of exactly what happens under her window, revising its perceptions as it goes along, considering how something that was absent is now present. At first the poet sees what seems to be a bunch of laundry moving by itself about three feet off the ground. Then there is an exclamation of recognition: "Oh, no — a small black boy is underneath."[28]

The poem continues with this air of rational consideration of the visible world right to the end when Bishop sees oil that has seeped into "the ditch of standing water." She says that it "flashes or looks upward brokenly, / like bits of mirror," and immediately rethinks what she has just said (as though the poem were wholly spoken, not written): "no, more blue than that: / like tatters of the *Morpho* butterfly."[29] Bishop's virtues as a poet, as Moore describes them, are at the antipodes of those held by such as George Saintsbury (1845–1933) and Basil Bunting (1900–1985), for whom the value of poetry abides primarily in its sound, not in its sense.[30] Not that as a poet Bishop overlooks the pleasures of euphony; she merely renders them by way of an informal voice, more than in neatly measured diction.

We might also say that Bishop understands her friend and mentor very well when, in 1948, she notes with admiration how Moore has an "immediacy of identification" with what she is writing about, be it a badger or a butterfly, and asks: "Does it come simply from her gift of being able to give herself up entirely to the object under contemplation, to feel in all sincerity how it is to be *it*?"[31] There is no question here of passing from contemplation to action, as with those -*ing* words that come to mind when reflecting on what one is doing. Rather, there is an abiding in a steady identification with the object: a natural object, of course — a chameleon, a snail, a mongoose, a pangolin, or a fish — one that, if we accept St. Bernard's view of contemplation and apply it to a mundane being, Moore would have intuited and responded to without doubts that affect her when engaged in composition. Think of that extraordinary poem "An Octopus," from *Observations* (1924; rev.

1925). The book's title is significant, even more so than T. S. Eliot's *Prufrock and Other Observations* (1917). For Moore observes things, makes observations about them, and incorporates observations by others, all the time respecting their otherness. Sometimes these observations by other people are about quite different matters than the mountain; they are taken from books she has read, articles she has perused, snatches of conversation she has overheard. She does not simply behold what she sees, as happens far more often in Romantic lyric verse. In "An Octopus," Mt. Rainier is approached in various ways and from multiple perspectives: by foot of course (Moore ascends the peak) but also by way of quotations from all sorts of texts, summoned without regard for cultural hierarchies (a line from Newman's *Historical Sketches* [1872] sits beside quotations from the *Illustrated London News* and from Clifton Johnson's *What to See in America* [1919]). One quotation about happiness is taken from a Puritan work, Richard Baxter's *The Saints' Everlasting Rest* (1650), a treatise that partly derives from St. Bernard and commends consideration and to which Moore recurs several times in her poems. Along with the warmer spiritual exercises of soliloquy and prayer, Baxter thinks, consideration leads one to "heavenly contemplation."[32]

In Moore's poem, a highly edited passage from Baxter's reflections on the spiritual life of Christians is intriguingly assimilated to the Greek idea of happiness, the effect of which is to ratchet the spiritual life down from the heavenly heights. "The Greeks liked smoothness," Moore writes, "distrusting what was back / of what could not be clearly seen, / resolving with benevolent conclusiveness, / 'complexities which still will be complexities / as long as the world lasts,'" and

> ascribing what we clumsily call happiness,
> to "an accident or a quality,
> a spiritual substance or the soul itself,
> an act, a disposition, or a habit,
> or a habit infused, to which the soul has been persuaded,
> or something distinct from a habit, a power"—
> such power as Adam had and we are still devoid of.[33]

This does not apply to all the Greeks to whom Moore alludes, of course, only to those who prized θεωρία. Throughout the poem, Moore attends to the sensual world not in an attitude of religious piety, or with a trust in natural theology, or even with a desire to ascend to spiritual heights, but only in order to discover "Relentless accuracy," which she does in the figure of Henry James. If there is love prized here, it is not *amor purus* but "the love of doing hard things,"[34] as one finds in the finely nuanced moral shadings of James's late novels and, in another way, in the poem before us.

Moore's poem is an example of contemplation in two aspects of its modern mode: attention to the immediate present and the passing from parts (or, if you wish, profiles or perspectives or images or allusions or digressions) to a whole, always undertaken in quest of a more capacious understanding of a phenomenon, in all its complexity, in all the regions of being that are evoked. It is also an example of contemplation as Husserl would have us see it, the suspension of the natural attitude so that we can ponder the process of constitution. Throughout, the quotations prevent us from accepting the poem as an apparently pregiven work; it seems to be always in the process of being thought and written. Yet Moore helps us see in her representative use of the low-modernist manner something that could easily be left unseen.[35] For her, contemplation and consideration are far closer than they are for religious people, and far less is expected of them by her than by those who construe them as spiritual exercises or modes of prayer. She is concerned far less with the invisible than with something with which it is easily confused, the absent, which is noted by way of quoting other voices. She would be *baroque* in Croll's (and Bishop's) sense of the word, though not in the sense that people use when referring to Richard Crashaw (1612–49) as *baroque*, especially in a poem such as "The Weeper." She might also be *almost baroque* in something close to Stephanie Burt's coinage ("art that puts excess, invention, and ornament first," that "exhibits elaborate syntax and sonic patterning, without adopting pre-modernist forms"), but that would be a secondary sense, and one might demur over the claim of priority if only because it would be very hard to know how to establish or defend it.[36]

No doubt Moore uses the baroque "loose period" in her poem, giving the impression of having eschewed any predetermined plan of composition and being opened to experience as it comes, both one's own and that of others. It is consideration in action, as it were, looking up, around, down, and within, in no particular order, rather than mentally performing an orderly consideration and then composing. In "An Octopus," Moore writes about walking around the icy tentacles of the glacier on top of Mt. Rainier in one long sentence:

> Completing a circle,
> you have been deceived into thinking that you have progressed,
> under the polite needles of the larches
> "hung to filter, not to intercept the sunlight"—

met by tightly wattled spruce-twigs
"conformed to an edge like clipped cypress
as if no branch could penetrate the cold beyond its company";
and dumps of gold and silver ore enclosing The Goat's Mirror—
that lady-fingerlike depression in the shape of the left human foot,
which prejudices you in favor of itself
before you have had time to see the others;
its indigo, pea-green, blue-green, and turquoise,
from a hundred to two hundred feet deep,
"merging in irregular patches in the middle of the lake
where, like gusts of a storm
obliterating the shadows of the fir-trees, the wind makes lanes of
      ripples."[37]

The sentence slowly discloses a categorial intuition: the "reserved and flat" scene of Mt. Rainer, Washington, as it unfurls before Moore while she walks around it, which turns out to have significant parts (larch needles, spruce twigs, the depression, the lake, the wind), although one can be deluded in passing from one point to another. In fact, the sentence conveys two distinct categorial intuitions, for it threads together what is present with what is absent.

So one should not think of Moore as passively recording what she sees. She reaches out, as it were, with tentacles of her own to draw in any insights that might help lead her to the understanding she seeks, and, desiring as much openness as possible, she seems to close the period only reluctantly.[38] Her extensive and varied use of quotations is remarkable, for she keeps taking judgments made by other people, who sometimes have quite other ends in view, and making them her own, though always at a slight distance. There is almost no doxic variation in her manner of quotation here, no raised eyebrows or faintly amused irony, and never a flicker of gullibility in accepting or at least entertaining another's view, only a sense of almost fastidious verbal choice. So frequent and so diverse is the activity of quotation that much of the poem is outside itself, as it were, while also, at the level of composition, neatly self-contained. A little editing of what is taken is, as noted with respect to Baxter's treatise, sometimes required for that to be so.[39] Reading Moore's poem aloud, we notice how phonic and verbal elements become apparent when quotations are absorbed in her poem: the line of alliteration in "conformed . . . clipped . . . cold . . . company," for instance. More generally, the experience we are offered in the poem is a refraction of others' experiences as much as her own reflections on her experience, the result being that we never quite get Moore into focus as we read. She appears as an *I* that keeps retreating and advancing by means of the observations of others as well as her own. She looks around, beneath, and above, though not in in any direct manner. Yet we sense that she knows herself well.

Moore's poems—especially the longer ones—dip down to consideration, not by dint of a loss of intensity in her poetic gaze, but because the poetry is never far from a deflated mode of contemplation in the first place, one that is hesitant to claim access to the truth before writing and instead finds it as it goes along. Consideration, in "An Octopus," works in the service of not so much spiritual ascent as cultural ascent: the democratic impulse behind the use of quotations frays a little before the august presence of Henry James. Nonetheless, the poem under discussion touches on an insight or a truth and does so with an unusual exclamation ("Neatness of finish! Neatness of finish!").[40] Moore hovers for a while over the registration to which she has alerted both herself and us. Her recollection is no inward prayer but a gathering of sources. Two simultaneous intentional acts guide the poem in order to manifest the grandeur she values in nature (the mountain) and in culture (James).

*

The Vulgate is rich in verses that use one or another form of *consideratio*. One of the most familiar of them is Prov. 6:6: "vade ad formicam o piger et considera vias eius et disce sapientiam" ("Go to the ant, O sluggard; consider her ways, and be wise" [RSV]). It is the only time that an ant is mentioned in the scriptures, one less time than the snail, which appears in Lev. 11:30 and Ps. 58:8. Ants are praised in medieval bestiaries since they work for the common good.[41] Snails, however, are often regarded as aggressive; they appear in the margins of medieval manuscripts, often defeating knights armed for battle with them.[42] Or they are associated in medieval times with death and resurrection: a snail appears in the margin of the story of Jesus raising Lazarus from the dead (John 11:1–44), for instance.[43] Or, yet again, they are a figure of our slowness along the path to God, as one finds in a sermon of William of Auvergne (1190–1249).[44] There have been poems aplenty about ants, including the industrious ant in Proverbs, in English poetry.[45] In the eighteenth century, a cat—Jeoffry—is considered extensively by his owner, Christopher Smart: what is above him, what is beneath him, and what is around him.[46] Curiously, however, in the twentieth century several prominent poets have associated consideration with the snail, and, when they do so, the reference in *consider* to a star or constellation (*sidus*) or anything heavenly is completely or almost completely set aside. One looks downward or, at most, around oneself or at oneself in a thoughtful manner. Accordingly, I turn for a moment from birds to snails.

Moore's charming fable "To a Snail" begins by entertaining a quotation from Demetrius of Phalerum's *On Style* (ca. 270) and then immediately undercuts any high seriousness to which we might feel inclined with three brisk syllables on the second line that directly address the snail:

If "compression is the first grace of style,"
you have it. Contractility is a virtue
as modesty is a virtue.
It is not the acquisition of any one thing
that is able to adorn,
or the incidental quality that occurs
as a concomitant of something well said,
that we value in style,
but the principle that is hid:
in the absence of feet, "a method of conclusions";
"a knowledge of principles,"
in the curious phenomenon of your occipital horn.[47]

Here is "a mind thinking," ranging around right from the beginning (passing from an appeal to Greek rhetoric to plucking a word from the language of modern natural science, *contractility*), intent on grasping the εἶδος, "style." For Moore, style is "hid," not just "hidden"; and the difference in tense tells us more than one might think at first. We may remember from schooldays William Cowper's snail that simply "hides" in its shell.[48] The simple past tense, *hid*, suggests, however, that a principle of style can be made manifest only with great difficulty, if at all, despite what Demetrius propounds.[49] We should remember the insouciant *If*, so easy to overlook at the start of the poem. Without a clear principle readily available to determine what style is, one must therefore proceed inductively, as the Franciscan Duns Scotus (1266–1308) maintains about theology. For theology cannot fully be a science, Scotus argues (against Aquinas), since it is not based on deductive reasoning.[50] The two final quotations in the poem allude to Scotus, and we fully understand the lyric only when we tease them out.[51]

For Scotus, theology alone turns on "a knowledge of principles," as Henry Osborne Taylor, Moore's source, puts it. Its ground is divine revelation, which Scotus takes to be unshakable, though only in

the attitude of faith. Metaphysics, a quite distinct area of investigation for Scotus, proposes "a method of conclusions," one based on the
use of natural reason. The existence of God, for example, can be established in metaphysics by examining the absolute or perfect properties
of God, those that are not limited as properties are in creatures. We see
here, far better than in "An Octopus," how Moore sometimes lightly
ironizes quotations by placing them in unforeseen contexts: "method"
(μέθοδος: "inquiry," among other things) is formed from μετα- + ὁδός
("by means of" + "road"). The snail must have a mode of inquiry because of its limited power of locomotion: it crawls forward on its one
foot over a layer of slime that it secrets from a gland at the front of its
foot and that becomes the road it has traveled. Its method must relate
to "conclusions," to one or more provisional ends of its journey, just as
a metaphysician must conclude his or her argument about being or as
a poet must terminate his or her work in appropriate judgments about
a phenomenon reached by using an individual method, his or her own
slime, as it were. What about "a knowledge of principles"? For Scotus,
theology begins with revealed principles and, primarily oriented to the
will rather than to the intellect, is practical, not speculative: it inclines
us to love God and neighbor.[52] We do both metaphysics and theology
in our minds, of course, but Moore playfully imagines a snail doing
both in its "occipital horn," its long upper tentacles that are "curious"
in both senses of the word, eager for knowledge and unusual.[53] Revealed theology for Scotus becomes transformed into natural theology
for Moore. We are left considering less the infinite being of God than
the gulf between the snail's being and God's as well as the snail's (and
our) risible attempts to look so far above itself and attain such sublime
knowledge (by way of metaphysics) and love (by way of theology).

    Moore's snail also is always practical, pushing methodically ahead
on its path of slime, even though we have no reason to think it is seeking divine love or offering us an allegory for doing so, and nothing is
said about it contemplating its creator, either. (It is not perceived as a
"hermit," like Cowper's snail, e.g.) Without any direct intuition of the
truth, and therefore not being able to contemplate it, Moore herself engages in consideration, in this case passing from the natural world not
to God but to a highly prized adornment of culture ("style") that is almost invisible. The fable interweaves two intentional acts, which we
can see in its implied simile; it figures the snail as like a poem, although
one that does not have regular meter ("the absence of feet"). With regard to the snail, the observation is anatomically exact, as already
noted: a snail does not have feet, only one muscular foot. Induction,

along with the movement of the will, occurs by way of the eyes on the tips of the snail's upper tentacles. That this induction would be a painstaking process (like writing a poem) is evident since the snail has very weak eyesight. It can see barely ahead of itself, and for the poet this means looking at what he or she has been reading or hearing of late, whatever it may be, and including it in his or her poem.[54]

There could be no doubt that, when Thom Gunn (1929–2004) turns to regard a snail, he does so in what we might see as a low-modernist, even further scaled-down version of *consideratio* than one finds with Moore. The very title of his poem bears out his recourse to the lower mode of reflection—"Considering the Snail"—and there is no evocation, however ironic, of theology. There is no reason to believe that Gunn knew the tradition of *consideratio* that runs from Cicero to St. Bernard, and from St. Bernard to Baxter (or indeed from St. Bernard to Luis de Granada [1505–88]), and from either the Puritan or the Catholic to himself.[55] If he was aware of any of its manifestations, it would most likely be in its appearance in seventeenth-century poetry, George Herbert's in particular.[56] The ordinary English word *consider* and its various forms disclose its religious past mainly to classicists, medievalists, and theologians.[57] In fact, Gunn's poem is not at all oriented to what is above him (*supra eum*) and appears to look steadfastly toward something beneath him (*sub eum*), which of course is visible if one takes the time to look for it.

The poem begins by sympathetically adopting the perspective of a garden snail on its world, and the syllabic meter slows a reader to a snail's pace. (Each line consists of seven syllables so as to avoid a caesura falling continually after four syllables and to facilitate unexpected enjambement.) The half-rhymes (*abcabc*) are so light as they work with the run-on syllabic meter that they are barely noticed—again, much like a snail. But this snail *is* noticed:

> The snail pushes through a green
> night, for the grass is heavy
> with water and meets over
> the bright path he makes, where rain
> has darkened the earth's dark. He
> moves in a wood of desire,
>
> pale antlers barely stirring
> as he hunts. I cannot tell
> what power is at work, drenched there

with purpose, knowing nothing.
What is a snail's fury? All
I think is that if later

I parted the blades above
the tunnel and saw the thin
trail of broken white across
litter, I would never have
imagined the slow passion
to that deliberate progress.[58]

As the poem enters its second stanza, it passes from confident present observation, assigned to the snail's orientation in its wet, grassy world, to statements of epistemic distance from the creature. We slide from "a green / night," "heavy / with water" and "bright path" to "I cannot tell," "knowing nothing," and the modest claim "All / I think" and then the more decisive "never have / imagined."

When Gunn considers the snail, however, he looks for what is in principle invisible. He attends chiefly to its will, inferred from its persistence in motion and without the slightest theological resonance. He addresses himself to how it "pushes through a green / night," a task made harder by the dew that bends the blades of grass over the earth, and how "He / moves in a wood of desire," presumably because he can eat almost everything around him. What intrigues Gunn is the "power" that animates the snail, its saturated sense of "purpose," which even suggests to him the inner life of the snail, even its possible "fury." (The possibility is not arbitrary: as already noted, the doodles in the margins of medieval manuscripts sometimes represent fierce snails.)[59] The word choice is nicely balanced between natural violence — as in the common expression "the storm's fury"—and human anger or energy, and the lack of an answer in the poem keeps the ambiguity alive. The snail's willpower exceeds its intellect; it knows nothing but wills much. Having imagined the snail's single-minded determination, Gunn tells himself (and us) that, if he looked later at the snail, he would not have imagined what chiefly matters. "The slow passion / to that deliberate progress" will always have been greater or other than is possible for him to conceive.

Moving toward closure, Gunn says that, "if later // [he] parted the blades above / the tunnel," he would see evidence of the snail's persistent movement, the invisible appearing in and through the visible. The use of the conditional might be overlooked at first, for, on the basis of the final registration of detail at the end of the third stanza, one might mistakenly assume that Gunn has indeed returned to look at the snail. We know already that he is sufficiently curious about the snail's intensity of will and is also, perhaps, concerned about him and his progress or lack of it to do so. Yet the third stanza is about the snail being given in the mode of anticipation, and this empty intuition of the snail results in more perplexity than we have already witnessed. For with the appearance of the *I* in the second and third stanzas there also comes an acknowledgment of the otherness of the snail, and the *I*'s epistemic humility increasingly contrasts with the volitional power of the *he*. Nonetheless, in a final pirouette, Gunn takes himself to have successfully imagined something in the mode of anticipation, for the snail will have been experiencing, he thinks, "slow passion."

What actually is being considered in the poem? One approach to the question comes by noting that the snail is given the pronoun *he* twice: "*He* / moves in a wood of desire" and "*he* hunts" (emphasis added). One might see the snail's determination as an allegory of human existence, of the sheer willpower that is needed to persist in everyday existence in order to make ends meet. If we think first of Schopenhauer, we would do better to think of Sartre. Of course, the male pronoun is entirely conventional: we find it in Shakespeare's and Cowper's evocations of snails, for instance.[60] But, if the poem proposes an allegory of the human race or even of male behavior, why would the speaker register so pointedly the otherness of the snail? Gunn is a male human being and must be included in any such allegory. It could be, rather, that, as he imagines himself returning and looking from on high at the snail, Gunn would have a sudden, defamiliarized sense of creaturely existence that crystalizes his consideration. He would overcome the distance between his own inner feelings and the snail's, not just by fulfilling his intuition of the creature once again, but by having a sense of empathy with it. He would feel almost viscerally and for the first time the "slow passion" that the snail (and, by extension, some individuals) must experience day by day as they push through life. Yet the "slow passion" is given in imagination; the poet has not yet returned to view the snail, if indeed he ever does, and his evocation of the creature's inner life is a series of empty intuitions. It might be inferred that Gunn, connoisseur of gay sex, motorcyclists, rock guitarists, and street gangs, tends to "fast passion" and thus that "slow passion" is something new for him. At any rate, in imagination he comes to understand intimately what is involved when other individuals deliberate as they seek their goals.[61]

Another consideration of the snail appeared in France between the writing of Moore's fable and Gunn's lyric, and a brief examination of it will shed light on both poems and on our general theme. In his prose poem "Escargots," in *Le parti pris des choses* (1942), Francis Ponge (1899–1988) attempts to take the side of the snail by using words to prompt the creature to manifest its inner life, though we should not take that expression to denote or connote anything spiritual. Snails have "Plus de méthode" (more method) than any pig, Ponge says (reminding one a little of Moore), and then asks, as Gunn did after him: "La colère des escargots est-elle perceptible? Y en a-t-il des exemples?" (Is the anger of snails perceptible? Are there instances of it?).[62] Writing a roomier poem than "Considering the Snail," Ponge can do what Gunn does not, answer his own question:

> Comme elle est sans aucun geste, sans doute se manifeste-t-elle seulement par une sécrétion de bave plus floculente et plus rapide. Cette bave d'orgueil. L'on voit ici que l'expression de leur colère est la même que celle de leur orgueil. Ainsi se rassurent-ils et en imposent-ils au monde d'une façon plus riche, argentée.
>
> L'expression de leur colère, comme de leur orgueil, devient brillante en séchant. Mais aussi elle constitue leur trace et les désigne au ravisseur (au prédateur). De plus elle est éphémère et ne dure que jusqu'à la prochaine pluie.

> (Since it doesn't have gestures, it most likely manifests itself by a more downy and faster secretion of drool. That proud drool. We see here that the expression of their anger is the same as that of their pride. Thus, they reassure themselves and they impose themselves on the world in a richer, more silvery way.
>
> The expression of their anger, like their pride, becomes brilliant as it dries. But also it leaves a trace which shows those who would capture them [or prey on them] just where they are. Moreover, it's ephemeral and lasts only until it rains again.)

Again, the medieval notion of the fierce snail is tacitly engaged, while the snail's association with death and resurrection is silently declined.

Yet there is a Christian allusion. Ponge's snails are not like poets, as they are for Moore; instead, their very lives are a work of art, which (in a way) makes them more like saints than like anything else.[63] Could Ponge be reaching back to the proposals about *consideratio* ventured by his fellow Frenchman, St. Bernard of Clairvaux? Not wholly, as Ponge makes clear when he expatiates on his insight:

Mais saints en quoi: en obeisant précisément à leur nature. Connais-
toi donc d'abord toi-même. Et accept-toi tel que tu es. En accord
avec tes vices. En proportion avec ta mesure.

   Mais quelle est la notion propre d'homme: la parole et la morale.
L'humanisme.

(But saints in what? In obeying precisely their nature. Know yourself first. And accept yourself as you are. With all your vices in mind.
In proportion to what you can do.

   But what is man in essence? Speech and morality. Humanism.)

We return then to the first principle of *consideratio*, the difficult directive *Nosce teipsum* (Know thyself), but this self-knowledge, if attained,
will help keep us within our own sphere of activity, one marked solely
by morals and language, and will not prompt us to look for what is
above ourselves (*supra*). Thus chastened, we will look only from time
to time at what is beneath us (*sub*), the physical, doubtless for moral
lessons from ordinary things, for our proper sphere of regard is ourselves and those around us (*circa*). Where Gunn recognizes the otherness of the snail and imagines overcoming it to some extent, Moore
is less concerned with alterity than with the snail as a poet. She is unlike most people in her devotion to that patient (if at times intense and
bewildering) activity but finally not to herself as agent. Finally, Ponge
finds his snail surprisingly close to enlightened human beings, inheri-
tors of Bacon, Malherbe, and others, and this experience confirms his
sense of rational humanism. We might say that Ponge makes explicit
what remains of *consideratio* in its contracted mode in the twentieth
century and does so by way of a natural theology.

*

Yet *consideratio* is not invariably practiced in a curtailed mode in modern poetry. I will discuss two examples of it in its higher mode, one elevated in tone and manner, the other almost hymnic, by poets whose
longer work will feature in later chapters. The first of these poets is
Geoffrey Hill (1932–2016), and I choose his very early poem, "Merlin"
(1953):

   I will consider the outnumbering dead:
   For they are the husks of what was rich seed.
   Now, should they come together to be fed,
   They would outstrip the locusts' covering tide.

Arthur, Elaine, Mordred; they are all gone
Among the raftered galleries of bone.
By the long barrows of Logres they are made one,
And over their city stands the pinnacled corn.[64]

Here, the speaker almost forcibly turns his attention ("I *will* consider") to the many who have died long ago, particularly those who
once lived in King Arthur's realm, Logres, presumably around the fifth
century CE. The place itself presumably has a far deeper history, for
those monumental constructions, the "long barrows" next to "the raftered galleries of bone," belong to the early Neolithic period, and the
Arthurian dead are apparently buried beside them. The speaker gives a
reason for his disciplined mental act of consideration. Although these
dead are husks, no more than literary characters in works such as the
Morte d'Arthur (fifteenth century) and Tennyson's *The Idylls of the King*
(1859–85), they were once "rich seed": they flourished in their day and
now are mourned. Unlike others, the speaker will keep faith with their
memory, even if it might be painful for him for reasons that are not yet
entirely clear. Yet these "husks" are not altogether dead. Imaginatively,
at least, they are more threatening than a plague of locusts (thereby
giving weight to the expression "outnumbering dead") that consumes
any and all crops. Specifically, we learn, in the very last line of the lyric,
the corn grows over where they once lived and flourished. The corn is
"pinnacled," suggesting both the turrets of the Arthurian castles and a
culmination of natural growth. It too comes from "rich seed," perhaps
the very dead who are being mourned.

    Consideratio, here, begins with those beneath the speaker, the dead
(in general), but quickly specifies a group of actors well known to Merlin who were caught up in sexual passion and battles ("Arthur, Elaine,
Mordred"), now conceived as unified in death and, in the fantasy of
locusts, above him and around him as well.[65] The temporal range is
vast in one respect, ranging back to Neolithic times, and tightly limited
in another: we pass from the past ("was") to the present ("should"),
glimpse a possible past ("would"), and return to the present. The loss
of the dead and the dark prospect of them returning as a locust swarm
must be contained. It is perhaps too distressing to be considered for
long. The point is worth underlining, for we should not conceive that
consideratio is anything less than demanding, whether in the spiritual
life or in the hands of a poet as challenging (and self-challenging) as
Hill.

    But who is the speaker? That is something the reader is required to answer. It could well be Hill himself, often given, even at a tender age, to elegy. Or it could be Merlin, especially if Hill follows one of the later stories about the bard or magician such as in the *Didot Percival* (late twelfth or early thirteenth century) in which he will not die until the end of the world. Either way, *consideratio* is undertaken in an unusual manner, as poetry, whether it be Merlin or Hill who is the speaker (but certainly with Hill in the background as the poet and the one who bears final responsibility for the poem). The dead are recalled from their graves precisely by bardic powers, which recur to the reputation or fame of the one exercising them and court the danger of aestheticizing the pain and distress of others who cannot speak for themselves. Such will become a major theme of Hill's later poetry.[66] We begin to understand more fully the need forcibly to engage in the act of mental attention. It is one thing (ethical) to keep faith with the dead, another (aesthetic) to memorialize them in poetry, and, for Hill, who keeps the two dimensions of value theory strictly distinct, any elegy is morally equivocal by virtue of the contrary impulses to composition, impulses that are never resolved in the finished work. Although consideration here involves looking beneath, around, and up, it cannot properly conclude by looking within: the aesthetic and the ethical fail to coincide, with the consequence that self-knowledge eludes the speaker.

I turn now to a poem of *consideratio* that is more highly pitched rhetorically and, while not Christian in any definite way, deeply religious in orientation. I am thinking of "The City Limits" (1970) by A. R. Ammons (1926–2001):

When you consider the radiance, that it does not withhold
itself but pours its abundance without selection into every
nook and cranny not overhung or hidden; when you consider

that birds' bones make no awful noise against the light but
lie low in the light as in a high testimony; when you consider
the radiance, that it will look into the guiltiest

swervings of the weaving heart and bear itself upon them,
not flinching into disguise or darkening; when you consider
the abundance of such resource as illuminates the glow-blue

bodies and gold-skeined wings of flies swarming the dumped
guts of a natural slaughter or the coil of shit and in no
way winces from its storms of generosity; when you consider

that air of vacuum, snow or shale, squid or wolf, rose or lichen,
each is accepted into as much light as it will take, then
the heart moves roomier, the man stands and looks about, the

leaf does not increase itself above the grass, and the dark
work of the deepest cells is of a tune with May bushes
and fear lit by the breadth of such calmly turns to praise.[67]

This is no slow and steady mental act of deliberation, nothing like the poems by Moore, Gunn, and Ponge. In one long sentence, cascading over six highly enjambed tercets, the poet asks himself and the reader to consider the "radiance" twice and to consider three other things, each of which he points out is associated with light, even if we do not usually make the link ourselves: the bones of birds flying in the sky; all sorts of things we would prefer not to think about (flies, slaughtered animal flesh, and feces); and the air around diverse animals, vegetables, and minerals.[68] If we practice this natural *consideratio*, we will, we are assured, be transformed within and see the world about us differently than the ways our urban culture offers us. We too will be touched by the spring, and, however immense and complex the world seems when regarded in such an open manner, it will not frighten us for long and will bring forth praise from us for its bounty and order. But what is this "radiance"? And what is the nature of this "praise"?

One path to an answer to these questions goes by way of what Ammons receives from Emerson. Recall the Sage of Concord's impressive sentence in his lyrical essay "Nature" (1836): "I become a transparent eyeball; I am nothing; I see all; the currents of the Universal Being circulate through me; I am part or particle of God."[69] This passivity before nature, in all its diverse abundance, is as close as one reaches in Ammons's shorter poems to a contemplative stance, but it is Emersonian and Whitmanian, not Plotinian, and certainly not Christian.[70] For one thing, Ammons's attention is fixed on the visible, with little concern about the invisible, in whatever sense, being nudged to appear by reduction. The "weaving heart" is evoked, making Sir Water Scott's cautionary "tangled web" of deceit, so familiar from childhood, come to mind. But what illuminates the heart is entirely natural, not an invisible moral or spiritual presence.[71] The poet describes and extolls rather than moralizes or preaches. His gaze is anterior to the poem, bespeaking a prior act of consideration that has led to the poem. Yet the poem itself thinks as it proceeds; it is not entirely given over to being receptive. The virtues of reception are offered to be actively considered, not simply accepted. "The City Limits" does not lead to absorption into the One, then, but to a discerning admiration for the generosity and persistence of the radiance of natural life, despite the resistance it meets on our planet, including those who inhabit it, and to the ways in which the One becomes the Many. We are to consider that resistance and our part in it, among other things.

The title of the lyric alludes to a passage in Sherman Paul's *Emerson's Angle of Vision* (1952) in which Emerson is taken to have "two perspectives on nature . . . distant and proximate" that correspond to the country and the city.[72] Distant vision tends to equalize phenomena and is loosely associated with democratic values, while proximate vision leads one to distinguish, analyze, and dissociate phenomena that appear before it. Ammons's lyric is set at the city limits, where hierarchy begins to give way to equality. We hear that with the practice of natural *consideratio* "the // leaf does not increase itself above the grass" and that an equilibrium is possible between our inner biological workings and those of the natural world outside us. Indeed, the old Platonic and Christian hierarchy of the invisible and the visible has already given way, long before the poem begins, for the poet. His is a lyric of categorial vision: we see the radiance over everything that comes within our visual field, and we also see the particulars of shale, squid, lichen, and so on. But the vision has been deliberately lowered, even in the mode of praise.

We are prompted to "consider the radiance," to recognize that it pours over the world without regard for degrees of being, as Richard held, or human hierarchies or dualisms such as those between the inner and the outer, the guilty and the innocent. This consideration tacitly excludes anything Platonic or Christian, any phenomenality or revelation traditionally associated with light. When we ponder the radiance, we find that it is twofold, both light that is emitted from the sun and the glowing quality on surfaces, such as the leaves of trees and the feathers of birds. Early in the lyric, Ammons refers us to birds in lines that lightly return us to a vestige of the classical *templum*, although it is no longer a space of augury—the very idea would be incredible in the world of this poem—but only sunlit air. If we think about it, the bones of birds do not make an unpleasant sound as they fly above us, as planes and helicopters do. To be sure, birds' feathers sometimes make a clapping noise on taking off, and sometimes one hears a whistling as birds fly quickly through the air. But that is all. They make "no awful noise *against* the light" (emphasis added), Ammons says, making a slight crease in George Fox's remark, repeated by many after him, about decrying those who "speak against the Light."[73] Ammons has long since passed from the supernatural to the natural. These hollow bones, full of air sacs, "lie low in the light," we are told, which is to say that they make no display of themselves, not because of anything wrong that they have done, but solely out of silent awe for the radiance that they experience in their own way. As they bear the birds aloft, the light bones offer "high testimony," as though freely giving a profession of natural faith in the generosity of the physical world about him that enables birds to rise, swoop, and hover, to experience the joy of the radiance about them, to engage in θεωρία φυσική, although it is a θεωρία that does not seek to ponder anything above or beyond the visible.

Nor does the radiance of life shy away from disease and waste: everything is offered the effulgence to the extent that it can accept it. Ammons stands, then, at a fair distance from Dante's view of divine glory as given at the start of the *Paradiso*:

> La gloria di colui che tutto move
> per l'universo penetra, e risplende
> in una parte più e meno altrove.
>
> (The glory of the One who moves everything
> penetrates the universe, and glows
> on one part more and in another less.)[74]

If we bow to the principle of life, given in the present moment—for the poem never speaks of remembering or anticipating—then we are led to welcome and accept our place in the cosmos, the activities of our cells, whether their programming leads to a long life or a short one, whether we make of it a happy one or an unhappy one. Our response to the extent and generosity of the source of life, if properly considered, will not be neutral, nor will it be violently ecstatic. Consideration, in Ammons's modern American inflection of it, with a twofold vision of proximity and distance, "*calmly* turns to praise" (emphasis added). The calmness and the praise are equally weighted in the context of fear, both indices of an achieved toughness and an achieved wisdom. Praise, for Ammons, begins in consideration and touches on contemplation; it is praise for what is above us, around us, beneath us, and within us: the radiance of life itself, understood to be entirely within the limits of the natural.

CHAPTER 7

From Supreme Being to Supreme Fiction

A review of Wallace Stevens's *Collected Poems* entitled "In the Orchards of the Imagination" appeared in the *New Republic* on November 1, 1954, nine months before the poet's death. There, the reviewer, Delmore Schwartz (1913–66), told his readers: "The starting-point of Stevens' poems is often the aesthetic experience in isolation from all other experiences, as art is isolated from work and as a museum is special and isolated in any modern American community."[1] Several recognizable things are lightly pressed together here: the classical distinction between *otium* and *negotium*, the idea of the museum or gallery as a place of refuge and refreshment, and the Romantic view of the artist who abides in solitude. Schwartz's readers would have recognized in his words the familiar fin de siècle figure of the poet as aesthete or dandy that had been promoted by Charles Baudelaire as far back as his "Le peintre de la vie moderne" (1863).[2] The label had been attached to Stevens not long after the publication of *Harmonium* (1923), as reviews by Louis Untermeyer and Gorham B. Munson amply testify.[3] Unlike Baudelaire's dandy, however, Stevens had long been a successful bourgeois, a man of business. If, unlike the dandy, he did not set poetry and money in opposition—he even later declared in an aphorism, "Money is a kind of poetry"—he seemed to devote himself to art like one, and early readers made hasty inductions about the relationship to poetry that someone could have who was "well-fed and well-booted" and who enjoyed his "contentment."[4] Unlike Baudelaire, the American public tended to think of the dandy as a dilettante, perhaps even a skeptic, and not as an eternally superior person.[5]

Schwartz understood all this perfectly well, as is clear in the comments that directly follow his situating of Stevens's starting point for writing, and I will let him lead me into the dimension of Stevens's poetry that most interests me here. He continues: "And if one limits oneself to the surface of Stevens' poetic style, one can characterize Stevens as the poet of Sunday: the poet of the week-end, the holiday, and the vacation, who sees objects at a distance, as they appear to the tourist or in the art museum."[6] We might think of "Thirteen Ways of Looking at a Blackbird," "Peter Quince at the Clavier," and other poems familiar to anthology readers of the day, poems that contributed, rightly or wrongly, to entrenching the view of Stevens as a "conscious aesthete," practitioner of "the flambeaued manner," someone drawn to the decorative aspects of French culture and to chinoiserie.[7] Then Schwartz pivots and states his main case: "But this is merely the poet's starting-point. Stevens converts aestheticism into contemplation in the full philosophical and virtually religious sense of the word. The surface of his poetry is very often verbal, visual, and gay; beneath the surface, it is a deadly earnest scrutiny of attitudes toward existence, of 'how to live, what to do.'" He observes: "Stevens has been much underrated because readers fail to perceive this transformation."[8]

It will be noticed that Schwartz silently translates *aesthetic experience* into *aestheticism*, Pater's art for art's sake, and thereby restricts the former even more narrowly than he does when oddly insisting that aesthetic experience abides "in isolation from all other experiences." But his central point concerns another shift, one that is far more important, that can be rephrased in another key. Stevens performs in his poems a conversion of the gaze from a highly determined mode of aesthetic experience to the philosophical or even the religious, and we shall recognize it only if, as readers, we pass from surface to depth. We cannot content ourselves with verbal play, as in "Bantoms in Pine-Woods," or merely relish visual images such as "palms, / Squiggling like saxophones," in "An Old High-Toned Christian Woman,"[9] or openly enjoy a witty criticism of the general lack of imagination in America, such as in "Disillusionment at Ten O' Clock," if we are to reach the appropriate position required to offer a judicious estimation of Stevens's achievement in his poetry. Two questions are prompted here. The first is why aesthetic experience is not taken to be coordinate with an aesthetic attitude that gives rise to contemplation on its own accord. Is aesthetic experience not a good in and of itself? These concerns will reverberate throughout this chapter, although I will return to them more directly in the following chapter. The second question is what *philosophical* and *religious* might mean here, especially if one removes the aesthetic from philosophy, and I will address it first.

The general tenor of Schwartz's comments about Stevens's verse ("scrutiny of attitudes toward existence") inclines one to think of existential concerns that were still pervasive among educated readers on the East Coast of the United States in the 1950s.[10] The first English translation of Sartre's *L'existentialisme est un humanisme* (1946) appeared in 1948, and the philosopher's main work, *L'être et le néant* (1943), was to appear in English in 1958. For other readers, Stevens suggested philosophical or religious positions that were at odds with each other. Allen Tate suggested, early on, that "an intense Puritanism" lay beneath the surface dandyism of Stevens's verse—again, an encouragement of readers to pass from surface to depth—while Ivor Winters believed that he recognized a hedonist in the same poet.[11] One can see Stevens drawing, for his own ends, on distinctions such as those between the real and the imagined and between the natural and the celestial, one can trace a steady interest in material reality and in forces, and throughout one can see a lively interest in forms and ideas.[12] Never intrigued by Sartre, unlike some of the early admirers of his poetry, Stevens was more taken by other contemporary thinkers, especially those who were themselves disposed to noetics and poetics, including, from Europe, Maurice Blanchot, Benedetto Croce, Charles Mauron, Jean Paulhan, and Jean Wahl and, from the United States, William James and George Santayana.[13] Stevens's reading in this area was nothing if not eclectic; he drew from idealists and anti-idealists, pragmatists and nihilists, and almost everyone in between and around the two groups.[14]

None of these distinctions or attitudes makes a way of thinking that hangs together sufficiently well to justify calling Stevens a *philosophical poet* in the way that we might properly use that expression, with various reservations, when speaking of Lucretius, Dante, or (just possibly) Goethe.[15] In the composition of his poems Stevens is more interested in the manner—or indeed the mannerisms—of philosophical or at least scholarly discourse than in forensic or speculative thought with a view to establishing truth. We find a taste for the philosophical in the ways in which he draws distinctions, for example, more than in what he says or seeks to explain, and often enough the niceness of the distinctions either marks them with a tinge of irony or is a way by which he achieves closure or indicates his manner of thinking as he writes. At a pinch, some readers might wish to say, with T. S. Eliot, that there is a "philosophy" that can express itself only in the language of poetry, and I take it that here Eliot's scare quotes set aside any need for argumentative rigor.[16] It would be a matter of the feel of an individual philosophical culture being apparent in the poetry, a taste for philosophical ideas and speculation rather than narrow procedures.[17] Eliot's own *Four Quartets* (1943) would be a case in point. But Stevens does not seem to do this or attempt to do it; his remarks about "the first idea," "belief" and "reality" generate an air of philosophical reflection—indeed, of modalization—while he thinks in his verse in ways that are not quite philosophical, in any robust modern sense of the word.

It is tempting to look back to Eliot's earlier distinction in his weighty essay "The Metaphysical Poets" (1921) between intellectual and reflective poets, if only because the stakes seem less high than in direct appeals to philosophy. Is Stevens a reflective poet? The exemplars of this group are Tennyson and Browning, Eliot suggests, and he contrasts them to the advantage of Donne, in particular, for whom "a thought . . . was an experience; it modified his sensibility."[18] The Victorian poets do not feel their thoughts with the same immediacy. It is not clear how one might know whether or how someone feels a thought, for striking lines of verse can be written in cold blood or initiated by miswriting a word. Let us look elsewhere for illumination. Stevens's syntax in parts of "Notes toward a Supreme Fiction" (1942) suggests a process of thought in the moment, a restless drive for precision but of a kind that one would hesitate to call *philosophical* in any narrow sense of the word. Sometimes it comes in an apparent rush, as though to force a process of thinking through a tight channel that is being built as Stevens writes:

> There was a will to change, a necessitous
> And present way, a presentation, a kind
> Of volatile world, too constant to be denied,
>
> The eye of a vagabond in metaphor
> That catches our own.[19]

This might not be intellectual in Eliot's sense, but nor does it seem reflective in quite the way he has in mind with the Victorian poets. (Coleridge's sense of *reflective*—thinking over one's mental acts—might edge us toward firmer ground, as might a word we have pondered in the previous chapter, *consideration*, and, indeed, Schwartz's *scrutiny*.)[20] If we demur about there being a "full philosophical" sense of something, anything, in Stevens's poetry, we can agree that, especially in his longer poems ("Sunday Morning," "Notes toward a Supreme Fiction," "The Auroras of Autumn," and "An Ordinary Evening in New Haven" above all), Stevens is concerned both to observe and to behold mortal being. It is not all that the word *philosophical* can do for us when reading Stevens, but it is a useful first step along the path.

Before taking any further steps in that direction, especially along the lines that Schwartz suggests, we should recall that a "full philosophical" sense of contemplation is probably something Stevens does not have or would have claimed to have, if only because θεωρία is traditionally cued to a metaphysical approach to being and Stevens, as poet, does not think of being in quite that way. Poetry, he says in "The Figure of the Youth as Virile Poet" (1943), is "an unofficial view of being" (the official one being philosophical), and he entertains the thought that the poet might come on ideas that satisfy both reason (the realm of philosophy) and imagination (the modern poet's traditional homeland).[21] That his verse has a quality of attentiveness is apparent to any reader, and his attention is taken not only with surfaces and forces but also with mental movements, both his own and those of characters in his poems. That his verse has a certain coolness was spotted by Munson, although it would be hasty to think that it has no blood passion. Placing hot emotions in a cool place is a way of trying to understand them and appreciate their force and the direction in which it would have us move.[22] Finally, that this verse has a tranquil quality is something that Munson was also the first to notice.[23] Taken together, these three things—attentiveness, coolness, and tranquility—incline one to think of the poetry as contemplative. But one should still proceed with caution before using *contemplative* freely to describe Stevens's poems. The poet who says "There is no such thing as the truth" may well feel that the grapes he sees before him have become fatter in the absence of a rapport between declarations and reality, but we may wonder quite what he is saying.[24] Is this a disparagement of using reason alone to seek the truth, as in philosophy, or a denial of a creator God as Truth, as in theology, or a performative contradiction of the kind one finds in irony and in some humor?

It might be that Stevens does not so much deny the truth in a categorical manner as muse over a theory of weak truth in his own way. "We have been a little insane about the truth," he writes in "The Noble Rider and the Sound of Words" (1942). "We have had an obsession. In its ultimate extension, this truth about which we have been insane will lead us to look beyond the truth to something in which the imagination will be the dominant complement."[25] Stevens uses *true* and *truth* too often in his verse and prose for us to think with any assurance that this single remark in an essay summarizes his position on it. Many, but not all, of his views cohere around it. If he toys with a deflationary approach to truth or even is influenced by a pragmatist conception of truth akin to William James's, we will not think of him as continuing the contemplative tradition as it has been chiefly received and discussed by philosophers and theologians.[26] That is not to say, however, that he does not take a cue from elsewhere and reset the notion of contemplation in his writing. He does precisely that when he turns to George Rostrevor Hamilton's *Poetry and Contemplation* (1937). He quotes from the book in "The Noble Rider and the Sound of Words." "The object of contemplation," Hamilton says, "is the highly complex and unified content of consciousness, which comes into being through the developing subjective attitude of the percipient."[27] Contemplation, here, is not of the highest being or being itself outside or beyond consciousness, neither *ens creatum* nor God himself, but rather of being that has already been brought, as it were, into mental space by way of aesthetic experience. The mind revolves something that has been rendered immanent to it, whether it be psychological or transcendental. What it attends to is precisely itself, albeit in a changed state.

Immediately after quoting from Hamilton, Stevens turns for further support to Benedetto Croce's Philip Maurice Deneke Lecture at Oxford, "The Defence of Poetry: Variations on a Theme of Shelley," delivered on October 17, 1933. I quote his quotation:

> If . . . poetry is intuition and expression, the fusion of sound and imagery, what is the material which takes on the form of sound and imagery? It is the whole man: the man who thinks and wills, and loves, and hates; who is strong and weak, sublime and pathetic, good and wicked; man in the exultation and agony of living; and together with the man, integral with him, it is all nature in its perpetual labor of evolution. . . . Poetry . . . is the triumph of contemplation. . . . Poetic genius chooses a strait path in which passion is calmed and calm is passionate.[28]

It may be that Stevens takes more than he really needs when he looks to Croce after Hamilton, for the Italian idealist regards contemplation as a unity of feeling, sound, and image, and, in his view, poetry presumes contemplation on the part of the poet. To be sure, one might wish to say that all of Stevens's poetry, from short poems to long ones, is the result of *contemplation* in the sense that Croce gives to the word, although surely some will be less fully so, or less importantly so, than others. This prizing of poetry as a calming of passion might explain why Stevens was attracted to Croce's lecture. But what does "Poetry . . . is the triumph of contemplation" mean? It could mean that the poet contemplates something and then composes. Yet that is not always what happens: some poets snatch their poems from the air around them. And, if we take Croce also to suggest that poetry *is* the triumph of contemplation, that it is essentially contemplative, we might take pause. Would one wish to call Guerin's fabliau "Béranglier au long cul" *contemplative*? Or Jonathan Swift's satire "The Lady's Dressing Room"? Or Robert Browning's dramatic monologue "Bishop Blougram's Apology"?

All three works ask to be read as poetry, with the provision that there are many sorts of poetry and that they attempt different things. Croce would be left trying to insist on a stipulative definition of poetry that excludes many fine poems or forces them into a single mold.

Neither Hamilton nor Croce says anything about religious contemplation and poetry, at least not insofar as either enters Stevens's sphere of regard, and, before we go any further, we need to ponder Schwartz's claim that, when read well, the poetry is also "virtually religious" in its stance.[29] We have been aware from the beginning of this book that the lines separating the philosophical and the religious in contemplation are very often discontinuous and broken. We do not usually think of Stevens as having a religious view of life in any full-bodied or even positive sense, and it is easy enough to find evidence in his writings of a distaste for many things associated with Christianity, the Western religion in which contemplation looms largest.[30] We should not embrace firm conclusions too quickly, however. "Sunday Morning" (1915), for instance, is unfriendly to church and doctrine, but the seventh section converges on "a ring of men" who "chant in orgy on a summer morn" and perform a ritual that affirms "the heavenly fellowship / Of men that perish and of summer morn."[31] A basic religious impulse is acknowledged. To be sure, Stevens refers in his poetry no fewer than eight times to rabbis (once more than to priests) and even twice to kabbalah, but these references do not combine to suggest a deep appreciation of Judaism and do not bespeak any commitment to it. In his poetry, the rabbi is a metaphor of the scholar.

We can get clearer about Stevens's attitude toward religion and perhaps a bit closer to judging whether Schwartz is right to say that his contemplative attitude is "virtually religious" if we look at his essay "Imagination as Value" (1948). "If poetry should address itself to the same needs and aspirations, the same hopes and fears, to which the Bible addresses itself," Stevens writes, "it might rival it in distribution." Having said that, he says something slightly different while intending, it would seem, to summarize what he has just said: "Poetry does not address itself to beliefs."[32] We might recall the lines that open "Of Modern Poetry" (1942):

> The poem of the mind in the act of finding
> What will suffice. It has not always had
> To find: the scene was set; it repeated what
> Was in the script.
>   Then the theatre was changed
> To something else. Its past was a souvenir.[33]

What will suffice turns on human needs, aspirations, convictions, hopes, and fears but not on the beliefs in creation and redemption that often vitalize them. "Consequently," Stevens resumes, "when critics of poetry call upon it to do some of the things that the Bible does, they overlook the certainty that the biblical imagination is one thing and the poetic imagination, inevitably, something else."[34] The words *certainly* and *inevitably* suggest that Stevens is protesting a little too much, and *something else* says far too little about the poetic imagination to be of any help in recognizing it and its relationship with the biblical imagination.[35]

For aid in grasping what Stevens has in mind, we must turn to the last essay that he collected in *The Necessary Angel* (1951), "The Relations between Poetry and Painting" (1951). "The paramount relation between poetry and painting today," he says, "between modern man and modern art is simply this: that in an age in which disbelief is so profoundly prevalent or, if not disbelief, indifference to belief, poetry and painting, and the arts in general, are, in the measure, a compensation for what has been lost." After this well-aged Arnoldian sentiment there comes another in the crucial sentence: "Men feel that the imagination is the next greatest power to faith: the reigning prince."[36] Having read that remark, we may well recall something else in "Imagination as Value," namely: "Imagination, as metaphysics, leads us in one direction and, as art, in another."[37] The sort of imagination prized by, say, J. G. Fichte (1762–1814) differs from what was prized by Stevens himself. For Fichte, the *Wissenschaftslehre* (1794–95) would lead inexorably to the *Religionslehre* (1806). Yet, for Stevens, the imagination as used in poetry leads to a compensation, or an attempted compensation, for the felt loss of religious belief: "How much stature, even vatic stature, this conception gives the poet!"[38] Contemplation in poetry might well be "virtually religious" in an analogous way that German metaphysics might speak for what traditional religion has called *God* when it addresses the Absolute.

It is with all that Schwartz has enabled us to think by following his "In the Orchards of the Imagination" that I turn to one of Stevens's most abundantly flowering poems, "Notes toward a Supreme Fiction" (1942), which is roughly contemporaneous with "The Noble Rider and the Sound of Words" and "The Figure of the Youth as Virile Poet." Husserl alerts us to the passage from perception to thinking when we shift from a simple phenomenon to an articulated whole, and "Notes" is more or less a loosely articulated whole (more by way of form, slightly less by way of theme). Also, Richard of St. Victor tells us that contemplation "moves around with astonishing mobility," which prima facie makes it appropriate to longer poems, including the one that is to command our attention now.

*

A religious or virtually religious sense of *contemplation*, as I have been using the expression in this book, would presume love. And, for *love* to have sufficient weight here, it would have to come from the object of contemplation as well as from the one who gazes on it. Or, if that is not possible given the aesthetic sense of *contemplation* to which Stevens subscribes, there would have to be some sort of compensation for love that would make the act more than philosophical. There would need to be more than speculative interest and conceptual understanding, as happens with θεωρία. These concerns prompt any reader of "Notes" to spend more time than might otherwise be deemed worthwhile on the exergue of the poem, the eight unremarkable lines, with respect to the lusters of poetry, that follow the dedication and come before the first canto of "It Must be Abstract":

> And for what, except for you, do I feel love?
> Do I press the extremest book of the wisest man
> Close to me, hidden in me day and night?
> In the uncertain light of single, certain truth,
> Equal in living changingness to the light
> In which I meet you, in which we sit at rest,
> For a moment in the central of our being,
> The vivid transparence that you bring is peace.

The lines begin almost as an aside in a conversation to which we have not been privy, a conversation, soliloquy, or reflection that has been going on for some time before we are allowed to overhear it. A Supreme Fiction is addressed as Muse, which is far more than the poem that is to follow, three self-declared notes — brief records, testimonies — that are elaborated in groups of ten lyrics and point to something larger and more opulent than Stevens, or perhaps anyone, is able to achieve.[39]

If the first question presumes an answer in the affirmative, the second one is more elusive. The "extremest book of the wisest man" may well be something that offers its readers the deepest wisdom that is available to us; it would not be the work of someone who has become a "logical lunatic."[40] Does Stevens hug such a book or have it by heart? We have no ground to think so, and undoubtedly his not having such a work to hand is a prompt for him to search time and again for a Supreme Fiction, which would be, in Hamilton's words, "the highly complex and unified content of consciousness." "The extreme poet," Stevens tells Hi Simons in a letter of August 28, 1940, "will produce a poem equivalent to the idea of God."[41] It is hard to know what *equivalent* could mean here. Can a poem be equal in *value* to the idea of God? (If so, for whom?) Can it be equal in *meaning* to the idea of God? (It is hard to conceive theologians and philosophers of religion thinking so.) Can it *function* in the same way as the idea of God? (Presumably not in many respects, whether philosophical or religious.)[42] What seems to be proposed is that for the thinking person the idea of a supreme being can and should give way to that of a Supreme Fiction. Revealed theology has been defective; natural theology, it would seem, has been looking for the wrong thing; and antirealist accounts of God are unsatisfying. Stevens's hope is to be the poet who makes this possible. The third sentence is also perplexing. There is a "single, certain truth" that casts light, although this light is itself "uncertain," not quite definite and thereby able to facilitate meditation.[43] This certain truth is to be found by way of reason and imagination, which Stevens takes to offer a complete fulfillment for the human subject, a "vivid transparence."[44] The division between reason and imagination is largely a consequence of his deep-rooted naturalism, which leagues reason and matter (along with psychic force) while leaving the imagination in a separate realm. In some ways, we might say, Stevens's quest for the Supreme Fiction—and for regarding reading and writing poetry as contemplative—is a way of living with, if not quite overcoming, his own prephilosophical commitment to naturalism. What is true of Stevens is also largely true of some of his most important critics, although for them contemplation is not a possibility that their conceptual vocabularies can countenance, let alone motivate.[45]

Presumably, the light in which a Supreme Fiction is met is one that gratifies both reason and imagination. It is living and therefore subject to change, just as reason is, if philosophers (and not only Hegelians) will admit that what we take to be reason expands and contracts in history. What Augustine means by *ratio* is not quite the same as what Anselm means by it, nor what Leibniz makes of it, and certainly not how Coleridge construes *reason* in its positive sense.[46] I recur to "The Figure of the Youth as Virile Poet": "An idea that satisfies both the reason and the imagination, if it happened, for instance, to be an idea of God, would establish a divine beginning and end for us which, at the moment, the reason, singly, at best proposes and on which, at the moment, the imagination, singly, merely meditates."[47] The certainty offered by reason is ideally joined by the imagination, and in that instant the poet and a Supreme Fiction "sit at rest" and are one: an interval of refuge and refreshment. It is a unity not of the soul and God but of poet and Fiction, and for all one knows the poet absorbs no more of all the Fiction than the devout soul can of God. In "the central of our being," the composition or consummation of the poem, the poet experiences the peace of beholding an expansion or enrichment of his consciousness, a *dilatio mentis*, made possible by conducting, insofar as he can, a Supreme Fiction into a poem. Yet the poet's love ends in peace, not because the Fiction can love in return, but because an act of love results in something more than rational mastery. Stevens calls it "ecstatic freedom of the mind."[48] Yet in one respect we are not so very far from love, for there can be no love without freedom in the sense of *libertas*.[49]

What follows in the "notes" are three distinct profiles of a Supreme Fiction, each of which is given in the imperative mood: "It must be abstract," "It must change," and "It must give pleasure." The grounding of Stevens's choice of these three profiles and no others is left obscure. For instance, despite the final line of the introductory stanza, we are not told that a Supreme Fiction must give peace. We are not told that it must instruct us or rally us to improve our moral behavior or anything of the sort.[50] What justifies the obligation in each case is never stated, although we can attempt to do so ourselves. That a Supreme Fiction is abstract (in the sense of being withdrawn from the particular) can be accounted for insofar as it would not readily be embodied in the words of a natural language; it would be ahead of the poet, not something to be found readily in past literature. It would be an idea, an abstract object such as love or beauty or justice that could be owned by the poet. More particularly, the object would be in the imagination, not reason, from where the poet could draw in order to write a poem.[51] The same object might later appear in the understanding. There is a movement, then, from poetry about the supreme being (as by George Herbert or G. M. Hopkins, e.g.) to poetry about a Supreme Fiction: not God but a property detached from the deity and naturalized, something with which the poet's consciousness can be readily in relation.

Only a formidable poet could write a poem that would actually be a Fiction as Stevens conceives it; its supremacy would be partly justified by bringing a generation or more of readers under its sway, just as much as it would its author. (There is reason to recall here Shelley's idea of poets as the "unacknowledged legislators of the world.")[52] And, of course, the actual poem could be as concrete as the poet wishes. For the relevant distinction is between abstraction and particularity, not abstraction and concretion. We might say that Dante's *Divina commedia*

(1308–20) approximates what such a Fiction would have been for him, that *The Faerie Queene* (1590–96) lets us glimpse what Spenser's Supreme Fiction was, and that the prophetic book *Jerusalem* (1804–20) gives us a sense of what Blake's corresponding Fiction must have been had any of these writers thought about his art along these lines. That said, we should not put aside the very distinct possibility that such a Fiction may well be embodied, in its own way, in many short poems, not just in a single long poem, or might find its home in a collection, such as Stevens's *Collected Poems* (1954).[53] In many ways the Supreme Fiction is a Coleridgean Idea, and accordingly we might usefully recall one of his definitions of *Idea*: "that which successively we may be evermore realizing but totally can never have realized."[54]

That a Supreme Fiction would change makes notional sense, for each age has its own range of such Fictions, such human orders, that serve to orient its poets and are seldom, if ever, perfectly realized by dint of the concrete particular having to negotiate the abstract. And a Supreme Fiction might differ to a poet after an attempt to capture it in verse has taken place, and of course he or she might well change his or her Fiction over the years. More narrowly, Hamilton has already told us, doubtless with Stevens's agreeing with him, that the object of contemplation "comes into being through the *developing* subjective attitude of the percipient" (emphasis added). The unchanging supreme being has an asymmetrical relation with his creatures: we depend ontologically on him, and he does not depend ontologically on us. Not so with a Supreme Fiction, for it is modified in individual consciousnesses, and doubtless it also changes in them the more each person reflects on it. Change must be taken in tandem with continuity, however: the human order to which Stevens appeals must have significant duration to account for its dignity. That a Supreme Fiction must give pleasure, in the sense of happiness, also makes tacit sense and not merely because, as Stevens himself said, change and pleasure involve one another.[55] For, if a poem did not create pleasure, why would a poet devote himself or herself to trying to realize it (often failing to some extent to do so, sometimes succeeding beyond his or her hopes)? Why would a reader bother to read it, especially if it is rhetorically or cognitively demanding? A difficult pleasure is still a pleasure, perhaps a greater one. The word *pleasure* suggests satisfaction, which is at the root of Stevens's aspiration that reason and imagination would converge, that neither would be in debt to the other, and this may explain why he chose the word for the third note rather than *peace* or *joy* or *freedom* or *ecstasy*. Of course, the word also suggests entertainment and sensual gratification, which briefly returns us to Stevens as aesthete or dandy.

The poem also stages, with more than a degree of irony, a scene of instruction, and thus in its own way it goes back to Horace's *Epistulas ad Pisones* or *Ars poetica*, specifically to the injunction *docere et delectare*, "instruct and delight."[56] Here, however, it is not the reader who is being instructed but a young poet. Reflection on one's own subjectivity can also go by way of others, real or imagined. Stevens draws the terms of his imaginary pedagogical scene from long before Augustan Rome, in ancient Athens, referring to the institution of the ἔφηβοι, and, since this has puzzled many readers, it is worthwhile to begin by reading the first canto of "It Must Be Abstract":

Begin, ephebe, by perceiving the idea
Of this invention, this invented world,
The inconceivable idea of the sun.

You must become an ignorant man again
And see the sun again with an ignorant eye
And see it clearly in the idea of it.

Never suppose an inventing mind as source
Of this idea nor for that mind compose
A voluminous master folded in his fire.

How clean the sun when seen in its idea,
Washed in the remotest cleanliness of a heaven
That has expelled us and our images. . . .

The death of one god is the death of all.
Let purple Phoebus lie in umber harvest,
Let Phoebus slumber and die in autumn umber,

Phoebus is dead, ephebe. But Phoebus was
A name for something that never could be named.
There was a project for the sun and is.

There is a project for the sun. The sun
Must bear no name, gold flourisher, but be
In the difficulty of what it is to be. (1.1)

After the end of the Peloponnesian War, Epicrates proposed a way of preparing the young men of Athens to become full citizens. Originally, an ἔφηβος would, from the ages of eighteen to twenty, have six teachers who would instruct him in the martial arts and religious duties; after a year, he would receive a shield and a lance and take a solemn oath in the Temple of Artemis Aglauros to serve the city and then spend another year patrolling the coasts and frontiers of Attica. Thereafter, he would enjoy all the rights and responsibilities of a full citizen. The college of ἔφηβοι slowly faded in military and civic importance, and by the end of the second century BCE it had become diversified: young men were still trained in the martial arts and instructed in the religion of the city-state, but they were also taught literature and philosophy. It is this latter stage of the ἔφηβοι to which Stevens, with a smile, alerts us. He instructs a contemporary ἔφηβος in the movement from supreme being to Supreme Fiction. The modern ἔφηβος, a youth as virile poet, lives in an inexpensive attic apartment with sloping walls where he plays a rented piano and looks out over the cityscape (1.5). It is clearly not Stevens himself, at least not as he has been since his early days in New York.

In a letter to Henry Church of October 18, 1942, Stevens explains what he means by "the first idea": "If you take the varnish and dirt of generations off a picture, you see it in its first idea. If you think about the world without its varnish and dirt, you are a thinker of the first idea."[57] Immense philosophical and theological challenges are channeled into these words: Bonaventure, Schopenhauer, Peirce, and Husserl would need to be invoked and discussed even to specify the challenges with requisite precision. But it is unlikely that Stevens had any special philosophical process in mind of bracketing or leading back to firstness or pure intuition when he wrote the poem or the letter. The opening canto of "Notes" apparently sets the ephebe the exercise of reducing the sun to its first idea; he must perceive "the idea . . . of the sun" to see it "with an ignorant eye," and this perception apparently must pass by way of "this invented world."[58] It should be pointed out, right at the start, that this procedure is quite different from the emptying of the mind that prepares the way for religious contemplation or even petitionary prayer, in some accounts of that practice.[59] If "Notes" is to be heeded as a contemplative poem, it will have to be in another key than the one we are used to hearing in the discourse of religion, one we have sounded in chapters 2 and 3.

The tone and vocabulary of the opening canto are nothing if not unusual in poetry, not least of all because of the use of the philosophical word *idea*, which occurs four times in the lyric. Usually, we think of the word's meaning as given to it by David Hume (1711–76). Impressions, for Hume, are sense perceptions that strike us with "force and violence," while ideas are "the faint images of these in thinking and reasoning."[60] The very notion of abstraction might lead us to associate Stevens's sense of *idea* with Hume. However, there is another heritage of meaning linked to the word, one that is common in some strains of aesthetics, and it goes back to Coleridge. We have touched on it in chapter 2. For Coleridge, at least from the early years of the nineteenth century, *idea* denotes something very far removed from the senses and available to the mind only through the imagination. Ideas abide in God's mind, as they did for Christian Neoplatonists, and can therefore only be contemplated, yet they can be seen to be imperfectly realized in certain human institutions.[61] So the ideas are changeless, even though we can discern them through changes on earth if we are sufficiently attentive. Stevens is drawn more to Coleridge than to Hume, but he is more surely attracted to an earlier philosopher, one whom Coleridge valued above all others. The choice of a Greek word, ἔφηβος, even in its anglicized form, prompts us to think along Greek lines so that we recall the etymology of *idea*, namely ἰδεῖν (to see), and of Plato's image of the sun as the Good in *The Republic*, 507b–509c. Stevens is more likely to have known these latter things, even if not in detail, than any technical procedure of reduction or any particulars about Hume or Coleridge. His recourse to the *Oxford English Dictionary* when writing poems is well attested.[62] The somewhat donnish tone of the speaker invites us to think about the sense and provenance of *idea* while, at the same time, we are unsure of the appropriate level by which to engage what we are meant to overhear. There might be more than one possibility.

Most basically, the ephebe is asked to become conscious of the world that has come into being before him and around him (*invention* comes from the Latin: *in* + *venire*) and of the sun by which one can see and therefore understand phenomena. The sun itself appears to be outside or beyond the world of phenomena, equally illuminating the whole of it, all the more so if one is seeking to strip oneself of modern knowledge and become "ignorant." Were one successfully to divest oneself of all scientific knowledge of the universe, one might begin to think of the sun as the source of all life, itself unable to be conceived (as one being among others or as part of a plan) by anything higher. The ephebe is enjoined not to go further than this, specifically not to reach toward a religious explanation in the bypassing of a scientific one. This includes Neo-Platonic Christianity along with its Coleridgean inflection ("an inventing mind"), Blakean art ("A voluminous master folded in his fire"), and pagan deities (Phoebus Apollo). The pupil's task is a very thorough demythologizing of reality. The sun is not to be given one of the "rotted names" from classical mythology or even from Christianity (*Son*, e.g.); it is not to bear our projections;

its task is simply to illuminate the earth with all the problems of living here and thus to be "In the difficulty of what it is to be" ("Notes," 1.1.21).[63] What we have, in the ephebe's appointed exercise, is the familiar Greek procedure of ἀφαίρεσις, "taking away" or "separating" or, for Stevens, abstracting, which for him involves removing a phenomenon from perception and placing it in the imagination.

Of course, a problem remains, for we are also entitled—more, invited—to take the pronoun *this* to indicate the poem that we, including the ephebe, have started to read or hear. So we might readily take the sun to be an emblem for a Supreme Fiction, the idea of it being inconceivable because it is almost impossible for a poet effectively to represent it in lines and stanzas. (We remember, as Stevens himself surely did, that Keats calls Phoebus Apollo "the Father of all verse.")[64] A Supreme Fiction abides as an abstraction in the poet's imagination, and great artistic force would be required to form it there and, even more, bring it onto a page. A poet can only negotiate the abstract and the particular, invent a world of words in which the Fiction is embodied more or less adequately. The first canto will then be not only a diagnosis of the failure of religion but also the commencement of a thinking of a Supreme Fiction as compensating for that very failure, perhaps being what Stevens once called "the great poem of the earth."[65] Once realized, imperfectly or perfectly, the Fiction will not solve or even clarify our social and political problems, but it will encourage us to live without so many illusions, especially religious ones. It will help us live our lives, hard though that might be to do at times. It will offer itself to us not as a mirror reflecting our lives but, rather, as a place we might inhabit for the duration of those lives.[66]

There is a clear sense in which Stevens's rethinking of the emblem of the sun situates his poem at a far remove from the Western religious tradition of contemplation. Stevens goes to considerable lengths to dissuade the ephebe from regarding the sky above him as being anything like a *templum*. (We may recall the end of pt. 3 of "Sunday Morning" where he laments "this dividing and indifferent blue" and hopes for a less alienating sky, not one that encourages contemplation of a religious kind. Another mode of contemplation is countenanced in the delicate image of "casual flocks of pigeons" that "make / Ambiguous undulations as they sink, / Downward to darkness, on extended wings.")[67] The ephebe looks only across the sloping roofs of his borough, not up into the heavens. He is not a monk, as might have been the case had he lived in an earlier age, but a young artist: he is enjoined to seek a Supreme Fiction, not God. Even before we see him languishing on his bed, having completed the exercise or having failed to do

so, having neither *otium* nor *negotium*, we find Stevens the master offering a caution about the very procedure of returning to the first idea,
which is what he believes sparks the life of "Notes." The truth's "rav-
ishments" are "poisonous" (1.2.3–4): a check on the necessity of abstraction. Each seductive in its own way, reason and imagination need
one another in order to yield a truth that can satisfy the one quest-
ing for it. The philosopher, who relies wholly on reason, will not find
what he or she seeks and will become listless or will find it and become
lifeless, having lived "a skeleton's life," as Stevens will say much later.[68]
The poet, looking to the imagination, will become similarly frustrated,
for the first idea—reality perceived without embellishment—will inevitably be missed by his or her metaphors, which the young poet will
prefer to the first idea because of the immediate delight they give. The
poet misses the real and grasps its shadow, which means that the first
idea is at best beside or among the poet's metaphors, like a hermit who
shuns society in order to live face-to-face with ultimate reality. The
first idea cannot be captured by the poet, and it would be a poverty for
him if it were found. If the sky wants more than winter, as Stevens viv-
idly testifies, if it "hears the calendar hymn" (1.2.18), the first music of
spring, it is content with merely becoming blue, not with augers staging a *templum* into which birds might fly or, as with Hopkins, a single
bird becoming a symbol of the religious ecstasy one may enjoy if one
does not hide from Christ.

One way of reading "It Must Be Abstract" would be to chart the proposals, retractions, and revisions of the relation of the poet to the first
idea: its modalizations. This would be a part of the inevitable process
by which Stevens writes a contemplative poem that readers will benefit by recognizing as such. As with any poem, we are forever projecting ourselves forward to an imagined whole while reading "Notes," taking notice of depths and vistas opened, and no sooner have we started
than we are casting ourselves back to earlier sections of the poem. The
very fact that it is called "Notes" and does not presume to be a whole
means that the task is even more endless than it would be ordinarily.
The poem is reflexive in that it embodies the Supreme Fiction it hails,
though in an ironic mode as mere notes. Our task, imposed by Stevens, is to find a whole that takes account of the Supreme Fiction. This
whole is not a linear or dramatic unity. Nor is it a totality since each
reading will gather more meaning, more rapports between earlier and
later cantos, and recognize more subtle rhetorical strategies at work
in the poem.[69] The whole changes, as Stevens alerts us in the second
part of "Notes." Yet, in the first note, this overarching problem of fitting
parts into a provisional whole that itself opens onto a greater whole is

negotiated by way of responses to the first idea. Also, we need to re-member throughout that *part* does not and cannot denote any separa-ble portion of the poem; each section of the poem depends on the oth-ers, even when we might wish it otherwise.[70]

Immediately after ending the second canto, Stevens reaffirms the poet's ability to grasp the first idea. If a poem does not utterly strip away the varnish and dirt of our conception of the world, it must come close for us to "share, / For a moment, the first idea" (1.3.2–3) and live in a projection from experiencing it to experiencing its reimaginings much later. Religious contemplation, we have seen, results in humil-ity, even and only for a moment sometimes in a mode of death (*mors mystica*), but for Stevens, with his idea of contemplation as enriching awareness, it provides "An elixir, an excitation, a pure power" (1.3.10). This physical strength does not always manifest itself in worldly action or subtle acts of making or even attention to being. For the quest for the first idea takes us back even before the ascription of sense to phe-nomena. The moon, which orbits the earth counterclockwise, comes to the East Coast of the United States from Arabia and, with its light, scribbles signs on the walls that we cannot decipher; the wood doves chant sounds we cannot interpret; and the ocean howls unintelligibly in the distance. It is an apology, of sorts, for the streak of nonsense in Stevens's poetry at large, especially in *Harmonium* (1923). More impor-tantly, it is an index that contemplation is no longer always to be cued to being or even to meaning. The point needs expanding just a bit, for it concerns contemplation, on the one hand, and the program of pass-ing from supreme being to Supreme Fiction, on the other.

Later in his writing life, Stevens will tease his readers a little by say-ing, as we have heard earlier: "The poem must resist the intelligence / Almost successfully."[71] Contemplation, for him, does not end in a simple moment of understanding; if anything, it seeks to delay such a moment, if it ever comes, for as long as possible. Instead, contempla-tion is a process of reflection, not one that seeks to escape from history but one that resists the pressure of imposing external events precisely by being fortified whenever needed by the irrational, one of the ener-gies of poetry.[72] Another recourse to contemplation occurs when the poet pauses in order to take in the correlation between what he consti-tutes when writing the poem and what is actually constituted or mani-fested there. From time to time, he observes, as he puts it, "The hermit in a poet's metaphors" (1.2.6), which he thematizes as the gap between fact and miracle.[73] This is a long way from anything like religious con-templation. The divinity whom we cannot grasp because he transcends our cognitive abilities has, like all the gods, left us alone in a world that seems empty.[74] He cannot be simply replaced by a poet, but in some measure his departure can be overcome by poetry, which, for Stevens at least, must take account of another mode of ineffability, one that is prehuman, not more than human. Here, the kingdom, which coheres around the figure of God and neighbor, goes out of focus while we attend in the aesthetic attitude to that which makes no sense but, nonetheless, has primal kinship with us.

Could the ephebe ever successfully complete the exercise assigned to him in the first canto? Stevens seems to reveal that it is more of a paradox than an injunction that can be followed, although the paradox might itself have pedagogical value for a young poet. Now, in canto 4, we are told: "The first idea was not our own" (1.4.1). We do not find reality and then apply consciousness to it. Rather, we impose our ideas on reality from the very start: Adam shaped reality with his reason just as forcefully as Descartes did when writing the *Meditationes de prima philosophia* (1641). Eve and her children looked into the heavens as in a mirror and saw themselves there, whether obscurely or clearly—obscurely if consequent to the Fall (1 Cor. 13:12) and clearly if before the Fall—and so commenced thinking of God in anthropomorphic terms. In fact, if we trace the first idea to its beginning, we find that it has no beginning: we would be required, impossibly so, to go back before human intelligence in order to track it and know its firstness. If Eve enjoyed the illusion of looking into the sky and seeing the meaning of life in a deity who resembled her and her kind, we have other horizons. Our life is more like acting on a stage, as Shakespeare's Jaques proposed in *As You Like It*, without any *templum* in the sky, pagan or Christian.[75] Even in the human comedy, which is far more than our experience of nonsense, we add meanings to the events of life and do not behold these events as containing pregiven meanings. No wonder the ephebe writhes on his bed without being able to speak, as we read in canto 5. No wonder he entertains himself with writing poetry like a circus performance, specifically working against "the first idea" that has been advocated for his benefit.

Anteriority with respect to the first idea is attributed to the clouds, not persons, in canto 4, and the air itself is devalued in canto 5. Despite this, in canto 6 the weather becomes more prominent as a metaphor of desired concretion.[76] The power of art to let phenomena manifest themselves is held to be exemplary in Franz Hals (1580–1666), as in the weather depicted in the background of *Fisher Girl* (1630–32). The choice of the Dutch artist is noteworthy, for Hals was primarily a painter of portraits (including one of Descartes in 1649) in which landscape and weather conditions are sometimes apparent behind or around the individuals. Those individuals have a sense of being quite at home, whether in a house, in a tavern, at the shore, or in a garden, when they are painted. At times there is fruit on the table (as in *Vegetable Seller* [1630]), birds most likely singing, producing notes like those from a spinet, and often a feeling of nature in discreet ease, not abandonment. The names of certain persons portrayed are unimportant: would our appreciation of the canvas increase if we knew that the name of the fisher girl was Evi or Lotte? What matters is that it is a fisher girl (and not, say, Kymothoe, Speio, Glaukonome, or any other sea nymph from classical literature), the concrete realization of a specific scene, such as the weather—clouds, wind, and sky for Hals and sunlight on the magnolias for Stevens—which is accomplished by the imagination. Even if one incorrectly sees a flick of the flower in a breeze, or misjudges its form from the shadow it casts, one shares a certain kinship with it because the imagination has been at work and brought the phenomenon into "a strange relation" with oneself ("Notes," 1.3.21).

By virtue of the lively concretion of the clouds, the wind, and the sky in his paintings, with the loose brush strokes that characterized his later style, Hals is a "giant of the weather" ("Notes," 1.6.19) and "A thinker of the first idea" (1.7.2): he sees the world freshly. If this scene were presented in order to encourage the ephebe, the reassurance would not be long-lasting, for Stevens ultimately elects only "the weather, the mere weather, the mere air" (1.6.20), reality itself and not as it is represented: it is the material particulars of the world that have life in them, just as we have life in us when our mind is animated. A division between the two opens as the canto ends; only the imagination will be capable of closing it and then only for a brief time. If Stevens entertains the value of the invisible, it is not that which roused Richard of St. Victor, a spiritual reality above and beyond the world, but only that which is not visible at any given time and for which one requires the artist's eye: a wind, for instance, that is seen and almost felt in the movement of a girl's hair. The truth is not to be found in contemplating the heavens; it is more likely that it "depends on a walk around a lake" (1.7.3) during which one might see and hear distinct things, such as hepatica, pine trees, and a crowing cock. We might also glimpse the gaps between our constituting and what is constituted. Contemplation, here, is flush with the natural world, not seeking to ascend above it. There is no need for the reader to pass from surface to depth. Or to put it negatively, as Stevens preferred: "There is no difference between god and his temple."[77]

Nonetheless, there are "balances that happen" and "moments of awakening . . . in which / We more than awaken" ("Notes," 1.7.17–19).

They do not nudge us to behold simple, divine being; in fact, they prompt us to ponder something faint, as though discerned beneath tracing paper: "The academies like structures in a mist" (1.7.21). Presumably, these are the academies in which the clouds are pedagogues, teachers—"Gloomy grammarians," as Stevens once called them—closer to the first idea than we shall ever be, no matter whether we are MacCullough, Nanzia Nunzio, the Captain, or the Canon Aspirin.[78] The affirmative occurrences that Stevens freely evokes occur without the first idea, which, we are told in canto 8, is "an imagined thing" (1.8.4). Is this the lesson that the ephebe was meant to learn? If so, the lesson is to trust his imagination, not to place all his faith in what Stevens will call, in canto 9, "reason's click-clack," which is not reason itself but only "its applied / Enflashings" (1.9.4–5), its tendency to become mere rationalization, employed after the fact, rather than to aid the imagination in shaping a contemplative spirit from the very beginning. The ephebe has become no more than an implied reader here. The character with whom we chiefly have to contend is a plain man, MacCullough, sometimes called "the MacCullough," not to make him like a laird, but in order to give him a representative status in humanity or, rather, the advancement of humanity that Stevens envisages in a hypothesis that is crystal clear to him, if not always to his readers.

MacCullough can benefit from being acquainted with anyone who has thought the first idea. For is it not possible that he (and not an artist such as Franz Hals) is the true "pensive giant" (1.8.5)? So speaks Walt Whitman through Stevens. If MacCullough "lay lounging by the sea" (1.8.12), the wave or the book he was reading, which could even be *Notes toward a Supreme Fiction*, might begin to transform him, making him not more of a giant but, if anything, less of one. Moreover, in that gentling of his spirit, as once happened in other ways in "The Plot against the Giant," he might become an exponent of "the major abstraction," which is "the idea of man."[79] The coast is the place for him, as it was so often for Whitman, for one of the medieval French towns or grand houses restored by Eugène Viollet-le-Duc (1814–79), such as Carcassonne or Château de Pierreronds, would not suit his temperament or style.[80] MacCullough might "take habit" (1.8.15), we are told, that is, might get a vocation for seeing the continuity of the world and become able to grasp the language of the book or poem with a fluency not noticed before or not even possible before. It is MacCullough, not the ephebe, who, so far as we are allowed to see, better learns the lesson that the Master teaches. As we begin to acknowledge this surprising change of pedagogical scene, we also grasp that, as readers, we are being taught to contemplate in the very act of reading the poem: we search restlessly to join dependent part to dependent part in quest of a whole that delights and swells our consciousness while all the time escaping it as a complete whole. In the process, each reader seems to have a choice: whether to align himself or herself with the ephebe or with MacCullough or even to pass from the one to the other.

When "It Must Be Abstract" draws to a close, it becomes evident that Stevens prizes everyman, MacCullough, over the sophisticated modern ephebe, who is told, right at the end of the first note: "It is of him [i.e., MacCullough] . . . to make, to confect / The final elegance" ("Notes," 1.10.20). Major man has nothing Romantic about him, nor is he in any way a supernatural elevation of the human to the more than human. The elevation of the person who is to be prized is nothing if not a rational endeavor, the product of late-night research in order to see an anthropic possibility to which others have been blind. The concept of major man is "Compact in invincible foils" (1.9.7); it has been prevented often in recent history, whether as proposed by Hegel (by way of "the world-historical individual") or Marx ("actualized man") or Nietzsche (*der Übermensch*), each of which theory has significant flaws that stop it from being realized. It seems that the idea is composed of setbacks, and it seems unlikely that it will ever be taken seriously in a modern democratic country. When the idea has come up in the past, it has been left as a foundling: in other words, it has been a neglected idea in books of philosophy. MacCullough has been no more than "The impossible possible philosophers' man," "the man of glass."[81] Nonetheless, MacCullough, this representative of an emerging humanity, one marked by poetry, prophecy, and philosophy, comes to light when he reads by the ocean. He does not advance by his own merits but allows "a leaner being" (1.8.17), trimmed down as regards metaphysics and theology, to come on him from what he reads and from the ocean's waves that move toward him.

When I say *research,* I do not mean to elect the philosopher or even the scholar to the exclusion of others. It could just as well be a poet, such as Whitman, whose muse would be the "breast forever precious" ("Notes," 1.9.12) because it nurtures the possibility of the new vision of humanity. We remember Whitman in "Song of the Exposition" saying in lines that would have appealed to Stevens: "Come Muse migrate from Greece and Ionia, / Cross out please those immensely overpaid accounts, / That matter of Troy and Achilles' wrath, and Aeneas's, Odysseus' wanderings. . . . For know a better, fresher, busier sphere, a wide, untried domain awaits, demands you."[82] However, philosophers and scholars have muses too, even if they are not often named these days. It little matters from exactly where major man comes, for he does indeed come, and we heed a moment of rare excitement in Stevens's voice ("oh! he is, he is" [1.9.16]). Stevens hails his muse ("My dame" [1.9.15]), asking her to sing "accurate songs" (1.9.15) for MacCullough, not hymns that would exalt him as a savior. One is not to form a cult of personality around major man or look to him as a messiah. If he has a name, he is to have no title. It is the warmth that we feel for the idea or ideal of him that counts most. That, along with the ability to discern his potential, for right now he will not have any signs of distinction about him that will disclose it. He may well be a tramp, like the one played by Charlie Chaplin in *The Tramp* (1915) and *The Bank* (1915), or self-conceived by Whitman, who sings: "I tramp the perpetual journey / My signs are a rain-proof coat, good shoes, and a staff cut from the woods."[83]

The introduction of MacCullough as major man in the closing canto of "It Must Be Abstract" effects a shift that the reader would not have been able to anticipate when beginning the poem. It is not the ephebe, the dandy, who embodies or conducts a Supreme Fiction, nor is it the "philosophers' man"; it is MacCullough, the tramp who lazes by the ocean. We have passed from a supreme being, seen as Phoebus Apollo, to an ordinary man who, in his openness to nature and culture, will come to exemplify a new Supreme Fiction and do so in America, where democracy will help enable the Fiction. The first canto of the first note ended with an injunction that the ephebe and the reader give "no name" to the sun, not to engage in natural or revealed theology but to let it be "In the difficulty of what it is to be" ("Notes," 1.1.20–21). The same note approaches its end by telling us of major man: "Give him / No names" (1.10.19–20). He is not to be consoled for his poverty or sanctified for any supposed messianic spirit people might intuit in him, but the rational principle, supported by the imagination, which he represents—that of a new, vital humanity—is to be propounded by the ephebe. All the master can do is supply notes. Our contemplation is to be directed not at Phoebus or even at what remains when he is reduced to the sun at the center of our planetary system. That is needed for us properly to see "The man / In that old coat, those sagging pantaloons" (1.10.17–18), and also it is needed that we richly imagine his future. We cannot name him, but with reason and imagination we can behold him in the abstract and see his potential for "The final elegance" (1.10.20).

CHAPTER 8

Contemplation with Noisy Birds

If the animating spirit of "It Must Be Abstract" finally reveals itself in its last cantos to be Whitman, its counterpart in "It Must Change" is Shelley. The tutelary spirit that hovers over the second note is not the entranced author of "To a Skylark" (1820) but the darkly inspired poet of "Ode to the West Wind" (1819) and the melancholy speaker of "Ozymandias" (1818). The second note is replete with birds and other flying beings, from angels to bees. It begins with an "old seraph" contemplating not God but only the fallen earth. He is not even able "To contemplate time's golden paladin," for he sees only doves that rise up "like phantoms from chronologies" and pigeons that "clatter in the air" ("Notes," 2.1.3, 18).[1] The second note dilates on the squabbles of sparrows, wrens, jays, and robins; and at the end, in a circular motion, it refers to swans that glide over the water like seraphs.[2] In two memorable passages, we are presented with bees. Stevens is not delighted by the birds he hears, and he nowise entertains the thought of them being unseen, coming "from Heaven, or near it" and "Singing hymns unbidden."[3] Shelley's skylark is also a teacher, but the Stevens of "It Must Change" will not cede his role as pedagogue, not even any longer to the clouds. His lesson in this note is not reduction to the first idea, with all its equivocal gestures, so much as the inevitability of repetition and the fear of it. In developing this theme, Stevens sometimes departs a little uneasily from his declared argument, the need for a Supreme Fiction to change. Instead, we look with him at the need for positive change instead of mere repetition of the same.

The second note begins in spring with violets and concludes with the west wind, tamer than in Shelley's ode, blowing irises on the banks of a lake in Hartford. This spring is no *reverdie*, however, and the Italian girls with jonquils in their hair have all been seen before. They are not

like MacCullough, who embodies a new sort of hope. We survey the
scene from the old seraph's viewpoint, and he too suffers from change.
Heaven, also, is aging. His gilt has partly worn away, and the odor
of the violets is for him merely "appointed" ("Notes," 2.1.2): he has
smelled it all too many times before. The girls grow into mothers, and
their own daughters will come to be much like them. The blooming hy-
acinths of March and April recall the previous year's flowers, going all
the way back to Hyacinthus. Stevens is not fond of "the rotted names,"
as we have seen, but here he surely alludes to the sorrowful myth of the
Spartan hero accidentally killed by Apollo who had previously taken
the beloved boy with him around fabled lands in a chariot pulled by
swans. Thereafter, *Hyacinth* bespeaks the birth and death of nature and
the flower associated with him, which grew from his spilled blood,
connotes sorrow. The Greek festival of Hyacinthia lasted for two days,
the first of which was solemn, the second joyous. Whatever celebration
there is must be preceded by an acknowledgment of loss, and even this
cycle is subject to the tedium of repetition. "We say / This changes and
that changes" observes Stevens rather flatly (2.1.8–9), from a prospect
he shares with the world-weary seraph, and so do we, but change is itself deeply equivocal in value: things change for the worse as well as
for the better. And sometimes we merely say, "This changes, and that
changes," when, in the debilitating grip of a long perspective, it is closer
to the truth to say that things merely repeat themselves.

The highest rank of the angelic hierarchy, the seraphim are angels
of fire (Heb. *Seraph*, "fiery serpent") but also of love and light. Lucifer is traditionally taken to have been a seraph, not unlike the serpent
who tempts Eve, even if the common Christian identification is based
on a misunderstanding of scripture.[4] There is no justification for taking the old seraph of "Notes" to be Lucifer or thinking that Stevens is
evoking any particular angelology. The central point is that, even for
the spirits supposedly closest to divine love, time is change, and its
value abides only in shifts to freshness and vitality. Mere repetition of
the same, albeit with variations that seem bigger or smaller and more
or less consequential as the years go by, is simply tedious. No angel "of
rain and lightning," such as Shelley's west wind, the seraph has less zest
for life than that impetuous spirit or indeed than MacCullough. The
landscape and its population present for him only a "withered scene"
(2.1.15), even though it is spring, except for the bee that booms around
the flowers. If birds and bees were long associated with religious contemplation, for Stevens they are, if anything, agents of frustration for
the aesthetic counterpart to religious contemplation. I will return
to the birds shortly, but before that I need to address the bee, once the

very image of the good monk for Evagrius. Stevens's is an unusual fig-
uration, to say the very least, and one that prizes the bees far above the
birds.

"The President ordains the bee to be / Immortal," begins canto 2
of "It Must Change," about which the least that can be said is that it
is a denial of the very possibility of change for the bee. The country
is the United States of America with Old Glory "in a red-blue dazzle"
smartly blowing in the wind ("Notes," 2.2.14). Only one president of
the United States could conceivably be imagined as having the power
to do as Stevens suggests, and that is the George Washington of Con-
stantino Brumidi's fresco *The Apotheosis of Washington* (1865), painted
on the eye of the rotunda of the Capitol Building in Washington, DC.
But, in the poem, we see the father of our country very much at home
in Virginia, not in heaven:

> The President has apples on the table
> And barefoot servants around him, who adjust
> The curtains to a metaphysical t. (2.2.10–12)

We know that Washington kept bees (and drenched his breakfast pan-
cakes in butter and honey), that he liked apples, especially Yellow
Newton Pippins, and that he kept barefoot slaves at Mount Vernon.
Nonetheless, it is better to applaud Stevens's amusing fantasy of political power by way of the verb *to be* rather than to search for scraps of
historical evidence that might have led him to take the flight of fancy
in the first place. If anything escapes mortality, it is being. The bee's
immortality consists not in any presidential overreach or Stevensian
humor but in the sheer vitality of love. For the lover's experience of
being in love is always intense, always felt as a genuine new beginning,
and it is love that makes the human race continue in being, always attentive to birds and bees in spring. Birds do not appear in a *templum*
here, however; they tell us nothing about the future or about the divine
realm. They are there before our eyes, miring us in repetition, not releasing us from it.

And they are in our ears, Stevens insists in his complaint against
birdsong in canto 6, which removes him from all romantic sentimentality. Before he gets to this canto, however, he dismisses political and
military heroes as not worth any sustained human contemplation these
days. There has been a Supreme Fiction based on military heroism; it
goes back to Homer and Virgil and encompasses the age of the ἔφηβοι.
Attention has shied away from it, however. Troy is no longer at the center of our imaginative lives: wars continue, but no hope or consolation

is to be gained by referring back to the exploits of Achilles and Aeneas. More recently, there was a Général Dominque Martin Dupuy
(1767–98), and he is commemorated by a statue in Toulouse, but Stevens's dated military hero is American, of his own imagining, along
with the horse on which he sits.[5] (The Monument au Général Dupuy
is a bronze statue of the winged "Dame Tholose," an allegorical figure
of Toulouse.) The bronze statue of General De Puy is so rigid that he
looks "a bit absurd" ("Notes," 2.3.12)—he is incapable of change, of
resonating with a world with other imaginative centers, one that promotes quite distinct values—and it is certain that the statue will collapse one day. (It is a lesson for the ephebe if he invests too heavily in a
military career as well as for his possible double, the American soldier,
fighting in the Second World War, who is addressed in the final canto
of the poem.)

When, in canto 4, Stevens addresses "the origin of change" ("Notes,"
2.4.4), he seeks more than how things change locally by the quiet, if
relentless, power of time. Now, reclaiming his argument, he claims a
deeper level of analysis from which it can be explained how Supreme
Fictions change. Our world is divided into dualities—male/female,
day/night, and imagination/reality are named first—and these interact in diverse ways according to varying ages and the great minds at
work in them. (We might recall the way in which reason and imagination rely on one another in pt. 1.) Each time, a new unity is found,
even if it does not last for long. This applies to local changes, generative, climatic, and seasonal, as well as to changes of Fiction, which can
be heralded by something easily unnoticed, for "A little string speaks
for a crowd of voices" (2.4.15). At the end of "Notes," the dependence
of opposites will be refigured, almost in Heraclitean terms, as a perpetual war: "Soldier, there is a war between the mind / And sky, between thought and day and night."[6] The poet must return to "his Virgilian cadences," ("Notes," coda, lines 1–2, 5), which are appropriate to
war (and to an earlier Supreme Fiction), even if it is not a war that will
lead to imperial power and be celebrated by a poet, as happens in the
Aeneid. It is a struggle, rather, between the rival claims of the aesthetic
and the religious and the different modes of contemplation appropriate to them.

Stevens abides in and works within a fiction that differs from Virgil's, one in which there are no gods to guide the hero, in which the
poet must do as best he can to supply "the bread of faithful speech,"
which is all that can be offered in lieu of Eucharist by a poet with no
Christian faith. There is no redemptive Logos, only language, which
he will later ironically downplay as "the poet's gibberish" (2.9.1). Nor is

there an ecclesial communion of souls. At best, there is a limited union
of will and task for everyone involved in the war effort, and inevitably
it is Whitman whose voice momentarily returns, for one will not find
in Shelley any ground for comradeship in lines such as "The captain
and his men // Are one and the sailor and the sea are one" (2.4.18–19).
In a slightly strained rhetorical manner, all the poem's readers are gathered together despite our differences and enjoined to strive to achieve
the same union of wills: "Follow after, O my companion, my fellow, my
self, / Sister and solace, brother and delight" (2.4.20–21). The poet and
the soldier, including the ephebe, must live as one in a Supreme Fiction
that touches the martial one of classical times, even if they play quite
specific roles, as soldiers and poets do, whether in the war that is reality or a local war between countries vying for political and economic
power. The poet is not concerned with contemporary events so much
as "the poetry of the contemporaneous"; and, as Stevens also says,
"The poet who wishes to contemplate the good in the midst of confu-
sion is like the mystic who wishes to contemplate God in the midst of
evil."[7]

Yet the rhetoric is hollow, both in the middle of the poem and at its
end, when Stevens exalts the poet's vatic stature. He seeks there a balance other than the one looked to by those with religious faith, who
themselves may construe reality in terms of a war between good and
evil, albeit one in which the outcome is already assured. Any trium-
phalism, sacred or secular, is empty, for no human gaze can take in an
eschatological whole, while secular attempts to do so will inevitably
overextend themselves. Hence the lowering of the poet's voice in canto
5, the very center of "Notes," in which a Caribbean homesteader, far
from any theater of war, lives out his life in modest, good ways, establishing a grove of lime and orange trees that lasts beyond his natural
term of life. Nothing abides in the sky above the planter's house and
trees, only a sun that provides energy for his plantation. His contemplations are not of the beyond but of "an island beyond him" that en-
tices him to ponder another island, farther south, more fabulous, fea-
turing "the great banana tree" of mythic proportions (2.5.10, 14). The
planter lives with illusions, to be sure, but they are relatively innocent
ones, as Stevens judges them, and they do not distract him from the
pleasures of life, as would other trees, such as Yggdrasil and the cross.
For the most part, to borrow the words Stevens says in the final section
of "Sunday Morning," the planter enjoys an "island solitude, unspon-
sored, free." Indeed, some illusions are needed to sustain a life of labor.
(Stevens will go on in the third part of the poem to propound that
one must believe in fictions while knowing perfectly well that they are

fictions, a position that calls for explication later.) For all his framing by way of negatives ("unaffected . . . ," "negative . . . ," "Could not . . . ," "nor . . ." [2.5.19–20]), the planter is warmly appreciated by Stevens. He dies "Sighing that he should leave the banjo's twang" (2.5.21). Art has its illusions as well, no doubt, though they are difficult to give up and perhaps to do so would be fatal in itself: they console us for our losses, past, present, and to come. The banjo's notes also serve as a recursive image of the three notes that constitute the poem that we are reading and already announce the end of the poem before its third part is even in sight.

This brings us to the noisy birds of canto 6, which echo Shelley's "Ode to the West Wind" in a parodic manner. "Be thou, Spirit fierce, / My spirit! Be thou me, impetuous one!"[8] cries Shelley to the west wind in his bid to become a prophet of destruction and preservation. "Bethou me, said sparrow, to the crackled blade," we read in Stevens's poem: we have passed from a strong wind to slight cracking noises made by blades of grass. Then we hear: "And you, and you, bethou me as you blow" ("Notes," 2.6.1–2). With this, nature returns Shelley's cry, although it is only a sparrow that ceaselessly desires intimacy with its surroundings, not the west wind, nature without human qualities. This is not the "banjo's twang" but an "idiot minstrelsy" (2.6.7), notes without abstraction, change or pleasure that "compose[s] a heavenly gong" (2.6.9), much like the voice of God in Exod. 20:18. Any contemplation of the natural world must put up with noisy birds. These birds have theological significance, albeit a completely negative one, for their endless, irritating cry of "ké-ké" yields "A single text, granite monotony" (2.6.12), a secular counterpart to the tablets of the law given by God to Moses for the children to Israel always to follow, without change or deviation. In the perpetual racket they make, the many birds become just one bird; and when all individuality is lost, we see "One sole face" (2.6.13). It is not the same as when the rabbi or the chieftain looks over many separate figures and sees just one, "The man / In that old coat, those sagging pantaloons" (1.10.17–18), but a complete suppression of individual differences:

> like a photograph of fate,
> Glass-blower's destiny, bloodless episcopus,
> Eye without lid, mind without any dream—
>
> (2.6.13–15)

All variety is reduced here: all faces become as one, as do all molten glass bubbles, and what looks over us from the trees does so without blinking or pausing to dream. (Stevens could be recalling the startled face of the angel in Paul Klee's monoprint *Angelus Novus* [1920].)[9] We are invited to refer back to the statue of General Du Puy, which will eventually become rubbish, and we are being prepared to meet an Ozymandias of Stevens's own making. Both are idols, unworthy of contemplation in any religious sense, and the risk still being considered by Stevens is whether there is a mode of aesthetic contemplation that can replace dependence on idols and on divinity alike.

The beauty of the earth and of mortal love takes away "the need of any paradise" and "the need of any seducing hymn" ("Notes," 2.7.2–3). We are directly told that in the following canto, which extends and renders concrete what we were earlier told in canto 4: "a man depends / On a woman" (2.4.2–3). If we entertained the possibility that the firmness of these statements might be modulated into something more religiously acceptable as the canto develops, we are quickly disabused by the blunt statement "It is true" (2.7.4). It is our capacity for love—"the lover that lies within us" (2.7.6)—that has value, even if it has no object other than the lilacs that have no associations, nothing that conditions our affections, while still enflaming us. The bliss that we can attain is the perfume of the lilacs, not anything spiritual; the heavens have nothing to offer us, not even if we were to perch ourselves on "the top-cloud of a May night-evening" (2.7.16). Having bravely tried to go back to the first idea and thereby become an ignorant man, the ephebe is intent on the modalizations that occur in honest writing; it is a part of contemplation to attend to those shifts from certainty to uncertainty, to questioning, to doubt, and so on, in both directions, back and forth, as well as the degrees of perception, inner as well as outer, that change as the author or reader works late into at night, much like Milton's Penseroso.

Equally, if differently, a woman depends on a man and the spiritual on the physical, and this is the burden of canto 8, in which a female angel goes in quest of Ozymandias. The Italian *Nunzio* is the masculine abbreviation of *Annunziata*, anglicized as *nuncio* (papal ambassador). Nanzia Nuncio, however, is female, presumably sent from heaven to find her earthly counterpart, and she is less world-weary than the seraph. We have cause to recall Shelley's ruined statue of Ozymandias, of which the statue of General Du Puy is a later and more benign iteration. Before this ruined statue, which, as Shelley tells us, has a "sneer of cold command,"[10] the angel undresses and offers herself to the male gaze. The note begins with a seraph contemplating the fallen world, and now it includes an angel being contemplated by an idol. "I am the contemplated spouse" ("Notes," 2.8.12), the angel says, having already played on the divine name "I AM," which for Aquinas alone determines the sole, proper object of religious contemplation.[11] If the celestial hierarchy is one "inflexible / Order" (2.8.11–12), another is the social and political order of ancient Egypt, where Ozymandias was once pharaoh. Egypt's Supreme Fiction was assuredly abstract, but it resisted all manner of change, including the introduction of other Fictions that might compete with the conservative old religion: that of Akhenaten (d. 1335 BCE), for instance. Nanzia Nunzio's annunciation to Ozymandias is not of a redemptive messiah to be born, only of the attraction of change in the Fiction that he represents. The very act of undressing, however, does not leave the angel naked, at least not to the broken statue, for her speech acts ("Speak to me," "Set on me," "Clothe me") cover her, although whether impeding or encouraging the statue's erotic gaze is not said.

"It Must Change" approaches its end with a canto that, like canto 4, conceives its subject matter by way of several dualities: flittering/concentration, wordless/wordy, peculiar/general. Unlike in canto 4, however, these counterparts do not readily resolve themselves and offer the resolution as an explanation of change, and Stevens speculates whether poets (including himself) actually evade the reader's gaze: their poems seem always to be between terms and not terms themselves. He then briskly cuts through the questions and provides three conclusions. First, the poet seeks "the gibberish of the vulgate" ("Notes," 2.9.2); it goes in the direction of MacCullough and the homeworld, as we might have come to expect. Second, the poet uses a particular speech— his or her own idiom—"to speak // The peculiar potency of the general" (2.9.18–19). We are reminded of the line in canto 4: "A little string speaks for a crowd of voices" (2.4.15). Third, there is an overcoming of another presumed duality, though one not mentioned earlier in the canto, one between the imagination and pidgin (the language of trade). The imagination is the "high" language (Latin), and the lingua franca is the "low" language (pidgin, rough-and-ready English or French, the "gibberish of the vulgate"). But the poet needs both the purity of the high language and the ebullience, the *jocundissima*, of the low language in order to present the "essential gaudiness" of poetry at a level that will communicate broadly to readers, both now and to come.[12]

The second note ends formally with a scene of the poet not so much contemplating the pond before him in Elizabeth Park, Hartford, as being in a more diminished state—"catalepsy"—there. It is as though he has become rigid, somewhat like General De Puy in "Notes" 2.3, but unlike the general the poet discerns "a will to change" in what he sees (2.10.8). As the note seeks its closure, it gathers together several motifs from the first note of the poem: the elusive metaphor (once a hermit, now, perhaps in another era, a vagabond) of 1.2, the clouds of 1.6, and the theater of 1.4. Earlier, we had been told that "Perhaps / The truth depends on a walk around a lake" (1.7.2–3); now, sitting before a lake, he sees not the truth in any definite sense but a theater of trope. Being in the open air does not tempt him to ascend mentally: the sky is reflected in the pool, a *templum* at eye level, and it is there, in front of him, that he sees swans become seraphs and saints and then Supreme Fictions passing before his eyes. The transformations are not simply taking place in a world; they are of the world itself, and we can see this happening here and now, by rubbing the enigmatic glass before us, as Paul says in 1 Cor. 13:12, and do not have to wait until we are face-to-face with the God in whom Christians believe. The hint of transformation given by staring at the pond is small but sufficient for us to "propose / The suitable amours" (2.10.20–21), the Supreme Fictions that rouse, engage, and order human life. We may not be able to embody them in words here and now, but there is a consolation: "Time will write them down" (2.10.21). That is, artists to come will grasp them, if they can.

*

"The belief in poetry is a magnificent fury, or it is nothing."[13] So writes Stevens to Henry Church on March 30, 1943, and in the third note, "It Must Give Pleasure," we find ourselves caught up in a thinking about belief so that we must reflect again on Stevens's prose remark: "Poetry does not address itself to beliefs."[14] Belief in poetry, however, does not involve God or the gods but a Supreme Fiction or, if you wish, the principle of major man.[15] If anything is at the antipodes of contemplation, it would be fury, but, if there is fury in the third part of the poem, it is directed against the institution of religion and has been largely sublimated in the presentation of poetry as a human happiness, as that which redeems us from the "bitter aspic" of life.[16] The third note begins by situating itself at odds with liturgical expressions of joy. I take as my guide to this note Stevens's own remark in *Adagia*:

> Religion is dependent on faith. But aesthetics is independent of faith. The relative positions of the two might be reversed. It is possible to establish aesthetics in the individual mind as immeasurably a greater thing than religion. Its present state is the result of the difficulty of establishing it except in the individual mind.[17]

One reason why Stevens might go awry in this project is apparent here. Religion—or at least Christianity—is indeed dependent on faith, but faith presumes love, which opens the space wherein faith may be exercised.

The possibility that Stevens entertains in this aphorism would turn on a very thorough discrediting of religion at a fundamental level: there is no God and hence no creation and no redemption. One difficulty envisaged here would turn on ethics being readily separable from religious belief, which had long been admitted as viable, although it is a view that was not widely held in Stevens's America. More challenging would be educating the general populace in the cultivation of aesthetic attitudes, and that, presumably, is part of what is in play in the evocation of major man toward the end of "It Must Be Abstract." In all probability, it would take a very long time. In its own ways, "Notes" addresses itself to the social and intellectual difficulty that Stevens perceives, and to do that it must give substance to the claim that the aesthetic is "immeasurably a greater thing than religion." Even if we grant that the idea makes tacit sense, we would need to know in what way or ways it is greater.

"It Must Give Pleasure" commences, then, with a canto that registers and then sharply undermines the joys and consolations of religious liturgy, both Christian and the pre- or post-Christian religious impulse already identified in part 7 of "Sunday Morning":

> To sing jubilas at exact, accustomed times,
> To be crested and wear the mane of a multitude
> And so, as part, to exult with its great throat,
>
> To speak of joy and to sing of it, borne on
> The shoulders of joyous men, to feel the heart
> That is the common, the bravest fundament,
>
> This is a facile exercise. ("Notes," 3.1.1–7)

The classical Latin *iubilatio* denotes wild shouting or whoops, but by the time of Augustine's *Enarrationes in Psalmos* (392–422) it has become the singing of a praise that overflows the meaning of words.[18] In the Vulgate, undertaken at the same period as Augustine's commentary, Psalm 99 begins: "Jubilate Deo omnis terra: servite Domino in Laetitia" (O be joyful in the Lord all ye lands: serve the Lord with gladness). And the psalm—duly renumbered as 100 outside the

Vulgate—is given as an alternative to the *Benedictus* in the office of Morning Prayer in the *Book of Common Prayer* (1559). For Gregory the Great (d. 604) or perhaps someone associated with his name, *jubila* came to mean "rejoice" in a more determined manner, as in a prayer we associate with his name, *Regina caeli, jubila* (Queen of heaven, re- joice!). We have already met a lion roaring in the desert and then being lashed by those who are bred against the first idea in 1.5. (And we have already been introduced to an exercise that Stevens rates as salutary, re- duction to the first idea, which, even though it reaches a limit, stands in contrast to the "facile exercise" of singing psalms and the like.) Now the animal stands for the multitude of the faithful, maybe drawn from the familiar image, going back to Vincent of Beauvais's *Speculum his- toriale* (ca. 1240), of Jerome (347–420) helping an injured lion who thereafter remained docile and faithful to the scholar.[19] The saint may not have lashed the lion, but its roar has been thoroughly domesti- cated.

It is Jerome, Stevens tells us in faux biblical language, who "Begat the tubas and the fire-wind strings, / The golden fingers picking dark blue air" ("Notes," 3.1.8–9). Here, the Latin *tuba* means "trumpet" (our modern tuba being a nineteenth-century addition to the orchestra), and the trumpets are presumably the books of the Hebrew Bible that Jerome put into Latin, which are now part of the Vulgate. Rendering the Hebrew scriptures into more elegant Latin than was available in the Vetus Latina spread a fire across the known world, especially later, once the Psalms were sung, at first in the liturgy of the hours, as specified by the *Regula* of St. Benedict (516), and then by later composers. We think of pieces by Loys Bourgeois (ca. 1500–1559) and inevitably by Monteverdi (1567–1643), Vivaldi (1678–1741), and Mozart (1756–91), among others. The difficulty that religion presents for Stevens here is given not in its sensual or more than sensual liturgies but rather in the image of the natural world about us, which seems not to be grounded in any rational act, including "an inventing mind" as rejected in 1.1.7. Our immediate pleasure in the natural world has the effect of muting any reasoning we do by way of projecting a Creator as the ground of it: the *quinque viae* of Aquinas, for instance.[20] Even a consecrated vir- gin devoted to divine contemplation sees the moonlight on her cell wall and, being human, is moved by it. The "irrational" is a figure of po- etic energy, Stevens thinks.[21] The rising sun, the ocean's tides, and the moonlight scribbling on our walls at night (as in 1.3.15) are all entirely natural and have remained so since the earth began, even though we think about them in ways we have later devised, both religious and sci- entific.

Canto 2 passes from a nun to a blue woman, that is, a clear blue sky without any *templum*, looking in at the poet's window. There is not the slightest hint of a positive reference to the Virgin Mary. Later, in canto 4, we will witness a "mystic marriage" of the maiden Bawda and a Captain in the land of Catawba. The theme of a mystic marriage is familiar to readers of Stevens.[22] It is the least successful of the poem's fables; nonetheless, it serves to recapitulate 2.4, and thematically the adjective *mystic* is sharply ironic at the nun's expense.[23] The imaginary couple are not exactly "cold copulars" like the spring and winter of 2.4.5, which is about as chilly an evocation of lovemaking as one can imagine. Theirs is not an inescapable passion for one another, however; they wed "because the marriage place / Was what they loved. It was neither heaven nor hell" ("Notes," 3.4.20). Indeed, Catawba is no more than *Captain* and *Bawda* vaguely run together. If there is any *templum* at all in the poem, it is, we begin to realize as the third note progresses, the poet's cleared consciousness where questions of belief appear to be answered only in the aesthetic, not the religious-mythic, attitude. There is no deity in the sky, Stevens tells us, who gave a silvery color to those smelts we call *argentines* or who guides them to where they spawn in the Mediterranean, and so on for all the natural phenomena that he lists: they simply are what they are, without any transcendent designing mind behind their being or regulating their actions. Only the human eye plays on them, as Stevens has told us earlier, in "Tattoo," in his lines about seeing the light on things: "There are filaments of your eyes / On the surface of the water / And in the edges of the snow."[24] Eyebeams go forth into the world, but not as a consequence of the *malus oculus*.

Entirely consequent, Stevens now recalls his picture of Nanzia Nunzio's visit to Ozymandias in 2.8 and, resituating the statue in a jungle, renders it first terrifying and then antiquated. The story of Yahweh in the burning bush, as given in Exod. 3:1–4, is one of the deepest sources of aniconic Judaism, yet in a fierce fantasy Stevens has it pass directly into an idol, not of a golden calf, and probably not of the Canaanite god Moloch, but of something as frightening and as cruel as the latter. We see "A face of stone in an unending red" ("Notes," 3.3.2). The idol has been abandoned by its cult and has eroded badly, with vines clutching it about the throat, signifying the final power of nature over religion. It was once a means of attracting and focusing religious feelings and ideas, crude though they surely were, and it could well have continued. "The eye could not escape" (3.3.13); its fascination is absolute, unlike the more relaxed attitude adopted toward the dogwood at the end of 3.2. The religion of cruelty and fear is over, blessedly, and

Stevens sweeps from the cult to a new religion, presumably introduced by missionaries, that overthrows it. It is centered on "A dead shepherd" (3.3.15). The allusion is to John 10:11 ("I am the good shepherd. The good shepherd lays down his life for the sheep" [RSV]), presented in the frame of Easter Saturday when Christ descended into hell and released those children of Israel who had remained faithful to Yahweh, who responded with songs of praise:

> A dead shepherd brought tremendous chords from hell
>
> And bade the sheep carouse. Or so they said.
> Children in love with them brought early flowers
> And scattered them about, no two alike. (3.3.18–21)

Formal *jubilas* emerge from mere carousing, for Stevens, an inebriation at the promise of personal immortality that is given ritual shape by the "love feast." That this meal was abused in the early church is clear from St. Paul's first letter to the fledgling community in Corinth (1 Cor. 17–22). Like the ancient Greeks, the Romans scattered flowers on the graves of fallen soldiers (*Parentalia*) and their loved ones (*Inferiae*). Early Christians of the simpler sort persisted in the pagan practice, which was neither commended nor condemned by Jerome, Ambrose, and other church fathers.[25]

The cure for carousing is usually aspirin, so we find three cantos devoted to the Canon Aspirin, a comic name for what Stevens takes Christianity to have become: a mild sedative for the pains of everyday life. We have come a long way from that notable canon regular Richard of St. Victor and his *The Ark of Moses* with whom we started thinking about contemplation. The fantasy of the almost allegorical figure of the Canon Aspirin appears not after any carousing but only after a very fine dinner of "lobster Bombay with mango / Chutney" ("Notes," 3.5.1–2), washed down with Meursault. Evangelical poverty is presumably not his charism. And, when he does appear, it is not of religious belief that he speaks but of his sister, in particular of the "sensible ecstasy" with which she ekes out her widowhood. That she lives sensibly is clear from what the canon tells of how simply she dresses her daughters, and the oxymoron—"sensible ecstasy" (3.5.3)—is borne out only in that she never rises higher than the sensory world and holds her children "closelier to her by rejecting dreams" (3.5.12), her own first, and that she wishes for them that they have dreamless, rather deathly rest at night. Not so the canon himself: he has not ventured so perilously close to the first idea so as to see even her children as they actually are without the "fictive covering" with which parents fondly indulge themselves and their progeny (2.8.20). By contrast, he ventures far when night comes; it is an inner voyage, one that harks back to the "ascending wings" of Ps. 120:34 and the early church in its discernment of mental ascent, which is available to the canon only in sleep.

Once asleep, the canon experiences more than the sensible ecstasy of his sister, although he too is concerned about his nieces. His ecstasy has the air of a cosmic or spiritual adventure, of the sort that goes back to Cicero's *Somnium Scipionis*:

> So that he was the ascending wings he saw
> And moved on them in orbits' outer stars
> Descending to the children's beds, on which
>
> They lay. Forth then with huge pathetic force
> Straight to the utmost crown of night he flew.
>
> ("Notes," 3.6.10–14)

It is Milton more than Cicero who stands in the background of these lines, however, *forth* being one of the poet's favored words, and the fear of nothingness being something that pierces Belial in *Paradise Lost*:

>   for who would loose,
> Though full of pain, this intellectual being,
> Those thoughts that wander through Eternity,
> To perish rather, swallowed up and lost
> In the wide womb of uncreated night,
> Devoid of sense and motion?[26]

The canon flees from nothingness only to find it again at "the utmost crown of night" (3.6.14). His ascent is not higher in a cosmos populated by spirits and allegorical figures, like Milton's, but one that he has "conceived" only by way of the books he has read in seminary and thereafter. The fact of sleep leads to fantasy; the pathos he feels in his dream might spur him to escape death, but there is no heaven to receive him. His situation is unthinkable, at least for a canon, for he will be "swallowed up and lost / In the wide womb of uncreated night." He must choose, it seems, between one or another mode of nothingness, but in his dream he opts, finally, to direct his pathos into his imaginative feat. Poetry overcomes theological fantasy or, perhaps, shows this fantasy to have been no more than poetry in the first place; accordingly, he embraces "the whole, / The complicate, the amassing harmony" (3.6.20–21). It is another way of saying what Stevens has already stated in an earlier poem: "Poetry // Exceeding music must take the place / Of empty heaven and its hymns."[27] Here, however, we have something grander than merely taking the place of something that happened to be there first.

The canon's choice does not lead him to any effective contemplation of the world, let alone beyond it, certainly not the aesthetic gaze that Stevens extols as offering the only redemption available to us. For he imposes the contents and the forms of his mind, untested by any attempt to go back to the first idea, on the object of his gaze and thus remains alienated from the very harmony he has elected given his choice of nothingness or nothingness. He does not find the "major weather" (3.7.12), reality, when he flees the void, so his tremendous effort and the pathos associated with it are all for naught. The possibility of doing so remains, almost intransigently, which nonetheless leads Stevens to a definite statement of his settled desire:

> To find the real,
> To be stripped of every fiction except one,
>
> The fiction of an absolute— (3.7.17–19)

The first idea, reality unencumbered by human interpretation, is, as we have sensed from Stevens's caveats as early as 1.2, an enabling fiction, not anything that leads to naked contact with what truly is. Such contact would be ruinous to the Master, the ephebe, MacCullough, and the reader, and for all that we cannot do without it. "We believe without belief, beyond belief," we have been told in "Flyer's Fall," even if, in the end, we are left with "Darkness, nothingness of human afterdeath."[28] Two questions arise from these lines about the real. How can "the real" and "fiction" comport with each other in Stevens's statement? And what are we to make of that dash at the end, by means of which Stevens pivots to the angel, telling him: "Be silent in your luminous cloud and hear / The luminous melody of proper sound" (3.7.20–21)? I will consider each in turn.

The infinitive mood of Stevens's statement at the end of 3.7 is governed by *to find*: the impetus for discovery must come from the subject, and we must acknowledge that Stevens's emphasis in the sentence is on the quest for the real, not on possessing it. We can presumably go about finding the real by way of judgment, made with a greater or lesser degree of confidence, depending on what it is taken to be, how it is reached, and the process of self-evidence that is proper to it. We can find logical or mathematical truths by mental deduction and enjoy a high level of epistemic justification; empirical truths offer lower levels; the memory gives still lower levels; and anticipation gives us very low levels, if any at all. It might be that some beliefs entertained in the mythical-religious attitude could be justified over a season of prayer, and one would take them to be grounded by God. To be sure, as Stevens says, "poetry is like prayer," but here the *like* also carries a very strong countercharge of "unlike," for the likeness that is claimed is extremely limited ("it is most effective in solitude").[29] An inner quest for God, as ground of all being and knowing, is not even entertained. Stevens's judgment turns, rather, on one's experience of poetry, and we recall the exergue of the poem, in which he addresses the Supreme Fiction as giving a "certain truth" that casts an "uncertain light" and the presence of which is authenticated by a feeling of peace.

No doubt the strong language of being "stripped of every fiction" (3.7.18) recalls the opening canto of "It Must Be Abstract": "You must become an ignorant man again" in order to make contact with the first ideas (1.1.3). No more here than there, however, is this a self-emptying proposed in order to behold the divine, and now the ground of that conviction is evident: the absolute, the unconditioned, is itself held to be a fiction. The word choice is deliberately provocative, distancing Stevens from all philosophers (except Nietzsche, whose works he perused when young).[30] For philosophers would tend to speak quite differently. Kant, for instance, writes of regulative principles that can offer no constitutive grounding when it comes to theoretical knowledge, so noumenal reality always escapes our attempts to find it.[31] Dogmatic religion, outside the narrow circle of rational religion, would itself not be justified by the court of reason, but Kant would not consider using the word *fiction*.[32] More recent philosophers might point to the ways in which language generates puzzles about reality that we must finally set aside as pseudoproblems or that are at best approached through symbols, but no more than Kant would they have recourse to the language of fiction. Husserl uses the word, as we have seen in chapter 3, but to quite other ends.

When Stevens announces his quest for the real, however, he is not proposing that we hold as true something we know full well not to be true.[33] That happens only when reading a poem, and it dissipates almost immediately after. Instead, he has in mind a Supreme Fiction, high art as effectively replacing religion and philosophy as a guide and consoler for the troubles in our lives, while nonetheless drawing on their impulses when needed. Indeed, a few years after completing "Notes toward a Supreme Fiction" Stevens wrote "Description without

Place" (1945), in which he proposes the thesis that primarily we live in descriptions (read: fictions), not places. He goes so far as to affirm there "Description is revelation." Such is, he thinks, "The thesis of the plentifullest John," the author of the Book of Revelation.[34] A less bold claim is made in "Notes," easily the stronger poem of the two. The particular Supreme Fiction that concerns him there is the poem he is now writing, which will be notes toward the great poem of the earth. Stevens's mind is not searching naturally for God; it is searching for a Supreme Fiction that will replace God with the natural world. It is a deflation of natural theology. The Supreme Fiction seems to have absolved itself from everything that has made it possible, and now it revolves, complete in itself, a *templum* on the page through which birds and angels pass.

When Stevens swivels to address an angel, he is evoking the old seraph of 2.1, who, though one of the highest order in the celestial hierarchy, is nonetheless an angel, and it is all the more appropriate to call him such because of his weary familiarity with the earth, which is traditionally visited only by those in the lowest order of the hierarchy, angels.[35] Earlier, we had been told that "Clouds are pedagogues" ("Notes," 1.4.16), but here it is Stevens, the Master, who retrieves the role of teacher, silencing the seraph on his cloud before he can complain about the tedium of change and point us to the delights of the heavenly heights. The angel contemplating our world is instructed to hear the "luminous melody of proper sound" (3.7.20) in the very poem we are reading, not the celestial hymns he has been used to hearing. His age—the age of belief—is coming to an end. The ephebe, MacCullough, and now a seraph, all take their place in a scene of instruction for which notes are provided, and the reader resumes his or her seat as well. Even the Master will be seeking further education before his poem is complete.

For the Master quickly reveals himself not to be in full possession of all that he needs to teach us and all that he needs to know as man and poet. "What am I to believe?" he asks ("Notes," 3.8.1). The question has a limited scope; it is not about the articles of religious belief, or even about the meaning of *belief*, natural or supernatural, but about the power of the imagination as it operates in him and not as it guides his fictional character, the Canon Aspirin. Can it replace such beliefs? With what losses and gains? Over his lifetime Stevens rehearses his general position time after time, chiefly in letters and aphorisms, this remark in *Adagia* being characteristic: "After one has abandoned a belief in god, poetry is that essence which takes its place as life's redemption."[36] As is this one: "God is a symbol for something that can well take other forms, as, for example, the form of high poetry."[37] Only later do we find the more evasive line: "We say that God and the imagination are one."[38] For we say many things without being wholly committed to them, and unity can be achieved in all sorts of ways, replacement being only one of them. Perhaps it is best to say that, for Stevens, the "true imagination . . . is the sum of our faculties" and that these faculties are the means by which we project an image of God.[39]

Stevens's angel beholds the abyss, like Milton's Satan, but, in his imaginative gaze on the angel, Stevens holds him steady in an aesthetic contemplation. If we think of Hopkins beholding the kestrel-saint in a single categorial act, we will not be entirely mistaken, but Stevens has quite other concerns than those of the young Jesuit. He grasps an angel in himself, not a saint in a bird. The harp, the wings, the gliding in space, are all held in the poet's awareness, and it is the act of composition that supplies the "expressible bliss" he feels ("Notes," 3.8.12). This is the "vivid transparence" evoked in the exergue that, he testifies, satisfies him—and we remember the importance of the verb *satisfy* in the argument of "The Figure of the Youth as Virile Poet"—and not any "solacing majesty" of "A voluminous master folded in his fire" (1.1.9). It is this sense of peace in steady aesthetic contemplation of a Fiction, experienced in composition and in musing on the completed work later ("an hour," "a day," "a month," "a year" [3.8.15–16]), that sanctions the use of the word *redemption* in *Adagia*. It is a temporal freedom from the troubles of life, both in business and at home, along with the constant threat of death; and, along with this freedom, there is a sense of achieved wholeness. (We may well recall Schopenhauer.) Stevens cannot entirely possess what he imagines, so desire always remains: "Notes" is not his last poem, for which we can be thankful. Yet he is what he is, and with Coleridgean confidence his "I am" takes the place of the divine "I AM" of Exod. 3:14.[40] If the ephebe was comically pictured as engaged in no more than a circus act in 1.5, the Master himself shares traits with Cinderella, who because of her fairy godmother is able to attend the ball and dance with the bedazzled prince. The Muse as fairy godmother!

Assured now of the viability of his vatic position, of a broadened consciousness and the tranquility that comes from it, Stevens now turns from the angel to a wren, from an imagined heaven to a material earth, and delights in his scaled-down redemption. There is no Horatian boast, no *non omnis moriar* (I shall not wholly die), only an endorsement of enjoying life as it is lived.[41] His view of the noisy birds—wren, cock, robin—is far more conciliatory than in 2.6, for their repetitions are conceded to have a role to play in life, freshly understood: "These things at least comprise / An occupation, an exercise, a work, // A thing final in itself and, therefore, good" ("Notes," 3.9.8–10). Seen fairly, life is largely a matter of repetition, and what is poetry itself but judicious repetition of sounds, figures, and themes? One must live like human beings, not as imagined gods, and thus appreciate, not lament, existence, even when its cycles seem almost Sisyphean: "the going round // And round and round, the merely going round" (3.9.12–13). The true master is the one who controls repetition, as in the writing of poetry, and is not brought low by the force of that *merely* in "merely going round." Reconciled to the earth, and holding as much of heaven as he can deep within himself, Stevens finally addresses our primal mother, always expecting new life, in comic-intimate mode as "Fat girl" (3.10.1).

The fat girl is familiar "yet an aberration" ("Notes," 3.10.4), apparently waddling around the solar system because, as we know better than Stevens ever could, she is swollen at the equator and because she has a slightly elliptical course. Too large, she is never able to be embraced wholly as she is. The real is finally found (we are briefly returned to 3.7), not in a philosophical or theological procedure, but in the differences of meter, trope, and tone. There is a "fictive covering" that is "always glistening from the heart and mind," as we recall from 2.8.20–21. This is not a lessening of the natural but an enhancement of it: She remains "the more than natural figure" ("Notes," 3.10.11) for the poet, for all poets, because she is always conceived as more than she really is, for such is the power of the imagination when it broods on the natural world. Neither an Italian girl with jonquils in her hair nor a fairy grandmother, she is the fat girl, the mother of us all, distended through many births, whom one must respectfully call *madam*, as well as the muse who is ceaselessly represented just like a human woman, "strong or tired, // Bent over work, anxious, content, alone" (3.10.9–10). If the imagination adds to what we think of as properly basic reality and thus distorts it, it thereby renders it not less than rational but more than rational. The realization seems to surprise and please Stevens even as he formulates it: "That's it: the more than rational distortion, / The fiction that results from feeling. Yes, that" (3.10.14–15). This would be the Supreme Fiction that, unlike Dante's *Commedia* or Milton's *Paradise Lost*, great poems of the supernatural world, is the great poem of the earth, one that is modestly given only in three notes, offered to an ephebe, perhaps to be developed by MacCullough, and will be continued in later poems by Stevens.

In the final line of "Notes," except for its less than successful coda, the fat girl will have "stopped revolving except in crystal" ("Notes,"

3.10.21). Why? Not because a French professor of philosophy at the Sorbonne—the idealist Léon Brunschvicg (1869–1944), for example—has established that "the irrational is rational" (3.10.18). The amusing line brings back the nonsense that pieces us with "a strange relation" (1.3.21), not least of all because it marks poetic energy, the "irrational moment" of 3.1.16 and of course the irrationality of the "soft-footed phantom" of the same canto (3.10.12). Could poetry be assimilated to an amplified sense of reason, as happens in various philosophies of art? That might please us, but it will not satisfy us. Not because the planet has ceased to orbit the sun. Rather, the earth stops revolving around any figure of the sun as divine or any divinity as a sun (as in 1.1); it is what it is, and what we can imagine it to be, and no more than that, nothing created by the "inventing mind" that was dismissed in 1.1.7. Also, it stops revolving because after the lecture, walking home through the twilight streets of the fifth arrondissement, the poet is touched and emboldened to name the earth, with which he has become finally reconciled, despite its ceaseless repetitions. The poem that began by saying "No names!" for the sun and for MacCullough now reaches its end with the confidence to name the planet on which the poet stands. Yet he describes rather than names: "my green, my fluent mundo" (3.10.20). And in doing so he completes his poem with its crystalline structure (three notes, each of ten cantos, each of seven tercets).[42] "Notes toward a Supreme Fiction" does not thereby become a static object, however. It still revolves, showing its glittering facets, whenever it is read, and crystals are themselves subject to growth. A poem is not a thing but an event: it must change, as we have been taught. To read it contemplatively, in a modern sense, is, among other things, to grasp it freshly in its openness and its changes. We cannot expect a final, simple intuition of a Supreme Fiction.

The coda is less than successful not because it introduces extraneous material or distracts us from the whole we have been projecting and recalling but because it fails to do justice to the soldier whom it addresses. The ephebe or MacCullough returns, now a soldier having to serve the state in a time of world conflict who needs to be reminded of other, more permanent battles. The first of these is "between the mind / And sky," the former of which now lays claim to be the true *templum*, the space of aesthetic contemplation. The poet is always "in the sun" as he conceives it, maybe not fully reduced to the first idea, but in a struggle to resist the allurements and poisons that accompany any severe project of reduction to the first idea. And the poet always depends on the soldier's war, if only for his "Virgilian cadences."[43] It may be that the old Supreme Fiction of Homer and Virgil is not quite over and that

Stevens's must still participate in it to some extent. It is no mistake that "Notes" commences with "Begin, ephebe," and the modern ἔφηβος always knew that one day he would be called on to leave his literary and philosophical training and serve his country, as did MacCullough. If he returns alive, he can, after a splendid welcome home, resume life in his attic with its rented piano and continue his studies or laze once again by the shore, but already he has been enhanced by the very poem we have been reading. "How gladly with proper words the soldier dies, / If he must," we hear as the poem closes. This is not Horace's "dulce et decorum est pro patria mori" (It is sweet and fitting to die for one's country) but something slightly different.[44] The soldier who must die in battle (and nothing is said either to show or to hide its horror) is at least consoled by the poet's words, which have been spoken to him from 1.1. He receives no *viaticum*, as we must expect by now, only "the bread of faithful speech." The most that *faithful* can mean here is "loyalty." It may be that Stevens is cheered by poetry replacing God, by the thought of the "fictive hero" becoming "the real." It is perhaps another thing for the soldier in extremis, for whom temporal redemption could mean little or nothing. If this is the final lesson that the Master has to teach the ephebe, it is a bleak one indeed.

*

In "The Noble Rider and the Sound of Words," Stevens takes comfort from George Rostrevor Hamilton's words in *Poetry and Contemplation*: "The object of contemplation is the highly complex and unified content of consciousness, which comes into being through the developing subjective attitude of the percipient." Hamilton distinguishes several attitudes that can be adopted in contemplation and is quite clear how he sees their differences: "In aesthetic activity emphasis falls most on the object and least on the subject; in practical activity it is exactly the reverse, while in speculative activity, though there may be more emphasis on object rather than subject, the main weight falls on the pursuit itself." Under practical activity, he includes human happiness (and hence much of the traditional territory of religion) and, under speculative activity, both elevated philosophical concerns and "all sorts of humble activities of the restless intelligence."[45] Only aesthetic experience does not distract us in the direction of the practical or the speculative, so only aesthetic experience gives us contemplation in its purest state.

Doubtless Stevens would have been in general agreement with Hamilton, with the rider that aesthetic contemplation leads to pleasure and peace. He may have wished to add that in modern times—in which, by virtue of the achievements of science, reason has claimed the high road to knowledge and mainstream Christian faith has become an impediment to grasping reality—only aesthetic contemplation, based on reason and imagination, gives us true understanding and supplies a concomitant sense of peace.[46] It does what religion used to do, but it does so in another attitude. He may well have wrinkled his brow when reading Schwartz's words about aesthetic experience being merely a starting point for his poetry. For it was that experience that led him into the aesthetic attitude, and that was, for him, a good in itself. And he would have demurred at Hamilton's final words:

> The contemplative experience of poetry—and not of tragic poetry alone—has a special stability, unity and clarity. It is a world apart, in which we may rest. It is complete in itself and is unlike religious contemplation, which creates the need for action. If only for that reason, it can never satisfy all our spiritual needs. Its rank, without any such claim, is sufficiently exalted.[47]

The aesthetic attitude might be "virtually religious," offering what Coleridge called one of those "brief Sabbaths of the soul," but never any more than that.[48] Within Christianity, the contemplation of God leads to work for the kingdom, and that work points us back to the desire for deeper contemplation of God. Stevens's fables of MacCullough, the Planter, Nanzia Nunzio, and the Canon Aspirin, not to forget the figure of the ephebe, replace the myth of Phoebus. They show Stevens thinking around a Supreme Fiction, approaching it one way and another, as is common in seeking the truth (consideration) and in finding it (contemplation). They toy with piercing the aesthetic attitude that he adopts throughout the poem, but they do not satisfy a spiritual need for the kingdom. His final gesture of poetry offering a dying soldier "proper words" and "the bread of faithful speech" marks something of a retreat, in the very movement of a tentative advance, from the kingdom back to the aesthetic attitude that occludes it. In "Notes," the *templum* has shrunk from the sky, metaphor of the divine realm, to the poet's consciousness, which dilates when ideas for poetry pass through it and are realized in composition or admired when read on later occasions. "The world of the poet depends on the world that he has contemplated," Stevens writes in *Adagia*.[49] It is true, but one must add a caveat in the form of a question. How has he contemplated it? The aesthetic attitude both enables and limits the conception of a world. It marks the closest that contemplation comes to fascination.

CHAPTER 9

Contemplating
"the True Mystery"

Sometime around 1972, A. R. Ammons (1926–2001) saw on television an early photograph of the earth floating in the darkness of space, and it became the prompt to write his finest long poem, *Sphere: The Form of a Motion* (1974).[1] It would not have been the famous image known as "Blue Marble" taken by Harrison Schmidt on Apollo 17 in December 1972 because Ammons explicitly mentions Apollo 16 being launched in *Sphere* 39.463. It is possible that an image of a nearly full earth captured by the crew of Apollo 15 on July 26, 1971, was shown on television the following year.[2] "There was the orb," Ammons says in a 1994 interview. "And it seemed to me the perfect image to put at the center of a reconciliation of One-Many forces." He had evoked that old philosophical conundrum before, but now he wished to marry "the One-Many problem with the material earth."[3] Two things are worth commenting on here by way of orienting ourselves to the poem.

First, Ammons situates his poetics, at least in part, by way of mereology, the study of parts and wholes, or, as he likes to put it, "the One and the Many." This branch of philosophy begins with Parmenides, is developed by Plato, Aristotle, and Plotinus, receives narrow attention throughout the Middle Ages (including by Achard of St. Victor in his *De unitate*), and becomes a prominent theme in Husserl's *Logical Investigations* (1900–1901) and, as such, is a major theme of early phenomenology.[4] It is also part and parcel of contemplation, both natural and religious. I recall from the first chapter that Aquinas distinguishes three aspects of contemplation: height, fullness, and perfection. To be sure, Ammons evokes height, which for Aquinas is God, who is to be approached by way of metaphysics; but the poet has nothing like Aquinas's view of God. Nor does he have much to say about perfection, which for Aquinas is a matter for the moral sciences. The Christian seeks to gather his or her many cares and offer them as one in prayer to God and then align his or her will with God's so that the mystery of divine love is all. Not so for Ammons.

The American poet restricts himself to natural contemplation, θεωρία φυσική, which he does mainly by way of the third of Aquinas's aspects of contemplation, fullness. It is very much his concern since it is linked to the natural sciences.[5] (Ammons would sympathize with Marianne Moore: "Too much cannot be said for the necessity in the artist, of exact science.")[6] He is intrigued by "the sight of the small events / happening in fullness."[7] Natural contemplation, or what Aquinas calls *speculatio*, often goes, for him as for others, from smallness to fullness.[8] In one of its modern formulations, contemplation seeks to integrate parts into wholes, and vice versa.[9] Such would be a principal meaning of *reconciliation* in Ammons's project of bringing together the One-Many forces. Yet we need to be aware from the beginning that his relation of part and whole is not neat: as we read the poem, parts do not melt into a single, absorbing whole. Rather, we see transformation and disjunction, and only at the end of the poem do we find anything like a vision of a whole.

Second, Ammons's adjective *material* along with the noun *forces* requires comment. He is said to be a Lucretian poet, and Lucretius commends contemplation of the gods. Also, *Sphere* certainly attends to a number of themes that traverse *De rerum natura*, including how organisms come into being and are changed throughout their existence, the mortality of the soul, the relative absence of the gods, and the forces that produce, sustain, and change phenomena.[10] We might think twice before calling *Sphere* an *Epicurean poem* and prefer to look to the author's modern scientific education at Wake Forest University. If we do so, we will begin to find an Aristotelian stratum in *Sphere*, especially that of the father of biology and the author of the *Physics*. We are likely to hesitate before calling *Sphere* a *philosophical poem*, except in the most general sense that it is loosely concerned with the One-Many problem and proposes "to make the essential fashionable" (54.1). But we may well incline, after a while, to take it as a didactic poem, at least in stretches.[11] At the same time, we will surely see the poem as reversing the Christian understanding of divine sight being spherical; the sphere of regard is resolutely human.[12] We may very well recall the Emerson of "Circles":

Nature centres into balls,
And her proud ephemerals,
Fast to surface and outside,

Scan the profile of the sphere;
Knew they what that signified,
A new genesis were here.[13]

Also, there is not a little of what Thomas Carlyle in *Sartor Resartus* (1836) calls *natural supernaturalism*, the Romantic project that, as M. H. Abrams succinctly puts it, seeks "to naturalize the supernatural and to humanize the divine."[14] In some respects, it is a counterpart to natural theology.

My concern in this chapter and the one that follows it is to see how contemplation is refigured by Ammons by way of what he calls *the true mystery*. It is not a straightforward task for the poet since he finds himself frequently absorbed, emotionally if not intellectually, by what he calls the "mere disguises" (*Sphere*, 1.2) that angels adopt and what is for him an enticing, though false or delusive, mystery, that of the gods. Although he reaches toward the sublime from time to time, Ammons does not subscribe to a high view of religious experience. He is as concerned as much with weak phenomena as with strong ones that bespeak the glory of God, namely, those that quickly pass away or are fragile or assimilated to other phenomena or are easily overlooked, and these are brought into his contemplation, which is always cued to nature. As in earlier chapters, I will take contemplation both as a topic, figured on occasion in the poem, and as a movement that leads from time to time to *dilatio mentis*. Yet, with *Sphere*, more than other poems so far read, the question arises whether it can be contemplative in mode, given its adherence to the naturalistic attitude (and, from time to time, "the view from nowhere"), the disorienting and garrulous nature of the text, and its attention to the everyday rather than the transcendent in whichever of its many modes. We are in the realm of counterexample.

*

Ammons refers to mystery several times in the poem, the first occasion being in his opening sweep of "The sexual basis of all things rare" (*Sphere*, 1.1). In *Sphere* 4, the One-Many problem is pictured as a triangle, isosceles or equilateral, and this general structure equally applies, he thinks, to rocks and gas, which, unlike insight and knowledge, are not at all rare in any sense of the word: "one feels up the two legs of possibility and, ever / tightening and steered, rises to the crux, to find // there the whole mystery" (5.50–52).[15] The "whole mystery" of existence is perhaps in the crotch, he winks. Later in the poem, he is somewhat less reductive of mystery to sexual desire and female reproductive biology in particular. We find him channeling the view of Xenophanes of Colophon (d. 475 BCE) that humans created the gods in their own image, which is always a problem for some natural theology: "make a mighty / force, that of a god: endow it with will, personality, whim: / then, please it, it can lend power to you" (49.580–82).[16] The danger is, as he says, that you can become a slave of your own creation. However, "the forces are there all right" (49.588), even if they are not persons. And we remember that Theagenes of Rhegium (fl. 529–22 BCE) was reputed to have made a similar observation in his allegorical reading of Homer.[17]

Reflecting on the creation of gods by human beings, Ammons tells us "a darkness in the method, a puzzling, obfuscating surface, / is the quick (and easy) declaration of mystery" (*Sphere*, 50.593–94). As we saw in chapter 6, *method* is a Greek word (μετ' [by means of] + ὁδός [way]); we think more deeply about it, however, when we regard it as a way of ordering reality.[18] A particular way of ordering reality marks the success of modern natural science, in which, at least since Francis Bacon (1561–1626), method (i.e., the scientific method) has been prized over contemplation almost to the point of eclipsing it. It was not so for Aristotle, for whom θεωρία came gloriously into play after method had been followed and the structures of reality had become apparent.[19] For Aristotle and Aquinas, unlike Bacon, there was such a thing as final cause, a purpose to which an action or a being is oriented, and, when Bacon eliminated it from scientific method, contemplation was set adrift with respect to natural science.[20] For Ammons, since mystery is not inherent in anything, divine or human, good or evil, but cued to method, a mystery can be dissolved, degraded into a mystification, just as readily as it once imposed itself on us "should the method come plain" (50.595), and that is exactly what happens with the criticisms of Xenophanes and Theagenes. Then Ammons proposes a final dialectical step, one that distances him from Greek criticism of cultic religion and from contemporary eliminative materialism alike: "of course, under the quick establishment of difficult // method" one would find that "the true mystery survived" (50.597–98). Here, the method itself is inadequate to the richness of the reality it is to explain, or the reality resists understanding, or it generates problems of its own, thereby disallowing any complete reduction of mystery. Besides, as Ammons indicates later, we are within what we seek to explain (74.885–75.889); we participate in it rather than neutrally viewing it from above.

Not that being within the cosmos prevents scientists from examining it objectively. Nonetheless, the scientist, for Ammons, appreciates that the cosmos is at heart a mystery, not a problem.[21] For we ask, Why is there something and not nothing? Science runs up against a limit in trying to give an answer, perhaps especially when one leaves the lecture on astronomy and looks up in wonder at the night sky.[22] Nonetheless, the sense of *mystery* that survives for him is far more limited than what Christians affirm of God. When a scientist consigns a phenomenon—or the origin or the presumed unity of the cosmos—to the status of mystery, it is (unless religious beliefs are involved) generally with the expectation that the mystery will resolve itself into positive knowledge sometime in the future. It is provisional, something hidden that will become visible in the language of chemistry, math, or physics: that something is a *mystery* means no more than that something cannot be explained at the moment (UFOs, geoglyphs, the pyramids on the Gaza plateau correlating with the three stars of Orion, and so on). A scientist might not believe fully in a working theory at any given time—it might be regarded day by day as the best and only means one has available for doing research—but he or she will always be open to a better hypothesis and more data to support another theory.[23] A Christian, who may also be a scientist, holds that the divine mystery is irreducible by virtue of the transcendence and the simple nature of God, which hide him from view, and that our lives are pervaded by mystery because we bear the *imago dei* and already participate here and now in the divine life. Our truths are provisional until they stretch into the mystery of eternal love.[24]

Even with an appreciation of Ammons's nuanced view of mystery, we must still tread with care lest we unknowingly abuse it. Ammons himself takes a further step and talks of mysticism, not to dismiss it, but to value it if and only if it falls within the bounds of natural science, which he thinks it does: "the heights and depths somewhere join in a near-complete / fizzle of the discreet" (*Sphere*, 10.109–10). Certainly, the reconciliation he seeks is not of the Many being mystically dissolved into the One: human beings remain in the sphere of experience. Nor is it a union of wills (although it does involve the bringing of the human will into harmony with natural law).[25] Ammons will often refer to touching a limit as yielding "radiance," as we have seen with respect to that powerful lyric of *consideratio* "The City-Limits" in chapter 6. Experience of the radiance is, he thinks, what people have always encountered when they talk of "religion" (6.64). However, the truth of the matter, he says later, is that "all movements are religious" (52.616), that radiance can be found everywhere, high and low. And, when he tells us that "prayer is the working in the currents, // hallelujahs dive and sculp the mud" (52.618–19), we are back in the world of his early poem "Hymn" (1), a natural theology that ends in reverence for nature, not in finding a supreme being.[26] A little later, he will speak of "the mystery, if reasonable, that // when the one item stands for all, the one item is so lost / in its charge that it is no longer bounded but all radiance" (*Sphere*, 65.771–73). The qualification says everything: the mystery, *if reasonable*. He is evoking contemplation in the context of Kantian reflective faith.

Yet it is poetry, not religion, that is deemed best suited to deal with this sense of awe (*Sphere*, 120.1431–36). Knowing that, we might then be surprised by the frequency with which the gods, including the Most High, appear in the poem. At first, Ammons is tentative, telling us, in terms about the sublime made familiar by Burke and Kant, that "the shapes nearest shapelessness awe us most, suggest / the god" (13.145–46). Then, in the very next section, "the real gods" are acknowledged, in good Epicurean fashion, as "unavailable" to us, although they give us reason to affirm them, for "they appear in our sight when they // choose and when we think we see them whole, they stall / and vanish or widen out of scope" (14.165–67). The unexpected word here is *choose*, emphasized by the enjambment, but the drift of Ammons's sentiment inclines us to take it as a figure, not a reality. This will be confirmed in due course when we are told not to remember the "coelum empyreum that dries up gods / into luminosities, radiances, cooling into sightlessness" (24.280–81). The fire that once marked the holiness of the gods now serves only to wither them.

Notwithstanding all that we have just witnessed, there are times in the poem when one might almost think that Ammons believes in the biblical God, especially when he invokes the title of the Most High. One might *almost* think that, for we will also recall being told, as in a secondary school science class, what belief is. It is put negatively: "to believe what runs against the / evidence requires belief— concentration, imagination, stubbornness, // art, and some magic" (*Sphere*, 56.668–70). Natural belief does not go beyond what sound evidence and a well-formed hypothesis can support; it turns on expecting future events to resemble past events in essential ways made clear by the laws of chemistry and physics, and only when there are no general grounds to which one can appeal does it reach a limit. Then one passes from science to testimony.

By contrast, supernatural faith is held by Christians to be a gift that comes with baptism, one that will be realized in time in and through love, and we need to be aware that Ammons's description of it is taken from outside the faith. In the sections I have in mind, however, Ammons no longer takes the lead provided by Xenophanes and Theagenes that had directed him earlier in the poem, and he has passed from Greek to Hebrew. *El Elyon* is used in Genesis and the Psalms, and the shorter form, *Elyon*, occurs often in the Psalms. Almost halfway through the poem we read, in a rather prosaic passage,

> what is to be done, what is saving: is it to come to know
> the works of the Most High as to assent to them and be reconciled
> by them, so to hold those works in our imaginations as to think
>
> them our correspondent invention, our best design within the
> governing possibilities: so to take on the Reason of the Most
> High as to in some part celebrate Him and offer Him not our
>
> *flight* but our cordiality and gratitude
>
> (*Sphere*, 69.820–26; emphasis added)

"What must I do to be saved?" asked a jailor of Paul and Silas when they were miraculously freed from their chains in Philippi (Acts 16:30–31 [RSV]). Ammons ponders the same question in a roomier way about life in general, and not for the first time in the poem he raises the question of redemption (see 33.390). His answer would not satisfy anyone with orthodox Abrahamic beliefs, and social redemption does not seem to be a candidate for him either, at least not here. We can celebrate the Most High by taking the reason with which we are naturally endowed as creatures (and not the Λόγος of Johannine Christianity) as enabling us to make the most of the possibilities given to us in nature. There is no mystical "flight from the alone to the Alone," as Plotinus, thinker of the One and the Many, beautifully figures θεωρία in *Enneads* 6.9, but it is nonetheless fitting to show a sense of gratitude to being as a whole for one's span of life.[27]

That Ammons's voice is replete with religious sentiment while his mind is seeking a new home for it is evident in the following section.[28] This is very far from what we read when Lucretius begins *De rerum natura* with an invocation to the goddess Venus: "Aeneadum genetrix, hominum divomque voluptas, / alma Venus" (Mother of Romans, delight of gods and men, dear Venus).[29] The Roman poet appeals to a literary convention, for he knows full well that Venus, like all the gods, is far away from the world and not interested in anything he writes.[30] Ammons might not believe in the Most High, but he writes as though he almost wished he could:

> but if we are small
> can we be great by going away from the Most High into our own
> makings, thus despising what He has given: or can we, accepting
>
> our smallness, bend to cherish the greatness that *rolls through*
> our sharp days, that spends us on its measureless currents: and
> so, for a moment, if only for a moment, *participate* in those means
>
> that provoke the brief bloom in the eternal *presence*: is this
> our saving: is this our perishable thought that imperishably
> bears us through the final loss: then sufficient thanks for that.
>
> (Sphere, 70.830–40; emphasis added)

The anxiety here is specified later when, like Yeats, Ammons worries out loud about "how // to give up the life of words for life" (109.1299–1300).[31] Of course, we must not expect there to be a clear, even line separating writing from living. That is precisely what is registered by Ammons's *how*. It is difficult to stop writing when writing permeates all one does and serves as a tonic for daily life.

Then Ammons turns, in high Romantic fashion, "to cherish the greatness that *rolls through* / our sharp days" (emphasis added), and we cannot overlook the ripe allusion to a very well-known passage in Wordsworth, a poet who is close to him, not least of all in that the Romantic was also at times invested in Newton and in all that contemporary science had learned from him. This familiar passage from "Lines Composed a Few Miles above Tintern Abbey" (1798) has another interest, however:

> And I have *felt*
> A *presence* that disturbs me with the joy
> Of elevated thoughts; a sense sublime
> Of something far more deeply interfused,
> Whose dwelling is the light of setting suns,
> And the round ocean and the living air,
> And the blue sky, and in the mind of man:
> A motion and a spirit, that impels
> All thinking things, all objects of all thought,
> And *rolls through* all things.[32]

Wordsworth testifies to a presence in and beyond nature that presses on his consciousness and thus is felt there; it is no pure intellectual principle, as one would find in Aristotle and the Scholastics, for it gives him "a sense sublime." When he tries to peg what gives him this sense, he does so in terms that seem almost to be those of *Sphere*: "A motion and a spirit."[33]

In "Tintern Abbey," the young Wordsworth, strongly influenced by Spinoza, speaks as a pantheist, believing that nature has an objective reality but that nothing is guiding it: consciousness can determine itself, but there is no separate divine consciousness, no "Spirit" rising above and beyond phenomena. Both Wordsworth and Ammons maintain that one can take part in nature, as they understand it, but the English poet testifies to "something far more deeply interfused." What is this "something"? With what is it "interfused"? And "more deeply" than what? I take it that the "something" is the consciousness (or spirit) of nature, that it is felt and presumably interfused in human consciousness and more deeply than one finds in lower principles that are commonly available to human cognition. There is a sense here of the μέθεξις (participation) of which Iamblichus (245–325) speaks with regard to higher principles informing lower principles and thus giving rise to the transcendental form that is immanent in nature, but it is only a sense, and one should not reach for specific Neo-Platonic sources or confidently use them as keys for entering the poet's world.[34] Ammons, by contrast, thinks of our place in the cosmos by way of participation but not in any Platonic sense. For him, nature is figured more by way of processes—forces, motions, waves—than by the settled presence of immanent, if dynamic, spirit. We take part in processes, small as well as large, more so than essences, and this is all that we have between ourselves and nothingness. Even so, there is the thought that "our saving" might well turn on a moment's participation in something higher than ourselves in which we are raised beyond the everyday, "for a moment, if only for a moment." (We might recall Aquinas on the simple apprehension of the divine.) Ammons will seek further metaphors for this existential situation in his poem, finding consolation that we (who are Many) can at least participate for a while in the cosmos, which is One. It is a starkly different encounter with death than one finds in Larkin's "Aubade," as discussed in chapter 5.

Having gotten halfway through the poem, we are likely to gloss the Most High as the highest principle of existence, the Heraclitean Ἕν, or Aristotle's τό ὄν ᾗ ὄν or his θεῖον, or the Cosmological Principle, or the Tao, or what Robinson Jeffers (1887–1962) called the *omnisecular spirit*, and there is no way we would attribute any personhood to it.[35] When Ammons returns to the same issue, however, his tone is more urgent than before:

do we *celebrate*
most truly when we fall into our limitations, *accept* our
nothingness of years, spawn, beget, care for, weep, fail, burn,

slobber, suck, stroke, dream, shake, sleep, eat, swim, squirm:
does He *forgive* us, does he *accept* our celebration, when we turn
away from the fruits given and *hunger* after Him.

(*Sphere*, 93.1108–13; emphasis added)

We might well celebrate life, even without believing in a creating and redeeming deity, and learn to accept our genetically disposed allotment of time as well. Nonetheless, it is difficult to see for what forgiveness and acceptance might be metaphors and what it means to hunger after "Him" if "he" is no more than being itself, or the highest principle of existence, or the Unity of the cosmos, all of which would be entirely neutral with respect to the poet.[36] It is as though Ammons has a religious sense for which he can find no adequate outlet in his world. Several sections later, he jokes about a solution: "this afternoon I thought Jove had come to get me" (98.1168); it is merely a pleasantry. The event that prompts the remark is that he "walked / into a corridor of sunlight swimming showering with turning shoals / of drift pollen" (98.1168–70) and was reminded of Jove and Danae. Amusingly, he also thinks he might be being "beamed aboard" a spaceship, as in the original of the television series *Star Trek* (1966–69). The one scenario belongs to mythology, the other to science fiction, two of the many shifting borders of religion. Soon we are referred to "the Lord of the treetops" (106.1266), which may well be no more than wind in the high leaves, and then, in Gnostic fashion, to "a spark of divinity" (117.1398). As the poem draws to a close, we find ourselves back with the demystified deity with which the poem started, this time with more of a Romantic inflection—it is a "god / of a kind, traveling wave of the imagination" (148.1772)—and then we are back with a thoroughly pantheist spirit, "the grass gods, the / god of the killdeer . . . and the old god of the forest" (149.1781–82).

There is not enough here, then, to speak strictly of a natural theology in *Sphere*, though there is plenty to support a discussion of something very close to it, natural supernaturalism. However, Ammons will return to the gods, plangently, in lines that will concern us later. That there may be a longing for something more than what is offered in everyday life pervading the poem, however, is something to which we have been alerted in the dedicatory lyric of the book: "I looked into space and into the sun / and nothing answered my word *longing*." (We might recall Augustine asking the sun, moon, and stars whether they are the objects of his love.)[37] But there is no *templum*—not yet. The image for which Ammons searches, however, is "the image of myself," which cannot be found anywhere in nature, not even on a mountaintop, whether it be Mt. Sinai, Mt. Parnassus, or one of the local peaks that feature in his poems. He has been brought far by nature, it is true, so far in fact that, as he extends a Yeatsian moment, he claims accomplishment where Yeats merely expressed postmortem desire: "I have been / brought out of nature."[38] In this state of profound alienation from the natural world, in which there is no creator God, only the poet can make an image of himself. For none is to be found around him. He tells us, "so I went back down and gathered mud / and with my hands made an image of *longing*," and inevitably recalls the interdiction against making graven images in Torah. Having made the image in defiance of (and in competition with) the Most High, Ammons has to ask himself "Where to place it?":

> I took the image to the summit: first
> I set it here, on the top rock, but it completed
> nothing: then I set it there among the tiny firs
> but it would not fit:
> so I returned to the city and built a house to set
> the image in
> and men came into my house and said
>   that is an image for *longing*
> and nothing will ever be the same again.[39]

Several things call for attention here. I will take them one at a time.

In the first place, the image is not of a god but of himself and of himself in just the one profile, that of longing, which includes religious yearning but is nowise limited to it. If *Sphere* is a poem of longing, for what does Ammons crave? That sexual desire marks him and every living thing in the cosmos is announced from the very beginning of the poem, and the importance of love is registered later, as is that of poetic creativity. But, more than local yearnings, moments of restlessness seem to be at issue. Longing is an ontological state for Ammons, as for all of us. He makes an image not of himself as a god but of himself as a human, one among many, yearning to return to the One. Having extended himself in nature, he now reaches beyond it, presumably to connect with a visionary mode of poetic composition. It cannot complete anything in nature—it is very far from being Stevens's jar placed on a hill in Tennessee—not even as it is revealed from the tops of mountains, nor does it fit in anywhere else that nature offers.[40] The right place for the image turns out to be private and domestic (no museum, no temple), though one that must be newly built. And it is there that the nonnatural image is recognized. But what does Ammons do with the image, his Genius (in both the classical and the modern senses of the word)? It would seem to be set in the house in order to be contemplated by himself and others who come to visit.

*

Contemplation is expressly raised twice in *Sphere*, once in a perfectly ordinary way in section 139, in which he dreams of walking through the stars and musing on the universe as he does so, and once in a more unusual context in section 67.[41] In this earlier occurrence, natural contemplation is mentioned by way of a contrast with being hypnotized, which allows him to show that poetry is found to be between the two states. The mind is awakened in poetry but not in order to do anything. Immediately before this contrast is staged, an attenuated *templum* briefly and quite unexpectedly appears in the poem. Spring is late in coming, he says, but then something unusual happens: "suddenly as if a / bright bird had passed, one is old" (66. 787–88). He looks into the sky, sees a bird, takes it as an augury, and grasps its meaning; he knows exactly what will happen in the future. He has always known, of course, but now he has had a confirming sign.[42] The result is that "one dozes forgetful of what / one was for," there is "a suspension of interrelationships," and the author as tutelary genius of the page momentarily fades from view: "the reader is / the medium by which one work of art judges another" (66. 788–90). It is as though tradition has already absorbed his individual talent or he has already become his admirers.[43]

Then, in an abrupt change of direction, to which we have become habituated merely by reading the poem for a spell, we are told, "hypnosis / is induced by focusing the attention" (*Sphere*, 66. 790–91), and we find Ammons more or less agreeing with Yeats on how rhythm can lull us into a quiet state: "the poem, its rhythm, is exclusive and hypnotic, / too, but the poem keeps enough relevant variety going to interest // the mind from sleep but enough focus to disinterest it in / external matters" (67. 794–97). In that focus, the conscious mind is fully occupied but not to the point of excluding absolutely everything else. Identifying this mental state between wakefulness and interest allows Ammons to stipulate the purpose of poetry:

> the purpose of the motion of a poem is to bring the focused,
> awakened mind to no-motion, to a still contemplation of the
> whole motion, all the motions, of the poem. (67.7–9)

It is one of the few moments in which *dilatio mentis* is figured in the poem, and it is an unusual one, for traditionally the object of contemplation is static, not dynamic, and here only the contemplation itself is steady. Gazing into the *templum* has induced Ammons to reflect not only on his own mortality but also on what a poem is for, a bringing of the mind (the reader's and the writer's) to rest for a moment in a state of stillness so that the poem can be beheld all at once. "(The poem reaches a stillness // which is its form)" (79.947–80.949), Ammons tells us, explaining the poem's subtitle, *The Form of a Motion*.[44]

Of course, it is the mind that has reached a stillness, albeit a mind that is now largely filled with the poem. This insight into the mind resting in order to reflect on the poem allows us to measure Ammons's distance from Christian contemplation in at least two ways. In *lectio divina*, we must say that, while the devotion is not tightly ordered and certainly not methodical, in its fullest stretch it enacts a progression of *lectio* (reading), *meditatio* (reflection), *oratio* (prayer), and *contemplatio* (loving suspension before God).[45] And in mental prayer, undertaken on its own, once again there is no narrow method, apart from spiritual preparation, the positioning of the body, the regulation of breath, and the focusing of attention. The modern appropriation of contemplation, of which Ammons is a prime example, extends the idea of θεωρία as a natural capacity. One sees without divine aid into the depths of nature, οἱ λόγοι, which are themselves divine or, as we would say today, properly basic.[46] Also, the modern use of *contemplation* tends to conflate *meditatio* and *contemplatio* and drop *oratio*, except, as we have seen in *Sphere*, as a tenor without a definite vehicle. In the monastic tradition, the reading of scripture is tied to prayer, rises to contemplative prayer, and over a protracted period deepens a life with what we call *spiritual experience*, an awareness of the mystery of love; while, in the stream of modern poetry that runs from Emerson to Ammons by way of Stevens, contemplation offers peak aesthetic experience, here of nature, which may well include mathematical or physical elements.[47] A deepening relationship with the Spirit leads to action, to bringing on the kingdom, while aesthetic experience leads one in darker moods to ask what poets are for. Hölderlin posed the question in his elegy "Brot und Wein" (1801), and like a tapeworm it lives inside each poet who recurs to the aesthetic attitude and sees the world only from there.[48] The kingdom tends largely to slip out of view, as we have seen with Stevens, but not altogether. We have still to see how Ammons lets it appear, in a limited way, later in his poem.

In the second case, where a Christian reader, monastic or not, who is engaged in *lectio divina* or formal mental prayer or any sort of *reductio in mysterium dei* finally rests in the presence of the Spirit and tastes the goodness of God, the reader, as Ammons sees things, remains in solitude and communes only with the text, understood as a nexus of psychic forces.[49] At most the reader attains a still point in his or her mind where he or she can take in all the many movements of the poem, including, perhaps, those that come from other poems and other areas of thought. Indeed, for Ammons, the thought of the cessation of life leads to a temporary abeyance of thought. Death exerts no fascination here, in part because of the state of abstraction in which one is placed, but the act of contemplation is free only in a limited sense, for it can play solely over an image that has been made. More importantly, contemplation is primarily associated in the poem not with ascent but with descent; the conscious mind finds itself lowered "down the ladder of structured motions" (*Sphere*, 68.806). It is as though Ammons replays the melody of Christian tradition that leads from Plato's *Symposium*, as read in one or another doxography by the Platonizing fathers, to Guido II's *Ladder for Monks* (ca. 1150) but in reverse. Where the monk seeks to rise to God by purifying himself of sin and ascending in the darkness of unknowing, Ammons descends into his psyche in order to find his "deeper self," which is deemed to be of value precisely because its description (*deeper*) is also a covert evaluation.[50]

Directly after explaining how a poem elicits contemplation, Ammons turns to ask what use this process might serve. For Aristotle, θεωρία has a limited utility, and, for monastic Christianity, it has none at all. Becoming more like God is beyond all possible use value, including the gaining of merit, which is not anything countenanced by spiritual exercises.[51] One prays for Grace, not recognition. But Ammons is American; everything must serve a purpose, even if it is no more than a passing experience of heated or chilled emotion. We might think that an answer has already been given, not once but twice. We may well suppose that contemplation is needed so that a poem can be beheld in all its parts and as a whole and thereby appreciated in its integrity. Second, we are put in touch with "the / refreshing energies of the deeper self" (*Sphere*, 68.806–7). Not so for the first answer, and not quite for the second. Why are we "brought through organized motion from chaos and / ephemerality to non-motion" (68.808–9)? His answer:

                        to touch the knowledge that
        motions are instances of order and direction occurring

    briefly in the stillness that surrounds to touch, to know,
    to be measured and criticized by the silence, to acknowledge
    and surrender to wholeness and composure: the non-verbal

    energy at that moment released, transformed back through the
    verbal, the sayable poem: spirit-being, great one in the world
    beyond sense, how do you fare and how may we fare to Thee.

                        (68.809–16)

The aim of contemplation here, it seems, is to appreciate "order and direction," parts converging on a projected whole, and we do so by way of a nontheoretical sense (touch), just as a Christian contemplative is also granted the use of another nontheoretical sense (taste) by which to know God (Ps. 34:8). Where the Christian rests in the Spirit, the reader, for Ammons, yields to the available comforts of a secular counterpart, "wholeness and composure." In doing so, there is a release of "non-verbal / energy" that we experience, a discharge that resembles orgasm, which is then conducted by the words of the poem itself.[52] The poem gives new life to author and reader alike, and, once again, Ammons points us to what seems, on a first reading, to be a religious dimension of his experience. It is as though the poem puts us in touch with a "spirit-being," the "great one in the world / beyond sense." We touch him and long to know how we may come to him. Withal, we know, deep down, that this "spirit-being" is no more than the One of which we, author and reader, are no more than instances of the Many.

                                *

Before going any further, one must acknowledge that there is a tension between what Ammons tells us about poetry leading us to contemplation and our experience of reading *Sphere*. We would more readily regard any number of lyrics by him as contemplative in part because of the limpid nature of the verse, the brevity of the lyric, and the invitation to share and prolong a rich moment of attention. Consider, out of many possibilities, "Day," composed just before *Sphere* in 1970:

    On a cold late
    September morning,

wider than sky-wide
discs of lit-shale clouds

skim the hills,
crescents, chords
of sunlight
now and then fracturing

the long peripheries:
the crow flies
silent,
on course but destinationless,

floating:
hurry, hurry,
the running light says,
while anything remains.[53]

A crow flies in a Fall morning, most likely in New England. No *I* is introduced in this report of experience, the speaker being wholly absorbed in contemplating an utterly ordinary day and an unremarkable
event, and we follow his line of attention. Immense clouds exceed the
vanishing points of the scene, and the horizon becomes visible only
when sunlight passes through them. Everything is silent: the sunlight is
a "Musicienne du silence," to recall a line from one of Mallarmé's early
poems.[54] In this cold world, there is a single crow, also silent, foraging
for food, itself attentive and open to any opportunity that presents itself (insects, snails, eggs, roadkill, mice, berries, etc.). Despite the possibilities of sublimity in the wide sky and the "chords / of sunlight,"
Ammons contents himself with an event that is easily overlooked, bypassed, or regarded as invisible and of no epiphanic significance. The
crow itself is "floating" on the currents of the air, much as the birds
were when Richard of St. Victor saw them in the twelfth century and
made them a figure of contemplation. Here, however, the crow is not
allowed to enjoy its suspension above the land; the light, destined to
run out, quietly tells it to hasten if it is to find food before dark. The
poet and the reader learn the same lesson: we too must do what must
be done. Ammons might seem to differ from Richard of St. Victor:
contemplation may have its proper time, but it has its limits also, one of
which is physical survival. Yet Richard knew that as well.
    We might recall the little poem that Ammons evokes, tongue-in-

cheek, in *Sphere*; it is a poem that he supposedly wrote while visiting
Baltimore, though one without the snap of his "really short poems":

> when I go up into the mountains, I like to go up into the
> mountains: when I come down from the mountains, I like to
> come down from the mountains. (73.874–76)[55]

Ammons offers these flat lines as an index of his desire to anticipate
different things to come, but we may also take them to suggest that,
as he sees it, the aesthetic is not only exhausted by the sublime (as it
is for Bloom) but also concerned with weak phenomena. Religion is
not only a matter of the radiance that comes from the Most High, albeit conceived in an unusual manner; it also turns on the radiance of
small things and events, the very being of which is in danger of being
bypassed or overlooked.[56] These too can be contemplated, and, like
the crow of "Day," the contemplation might be without a destination.
There is no reason to think that it ends in a mystery. The crow seeks out
what hides itself, and so does Ammons.

Such short lyrics are not the only possible models for contemplative
verse, however. If we want a more capacious work, one given to verbal luxury, we might wish to regard some of John Ashbery's drawn-out
poems as inducing a peculiar state of reflection. As we read *Three Poems*
(1972) or "A Wave" (1984), for instance, we might follow the poet's associations, apparently released by his unconscious, less closely than we
would in many another poem (including some of his own) and allow
our minds to rest above the mental flow. The particularity of his personality is less important than a sense of a deeper self that is opening itself to us and that is, we recognize, close to our own deeper selves. We
are not attuned to any confessions or psychological insights that might
occur in the verse, even though we will encounter memorable passages
of pathos, humor, and joy. Slow reading here does not work in the same
way as when verse turns on double genitives, paradoxes, ambiguities,
and the like; it turns, rather, on mulling over what is said. We realize,
more than when reading *Sphere*, that we are not encountering an aesthetic object at all: the poem is a flow that overruns any frameworks we
seek or impose. The analytic aspect of the mind is allowed to idle for a
while. These poems by Ashbery are not experienced by the reader as
especially fast, however, even if we are not required by our critical su-
peregos to slow down. We can stop as we wish, between extensive paragraphs, in prose or verse, or even between sections of a poem. This is
very different from what happens when reading Ammons's long poem.

It cannot be denied that, especially on a first or second reading,

Sphere is a fast-moving poem and in its turns of attention at times a bewildering one, not likely to induce a contemplative state, as Yeats conceived it. There is no quantitative or qualitative meter; each line crams in words until the notional end of the line (coming soon after when the typewriter bell rings) and then swings down to begin a new line. The poem throbs like a pulse through its numbered sections, which resemble calibrations more than organic divisions. For all Ammons's interest in the One and the Many, the numbered sections do not serve as discrete parts of a whole. More often than not, the line breaks are sharp, unmotivated by grammar or sense, and not even the ends of stanzas or sections coincide with a pause. This is nothing like "Corsons Inlet" (1962), for instance, in which the lines flow as if they were in an organic relation with perceptions and thoughts. Where traditional meters make us look along a line, anticipating its end (and whether there will be an enjambment), Ammons's rhythm pushes us ever down a page and over the next page, all the way until we glide toward the end. Strictly speaking, *Sphere* is one protracted sentence punctuated mostly by colons, offering us nowhere to draw our breath, let alone an opportunity to put the book down. It offers itself as a single rush of experience, one that of course takes in a great many events, some elevated, others banal. We tend to be sped up as we read it, with a sense that we are being sucked into a whirlpool or caught on currents of the air, which perhaps makes us less attentive to detail as the poem goes on and more intrigued by the speaker who has buttonholed us. It is a more exhausting experience than the one the wedding guest undergoes with the compulsively talking ancient mariner.

In addition, the poem proceeds by way of sudden transitions; no sooner has one perception or observation or faux aphorism been made than we are redirected to another. It is a poem apparently given to distraction more than attention, one that Ammons reminds us need not be read continuously ("dip in anywhere" [*Sphere*, 44.522], he says, disarmingly). Recall the following lines from early on in the poem. I quote Ammons in section 6, midway through a flow of words about a professor unwittingly using sexual metaphors:

> he invokes a woman: he wants
> shapeliness intact, figure shown forth: dirty old
> man hawking order and clarity: but if he would not
>
> be dark, what a brightness! though I am not enjoying the
> first day of spring very much, it is not with me as it is
> with my friend George, spending his first spring in the grave:

7

windbaggery, snag-gaggling, yakety-yak, fuss: if you dig
a well, steen it well: earth's fluid: it moves: any
discontinuity imposed, opposing the normal intermingled sway.

(6.67–7.75)

On a first reading, the passage is disorienting, passing, as it does, in
just nine lines from a diagnosis of a professor's metaphors, to the first
day of spring, to a touching allusion to a dead friend and the difference
between living and being dead, to mere chatter, to movements in the
earth, to digging a well. On a second reading, however, the sheer diversity of the observations reduces somewhat, for we see that Ammons is
continuing his theme about the "sexual basis of all things," reflecting on
the death of the soul, speaking about the poem itself, which seems to
be motivated by what the French call *tout dire* (saying everything), and
even about the technique of the work that we are reading ("discontinuity imposed, opposing the normal intermingled sway"). We also begin
to see that Ammons's speech occupies a border between the interior
and the exterior, between stream of consciousness and ordinary talk.

*

Given all this, while not forgetting that *Sphere* is announced as a poem
of longing, how can it possibly induce the quiet of mind that Ammons
holds to be essential to poetry?

Outside religious practice, we tend to think of contemplation, first,
as extensive, rapt attention and see, with Yeats, that in their chosen acts
of excellence Caesar, Helen, and Michel Angelo each has a mind "Like
a long-legged fly upon the stream" that "moves upon silence."[57] The
balance of activity and passivity is worth noting. More, Yeats's accent
on silence sits well with a lyric such as "Day" but oddly with a poem
such as *Sphere* that talks incessantly. And, with the same proviso invoked with regard to attention, we think of it especially as inherited
from Coleridge. It involves an endless process of reflecting backward
and forward in search of a whole, one that will always escape us, even
if we find a richer or fuller whole on a later reading.[58] It is difficult to
keep track of what happens in *Sphere*, although, as already seen, some
of the most disorienting turns of attention are, on a second reading,
less abrupt than they first seemed. (As we read it, the poem convinces
us of its ability to "evolve and adapt," as Catherine Malabou says when
speaking of *plasticité*; we are never sure of what is coming, only that the
poem will open out by way of sudden changes of attention, the specific

objects of which we cannot tell in advance.)[59] Nor can we anticipate what we are to hear, partly because of the sudden shifts, and partly because, as we finally realize, the poem is not a transitive text; it does not lead us, by highways and byways, to a conclusion that satisfies us in a narrative and thematic manner. Wholes are projected or conceived recursively, but none is offered as definitive.

To be sure, the final section, 155, is rhetorically structured to give us a "sense of an ending," an image appropriate to the vast scale of the poem, and to supply a thematic unity to what we have been reading.[60] There is an affirmation of our brief span of years in the Milky Way being like a ride on a Ferris wheel that eventually must stop. We are not led to feel that the poem as a whole is motivated to end at line 1860; it stops rather than concludes, even if not as abruptly or coyly as other of Ammons's long poems.[61] And we do not feel cheated. For, at some stage of reading the poem, we begin to accept that we are asked to experience a continuous living present in which thoughts and feelings are perpetually subject to transformation. We become reconciled, at least temporarily, to witnessing a certain plasticity of thinking, one that operates beneath the level of conscious observation or even argument.[62] The One seems for a while to become regulative rather than constitutive.

We might get closer to answering our question by looking at a short paper that Ammons read to the International Poetry Forum in Pittsburgh in April 1967. It is entitled "A Poem Is a Walk." We can begin at the end of Ammons's reflections, which will seem familiar to readers of *Sphere*:

> Poetry is a verbal means to a nonverbal source. It is a motion to no-motion, to the still point of contemplation and deep realization. Its knowledges are all negative and, therefore, more positive than any knowledge. Nothing that can be said about it in words is worth saying.

The first two of these dark sayings more or less found their way into *Sphere*, but the latter two did not. Before I venture to ponder what, if anything, we can learn from them, it is worth noting the burden of the entire paper, namely, that walks are useless (and hence that poems are strictly useless as well) and that they are meaningless (and hence that poems are meaningless as well). Ammons's argument for these conclusions is less than compelling. He gives a wide range of plausible answers to the question "what walks are good for"—"to settle the nerves, to improve the circulation, to break in a new pair of shoes, to exercise the muscles," and so on—but is unsatisfied by extensional definition or appeals to a final cause. The second question, "what walks mean," is not answered by way of so many examples. No doubt we will wish to say that certain actions bear meaning, depending on their role in social situations, and that they have purposes we can usually identify. What Ammons seems to have in mind is not that walks (and hence poems) have no ends or meanings but that they have no *final* ends or *final* meanings, nothing that can be expressed in words and concepts. (Again, we might recall Bacon on natural science not needing to appeal to final causes.) The purpose of a poem, he writes at the start of the paper, "is to go past telling, to be recognized by burning."[63]

Presumably a poem is a verbal means to experience this "burning," which a mystic such as Richard Rolle (1300–1349) might well call "a counterfeit 'fire of love.'"[64] In any case, this burning is a figure of *dilatio mentis* or even *sublevatio mentis*. Having reached this heightened emotional and intellectual state, the poet is able to contemplate the poem as a whole, as a flow of writing that is able to balance or reconcile "opposite or discordant qualities" without a final figure at the end.[65] A poem does not have any final single meaning; it is a tissue of "contradictions, inconsistencies, explanations and counter-explanations" and nonetheless a flowing whole.[66] So it is not a totality; it is always open and, despite its fixed appearance on the page, forever in motion. A poem is like a walk, Ammons suggests, in that it begins somewhere and ends somewhere, not necessarily at the same place. (We might think of *essai* in Montaigne's sense and thus recall several of Ammons's verse essays.) A poem is also like a walk, Ammons continues, in that it is relatively singular, involves movement, and exercises the body. He does not specify that what he means is a solitary walk, much like those of Rousseau and Whitman.[67] Nor does he say directly that walking, and not only standing still, is one of the ways in which people have traditionally contemplated the world about them and reflected on the problems that beleaguer them.[68] If a poem is like a walk, it is partly because it involves our bodies (at least our breath, our eyes, our ears, and various appeals to our senses) while freeing the mind to ponder what passes through it.

The point of taking a walk is not the walk itself but something that exceeds any intensional definition of *a walk*. The body moves, but there is some part of the mind that rises above the body or stands to its side and views what is occurring. As Ammons writes of his most memorable stroll, the one to which "Corsons Inlet" is dedicated, after starting another exploration of the dunes at the Jersey Shore he found

the walk liberating, I was released from forms,
from the perpendiculars,
      straight lines, blocks, boxes, binds
of thought
into the hues, shadings, rises, flowing
   bends and blends
         of sight.[69]

Releasement here is from straight lines to curves, from attending to culture to encountering nature; it is a passage from abstraction to the concrete. Ammons goes on to testify that in not willfully imposing concepts or images on the scene around him, in not seeking a totality, an "Overall" summation of things, "there is serenity." So serenity is not to be sought by ascent or descent, only by steady looking. More, in the freedom he experiences, he realizes "that there is no finality of vision."[70] (Again, we see an emphasis on dissolving experience as ultimately transitive in favor of the ultimately intransitive.)[71] Actively or passively, the quiet mind is intent on reconciling tensions, joining part to part in order to make a whole that will be slightly or significantly different the following day. As Ammons tells us at the end of "Corsons Inlet," "tomorrow a new walk is a new walk," and he speaks with authority since, as he tells us in the poem's first line, he has already explored the dunes before.[72] *Sphere* is one of those walks, although it has a distinctive gait of its own and mentally rambles over the world, *his* world, not over the dunes of the Jersey Shore. It is a contemplation that remains "on course but destinationless," without any simple intellective intuition in sight.

CHAPTER 10

"On Course but Destinationless"

In "Corsons Inlet," one can almost feel the body of the speaker in steady motion by virtue of what and how his eye sees. He moves at a normal walking pace, noting that "by *transitions* the land falls from grassy dunes to creek / to undercreek," and he sometimes stops to observe events in detail, such as the gull that "cracked a crab, / picked out the entrails, swallowed the soft-shelled legs." He declares that because of the black mudflats he cannot see what the white black-legged egret is doing, and he gains "the top of a dune" and from that vantage point is able to watch swallows.[1] In *Sphere*, by contrast, there is no setting, and the speaker's eyes and voice seem disconnected from his body. It is a poem of a mind thinking more than of a body walking, and Richard's sense of *thinking* is relevant here ("Thinking wanders through whatever by-ways, with a slow pace, without regard for arrival"). It is a whole being that is articulated, not natural phenomena being perceived. The voice, in particular, talks and talks with barely a pause for breath, offering us no development of thought and nothing like a record of emotional or spiritual growth. After several pages, we begin to sense that one of the longings at the heart of *Sphere* is a hunger to talk. "I'll have to say everything," Ammons notes in a poem of 1969, while in another, dating from 1965, he evokes himself as "a posing man who / must talk / but who has nothing to / say."[2] The mind thinks best when the hand writes, even when the thinking is not remarkable.

I have already mentioned the French expression *tout dire*, and perhaps it will help us situate what is going on in the poem and in what way, if any, the poem can usefully be seen as contemplative. For it seems as though *Sphere* talks and talks in order to avoid contemplation, thinking everything, as much as to fit part to part in order to disclose a whole and thus be contemplative. At the same time, we need to remind ourselves that, unlike Stevens and Ashbery, there is no French dimension to Ammons's literary life, and we need to be aware of the dangers of importing foreign ideas somewhere they cannot take root. French writers, philosophers, and critics have taken a narrower interest in the topic of "saying everything" than their American counterparts, who, to be sure, have more than enough texts at their disposal—both in their European heritage and their own literary history—to reflect on the phenomenon if they wish to do so.[3] At least in one respect, *tout dire* needs to be distinguished from contemplation. A person who engages in religious contemplation circles before God and might compose a long commentary or testimony of intimacy with the divine that has been gained in the process: St. Hildergard of Bingen's *The Book of Divine Works* (completed 1172–74) or Mechthild of Magdeburg's *The Flowing Light of the Godhead* (completed 1281), for example. And someone who practices θεωρία φυσική with respect to a landscape, a hemisphere, or an artifact might do the same thing: Wordsworth's first version of *The Prelude* (1798), Pablo Neruda's *Canto general* (1950), or Francis Ponge's *Le savon* (1967), say. An individual who says everything also engages his or her topic by way of expansion, but not in a quest for understanding something inherently mysterious or beautiful. It may be an attempt to confess faults (des Forêts), to evade other work (Henri-Frédéric Amiel), to recover the past (Proust), to transgress social norms (Sade), or to respond exhaustively to everyday life in a particular place (Georges Perec).[4] It is oriented more surely to fascination than to contemplation. We can distinguish two elements in it.

First of all, the desire to say everything involves a reaction to censorship from whatever quarter, and it is linked with a modern determination of literature that reserves for it the right to speak freely on religion, sexuality, politics, or whatever.[5] This angle of desire is not my immediate concern, however, despite Ammons's emphasis on the sexual basis of all things, which, in *Sphere* at least, runs between the biological and the boorish (as in 5.50–52).[6] The second element is general: the quest to say everything about oneself or one's world by one means or another, for one reason or another. Restricting ourselves to the West, we might think of Gregory the Great's *Moralia in Job*, Aquinas's *Summa theologiae*, Dante's *Commedia*, and Hegel's *Enzyklopädie* (1830), each of which adopts a wide-angle view of reality while pursuing finely grained analysis. In the more recent past, we will think of Proust's *À la recherche du temps perdu* (1913–27), in which the narrator's childhood is lovingly caressed, and Joyce's *Ulysses* (1922), which is not just a lengthy novel but one that tries by a continuous parallel with Homer's *Odyssey* to condense the whole of human experience, both historically and spiritually, into one story at once banal and extraordinary (Leopold Bloom, for Schopenhauer, would serve as the Idea of Man) and, in a quite different vein, also Neruda's *Canto general* (1950), which ventures to include all the Americas. More locally, we will think of Whitman's immense *Song of Myself* (1855), Pound's sprawling *The Cantos* (1962), Williams's exhaustive celebration of his hometown in *Paterson* (1946–58), and Zukofsky's *A* (1978).

These texts can all be placed under our chosen rubric only with difficulty, for they seek to say everything in quite different ways, about various objects, from unique perspectives, for distinct reasons, and with differing degrees of success. A line sometimes runs between saying everything and saying everything that is worthwhile. For a believer to comment on Job is to come into the presence of the divine, which will overflow even the most extensive interpretation. As copious as the *Moralia* is, especially in its initial design, the assumptions that Gregory has firmly in place could always justify a more lingering work. To compose a *summa* in the high scholastic manner is not to produce an encyclopedia of theology but, more subtly, to determine the principles of Christian life and thought and show their interconnections, both apparent and hidden. The *Summa theologiae* is a massive fragment, and if we are struck by its bulk, we will even more applaud its concision when reading individual articles. To view the entire vista of hell, purgatory, and paradise, as Dante does, is to tell us all that one person can about being human. And so on, all through the list of more recent works, though each of them would call for its individual nuances to be noted. In each case, one says everything not by attempting to capture the sheer diversity of life, its many forms, its distinct feelings and varied styles of thinking, but by finding a viewpoint and a range of strategies from which one can account for as much of an open whole as possible.

Not that one must write an immense work in order to try to say everything, for it is also possible to bunch interminable sequences of literature, philosophy, and theology (not to mention the natural sciences, which are so important to Ammons) into short poems so that, when we read them with all due attention and with enough erudition we can, as it were unfurl all that is contained in those sequences. Sometimes, this critical process will involve opening deliberate and quite complex folds made by the poet. At other times, it will be a matter of seeing how schemes of maximizing the equivocal in language have led to a vast field of possible meanings. At further times, it will be a question of the reader making appropriate associations so that what has been left unsaid by the poet is actually thought or said by the reader.[7] In principle, then, even a short lyric by Stéphane Mallarmé (e.g., "Le vierge, le vivace, et le bel aujourd'hui"), Paul Celan (e.g., "Todesfuge"), or Geoffrey Hill (e.g., "Annunciations") might, each in its own way, seem to say everything about a situation or theme if only one could exfoliate all it contains, hear all the resonances of all the words, and write a commentary sufficiently detailed to show it. With Ammons, however, it is otherwise. His shorter poems are not concatenated in quite that way. More particularly, *Sphere* is not a poem into which the poet has crimped ambiguities, paradoxes, and the like; it is a poem that opens out from section to section, sometimes from stanza to stanza, even from line to line, in an unpredictable way, projecting wholes that often do not guide the poem for long as we continue to read it. Reconciliation is no more than an enabling fiction. For *Sphere* is not a poem in which part adds to part and makes a final whole; it is a poem in which contemplation is "on course but destinationless," if I may return to "Day." The long poem plays recursively with parts and wholes, going up ("into the mountains," as Ammons jokes) and then coming down ("from the mountains") (*Sphere*, 73.874–76).

In France, there is reason to begin thinking about *tout dire* with Rousseau's *Confessions* (1782), in which the author wishes to relate his entire life's story, not leaving out anything, partly to keep his self wholly before his view, and partly to show himself as he truly is to his public.[8] One might also look a little to the side of Rousseau, to the Marquis de Sade (1740–1814), whose voluminous narratives have been aptly seen to share a peculiarity that accounts for their length: "At every moment, his theoretical ideas release the irrational forces that are bound up with them. These forces at once animate and frustrate his ideas, and then yield to them, seeking to master this impetus, which effectively they do, but only while simultaneously releasing other obscure forces, which will lead, twist, and pervert them anew."[9] The result of this conjunction of ideas and forces, both sexual and political, is that at any given moment we think we know what Sade is telling us, only to have something added a little later that must be incorporated into what we already know and so on, until we realize that, precisely in this way, Sade tries to tell us everything that he knows, fantasizes about, or will ever fantasize about. Moving away from the eighteenth century, one can approach *tout dire* by way of Raymond Roussel's poem "La vue" (1904), in which over the course of four thousand lines—well over a thousand lines longer than Tennyson's *In Memoriam* (1849)—the speaker minutely describes every last thing that he can see of a miniature beach scene painted on a souvenir pen stand.[10] Or one might go to Henri-Frédéric Amiel's vast *Journal intime* (1884) or to Paul Claudel's *Cinq grandes odes* (1907).

Not even those philosophers who gravitate to the idea of saying everything agree, even in general, about whether it leads to contemplation or fascination. Jean-Louis Chrétien, for one, explicates the joy of reading spacious works, which offer us "open roads" or "mystical dilations" or "voyages without limits" or "cosmic respiration."[11] It is easy enough to see how one could read *Sphere* in related terms. It is a poem that multiplies its intentional rapports with the world, large and small, both outer and inner. If we see profiles of the planet and of all sorts of events on it, we also see varying profiles of the author in the act of following his daily life and occasionally venturing close to the sublime. We would find parts leading to a provisional whole that opens onto another whole and so on. But there is another theory, from the same sources, that asks for attention. Maurice Blanchot contests one of the principal motifs of phenomenology (the generality of manifestation, apart from special sorts of limit phenomena) in order to uncover an obscure dispersal of the present that stagnates in literary texts. It can be discerned in an exemplary manner in the works of Samuel Beckett, René Char, and Franz Kafka, among other modern writers whose works exert a fascination on the reader. We need to see whether this theory helps us come any closer to the obsessive talking that is *Sphere*.

We can begin by listening to Blanchot characterizing a narrative work by Louis-René des Forêts, "Le bavard" (1946), since, in some respects, it approaches our experience of reading *Sphere* or, perhaps it would be more accurate to say, our experience of being detained to listen to *Sphere*, which is so very different an experience from reading Gregory, Dante, Aquinas, Joyce, or anyone I mentioned a minute ago. Not all lengthy works, including substantial poems, need be garrulous. For not all works that surround us with voice need do so in Ammons's manner.[12] The narrator of "Le bavard" talks incessantly of an evening's outing and his outrageous behavior in a bar, then confesses that it is all lies, that snares have been laid with care for the reader to trust him: he has spoken out of a need to speak when he has nothing at all to say. Blanchot reflects on this work that has "neither beginning nor end" and characterizes it as "this speech that does not speak, entertaining speech that is always going from here to there, with which one passes from one subject to the next without knowing what is at issue, speaking equally of everything—of things serious, of things insignificant, with as much interest, precisely because it is understood that one is speaking of nothing."[13] Now, if one brackets the mendacity of des Forêts's narrator, one could almost think that Blanchot were describing one's dizzy experience of reading *Sphere* where Ammons tells us that "garrulity is harm enough even when, as here, it // finds harmless way" (62.6–7). But

Ammons thinks he is speaking of something, the One-Many Problem, as well as all sorts of events and individuals met in daily life that themselves are parts to be formed into one or another whole. Is there anything else to make us place these two books side by side?

Des Forêts's narrator is a chatterbox; he has an unremitting desire to speak, indeed, an urgent need to empty himself of words, while thinking poorly of himself for even seeking to speak and being well aware of how to multiply strategies of speaking while apparently denying himself the rhetorical means of doing so. A brief passage from near the beginning of the narrative is indicative of the whole while also indicating the problem at hand:

> I suppose most of you have had the experience of being button-holed by one of those garrulous fellows [*ces bavards*] who, longing to make their voices heard, seek out a companion whose only function is to lend an ear, without any obligation to utter a word; and indeed it's not even certain that the bore insists on being listened to, it's enough to assume an air of being interested, either by giving an occasional nod or what novelists call a murmur of approval, or by valiantly enduring the poor beggar's insistent gaze despite the exhaustion inevitably ensuing from such a muscular strain. Let's take a closer look at such a man. That he should feel the need to speak and yet have nothing to say, and moreover that he cannot satisfy this need without the more or less tacit complicity of companion chosen by him, if he's been free to choose, for qualities of discretion and endurance, these facts are worth pondering over. This fellow has nothing whatsoever to say, and yet he says a thousand things; he doesn't really mind whether his interlocutor agrees with him or dissents from him, and yet he cannot do without him, although he wisely requires from him only a purely formal attention. It all takes place as if he were affected by a disease for which he can find no remedy or, to borrow a familiar comparison, as if he were in the same dilemma as the Sorcerer's Apprentice: the machine goes round and round to no purpose, and he is unable to control its wayward movements. Now I make bold to say, at the risk of alienating all my readers, that I belong to this particular brand of talkers [*bavards*].[14]

To speak is to adopt one facade after another, the narrator thinks. Bad faith helps him overcome the banality of his life, and the very idea of uncontrolled talk fascinates him—that is to say, it both absorbs him and repels him—as does his reflection in the mirror.[15]

If we place *Sphere* next to "Le bavard," we will find that the American poet is also a chatterbox but not someone with a clinical problem, as is the case with the unnamed narrator of the French narrative. Chatter is linked in *Sphere* not to deceit but to having no destination, no final cause, which, on a first reading, seems to make the poem all deflections. The avowed aim of the speaker is to hold the reader (44.521), at least for a while. He or she is not denied aesthetic distance from the work and is allowed the distraction from ordinary life we have come to expect from reading poetry, albeit at the cost of another sort of perpetual distraction. This first distraction is what Blanchot will call *contemplative irresponsibility*, which removes us from social and political engagement with the world by allowing us to indulge in aesthetic repose.[16] One reason why we should attend to the works he esteems, Blanchot suggests, is that they deny or worry at the positing of aesthetic distance; the fascination we experience in reading them points us to the Outside, which will draw us away from the privileged social, political, and religious world in which we have lived and invite us to make another world more solidly rooted in our common humanity.[17]

Ammons, however, wishes to hold attention and distraction in harmony, allowing us a measure of aesthetic distance and the contemplation that accords with it. The reader is required to be a still center around which the speaker dances, jumps, and occasionally slumps, and his or her reward will be being brought "to no motion, to still contemplation of the / whole motion" (*Sphere*, 67.800–801). For Ammons, there is no confession, not even of anxiety as a stimulus for writing, no need to fabricate reasons to interest the reader; if anything, he is foursquare in his confidence both in himself as a captivating speaker and in a reader who will appreciate what he has to share even if he claims not really to understand some of his readers' reactions to his writing (§ 122). Yet there is another step that we need to take toward Ammons with Blanchot, if only to show that the Frenchman can help us only so far.

*

For Blanchot, there is a fine but thoroughgoing distinction between the category of aesthetic disinterest, as inherited from Kant's *The Critique of Judgement* (1790) and expanded in psychology, and what he calls the *nonconcerning*, which he ascertains in the narratives of Sade, Kafka, and Beckett, among others. The former requires the author and the reader alike to bracket any interest he or she might have in what is being presented. We recall from chapter 2 that a judgment of taste, Kant argues, "is simply *contemplative* [*kontemplativ*], i.e., . . . a judgment which is indifferent as to the existence of an object, and only decides how its character stands with the feeling of pleasure and displeasure."[18] Aesthetic disinterest allows for the writer and the reader to sit at a remove from a representation and to ponder it as a representation in his or her own way. We are not to ask whether Ammons really "walked / into a corridor of sunlight swimming showering with turning shoals / of drift pollen" (*Sphere*, 98.1168–69); we are only to delight in his description of the event. On Blanchot's understanding, the ruling metaphor of aesthetics, hidden or not, is irreducibly visual (e.g., *gaze*), and it has been used to turn writing into so many cultural monuments, what we call the canon of *literature*. Post-Kantian aesthetics has promoted this metaphor and tended to conceal its power. But it is beginning to be overcome, Blanchot thinks, by a quite different set of assumptions about writing and reading that one can detect operating in his own writing and in that of those who have influenced it. Aesthetic distance can be used in two ways, Blanchot tells us, either dialectically, in order to generate meaning, or by being abolished in a fusion of subject and object, as in a mystical experience, natural or not. Such would be the two senses of θεωρία, observation and beholding.[19]

What of the second category, the nonconcerning? It is resolutely not a question of contemplation in any natural or Christian sense, in part because it looks to writing, not vision, for its base metaphor, and in part because it looks to neither admiration nor love. It is neither dialectical nor fusional. Blanchot will speak of it as nonrelational or neutral because any text in which he uncovers it will give the sense that "what is being recounted is not being recounted by anyone."[20] More than that, any substantial selfhood that we might wish to attribute to an *I* (a character, an author, a reader) has always and already been hollowed out by the act of writing itself. The text supplies a voice we hear, a ghostly murmur that is not that of a living *I* speaking to us. A voice abides within the confines of the writing that obsessively talks to anyone who cares to listen. Even if an author is long dead, a trace of his or her consciousness remains "in" the words as *irreal* and does so as an "impersonal spontaneity."[21] What is affirmed in this voice is strictly of no concern to anyone since there is no anyone, no substantive self, writer or reader, for whom it could matter.[22] Searching for an example, we might think of a novel such as Beckett's *L'innommable* (1953), in which a bodiless narrator seems to be generated by the voices that belong to his monologue, and what makes us settle on this novel is that in it narrative voice and theme converge, at least for long stretches: "a voice that never stops," "this meaningless voice which prevents you from being nothing," "The subject doesn't matter, there is none."[23]

Does *Sphere* speak to us in a narrative voice or in a narrator's voice or both, assuming, of course, that it makes sense to speak of a narrative here in the first place? There is no question that the poem neither begins nor ends in any motivated manner and that it is thoroughly nontransitive in its textual grammar; it does not propose to offer us any final meaning, any eschatological whole. We may think that it will, eventually, but it keeps twisting away from what we have expected at any given moment. (Yet the last image of the Milky Way as a Ferris wheel comes close to doing so.) The poem may not give us a body, but it certainly gives us a voice. *Sphere* insists, section by section, on the presence of a secure speaker whom we can determine in several ways — male, white, North American, educated in the natural sciences, with a taste for classification, middle-aged, and so forth — who speaks on and on, passing from percept to percept, theme to theme, aphorism to aphorism. He speaks of the cosmos about us, of which we are a part, and in the existence of which we must surely have an interest; it is to do not with taste or with the good but with the brute fact of our existence, where we have come from and where we are heading. In this, the speaker is totally unlike the of "Le bavard," who is not situated at all, quite deliberately, so as to further his dark intentions with respect to misleading the reader. In part the poem is about a sphere, our earth, and in part it acts as a sphere itself, constantly turning and, as any reader will testify, doing so at a much faster speed than the planet and in several directions over a short period.

It seems clear that we should speak of Ammons's talk rather than his diction in the poem. Yet it is a delicate question whether we should speak of his talk or his chatter, or perhaps chitchat, in the poem, for there seem to be significant stretches of idle speech in it. The expression needs to be used with care. There are passages of small talk — observations and reportage — that seem both prosy and aimless and that seem not even designed to charm the reader into a feeling of intimacy with the author, warts and all, in the way that James Schuyler does in his sustained self-revealing poem "The Morning of the Poem" (1980) or that Frank O'Hara (1926–66) does in his "I do this I do that" poems such as "A Step Away from Them" and "The Day Lady Died."[24] If we talk of *idle speech*, especially in Ammons and Schuyler, it will be in a way that is different than the technical sense that Heidegger gives to the expression (*Gerede*) in which rumor and gossip are relayed from person to person with no one ever taking responsibility for the veracity or even value of what is said.[25] That is not Schuyler's way and not Ammons's either. Nor is it Ashbery's. As noted in the previous chapter, we do not find a stable psychological self in Ashbery's poetry, let alone a Cartesian *ego cogito*. We nonetheless find a deeper self that we might figure by way of the transcendental ego as elaborated by Kant, a *cogito* distinct from the *sum* and thoroughly enjoying its freedom, which in composition is marked by a liberation from a specific empirical personality tethered to a narrative or lyrical *I*.[26] The closest Ashbery gets to telling us anything about himself, at least in his earlier poems, is perhaps "Soonest Mended" (1966), but throughout this poem he adopts the plural pronoun: everything he says about himself growing up applies to the reader as well. He presents us with an experience of experience.[27] Clearly, however, there is nothing in *Sphere* to make us go in the direction of Ashbery's poetics of the subject.

We could think of Ammons's instances of small talk as evincing a sense of everyday life by way of what the French call *l'effet du réel*.[28] Consider section 40 and the start of section 41, which are about Sunday, April 16, 1972. We know the day because Ammons has just told us that Apollo 16 has been launched:

John and I drove out to check the paint job on the propjet,
Mohawk merging with Allegheny and losing its emblems and
identifications, such as colors, black and gold, and the

head of the Indian chief on the tail assembly, to the white
and blue streaks, with red lettering, of Allegheny: as
part of his commitment to the baggage man, John stood out

by the wire fence in the pouring rain until the second
engine started to spin and the passenger door went up: then
we stood under a shelter with our hands over our ears while

the plane taxied out on the runway: just then it occurred
to me how much I dislike weekends and how pleasant it would
be to pull Sundays in particular out of the calendar and

41
add a longish month to June. (*Sphere*, 40–41.481)

Thinking over the whole of *Sphere*, one might say that this rather drab passage and others like it (e.g., sec. 91) form the ground against which more lyrical, intense, dilated, or humorous passages cut their figures. Call that ground *the everyday*.

It is a curious phenomenon that the everyday resists becoming a figure itself. As soon as there is a bid to do so, it disappears and leaves us with a banal list of opinions, routines, and circumstances. (Even in the sitcom *Seinfeld* [1989–98], the everyday has to be highly selected, usually by way of intersecting narratives and made to sparkle by way of amusing coincidences.) We recognize them as part of the everyday, but they seem suddenly disconnected from the stream of life as we experience it, even as background. We live the everyday unreflectively, in the natural attitude, outside both poetry and science, and, as soon as we take an interest in something that obtrudes in this attitude, we tend, even ever so slightly, toward science (Why is this happening?) or religion (Which deity is making this happen?) or a good deal of modern poetry (How is this happening?) The bend toward science involves a move from the natural attitude to the naturalistic attitude (or, at times, the theoretical attitude), and it is worth our while to recall that the former is prior to the latter: the naturalistic world is not the world in which we concretely live, and one of the values of passages such as section 40 is to remind us of the priority of our personal, everyday life, unremarkable as it sometimes is, which includes much of our experience of nature.[29] A turn to religion requires a pivot to the religious-mythical attitude (as Ammons and Husserl both see it but with different valuations of it), and we have already noticed how this occurs in the poetry. A shift to poetry involves a slide, usually incomplete, from the natural attitude to the phenomenological attitude in which the poet's intentional consciousness correlates in manner with how the world gives itself. But things are often more complex in *Sphere*, with the poet speaking from within a complex of attitudes. When regarding nature, as happens throughout the poem, Ammons will at times speak in the naturalistic attitude, stating scientific facts as so many theses (e.g., "man waited / 75, 000 years in a single cave" [45.538–39]), and, when this happens, we might well wonder whether he can contemplate in the naturalistic attitude.

He does not remain there, however, for sometimes Ammons sees, by way of those lenses we call *tropes*, how natural processes are working. Bear in mind these lines about midway through the poem:

> when the grackle's flight shadows a streak of lawn, *constellations*
> *of possibility break out*, for example, the multitude of
> glassblade shadows subsumed in a sweep: *for example*, an aphid
>
> 76
>
> resting in bugleleaf shade must think lost his discretion of
> position: (his feelers notice, his eyes adjust): an ant
> struck by the flashed alternation stops, the friction of which

event *gives off a plume of heat, a small invisible boom*:
myriad chloroplasts circling the cell peripheries *kick out*
of photosynthetic gear and coast in a slough and many atoms

of carbon and nitrogen miss connection.

> (*Sphere*, 75.898–76.906; emphasis added)

How quickly Ammons passes from the natural attitude, in noting the flight of the bird, to the essential structure of the phenomenon that he makes manifest: "constellations / of possibility break out." We slide toward the theoretical attitude ("for example"), then into the phenomenological attitude ("gives off a plume of heat, a small invisible boom"), back to the naturalistic attitude ("myriad chloroplasts circling the cell peripheries"), only to twist back into the phenomenological attitude by one carefully chosen metaphor ("kick out / of photosynthetic gear"). This is not scientific writing spiced with metaphor; it is the poet changing mental frames with speed and ease, and the attitudes I have named, which have their point in philosophy, seem somewhat lumbering when used with respect to poetry.

To return to the problem of the flatness of sections 40–41. It is only in the final remark of this passage that the speaker shifts from the natural attitude to fantasy, from the mode of "it is" to the mode of "as if." With a stretch of additional holiday over the summer—fifty-two or fifty-three days!—one might be able to write another long poem.[30] As though inspired by the idea, Ammons continues, praising his chosen measure of verse:

> this measure, maw, can grind
> up cancers and flourish scarfs of dandelions, manage the
> pulp of hung ticks and be the log the stream flows against
>
> for a whole year: its mesh can widen to let everything
> breeze through except the invisible: it can float the
> heaviest-bloodied scalding dream and sail it into the high
>
> blue loops of possibility: *it can comprise the dull*
> *continuum of the omnium-gatherum*, wait and wait, without
> the alarm of waiting, getting as much being out of motion
>
> as motion out of being: multiple and embracing, sweet
> ingestion, the world bloat, extension pushed to the popped
> blossoming of space, the taking of due proportion's scope.

> (*Sphere*, 41.481–92; emphasis added)

Ammons's preferred verse form is a maw, a greedy mouth feeding on everything that comes its way. Nothing is filtered out on the ground that it is unsuitable for poetry. This is not to say that it does not also generate lyricism from time to time. What a reader also needs to admit, however, is that probably not since Robert Browning (1812–89) has there been a poet of such forward drive in his or her poetic line when Ammons is writing at his best in this style.

Ammons does not acknowledge that the greed at issue is marked for the reader less by what the poem can absorb than by what it keeps telling us. To be a greedy writer in the way that Ammons enjoys is also to generate a greedy speaker and hope for a greedy reader. The only resistance that the verse form meets is that each tercet is like a log over which the stream of experience flows. Part of his consumption is, Ammons cheerfully admits, "the dull / continuum of the omnium-gatherum," the mock-Latin expression telling us that, in its own way, *Sphere* is a miscellany. It is not, then, a deliberate *selection* of anything but an artfully devised *collection* of everything over an arbitrarily chosen period of time; it aims to include rather than exclude, to give the sense more of life than of autobiography, to preserve aspects of the poet's experience that the stewards of literature—anthologists, as well as professors—might consign to the ephemeral or marginal.[31] And it is this aspect of the poem that needs to be taken into account when associating it with the everyday. Understood in this way, *Sphere* would involve a revaluing of the miscellany; indeed, it would offer itself as a continuous *self*-miscellany and hence challenge one of the usual canons of literary composition. The poem invites us to contemplate it not as a polished work of art—"I'm sick of good poems," Ammons exclaims (*Sphere*, 138.1652)—but as "dumb, debilitated, nasty, and massive" (138.1654), and in doing so it also asks us to adjust the meaning of *contemplation* as used in section 67. If contemplation has generally been patient and, in a way, selective, looking to "the / whole motion," Ammons asks us to expand it so that it includes "all the motions," including the unattractive ones, and invites us to reflect on them as we go along. The Many is not to be subsumed too neatly or too readily into the One. Nor is there, perhaps, a single, identifiable whole into which they will eventually fold, even after veering in one or another direction any number of times. All the same, the deflation of poetry always harbors a risk of Ammons writing badly and excusing himself by way of an appeal to an alternate poetic. Might it be that the reader is not "sick of good poems" and has no reason to be?

*

Aesthetic contemplation often resembles religious contemplation, but the differences between the two are significant. A Christian engaged in contemplation participates in the living mystery of Christ and over time is decisively changed by it: love of God nourishes love of the kingdom. Yet in its main current aesthetic contemplation requires a distance to be maintained between the beholder and the beheld, a distance that Kant thematizes by way of disinterest.[32] We can be moved by poems, but we are seldom moved to act justly with respect to others by reading them. In *Sphere*, Ammons brushes up against that high instance of aesthetic contemplation, Stevens's idea of a Supreme Fiction, and inevitably he recapitulates the master's way of distinguishing religion and poetry, though in more colloquial manner:

> when poetry was a servant in the house of religion,
> it was abused from all angles, buggered by the fathers,
>
> 120
> ravished by the mothers, called on to furnish the energies
> of entertainment (truth) for the guests, and made, at the
> same time, a whipping-post for the literal: poetry is not
>
> now a servant in the house of religion, the matter having
> become clear who got what from which: if you wish to get
> religion now you will have to come and sit in poetry's
>
> still center, bring your own domestic help, and resort to
> your own self-sustainment: if, leaving center, you make
> uses of poetry, you must represent them as uses, not as the
>
> true life, and in recognition of that you must dress your
> uses in rags as an advertisement that violations are underway:
> no more hocus-pocus derived from images and lofty coordinations.
>
> (*Sphere*, 119.1427–120.1440)

The "sexual basis of all things rare" becomes violent when religion and poetry meet in a hierarchical relationship, with the latter required to be *ancilla religionis* or *puer religionis*.

Not all hierarchies involve violence—Ammons himself refers to pyramids and mathematical sets with equanimity—but this one brings forth extreme sexual metaphors because for Ammons the hierarchy is inverted and because both religion and poetry lay claim to the same terrain. On Ammons's reckoning, poetry is transcendentally prior to religion, and this situation has finally been realized in the twentieth century. He moves too quickly to look fairly and evenly at the situation, for he is not at all bothered that poetry could mistreat religion by seeking to absorb it unproblematically (as in some examples of theological modernism) by forcibly reducing it to symbols of our condition and our desires.[33] Yet there remains "poetry's / still center." The conviction that poetry offers opportunities to be contemplated remains secure in the poem. There is to be "no more hocus-pocus." The old expression once used in the Middle Ages by magicians deforms the Latin *hoc est corpus meum* (This is my body), which marks the instant of transubstantiation during the Eucharist. Ammons's lesson is evident: we can contemplate but only if we do it naturally, without the consolations of religion, and without using poetry as a substantive substitute for religion.

Poetry is our means of contemplating nature, Ammons thinks; and, in *Sphere* at least, it is done in a voice rather than a sense of flesh or even a complete body. We adopt a Kantian attitude when it comes to beholding anything in poetry. Earlier in the poem, Ammons wittily tells us:

> I know Matthew Arnold is not

> far off: he's going to come roaring out of the woods, deeply
> offended by the briars of limber limbs, and mount up on a
> high stone chair and declaim to the woods: he's going to

> reinaugurate the distinctions and subordinations that make
> sense: he's going to turn the lofty lofty and broad and
> force the miniscule into its residence. (30.354–60)

Arnold has not been far off at all, it seems; perhaps he has been declaiming to Ammons from his "The Study of Poetry" (1880), in which he declares that the future of poetry consists in its effective replacing of religion in society. Nor is Wallace Stevens, the architect of Supreme Fictions that he hopes will replace religion, very far away.[34]

We meet Stevens glancingly in the poem before this passage, however, in section 57, when Ammons tips his hat to "Notes toward a Supreme Fiction," and there has been a sly allusion to his "Anecdote of the Jar" in the introductory lyric. Ammons encounters Stevens here by approaching the poem stealthily, by defining belief, as we have seen, in a negative manner, but then he makes a dialectical pirouette, "the need to disbelieve belief so disbelief / can be believed" (*Sphere*, 56.670–71).

In other words, one must trust in a world of positive fact: "there are in-
fidels only of fictions: not / a single temple has been raised to the fact
that what is raised // falls" (56.671–57.673). Like Lucretius, and also
like late Stevens, Ammons insists that reality for human beings is experienced as force and form:

> when you come
> to know the eternal forces realizing themselves through form
> you will need to lay on no special determination to assent
>
> to what demands none. (57.676–79)

If this seems like a bleak world, it is because the world is bleak. A poet,
however, can do something to ameliorate the situation, as Stevens
surely does:

> but if truth is colorless, fictions
> need be supreme, real supreme with hot-shot convincingness
> and lashes laid on lavishly for the doubter, and, per
>
> usual, regular dues: gentlemen of the *naked vision*, let us
> see straight: here we are today and here we are not tomorrow:
> if you kick the sand you are likely to raise some dust.
>
> (57.679–84; emphasis added)

Of course, this is not quite what Stevens says since, for him, Supreme
Fictions suspend the claim of truth: we willingly believe in something
that we regard as a fiction.[35] But Ammons's scientific training has made
him more hardheaded than Stevens. Modern science seeks to replace
our model of reality, one based on experience, with one it has itself developed, a model based on method. It seeks to be "supreme" but not a
theology or a Fiction. Fictions are like makeup; they can and should
seduce us, as John Coltrane does in his jazz album *A Love Supreme*
(1964), which Ammons quotes here in order to deflate Stevens just a
little.

Similarly, Ammons distances himself from another sort of aesthetic
contemplation drawn from religion, that of the "naked vision," as proposed by Dylan Thomas (1914–53). "Poetry is the rhythmic, inevitably
narrative, movement from an overclothed blindness to a *naked vision*
that depends in its intensity on the strength of the labor put into the
creation of the poetry."[36] For Ammons, unmediated vision must be led
back to simple straight seeing in poetry as in what passes for religion;

otherwise, one might miss what is right in front of one's face.[37] Θεωρία
as contemplation of the heights, in which union presumes death, might
well exact too much from him and must be ratcheted down to observation.[38] Nonetheless, Ammons is more ambivalent about visions than
he suggests when Dylan Thomas comes to mind. He turns his attention
to them in section 85. The segue is television, but the impetus is unfin-
ished business with the gods:

> you can't keep visions selective enough: they
> fill up with reality, too gravid grown to keep off the ground:
> as we return to the dust from which we came, the gods die
>
> away into the sky, the womb of gods: from the common
> universalized materials we ascend into time and shape, hold our
> outlines and integrations a while, then stiffen with the
>
> accumulations of process, our bodies filters that collect
> dross from the passages of air and water and food, and begin
> to slow, crack, splinter and burst: the gods from the high wide
>
> potentials of aura, of encompassing nothingness, flash into
> concentration and descend, taking on matter and shape, color
> until they walk with us, but divine, having drawn down with them
>
>   86
> the reservoirs of the skies. (*Sphere*, 85.1009–86.1021)

Visions are not of a permanent spiritual world, and after death we do
not ascend to any gods there. If anything, the divinities are so heavy
with reality that they spend their days with us on earth as avatars of
light. The *templum*, that reservoir of the skies, is where we turn our
heads, looking for a sign, until we pass away, and it has a lasting effect
on us. The gods "have communicated something of the sky to us making us / feel that at the division of the roads our true way, too, / is to
the sky" (87.1035–37).

Once again, Ammons's view of how the gods manifest themselves,
exposing themselves to our beholding, resembles that of the Greeks, at
least Homer. We remember the opening of the poem, with its rewrit-
ing of a commonplace: "fools crop up where angels are mere disguises"
(*Sphere*, 1.2). And we remember too that the presence of the gods is
recognized in ordinary human beings by a sparkle in their eyes or some

other physical feature. Thus, Helen perceives Aphrodite, who has taken on the appearance of an aged woman:

> She, as she recognized the round, sweet throat of the goddess
> And her desirable breasts and her eyes that were full of shining,
> She wondered, and spoke a word and called her by name.[39]

Ammons, surprising the more skeptical of his readers about the gods, says: "they will return, quick / appearances in the material, and shine our eyes blind with adoration // and astonish us with fear" (*Sphere*, 86.8–10). (The adjective *quick* is nicely placed here: the gods are briefly testified as alive before they are deflated into sudden glints or flashes in material things.) Notice that Ammons reverses natural theology. Instead of passing from nature to the gods, he attends to the gods returning to nature. Why will the gods always return? Why can we not demystify them completely, once and for all? Because human beings think both concretely and symbolically, and therefore we cannot help but see more in the world than is strictly there. Our challenge "is that in the future we can have the force to keep / the changes secular," and the "one: many problem" is one resource by which we may do that, along with "set theory, and / symbolic signifier, the pyramid, the pantheon" and so on (87.1039–41).

*

We have noticed Ammons's unease with one hierarchy, that involving religion's claim to primacy with respect to poetry, though that is not the case with another, that of male and female, presented as a polarity but treated as a hierarchy in section 145; and we have seen that Ammons appeals to pyramids and sets as models of hierarchy (as in John von Neumann's hierarchy of sets). Also, we have seen that he rejects contemplation as spiritual ascent while affirming it as descent to the depths of the unconscious. In general, however, *Sphere* is a poem that directs its author and we its readers to look horizontally, much like Aristotle in Raphael's fresco *The School of Athens* (ca. 1510) and Ammons's own "Corsons Inlet." The "true mystery," we have been told in section 50, is what survives an overly simple method of investigation. Earlier, I took this to mean that, for Ammons as for scientists in general, mystery is no more than something unexplainable in terms of the viable theories of the day: its complexity cannot be comprehended at the moment. In principle, there is nothing hidden in the cosmos. But it can also mean the mystery of what is true, that which is flush with the natural world about us. We remember Wittgenstein telling us in the *Tractatus Logico-Philosophicus* (1921): "Not *how* the world is that is the mystical, but *that* it is."[40] The sheer fact that there is something rather than nothing is, for the younger Wittgenstein, what cannot be explained by reference to the principle of sufficient reason. No interest is shown in how the divine approaches the soul. Ammons would incline to Wittgenstein's view, yet for the most part he is less interested in contemplating the world about him, the earth and its place in the cosmos, than in poetry as affording a still moment in which one can ponder the motions that pass through a poem. Until the very end of the poem, contemplation is less the adoption of an aesthetic attitude than attention to an aesthetic process, an imagined coming together of diverse parts and integrating (if often delusive and finally vanishing) whole.

One of those motions to be pondered is sexual, as we have seen; another is political. When politics finally appears in Ammons's sphere of regard, it is not a question of the whole planet or the politics of local place—a prefiguring of the slogan "Think globally, act locally"—as one might have imagined from the title *Sphere*; it is restricted mostly to the United States and the level of the nation-state, although, as noted, there is a gender politics that runs throughout the poem. Otherwise, there are commonplaces, with all the vagueness of *idle talk* in Heidegger's sense, such as "they say when egalitarianism is legislated into ultimate / ramification, legislation and effect click / heels into totalitarianism" (12.133–35). America comes to the fore only in sections 122 and 123 and is introduced by anxieties about the reactions of those who read Ammons's poems:

> I can't understand my readers:
> they complain of my abstractions as if the United States of America
> were a form of vanity: they ask why I'm so big on the
>
> one: many problem, they never saw one: my readers: what do they
> expect from a man born and raised in a country whose motto is *E
> pluribus unum*: I'm just, like Whitman, trying to keep things
>
> half-straight about my country: my readers say, what's all
> this change and continuity: when we have a two-party system,
> one party devoted to reform and the other to consolidation:
>
> 123
> and both trying to grab a chunk out of the middle: either we
> reconcile opposites or we suspend half the country into
> disaffection and alienation. (122.1456–123.1467)

All through the poem, the concern with parts and wholes has been seen abstractly, mostly by way of natural science, but now it is held up as inevitable because of the original thirteen colonies being united into the one country: *E pluribus unum* (Out of many, one: but the Latin is sharper, since it has thirteen letters) became the motto of the United States of America and was inscribed on the Great Seal—along with, on the reverse side, *Annuit coeptis* (He [i.e., God] favors the undertaking) and *Novus ordo seclorum* (New order of the ages)—after being approved by Congress in 1782. Since 1956, however, the official motto of the United States has been not *e pluribus unum* but "In God we trust."

Whitman appears in section 122, again in 123, once again in 125, and finally in 145, where we have already noted Ammons declining the role of being a "whit manic" (*Sphere*, 145.1738) and thereby separating himself all the more surely from Stevens. If we expected Ammons to hail Whitman as an early poet of the whole earth—"I see a great round wonder rolling through space"—we will be disappointed.[41] Our great poet of democracy directly appears only within the frame of being American, first as a responsibility for a citizen of the Republic ("trying to keep things / half straight about my country") and second as the sort of poet Ammons aspires to be ("I'm the exact // poet of the concrete *par excellence*, as Whitman might say" [123.1470–71]). (The French is doubtless a dig at Whitman's "too-extensive acquaintance with the foreign languages," as Henry James put it to Edith Wharton.)[42] Yet in his song of himself Ammons refuses any public or political role: not a word is said about Bloody Friday (July 21, 1972), America's involvement in the Vietnam War (1965–75), or the Watergate scandal (June 17, 1972). Rather, the poet represents himself as "for years singing // unattended the off-songs of the territories and the midland / coordinates of Cleveland or Cincinnati" or prizing "multeity and difference down to the mold under the leaf" (123.1473–76). Nonetheless, he has ideas about community:

I want you to be a poet: I want, like Whitman, to found

a federation of loveship, not of queers but of poets, where
there's a difference: that is, come on and be a poet, queer
or straight, adman or cowboy, librarian or dope fiend,

housewife or hussy; (I see in one of the monthlies an astronaut
is writing poems—that's what I mean, guys). (125.1491–96)

Whitman sang of "the love of comrades" in "For You, O Democracy" (1856) and also declared in the preface to *Leaves of Grass* that "the United States themselves are essentially the greatest poem," but he did not propose political unity by way of the aesthetic, as Ammons does here, though very much tongue-in-cheek (and giving women very few roles to play with respect to it).[43]

Far more moving than Ammons's identification of "my self, my work, and my country" (*Sphere*, 124.1486), however, are his earlier words on the formation of groups. At first, he allows metaphors of organisms to lead the way ("agglutinations," "binding syrup"), as though looking at the earth from far above it in the manner of Lucian's "Icaromenippus."[44] Then he turns to look on living individuals and their problems and does so less in the key of the kingdom than in the familiar tones of Whitman:

                                                                    I
know my own—the thrown peripheries, the strugglers, the cheated,
maimed afflicted (I know their eyes, pain's melting amazement),

the weak, disoriented, the sick, hurt, the castaways, the
needful needless: I know them: I love them: I am theirs. (17.199–203)

In the very next section, however, he adopts an aesthetic stance once again. "I do the ones I love no good," he writes, "I hold their pain in my hands *and toss it in moonlight*" (18.209–10; emphasis added). *Song of Myself* keeps opening toward other people, while *Sphere* keeps closing around Ammons, and, in the end, it is the individual "Ammons" (taken as a metaphor for unity), not America or the earth, that holds the poem together. And, when he speaks, toward the end of the poem, of "a united capable / nation, and a united nations! capable, flexible, yielding, / accommodating, seeking the good of all in the good of each" (154.10–12), there has simply been insufficient evidence of true fellow feeling in the poem to make the rhetoric seem anything but hollow.

Ammons is on firmer ground, at least as a poet, when, like a Stoic, he expands the context in which he meditates to such an extent that all our problems, no matter how grievous, seem trivial. Parts slide into a whole that opens onto a greater whole or even, after a twist, just another whole. Having found contemplation by way of descent into the mind, Ammons now turns to ascent, leaving the planet on which we all live. The expansion begins in section 149: "from other planets, / as with other planets from here, we rise and set, our presence, / reduced to light, noticeable in the dark" (*Sphere*, 149.1783–85). We pass from

Stevens's fat girl to a great many fat girls (even if they are "feather-light" at the center [22.262]). We see ourselves as we might be seen from Uranus or Neptune. The process quietly begins early in the poem: "sail, sail on, oblate spheroid" (22.261), he says immediately after a macabre imagining of a man being buried with a sandwich to eat. Right at the end of the poem, after he has extolled "the good of all in the good of each," he raises his eyes and his voice to something that encompasses all human goods and evils, desires and disappointments, the final resolution of the Many into the One. No surprise that he embraces all readers with the inclusive *we* in the poem's final lines.

We have already witnessed Apollo 16 venturing into space in section 39, and now we are invited to follow it, indeed, to go far beyond the lunar surface where it landed:

> with the
> mind thereto attached, to float free: the orb floats, a bluegreen
> wonder: so to touch the structures as to free them into rafts
>
> that reveal the tide: many rafts to ride and the tides make a
> place to go: let's go and regard the structures, the six-starred
> easter lily, the beans feeling up the stakes: we're gliding: we
>
> *are* gliding: ask the astronomer, if you don't believe it: but
> motion as a summary of time and space is gliding us: for a while,
> we may ride such forces: then, we must get off: but now this
>
> beats any amusement park by the shore: our Ferris wheel, what a
> wheel: our roller coaster, what mathematics of stoop and climb: sew
> my name on my cap: we're clear: we're ourselves: we're sailing.
>
> (*Sphere*, 155.1850–60)

This final section of *Sphere* is one of its most striking, in part because it offers a last image of contemplation, of *dilatio mentis*, although it does so without using the word.[45] This happens in several ways, beginning with the astronomer's θεωρία of gazing into the stars, which goes back to Plato's absorption with the "first things" (τα πρώτα).[46] These days we may not listen for "the high ranges of music" (153.1) that come from the spheres since we are no longer "oriented geocentric (with our heads in the harmonious / skies")" (20.235–36), but we know that the planets continue in their "holy roads" (153.1827). We see that the mind is set to "float free" as one rides on a galactic tide, an image nicely anticipated by the previous section's evocation of "the common tide of feeling"

(154.1841). Also, we are invited "to regard the structures": an allusion to Plato's *Phaedrus* where the gods travel in order to view the Forms and enjoy the blessed sight.[47] Finally, we are told that we are all "gliding," much like the birds of the air, including the crow in "Day": not before God, as Richard of St. Victor thought, but in a groundless nothingness of time and space. Ammons ponders the abyss, though differently than how Milton's Satan brooded on it. The very grammar of the final stanzas, centered on infinitive verbs, makes the lines we read seem to glide.

Ammons summons us to "go and regard the structures," which Plato once thought were ideal Forms but we now mostly take to be material forms. He calls them "the six-starred / easter lily" but not because our galaxy bespeaks the resurrection of the cosmic Christ. (Lilies were piously believed to have grown after the Resurrection from drops of Jesus's blood in Gethsemane.) Instead, he returns to the Greek myth of the lily springing from Hera's breast milk, spilled when she pushed the infant Hercules away from her when she realized that Zeus had tricked her into suckling a child of his infidelity. Some of the milk fell to earth and became lilies; some became the Milky Way.[48] Easter lilies have six petals, and for Ammons the Milky Way is an Easter lily with its four arms and the two protuberances of the center bulge. More Greek thought is gathered into what immediately follows: the Pythagorean belief that beans resemble the shape of the universe and that they link the living and the dead. The beans may indeed feel "up the stakes" (and we remember the sexual imagery of *Sphere*, 5.50–52), but there is no ascent, only a descent to Hades. Greek thought then yields to modern science, specifically to Einstein's special theory of relativity, which posits the identity of space and time relative to the motion of the frame of reference. And then this too yields to childlike entertainment with the image of the Milky Way being like a Ferris wheel or a roller coaster at a seaside amusement park. We can enjoy ourselves, giving ourselves over to "wonder," for as long as we live. This wonder, θαῦμα, is the beginning of philosophy, of friendship with wisdom; it is also the beginning of natural science, and, even more than the descent into the unconscious, it is the deep meaning of *mystery* for Ammons, the mystery of the cosmos that he contemplates in *Sphere* and that gives him and us, at best, a mode of natural contemplation that is always in process, never complete.

Mystère and Mystique

An unusual and memorable formation of contemplative poetry is to be found in Geoffrey Hill's masterwork, his one-hundred-quatrain poem *The Mystery of the Charity of Charles Péguy* (1983). Many readers may approach this poem, as with others by Hill, keeping in mind his remark that, when composing poems, he has a sense of "hovering" before what is being written.[1] This "hovering" is partly explicated by Simone Weil's observations on poetic composition in *The Need for Roots* (1949). "Simultaneous composition on several planes at once is the law of artistic creation, and wherein, in fact, lies its difficulty." Weil continues (and Hill follows her with appreciation):

> A poet, in the arrangement of words and the choice of each word, must simultaneously bear in mind matters on at least five or six different planes of composition. The rules of versification—number of syllables and rhymes—in the poetic form he has chosen; the grammatical sequence of words; their logical sequence from the point of view of the development of his thought; the purely musical sequence of sounds contained in the syllables; the so to speak material rhythm formed by pauses, stops, duration of each syllable and of each group of syllables; the atmosphere with which each word is surrounded by the possibilities of suggestion it contains, and the transition from one atmosphere to another as fast as the words succeed each other; the psychological rhythm produced by the duration of words corresponding to such and such an atmosphere or such and such a movement of thought; the effects of repetition and novelty; doubtless other things besides; and finally a unique intuition for beauty which gives all this a unity.[2]

A poet may well compose with the kind of structured contemplative openness suggested here and do so with even more planes in play, showing a receptivity that resembles a deeply skillful suspension before the lines appearing on the page, yet not offer readers a poem that is contemplative in any robust sense. It might be amusing, informative, or satirical and no more (although some contemplative poems will surely have these elements). There may be no attempt to press into a living mystery or understand a whole, let alone appreciate it or love it. Yet Hill's verse characteristically turns around what Weil calls "the possibilities of suggestion" that each word contains; it dilates on ambiguities of situation, meaning, and attitude, exposing different facets of a phenomenon to our contemplation of parts and wholes. We might recall Richard's attention to the birds hovering in the air. The word he uses is *suspendo*, which, when used participially, means "doubt," "uncertainty," and "ambiguity."[3] One contemplates amid these things and through these things. For Hill is definite that reflection involves language and does not float above it.[4] The poem before us is concerned with both *mystère* and *mystique*, each of which seems, at first, conducive to contemplation in the sense of the practice of κένωσις followed by ἐπέκτασις.

On beginning to read *The Mystery of the Charity of Charles Péguy*, however, the object of its contemplation is not immediately clear, nor is its mode of contemplation or how we are to read it contemplatively. It does not seem contemplative in Yeats's sense, being somewhat rough in its opening movement. The first jolts that we experience in reading it come from broaching the border between English and French. For the title of his poem Hill adapts the title of Péguy's *Le mystère de la charité de Jeanne d'Arc* (1910), but far more is involved than replacing "Jeanne d'Arc" with "Charles Péguy," although, to be sure, much is suggested by that insouciant transposition, and I will weigh some of it later. It is noteworthy that the venerable French word *charité*, which remains close to the Latin *caritas*, is rendered in the title by *charity* rather than *love*.[5] Hill's preferred word has not always been received with equanimity in English as an appropriate translation of ἀγάπη, the self-sacrificial love that Jesus exemplifies and commends. Both *loue* and *charite* were used by John Wycliffe in his English Bible (1382–85), but William Tyndale eliminated *charite* from his version of the New Testament (1526), regarding it as skewing the original sense of scripture. Had he wished to do so, he could have pointed his finger at Aquinas, for whom charity (*caritas*) is a theological virtue and love (*amor*) a passion, and for whom charity is a perfection of love.[6] Tyndale's scruple was influential, being accepted by Myles Coverdale (1535), Matthew's Bible (1537),

the Great Bible (1539), and the Geneva Bible (1557), but his appeals to
the original Greek were eventually seen to be theologically motivated
by his inflection of Protestantism. That model of high and low church
compromise, the King James Version of the Bible (1611), keeps both
charity and *love* as renderings of ἀγάπη, using one or the other depending on the context.[7]

In any case, the title of Hill's poem maintains both senses of *charity*,
"virtue" and "love," which discloses a theological choice on the poet's
part with regard to the divisions of the Reformation, one that is sympathetic to the Catholic Christianity of Jeanne d'Arc and Charles Péguy.
More, in translating the French word *mystère* as *mystery*, Hill has his
title swing in two quite different directions over the poem. There is the
threefold Christian sense of mystery, which indicates different ways in
which something is hidden. First and foremost, mystery is a property
of divine love, both the trinitarian life of God and the motivation for
creation and atonement; second, it bespeaks the hiddenness of divine
permission whereby evil is allowed; and, third, it points to the theological virtues (faith, hope, and charity). To these senses we may add the
nineteenth-century genre in which a murder is investigated with a view
to the crime being solved by a detective, the police, or the reader. The
second allusion works solely in English since in French this popular
genre is known as *roman à suspense* or *roman policier*. Both English and
French forms of the word are used to evoke the medieval mystery play,
however, as in the York Cycle, the Chester Cycle, and the Wakefield
Cycle in England and the *Passion d'Arras, Sainte Venice, Les actes des
Apostres* and *Le mystère du Viel Testament*, among others, in France. In
some ways, Péguy's *Le mystère de la charité de Jeanne d'Arc* harkens back
to the French mystery play in general, and we may recall the *Mystère du
siège d'Orléans* in particular. We begin reading *The Mystery of the Charity of Charles Péguy* with its generic markers moving before our very
eyes and are not quite sure of its relation to Péguy's original poem or
what to expect in what is to come.

When we open the original book publication of Hill's poem, we see
its first five stanzas printed on the recto and, on the verso, an epigraph.[8]
Only the name of its author, Charles Péguy, is given, and no reference
to the text from which it is taken is made. Accordingly, we turn our
eyes, read, and silently translate:

Nous sommes les derniers. Presque les après-derniers. Aussitôt
après nous commence un autre âge, un tout autre monde, le monde
de ceux qui ne croient plus à rien, qui s'en font gloire et orgueil.

(We are the last. Almost the ones after the last. Directly after us begins another age, a wholly other world, the world of those who no
longer believe in anything, who pride themselves on it.)[9]

The passage comes from "Notre jeunesse," which appeared in Péguy's
journal *Cahiers de la quinzaine*, on July 17, 1910, six months after the
publication of *Le mystère de la charité de Jeanne d'Arc* in the same organ.
Jeanne had variously haunted Péguy since his youth, and (for the most
part) the poem leans lightly on the essay, while the essay highlights
certain themes of the poem.[10] In the powerful testimony from which
Hill quotes, Péguy reiterates his intense fidelity to the ideals involved
in affirming the innocence of Alfred Dreyfus (1859–1935) and, more,
his unreserved investment in the *Cahiers* as a *journal vrai*, a periodical
that not only tells the truth but also tells all the truth, no matter how
wounding it might be to some of its readers.[11] Such was the position
that Péguy took in his "Lettre du provincial," the opening text of the
first *Cahier*, which appeared with the new century on January 5, 1900.[12]

The story of Dreyfus is well-known. He was a French army officer of Jewish lineage who was falsely accused of betraying France to
Germany and condemned to perpetual imprisonment on December 22, 1894. He was ceremoniously stripped of his rank on January 5,
1895, and deported to Devil's Island. His cause divided France. After
new evidence in his favor was found and a press campaign launched in
his support (initiated by Bernard Lazare [1865–1903]), a second trial
took place in 1899, and again he was found guilty. There was social unrest. He accepted a pardon from the president of the Republic, Émile
Loubet, which disconcerted his more ardent supporters, who thought
he should have declined the pardon and insisted on his complete innocence.[13] He was finally exonerated by the Cour de cassation only in
1906. "Notre jeunesse" affirms that it is Péguy and his friends, all associated with the *Cahiers*, who alone have been truly faithful to the republican and socialist allegiances of their youth, not the entrenched politicians and cultural writers of the day, who have capitalized on the efforts
of the pure Dreyfusards: "Toute la génération intermédiare a perdu le
sens républicain, le goût de la République, l'instinct, plus sûr que toute
connaissance, l'instinct de la mystique républicaine." (The entire intermediate generation has lost the republican sense, the taste for the Republic, the instinct that's more sure than all knowledge, the instinct of
republican "mystique.")[14] In that sweeping judgment are included the
pacifist Socialist leader Jean Jaurès (1859–1914), the vehement antimili-
tarist leftist Gustave Hervé (1871–1944), the anticlerical Émile Combes
(1835–1921), and the syndicalist Georges Sorel (1847–1922).

All these names are associated with the weakening of the shared high ideals of Péguy's youth, ideals summarized as *la mystique républicain*. We hear that Daniel Halévy (1872–1962) is wrong to argue, as he did in "Apologie pour notre passé," the *Cahier* for April 1910, that there was no reason for the Dreyfusards to claim to have been heroes. The proper lesson to be learned from the Dreyfus Affair, according to Péguy, is that truth and justice demand integrity and self-sacrifice for those who perceive them and that this demand is at one with patriotism.[15] The premise of the argument is evident, although surprising: "Notre dreyfusisme était une religion, je prends le mot dans son sens le plus littéralement exact." (Our Dreyfusism was a religion, I use the word in its most literal sense.)[16] Indeed, the pure Dreyfusism of Péguy and his friends, especially Bernard Lazare, stands as an "exemple unique" (unique example) by which we can try "connaître un mouvement religieux dans les temps modernes" (to understand a religious movement in modern times).[17] How will we know it? By seeing in its depths not love so much as "la virtu du charité" (the virtue of charity).[18] The Socialists did not have it; for them, the mistreated workers were more deserving of sympathy than an abused army officer was.[19] They could not see, as Péguy could, that the issue had to do with justice and truth, not sympathy. The lesson Péguy draws from the Dreyfus Affair will reverberate in the discussion of Hill's poem: "Tout commence en mystique et finit en politique." (Everything begins in mystique and ends in politics.)[20] The word *mystique* has already appeared several times in this chapter, but I will continue to leave it untranslated; it calls for significant precautions before it can be rendered as *mysticism*, as is commonly done, and as Hill does himself.[21] To be sure, Hill takes a clue from Péguy, who plainly thinks of *mystique* by way of certitude ("plus sûr que toute connaissance [more sure than all knowledge]"). Yet we must respect the word's place in the family group *mystère*, *mystique*, and *mysticisme*, each of which is associated with one or another mode of contemplation.

As we silently translate the lines from Péguy's essay just to the left of the start of Hill's poem, we form the words "We are the last" and "after us" and know that, since Hill has chosen the words and placed them in such a prominent position, we are discreetly encouraged to see him inhabiting that first-person plural, if only on its borders, and accept or decline the invitation to abide there ourselves, at least while reading the poem. Not that Hill is thereby aligning himself in any definite way with republican or socialist principles ca. 1910 or even with Péguy's side of the Dreyfus Affair, although he would surely prefer to support a group he understands to be "regenerative and sacrificial" as distinct from one composed of clerics, military officers, and government officials, whom he characterizes as "cynical and reactionary."[22] If we are familiar with Hill's earlier poems and criticism, we will see that, together with Péguy, he sees himself as belonging to a remnant in society, one that, among other things, cherishes respect, craft, and honest toil, which have been overshadowed in modernity by other values.[23] His position is not quite the same as Péguy's, though.

For one thing, Hill's concern with linguistic acts is not shared by the Frenchman or his generation. One would not expect Péguy to bristle at our moral judgments being eroded or deflated because the same language in which we make them is also used in a more colloquial way, often cheapening them, so that it can be difficult to tell the serious from the sentimental.[24] More broadly, taking a cue from the poet himself, we might speak of Hill as a "radical Tory," inheriting conservativism from Coleridge more than from Burke, and being exemplified best in someone such as Richard Oastler (1789–1861): an advocate of factory reform and humanitarian causes who nonetheless respected conservative values.[25] We should not expect Hill to identify with all Oastler's views (resistance to Catholic emancipation, e.g.). He receives nineteenth-century radical Toryism in his own way, positively in terms of identifying with the working classes, and negatively by resisting the cheapening of traditional values, whether by linguistic laxness or by moral laxness, in the name of one or another modernity.

Again, a caveat: in his poems Hill does not usually affirm, in a direct manner, distinct positive beliefs, natural or revealed, as a "committed individual." The views he holds are not so much openly endorsed as witnessed or staged in poems in which the divergent passions and thoughts of the actors, which are in each case often internally divided, can be seen to act on one another and are presented to be understood and evaluated, with all due care, by the reader.[26] Hill's Péguy himself was beset by contrary impulses, at once exhibiting, as Hill sees things, "the most exact and exacting probity, accurate practicality, in personal and business relations, a meticulous reader of proof," and being "moved by violent emotions and violently afflicted by mischance."[27] He is no model of balance.[28] Presumably Péguy saw something of his character and evolving situation around 1910 in the distorting mirror of his fellow countrywoman Jeanne d'Arc. Le mystère, however, attends only to Jeanne's situation and her vocation, not to her battles, capture, and death, which he considered in his earlier play, the unwieldy twenty-four-act drama Jeanne d'Arc (1897) with its many blank pages left for our reflection on what was happening or not happening in it.[29] Perhaps too Hill sees elements of himself and his situation in the broken mirror of Péguy, although he takes in a sweep of the Frenchman's life (but not all of it), including snippets of other voices, seeking all the while to understand the spring of his responses to human and divine suffering, his "charity."[30]

Speculation about Hill's motives when writing of Péguy and, behind him, his uses of Jeanne d'Arc as a national saint and warrior is not my brief in this chapter and the one that follows it. How Hill orchestrates his long poem as a contemplation is, however. This dense work involves the religious senses of *mystery* in an unusual way, one that we should not presume to be identical with Péguy's sense of *mystique*. For Péguy, the latter word denotes unconditioned moral adherence to an ideal, and, because of that, it can apply to both secular and religious absolutes, each of which can devolve into policy (*la politique*), which is of another and lower order than *mystique*.[31] (With respect to adherence to an ideal, we might recall from chapter 3 Hopkins's devotion to the chevalier in "The Windhover.") For the most part, Hill's poem views a *templum* drawn not in the sky but in a "radical soul" (*Mystery*, 5.6) as it experiences its own ambivalences and anguish in clinging to high moral standards while also drawing his poem as a *templum*. Yet there are also modes of contemplation in play that respond to several landscapes: *l'ancienne France*, Paris, the scene of one or another war (Sedan, Sudan, etc.).

My task is to make sense of a doubled object of contemplation— Péguy for Hill and the poem organized around him for us—each of which continually wavers rather than holds steady, and each of which looks, from different vantage points, to a virtue or a landscape instead of God as such, actually a theological virtue and several landscapes associated with someone far from being a Catholic in good standing with the church, someone committed to "a kind of truth, / a justice hard to justify" (*Mystery*, 5.83–84). Contemplation, if the word holds here, will not be an affective gaze, as it is for G. M. Hopkins, at least not primarily.[32] Nor is it an aesthetic regard, as it is for Wallace Stevens, or an attempt calmly to behold all the motions that go into a poem, as it is for A. R. Ammons; it will be a knotting of the moral and the religious, such as in *la mystique*, with its act of faith, natural or supernatural, its fierce protestations of love, and its equally intense disappointment when love fails and becomes *la politique*. Contemplation will hover over ambiguity and paradox, among other things. Nor will the poem's rhythms lull us into a meditative state; if anything, the roughness of enjambments and the half rhymes will interrupt such a state, if one ever establishes itself.[33]

Before embarking on reading Hill's poem as contemplative, I must return for a minute to the border between English and French. I take a first step into the poem, bypassing, for the moment, several large questions tightly coiled in the first stanza:

> Crack of a starting-pistol. Jean Jaurès
> Dies in a wine-puddle. Who or what stares
> Through the café-window crêped in powder-smoke?
> The bill for the new farce reads *Sleepers Awake.*
>
> (*Mystery*, 1.1–4)

The detail I have in mind stands out only if one brackets the English of the poem, the demands of the (admittedly flexible) rhyme scheme, the convention of silently translating from foreign languages so that one magically understands them just as well as one does English, and the passage from French to English as already experienced in reading the epigraph. It is straightforward: the bill for the "new farce" on the window of the Café du Croissant, 146 Rue Montmartre, where Jean Jaurès was shot at 9:40 p.m. on July 31, 1914, would have read *Dormeurs réveillez-vous*, not *Sleepers Awake.*

That there was no such farce, in French or English, playing in Paris in 1914 might make us uneasy about the historical reliability of the poem, as though a rhyme could supervene with respect to truth, but only a historian of modern French theater would be expected already to know a detail like that. A vigilant reader, however, will quickly see that, in giving the English title of a French farce playing in Paris, we are lightly warned that a broken line, conventional enough when dealing with a poem involving speakers of a foreign language, runs between fact and fiction in the poem, a line that quietly signals an emerging theme. Such a reader would likely recall that "Sleepers Awake" derives from the scriptures (Isa. 51:17; Eph. 5:14) and refers to the English translation of Philipp Nicholai's hymn "Wachet auf, ruft uns die Stimme" (1599), which is based on the parable of the ten virgins (Matt. 25:1–13); it was set to music by J. S. Bach in a choral cantata (1731) that became one of his most beloved compositions. The same reader might also recall Blake's "Awake! Awake O sleeper of the land of shadows!" from *Jerusalem: The Emanation of the Giant Albion* (1804–20) and know how surely Blake's imagination presses on Hill's, even when the latter crosses linguistic borders, as in the call "You sleepers, wake!" in Hill's stage version of Henrik Ibsen's *Brand* (1865).[34] The bleak visionary priest Brand is intransigent, much like Péguy. He says to his wife, Agnes: "in my book / the first commandment says, / 'You shall not compromise.'"[35] He demands of his dying mother that she give all her money (stolen from her dying husband) to charity, money that he would be in line to inherit; otherwise, he will not hear her confession and offer her the consolation of the Eucharist. She finally agrees to give nine-tenths, not more, and Brand does not shrive her. He invokes God's "redeeming wrath: 'You sleepers, wake!'"[36]

Apart from its religious senses—of stirring from one's slumbers to hear the gospel and of Christ coming when one least expects it—the title of the advertised farce has a political meaning. It was the Socialist rallying cry to workers who metaphorically sleep throughout their lives and do not see the glimmerings of a dawn of a new egalitarian society in which they have a decisive role to play. The new society, which Péguy called *la cité harmonieuse* (which is not quite the stricter *cité socialiste* of which he had dreamed earlier), and the Christian hope for the kingdom or the *civitate dei* are represented by Hill as held up to ridicule in the heady culture of *la belle époque*.[37] This special farce, mocking what it takes to be the false hopes of socialism and Christianity alike, is "new," but we know that there have been farces going back to the twelfth century in France. We also know that, for Hill, Clio, the muse of history, will be forever turning serious events retrospectively into farces.[38] Further, we know that farces gain their traction by treating situations that, if seen fairly, have their own pathos. The poem will return to sleepers at several points and with different ends in view: soldiers falling asleep (sec. 2), the dream of *la vieille France* (sec. 3), the dream of an agrarian army (sec. 3), the sleep of the French after the Franco-Prussian War (sec. 9), and the dead Péguy apparently asleep on a battlefield (sec. 10).

When Péguy wrote, "Tout commence en mystique et finit en politique," he was thinking of religious and secular ideals and how they are both forsaken in shabby accommodations of elevated moral standards to social and political circumstances. At least one might think so if, given his sense of *religion* in 1910 ("Notre dreyfusisme était une religion"), he could accept a clear distinction between the religious and the secular. Belief in the elevation and moral rightness of the Republic is *mystical*, but in a special sense of the word. In modern times, we usually reserve the adjective *mystical* to qualify experiences such as auditions, locutions, or altered states of consciousness that arise from direct awareness of the deity, and in this general sense visions fall under the heading *mysticism*. Yet the word has an older stratum of meaning in mystical or apophatic theology, in which God's essence finally escapes our predications, both positive and negative. We ascend to God only in and through the darkness of self-sacrificial love. Péguy reverses the etymological meaning of the word, which turns on μου (the closing of

eyes or ears), so that everything begins with *mystique* in the sense that
we must honestly respond to what we behold and what convicts us.
The response is mystical only insofar as it denotes a conversion of religious depth and intensity to an absolute, the eternal breaking into the
temporal, a conversion that should have ineluctable consequences for
the one who has made it.[39] We can think in these terms of Jeanne's firm
belief that saints have spoken with her and that her promise to Christ
requires her to give her day's food to poor children along with forming
an army to fight the English.[40]

We can also think of Jean Jaurès, but with a reservation. In his
younger days, he was a socialist prophet and philosopher admired by
Péguy, for whom he quickly became the very εἶδος of the pure Dreyfusard, but for Péguy he betrayed his intial calling (unlike Jeanne and unlike Bernard Lazare). He joined the parliamentary Bloc republicain in
1901 and supported Prime Minister Combes in his bid of 1902 to close
down twenty-five hundred religious schools as well as in his repressive
1904 bill on religious congregations. This Caesarism with regard to an-
ticlericalism was just as offensive, in Péguy's eyes, as reactionary positions that had been urged by the church.[41] Jaurès's attempt to prevent war between France and Germany in 1914 was centered on pacifist
workers in both countries being called to strike, yet, if this strategy
were successful, it would be as if France were capitulating to the annex-
ing of Alsace-Lorraine after Germany's victory in the Franco-Prussian
War of 1870.[42] Extreme French nationalists wanted revenge on Germany, not peace with it. In Péguy's view, *mystique* was succumbing to
politique in the very person of Jaurès.[43] It might be added that, when
for fear of being associated by the church with a heretic or, worse, a
witch, Charles VII did not attempt to rescue Jeanne from the English
after she had been brought to Château Bouvreuil, the *mystique* associated with belief in the divine choice of Charles as King of France col-
lapsed into *politique*.

The Mystery of the Charity of Charles Péguy presents itself then as a
poem that contemplates a man, or at least something he partly and perhaps unexpectedly embodies, in whom the traits of visionary and warrior cannot be separated, each being bound tightly in the other from
early on in his life and attached to one or another landscape; whose
love for the poor was both socialist and Catholic; whose firm vow
made in his secular marriage forbade him to participate in the church's
sacramental life; and whose fervor led him to write inflammatory prose
that perhaps prompted—or helped prompt—the assassination of Jean
Jaurès.[44] From its very framing and opening, *The Mystery* is not a poem
that seeks to judge cleanly between Péguy and either his apologists or

his detractors. And this is not because Hill does not admire the French-man, which he does despite some prudent reservations, but because the line separating history and fraud, integrity and zealotry, tragedy and farce, literality and metaphor, has been breached time after time in his case, as in those of many others before him.[45] Even Hill himself crosses those lines in the poem, if only to bear witness to the difficul-ties of making defensible moral judgments in intractable and overde-termined circumstances and in writing poetry that is not perjury.[46]

As we shall see, no relaxation of scrutiny is countenanced by Hill, nor is the broken line between fact and fiction taken to justify the thor-oughgoing rhetoricity of all factual statements and thereby transform deliberation into an exercise of the will to power. For Hill, human be-ings are weighted with responsibility and all too often marked by suf-fering because of that burden. The poem asks us to behold a "radical soul" as steadily as we can and, further, to acknowledge it as exem-plary while knowing that we do so standing on shifting ground and that the soul is also moving before our eyes or is hidden by the smoke of circumstance. Contemplation is summoned in a world in which a poet must negotiate language with scrupulous care, resisting debased cadences at least as firmly as he seeks freely and honestly to speak in his own idiom.[47] The kingdom concretely comes to us, in one or an-other of its profiles, in moments of resistance to misused secular and religious powers, not as something that will directly remove us from them.[48]

*

Uppermost at the start of the poem is *mystery* in the sense of solving a crime, although the death of Jean Jaurès on the last day of July 1914 cannot be separated from the start of the First World War at the begin-ning of August. Hence the "starting-pistol," which presumably begins a race of events. It is not, of course, the first shot of the war: that dubious honor would go to the assassination of the Austrian Archduke Franz Ferdinand on June 28, 1914, by Gavrilo Princip, a member of the rev-olutionary Young Bosnia group. Had Jaurès, a pacifist, not been shot, he would have done his best to prevent war between France and Ger-many. Hindsight tells us that unquestionably he would have failed, but his young assassin, Raoul Villain, could not have known that. Start-ing pistols can be adapted, illegally, to shoot live ammunition, but there is no reason to think that Villain did not have a handgun, so, if we read it literally, the poem begins with another slight departure from historical fact. Already open, a fissure will continue to widen as the

poem develops and, for all the action of the poem, call forth the reader's reflections on the differences between history and fiction, including the false start of the poem, which, it will turn out, is no murder
mystery written for our entertainment.[49] We know or think we know
just who is the "guignol" (*Mystery*, 4.25), the political puppet who appeared at the window frame. If we are mistaken, it will not be because
of an unexpected twist in a plot. Indeed, the assassin Villain is immediately doubled by Hill with "History": the who and the what both
stare through the café window, each holding "a toy gun" (1.5), trying
to make out through the gunpowder, which looks like powdered sugar
on a crêpe, whether Jaurès is truly dead.[50] Villain fired two shots, and
only the second hit the Socialist leader as he was leaning forward to
look at a photograph of the little daughter of his dinner companion.[51]
Doubtless Hill's Villain thought he was sweetening France by removing Jaurès from it.

Given the phrasing of the second stanza, we might think that two
crimes have been committed in a single shot, one by Villain (the death
of Jaurès) and one by History (the entry of France into World War I),
were History not using the assassin to do its business. If we appeal to
"the cunning of Reason" (*List der Vernunft*), as Hegel called Reason's
(or the Spirit's) ability to turn individual purposes to the will of History, we would be making a false step, for Hill punctures any such grandeur.[52] History is merely an actor wearily "rehearsing another scene"
(*Mystery*, 1.6) in a play that will be followed by another play and so
on ad infinitum. The death of Jaurès is not even in the opening performance of the play, which is more likely to be the Battle of the Marne,
just before which Péguy himself will be shot in the head, like Jaurès.
History as "supreme clown" (1.8) quickly becomes History as "dire tra-
gedian" (1.8), and we shift from *Sleepers Awake* to Shakespeare's *Julius
Caesar*. There, Brutus calls for the murder of Caesar, and in death Caesar becomes a martyr and a mountebank. He is a martyr to Rome (and
his ambitions) and a mountebank because his remedy for Rome's dis-
order, the bruiting about of him becoming emperor, would have cured
none of the state's ills. We remember Plutarch in his life of Caesar,
Shakespeare's source for his play (along with the lives of Antony and
Brutus), reporting a view of the day that arose after the death of Cras-
sus. It was that "there was now no other possible remedy for the disease of the state except government by one man," a view that was as be-
guiling to Pompey as it was to Caesar.[53] A classical republic in a time of
crisis frames our understanding of a modern one, and Jaurès becomes
a martyr to the Socialist cause and a mountebank in addition, for his
solution to keeping peace—a massive strike of workers in France and

Germany—is felt by some—radical French nationalists in addition to
the *Cahiers* group, though each for his own reasons—to be woefully
inadequate to the malady of the time.

This leads Hill to introduce Péguy. We first hear his name in conjunction with his inflammatory words against Jaurès in "L'argent suite,"
the *Cahier* for April 27, 1913, in which the Socialist leader is polemically
identified with Louis XVI being led to the guillotine in order to preserve the Republic:

> Je suis un bon républicain. Je suis un vieux révolutionnaire. En
> temps de guerre il n'y a plus qu'une politique, et c'est la politique de
> la Convention nationale. Mais il ne faut pas se dissimuler que la po-
> litique de la Convention nationale c'est Jaurès dans une charrette et
> un roulement de tambour pour couvrir cette grande voix.

> (I am a good republican. I am an old revolutionary. In times of war
> there is only one policy, that of the National Convention. But let no
> one hide the fact that this policy of the National Convention means
> Jaurès in a cart and rolling drums to block out his powerful voice.)[54]

Three questions come in a rush without waiting for answers. The
reader will have to live with them and perhaps try to answer them,
solve the mystery by going back and forth while reading the poem. For
Hill, the questions are open, which is part of his contemplative procedure; but the reader is doubtless tempted to seek answers:

> Did Péguy kill Jaurès? Did he incite
> the assassin? Must men stand by what they write
> as by their camp-beds or their weaponry
> or shell-shocked comrades while they sag and cry?
>
> (*Mystery*, 1.13–16)

The first question must be answered in the negative unless one takes
History to have suborned Péguy along with Villain. The second is
likely to be answered affirmatively—we cannot ignore the rhyme of
incite and *write*—with the caveat that the incitement was metaphoric,
not directed to anyone in particular, and was published over a year before the assassination took place.[55] Yet Péguy's words stirred up passions that were already inflamed by the circumstances. "So you spoke
to the blood" (4.31), Hill pointedly reflects at the end of section 4, adding that Jaurès was "killed blindly, yet with reason" (4.29) (not *by* reason, note), a judgment that sits awkwardly with his later exculpatory

remark: "The guilt / belongs to time" (4.28). The lines open out in two directions: the guilt is consigned to the past (including as gilt), and it is a matter of the zeitgeist. The contemplating mind goes back and forth until a whole is found that will hold the two things together.

More complex, and more moving, is the third question. Must one adhere to one's words? Of course: one's word is one's bond.[56] Yet many merely "stand by" what they have said in the sense of putting a distance between themselves and their words. One might well ask whether one is responsible for acts based on the literalization of one's metaphors, especially when performed by a political extremist? After all, to what extent must one adhere to the consequences of one's words when those consequences make their way down unexpected pathways of the past into the present? If they helped in any way or to any extent lead the nation into war, must one therefore be loyal to soldiers at the front and assist them in their distress, to which one has contributed? This final question is almost beside the point, for Péguy was already in uniform on the day that Jaurès was murdered. He left for Coulommiers and then for the Eastern Front on August 4, 1914, the day on which Jaurès was buried.

The following stanza is set in the brief time between Jaurès's death and before Péguy's mobilization and poses a further, more searching question:

> Would Péguy answer—stubbornly on guard
> among the *Cahiers*, with his army cape
> and steely pince-nez and his hermit's beard,
> brooding on conscience and embattled hope?
>
> (*Mystery*, 1.17–20)

The rich conjuration of the author and editor standing in his shop, Boutiques des Cahiers, 8 rue de la Sorbonne, emphasizing the literary-military-religious traits of his character and perhaps reminding us that the windows of the establishment were sometimes smashed by his political opponents, does not allow us to forget the start of the question or gloss over all that the dash stops from being said. Would Péguy answer *to* the situation he has perhaps precipitated? Would he answer *for* it? As already seen, he answers to the situation, for he immediately responds when called to join the war effort, and we are left to anticipate whether his death, as the nation receives it, will show that he also answers for it, in one or another mode of expiation and leave us to wonder whether the nation also answers for Péguy's death in order to gain something from him. Will he die for being faithful to the truth as he sees it or for distorting the truth? The question cannot be avoided when we read that Péguy is "Truth's pedagogue," at once the self-appointed teacher in the *Cahiers* of a definite truth, one that any honest, rational person should be able to see, and the one who willfully takes it on himself to teach Truth what is surely true. If we are to contemplate Péguy, we will find it difficult to get him into focus in order to do so with satisfactory clarity of mind. What we see is, as we learn later, "a kind of truth, / a justice hard to justify" (5.83–84). We have come a long way down from θεωρία and its Christian developments. We are not to contemplate the heights of being with sure intuitions but rather to consider the gaps between reality and its representations.

Like many a filmmaker before and since, Hill's action after posing a defining contrariety in a character is to pan out from the scene and offer a long perspective in which the actions of the hero might be justified (or at least be partly explained) or revealed in the full magnitude of their consequences (or exposed as finally trivial) by being set in a broader context.[57] We pass from 1914 to 1916 and view, panoramically, the march of French soldiers to the debacle of Verdun, and we do so by way of silent film, which turns the tragedy of thousands of men about to be killed by Gatling guns into a farce: the slowness of only sixteen frames a second passing through the projector makes the soldiers stagger like drunken cartoon characters. The "violent" inconsistency between the soldiers inebriated on patriotism and the horror to which they march is rendered "calm" by the mode of representation, which enables us to see the march over and over again, and Hill tries to keep both reality and representation in tension by virtue of his panning technique and the "juddery" rhythms of his stanzas. The flicker of light captured by the old film looks like St. Elmo's fire (yet we know the real fire of which they will soon become victims), while the scratch marks on the film (known as *rain*) change the appearance of even the weather. The reel of film does not neutrally record the facts of history so much as distort them so that the soldiers "go reeling towards Verdun" (*Mystery*, 1.32). Representation gains the upper hand over historical presence. They are shot by film passing through the gate of a projector before they are shot by the Germans with bullets being fired, many times faster than the frames of film can pass through the camera. (Gatling guns fired two hundred rounds of 0.5-caliber ammunition or four to nine hundred rounds of 0.30-caliber each minute.) The *mystique* of the Republic is quickly mown down by what Péguy judged to be its direst enemy, modernity. Two sorts of machine lay claim to "victory," despite D. H. Lawrence's assurance that such a thing would never happen: the camera and the Gatling gun.[58] In the end, "victory"

is snatched by modernity, not by Germany or France, first in the mode
of farce and then in that of tragedy. Hill reverses Marx's well-known
quip against Hegel that history follows tragedy with farce.[59]

*

When Hill replaces "Jeanne d'Arc" with "Charles Péguy" in the title
of his poem, he sets us to envisage in what way or ways the irascible
twentieth-century French author is both like and unlike the visionary
fifteenth-century French maid. Both hail from Orléans, as we know,
and both have military-religious traits in their characters. *The Mystery
of the Charity of Charles Péguy* does not contain distinct textual surfaces or even separate layers addressing the poet's relation with La pucelle; instead, its concern with Péguy allows us to see, once or twice,
what the French writer retains of the maid as he has depicted her in his
writings of 1897 and 1910: her charity, her dedication to king and country, and her suffering for her beliefs.[60] It is not the deepest historical
reference in the poem. We have seen that the Roman Republic plays a
role in its first section, and it will do so, more discreetly, in the second
when Péguy is promoted by Hill from being a sentinel to a military tribune overseeing the "sun-tanned earth" (*Mystery*, 2.9) of August 1914
that serves as his centurion.[61] The very earth of France, with its hills
and valleys, its woods and rivers, is an active part of the battle against
the invading Germans.

French soldiers will find their home in the earth just as Roman soldiers did when they died in Caesar's conquest of Gaul (58–50 BCE).
For the Romans, "old Rome" was the Republic, the stability of which
Caesar disturbed, while for a Frenchman like Péguy the Republic has
an uneasy relation with *l'ancienne France*.[62] Is it a redirection of France,
one that also preserves tradition, as he thought, or a completely new beginning, as he believed was being taught at the Sorbonne? We will also
see that Hill elicits a still deeper historical reference to Joseph, who, in
the story related in Genesis, was sold into slavery by his brothers and
came into his own only in a foreign land. There, he interpreted Pharaoh's dream of the seven lean cows that devoured the seven fat cows
(Gen. 41:15–37). In the poem, the story is summoned by the allusion to
"the lean kine" (*Mystery*, 4.8) seen by Péguy in the mist of dawn. In his
editorial life in Paris, closer to what Husserl called *die Fremdwelt* (the
alien world) than *la cité harmonieuse*, Péguy will suffer at least seven
lean years, and he will also correctly prophesy a bleak future for France.

Also, we glimpse moments when Péguy and Jeanne haplessly converge in how History treats them, if in no other way. Were they heroes,

fools, or knaves? Were they self-deluded in their hope, if not in their faith and charity? The second question hovers over much of the poem, which, centered on charity, also recalls the other theological virtues, hope and faith. In the first section, we hear Hill paraphrase a line from the Frenchman's *Le mystère des saints innocents* (1912): "still Péguy said that Hope is a little child" (*Mystery*, 1.24). Actually, the Frenchman wrote: "Mais l'espérance est une toute petite fille" (But hope is a very small girl).[63] (In Hill's poem, the allusion is bitterly ironic, for Jaurès was shot, as we saw, when he leaned over to see the photograph of his companion's little daughter.) The half rhyme of *child* and *world* is allowed to let something fall out of focus that will try to snap back in the following section of the poem (and that will be picked up again at the start of sec. 10). But not before Péguy is once more presented in the light of his true paradox: "Footslogger of genius, skirmisher with grace / and ill-luck, sentinel of the sacrifice, / without vantage of vanity" (2.4–7). An indefatigable editor of the *Cahiers* for fourteen years, though one who did not impose his views on any text he accepted for publication, none of which, excepting his own "Notre jeunesse," was ever a towering achievement, Péguy was perhaps no more than a "footslogger" in the literary world, forever trailing authentic genius, even in his original writings such as *Le mystère de la charité de Jeanne d'Arc*.[64] (On beginning active duty in the French army and thereby being given an opportunity to die for his country, he was, if seen in retrospect, promoted up the ranks of Frenchmen.)[65] Still, he was a genius in his selfless editing and exacting proofing of the *Cahiers*; he had a strong natural aptitude for the work.[66] Small, irregular battles with divine Grace occurred throughout his life, and his writings sometimes achieved literary grace, despite (or because of) his departures from *le style bon français*, shown chiefly in his digressions in prose and his rhythms of repetition with slight variations in verse.[67] His ill luck is like playing the difficult game of *jeu de grâces*, in which a hoop is thrown and caught by two sticks, and on which he puns in *Le mystère des saints innocents* (1912).[68]

No doubt Hill's diction, centered in ambiguity, oxymoron, paradox, and allusion, provides one way in which his contemplation of Péguy is able to condense many features of his subject and requires a new attunement of our gaze—the poem keeps amplifying itself before our very eyes—but it is not the only way or always his most impressive manner. Consider the stanzas that follow the vision of the childlike soldiers who are "taken home" to the grave in the soil of their native country. The first two lines, especially, exhibit a calm gravity when faced with human suffering and are spoken without evasion or ornament:

Whatever that vision, it is not a child's;
it is what a child's vision can become.
Memory, Imagination harvesters of those fields,

our gifts are spoils, our virtues epitaphs,
our substance is the grass upon the graves.

(*Mystery*, 2.14–18)

The child is Hope, of course, but also Jeanne, who had her first vision at thirteen years of age in her father's garden.[69] She claimed to talk with Saints Catherine, Margaret, and Michael, who told her to fight the English and have the dauphin Charles consecrated king in Reims, and she was only sixteen when she set out to do what they required. Péguy's vision, which is that of a mature man, is most poignantly expressed in *Ève* in the lines "heureux ceux qui sont mort pour la terre charnelle" (happy those who die for the carnal earth), which Hill will cite as a poem "We still dutifully read" (7.16): apparently, in his estimation, it is not a work of genius.[70]

Péguy's Horatian sentiment is not part of Hope's vision or Jeanne's either, but as Hill says, with a pathos more compelling than in his cultivation of double genitives and tropes: "it is what a child's vision can become" (*Mystery*, 2.15). War is a consequence of Jeanne's angelic vision or Hope's vision. *Mystique* becomes *politique* in its military mode, and we see the death of Jeanne's soldiers along with those of Caesar's, those fighting against Prussia, and the twentieth-century French in the Marne, Verdun, and elsewhere.[71] (Later, they will all become toys, "tin legions lost in haystack and stream!" [5.48].) We remember both military campaigns, among others, and we can only imagine the hopes and pains of the soldiers. Efforts of memory and imagination are all the spoils we gain from such suffering, along with the life and peace we enjoy, and the conventional epitaphs we chisel on the gravestones of the soldiers and memorials are an index of our limited virtue. Our gifts are not truly our own; we have taken them from the dead, as when we walk freely or when we benefit from elegies we write at our desks. For we are "embusqués" (6.5), as Hill will sharply remind us in section 6; we have office jobs and armchairs and can speculate on somber affairs in comfort. Or as he says in the passage quoted: "our substance is the grass upon the graves" (2.17). The line suggests several things at once: our essence is ephemeral, our wealth is transitory, and even when alive we stand on no solid ground. By now, however, we have learned how Hill mines English in writing his poem, and we may well feel that the play of *sub-* and *upon* is no more than a verbal reflex on his part.[72] It is as though we hear the steady humming of a paradox machine in the background, just as we sometimes hear the whirling of an ambiguity machine turned to its maximum setting.[73]

A voice interrupts Hill's solemn meditation—"Du calme, mon vieux, du calme" (*Mystery*, 2.19)—along with our own, and we recognize Péguy's cadence ("Ah, mon vieux, les mots! Les mots!") and thus hear a justification for Hill's peculiar mode of linguistic attentiveness.[74] The second section ends with four masterly stanzas in which several threads are tied together without losing their individuality and several leaps are perfectly performed:

> How studiously
> one cultivates the sugars of decay,
>
> pâtisserie-tinklings of angels "'sieur-'dame,"
> the smile of the dead novice in its plush frame,
> while greed and disaffection are ingrained
> like chalk-dust in the ranklings of the mind.
>
> "Rather the Marne than the *Cahiers*." True enough,
> you took yourself off. Dying, your whole life
> fell into place. "'Sieurs-'dames, this is the wall
> where he leaned and rested, this is the well
>
> from which he drank." Péguy, you mock us now.
> History takes the measures of your brow
> in blank-eyed bronze. . . . . (2.19–31)

"Sugars" draws us back to the very start of the poem, with the "café-window crêped in powder-smoke," but this is not a violent act that might sweeten France's future, merely a diagnosis of how we make the past more palatable through nostalgia; for example, by retroactively forging a national culture by popularizing the story of Jeanne d'Arc. The voices that Jeanne hears become no more than the tinkling of a bell on entering a patisserie, such as Angelina Paris, 226 rue de Rivoli, Paris, and Jeanne addresses Saints Michael, Catherine, and Margaret as she would a man or a woman behind the counter wearing an immaculate white apron. (Six lines later, those polite forms of address will shift from angels to tourists summarily seeing the sights associated with the last days of Péguy, whom History has now installed as a patriotic hero and a canonical author.) The saccharine image of a shepherdess talking with angels in her father's garden might lead an impressionable young

man to think he has a calling to a religious order, but it does not nourish those who consume it, no matter how often they turn to it.

The parliamentary authorities in Paris have lost whatever *mystique*
they had, and all is now *politique*; it is just as Péguy, truth's pedagogue,
has taught the readers of the *Cahiers*. The lesson is over, the chalk has
been put down, but clear though the instruction has been that nothing has changed; there is politics as usual and the obligation to tell the
whole truth about it.[75] "Rather the Marne than the *Cahiers*," as a voice
from the *Times Literary Supplement* interrupts (*Mystery*, 2.25): at least
in battle one might be in closer touch with *la mystique* and away from
the endless chores of editing.[76] Indeed, it is being shot in the head (like
Jean Jaurès) on September 5, 1914, just before the Battle of the Marne,
that redeems Péguy, turning him into a canonical author and a national
hero, one who has expiated any responsibility for the assassination of
Jaurès and for any flaws in his character. He falls down dead in a field of
beetroots, as in slapstick, and rises, as it were, a monument of French
culture, with his bust cast in bronze in the corner of a park in Villeroy.[77]
The "strange Christian hope" (5.39) of resurrection, presumably an allusion to 1 Cor. 15:35–44, becomes no more than a civic act of one's
image being erected as a public statue in a secular state. We have passed
from a farce that mocks Christianity and socialism to Péguy mocking
the tourists who stop for a minute before his image, that of a socialist
hero and almost a saint. But can one honestly believe in such a transformation? Apparently, the statue of Péguy, for one, does not.

*

Religious contemplation is often nourished by dilation.[78] Is a contemplative poem therefore required to be a long one, let us say one such
as Péguy's *Ève*, which extends to 1,911 quatrains? Might it be of a more
modest length, such as *The Mystery of the Charity of Charles Péguy*,
which runs to 400 lines, not counting its possible addenda, the twenty-
one lyrics that constitute "Hymns to Our Lady of Chartres" and the
five lyrics entitled "Mysticism and Democracy"? Modern readers
might argue that, in poetry, it is the lyric that lends itself most fully to
cognitive and heartfelt attention: its concentration disciplines the reader's eye, which moves back and forth, from beginning to end, always
with the task of making a fuller, richer whole, which is precisely what
a longer poem will resist. It exceeds our regard, wearies it because it is
offered more and more dependent parts to be held together, not a simplicity that is inherently mysterious (or a set of intentional relations
with a text that are *rich*, *rewarding*, or *engaging* or however one wishes

to phrase matters). Even if we adopt an aesthetic attitude and seek satisfactions in fulfilling the imagination, not one's whole being *sub specie aeternitatis*, we will need an object that remains steady, at least in principle, so that we may take in its profiles one after the other, even if all of them are not offered to us. With a poem that tells us and shows us, time after time, that what seems to be its εἶδος is a matter of retroactive cultural and historical decision, a national fiction blithely presented as truth, one whose subject tried to teach the truth what was true, we might feel that contemplation itself is being frustrated at every turn. Yet we might also reflect that we are being invited to ponder the gaps between truth and representations of the truth and mull over what takes place there.

The Mystery of the Charity of Charles Péguy is a fairly long poem, certainly by the standards of English verse in the twentieth century. It is also a very dense poem, not a group of compacted lyrics leagued together by theme, structure, or narrative (as "Lachrimae" is, for instance), yet not a continuous poem, either, as Ammons's *Sphere* is.[79] We have perhaps seen enough of Hill's style of mining grammatical structures and rhetorical forms, how he thinks by way of the semantic thickness of language, including its parasitic uses, in order to read the poem; but to see how contemplation is leagued with this thinking is a task still ahead of us. The assignment cannot be avoided, for we are told, toward the middle of the poem, that we are "to step aside" from the evidence of war and, more, "to turn away" and "contemplate the working / of the radical soul" (5.5–6). Where Moses, faced with the burning bush, says to himself, "I will turn aside and see this great sight" (Exod. 3:3 [AV]), Hill asks us to turn to contemplate not God but a soul, one that is rooted in one or another landscape and must be uprooted to be beheld properly. We are to brood on the *working* of a soul, note, its action and not its leisured continuing attention, to which we are directed. We remember, however, that Péguy insisted that men of action are also men of contemplation.[80] In addition, it is not Péguy's own reflections that are at issue—his melancholy view of his lost youth or of his aging body, in both of which he thought he saw the kingdom begin to appear—but our reflection on how his soul toils and, if there are any, how other souls that resemble his perform also.[81]

We approach the center of gravity of Hill's poem when we recognize that for him contemplation is linked primarily not to mysticism, as it would be for many a medieval Christian, including Jeanne, but to *mystère* and *mystique* in Péguy's sense of the words. Howsoever the latter word is used, it never has the sense of one blessed individual beholding a vision of changeless transcendent truth over and above reason and to the exclusion of other people. And, as he admits, *mystique* always ends in *politique*, whether it be parliamentary, university, or socioliterary acts of convenience or compromise, even if it sometimes avoids being completely devoured by it.[82] Contemplation is not necessarily undone in countenancing that downward slide, but it is complicated by it and somewhat diverted from the main sweep of its tradition. Only somewhat, however, for Hill's moral-political gaze seeks to be an abiding reflection on the "radical soul" by way of Péguy, and the tradition prizes not only the discipline of sustaining a gaze when set on a suitable object but also the prizing of that regard as having, in its own way, a redemptive quality.[83] In religion, this quality consists in one's response to God's promise of redemption. In poetry, one can redeem a person who is irreducibly complex from political and religious processes of simplification and what is exemplary from what is particular. For the poem directs us not to a "radical soul," Péguy, so much as to "*the* radical soul" (5.6; emphasis added). The particular crosses the general; our eyes might have to turn away from war, but eventually they will also have to turn away from Charles Péguy in all his personal and historical individuality, including his vexed relations with the church, if we are to follow Hill's directive and consider the Frenchman as exemplary. But of what? Before beginning to answer that question, we need to know what *radical* means.

First of all, *radical* denotes someone whose thoughts and acts go to the root of a matter, usually when religion or politics is the concern. Péguy is unreservedly oriented to *la mystique*, understood both as truth and as value, indeed, the supremely true value of an honorable cause, and he is absolute in this undertaking, whether it be to socialism or Catholicism. His work is to preserve *la mystique*, even when all others backslide to the exigencies of *la politique*. Yet, as we recall from Richard Oastler, radicality need not be deracinated. For, second, Péguy's roots are in the peasant life of *l'ancienne France*, and it is there that his Catholicism and socialism were born and took their basic shape. (In a moment of dark comedy, he becomes fully one with his roots by, as we have seen, dying in a field of beetroots.) He must draw from the past, *his* past, in order to become a true radical, Hill's "radical Tory."[84] What this means is partly suggested some lines later when Hill evokes "seminal verdure from the roots of time" (5.24): a radical is in touch with the lushness of origins but is not thereby a Romantic in love with a glorified view of the Middle Ages.[85] A man of the country and a defender of its values, Péguy is an exile in Paris, home of the *parti intellectuel*, much as Joseph was in Egypt. Not that one should cleanly assimilate Péguy to *l'ancienne France*. His radicalism is thoroughgoing, his commitment to truth (as he sees it) involving "an apostasy and a perpetual renunciation."[86]

The reader's eye is gradually educated in reading Hill's poem; it is led into the cracks of words, which bespeak the polarities of a life that seeks to be moral in intractable situations that, were they abridged, would offer more comfortable paths, and the perception is beautifully drawn out to vistas of a moral or religious landscape. We first see this dilation in the third part of the poem, in the tender evocation of Péguy's home in the Faubourg Bourgogne, Orléans. Again, representation shapes reality: "Here life is labour and pastime and orison / like something from a simple book of hours" (*Mystery*, 3.11–12). Then, by extension, we see the land where he grew up, Château de Trie, where he stayed with the actress Simone Casimir-Périer, and Colombey-les-deux-Eglises, where his admirer Charles de Gaulle retired and where the ageing statesman read and reread *Le porche du mystère de la deuxième vertu* (1912). To these are added Chartres, which he first saw in 1900 and where he went on pilgrimage in June and September 1912, the second time to consecrate his children to Our Lady; the cathedral at Gisors, where, just before the start of the war, he meditated on the Day of Judgment; and St. Cyr's, the military academy where his fellow officers were trained.[87] Péguy's wealth as a person (which is distinct from his meagre personal wealth) is to be judged not only by what he has made his own in the land but also by its spiritual, intellectual, and military depths: "It is Domrémy / restored; the mystic strategy of Foch / and Bergson" (3.29–31). Here, we find Hill using the adjective *mystic* for the first time, and we wonder whether it is meant to translate *mystique*. It is worth pausing to see just how it is being used.

No doubt *mystic* looks back to restoring Domrémy, where angels told Jeanne that she must drive the English out of France: the slightly off rhyme of *Donrémy* and *army* says it all. And, of course, *restored* is hardly an innocent word here; if it implies restoration through Grace, it also conjures the Bourbon Restoration (1815–30) and its reactionary politics. Péguy is more interested in not losing touch with *l'ancienne France* than in retaining the heritage of Louis XVIII (1755–1824) and Charles X (1824–30), however. Then *mystic* is directly used to qualify Foch's military strategy in the war. To be sure, Péguy reassured his skeptical and weary troops when on retreat from the Germans and resting in Ravenel that "Joffre has a plan," and he surely believed in General Ferdinand Foch's overarching tactics into the bargain.[88] But far more than offense and defense appealed to Péguy. As Barbara Tuchman explains in *The Guns of August* (1962):

Foch's mind, like a heart, contained two valves: one pumped spirit into strategy; the other circulated common sense. On the one hand Foch preached a *mystique* of will expressed in his famous aphorisms, "The will to conquer is the first condition of victory," or more succinctly, "*Victoire c'est la volunté,*" and "A battle won is a battle in which one will not confess oneself beaten."[89]

Tuchman lets us see that Hill translates *mystique* as *mystic*, although we should hear the French word in the English if we are to understand Hill at this point. One might suffer martyrdom by virtue of being chosen by God to have converse with angels, as Jeanne did, but rank-and-file soldiers will die for the *mystique* of their general.

If we move on to the start of the next line, we hear that the philosopher Henri Bergson (1859–1941) is also accorded a "mystic strategy" (*Mystery*, 3.30). We must be careful here not to import Bergson's later interest in Christian mysticism from his *The Two Sources of Morality and Religion* (1932) into Péguy's thoughts before the First World War. The poet was entranced by the Bergson of *Creative Evolution* (1913) who affirmed the wholeness of life, how the events of our childhood converge on our adult days.[90] This is what Hill nicely calls "time-scent" (3.31). More generally, there is no doubt that, like many another of his generation, Péguy was attracted to Bergson's welcome emphasis on intuition, understood not as a cognitive act but as an experience of sympathy, for it breathed life into a university world effectively drained of it by the disciples of Renan and Taine. The Sorbonne was the "enemy's country," after all; its professors are aptly called the "lords of limit and contumely" (4.2), at once narrow and nasty, screening out the mystique of *l'ancienne France* in favor of historical and sociological method and, ultimately, their view of France truly beginning only with the Republic.[91] Bergson had himself been relegated to the Collège de France, where he could have less of an impact on students dutifully absorbing the prevailing doctrines of reductionism in the university world. Yet his philosophy was not the assault on rationality it was taken to be. For him, intuition could not be separated from the intellect. Péguy himself assures us: "Le bergsonisme n'a jamais été ni un irrationalisme ni un antirationalisme. Il a été un nouveau rationalisme." (Bergsonism has never been an irrationalism or an anti-rationalism. It has been a new rationalism.)[92] After evoking Bergson, Hill ponders a peasant army. Only from an organic peasant culture, he thinks (by way of Péguy), can one derive the "militant-pastoral" intuition that countries are truly defended only by the poor and destitute. This is the army "of poets, converts, vine-dressers, men skilled / in wood or metal, peasants from the

Beauce" and so on (*Mystery*, 3.41–42). Péguy sensed, as early as 1905, with the First Morocco Crisis, that war with Germany was inevitable: his *Cahier* for October 22, 1905, *Notre patrie*, was very plain in that respect.[93]

We are asked to contemplate Péguy's soul in its moment of mature awakening, in its final self-appropriation by way of "earth and grace" (*Mystery*, 5.10), during which Péguy overcomes the beguilements of imagining being accepted one day, with whatever degrees of condescension, by the Académie and the Sorbonne and becomes most truly himself. (We have been told earlier, at the start of sec. 4, that his country had been taken by his enemies before he woke, by which we are to understand the Sorbonne's disregard of old France and its values.) The inheritance of his soul is twofold, "its landscape and inner domain" (5.9), the recovery of countryside, road and village to say nothing of an internalization of the traditions and values of the Beauce. Once again, we approach the meaning of *mysticism* by way of *mystique*, although this time neither word is used. The army of France's rural poor is replaced by a version of the same people, now doubly transformed in Catholic terms. They are the biblical wise men, imagined to be on pilgrimage to Chartres, and "in a bleak visionary instant" (5.16) they become seraphim, angels enflamed with the love of God. True wisdom abides in holding to the Catholic faith, for Péguy, not in the political insights of Franco-German relations as developed in *Notre patrie*. Chartres can reasonably stand for Bethlehem because of the relic venerated in the cathedral, the Santa camisia, the chemise worn by the Virgin Mary when she gave birth to Jesus. The "landscape and inner domain" are caught up and more sharply accounted for in the lapidary statements later in section 5, the first of which is a rare moment when Hill brushes against Wallace Stevens. He does so only to recoil from him: "Description is revelation," the American poet wrote about Supreme Fictions, as we saw in chapter 7.[94] "Landscape is like revelation; it is both / singular crystal and the remotest things" (*Mystery*, 5.25–26), writes the English poet in sharp disagreement with that approach. His two claims need to be delicately separated and treated one at a time. Even though the second seems to explain the first, we cannot grasp the explanation without prior inspection of the simile.

"Landscape is like revelation": as always, we need to judge in which ways the first term is like the second and in which ways it is unlike it. Of course, landscape does not of itself communicate anything general or special of the divine to believers or unbelievers. It is a late medieval belief, however, that "the book of nature" has a legitimate place beside the Bible, if the former is read with the latter as guide. Such is natural theology, as usually understood within Catholicism. Hill goes somewhat further than this traditional view, contending that both natural theology and revealed theology can stimulate contemplation. For landscape makes something manifest that is more than the sheaves, furrows, and trodden ground. It can be read by the people as a network of signs and symbols precisely because the sacraments and teachings of the church have been sedimented, generation after generation, in the people and their rhythms of farming the land.[95] The different village bells announce mass, festivals, births, fatal sicknesses, deaths, the coming of the tax collector, the opening of the markets; they frighten away demons and invite angels to descend; they establish an "auditory landscape" in which the people live; and they give a sense of rootedness.[96] For the "Hedgers and ditchers, quarrymen, thick-shod / curés de campagne" (*Mystery*, 5.13–14), it has become second nature to see the sheaves as spires, the cathedral's ogives as wings, and the trodden ground as endlessly marked with the sign of the cross.[97] The angelus rings across the fields at six in the morning, noon, and six in the evening, as we hear several stanzas later, and everyone stops to pray; and, in a countryside in which "walled gardens" are "espaliered with angels" (5.48), it is hinted that it is perhaps understandable that an unlettered country girl might believe that angels have spoken to her. Péguy's nostalgia for the premodern world of *l'ancienne France* is channeled by Hill with only that slight check of skepticism.

Directly afterward, however, Hill is more forceful in drawing attention to how later representations can supervene with respect to historical presence. People read about Jeanne d'Arc in their homes and in libraries and experience "solitary bookish ecstasies" (*Mystery*, 5.49). The imbrication of religion and politics has been deflected into literature, doubtless tinged by patriotism, and not, we might suspect, literature of the highest kind: *ecstasies* is clipped coinage. Or sentimentality intervenes, as when the Battle of Sedan is remembered and France's loss compensated by people quoting Wilhelm I's generous remark on seeing the French soldiers in battle: "oh les braves gens!" (5.51).[98] Admiration for military leadership extends moreover to the British in what at first seems to be Clio's stutter in which *Sedan* becomes *Sudan*, the African country that was a French colonial territory from 1880 to 1960. We glimpse Charles George Gordon (1833–85), who was made *chevalier* of the Légion d'honneur by the French government in 1856; the motto of the legion is "Honneur et Patrie." Yet Gordon's genuine bravery is sentimentalized by history in the painting *General Gordon's Last Stand* (1893), now housed in the Leeds Museum and Galleries, where Hill would have seen it during his tenure at the University of Leeds.

There, the painter, George William Joy, represents Gordon in Khartoum, the capital of Sudan, in full-dress uniform, unarmed apart from a rattan stick, about to be killed by the Ansar. He is depicted "stepping down sedately into the spears" (*Mystery*, 5.52).[99] As interpreted in the painting (and with a half twist in the poem), his is an innocent, sacrificial death. As with the statue of Péguy, we are invited briefly to consider the gap between artistic representation and historical presence, which involves realizing that the gap itself stimulates contemplation as to what it engulfs: the differences between art and sentimentality, history and fraud, tragedy and farce, literality and metaphor, and so on.

Achard of St. Victor would have intimately known the rural world that Hill evokes here, and his "lands of likeness," in which the practice of contemplation makes us less and less unlike the God to whom we pray, are in effect recast by Hill as both earthly and ecclesial, with no firm distinction being able to be drawn between the two terms. Contemplation is chiefly horizontal for the Hill of *The Mystery of the Charity of Charles Péguy*, a matter of weighing the *like* in "Landscape is like revelation," a deepening of one's sense of reality, which does not prevent the common people he imagines to be cultivating the land from looking upward to receive "the gaze of God" (*Mystery*, 5.29) or downward to recognize "the roots of time" (5.24). Nor will it prevent Hill from lauding hierarchy in a special sense, as we shall see in the following chapter. Landscape, for the peasants of old France, is "singular crystal and the remotest things" (5.26). It is unique, and it is tightly ordered, a compressed version of the immense revelation from Creation to Apocalypse, about which they hear Sunday after Sunday at Mass: the truth as such, or gripping theater. (But is it tragedy or farce?)[100] And it concerns that which is remote, barely conceivable on the horizon of thought and belief, such as the transcendent Trinity, angels who bring messages to God's chosen, the lives of biblical persons (such as Joseph), the Crucifixion of Jesus, true God and true Man, and Creation itself.

This is how Péguy himself saw the landscape of the Beauce, we are reminded; he was at heart, and proudly so, one of those silent peasants on pilgrimage, never one to justify his views or his values. An anecdote from his school education at Lakanal Lycée, Sceaux, in which he declined a teacher's request to elaborate his correct gloss on a sentence from Jean de La Bruyère, reminds us of his intransigence: "Having // spoken his mind he'd a mind to be silent" (*Mystery*, 5.84–85).[101] This, Hill says, is his "one talent" (5.86), the ground of his single-minded adhesion to the *Cahiers* and his unconditioned fidelity to mystique. We are directed to the parable of the talents (Matt. 25:14–30), one of the parables of the kingdom. There, Jesus tells how the man who was given just one talent hid it in the ground for fear of losing it, only to receive the very rebuke of the master that he had sought to avoid. For Hill, however, Péguy digs up the talent himself and adds value to it over the course of his life before returning it to the ground where he dies defending France. He has enriched what he first received, "love, honour, suchlike bitter fruit" (*Mystery*, 5.88). Such is Péguy's contribution to the kingdom, "le royaume d'une incurable inquietude" (the kingdom of an incurable unrest), and it is no small thing.[102]

CHAPTER 12

"To Contemplate the Radical Soul"

Inevitably in a poem such as *The Mystery of the Charity of Charles Péguy*, which is partly centered on *mystique* and its slide into *politique*, we must witness the crucial scene of Dreyfus's military degradation. It stands as a counterpoint to the erection of Paul Niclause's bust of Péguy in the park at Orléans (*Mystery*, 2.29–36): the one Frenchman is absolved by the culture, the other is condemned by it. The degradation is introduced by way of French *laïcité*, which in effect rendered the state "the catholic god of France" (6.2). The nation receives a capital letter, and two lowercase letters in effect replace the deity with no more than a common idol. The *mystique* by which social justice presumes that one has participated in the mystery of divine justice is set apart. Everyone is to be treated equally under French law, according to the motto officially instituted in the Third Republic, *Liberté égalité fraternité*. Yet the Dreyfus Affair shows all too sharply how such abstractions can be abused. France, which should "dispense, with justice," instead acts with regard to a distinguished Jewish officer so as "to dispense / with justice" (6.1–2). A mere comma separates rectitude from indecency. As Dreyfus is disgraced, "There is no stir / in the drawn ranks, among the hosts of the air" (6. 16). The final phrase echoes St. Paul's invocation of the power of evil spirits in Eph. 6:12, to which I will return in a moment.

If there is anything like a classical *templum* in Péguy's France, as Hill conceives it, it is that which formed of itself in the sky over the Morian Court of the École militaire in Paris on January 5, 1895, when the Republican Guard tore off all the insignia of Dreyfus's commission. "A puffy satrap" breaks Dreyfus's sword over his knee with "ordered rage" (*Mystery*, 6.12–13): he is doing precisely what his superiors have told him to do, and he does it in a conventional order of events, thereby making his "rage" something of a show. (A prison tailor had removed all Dreyfus's buttons and stripes and replaced them using a single stitch the day before, allowing them to be torn off readily, and his sword had been filed so that it could easily be broken in two.) An augury is evident, according to Hill, but only indirectly, seen by way of representation, not presentation; it is "the weird storm-light" (6.16) that one finds in several periods of history. It is depicted in cheap visual representations of battles at Mars-la-Tour and Sedan, both of the Franco-Prussian War of 1870, the reverberations of which lasted throughout the Dreyfus Affair, right up to, and including, the entry of France into the First World War. The same eerie light can be found in the background of many of the engravings accompanying the novels of Jules Verne (1828–1905), some of which are set in a France of the future.[1] Also, there is a biting reminder that, like Dreyfus, the innocent Jesus was Jewish, and it was deemed that both should be sacrificed to save the nation (John 11:50). The very same stormy light can be found in Gustave Doré's depiction of the Crucifixion in his illustrations to *La sainte Bible* (1866). We contend, St. Paul told the church at Ephesus, "against the spiritual hosts of wickedness in the heavenly places." And we contend against events that appear destined (as with the Old English *wyrd*, "fate," from which we derive *weird*). In Hill's poem, even the hosts of wickedness remain still when they look down, fascinated, on what is happening in the Morian Court. They do not need to fly through a *templum* and be seen; the storm light is more than sufficient to intimate bad days ahead, if we only knew it at the time, and the hosts of the air know, as we do, that Dreyfus will be sent to Devil's Island in French Guiana.

Revelation is now no longer like the landscape of the Île de France, or, rather, it is like it in one respect only, for it brings some of the "remotest things" (*Mystery*, 5.26) close: not angels, as for Jeanne, but demons. They appear over Dreyfus as he stands rigidly at attention in the École militaire. We see the whole of Christian revelation come at last to its final book, which is known from its opening word: "The revelation of Jesus Christ" (ἀποκάλυψις Ἰησοῦ Χριστοῦ). The Greek ἀποκαλύπτω (ἀπο [away from] + καλύπτω [I uncover]), from which we get *apocalypse*, refers to uncovering, unveiling, or revealing. The Jewish traitor has been revealed for who he really is! (For some, there was rejoicing: people at the Folies Bergère sang "Vive l'armée!" and waved their hands in the air.) Of course, *apocalypse* connotes the events described in the book that are regarded as bringing about the end of the world. Yet what is actually uncovered in Paris, with Dreyfus's degradation, is violent anti-Semitism. A mob gathers on the Place de Fontenoy, outside the École militaire, to witness the treasonous Jew's disgrace, the end of his world. Their cry is like that heard in the early days of the Revolution when aristocrats were summarily lynched on lamp posts: *Les aristos à la lanterne!* Now a mob shouts: "À mort le Juif! Le Juif / à la lanterne!" (6.22–23). Hill represents the scene as a representation, with speech scrolls (or banderoles), as often used in Gothic paintings of biblical scenes, such as Gabriel's annunciation to Mary, and in theatrical frontispieces.[2] The silent film of part 1 has become "silent mouthings" in part 6. There is nothing modern about anti-Semitism: "Serenely the mob howls, / its silent mouthings hammered into scrolls // torn from *Apocalypse*" (6.23–25). There is only one scroll mentioned in the final book of the Christian Bible, the one with the seven seals that only the Lamb can open, but the text alluded to here is most likely the *Apocalypse of Moses*, the apocryphal story of what happened to Adam and Eve after they were exiled from Eden.[3] The entire book is torn into pieces by Christians howling for Jewish blood: Dreyfus is seen as the Anti-Christ. Serenity appears only by dint of how the crowd is represented with banderoles, and it prompts the contemplation of evil.

O felix culpa! Catholics sing at the Exultet each Easter Saturday before the Paschal Candle, "O happy fault!" For without Adam's sin Christ would not have been sent to redeem us. There must be a fall before there can be a restoration, a debt before it can be redeemed: such is one version of the theological metaphor "the economy of salvation," which Hill, like many another before him, cashes out in fiscal terms. In the Catholic system of sacraments, we are endlessly forgiven our sins, restored to a state of Grace we cannot merit, established once again in the Book of Life, "beyond the dreams of mystic avarice" (*Mystery*, 6.28). Greed, which is inherently sinful, is figuratively recapitulated in another mode in receiving more Grace because of repenting the sin.[4] But the paradox is not perfectly formed, for the sin is not forgiven unless one is truly contrite, which, as Hill knows, is presumably not the case for the mob or, all too often, for any of us. The mystic desires God, but the love that unifies him or her with the deity must be pure, drained of all self-interest, and untouched by the longing to possess its object. To enter the lands of likeness and receive pure love is, precisely, is what some call *mystical experience*. Later on, in section 8, Hill will use the same economic understanding when considering secular duty: "Poilus and sous-officiers who plod / to your lives' end, name your own recompense, / expecting nothing but the grace of France" (8.17–19). Yet this secular Grace gives nothing to the soldiers. The goodwill and "august plenitude" (8.20) that France has to offer its soldiers as they approach death (and the supposed meaning of their lives) is no more than the guns of August.

We are brought into a dark moral world not because we act disgrace-
fully but because we regard the fall-restoration logic of Christianity in
too light a manner. We seduce ourselves into thinking that we can act
badly now and repent later, not realizing that desire for God and desire
for divine love are not the same thing and that the latter is supremely
hard to cultivate, especially if we have been hardened by sin. "We" cannot claim immunity from negative moral evaluations, including those
we must make about ourselves; nor can we control History (Clio) or
expect not to be treated unfairly in retrospect. When it comes to judgment, the poem tells us, it is History, not God, who performs it, so
far as we can tell. The individual is easily subsumed into the zeitgeist,
as we have learned from the start of the poem when Hill asks: "Who
or what stares / through the café window . . . ?" (*Mystery*, 1.2–3). (As
the poem progresses, Péguy's figure of Clio, adopted by Hill, makes it
harder to specify who or what with any confidence.) Usually, one has
recourse to scare quotes around *we* to indicate the dangers of including
others because their gender, race, or social class marks them as different from oneself; here, however, Hill uses scare quotes in order to include everyone. So "we" are "crucified Pilate," torn by his conviction of
Jesus's innocence, on the one hand, and his bowing to the murderous
demands of the crowd, on the other. "We" are also Caiaphas, quint-
essential model of the man of *la politique*, for he proposed that it was
better for the innocent Jesus to die than for the nation to suffer (John
18:14). "We" do no better than either, or even Judas, for we all betray *la
mystique* to *la politique* sooner or later, unless we are truly radical souls.
Péguy is included in the condemnation as an "élite hermit" in his book-
shop (6.43)—we remember his "hermit's beard" (1.19)—whose secret
oratory, often written late at night, is heard so often in the pages of the
Cahiers. Our ability to contemplate what is set before us is once again
shown to be compromised, for we do not have the moral purity "to
step aside" in order properly to behold the radical soul, and even the
example of the soul put before us, Péguy's, is far from pure.[5]

The question of exemplarity has quietly run throughout the poem
since we encountered Bernard Lazare in our commentary as an example of the pure Dreyfusard in "Notre jeunesse" and since we were
directed to contemplate "*the* radical soul" (*Mystery*, 5.6), not "*a* radical soul." It has been nudged into view from time to time by allusions to the parables of Jesus. It is a difficult task that Hill requires of
us, for Péguy must be presented and received as particular, with a specific chronology of years, events, personality, and relations, but not as
wholly particular since he is accorded a representative status.[6] He is
both bound to history and not bound to it. We are quietly asked to

ponder what happens when Jeanne d'Arc becomes a national figure and a saint (just herself and yet exemplary of being Catholic, French, and visionary) and whether what occurs to Péguy in death is simply a repetition of that process. The question of exemplarity comes up against a very challenging case in the general condemnation of the "we," which of course includes both Hill and the reader, for

> We come
> back empty-handed from Jerusalem
>
> counting our blessings, honestly admire
> the wrath of the peacemakers, for example
> Christ driving the money-changers from the temple.
>
> (6.35–39)

The scare quotes disappear from the *we*: the point about everyone being complicit with evil has already been made. The prosaic "for example" is a risky choice in a poem, one that we associate with Auden, who handled the gesture with poise ("In Breugel's *Icarus*, for instance").[7] But can Christ be an example of anything?

In a clear theological sense, the answer must be no. For, if Christ is the Second Person of the Trinity, he is God and therefore absolutely singular and does not belong to any genus. He cannot exemplify anything at all. Yet there is another sense in which Christ's human soul—seen in his compassion and self-sacrifice for others—together with the doctrine of the Incarnation is the very basis of the *imitatio Christi*, not necessarily in the world-weary sense that Thomas à Kempis was to give this expression in the fifteenth century.[8] In his humanity, Christ is relatively singular, like all of us (except in sin), and the events of his life give us many opportunities for meditation on how to become more like him. But we can take Christ as an example of something, include him as one in a series (e.g., great religious teachers: Moses, Christ, Buddha, Muhammad; or influential individuals in history: Socrates, Christ, Napoléon, Lincoln). In doing so, however, we lose Christ's principal claim on us, which turns on his absolute singularity with respect to salvation. Part of what Hill suggests here is that "we" are perhaps people who take the *mystique* of Christ and, when circumstances prevail, allow it to become no more than *politique*, as in the two series I have given. When that happens, the absolute disappears in the relative. The only wounds we receive are those of being pierced by the crown of thorns as we put it on Christ's head. We begin to discern a truth about ourselves. We wound ourselves in our exercises of *la politique*,

although the wound expiates nothing, and that insight is offered to our
self-contemplation. Yet this is a futile act, one made while sitting at a
desk, without anything being consequent on it. We may come closer to
the truth about our times and our reluctance to engage in them, yet we
quickly divert truth into journalism or poetry, which themselves have
consequences we cannot control: "Did Péguy kill Jaurès? Did he incite / the assassin?" (*Mystery*, 1.13–14).

*

In Christianity, the contemplative gaze returns the loving regard of
God, who initiates each and every relationship with him. Christ performs κένωσις and follows it with ἐπέκτασις, and his followers must do
the same if we are to be like him. With the start of the seventh section
of *The Mystery of the Charity of Charles Péguy*, this elevated situation
is reset in the mode of popular piety: we see a statuette of Christ—
with hand raised in blessing, or on the cross, or with open arms—in a
roadside shrine, glanced at all too quickly so that it seems to be saluting those who pass by. Once again, the absolutely singular Christ appears as relatively singular; such shrines are commonplace. He gives
a greeting, a blessing perhaps, but also a military salute. In his shrine,
Christ is imagined to be undergoing a long vigil, much as at Gethsemane, but he is also on sentry duty and has fallen asleep or has died
and must be relieved by "some boy-officer" (7.3), presumably a young
man conscripted late in the war. The Great War has proved to be a long
wait for the denouement, and it too has its Passion. The "polled / wil-
lows" (7.5–6) recall the landscape of Flanders, and *Passion* suggests the
disastrous Battle of Passchendaele (1917). The ruin brought about by
war does not afford many opportunities for beholding Truth; the "rut-
ted" paths (7.8) are not the "criss-cross-trodden ground" (5.20) once
walked on by the peasants on their pilgrimage to Chartres. Under fire
in dugouts or in upper rooms of former cafés, snipers have only a relic
from the Franco-Prussian War with which to defend themselves and
launch attacks, a Tabatière rifle, its incense and snuff being gunpowder,
not the myrrh of "the wandering kings" (5.28) or the snuffbox "won at
Austerlitz" (3.16), maybe in a game of cards. The resurrected Christ appeared in the upper room to his disciples (John 20:19–23), who were
frightened of what the Jews might do to them. He showed Thomas his
wounds. But the only resurrection for the injured soldiers entertained
by Hill is, after being shot by the Germans, becoming a name on a memorial or being generically depicted in battle on a public monument.
Only in this way and in memory do "these presences endure" (7.18). As

we glumly hear in the following section, at the moment of death, "the mind leaps / for its salvation, is at once extinct" (8.21–22).

As in a film set during the First World War, we cut from a statuette of Christ along the road to a village memorial to the war dead and to "those who worship at its marble rote" (*Mystery*, 7.21), those, that is, who bend over to lay flowers before the ceaseless repetition of names much as the soldiers crouched when under German fire. It is as though the "*dur*ation" and "en*dur*ance" of the war is marked in the engraved names of the dead, as is the "ob*dur*ate" memorial that blindly keeps vigil over the village square (7.23–24; emphasis added). Yet the worship of Christ gives way, for some, to a mourning of sons and grandsons that resembles idolatry. As for the soldiers themselves, now memorialized, explosions and flashes of battle once blinded them (like Saul on the road to Damascus), or, if one was in a bad state owing to shell shock or fear ("far-gone" [7.26]) he might have seen a ghost (like the disciples on the road to Emmaus).⁹ Singular events from sacred history become displaced and repeated in secular history. Much of the poem is concerned with this sort of deflection from the absolute to the relative: the snipers who are "watchmen of the Passion" (7.13) and the "men of sorrows" who "do their stint" and "whose golgothas are the moon's trenches" (10.30–31). Contemplation is deflected from the divine mystery and concerns only the mystery of charity (or radicality) and of course the mystery of evil as it manifests itself in war.

Two distancing procedures are used in the following stanzas, for it is one of the burdens of the poem to remind us that "History . . . has raged so before / countless times" (*Mystery*, 1.6–7) so as both to enlist our contemplation of it and to deny the requisite distance for it because of our complicity with History, past and to come. One occurs at the start of sections 7 and 8 and another at the end of section 7. Both are bitterly ironic. Let us look first at the passage at the end of section 7. Hill inflects the soldiers' advance into smoke by way of an allusion to the anonymous fourteenth-century guide to contemplation *The Cloud of Unknowing*, in which the cloud of what we cannot know of the divine separates us from God. It is an original inflection of the classical *templum*. We must abandon our thin knowledge of God and seek him, rather, in the darkness of love. This cloud can best be pierced by frequently praying heartfelt ejaculations, such as *Jesus!* The terrible irony is that the wounded soldiers would have shouted the word as an expletive, not as a prayer.¹⁰ If they once longed for paradise after death, now they would be content with oblivion.

Second, Hill has the soldiers in the First World War say, "Salute us all, Christus" (*Mystery*, 7.1), with the Latin word for *Christ* taking us back to Roman times and one of the older strata of the poem. In 52 CE, the Emperor Claudius organized an entertainment for himself, a naval battle on the Fucine Lake, in which captives from military campaigns, along with criminals of all sorts, were compelled to fight, most of them to the death. *Ave Caesar*, the condemned cried, *morituri te salutant* (Hail Caesar, we who are about to die salute you).[11] In section 8 of the poem, Hill writes *vos morituri*, "you who are about to die" (8.7), thereby turning the old expression into a military order. On the one hand, it is Christ who is to die for us, while, on the other hand, the soldiers who are to die in combat walk past a statuette of Christ saluting them from a roadside shrine. The Passion continues: not as a participation in the divine mystery of the atonement but as a repetition of suffering by ordinary soldiers. There is an "irony of advancement" (8.27), for a skirmish often gives at best a few feet of land, which are easily lost, and the Enlightenment bequeaths us Gatling guns and the like ("Victory of the machine!" [1.28]) as well as suffering with no hope of redemption. Even more difficult is the spiritual truth that we are nothing and that it is only in recognition of our own nothingness that we can receive the love of God.

"Landscape is like revelation," Hill told us in *Mystery* 5.25 in a powerful statement of natural theology vying with revealed theology. One thing that is revealed in the landscape of the Île de France is a certain beauty, the effect of an agrarian culture acting over the centuries on nature: Péguy extols the world of *l'ancienne France*, as we have seen, and it is hard to distinguish his love of nature from his admiration of the Catholic culture that has shaped it.[12] This culture of his home world (*Heimwelt*), as Husserl calls it, goes back to Jeanne d'Arc and back further still.[13] Hill reminds us now and then that the same landscape had been enjoyed by the Bourbons. He evokes them "view-hallooing" (9.16) not for a fox their dogs have unearthed on a chase but for regret since the restoration did not last, and France is haunted in other ways by the loss of the Franco-Prussian War of 1870. History is revealed by landscape, both its periods of peace and its episodes of war, its agrarian system and its symbolic order. One key meaning of "Landscape is like revelation" is that landscape is always open to our contemplation: it may not respond as God does, making our contemplation an endless ἐπέκτασις, but it offers itself by way of a ceaseless attempt to piece part to part in order to make a whole that always escapes a final determination as well as inviting us to muse on differences between reality and representation.

As the poem shows us, nature and culture cooperate in different ways. There is a religious culture of churches and bells, of pilgrimages, and an ordered life "like a simple book of hours" (*Mystery*, 3.12); and, intersecting with it, there is a social culture of *l'ancienne France*, in which the Bourbons were once very much at home; and there is a po-litical culture, marked by the nastiness of the *parti intellectuel* and anti-Semites and by the devastation of one war after another (landscape as apocalypse). All these revelations are encoded in French landscapes in Hill's poem, and each is offered to us to behold. No sooner do we begin with one facet of the land than we find ourselves led to ponder another. The "terre charnelle" is gazed on by God, and believers "go down / into the darkness of resurrection" (5.40): down, not up, note. The revela-tion of resurrection is not distinct from the landscape in which ordi-nary life takes place, including, when it must, war. If there is ever a spir-itual ascent, it will be from the land.

Only one of the landscapes, however, is deemed to be perfect, and it is the one that is evoked in Péguy's *Le mystère de la charité de Jeanne d'Arc*, which itself is marked by war with the English and represented in the play as less historical than theological: it is touched by the mys-teries of Faith, Grace, and Sacrament.[14] With the Hundred Years' War long finished, covered over by generations of peasant culture, the order and beauty of the land could be experienced even in Péguy's childhood and youth. Hill notices the men with iron muscles "who bell the hours" (*Mystery*, 9.11) and indeed don armor in order to ring bells to mark the mobilization order of August 1914 and others who stiffly carry them-selves as though they were military *maréchals* of France when it comes to admitting the coaches of visitors into the grand châteaux whose lords they serve.

This old world "is indeed perfection," Hill tells us; more, "this is the heart / of the mystère" (*Mystery*, 9.13–14). Notice that it is not the heart of any *mystique*: the natural category gives way to the nonnatural one. Notice also that neither remark is offered as a simple declarative statement; both are addressed to the bell men and the door men whose lives are rooted there, who participate in it and draw significance from its historically dense hierarchy of symbols, just as Péguy has done. If this world can be prized as "perfection," it is because what was once natural has been elevated by beliefs and rituals, by narratives and sym-bols, by recollections and hopes: it is not so much perceived as loved. For a believer, it is, as Péguy writes, "l'insertion de l'éternel dans le temporal, et pour tout dire c'est le mystère même de l'incarnation" (the insertion of the eternal in the temporal, and to say everything it's the very mystery of the incarnation).[15] For Péguy, however, saying every-thing involves pointing to the mystery being one with the Republic, not with a lost Bourbon world, which is something that drops out of focus in Hill's lines.[16] We notice that Hill writes *mystère* and not *mystique*: the heart of the mystery of Péguy's charity, for him, is socio-religious, less a matter of social inequality than of an organic hierarchy, less a question of nature perfected by Grace than of lived cycles of suffering and redemption.

The loss of this hierarchy is differently experienced by the peoples of France. For the bell ringers and the gatekeepers guiding the coaches into the grand houses, it was a way of life that passed with them. For the Bourbons, whose sovereign French line ended in 1883, it was a felt loss of a dream "of warrior-poets and the Meuse / flowing so sweetly" (*Mystery*, 9.18–19). And for Péguy it was a "defeat" and an "affliction" (9.15) in the very experience of the First World War, which had been brewing for decades, certainly since Bismarck won the Franco-Prussian War with the Battle of Sedan (September 1, 1870). After its defeat, France slept, at least with respect to Germany, for it had had social troubles enough: Germany was finally unified on January 18, 1871, in a ceremony held at Versailles, and this event was followed by the Paris Commune (March 18–May 28, 1871). But Hill's attention is elsewhere, with Rimbaud, who wrote to his teacher Georges Izambard in May 1871, "*Je* est un autre," thereby declaring a new insight for the writing of poetry: expression is recognized as distinct from self-expression.[17] To figure the communication as a telegram is to associate it with bad news. Yet the Bourbons had already intuited a version of the telegram's import, without having the slightest interest in its literary implications.

Who were they, after all? After the Franco-Prussian War was a Bourbon's *Je* to signify a Bourbon or a republican? Late in 1871 there was a brief period when the answer could have gone either way. With the end of the Napoléon III's regime, the Third Republic had a monarchist majority, and both sides of the Bourbon cause—the Légitimistes (supporters of Henri, Comte de Chambord [1820–83]) and the Orléanistes (supporters of Philippe Comte de Paris [1838–94])—agreed on October 27, 1871, to invite Henri to become Henri V of France. Had that happened, the Bourbons would have remained in a France that was, in some respects, essentially Bourbon for the time being. It seemed a very small thing. "If we but move a finger, France is saved" (*Mystery*, 9.45), Hill's Bourbons murmur to themselves, as though in sleep (and we magically hear them, as though we know French as well as we know English). "Sleepers awake" we remember from part 1 of the poem. We also recall that Henri declined to accept the throne if the Assemblée nationale insisted on preserving the revolutionary Tricolour over and above the old Fleur de lys. No change would be possible; the Tricolour would remain, even if Henri used the Fleur de lys for his personal flag, in part because the army prized the revolutionary flag.[18] So not a finger was moved, and the senior male-only line of Louis XV no longer had a French claimant to the throne. History waited only "a blank instant" (9.44) and then moved on. President Adophe Tiers (1797–1877) had already noted that the Republic was the form of government that divided the French people the least, and, by the time of Henri's death, most French citizens had come to agree with him. Time inexorably moves ahead, like a cadre of soldiers marching. There are three advances named in the poem and notably the only one that always progresses is time ("the small hours advance" [9.30]).

The Bourbons wished to save France for the monarchy, who would in turn save France from itself, but Péguy was a true republican, one who also saw that the ancient aristocracy had become no more than "une bourgeoisie d'argent" (a moneyed middle class).[19] His attempt to save France was partly cultural (he fought intellectually for the values of l'ancienne France) and partly military (he fought for France at the Marne and died there). His demise in the field of beetroots is described with restraint: "Péguy's cropped skull / dribbles its ichor, its poor thimbleful, / a simple lesion of the complex brain" (Mystery, 10.6–8). Lying dead on the battlefield, he seems nothing special: "he commends us to nothing, leaves a name // for the burial-detail to gather up / with rank and number, personal effects, / the next-of-kin and a few other facts" (10.16–19). Yet the truth, his "true passion," is found beneath these surface details; it is an ardor "for Chartres / steadfastly cleaving to the Beauce, for her / the Virgin of innumerable charities" (10. 22–24). Péguy's own charities might not have been "innumerable," but his cleaving to Notre-Dame de Chartres is acknowledged to be one of them. He participates in the mystery of the Virgin, the icon of many votaries, including Péguy.

"Take that for your example!" thunders Hill in the final stanza of the poem in mock serious fashion (Mystery, 10.41). Inevitably, we recall those who visited Jerusalem and who, returning, "honestly admire / the wrath of the peacemakers, for example / Christ driving the money-changers from the temple" (6.37–39; emphasis added). But the example we are enjoined to follow is Péguy's, not Christ's: we are only human, even if we are not radically so, and we might not be believers. It is as though Hill strikes us with Péguy as a special case of the "radical soul" that we are left to generalize, understand, and presumably apply to ourselves. It can be objected that this is not an easy thing to do for any soul. One might say that Péguy's inner life cannot readily be contemplated; for a believer, it is mysterious at the level of the imago dei, but at other levels closer to the surface of selfhood it is deeply frustrating in the contraries, even contradictions, that beleaguer it and shape it and that Hill draws to our notice. One can contemplate a mystery, one might say, but not a series of contrarieties that are variously oriented to one or another end. If we accept this line of reasoning, we have a twofold task. We may behold a mystery at the base of Péguy's soul, and we may also behold the shifting tensions of reason and will, belief, and desire that characterize what we have witnessed of the man. A "radical soul," however, would be one in which the contrarieties are ultimately oriented to the one end, so we can contemplate its dedication to the one end, though perhaps not anything else.

The death of Péguy, fallen on the battlefield, "his arm over his face as though in sleep" (*Mystery*, 10.20), returns us to the beginning of the poem with the advertised farce "*Sleepers Awake*" (and does so by way of an allusion to Siegfried Sassoon's "The Dug-Out").[20] Is Péguy's death a fact or a figure? Still, the genre of history has not fully resolved itself. It may not swing wildly between farce and tragedy anymore but there is still a struggle for command between "Low tragedy" and "high farce" (10.37), the terms of Marx's distinction having been adjusted. The metaphors of theater remain heavily marked in the final stanza: praise and elegy for Péguy are "so moving on the scene as if to cry / 'in memory of those things these words were born'" (10.44).[21] A combination of praise and elegy, it is a speech spoken, perhaps by Clio, as she treads the stage that Hill has erected in his poem and on which his characters have performed. She does not cry out a testimony of those times, from the Franco-Prussian War to the Dreyfus Affair to the First World War, but speaks "as if" to do so, and her witness is itself a quotation adapted from a volume of literary history. It seems that History is indeed "rehearsing another scene," albeit the final one of this particular play.

*

Religious contemplation usually attends to the highest mystery, divine love, and for the last century or so it has mostly been ushered under the heading *mysticism* and addressed in psychological and epistemological terms. An earlier sense of divine mystery figured it as a way in which God was hidden from us, by way of knowledge, but given to us in and through love. Yet Hill's poem asks us to focus on *la mystique* and the quality of moral attention that is appropriate to it, and that is quite another thing. For *la mystique*, as Péguy uses the word, applies to secular as well as sacred ideals and is ineluctably associated with a downward pull to *la politique*, which differs qualitatively from it. One might say that *la mystique* is a profile of mystery, one that presents its institutional and biographical moment and nothing more. And one might note that Péguy's and Hill's charting of *la mystique* in its inevitable fall into *la politique* is a deflated counterpart to the hermeneutic of suspicion. For them, there is nothing positive to be gained in finding politics at the heart of mystery, only an abiding loss of adventure, empathy, and intensity on the part of the one who experiences the decline. It is almost as though Hill is dangling a bait for a passing hermeneut of suspicion who might chance on his poem, and I have already given him or her a thread to follow in the word *perfection*, even though the thread is not quite hanging from the text as one might suppose it to be.

Another difference between Hill and the tradition: *contemplatio* directs us to God himself even if we linger on the way to enjoy him in his creation, while Hill commends us to contemplate (not just consider) the "radical soul," not only Péguy but also something that Péguy exemplifies, though in an unexpected way, and the landscapes through which he walked. For we are invited to contemplate not *the virtuous soul* or the *charitable soul* but the *radical soul*, which is, as we have seen, a conservative radical. The mystery of Péguy's life and actions is contained in the unity of *charité* and *radicalité*: divine love calls forth extreme commitment, and extreme commitment draws on a mystical love for nourishment. We would be mistaken to think that Hill's Péguy is a saint, however. *The Mystery of the Charity of Charles Péguy* remains skeptical about the process of secular sanctification, performed by History (Clio), who is fickle enough in her choices and methods. Nothing is expressly said in the poem about ecclesial sanctification, but we have no reason to think that Hill regards it differently. The authority of *la fille aînée de l'église*, along with her excesses and failures, is not a theme that appears in the poem, except insofar as she is honored by the rural poor. At the most, one finds a deflationary remark, in which the secular and the sacred are allowed to converge, when the dead Péguy has to face "the last rites of truth, whatever they are, / or the Last Judgment which is much the same" (10.13–14). The final cadence suggests Hill's eschatology: the mercy of a loving God does not appear, only the unyielding truth about a person. The apparent finality of that cadence is quickly undercut, however, by the very next words: "or Mercy, even" (10.15).

Yet we would be mistaken not to think that Hill's Péguy, like Péguy's Jeanne, has genuine charity, the virtue as well as the love that comes from its exercise, and that Hill admires it without reservation. Nowhere in the poem does he explicitly identify the root of Péguy's charity, as the title of his poem might encourage us to anticipate, although he does indicate "the heart / of the mystère" (*Mystery*, 10.13–14), at

least for those who participate in it. If we are tempted to read the poem
too piously, we might expect this expression to gesture toward the orthodox belief that Péguy came to profess, even if it is not affirmed by
Hill himself, namely, love of God and neighbor. But we would be disappointed, for the heart of the *mystère* is represented quite otherwise.
To begin with, it should be underlined that the word is French, not English: Hill is talking about the heart of the *mystère* for Péguy, not for
himself, at least not primarily. Yet this "heart" is given only in a single
profile, by way of the hierarchies of society and the church, which we
might better think of by way of *mystique*. The stability of those hierarchies has been shaken by the seismic events experienced by modern
France—the Franco-Prussian War, the Dreyfus Affair, and the First
World War—and, indeed, by modernity itself, and we witness Péguy's
responses to those events, not to mention his own active participation
in some of them. We may well leave the poem with a sense of what Hill
elsewhere says: "everywhere / Dismantled hierarchies."[22] And we may
well have reason to ponder further any shared ground between Péguy
and Hill with respect to views of hierarchy.

   In section 10 we witness the death of Péguy for the fourth time. We
encountered it first at the end of section 2, when he was raised from the
dead with his fellow soldiers "covered in glory and the blood of beetroots," again at the start of section 5, and yet again at the end of that
section when he is returned to "the claggy Beauce" (*Mystery*, 5.87). In
the same way, the death of Jean Jaurès is repeated: we see it first right
at the start of the poem and then again in the middle of section 4. And
resurrection, in one or another mode, is figured time and again: death
into a statue by way of "strange Christian hope," death into a ghost, and
as the specter of Christ at Emmaus. Reading through the poem, one
experiences not Hill thinking through the question of Péguy's charity
in a linear fashion but rather the poet hovering over the question, over
different sorts of love, possible modes of revelation, distinct modes of
mystery, and considering the shifting gulf between reality and representation. Péguy appears in a manifold of presentations and indeed
transcends that manifold, becoming richer as the poem continues: we
can never specify completely what his name means in the poem. The
poem circles and circles around its centers of gravity, a contemplation
that cannot push ever more deeply into divine mystery but invites us to
go further in mulling over the mystery of evil and the mystery of charity. It invites us also to make many disparate things—literary, political,
religious—into a whole.

   To be sure, we must take great care in judging the values assigned
to Hill's use of *hierarchy*. One of his aphoristic lines, written in a poem

composed some years after *The Mystery of the Charity of Charles Péguy*, points us in the general direction he wishes us to take—"Bless hierarchy, dismiss hegemony"—but the dichotomy is so sharp, as befits aphorisms, that it needs to be puzzled out a little before it can help us understand his position.[23] When Hill speaks of "broken hierarchies," he is not lamenting the collapse of any class system or the structures of empire or anything basic to democracy as he understands and prizes it. Nor is he merely following Shakespeare's Ulysses when he speaks quite generally about the link between order and social rank: "Take but degree away, untune that string, / And hark what discord follows."[24] Hill's concern, rather, is with the breakdown of a shared order of aesthetic, moral, religious, and social values that has variously come about through repeated abuses of an unregulated market and today informs Tories as fully as Whigs.[25] Simone Weil is just as useful here and just as close to Hill as she was when we were beginning to approach the poem. Earlier in *The Need for Roots* she has been talking about the human need for work, for respect, along with other things. Now she includes hierarchy in that list of essential needs:

> Hierarchism is a vital need of the human soul. It is composed of a certain veneration, a certain devotion towards superiors, considered not as individuals, nor in relation to the powers they exercise, but as symbols. What they symbolize is that realm situated high above all men and whose expression in this world is made up of the obligations owed by each man to his fellow men. A veritable hierarchy presupposes a consciousness on the part of the superiors of this symbolic function and a realization that it forms the only legitimate object of devotion among their subordinates. The effect of true hierarchism is to bring each one to fit himself morally into the place he occupies.[26]

Looked at from sufficiently far away, Weil gives us a modern version of *consideratio*, a looking up, down, and around in order to find one's proper place in the world and examine one's moral place in it.

In Hill's view, such *consideratio* has been utterly ignored, if not purposively debased. The lowest common denominator in modernity has become exchange value, understood as the whole story about value, a belief that, in practice, has imposed its hegemony, from beneath as it were, over all forms of social and intellectual life today. One crucial dimension of this situation is the way in which our talk about value, made in aesthetic and moral judgments, is constantly parasitized or even debauched by institutions and individuals committed or acclimated to value considered exclusively by way of exchange.[27] This occurs not only in the market but also, as Hill sees things, in discussions of culture, both inside and outside government and education. The market has thoroughly absorbed culture, rendering high culture a minority culture, even in the university. Nonetheless, it must be admitted, as Hill apparently does not here, that social hierarchy has long been responsible for great social injustices. Hierarchies need to be broken to allow social justice to manifest itself. Only then can *consideratio* have point and purpose.

To survive, let alone flourish, poetry of the sort that Hill commends, writes about, and writes himself, needs a shared public order, a sense of civic justice, an awareness of the sacred, and an affirmation of the value of learning. If this is not the kingdom, it is a secular imagining of the same. By contrast with the malady that he diagnoses as coming with liberal modernity, an amalgam of brash egalitarianism, debased usages, and meanness, Hill tells us that poetry, properly conceived, is "hierarchical, democratic, erudite."[28] We have a political word placed between a religious one and an intellectual one. Yet Hill has his reasons for choosing that middle word and for framing it as he does. A true democracy presumes that everyone is willing and able to acquire knowledge and appreciate and benefit from shared values, and, for Hill, our current experience of democracy means that everything produced in a society is (or should be) accessible, able to be attained with little or no effort and consequently neither prized nor valued. It is less democracy than egalitarianism, and less the egalitarianism of Locke or Marx than that of those, our contemporaries, for whom all value is a matter of what the market will bear. Understood as Hill would wish, the word *hierarchy* remains close to its original Greek: ἱερός (sacred) + ἄρχω (I rule). The word was coined in the late fifth or early sixth century by Pseudo-Dionysius the Areopagite, the most influential of writers in mystical theology.[29] In another aphoristic remark in the same vein, Hill appeals to the visionary Blake, not to the Areopagite, although an emphasis on the sovereignty of the sacred is maintained by both. In the poet's own words, "Hierarchy yet: Blake's lordly plates to *Job* / And he was a sworn Leveller," this last word presumably being used in the original sense of arguing for equal claims to justice for all people.[30] The placing of the adverb *yet* neatly bespeaks Hill's dedication to hierarchy and his hope against hope of its survival.

Blake's allegiance to religious radicalism, including the value of religious toleration, was inherited from the turmoil of the English Civil War (1642–49). In his *Mysticism and Democracy in the English Commonwealth* (1932), Rufus M. Jones proposes that we call dissident religious groups in the seventeenth-century Commonwealth (1640–60) such as the Seekers and the Brownists *mystical,* radical souls all. Jones stipulates a quite different sense of the word *mystical* than we have inherited from apophatic mysticism, which, in a conservative estimate, runs from Gregory of Nyssa and the Pseudo-Dionysius to Aquinas and Jean Gerson and then ventures far beyond in art as well as theology.[31] The English dissidents are *mystical,* Jones says, in the sense of having "the *conviction of certainty* that the person's own soul has found its goal of reality in God."[32] In other words, it is a profile of *mystique,* one in which a dissociation of mysticism and contemplation takes place. Jones argues that these nonconformist mystical groups organized themselves along congregational principles that, in time, would be transformed into democratic principles and extended to the state itself.[33] Among other manifestations of this sense of truth having a democratic spirit, we might think of Milton's *Areopagitica* (1644) with its affirmation that truth should be freely published over and against state censorship of literature and pamphlets.[34] For Jones, then, modern British democratic institutions begin in *mysticism.*[35] This "mysticism" is not quite the same as Péguy's "mystique," but they share some common ground, which is explored by Hill, not explicitly in *The Mystery of the Charity of Charles Péguy,* but in several poems dispersed through the book that follows it, *Canaan* (1996). These later lyrics are nowhere near as strong as "The Mystery of the Charity of Charles Péguy," which is one reason why they have been overlooked. Nonetheless, they can help us determine by way of a coda some of what subtends Hill's passion for the figure of Péguy in his long poem. They do so much better than the lyrics that comprise "Hymns to Our Lady of Chartres."[36] Each of the five poems is called "Mysticism and Democracy."

*

These shorter poems hew closely to Jones's thesis about the relation of religion and politics while bitterly lamenting what Westminster democracy in Britain has become now that its "mystical" order has steadily been ignored, eroded, and degraded. They offer us, in effect, a new profile of *mystique,* one removed from *mystère* and the practice of contemplation, natural or religious. In the fourth lyric, we hear of "mystical democracy, ill-gotten, ill-bestowed, / as if, long since, we had cheated them, / our rightful, righteous / masters, as though they would pay us back / terrific freedoms."[37] Characteristic of Hill, the last expression looks in two directions at once and makes the preceding lines, themselves historically compressed, conduct a force field of meanings. We have inherited large freedoms from the organizational models of the dissident religious sects of the seventeenth century, which were themselves awkwardly brought into existence by forcible separation from the established church. Those freedoms are summed up in our modern experience of democracy, both our freedoms from and our freedoms to, although one might wonder in retrospect whether they were wisely bestowed on us. For Hill thinks we have cheated our "righteous / masters," taken "terrific freedoms" with respect to our inheritance, so much so that we have weakened what was originally good in the political order they bequeathed to us. Why have we acted in this way? Out of unreasonable fear ("as though they would") that, despite its appeal to equality, the "mystical" order nonetheless has a hidden reliance on a hierarchy (in the original sense of the word) that might come to haunt us. There is a fear that adherence to the seventeenth-century sense of *mystical democracy*, whether coming from the Left or from the Right, will somehow allow that adherence to take liberties with us. It might remove or truncate some of the liberal democratic freedoms to which we have become accustomed, that we wish to flourish, and that are themselves in tension with the mystical democratic freedom that precedes it, both historically and (for Hill) in the order of priority.

John Bunyan's *The Pilgrim's Progress* (1678) is the warp across which Hill will weave his woof in the first and the third lyrics. I restrict myself to the final lines of the third lyric, which intersect my train of thought here:

> Exhaustion is of the essence, though in the meantime
> What song has befallen those who were laggard
> Pilgrims, or none. It is as you see. I would not
> Trouble greatly to proclaim this.
> > But shelve it under Mercies.[38]

Again, we encounter the problem of exemplarity, although this time given by way of the symbolic mode of allegory: Bunyan's Christian is at once particular and, as his name says, representative of those who adhere to the faith.[39] The pilgrimage is exhausting, not least of all when climbing the Hill known as Difficulty (which elsewhere gives the poet a heavy-handed pun), but what of those who, like Formalist, Pliable, and Talkative, do not persevere as Christian and Faithful do?[40] All we have to do to find out is to look about us as well as stand before a mirror. And then we should know what to do, for the church points us to the category of corporeal and spiritual works of Mercy.[41] As Hill's phrasing suggests, however, we are all too likely to "shelve" the very deeds that we should perform in order to lighten the burdens that others carry. The poem goes further than this, however, in outlining an allegory of its own. It can be related in two ways. First, the human pilgrim becomes exhausted in continuing on the path of mystical democracy and succumbs to the attractions of liberal democracy, which it extends as far as it will go. Second, the same human pilgrim slides from *la mystique* to *la politique*.

Unlike Christian in Bunyan's crowded allegory, the modern pilgrim does not stay the course over the last three hundred years of British culture and politics. The last of the five lyrics, the one beginning "Great gifts foreclosed on," looks grimly on our moral exhaustion, what we have done and have not done with our inheritance of the mystical democracy of the seventeenth century; it is a matter of "loss and waste offset / by thrifty oddities of survival." Hill attends to two elements in the nation's pilgrimage from the mid-seventeenth century to the late twentieth century, which of course crosses several wars:

> Flesh has its own spirit, confused with torpor,
> deeper than most rooted faiths, deeper than Passchendaele.
> Piety is less enduring though it endures much
> and with its own stiff diligence keeps the ground
> > set for humiliation.[42]

The flesh has a stubborn will to self-preservation, but its *conatus essendi* is hardly the same as torpor. With reason, Hill takes this native will to endure to be more tenacious than that of learned piety, sacred or secular, even that religious faith that is rooted in the gospel and in the rhythms of one's life at home. It will survive even a military disaster such as Passchendaele (1917), if only because soldiers are rigidly trained, right down to their flesh and bones, to fit into the military hierarchy, which had punitive measures on which it could and did call, including execution in the field for cowardice. Both pieties, religious and secular, are motivated by love, to be sure (*diligence* is from the Latin *diligere*, one of the language's words for *love*), even if this love is misunderstood. Certainly, religious piety has not been nourished in recent decades by even ordinary learning, notwithstanding the fact that a fingertip's knowledge of scripture (here 1 Sam. 7:12) might now strike some people as quaint at best: "There was a time, any Methodist could have told you / Ebenezer means stone of help."[43] And the same piety has been misunderstood by those who attack it, with the result that the cultivation of Christian humility through exercises of self-knowledge is mistaken for preparing for scenes of self-humiliation (or, worse, the humiliation of others). Perhaps needless to say, for Hill the mistake is also made by Christians who confuse humility and self-humiliation. There is little reason these days, it seems, for a stone to memorialize divine aid.

Having set up what the heritage of mystical democracy has sadly become in our times, Hill then turns to "the rabble," the equivalent today, perhaps in his mind, to the "mob" that tormented Dreyfus and needs to be woken to the injustice of its acts. *Rabble* is a harsh word to have chosen, even if it is presumably used not to enforce social difference but to stress the need for a properly educated populace in a democracy. The lyric ends in a terse display of vitriol barely disguised by classical and ecclesial erudition: "As for the rest, / ruunt in servitium, crammed vacancy's rabble— / this also is admitted: *introit turba*."[44] The first passage of Latin alludes to Tacitus's remarks in the first book of his *Annals*:

> At Romae ruere in servitium consules, patres, eques, quanto quis inlustrior, tanto magis falsi ac festinantes, vultuque composito ne laeti excessu principis neu tristiores primordio, lacrimas Gaudium, questus adulationem miscebant.
>
> (Meanwhile at Rome consuls, senate, knights, precipitately became servile. The more distinguished men were, the greater their urgency and insincerity. They must show neither satisfaction at the death of one emperor, nor gloom at the accession of another: so their features were carefully arranged in a blend of tears and smiles, mourning and flattery.)[45]

People of all classes are rushing into slavery, just as in the aged Augustus's Rome, but nowadays it is the slavery of cultural democracy, no matter how intellectually empty it might be.

If anything, things are worse today, Hill concedes, for the people's priests commence their ritual of sacrifice by processing to the altar, intoning a psalm that has been trimmed to what the crowd wants to hear. The church has not maintained the mystical democracy of the seventeenth century, arising from congregationalism, but has capitulated to the later liberal democracy of Locke (and in doing so "admitted" the rabble in both senses of the word: it has allowed them in and countenanced their beliefs), which Hill's mob has pushed far beyond the philosopher's principle of equality in the *Two Treatises of Government* (1690) into the realm of cultural democracy with its heavy emphases on pluralism and equity.[46] For Locke, equality turns on natural rights, which are constraints and do not require everyone or everything to be equal in all ways. Sacred doctrine itself is being compromised by democracy. In Péguy's terms, it is the complete and utter collapse of *la mystique* into *la politique*, one movement in the public accomplishment of de-Christianization.[47] We remember Péguy's somber words, which Hill uses as the epigraph to *The Mystery of the Charity of Charles Péguy*:

> Nous sommes les derniers. Presque les après-derniers. Aussitôt après nous commence un autre âge, un tout autre monde, le monde de ceux qui ne croient plus à rien, qui s'en font gloire et orgueil.

> (We are the last. Almost the ones after the last. Directly after us begins another age, a wholly other world, the world of those who no longer believe in anything, who pride themselves on it.)[48]

The sadness of these lines in "Notre jeunesse" becomes bitter when digested in the final lyric of "Mysticism and Democracy."

The idea of a modern, free French state derives largely from Montesquieu and Voltaire, who built on Locke's proposals for a liberal democracy, and, when the social world of late eighteenth-century France could bear absolutism no more, that idea erupted, horribly distorted by many pressures, in the Revolution (1789–99). There is no native French tradition of mystical democracy from which Péguy could draw. His *mystique* is entirely hierarchical, centered on absolutes rather than authority, and his beloved world of *l'ancienne France* offers nothing other than religious absolutes of a hierarchical kind long internalized (and in some cases applied to other ends) by a hardworking peasant culture. His radicality consists in the clear-sightedness with which he sees ideals, whether socialist, republican, or Catholic, all organized around truth for truth's sake, honor for honor's sake, and the tenacity with which he clings to them, even in adversity and in isolation. And his charity consists of actions freely consequent on his fidelity to his chosen standards, from his support of Dreyfus right down to scrupulous proofreading. In all this, he differs from his dramatic character Jeanne d'Arc, whose charity derives from her allegiance to the mystery of God's love, which can suffer no accommodations, ecclesial, national, or military. What compels Hill's attraction to Péguy is the struggle of a flawed man who prizes absolutes, even if he must suffer for his convictions, and resists any tampering with the hierarchy of which they are the summit. When Hill turns to his own country, he discerns such radical souls in the seventeenth century and in those who prized them (Coleridge among them) and their work in the seeding of mystical democracy.[49] In looking to modern Britain in "Mysticism and Democracy," he finds more of a history of betrayal and decay than moments of principled resistance to it. Liberal democracy has eclipsed mystical democracy, and the abuses relentlessly committed in its name by the Left and the Right offer little by way of hope, except to the remnant (of whom Hill is one) who can say with Péguy: "Nous sommes les derniers." Anything good accomplished in the name of liberal democracy is allowed to drop out of focus, and, in the same manner, nothing bad about mystical democracy, including any tendency it has toward anti-intellectualism, is countenanced. Nor is any other way of elaborating *la mystère* explored.

In terms of contemplative poetry, *The Mystery of the Charity of Charles Péguy* marks an original difference from other instances of the tradition, even those that prize aesthetic over religious contemplation. For Hill admits and exposes the wavy line between truth and fiction, integrity and intransigence, commitment and zealotry. And he does so while refusing to separate an aesthetic attitude from an ethical one. He asks us to contemplate "the radical soul," not the eternal God, a Supreme Fiction, or the material world about us, and we do so in part by pondering a gap that keeps appearing between presence and representation, in part by brooding on different landscapes, and in part by beholding a conservative radical. If Péguy is a model of theological aesthetics, as Hans Urs von Balthasar urges, Hill's Péguy asks us to look at him instead through the lens of moral and political theology.[50] Péguy was a radical soul, to be sure, his radicality consisting in his principled decision in favor of selfless charity (and vice versa) and in his stubbornness in arguing for it. But there is hope, including for Britain, in contemplating something more general than one Frenchman whose virtues vie with his crochets for domination, namely, "the radical soul," which we can infer from the distinct case of Péguy (and, indeed, in the cases of the seventeenth-century nonconformists of "Mysticism and Democracy"). Hill presents the Frenchman's soul as an exemplary *templum*, crossed by psychological flaws and contrary passions, from which we can generalize and thus learn from, each in his or her way, and in doing so perhaps forestall the complete victory of *le tout autre monde* that he believes is already well advanced, that he recoils from and rejects so fiercely in "Mysticism and Democracy." At the same time, Hill writes a poem that is itself a *templum* in which we see an example of radical human life and an exemplary way in which to live it. To read it with all due care would be to become more deeply human.

Poem as *Templum*

As we saw in the first chapter, the ancient Romans would look into the sky and draw a rectangle there. With great care they would watch to see which birds flew into the space they had defined, exactly where they entered the sacred space, and the direction from which they flew into it. In looking at the *templum* they believed that they could tell the likelihood of success in military campaigns and whether there would be abundant crops in the coming season. Not everyone was persuaded, but even the skeptical Cicero thought that the institution should be preserved. That it was perpetuated is well known, although it did not continue in the way that Cicero or any of the Romans thought it would. Christians came to practice contemplation, the raising of the mind to God, and some of its practitioners figured it by way of birds flying in the sky. Prediction fell away, and loving suspension before God took its place. This could happen in mental prayer, which required only a focus—a candle or a cross—for eyes and minds prone to wandering. It could happen also in *lectio divina*, which led the monk or nun from reading to meditation to prayer to a dilation of the soul and gliding before God. And it could happen in many forms of lay contemplation, most of which we shall never know how they have been and still are performed.

For some people today, listening to music or reading poems is one way in which the mind is disengaged from the world, and no one—certainly not the church—can say that it will not allow one to taste the goodness of God. The church advocates a system of sacraments, each of which is held to contain the Grace that it signifies for the person properly prepared to receive it. Yet since the twelfth century it has also commended sacramentals, ways in which one invites God to come to the soul. They cannot be numbered. For there is no limit to the ways in which God can enter time or, better, we can attune ourselves to God. In this book I have not broached the idea of reading poems in order to draw close to God. This would be a possibility within the orbit of an expanded natural theology, which is the theme of the Gifford Lectures, but my concern has been otherwise. I have wanted to think natural theology beyond a limited concern with proof, even beyond argumentation, and regard it within a different affective and cognitive horizon: contemplation.

I have tried to present contemplation in its natural (or philosophical) as well as its Christian modes and keep the category as open as possible. I have sought to develop a new hermeneutic of contemplation, quite different from the old four senses theory. That is a rather stiff way of saying that I wanted to be precise about how to cultivate spacious reading, a type of reading that is based on understanding, not interpretation narrowly conceived. In contemplation, we can learn to look *at* what is before us without forever trying to look *through* it to find something else, supposedly higher or deeper and therefore able to explain what we are reading by fixing it to a procrustean bed. Other people, with quite different educations, will point to Asian traditions and garner what they have had to say about meditation. Had I known those languages, I would have said more about Asian religious practices. For my part, I have concentrated on how Romantic and post-Romantic poems, so often associated with a natural religious impulse, can often be approached by way of natural theology. The category of natural theology is thereby expanded far beyond proof and argumentation about the deity, yet is also reduced very considerably at times, for many of the most intriguing poems to read in this manner touch on natural theology for only a moment or two and do so in unusual ways. But these ways are often potent and have been overlooked. One can admire the truth, and one can reflect on it as well as try to establish it.

There is little doubt that some poems engage in mystification of one sort or another; they idealize what poets are, what they say, and what poetry can do for those who devote themselves to it. The practices need to be identified and addressed. But mystery is phenomenologically distinct from mystification, and it is my experience that a great many poems evoke and respond to mysteries, whether coded as religious or not. That there are religious mysteries goes without saying, even for people without faith; yet religious poems can be read without faith and yet with understanding. One long poem I have discussed seeks to replace religious contemplation with its aesthetic counterpart in the hope of passing from any thought of a supreme being to the idea of a Supreme Fiction: a correlation between mind and world is

explored in different profiles. Another long poem figures contemplation in terms of a secular, scientific attitude but slips into aesthetic and
religious-mythical moments. And a further long poem asks us to contemplate an exemplary soul in the hope that we might remain open to
love at its deepest, even if it can be abrasive. Such are the exemplary
works on which I have focused. In each case, I have drawn from the sequence of Schopenhauer, Coleridge, and Husserl to enable me better
to understand what is written and how I should respond to it. I hope
that I have not forgotten lessons that I learned long ago from Marx,
Nietzsche, and Freud, and I trust that I have learned to situate them
within a more capacious hermeneutic. I hope too that I have shown
how a degree of suspicion can uncover contemplative rhythms in a text.

That there are poems that attend to fascination is true, and I have
written about two very powerful ones. Fascination is a deeply rooted
danger in our intensely visual culture, however, and contemplation can
edge us away from its excesses. To read contemplatively is to help regain a measure of balance in life, including the important lesson that
we can never properly reduce anything living, even a poem, to a totality. We are always in search of wholes, and they play hide-and-seek
with us. Adopting another perspective, St. Augustine was surely right
when in *De doctrina christiana* he distinguished *frui* from *uti*, enjoyment from use. Only God is beyond all use value. What we can gain
in the secular world may be a chastened contemplation, one that is
very close to what was once valued as consideration, though without
its strong moral sense; but that is really nothing new, except for seeing how it works in poems of the low modernist period. With contemplation we encounter ourselves, to be sure, and early Christians were
quick to point out that, when we approach our deepest selves, we also
find God by way of the *imago dei*. Similarly, when reading poems, we
hear human voices that we cannot reduce to our own. We reflect on
them and find likenesses between ourselves and others, real or imagined. We begin to see how other minds relate to the world about us all.
In doing so, we could detect a second general thesis and accordingly
come to see that the world might not be as it is generally presented to
us. We might learn not to trust those who tell us, with ready authority, that the world is pregiven by way of party politics and power, by social media and visual culture, by celebrities and secular idols; we can
begin to see instead that the world manifests itself to us in diverse ways,
some of them wondrous. None of us can hope individually or even in
groups to change the world quickly and decisively, but we can begin to
live more richly and more truly, which means looking to the planet and
those who share it with us.

Reading does not denote a single or a singular practice; we read at different speeds, in distinct ways, and for different purposes. With poetry, however, and much else, there is reason to read slowly, by which I mean contemplatively, in order to encounter voices that speak to us of home or where home might be found or how home might be made larger or how we might welcome others into our homes. We can also learn from those poems that confront us as alien, for if nothing else they also tell us about someone else's home or need for home. Anyone can learn broadly and deeply from such encounters, and we can let the soul breathe a little more freely than it does otherwise. We look at those neat or ragged rectangles on the page that we call *poems* and experience ideas and feelings passing through them, coming from foreign parts, or coming from the past, or coming from people who have suffered or delighted in ways we would not come to know had we not picked up a book. And then those feelings and ideas pass through us, sometimes with the peculiar sense that they come from deep inside. Some of them we have difficulty naming or even taming, but, if we read well, they call to us day by day and year by year. We go back to them, time after time, for the rich pleasures they give us, pleasures that are also challenges to see the world anew, from fresh perspectives, including some that alarm us, frighten us, or jolt us awake. We do not use them to guess at things that might or might not happen; but we grow more human by pondering them.

The *templum* has come down from the heavens to the page. Medieval monks and nuns knew that in their own ways as they sought the lands of likeness when practicing *lectio divina*. Some of us still seek those lands, just as they did, and we talk about them by way of the kingdom. More of us, students and teachers, along with anyone who can read, can learn how to enter those other lands of likeness, often far from divine simplicity, that we call *poems*, and, if we make good choices in what we read, we have the opportunity to grow in wisdom when dealing with others and ourselves.

ACKNOWLEDGMENTS

It is a pleasure to thank first of all the Gifford Committee of the University of Glasgow for the honor of inviting me to give the Gifford Lectures in 2019, which, interrupted by the COVID-19 pandemic, were concluded in 2023 and gave rise to this book. The kindness of the university community to my wife and son as well as to me remains a precious memory. In particular, I would like to thank Ramona Fotiade and Olivier Salazar-Ferrer for their solicitude and friendship when we were in Scotland. The eighth president of the University of Virginia, Professor Teresa A. Sullivan, generously granted me an additional semester of study leave that enabled me to write this book along with the book of my Étienne Gilson Lectures for 2000 at the Institut catholique de Paris.

Many people have helped me in gathering the sources for this work. Keith Weimer, the religious studies librarian at the University of Virginia, went to great lengths to track down several obscure references. Father Claude Pavur SJ cordially shared his knowledge of early Jesuit history. Greg Goering aided me in thinking about meditation in the Hebrew scriptures, and Ahmed Al-Rahim pointed me to work on Islamic meditation practices. Alexander Hampton helped me track down an elusive sentence of Friedrich Schlegel's. Several friends and colleagues read parts of the book in draft form. Constant Mews commented on chapters 1 and 2. My exchanges with him about medieval philosophy and theology gave new zest to checking email each morning. Jean-Yves Lacoste read chapter 3 and shared his immense knowledge of Husserl. Rick Anthony Furtak kindly read chapter 4 and shared his love of Hopkins and phenomenology. Stephen Artner read chapters 2 and 3 with the sharp eye of a Germanist. Jean Ward read an early version of chapters 11 and 12, and her close attention improved them considerably. Alexandra Aidler read several chapters in their early forms and offered bracing criticisms. Gavin Flood read chapters 11 and 12, sharing his admiration for Geoffrey Hill's great poem about Charles Péguy. Philip Gates read each draft chapter as it emerged, and his comments have improved every page of the whole. Not only did Walter Jost invite me to coteach his doctoral seminar on low modernism; he also read a draft of the first part of the book and was characteristically generous with his time and advice. Henry Weinfield also read the whole, and his skeptical questions were, as always, a spur to improve what I had done. Murray Littlejohn and Stephanie Rumza also read parts of the book, which is far better for their devotion to it.

Conversation with friends over the years on the themes of this book, even before I set pen to paper, have left their mark. To Jacques Derrida, Emmanuel Falque, Jean-Yves Lacoste, Jean-Luc Marion, and Claude Romano I owe a debt of gratitude for showing in their conversation and their writings the particular ways of posing questions and responding to them that only the French can display with ease. I mourn the loss of dear friends whose encouragement of my writing has always buoyed me up, now as much as when I could speak with them: again, I name Jacques Derrida, and along with him I think with thankfulness of time spent with Harold Bloom, Ian Donaldson, Geoffrey Hartman, and Stephen Prickett. Other friends, very much alive, were unstinting in their support of my writing: Francis X. Clooney SJ, Sir Michael Edwards, Anthony J. Kelly CSsR, John Nemec, and David Tracy, in particular.

An early version of some pages in chapter 1 was originally given as the Aquinas Lecture for 2020 at the University of Dallas, and I would like to thank my hosts for inviting me to speak there and participate in their vibrant intellectual world. Particular thanks are also due to Benjamin Fingerhut at St. Augustine's Press, who saw the expanded, written form of the lecture through the press as *Contemplation and Kingdom: Aquinas Reads Richard of St. Victor* (2020). A highly condensed version of chapter 3 was given as a lecture at Campion Hall, Oxford (2021): my thanks to my host, Gavin Flood. Different versions of chapter 4 were delivered at the Duke University Divinity School (2019) and at Hillsdale College (2020): my thanks especially to Thomas Pfau (Duke) and to the chapter of the Thomistic Institute at Hillsdale. Part of chapter 5 was read at the "Psychology and the Other" conference held at Boston College in October 2019, and I am thankful especially to Carolyn Stack for her thoughtful response to my treatment of Philip Larkin's "Aubade." An invitation to speak on landscape contemplation at Williams College in 2016 prompted reflection that, I hope, is apparent in the book. My thanks to Mark C. Taylor, who organized the event. Invitations to speak to the Chesterton Society and to the Virginia chapter of the Thomistic Institute at the University of Virginia helped me sharpen my thoughts in several areas. Students who took my graduate seminar "Contemplation" (2012, 2013) and my undergraduate seminar "Medieval Mysticism" (2008, 2021) prompted me to read particular texts more closely and weigh some arguments and conclusions presented in the scholarly literature. My visits as theologian in residence at Positive Connection in Taneyville, Missouri, one of the best places for theological research in the United States, remain a treasured memory. My thanks to its director, Dave Stefan.

For permission to quote from Wallace Stevens, I am thankful to Faber and Faber Ltd and to Random House. For permission to quote from Thom Gunn, Philip Larkin, and Marianne Moore, I warmly acknowledge Faber and Faber Ltd, Simon and Schuster, Farrar, Straus and Giroux, and the Literary Estate of Marianne Moore. For permission to quote from A. R. Ammons, I am indebted to W. W. Norton. For permission to quote from Geoffrey Hill, my thanks are due to Oxford University Press. For permission to quote from John Ashbery's *Three Poems*, my gratitude is extended to George Borchardt, Inc. For permission to quote from Francis Ponge, I am obliged to Gallimard. And for permission to quote Gustave Roud, I am thankful to L'Association des amis de Gustave Roud. Finally, I am very thankful to the Gifford Committee for defraying expenses relating to licenses to quote previously published material.

It is always a great pleasure to publish a book with the University of Chicago Press. I would like to thank Kyle Wagner and Kristin Rawlings for all their help in shepherding the book through production and the two anonymous readers of the typescript for their expert commentaries.

My final thanks are to my wife, Sashanna Hart, who read the whole, engaging me in conversation about points I had made that did not satisfy her. Her attention made the book much better than it would otherwise have been, just as her presence has made my life so much richer than it would otherwise have been.

GLOSSARY

ἀγάπη	*agape* (divine love as shown by God for human beings and by human beings for God and other human beings)
ἀφαίρεσις	*aphaíresis* (taking away)
βάσκανος	*báskanos* (envious)
βίος θεωρητικός	*bios theortikós* (the contemplative life)
βίος πρακτικός	*bios practikós* (the practical life)
γνῶθι σεαυτόν	*gnōthi seauton* (know yourself)
εἶδος	*eidos* (form or essence)
ἐπέκτασις	*epéktasis* (striving or straining toward something)
ἐποχή	*epoché* (suspension)
ἔστι	*esti* (it is)
ἔφηβος	*ephebos* (male adolescent in military training)
θαύμα	*thauma* (wonder)
θεωρία	*theoría* (contemplation)
θεωρία φυσική	*theoría physiké* (natural contemplation)
θεωροί	*theoroí* (ambassadors who observed sacred festivals)
ἰδέα	*idea* (idea)
κένωσις	*kenosis* (self-emptying)
κήρυγμα	*kerygma* (proclamation)
λόγος	*logos* (word, language, study; with an initial capital the Second Person of the Trinity)
μέθοδος	*méthodos* (method)
μετάνοια	*metanoia* (change of mind)
τα πρώτα	*ta próta* (the first things)
το ὄντως ὢν	*to óntos on* (the really real)
φάρμακον	*pharmakon* (remedy or poison or scapegoat)
φιλοσοφία	*philosophía* (the friendship of wisdom)
ὑπὲρ πάντα τὰ ὄντα	*hyper pánta ta ónta* (above or beyond all beings)

NOTES

Introduction

1. See "Lord Adam Gifford's Will" (August 21, 1885), https://www.giffordlectures.org/lord-gifford/will.

2. Alternative programs for natural theology have been entertained in recent decades. See, e.g., the project of "dialectical theism" as explored in John Macquarrie, *In Search of Deity: An Essay in Dialectical Theism* (London: SCM, 1984).

3. Aristides offers his natural theology after, he says, contemplating the creation. See *The Apology of Aristides*, ed. J. Armitage Robinson (1891; reprint, Nendeln: Kraus, 1967), 35. It is not to be supposed that natural theology was left uncontested. Aristides's contemporary Tatian distanced himself from any natural cognition of God; his own conversion was won by reading scripture. For the story of the conversion, see Tatian, *Oratio ad Graecos and Fragments*, ed. and trans. Molly Whittaker (Oxford: Clarendon, 1982), §§ 29–30. After Aquinas, one finds, among others, Denis the Carthusian finding a place for natural theology in his treatise on contemplation. See Denis the Carthusian, *Contemplation*, in *Spiritual Writings*, trans. Íde M. Ní Rian, with an introduction by Terence O'Reilly (Dublin: Four Courts, 2005), 1.39.

4. See Plato, *Timaeus*, 29a, 53a–b, 56c; David Hume, *Dialogues concerning Natural Religion and Other Writings*, ed. Dorothy Coleman (Cambridge: Cambridge University Press, 2007), pt. 9; Immanuel Kant, *Critique of Pure Reason*, trans. Norman Kemp Smith (London: Macmillan, 1933), A594/B622–A597/B625, A597/B625–A602/B630; G. M. Leibniz, *Philosophical Papers and Letters*, 2nd ed., ed. Leroy E. Loemker (Dordrecht: Reidel, 1969), 109–12, 477–85; and William Paley, *Natural Theology; or, Evidence of the Existence and Attributes of the Deity*, in *The Works of William Paley* (Philadelphia: J. J. Woodward, 1836), 387–487.

5. Isaac Newton, *Principia*, trans. Andrew Motte, rev. Florian Cajori, 2 vols. (Berkeley: University of California Press, 1934), 2:544.

6. See Edward Hitchcock, *The Religion of Geology and Its Connected Sciences* (Boston: Phillips, Sampson, 1851).

7. See A. J. Ayer, *Language, Truth and Logic* (London: Victor Gollancz, 1936).

8. See W. V. O. Quine, "Two Dogmas of Empiricism" (1951), in *From a Logical Point of View: Nine Logico-Philosophical Essays* (Cambridge, MA: Harvard University Press, 1964), 20–46.

9. See William Lane Craig and J. P. Moreland, eds., *The Blackwell Companion to*

Natural Theology (Oxford: Basil Blackwell, 2012). Eleven of the twelve chapters have the word *argument* in their titles. By contrast, in this respect, see Russell Re Manning et al., *The Oxford Handbook of Natural Theology* (Oxford: Oxford University Press, 2013). This prizing of argument over contemplation was not at first the starred feature of the English philosophical tradition. John Locke underlines the importance of contemplation, in a diminished sense, which he defines as "keeping the idea which is brought into it, for some time actually in view." See John Locke, *An Essay concerning Human Understanding*, ed. and abridged by A. S. Pringle-Pattison (Oxford: Clarendon, 1924), 79.

10. On this theme, see N. T. Wright, *History and Eschatology: Jesus and the Promise of Natural Theology* (Waco, TX: Baylor University Press, 2019), esp. 4, 30, 157.

11. One might object that it is impossible to think of Jesus as a natural human being without also thinking of him as divine. However, the Chalcedonian definition specifies that he is "truly man" and that "the difference of the Natures [is] in no way removed because of the Union." T. Herbert Bindley, ed., *The Oecumenical Documents of the Faith* (London: Methuen, 1899), 297. Historical analysis can speak only of the human being Jesus of Nazareth. Also relevant is the claim that were one to have observed the resurrection of Jesus, e.g., one would have had something as secure as proof. On this theme, see Arthur Gibson, *Metaphysics and Transcendence* (London: Routledge, 2003), 147–52.

12. It might be objected that the prophets and saints benefit from Grace, yet Grace perfects nature and does not abolish it or diminish it.

13. On this theme, see Victor Preller, *Divine Science and the Science of God: A Reformulation of Thomas Aquinas* (Princeton, NJ: Princeton University Press, 1967), 179–80.

14. A Christian skepticism with respect to proof in sacred matters is long-standing. See, e.g., St. Maximos the Confessor, "First Century on Theology," no. 9, in *The Philokalia*, ed. and trans. St. Nikodemos of the Holy Mountain and St. Makarios of Corinth, 5 vols. (London: Faber and Faber, 1979 [vols. 1–4]; n.p.: Virgin Mary of Australia and Oceania, 2020 [vol. 5]), 2:116. A stress that contemplation supplies intuition—for him, direct awareness—of what is contemplated is given in Joseph Pieper, *Happiness and Contemplation*, trans. Richard Winston and Clara Winston, with an introduction by Ralph McInerny (South Bend, IN: St. Augustine's, 1998), 74, 78.

15. On phenomena that give themselves by not giving themselves, see Anthony J. Steinbock, "Generativity and the Scope of Generative Phenomenology," in *The New Husserl: A Critical Reader*, ed. Donn Welton (Bloomington: Indiana University Press, 2003), 289–325. I take the expression *generative phenomenology* from Steinbock.

16. See Hesiod, *Theogony and Works and Days*, trans. Catherine M. Schlegel and Henry Weinfield (Ann Arbor: University of Michigan Press, 2006). The motif of natural theology was noted and discussed in Lewis Campbell, *Religion in Greek Literature: A Sketch in Outline* (London: Longman, Green, 1898), chap. 5. The early Greeks sometimes figured the stars as heroes in their afterlives, while Aratus of Soli (315–240 BCE) in his *Phaenomena* regarded the stars as a text that Zeus had composed. Philo in *De opificio mundi* 73 conceived the stars as alive, as did various early Jewish writers. See, e.g., Judg. 5:20; Job 38:7; Dan. 8:10.

17. It is worth noting that there has been a renewed interest in contemplation in recent years. See, e.g., Peter Cheyne, *Coleridge's Contemplative Philosophy* (Oxford: Oxford University Press, 2020); Zena Hitz, *Lost in Thought: The Hidden Pleasures of an Intellectual Life* (Princeton, NJ: Princeton University Press, 2020); Eleanor Johnson, *Staging Contemplation: Participatory Theology in Middle English Prose, Verse, and Drama* (Chicago: University of Chicago Press, 2018); and Rik van Nieuwenhove, *Thomas Aquinas and Contemplation* (Oxford: Oxford University Press, 2021). I draw on Cheyne in

the first chapter and van Nieuwenhove in the second chapter. I regret that I came across ✓ Lucy Alford's *Forms of Poetic Attention* (New York: Columbia University Press, 2020) only when this book was in production.

18. See Plato, *Republic*, 517d, and *Phaedrus*, 247b–c; and Aristotle, *Nicomachean Ethics*, 1178b25. Also see the commentary on the passage in Michael of Ephesus, *On Aristotle's Nicomachean Ethics 10*, trans. James Wilderding and Julia Trompeter, bound with Themistius, *On Virtue*, trans. Alberto Rigolio (London: Bloomsbury, 2019), 93. Also see Plotinus, *Enneads*, trans. A. H. Armstrong, Loeb Classical Library (Cambridge, MA: Harvard University Press, 1988), 1.2.1.

19. In some respects, my *L'image vulnérable: Sur l'image de Dieu chez Saint Augustin* (Paris: Presses Universitaires de Paris, 2021) is a preparatory study for this volume.

20. One way in which the thought was developed is in the direction of deification. See, e.g., Pseudo-Dionysius the Areopagite, *Ecclesiastical Hierarchy*, in *The Complete Works*, trans. Colm Luibheid, with a foreword by Paul Rorem, a preface by René Roques, and an introduction by Jaroslav Pelikan, Jean Leclercq, and Karlfried Froehlich (London: Society for Promoting Christian Knowledge, 1987), 1.4. For a recent version of the claim, see Illtyd Trethowan, *Absolute Value: A Study in Christian Theism* (London: Allen & Unwin, 1970), 123.

21. See Augustine, *Confessions*, trans. and with an introduction by Maria Boulding, vol. 1/1 of *The Works of Saint Augustine* (hereafter *WSA*) (Hyde Park, NY: New City, 2002), 7.10.16.

22. Achard of St. Victor, "On the Solemnity of Saint Augustine," in *Works*, trans. and with an introduction by Hugh Feiss (Kalamazoo, MI: Cistercian, 2001), 67. Also see the remarks on "illumination in likeness" in St. Bonaventure, *The Threefold Way*, in *Writings on the Spiritual Life*, with an introduction and notes by F. Edward Coughlin, vol. 10 of *Works of St. Bonaventure* (Saint Bonaventure, NY: Franciscan Institute Publications, 2006), 128. Étienne Gilson notes something similar in St. Bernard's reflections on Augustine. See Étienne Gilson, *The Mystical Theology of St. Bernard*, trans. A. H. C. Downes (London: Sheed & Ward, 1940), 45. Likeness to God and loss of likeness to God through sin is a strong theme of Russian Orthodox spirituality. See, e.g., Nicholas Zernov, *Three Russian Prophets: Khomiakov, Dostevesky, Soloviev* (London: SCM, 1944), 32.

23. For illuminating detail, see Bernard McGinn, *The Crisis of Mysticism: Quietism in Seventeenth-Century Spain, Italy, and France*, The Presence of God: A History of Western Christian Mysticism, vol. 7 (New York: Crossroad, 2021).

24. See Friedrich Schleiermacher, *On Religion: Speeches to Its Cultured Despisers*, ed. Richard Crouter (Cambridge: Cambridge University Press, 1996).

25. I am thinking primarily of Rush Rhees (1905–89), D. Z. Phillips (1934–2006), and Peter Winch (1926–97). Nonetheless, see D. Z. Phillips, *Religion and the Hermeneutics of Contemplation* (Cambridge: Cambridge University Press, 2001). *Religion and the Hermeneutics of Contemplation* is more interesting for what it says about individual philosophers of religion than for what it proposes about the hermeneutic of contemplation, as Phillips sees it. I would like to pay homage to three of my teachers: Bill Ginnane, Peter Herbst, and Kevin Presa.

26. Traces of *contemplatio* remain in England after the Reformation. John Donne, e.g., evokes contemplation in the sermon "Preached to the Lords upon Easter-day" (1619), in *The Oxford Edition of the Sermons of John Donne*, vol. 1, *Sermons Preached at the Jacobean Courts, 1615–1619*, ed. Peter McCullough (Oxford: Clarendon, 2015), 135. Also see Henry Vaughan's "The Night" (esp. the final stanza), in *The Works of Henry*

Vaughan, vol. 2, *Texts 1654, Letters, and Medical Marginalia*, ed. Donald R. Dickson, Alan Rudrum, and Robert Wilcher (Oxford: Clarendon, 2018), 610–12. On the change of *contemplatio* from mystical ascent to faith in Christ with Calvin and in Lutheranism, esp. with respect to Johann Arndt, see Bernard McGinn, *Mysticism in the Reformation, 1500–1650*, The Presence of God, vol. 6, pt. 1 (New York: Crossroad, 2016), 52–53, 161–62.

27. The passage from unlikeness to likeness involves renunciation. The point is made very plainly by Hendrik Herp in the fourth part of *A Mirror of Perfection*, which is itself influenced by Victorine spirituality. See Hendrik Herp, *A Mirror of Perfection*, in *Late Medieval Mysticism of the Low Countries*, ed. Rik van Nieuwenhove et al., Classics of Western Spirituality (New York: Paulist, 2008), 146. One early instance of contemplation becoming chastened and joining θεωρία and plainly not involving a likeness between contemplator and contemplated is Izaac Walton's *The Compleat Angler* (1653). Walton is chiefly concerned to argue that in angling contemplation and action meet. See Izaac Walton, *The Compleat Angler*, ed. with an introduction and commentary by Jonquil Bevan (Oxford: Clarendon, 1983), esp. 69.

28. William Wordsworth, "Preface to *Lyrical Ballads*," in *The Prose Works of William Wordsworth*, ed. W. J. B. Owen and Jane Worthington Smyser, 3 vols. (Oxford: Clarendon, 1974), 1:148.

29. For Coleridge on contemplation, see chap. 2.

30. The point is nicely made in Stephen Prickett, *Romanticism and Religion: The Tradition of Coleridge and Wordsworth in the Victorian Church* (Cambridge: Cambridge University Press, 1976), 19, 105. In an earlier generation, Vernon Storr testifies to the link between mystery and poetry in the early Romantics as well as the importance for them of natural religion. See Vernon F. Storr, *The Development of English Theology in the Nineteenth Century, 1800–1860* (London: Longmans, Green, 1913), 130, 132.

31. See John Keats to George and Thomas Keats, December 22, 1817, in *The Letters of John Keats*, ed. H. Buxton Forman (Cambridge: Cambridge University Press, 2012), letter 25; Mary Shelley, preface to *Posthumous Poems* (1824), in P. B. Shelley, *Poetical Works*, ed. Thomas Hutchinson, new ed., corrected by G. M. Matthews (Oxford: Oxford University Press, 1943), xxv.

32. Matthew Arnold, "The Study of Poetry," in *Essays in Criticism, Second Series, Contributions to "The Pall Mall Gazette" and Discourses in America*, vol. 4 of *The Works of Matthew Arnold*, ed. Thomas Burnett Smar (London: Macmillan, 1903), 2. In *Literature and Dogma* (1873), Arnold figures *Auberglaube*, extrabelief, as "the poetry of life." On the intimate connection of poetry and religion, but from quite another angle, see John Keble, *Lectures on Poetry, 1832–1841*, ed. E. K. Francis, 2 vols. (Oxford: Clarendon, 1912), 2:479–80.

33. With regard to Victorian authors, it needs to be remembered that J. S. Mill testifies to Wordsworth's poetry pointing him to the possibility of "real permanent happiness in tranquil contemplation." See J. S. Mill, *Autobiography* (1865; reprint, New York: Columbia University Press, 1924), 104. This is closer to aesthetic contemplation than it is to its religious counterpart.

34. T. E. Hulme, "Romanticism and Classicism," in *Selected Writings*, ed. Patrick McGuiness (Manchester: Carcanet, 1998), 71; M. H. Abrams, *Natural Supernaturalism: Tradition and Revolution in Romantic Literature* (New York: W. W. Norton, 1971). Of course, the religion of Romanticism was not always Christian. For an early complaint about this, see H. N. Fairchild, *Religious Trends in English Poetry*, vol. 3, *1780–1830* (New York: Columbia University Press, 1949). More generally, on early Romanticism's view

of literature and religion, see Jean-Luc Nancy and Philippe Lacoue-Labarthe, *The Literary Absolute: The Theory of Literature in German Romanticism*, trans. Philip Barnard and Cheryl Lester (Albany: State University of New York Press, 1988), chap. 2. For an example of what animates Nancy and Lacoue-Labarthe, see Friedrich Schlegel, *Dialogue on Poetry and Literary Aphorisms*, trans. and with an introduction and annotations by Ernst Behler and Roman Struc (University Park: Pennsylvania State University Press, 1968), 54.

35. Robert Duncan, "The Truth and Life of Myth: An Essay in Essential Autobiography," in *Collected Essays and Other Prose*, ed. and with an introduction by James Maynard (Berkeley and Los Angeles: University of California Press, 2014), 182.

36. Harold Bloom, "Poetry, Revisionism, Repression," in *Poetics of Influence: New and Selected Criticism*, ed. and with an introduction by John Hollander (New Haven, CT: Henry R. Schwab, 1988), 131. Also see Harold Bloom, "The Internalization of Quest Romance," in *The Ringers in the Tower: Studies in Romantic Tradition* (Chicago: University of Chicago Press, 1971), 13–36.

37. See Stopford A. Brooke, *Theology in the English Poets: Cowper, Coleridge, Wordsworth and Burns* (London: H. S. King, 1874); and Paul de Man, "Heidegger's Exegeses of Hölderlin," in *Blindness and Insight: Essays in the Rhetoric of Contemporary Criticism* (1983), 2nd, rev. ed., with an introduction by Wlad Godzich (London: Methuen, 1989), esp. 250.

38. Robert Ryan pointedly observes: "British Romanticism's historical milieu was at least as intensely religious in character as it was political." See Robert M. Ryan, *The Romantic Reformation: Religious Politics in English Literature, 1789–1824* (Cambridge: Cambridge University Press, 1997), 10. Doubtless it would be possible to explore the Romantic relation to religion in terms of the "secularization thesis," associated with David Martin and Charles Taylor, but this topic falls outside the scope of this volume.

39. See, e.g., Vicente Huidobro, "Arte Poetica," in *Selected Poetry*, ed. and with an introduction by David M. Guss (New York: New Directions, 1981), 2–3. Also see Jacques Maritain, *Creative Intuition in Art and Poetry* (New York: New American Library, 1953), 50.

40. See Jean Paulhan, *The Flowers of Tarbes; or, Terror in Literature*, trans. Michael Syrotinski (Champaign: University of Illinois Press, 2006).

41. As two indices only, see William Carlos Williams, "The Poem as a Field of Action," in *Selected Essays* (New York: New Directions, 1958), 280–91; and Jake Skeets, "Poetry as Field," *World Literature Today* 93, no. 4 (2019): 92–94. Williams does not explore the central metaphor in his essay.

42. Jean-Pierre Richard, foreword to *Pages paysages: Microlectures II* (Paris: Éditions du Seuil, 1984), n.p.

43. See, e.g., Maritain, *Creative Intuition in Art and Poetry*, 163.

44. T. S. Eliot, "The Use of Poetry and the Uses of Criticism," in *The Complete Prose of T. S. Eliot: The Critical Edition* (hereafter *CPE*) (London: Faber and Faber; Baltimore: Johns Hopkins University Press, 2021), 4:658.

45. See T. S. Eliot, "The Clark Lectures. Lectures on the Metaphysical Poetry of the Seventeenth Century with Special Reference to Donne, Crashaw and Cowley," in *CPE*, 2:652–54, and "The Percy Graeme Turnbull Memorial Lectures: The Varieties of Metaphysical Poetry," in *CPE*, 4:715–16. On March 16, 1926, Eliot wrote to Messrs. John Grant to obtain, if possible, several volumes of J.-P. Migne's *Patrologia latina*. Among the works he wished to read were those of Richard of St. Victor. See *The Letters of T. S. Eliot*, ed. Valerie Eliot and John Haffenden, 9 vols. to date (New Haven, CT: Yale

University Press, 1941–), 3:107. An electronic search of *The Complete Prose of T. S. Eliot* reveals many instances of *contemplation* and *contemplative*.

46. John Crowe Ransom, "Poetry: A Note in Ontology," in *The World's Body* (New York: Scribner's, 1938), 116.

47. I. A. Richards, *Principles of Literary Criticism* (London: Kegan Paul, Trench, Trubner, 1924), 248, and *Science and Poetry*, 2nd ed. (London: Paul, Trench, Trubner, 1935), 90.

48. See Friedrich Nietzsche, preface to *Daybreak: Thoughts on the Prejudices of Morality*, trans. R. J. Hollingdale, with an introduction by Michael Tanner (Cambridge: Cambridge University Press, 1982), 5.

49. See, e.g., Paul de Man, *Allegories of Reading: Figural Language in Rousseau, Nietzsche, Rilke, and Proust* (New Haven, CT: Yale University Press, 1979), 245.

50. See my *The Trespass of the Sign: Deconstruction, Theology, and Philosophy* (Cambridge: Cambridge University Press, 1989).

51. See the account of paleonomy—the science of old words standing for new concepts—in Jacques Derrida, *Positions*, trans. Alan Bass (Chicago: Chicago University Press, 1981), 71.

52. Deconstruction, as Derrida practiced it, is deeply indebted to Husserl's notion of sedimentation (*Sedimentieren*). His procedure is a regressive inquiry, a desedimentation, that grants no privilege to the present (*Gegenwart*), ontologically, ontically, or epistemologically.

53. Northrop Frye, *The Well-Tempered Critic* (Bloomington: Indiana University Press, 1963), 47.

54. Paul Ricoeur, foreword to Don Ihde, *Hermeneutic Phenomenology: The Philosophy of Paul Ricoeur* (Evanston, IL: Northwestern University Press, 1971), iv. For a detailed examination of the "hermeneutics of suspicion," see Alison Scott-Baumann, *Ricoeur and the Hermeneutics of Suspicion* (New York: Continuum, 2009). The slightly different expression *age of suspicion* was coined by Nathalie Sarraute in the title essay of her *The Age of Suspicion: Essays on the Novel*, trans. Maria Jolas (New York: George Braziller, 1963), 57. The French original of the collection appeared in 1956, and the title essay first appeared in *Les temps modernes* 52 (February 1950): 1417–28. Sarraute credits the first use of *suspicion* in a cultural sense to Stendhal.

55. On the fourfold meaning of scripture, see Henri de Lubac, *Medieval Exegesis: The Four Senses of Scripture*, trans. Mark Sebanc et al., 3 vols. (Grand Rapids, MI: Eerdmans, 1998–2009).

56. Geoffrey Hill, "The Mystery of the Charity of Charles Péguy," in *Broken Hierarchies: Poems, 1952–2012*, ed. Kenneth Haynes (Oxford: Oxford University Press, 2013), 147.

57. See Martin Heidegger, *Discourse on Thinking*, trans. John M. Anderson and E. Hans Freund, with an introduction by John M. Anderson (New York: Harper & Row, 1966), 46. For a discussion of the theme, see Ian Alexander Moore, *Eckhart, Heidegger, and the Imperative of Releasement* (Albany: State University of New York Press, 2019).

58. See, e.g., Paul T. Corrigan, "Attending to the Act of Reading: Critical Reading, Contemplative Reading, and Active Reading," *Essays in Reader-Oriented Theory, Criticism and Pedagogy* 65/66 (2012): 146–73; David Kahane, "Learning about Obligation, Compassion, and Global Justice: The Place of Contemplative Pedagogy," *New Directions for Teaching and Learning* 118 (2009): 49–60; and Charles Suhor, "Contemplative Reading," *English Journal* 91, no. 4 (2013): 28–32.

Chapter One

1. On this theme, see Andrea Wilson Nightingale, *Spectacles of Truth in Classical Greek Philosophy: "Theoria" in its Cultural Context* (Cambridge: Cambridge University Press, 2004).

2. For a discussion of the two senses, see David Roochnik, "What Is *Theoria*? *Nicomachean Ethics*, Book 10.7–8," *Classical Philology* 104, no. 1 (2009): 69–82.

3. See Plato, *Republic*, 517d, and *Phaedrus*, 247b–c.

4. See Plato, *Republic*, bks. 5–7; and Aristotle, *Nicomachean Ethics*, bk. 10.

5. See Aristotle, *Nicomachean Ethics*, 1178b25. Also see the commentary on the passage in Michael of Ephesus, *On Aristotle's Nicomachean Ethics 10*, 93. Also see Plotinus, *Enneads*, 1.2.1.

6. See Origen, *The Song of Songs: Commentary and Homilies*, ed. R. P. Lawson (New York: Newman, 1957), 369–70. Origen is also the first to note that Peter represents the active life. Early Christianity did not take over the distinction between πρᾶξις and θεωρία that had been so important—and variously so—for the Greeks. On the importance and complexities of this distinction, see Nicholas Lobkowicz, *Theory and Practice: History of a Concept from Aristotle to Marx* (Notre Dame, IN: University of Notre Dame Press, 1967), chaps. 1–2.

7. See, e.g., Cicero, *De officiis*; and Seneca the Younger, *De vita beata, De otio*, and *De tranquillitate animi*. The influence of Philo on Christian understandings of the active and contemplative lives needs to be taken into account. More generally, see Thomas Bénatouïl and Mauro Bonazzi, eds., *Theoria, Praxis, and the Contemplative Life After Plato and Aristotle* (Leiden: Brill, 2012). The division between the active and the contemplative lives goes back to Luke 10:38–42, the story of Mary and Martha, to which an allegorical interpretation of the story of Leah and Rachel in Gen. 29:16–20 was added in the Middle Ages. Augustine's reformulation of the classical understanding of the active and contemplative lives was decisive. See Augustine, *City of God*, 19.19. Also see Augustine, "The Lord's Sermon on the Mount," 3.10, in which the attainment of wisdom through contemplation brings peace to a person and establishes "a likeness to God." Augustine, *The New Testament 1 and 2*, ed. Boniface Ramsey, vols. 1/15 and 1/16 of *WSA* (Hyde Park, NY: New City, 2014), 27.

8. The issue of perpetual prayer became a problem with the Messalian movement. See Columbia Stewart, *"Working the Earth of the Heart": The Messalian Controversy in History, Texts, and Language to AD 431* (Oxford: Oxford University Press, 1991). It irrupted again in the seventeenth century with the notion of prayer as "one act," which meant that the soul was perpetually praying. The idea was proposed in Juan Falconi de Bustamante (1596–1638), *Castillas para la oración*, ed. Elías Gómez Domínguez (Madrid: Editores Fundación Universitaria Española, 1995), chaps. 7–10. In Greek and Russian spirituality, perpetual prayer is a major theme. See in particular St. Symeon the New Theologian, "How All Christians Should Pray without Ceasing," in *The Philokalia*, 5:327–31, and *The Pilgrim's Tale*, ed. and with an introduction by Aleksei Pentkovsky, trans. T. Allan Smith, and with a preface by Jaroslav Pelikan (New York: Paulist, 1999).

9. I would not wish to suggest that the Greeks practiced only two modes of life. A full account would also need to consider the life of pleasure (βίος ἀπολαυστικός) and the political life (βίος πολιτικός).

10. Augustine's name is linked to several rules: two texts known as the *Praeceptum* (one for men and another for women) and the *Ordo monasterii*. The *Praeceptum* for

monks is a major source for the *Regula Sancti Benedicti*, and another is the anonymous *Regula magistri*.

11. Gaius Marius Victorinus (290–364) had translated some books by Aristotle and also by the Platonists (perhaps Plotinus and Porphyry), as Augustine testifies in *Confessions*, 7. Augustine probably derived knowledge of Aristotle, except for the *Categoriae*, from Varro's *Disciplinarum libri*. The Western "rediscovery" of Aristotle's texts largely took place in twelfth-century Europe. His logical writings had been translated from Greek into Latin by Boethius, although only a slim selection of them was in wide circulation before the mid-twelfth century. A full translation of the *Nicomachean Ethics* was not available until 1246–47. With respect to this, see in particular Jon Miller, ed., *The Reception of Aristotle's Ethics* (Cambridge: Cambridge University Press, 2013). In general, Plato reentered philosophical and theological consciousness in the Latin tradition a century or so after Aristotle had done the same. Early Christian writers relied chiefly on doxographies, such as those compiled by Pseudo-Plutarch and Clement of Alexandria; many of these have been lost. For details, see H. I. Marrou, *Saint Augustin et la fin de la culture antique* (Paris: De Boccard, 1938); and Harald Hagendahl, *Augustine and the Latin Classics*, vol. 2, *Augustine's Attitude* (Gothenburg: Acta Universitatis Gothoburgensis, 1967), esp. chap. 5. Yet the Byzantine holdings of Greek learning have often been overlooked. See Speros Vryonis, *Byzantium and Europe* (New York: Harcourt, Brace & World, 1967), 108. The case for Byzantine holdings of Greek writings and against the commonplace view that Islam had sole ownership of the learning that was transmitted to Western Europe is forcefully put in Darío Fernández-Morera, *The Myth of the Andalusian Paradise: Muslims, Christians, and Jews under Islamic Rule in Medieval Spain* (Wilmington, DE: ISI, 2016), 71–78, 271 n. 65 (for detailed bibliographic support).

12. Denis the Carthusian offers an extreme example. His *Opera omnia* runs to 43 volumes.

13. Elsewhere, Gregory took pains to specify the different traits of the active and contemplative lives. See Gregory the Great, *Homilies on the Book of the Prophet Ezekiel*, trans. Theodosia Tomkinson (Etna, CA: Center for Traditionalist Orthodox Studies, 2008), 2.2.8. The notion of the mixed life (μικτὸς βίος) goes back to Aristotle, *Nicomachean Ethics*, 1172b, and one finds it sporadically thereafter, as in Arius Didymus (d. 10 BCE), passages of whose writings were preserved by Stobaeus. See Augustus Meineke, ed., *Ioannis Stobaei Ecologarum physicarum et ethicarum libri duo* (Leipzig: Teubneri, 1860), bk. 2.

14. Louis Martz supplies many examples in the seventeenth century. See, in particular, Louis L. Martz, *The Poetry of Meditation: A Study in English Religious Literature of the Seventeenth Century* (New Haven, CT: Yale University Press, 1954), introduction.

15. Aquinas does not make extensive reference to twelfth-century authors, far less so than Bonaventure does. Yet he mentions Richard of St. Victor in many places. The *Index thomisticus* gives fourteen citations in the commentary on the *Sententiae*, four in the *Summa theologiae*, two in *De veritate*, fourteen in *De potentia dei*, and others in further works. There is little commentary on the relation. See, however, Emmanuel Durand, "Comment practiquer la théologie trinitaire en pèlerin? Béatitude et trinité selon Richard de Saint-Victor et Thomas d'Aquin," *Revue des sciences philosophiques et théologiques* 92 (2008): 209–23. I confine myself solely to Aquinas's discussion of Richard in the tractate on the active and contemplative lives.

16. The Eastern church, however, is profoundly rich in accounts of mental prayer,

especially in the tradition of Hesychasm. See in particular *The Philokalia*, esp. vol. 5. In the Eastern church, the distinction between active and contemplative lives is sometimes formulated quite differently than it is in the Western church. For a late defense of the view that contemplation is itself action, see *The Pilgrim's Tale*, 211–12.

17. See Cicero, *De natura deorum*, 1.50. Also see Tacitus, *The Annals of Imperial Rome*, trans. and with an introduction by Michael Grant, rev. ed. (Harmondsworth: Penguin, 1973), 15.63.

18. One thinks, e.g., of *De finibus*, the *Tusculanae disputationes*, *De fato*, *Paradoxa stoicorum*, and the (mostly) lost *Hortensius*.

19. See Cicero, *De diviniatione*, pt. 2. Also see J. P. F. Wynne, *Cicero on the Philosophy of Religion: On the Nature of the Gods and On Divination* (Cambridge: Cambridge University Press, 2020). Wynne argues that Roman *religio* was less about right belief than it was about right practice and that Cicero was in favor of moderating religion by philosophical inquiry, preserving it from superstition, on the one hand, and impiety, on the other. See ibid., 72, 272.

20. See the illuminating discussion of Cicero's view of the gods in Michael J. Buckley, *Motion and Motion's God: Thematic Variations in Aristotle, Cicero, Newton, and Hegel* (Princeton, NJ: Princeton University Press, 1971), esp. chap. 11.

21. There were five ways in which auspices were determined: *ex caelo*, *ex avibus*, *ex tripudiis*, *ex quadrupedibus*, and *ex diris*. See William Smith, ed., *A Dictionary of Greek and Roman Antiquities* (London: John Murray, 1875), 174–79. With regard to *ex avibus*, the augur establishes his ritual space, his *auguraculum*, by aligning the cardinal points. He faces east: wild birds entering the sacred space to the augur's left, the north, is an auspicious sign from the gods, while birds entering the space from the right, the south, is a discouraging sign. On the importance of birds for the Romans, see Cicero, *De legibus*, 2.8, and *De diviniatione*, 2.34. Finding auguries from the flight of birds was well-known to the Greeks, although they also had recourse to oracles. The Greeks looked to the right for favorable signs, the Romans to the left. See Plutarch, *Themistocles*, 12.

22. See Cyril Bailey, *Phases in the Religion of Ancient Rome* (Oxford: Oxford University Press, 1932), 160–62. Varro tells us that *templum* derives from *tueri*, "to gaze." Varro, *De lingua latina*, 7.7. The construction of a *templum* is detailed in Pliny the Elder, *Natural History*, trans. H. Rackham et al., 10 vols., Loeb Classical Library (Cambridge, MA: Harvard University Press, 1938–62), 18.76–77. Seneca remarks that the human form, with a head on top of a body, is made for contemplation. See Seneca, *De otio*, 5.4. Livy documents the origin of marking out sacred areas where one could look for the will of the gods. See Livy, *Ab urbe condita*, 1. 6–7. For further reference to auguries, see ibid., 4.18. A *templum* was not required for all auspices. On military campaigns, e.g., a group of sacred chickens was consulted: if the chickens ate the food given to them, it was taken to be a favorable sign. See ibid., 10.40.

23. The importance of the eagle appearing is underlined in Tacitus, *Annals*, 2.17. For birds giving auguries, see Plutarch, *Coriolanus*, 32, *Marcellus*, 4, and *Mark Antony*, 5.

24. See Plato, *Theaetetus*, 185d–e. The discussion of the Forms in the *Seventh Letter*, 341b–345c, would lead one to doubt whether writing could ever allow the Forms to be understood. Of course, the authenticity of the seventh letter is in question. Also see John Chrysostom, *On the Incomprehensible Nature of God*, trans. Paul W. Harkins, Fathers of the Church (Washington, DC: Catholic University of America Press, 1984); and Gregory of Nyssa, *Against Eunomius*, in *Nicene and Post-Nicene Fathers*, vol. 5, 1.99, 2.256, 2.89.

25. On the differences between philosophical and Christian contemplation, see Jacques Maritain, *Théonas; ou, Les entretiens d'un sage et de deux philosophes sur diverses matières inégalement actuelles*, 2nd ed. (Paris: Nouvelle Librarie Nationale, 1925), 44.

26. Needless to say, the Romans engaged in purification before rituals. See, e.g., Cicero, *De legibus*, 2.19. Christians differed from Romans not in their regard for purity before sacrifice but in what *purity* meant to them and how to achieve it, namely, by a heartfelt moral reform of life, followed by study and devotion to prayer, all of which requires divine Grace.

27. Origen, *The Song of Songs*, 44. The translation is of Rufinus's Latin translation of the partly lost original Greek text.

28. See Gregory of Nyssa, *The Life of Moses*, trans. and with an introduction by Abraham J. Malherbe and Everett Ferguson and with a preface by John Meyendorff (New York: Paulist, 1978), 92.

29. St. Paul identifies faith, hope, and charity as special virtues in 1 Thess. 1:3 and 1 Cor. 13, and Augustine elaborates on the triad in *Enchiridion*, 8. Aquinas introduces the notion of the infused moral virtues in *Summa theologiae* (hereafter *ST*), 1–2 q. 63 art. 3. The idea was contested by Duns Scotus. See *Opus oxoniense*, bk. 3, dist. 36 n. 28. Incidentally, it should be noted that Augustine granted a limited role to auguries. See Augustine, *Sermons on the New Testament*, trans. Edmund Hill, ed. John E. Rotelle, vol. 3/4 of *WSA* (New York: New City, 1990), sermon 1, 12.4. Yet also see Augustine, *Confessions*, 4.2.3. William E. Klingshirn discusses the issue in "Divination and the Disciplines of Knowledge according to Augustine," in *Augustine and the Disciplines: From Cassiciacum to Confessions*, ed. Karla Pollmann and Mark Vessey (Oxford: Oxford University Press, 2005), 113–40.

30. Augustine, *The Trinity*, trans. and with an introduction by Edmund Hill, ed. John E. Rotelle, vol. 1/5 of *WSA* (Brooklyn, NY: New City, 1991), 1.17.

31. See Gregory the Great, *Moral Reflections on the Book of Job* (hereafter *MJ*), trans. Brian Kearns, with an introduction by Mark DelCogliano, 6 vols. (Collegeville, MI: Liturgical, 2014–22), 1.25.34, 2.7.10, 5.32.56, and 5.36.66. Gregory's work had extensive influence in the Middle Ages, as is suggested by, among other things, Peter of Waltham's digest of it, *Remediarium conversorum*, which is extant in seventeen manuscripts. See Peter of Waltham, *Remediarium conversorum: A Synthesis in Latin of "Moralia in Job" by Gregory the Great*, ed. Joseph Gildea (Villanova, PA: Villanova University Press, 1984). It is worth noting that the *Moralia* was read each year at table at the Abbey of St. Victor from the beginning of August until the beginning of September. Gregory reflects further on contemplation in his other biblical commentaries. See Gregory the Great, *On the Song of Songs*, trans. and with an introduction by Mark DelCogliano (Collegeville, MI: Liturgical, 2012), and *Homilies on the Book of the Prophet Ezekiel*. Coming before Gregory is *De vita contemplativa* by Julianus Pomerius (450–500).

32. On this theme, see my *L'image vulnérable*. Augustine also writes of *attentio*, a stretching out toward something beyond the soul. See the remarks on this in my *Kingdoms of God* (Bloomington: Indiana University Press, 2014), chap. 1.

33. See Gregory the Great, "Letter to Leander," in *MJ*, 5.

34. One exception is Hagar, who, after encountering an angel, testifies, "Thou art a God of seeing [ra'ah]," for she asks: "Have I really seen God and remained alive after seeing him?" (Gen. 16:13 [RSV]).

35. See Eccles. 1:13, 7:25; Pss. 94:11, 104:34, 119:97, 1:2.

36. See *Regula Sancti Benedicti*, chap. 48; and Rom. 10:8–10. More generally, see

Brian Stock, *After Augustine: The Meditative Reader and the Text* (Philadelphia: University of Pennsylvania Press, 2001), 105.

37. See William of St. Thierry, *The Golden Epistle: A Letter to the Brethren at Mount Dieu*, trans. Theodore Berkeley, with an introduction by J. M. Déchanet (Kalamazoo, MI: Cistercian, 1971), 31.121.

38. On the immediate influence of Eriugena, especially the *Periphyseon* and the *Homilia in Johannen*, see John J. O'Meara, *Eriugena* (Oxford: Clarendon, 1988), chap. 11.

39. See John Scotus Eriugena, *De caelesti ierarchia*, in *Patrologia latina* (hereafter *PL*), ed. J.-P. Migne, 217 vols. (Paris: J.-P. Migne, 1841–55), vol. 122, cols. 1037–69 (122.2.1.146c). Eriugena uses the word *reduceretur* when writing about our being led back to our original state of contemplative wonder.

40. See, e.g., Gregory the Great, *MJ*, 5.5; and Aquinas, *ST*, 2a2ae q. 180 art. 7 ad 2.

41. Nonetheless, see the late fourteenth-century text *The Chastening of God's Children*, in which temptations common to the contemplative life and the importance of spiritual direction are emphasized, in *The Chastening of God's Children and the Treatise of Perfection of the Sons of God*, ed. Joyce Bazire and Eric Colledge (Oxford: Basil Blackwell, 1957), esp. 174. Also see *The Remedy against the Troubles of Temptations*, in *Yorkshire Writers: Richard Rolle of Hampole, an English Father of the Church, and His Followers*, ed. Carl Horstmann, 2 vols. (London: Swan Sonnenschein, 1895), 2:109–13 (chap. 4).

42. Sometimes alarmingly so, as with Quietist teaching about nonresistance to temptation. See McGinn, *The Crisis of Mysticism*, 58–59.

43. See Origen, *Homilies on Luke; Fragments on Luke*, trans. Joseph T. Lienhard, Fathers of the Church (Washington, DC: Catholic University of America Press, 1996), 6.7; and Ambrose, *Concerning Virgins*, ed. Henry Wace and Philip Schaff (Seattle: Amazon, 2017), 2.2.10.

44. The treatise, entitled *De gratia contemplationis, seu Benjamin Major* by J.-P. Migne—see *PL*, vol. 196, cols. 63–192—is edited as the *De contemplatione (Beniamin maior)*, but it is also known as *De arca mystica* (*The Mystical Ark*) and *De arca Moysi* (*The Ark of Moses*). It is preceded in in the *Patrologia latina* by *De praeparatione animi ad contemplationem, liber dictus Benjamin minor*, which concerns itself with the preparations for contemplation. See *PL*, vol. 196, cols. 1–63. Richard of St. Victor's *The Ark of Moses* (hereafter *AM*) is translated by Ineke Van't Spijker and Hugh Feiss in *Spiritual Formation and Mystical Symbolism*, ed. Grover A. Zinn, Dale M. Coulter, and Frans van Liere, Victorine Texts in Translation, vol. 10 (Turnhout: Brepols, 2022).

45. See, e.g., Richard of St. Victor, *AM*, 2.9.

46. On canons regular, see Caroline W. Bynam, "The Spirituality of Regular Canons in the Twelfth Century," in *Jesus as Mother: Studies in the Spirituality of the High Middle Ages* (Berkeley and Los Angeles: University of California Press, 1982), 22–58. On the Abbey of St. Victor, see Frans van Liere and Juliet Mousseau, eds., *Life at Saint Victor*, Victorine Texts in Translation, vol. 9 (Turnhout: Brepols, 2021). For a general introduction to the Victorines, see Robert J. Porwoll and David Allison Orsbon, eds., *Victorine Restoration: Essays on Hugh of St. Victor, Richard of St. Victor, and Thomas Gallus* (Turnhout: Brepols, 2021).

47. Hugh introduces the distinction in the first of his homilies, *In ecclesiasten homiliae*. See *PL*, vol. 175, cols. 116d–117d. After Hugh and Richard, versions of the distinction recur. See, e.g., Walter Hilton, *The Scale of Perfection*, trans. and with an introduction and notes by John P. H. Clark and Rosemary Dorwood and a preface by Janel Mueller (New York: Paulist, 1991), bk. 1, chap. 15.

48. Richard of St. Victor, *AM*, 1.3.

49. Richard of St. Victor, *AM*, 1.3.

50. Richard of St. Victor, *AM*, 1.3. Bonaventure will develop the taxonomy so that it consists of meditation, prayer, and contemplation in his influential *De triplici via* (completed by 1260).

51. See Iamblichus, *On the Pythagorean Way of Life*, ed. John Dillon and Jackson Hershbell (Atlanta: Scholars, 1991), chap. 12. In the Latin West, Boethius says something similar. See Boethius, *De consolatione philosophiae*, 5.2. It should be pointed out that the motif was common in the ancient world. Seneca, e.g., writes of the intimacy of God and freedom in *De vita beata*, 15.7.

52. See Richard of St. Victor, *AM*, 1.1.

53. See Richard of St. Victor, *AM*, 1.4. Clearly, Richard is adapting the definition of contemplation in homily 1 of Hugh of St. Victor's *In ecclesiasten homiliae*, which he goes on to quote. For *In ecclesiasten homiliae*, see *PL*, vol. 17, col. 117a.

54. See Boethius, *The Consolation of Philosophy*, 5.4.

55. Richard of St. Victor, *AM*, 6. See, e.g., the seven subdivisions of the first level of contemplation. Ibid., 2.6. The Platonic origin of the division has been detailed in J.-A. Robillard, "Les six genres de la contemplation chez Richard de Saint-Victor et leur origine platonicienne," *Revue des sciences philosophiques et théologiques* 28 (1939): 229–33. Richard's distinctions surely influenced Bonaventure's *Itinerarium mentis in deum* (1259).

56. On the notion of ascent, see Richard of St. Victor, *De exterminatione mali et promotione boni*, in *PL*, vol. 196, cols. 1073–1114.

57. See Plotinus, *Enneads*, 1.6.9.24–25; and Augustine, *On Order*, trans. and with an introduction by Silvano Borruso (South Bend, IN: St. Augustine's, 2007), 2, *On Music*, in *The Immortality of the Soul, Magnitude of the Soul, On Music, Advantage of Believing, Faith in Things Unseen* (Washington, DC: Fathers of the Church, 1947), 6, and *Confessions*, 3.6.11.

58. For semantic ascent, see Paul Vincent Spade, "The Logic of the Categorical: The Medieval Theory of Descent and Ascent," in *Meaning and Inference in Medieval Philosophy*, ed. Norman Kretzmann (Dordrecht: Springer, 1988), 187–224.

59. See William of Ockham, *Summa logicae*, ed. Philotheus Boehner, Gedeon Gál, and Stephanus Brown, Opera Philosophia, 1 (St. Bonaventure, NY: Franciscan Institute, 1974), cap. 70, *De divisionibus suppositionis personalis*.

60. See Fyodor Doestoevsky, *Devils*, trans. Michael R. Katz (Oxford: Oxford University Press, 2008), 250. Richard points out that one should not begin with corporeal things that might pollute one's heart. Richard of St. Victor, *AM*, 2.1.

61. See Augustine, *On Order*, 1.9.27. Augustine speaks in more detail of ascent in several places, most notably in *The Magnitude of the Soul*, in *The Immortality of the Soul, Magnitude of the Soul, On Music, Advantage of Believing, Faith in Things Unseen*, 33.70–76, *Confessions*, 7 and 9, *On Music*, 6, *True Religion*, trans. Edmund Hill, in *On Christian Belief*, ed. Boniface Ramsey, vol. 1/8 of *WSA* (New York: New City, 2005), 50.98–99, and *Teaching Christianity*, trans. and with notes by Edmund Hill, ed. John E. Rotelle, vol. 1/11 of *WSA* (New York: New City, 1996), 2.9–11.

62. See F. R. Yeatts, "Tree Shape and Branch Structure: Mathematical Models," *Mathematical and Computational Forestry and Natural-Resource Sciences* 4, no. 1 (2012): 2–15.

63. See Augustine, *The Literal Meaning of Genesis*, in *On Genesis*, trans. and with an introduction and notes by Edmund Hill, ed. John E. Rotelle, vol. 1/13 of *WSA* (Hyde Park, NY: New City, 2002), bk 4.

64. On these two modes of knowledge, see Aquinas, *ST*, 1a q. 58 art. 6, 7.

65. See Richard of St. Victor, *The Book of Notes*, in *Interpretation of Scripture: Theory*, ed. Franklin T. Harkins and Frans van Liere, Victorine Texts in Translation, vol. 3 (Turnhout: Brepols, 2012), 310 (2.2). The idea that the Christian God can be contemplated in nature, not just in himself, precedes Richard. See St. John Cassian, "On the Holy Fathers of Sketis and on Discrimination," in *The Philokalia*, 1:96–97, and esp. St. Peter of Damoskos, "Contemplation of the Sensible World," in *The Philokalia*, 3:247–49. (Peter was Richard's Eastern contemporary.) Peter's orientation is quite different from Richard's: "Until our intellect has died to the passions, it should not attempt to embark on the contemplation of sensible realities." Ibid., 247. Also see St. Peter of Damoskos, "Conscious Awareness of the Heart," in *The Philokalia*, 3:277.

66. On the three modes, see Jean Châtillon, "Les trois modes de la contemplation selon Richard de Saint-Victor," *Bulletin de littérature ecclésiastique* 41 (1940): 3–26.

67. See Richard of St. Victor, *AM*, 4.2; and, more generally, Steven Chase, *Angelic Wisdom: The Cherubim and the Grace of Contemplation in Richard of St. Victor* (Notre Dame, IN: University of Notre Dame Press, 1995), esp. 116–19.

68. Note that the motif of suspension or gliding in contemplation is not universally adopted in the Middle Ages. In the late fourteenth century, e.g., one finds the figure of wrestling in the darkness as well as paring away an "encumbering lump." Both are proposed by the anonymous author of *The Cloud of Unknowing* in chap. 2 of his translation of the Pseudo-Dionysius's *The Mystical Theology*. See Pseudo-Dionysius the Areopagite, *The Mystical Theology*, in *The Cloud of Unknowing and Other Works*, trans. and with an introduction by A. C. Spearing (London: Penguin, 2001).

69. For the couple of Leah and Rachel as exemplars of the active and contemplative lives, see Augustine, *Answer to Faustus, a Manichean*, trans. Roland Teske, vol. 1/20 of *WSA* (Hyde Park, NY: New City, 2007), 22.52. Also see Richard of St. Victor, "Answers to Questions regarding the Rule of St. Augustine," in van Liere and Mousseau, eds., *Life at Saint Victor*, 290–92 (q. 14).

70. See Richard of St. Victor, *AM*, 5.7.

71. See, e.g., Denis Fahey, *Mental Prayer according to the Principles of Saint Thomas Aquinas* (1927; reprint, Fitzwilliam, NH: Loreto, 2018); Jean-Pierre Torrell, *Christ and Spirituality in St. Thomas Aquinas*, trans. Bernhard Blackenhorn (Washington, DC: Catholic University of America Press, 2011), esp. 6–18, 25–27; and, chiefly with respect to the speculative dimension of contemplation, van Nieuwenhove, *Thomas Aquinas and Contemplation*.

72. Denis the Carthusian examines Richard's views of contemplation while remaining sympathetic to Aquinas's criticisms of Richard. See Denis the Carthusian, *Contemplation*, 2.6. Yet see ibid., 1.66, where he considers nature as an object of contemplation.

73. Gregory is presumably alluding to John 8:25 as rendered in the Vulgate: "dicebant ergo ei tu quis es dixit eis Iesus principium quia et loquor vobis." Reference to Gregory is constant in the treatise on action and contemplation in the *Summa theologiae*. In the *Scriptum super Sententiis*, Aquinas makes the same point with reference to Aristotle, *Nicomachean Ethics*, 10. See Aquinas, 3 *Sententiae* d. 35 a. 2 q. 3. Also see Aquinas, *ST*, 1a q. 3 art. 5 *resp.*

74. See Aquinas, 3 *Sententiae* d. 35 q. 1 a. 2 q. 2 *resp.* Also see Aquinas, *De veritate*, q. 15 art. 1 *resp.* The view is not restricted to Aquinas. See, e.g., Bonaventure, *Itinerarium mentis in deum*, c. 5, n. 3.

75. See Aquinas, *ST*, 1a q. 2 art. 3 *resp.*

76. Gregory the Great, *MJ*, 17.9.11. Further, see ibid., 23.27.53. One might also point out that elsewhere Aquinas distinguishes three aspects of contemplation: height, fullness, and perfection. Of these, height is God, perfection is a matter of the moral sciences, and fullness is found in the natural sciences. See Aquinas, *Commentary on the Gospel of John*, trans. Fabian Larcher and James A. Weisheipl, with an introduction and notes by Daniel Keating and Matthew Levering, 3 vols. (Washington, DC: Catholic University of America Press, 2010), 1:3–4.

77. Gregory the Great, *MJ*, 2.6.37, 61. Further, see Aquinas, *Commentary on the Gospel of St Matthew*, trans. Paul M. Kimball (n.p.: Dolorosa, 2012), 5:10. Aquinas could well have cited Augustine, *De doctrina christiana*, 1.2, in support of his view.

78. The view is an early one of Aquinas. See Aquinas, 1 *Sententiae* d. 1 a. 1; and *De veritate*, q. 22 art. 2 ad 1. Also see the remarks on seeking wisdom in the contemplation of creatures in Aquinas, "Puer Jesus," in *The Academic Sermons*, trans. Mark-Robin Hoogland (Washington, DC: Catholic University of America Press, 2007), 103.

79. Also see Aquinas, *ST*, 2a2ae q. 175 art. 1 ad 1.

80. See Umberto Eco, *The Aesthetics of Thomas Aquinas*, trans. Hugh Bredin (Cambridge, MA: Harvard University Press, 1988).

81. Aquinas, *ST*, 2a2ae q. 180 art. 4 obj. 3.

82. See Aquinas, *ST*, 1a2ae q. 68 and 2a2ae q. 8 and q. 45. Aquinas is drawing on Isa. 11:1–2.

83. See Aquinas, *De veritate*, q. 15 art. 1 resp.

84. Aquinas, *ST*, 2a2ae q. 180 art. 4 ad 3. Aquinas often uses *consideratio* or one of its forms beginning with the *Scriptum super sententiis* and especially in the second part of the *Summa theologiae*.

85. Also see Aquinas, 3 *Sententiae* d. 35 q. 1 a. 2 q. 2. It should be noted that Aquinas does not always use *consideratio* in the sense outlined above. Sometimes he used it simply to denote mental reflection and not the practice advocated by St. Bernard. See Aquinas, *ST*, 1–2 q. 35 art. 5 ad 3, where he writes of contemplation being a consideration of truth: "contemplatio . . . nihil aliud sit quam consideration veri."

86. See Aquinas, *ST*, 2a2ae q. 180 art. 4 ad 4.

87. Richard also maintains that the soul rests at each level of ascent, but it cannot be, for Aquinas, the complete rest in the *principium* but only a lingering at a certain level of ascent.

88. See Hugh of St. Victor, sermon 72, in *PL*, vol. 177, col. 1131.

89. Aquinas, *ST*, 2a2ae q. 180 art. 3 ad 1.

90. Aquinas, 3 *Sententiae* d. 35 q. 1 a. 1 resp.

91. See Aquinas, 3 *Sententiae* d. 35 q. 1 a. 2 q. 3 resp.

92. For Augustine's theological anthropology, see my *L'image vulnérable*, esp. chaps. 2–4.

93. See Aquinas, *De veritate*, q. 15 art. 1 resp.

94. Aquinas, 3 *Sententiae* d. 35 q. 1 a. 2 q. 3 resp. Also see Aristotle, *Nicomachean Ethics*, 9.8. Aristotle is himself following Greek emphasis on contemplation as a way of life.

95. A slightly different yet relevant motif appears in the New Testament. See, e.g., 2 Cor. 2:15: "For we are the aroma of Christ to God among those who are being saved and among those who are perishing" (RSV). The idea of tasting bliss belongs of course to the teaching of the spiritual senses, which runs mainly from patristic times to the Counter-Reformation.

96. See Aquinas, 3 *Sententiae* d. 36 q. 1 a. 3 a. 5.

97. I draw from Aquinas's view of Christ's knowledge: "totam sed non totaliter."

Aquinas, *Truth* vol. 1 q. 20 art. 5 *prae*. Aquinas does not himself use the expression with respect to contemplation.

98. In 3 *Sententiae* d. 35 a. 2 q. 3 *resp.*, Aquinas distinguishes *contemplatio*, which is reserved for God, and *speculatio*, which pertains to looking for God in created things. Richard often uses *speculatio* in preference to *contemplatio* in the first four books of *The Ark of Moses*. On Richard's method of seeking ascent, see Dale M. Coulter, "*Per Visibilia ad Invisibilia*": *Theological Method in Richard of St. Victor (d. 1173)* (Turnhout: Brepols, 2006). On *speculatio* and *contemplatio* and their roots in Hugh of St. Victor's work, see Csaba Németh, "*Quasi Aurora Consurgens*": *The Victorine Theological Anthropology and Its Decline* (Tournhout: Brepols, 2020), 181–89. It is worth noting that later in the fourteenth century one finds from time to time a quite different emphasis in some devotional writing. Nicholas Love, e.g., commends that his readers contemplate the creaturely man Jesus, not the uncreated God whom he incarnates. See Nicholas Love, *The Mirror of the Blessed Life of Jesus Christ: A Reading Text*, ed. Michael G. Sargent (Exeter: University of Exeter Press, 2004), 10.

99. Also see Aquinas, *De veritate*, q. 12 art. 13 *resp.*

100. Aquinas, *ST*, 2a2ae q. 175 art. 1 *resp.*

101. Aquinas, *ST*, 2a2ae q. 175 art. 2 *resp.*, and *De veritate*, q. 13 art. 1–5.

102. Aquinas, *ST*, 2a2ae q. 175 art. 3 *resp.*

103. On this theme, developed in the direction of natural theology, see David Brown, *God and Enchantment of Place: Reclaiming Human Experience* (Oxford: Oxford University Press, 2004); and Mark R. Wynn, *Renewing the Senses: A Study of the Philosophy and Theology of the Spiritual Life* (Oxford: Oxford University Press, 2013).

104. Principal pre-Christian sources include Plato, Philo, Plotinus, the authors of the *Corpus hermeticum*, and of course the authors of the Hebrew scriptures.

105. See St. Peter of Damaskos, "A Treasury of Divine Knowledge," in *The Philokalia*, 3:108–43.

106. John Climacus's *Climax paradisi* (ca. 600) with its thirty steps, one for each year of Christ's life, is a model, although the book has little to say about contemplation. Of course, one can also multiply forms of contemplation by matching them to what is contemplated, e.g., God, the angels, created beings, the incarnation, and so on. See, e.g., St. Gregory of Sinai, "On Commandments and Doctrines," in *The Philokalia*, 4:248. Denis the Carthusian devotes the second book of his *Contemplation* to a recording of the stages of contemplation as proposed by various contemplatives.

107. Even in the case of Teresa of Ávila, the taxonomy offered in her *Autobiography* does not quite map onto the one presented in her *Interior Castle*.

108. The literature on affective piety is extensive, and my concern with it here is tightly restricted to contemplative practices. For recent work in the area, see, e.g., Sarah McNamer, *Affective Meditation and the Invention of Medieval Compassion* (Pittsburgh: University of Pennsylvania Press, 2009); and Michelle Karnes, *Imagination, Meditation, and Cognition in the Middle Ages* (Chicago: University of Chicago Press, 2011). For more detail about the different modes of mystical experience, see Bernard McGinn, *The Presence of God*, 7 vols. (New York: Crossroad, 1991–2021).

109. See Teresa of Ávila, *Interior Castle*, in *The Complete Works*, trans. E. Allison Peers, 3 vols. (London: Burns & Oates, 2002), 2:336.

110. See, e.g., St. John of the Cross, *The Ascent of Mount Carmel*, in *The Collected Works of St. John of the Cross*, trans. Kieren Kavanaugh and Otilio Rodriguez, with an introduction by Kieren Kavanaugh (Washington, DC: Institute of Carmelite Studies, 1979), bk. 2, chap. 14.

111. At the base of the view is Augustine's distinction between *uti* and *frui*, "use" and "enjoyment." See Augustine, *De doctrina christiana*, 1.21.

112. Robert Frost to Louis Untermeyer, January 1, 1916, in *The Letters of Robert Frost to Louis Untermeyer* (New York: Holt, Rinehart & Winston, 1963), 22.

113. See, above all, Martz, *The Poetry of Meditation*. Richard Baxter is the most significant Puritan who adopted and adapted meditative exercises. See *The Saints' Everlasting Rest* (1649).

114. Gustave Roud, *Air de la solitude et autres écrits*, with a preface by Philippe Jaccottet (Paris: Gallimard, 2002), 71–75.

115. See Jean Pouillon, *Temps et roman* (Paris: Gallimard, 1946), chap. 2, sec. 1 (b). Pouillon distinguishes narrators *avec, par derrière*, and *dehors*.

116. Gustave Roud, *Air de la solitude*, 72–73.

117. See W. H. Auden, "Caliban to the Audience," pt. 3 of "The Sea and the Mirror," in *Collected Poems*, ed. Edward Mendelson (New York: Random House, 1976), 325–40.

118. For influences on the prose poem in languages other than French, see Michael Benedikt, ed., *The Prose Poem: An International Anthology* (New York: Dell, 1976); and, more recently, Jeremy Noel-Todd, ed., *The Penguin Book of the Prose Poem: From Baudelaire to Anne Carson* (London: Penguin, 2020).

119. John Ashbery's prose is also influenced by Giorgio di Chirico. See Giorgio di Chirico, *Hebdemeros*, with an introduction by John Ashbery (Cambridge, MA: Exact Change, 2004).

120. John Ashbery, "Jane Freilicher," in *Reported Sightings: Art Chronicles, 1957–1987*, ed. David Bergman (Cambridge, MA: Harvard University Press, 1991), 242.

121. John Ashbery, "The System," in *Three Poems* (New York: Viking, 1973), 70, 71.

122. Ashbery, "The System," 72, 84, 73.

123. See Thomas Traherne, *Centuries*, with an introduction by John Farrar (New York: Harper & Bros., 1960). I am thankful to John Ashbery for a conversation in 1992 about the importance of this book for him in the writing of *Three Poems*. For an instance of this influence, see John Shoptaw, *On the Outside Looking Out: John Ashbery's Poetry* (Cambridge, MA: Harvard University Press, 1994), 141.

124. Ashbery, "The System," 75.

125. For the transcendental employment of understanding, see Kant, *Critique of Pure Reason*, A181–A182; and Edmund Husserl, *Ideas for a Pure Phenomenology and Phenomenological Philosophy: First Book: General Introduction to Pure Phenomenology*, trans. Daniel O. Dahlstrom (Indianapolis: Hackett, 2014), chap. 3.

126. See Angus Fletcher, *Allegory: The Theory of a Symbolic Mode* (1964), with a foreword Harold Bloom (reprint, Princeton, NJ: Princeton University Press, 2012), 107.

127. See Kevin Hart, "Eliot's Rose-Garden: Some Phenomenology and Theology in 'Burnt Norton,'" in *Poetry and Revelation: For a Phenomenology of Religious Poetry* (London: Bloomsbury, 2017), 41–80.

Chapter Two

1. The shift was not exclusively Christian, however. Plotinus, in particular, was concerned with union with the One, not only speculation about the One.

2. The figure of Christ as the true philosopher is widespread in the early church. See, e.g., Justin Martyr, *Dialogue with Trypho*, 8.1; Clement of Alexandria, *Stromata*, 1.28.3;

Augustine, *Contra Julianum*, 4.14, 72; and St. Neilos the Ascetic, "Ascetic Discourse," in *The Philokalia*, 1:200–201.

3. See Augustine, *Confessions*, 9.10.23–25. The living tradition is often called *the mystical body of Christ*, a notion that has roots in St. Paul (1 Cor. 12:12–14) and was ecclesially determined first in the bull *Unam sanctam* (1302) and much later in the encyclical *Mystici corporis* (1943). In the modern age, *contemplation* can accommodate group gazing. Henry James, e.g., writes of "communities of contemplation" that looked on certain Parisian shops and theaters. See Henry James, *A Small Boy and Others*, in *Autobiographies*, ed. Philip Horne (New York: Library of America, 2016), 229.

4. See Gregory of Nyssa, *Against Eunomius*, 2.89.

5. See, e.g., Abby Day, Giselle Vincett, and Christopher R. Cotter, eds., *Social Identities between the Sacred and the Secular* (London: Routledge, 2016). On the relations of the sacred and the secular with respect to translation, see Jacques Derrida, "De tours de Babel," in *Psyche: Inventions of the Other*, ed. Peggy Kamuf and Elizabeth Rottenberg, 2 vols. (Stanford, CA: Stanford University Press, 2007), 1 (chap. 8). Also see David Martin, *A General Theory of Secularization* (Oxford: Blackwell, 1978).

6. See Carl Schmitt, *Political Theology: Four Chapters on the Concept of Sovereignty*, trans. George Schwab (Chicago: University of Chicago Press, 2006), 36.

7. Kant does not reject positive religion so much as position it with respect to rational religion. See Immanuel Kant, *Religion within the Limits of Reason Alone*, trans. and with an introduction and notes by Theodore M. Greene and Hoyt H. Hudson (New York: Harper & Row, 1960), 47–48, and *Critique of Judgement*, trans. and with an analytic index by James Creed Meredith (Oxford: Oxford University Press, 1952), § 59. Also see the notion of *Aberglaube* as developed in Arnold, *Literature and Dogma*, chap. 2.

8. I briefly consider Croce's case in chap. 7.

9. See Maurice Blanchot, "Literature and the Right to Death," trans. Lydia Davis, in *The Work of Fire*, trans. Charlotte Mandell (Stanford, CA: Stanford University Press, 1995), 300–344; and Derek Attridge, "'This Strange Institution Called Literature': An Interview with Jacques Derrida," in *Acts of Literature*, ed. Derek Attridge (London: Routledge, 1992), 43–48. For Blanchot, literature (later widened to writing) exposes the reader to *le dehors*, while, for Derrida, literature, like all writing, opens onto *la différance*. For the former on the sacred, which for him is not distinct from the abyss, see Blanchot, "The 'Sacred' Speech of Hölderlin," in *The Work of Fire*, 111–31. More generally, see Kevin Hart, *The Dark Gaze: Maurice Blanchot and the Sacred* (Chicago: University of Chicago Press, 2004), and *Maurice Blanchot on Poetry and Narrative: Ethics of the Image* (London: Bloomsbury, 2023). Not all the relevant authors are French. It is worth recalling I. A. Richards, for whom some modern poetry, such as *The Waste Land*, seeks "a new order through the contemplation and exhibition of disorder." Richards, *Science and Poetry*, 71n.

10. On this sense of *interpretation*, see Susan Sontag, "Against Interpretation," in *Susan Sontag: Essays of the 1960s and 70s*, ed. David Rieff (New York: Library of America, 2013), 10–20.

11. See, e.g., Maurice Blanchot, "Mystery in Literature," in *The Work of Fire*, 43–60.

12. See, e.g., Bruno Latour, "Why Has Critique Run Out of Steam? From Matters of Fact to Matters of Concern," *Critical Inquiry* 30, no. 2 (2004): 225–48; Rita Felski, *The Limits of Critique* (Chicago: University of Chicago Press, 2015) (for reservations about "critique"); and Cheyne, *Coleridge's Contemplative Philosophy*, 346–47 (for observations about "suspicion").

13. See Jean-Yves Lacoste, *Être en danger* (Paris: Cerf, 2011).

14. For testimony about how reading poetry gives the flesh to itself, see Emily Dickinson, *The Letters of Emily Dickinson*, ed. Thomas H. Johnson and Theodora Ward (Cambridge, MA: Belknap Press of Harvard University Press, 1958), letter 342a; A. E. Housman, "The Name and Nature of Poetry," in *The Name and Nature of Poetry and Other Selected Prose* (New York: New Amsterdam, 1989), 193; and David Campbell, "Snake," in *Collected Poems*, ed. Leonie Kramer (Sydney: Angus & Robertson, 1989), 191–92.

15. See Wallace Stevens, "Man Carrying Thing," in *Collected Poetry and Prose* (hereafter *CPP*), ed. Frank Kermode and Joan Richardson (New York: Library of America, 1997), 306. Also see Wallace Stevens, *Adagia*, in *CPP*, 910.

16. This is not to say, however, that Schopenhauer is not uncritical of Kant. See Arthur Schopenhauer, "Critique of the Kantian Philosophy," in *The World as Will and Representation* (hereafter *WWR*), trans. and ed. Judith Norman et al., with an introduction by Christopher Janaway, 2 vols. (Cambridge: Cambridge University Press, 2010), 1:441–565.

17. On causality, see Schopenhauer, *WWR*, 2:332.

18. See Arthur Schopenhauer, *The Fourfold Root of the Principle of Sufficient Reason and Other Writings*, trans. and ed. David E. Cartwright et al., with an introduction by David E. Cartwright and Edward E. Erdmann (Cambridge: Cambridge University Press, 2012). In the preface to the first edition of his major work, *The World as Will and Representation*, Schopenhauer writes: "It is absolutely impossible to truly understand the present work unless the reader is familiar with this introduction and propaedeutic, and the concepts of that essay are presupposed here as much as if they had been included in the book." Schopenhauer, *WWR*, 1:7.

19. Schopenhauer, *WWR*, 1:40.

20. On the cognition of one's own willing, which cannot be an intuition (because intuition is spatial), see Schopenhauer, *WWR*, 2:207.

21. See Schopenhauer, *WWR*, 2:208–9. Schopenhauer's sense of will (and the coordinate notion desire) is more capacious than that of earlier philosophers, including Kant. There is no division between desire, in the sense of an intentional rapport with a representation, and action in the world. Instead, the will is immanent. Michel Henry takes Schopenhauer at his word when understanding *life* to mean "the will to life," but he develops the thought in a more affirmative direction. See Michel Henry, *Genealogy of Psychoanalysis*, trans. Douglas Brick (Stanford, CA: Stanford University Press, 1993), 134.

22. Schelling observes: "Will is primordial Being, and all predicates apply to it alone—groundlessness, eternity, independence of time, self-affirmation." Friedrich Wilhelm Joseph von Schelling, *Of Human Freedom*, trans. James Gutmann (Chicago: Open Court, 1936), 24. On Schelling's reliance on Böhme, see Cyril O'Regan, "The Trinity in Kant, Hegel, and Schelling," in *The Oxford Handbook of the Trinity*, ed. Gilles Emery and Matthew Levering (Oxford: Oxford University Press, 2011), 263.

23. See Arthur Schopenhauer, *Parerga and Paralipomena: Short Philosophical Essays* (hereafter *PP*), trans. and ed. Sabine Roehr and Christopher Janaway, with an introduction by Christian Janaway, 2 vols. (Cambridge: Cambridge University Press, 2014), vol. 2, chap. 10, "The Christian System," in *Religion: A Dialogue and Other Essays*, trans. Thomas Bailey Saunders (New York: Macmillan, 1899), 105–17, and *WWR*, 1:311, 302–3.

24. See the reflections on Schopenhauer's early melancholy as reported in David E. Cartwright, *Schopenhauer: A Biography* (Cambridge: Cambridge University Press, 2010), 4.

25. Schopenhauer, *WWR*, 1:201 (emphasis in original).

26. See Origen, *On First Principles*, 2.6.5. On boredom, see Schopenhauer, *PP*, 1:385.

27. See Schopenhauer, *WWR*, 2:146–56 ("On the Essential Imperfections of the Intellect").

28. Kant, *Critique of Judgement*, § 5. Also see § 12.

29. Yet see the use of the word in Schopenhauer, *WWR*, 2:387.

30. Such is one burden of Hans-Georg Gadamer, *Truth and Method*, 2nd ed., trans. Joel Weinsheimer and Donald Marshall (New York: Continuum, 1989). The following chapter continues this line of thought.

31. Schopenhauer also includes the negation of the will—in religious renunciation of life—as enabling one to escape the rule of the will. In addition, he concedes that in old age, when the will—especially sexual desire—ebbs, one is granted a more contemplative air. See Schopenhauer, *PP*, 1:431.

32. Schopenhauer, *WWR*, 1:201.

33. T. S. Eliot, "The Dry Salvages," in *Four Quartets* (London: Faber and Faber, 1943), lines 230–32. At Harvard, Eliot took courses in Sanskrit, Pali, and Philosophical Sanskrit. See Manju Jain, *T. S. Eliot and American Philosophy: The Harvard Years* (Cambridge: Cambridge University Press, 1992), 254–55. Also see Amar Kumar Singh, *T. S. Eliot and Indian Philosophy* (New Dehli: Sterling, 1990).

34. *Idea* in its several usages is defined in Kant, *Critique of Judgement*, § 57, remark 1.

35. Schopenhauer, *WWR*, 1:151.

36. Schopenhauer, *WWR*, 1:154. Nothing is said about the aesthetic ideas in Kant, *Critique of Judgement*, §§ 49, 57, although in some respects they are closer to Schopenhauer's sense of the Idea of pure reason.

37. Schopenhauer is certainly more open to cognizing the noumenal realm than Kant. "What we lack," he writes, "is only absolute and exhaustive cognition of the thing in itself." Schopenhauer, *WWR*, 2:208.

38. See Schopenhauer, *WWR*, 2:207.

39. Schopenhauer, *WWR*, 1:234.

40. Schopenhauer, *WWR*, 1:23.

41. Schopenhauer regards several phenomena as able to deflect contemplation: those things that stimulate our appetites, sensory or erotic, or that disgust us, along with those phenomena that confront us in a hostile manner. See Schopenhauer, *WWR*, 1:232ff. On a lack of clarity in Schopenhauer's conception of the artistic gaze in the passage under consideration, see Patrick Gardiner, *Schopenhauer* (Harmondsworth: Penguin, 1963), 204.

42. Schopenhauer, *WWR*, 1:209, 220.

43. Nietzsche contends, with some reason, that for Schopenhauer contemplation is chiefly required by the person of action. He contrasts Goethe's contemplation, which is "in the grand style," with Schopenhauer's. See Friedrich Nietzsche, "Schopenhauer as Educator," in *Untimely Meditations*, trans. R. J. Hollingdale, with an introduction by J. P. Stern (Cambridge: Cambridge University Press, 1983), 151–52. Nietzsche's early enthusiasm for Schopenhauer waned as early as *The Birth of Tragedy* (1872). Also see the criticisms of Schopenhauer in Friedrich Nietzsche, *The Gay Science: With a Prelude in Rhymes and an Appendix of Songs*, trans. and with commentary by Walter Kaufmann (New York: Vintage, 1974), §§ 99, 127.

44. See Schopenhauer, *WWR*, 1:218.

45. See Schopenhauer, *WWR*, 2:28, 444.

46. See Plato, *Republic*, bk. 10. Of course, Schopenhauer differs from Plato in seeing the Ideas through particulars.

47. Michel de Montaigne, "Of Repentance," in *The Complete Works*, trans. Donald M. Frame, with an introduction by Stuart Hampshire (New York: Alfred A. Knopf, 2003), 740.

48. Schopenhauer, *WWR*, 1:235 (also see §§ 63–64).

49. Schopenhauer, *WWR*, 1:205.

50. See Thomas Hood, "Sonnet" ("I had a Gig-Horse . . ."), in *The Complete Poetical Works of Thomas Hood*, ed. Walter Jerrold (London: Henry Froude, 1906), 236.

51. G. M. Hopkins, *Poems of Gerard Manley Hopkins*, 2nd ed., ed. with notes by Robert Bridges (London: Oxford University Press, 1931), 27.

52. For such Kantian monks, see Ulrich L. Lehner, *Enlightened Monks: The German Benedictines, 1740–1803* (New York: Oxford University Press, 2013).

53. See Schopenhauer, *WWR*, 1:401.

54. See Schopenhauer, *WWR*, 1:413–14, 2:628–30. Schopenhauer also sees wisdom in Pseudo-Dionysius the Areopagite and Eriugena and, in the latter, "a small drop of Indian wisdom." Schopenhauer, *PP*, 1:61. He is far more sympathetic to the spirit of renunciation in Hinduism and Buddhism than in Christianity.

55. See Schopenhauer, *WWR*, 2:626.

56. For Schopenhauer, the origin of the artwork is its conception, which presumably might occur when regarding a beautiful or sublime scene. See Schopenhauer, *PP*, vol. 2, § 215. For the difference between the beautiful and the sublime, see Schopenhauer, *WWR*, 1:226.

57. See Schopenhauer, *PP*, vol. 2, § 206.

58. Schopenhauer, *WWR*, 2:444.

59. For a discussion of this process, see Maurice Blanchot, *Lautréamont and Sade*, trans. Stuart Kendall and Michelle Kendall (Stanford, CA: Stanford University Press, 2004), 77.

60. The highest art for Schopenhauer is, however, music. Yet, in listening to music, one does not intuit an Idea, only the Will. So he does not include it in his classification of the arts.

61. Schopenhauer, *WWR*, 1:269. Also see the remark on abstract concepts as distinct from ideas in Schopenhauer, *PP*, 1:62.

62. I emphasize "in the modern era" since Plotinus (d. 270) proposes that in nature all things are engaged in contemplation of one sort or another. See *Enneads*, 3.8.

63. Samuel Taylor Coleridge, *Marginalia*, ed. H. J. Jackson and George Whalley, vol. 12 (in 6 pts.) of *The Collected Works of Samuel Taylor Coleridge* (hereafter *CC*) (Princeton, NJ: Princeton University Press, 1980–2002), pt. 5, 795. Coleridge is thinking of what he calls "Positive Reason" as distinct from "Negative Reason," which is merely formal.

64. Coleridge, *Marginalia*, pt. 5, p. 795. Coleridge does not note that the German writer may have been influenced by the emphasis on *Gefühl* in Friedrich Schleiermacher's *On Religion* (1799).

65. Coleridge retains the same view in 1829. See Samuel Taylor Coleridge, *On the Constitution of the Church and State according to the Idea of Each*, ed. John Colmer, vol. 10 of *CC* (Princeton, NJ: Princeton University Press, 1976), 165. He seems to have come on the Victorines only when reading Tennemann, perhaps as early as 1818, though certainly in the mid-1820s. He returned to Hugh sometime after July 2, 1829, and made cursory annotations to his *De sacramentis christianae fidei*. See Coleridge, *Marginalia*, pt. 2, pp. 182–83. Coleridge's distinction between "pseudo-mystic" and "Mystic" runs along very similar lines. See Samuel Taylor Coleridge, *Aids to Reflection*, ed. John Beer, vol. 9

of *CC* (Princeton, NJ: Princeton University Press, 2017), 389, and *On the Constitution of the Church and State*, 165. Cheyne argues that Coleridge correlates the Victorine model of contemplation with Böhme's "Seven Forms of Spirit." See Cheyne, *Coleridge's Contemplative Philosophy*, chap. 5.

66. See Cristina Flores, "'Contemplant Spirits': Ralph Cudworth and Contemplation in S. T. Coleridge," in *Coleridge and Contemplation*, ed. Peter Cheyne (Oxford: Oxford University Press, 2017), chap. 12. Douglas Hedley underlines the importance of Cudworth's natural theology for Coleridge. See Douglas Hedley, *Coleridge, Philosophy and Religion: "Aids to Reflection" and the Mirror of the Spirit* (Cambridge: Cambridge University Press, 2000), 29–33.

67. Louis Richeome, *The Pilgrim of Loreto*, trans. Edward Worsley, English Recusant Literature, 1558–1640 (London: Scholar, 1976), 49–50. I have modernized the spelling. Coleridge and Southey truncate the final sentence, which in Worsley's translation continues as follows: "who understand without discourse; although it may so happen, that the devout soul may enter into the divine wisdom that shall afford her inward objects, after the manner of visions, as it did often to the Prophets, and his most familiar friends and servants; or else where the party himself doth choose someone, where he feeleth greatest gust, and there stayeth without stirring." Ibid., 50. Another sentence following from this is also omitted in the *Omniana*: "It may happen also, that meditation may follow contemplation, as if one having attentively beheld an object, doth thereafter afterward ground some discourse, as *Moses* did, when having seen the vision of the burning Bush he approached, discoursing why it consumed not." Ibid., 50.

68. Samuel Taylor Coleridge and Robert Southey, *Omniana; or, Horae Otiosiores*, with an introduction by Robert Gittings (Fontwell: Centaur, 1969), 115–16. I give the passage with the punctuation of Richeome, *The Pilgrim of Loreto*, 50.

69. Coleridge and Southey, *Omniana*, 116.

70. Richeome writes: "contemplation do illuminate the understanding," "to discourse in the understanding," and "my understanding is delighted." *The Pilgrim of Loreto*, 48–49.

71. St. John of the Cross, *The Ascent of Mount Carmel*, bk. 1, chap. 13.

72. See Teresa of Ávila, *Interior Castle*. God draws the soul to himself from the fourth mansion right through to the seventh mansion.

73. Coleridge, *Marginalia*, pt. 5, p. 819.

74. For his part, St. John of the Cross is plain that the imagination plays no role in the apprehension of God. See *The Ascent of Mount Carmel*, bk. 2, chap. 8.

75. Coleridge, *Aids to Reflection*, 36.

76. Coleridge, *Marginalia*, pt. 5, p. 781. The angle brackets are part of the editorial apparatus of the edition.

77. See Samuel Taylor Coleridge, *The Friend*, ed. Barbara E. Rooke, vol. 4 (in 2 pts.) of *CC* (Princeton, NJ: Princeton University Press, 1969), *Logic*, ed. James Robert de Jager Jackson, vol. 13 of *CC* (Princeton, NJ: Princeton University Press, 1981), 13, 68, and *Aids to Reflection*, 217. On what Coleridge takes Plato to mean by ἰδέα, see *Marginalia*, pt. 5, p. 729.

78. Coleridge, *Aids to Reflection*, 224.

79. Coleridge, *Marginalia*, pt. 5, pp. 12, 743–44, 771. For Coleridge's view of Schelling's *Naturphilosophie*, see ibid., pt. 3, 286 n. 14 to line 5, and pt. 4, pp. 373–90.

80. Coleridge, *Marginalia*, pt. 5, p. 692. Coleridge is thinking of what he calls "Positive Reason" as distinct from "Negative Reason," which is merely formal.

81. For Kant's deflation of mysticism, see *Religion within the Limits of Reason Alone*,

162–63; and Immanuel Kant, "On a Newly Arisen Superior Tone in Philosophy," in *Raising the Tone of Philosophy: Late Essays by Immanuel Kant, Transformative Critique by Jacques Derrida,* ed. Peter Fenves (Baltimore: Johns Hopkins University Press, 1993), 117–71. For Coleridge's commentary on Böhme's *Works,* see Coleridge, *Marginalia,* pt. 1, pp. 553–686.

82. Coleridge, *Marginalia,* pt. 5, pp. 795–96. The strikeout indications that appear in some Coleridge quotes are an editorial convention indicating when Coleridge changed his mind about using a word.

83. See Samuel Taylor Coleridge, *The Statesman's Manual,* in *Lay Sermons,* ed. R. J. White, vol. 6 of *CC* (Princeton, NJ: Princeton University Press, 1972), 30.

84. Coleridge, *Marginalia,* pt. 5, pp. 780, 797.

85. Samuel Taylor Coleridge, *Notebooks,* ed. Kathleen Coburn, 5 vols. (Princeton, NJ: Princeton University Press, 1957), vol. 4, § 5210 f20. Cheyne usefully distinguishes between two senses of *idea* in Coleridge. There are primary ideas, which are transcendent and therefore timeless, and secondary ideas, which are historical and which one finds in human institutions such as the church. The historical ideas tend toward the eternal ideas, however, with varying degrees of success. See Cheyne, *Coleridge's Contemplative Philosophy,* 226–31 (8.1).

86. Coleridge, *The Statesman's Manual,* 114.

87. Coleridge, *Notebooks,* vol. 5, § 5685 f13.

88. Samuel Taylor Coleridge, *Opus Maximum,* ed. Thomas McFarland and Nicholas Halmi, vol. 15 of *CC* (Princeton, NJ: Princeton University Press, 2002), 223. Also see Coleridge's lament that Richard Baxter did not distinguish conceptions from ideas. Coleridge, *Marginalia,* pt. 1, p. 237.

89. The doctrine of trinitarian appropriation gains its impetus in the Pseudo-Dionysius's *The Divine Names.*

90. Coleridge, *The Friend,* pt. 2, pp. 173.

91. Coleridge, *Marginalia,* pt. 3, p. 460.

92. Coleridge, *Notebooks,* vol. 4, § 4524.

93. There are criticisms of the Ideas in the *Parmenides,* although since the protagonist is the young Socrates there is reason to think that Plato is being ironic and that the older Socrates will reconsider his and Parmenides's reasoning about the Ideas and be able to answer the older philosopher.

94. Henry James, *The Princess Casamassima,* in *Novels, 1886–1890,* ed. Daniel Mark Fogel (New York: Library of America, 1989), 484.

95. Coleridge, *Notebooks,* vol. 5, § 5495 f63.

96. Cheyne, *Coleridge's Contemplative Philosophy,* 349.

Chapter Three

1. Dorion Cairns, *Conversations with Husserl and Fink,* ed. Husserl-Archives, with a foreword by Richard M. Zaner (The Hague: Martinus Nijhoff, 1976), 47, 60. Husserl made the remarks on November 24 and December 23, 1931.

2. Edmund Husserl, *Logical Investigations,* trans. J. N. Findlay, 2 vols. (London: Routledge & Kegan Paul, 1970), 1:87. The same point is made in Edmund Husserl, *Introduction to Logic and Theory of Knowledge: Lectures 1906/7,* trans. Claire Oritz Hill (Dordrecht: Springer, 2008), 28.

3. Husserl, *Logical Investigations,* 2:861.

4. Husserl, *Logical Investigations*, 2:862. *Reel* refers to any phase of an experience. The word *real* is used to indicate something spatiotemporal. *Intentionality* denotes the idea that all consciousness is consciousness of something, internal or external. It includes many rapports with phenomena, including perception, memory, anticipation, and desire.

5. Husserl, *Logical Investigations*, 1:252.

6. Husserl, *Logical Investigations*, 2:862. Also see Husserl's remark: "Even transcendental psychology also is psychology." Ibid., 1:122 n. 1. The word *given* can sound odd to English ears in this context and can be silently glossed as "manifested." Similarly, the word *intuition* can be glossed as "awareness," without any relation to the colloquial sense of intuition as a sixth sense. Categorial intuitions are complex intentional acts directed at states of affairs, not at a simple phenomenon. Husserl does not explore any similarity between contemplative intuition, such as Pieper proposes, and phenomenological intuition, which is transcendental. Yet both the person contemplating God and the person contemplating phenomena are in search of *Evidenz*.

7. See Husserl, *Ideas . . . : First Book*, § 5.

8. Husserl often uses the word in its Latin form, *eidos*.

9. See Husserl, *Ideas . . . : First Book*, § 12.

10. See, in particular, Paul Natorp, "On the Question of Logical Method in Relation to Edmund Husserl's *Prolegomena to Pure Logic*," in *Readings on Edmund Husserl's "Logical Investigations*," ed. J. N. Mohanty (The Hague: Martinus Nijhoff, 1977), 55–66.

11. See Edmund Husserl, *Introduction to the Logical Investigations: A Draft of a Preface to the Logical Investigations* (1913), ed. Eugen Fink, trans. and with an introduction by Phillip J. Bossert and Curtis H. Peters (The Hague: Martinus Nijhoff, 1975), 25, 36. Also see Husserl, *Logical Investigations*, 1:330, 350, and *Ideas . . . : First Book*, § 22. Husserl returns to honor Lotze's insight in Edmund Husserl, *Ideas Pertaining to a Pure Phenomenology and to a Phenomenological Philosophy: Third Book: Phenomenology and the Foundations of the Sciences*, trans. Ted E. Klein and William E. Pohl (The Hague: Martinus Nijhoff, 1980), 50.

12. See the discussion of these words in David Carr, *Phenomenology and the Problem of History* (Evanston, IL: Northwestern University Press, 2009), 59–60. Robert Sokolowski favors the word *contemplation* for the stance of the disinterested observer. See, e.g., Robert Sokolowski, *Introduction to Phenomenology* (Cambridge: Cambridge University Press, 2000), 48. Jean-Yves Lacoste is in accord when he points out that *Ideas . . . : First Book* is "among other things a theory of contemplation, or almost." Jean-Yves Lacoste, *Recherches sur la parole* (Louvain-la-Neuve: Peeters, 2015), 273. I should add that Husserl does not think of positing a worldview (*Weltanschaung*) as having any part of philosophical contemplation.

13. Although there is no overt Christian resonance in Husserlian contemplation, there is a parallel with Buddhistic meditation, as Husserl makes clear in a short reflection dating from 1925. See Edmund Husserl, "On the Teachings of Gotama Buddha," in Fred J. Hanna, "Husserl on the Teachings of the Buddha," *Humanist Psychologist* 23 (1995): 367–68.

14. See Edmund Husserl, *Phantasy, Image Consciousness, and Memory (1898–1925)*, trans. John Brough (Dordrecht: Springer, 2005), 202, and "The Amsterdam Lectures," in *Psychological and Transcendental Phenomenology and the Confrontation with Heidegger (1927–1931)*, trans. and ed. Thomas Sheehan and Richard E. Palmer, Husserliana, vol. 6 (Dordrecht: Kluwer Academic, 1997), 247.

15. Also see Husserl, *Ideas . . . : Third Book*, 65.

16. Such would be Jacques Derrida's view when he proposes to interrogate philosophy, as conventionally understood, from its margins. See Jacques Derrida, *Margins of Philosophy*, trans. Alan Bass (Chicago: University of Chicago Press, 1982). Also see the interview with Derrida in Richard Kearney, *Dialogues with Contemporary Continental Thinkers: The Phenomenological Heritage* (Manchester: Manchester University Press, 1984), 111–12. One might also name Emmanuel Levinas here, for whom "first philosophy" is ethics. The metaphilosophical point would be that philosophy, as usually practiced, needs reflection on what it is doing and why it is doing it, a reflection that is animated by an ethical standpoint. See Emmanuel Levinas, *Totality and Infinity: An Essay on Exteriority*, trans. Alphonso Lingis (The Hague: Martinus Nijhoff, 1969).

17. Thus, Husserl develops from the mid-1920s a phenomenology of the reduction that amounts to a metaphenomenology.

18. See Edmund Husserl, "Philosophy as Rigorous Science," in *Phenomenology and the Crisis of Philosophy*, trans. and with an introduction by Quentin Lauer (New York: Harper & Row, 1965), 71–147, and "Fünf Aupsätz über Erneurung," in *Aufsätz und Vorträge (1922–1937)*, ed. Thomas Nenon and Hans Reiner Sepp, Husserliana, vol. 27 (Dordrecht: Springer, 1989).

19. Kant and Husserl both use the word *Anschauung* (intuition). For Kant, an intuition captures sensible impressions along with the forms of space and time; for Husserl, an intuition is the reception of an object or a category in its bodily givenness.

20. See Husserl, *Ideas . . . : First Book*, § 62.

21. See Edmund Husserl, *Cartesian Meditations: An Introduction to Phenomenology*, trans. Dorion Cairns (The Hague: Martinus Nijhoff, 1977), § 60.

22. See Husserl, *Ideas . . . : First Book*, §§ 51, 77.

23. On the general thesis and the natural attitude, see Husserl, *Ideas . . . : First Book*, §§ 27, 30. The word *attitude* suggests "cast of mind" or "mental framework" in English and does not connote any emotion, as is usual in the North American use of the word.

24. Kant, *Critique of Pure Reason*, B155.

25. Quite often, Husserl uses ἐποχή to mean "reduction." I follow the practice of distinguishing the two operations in Edmund Husserl, *The Crisis of European Sciences and Transcendental Phenomenology: An Introduction to Phenomenological Philosophy*, trans. and with an introduction by David Carr (Evanston, IL: Northwestern University Press, 1970), § 41.

26. This is the phenomenological reduction, not the eidetic reduction, which allows one to discern the laws that essentially characterize a phenomenon. For the latter, see Edmund Husserl, *Experience and Judgment*, rev. and ed. Ludwig Landgrebe, trans. James S. Churchill and Karl Ameriks, with an introduction by James Churchill and an afterword by Lothar Eley (Evanston, IL: Northwestern University Press, 1973), § 87, and *Ideas . . . : First Book*, § 5. Husserl also countenances "a sort of" reduction, such as when one passes from feeling something to reflecting theoretically on it. See Edmund Husserl, *Ideas Pertaining to a Pure Phenomenology and to a Phenomenological Philosophy: Second Book: Studies in the Phenomenology of Constitution*, trans. Richard Rojcewicz and André Schuwer (Dordrecht: Kluwer, 1989), § 11.

27. On phenomenologizing as "unhumanizing" man, see Eugen Fink, *Sixth Cartesian Meditation: The Idea of a Transcendental Theory of Method, with Textual Notations by Edmund Husserl*, trans. and with an introduction by Ronald Bruzina (Bloomington: Indiana University Press, 1995), 120. For Husserl, however, reduction does not unhumanize man so much as enrich him with the possibilities of rational advancement in life.

28. See, e.g., Edmund Husserl, "Attempt at a Distinction on the Stages on the Way to a Science of Transcendental Subjectivity," in *First Philosophy: Lectures 1923/24 and Related Texts from the Manuscripts (1920–1925)*, trans. Sebastian Luft and Thane M. Naberhaus (Dordrecht: Springer, 2019), 468–79. More generally, see Edmund Husserl, *Zur phänomenologischen Reduktion: Texte aus dem Nachlass, 1926–1935*, ed. Sebastian Luft, Husserliana, vol. 34 (Dordrecht: Kluwer, 2002). Also see Iso Kern, "The Three Ways to the Transcendental Phenomenological Reduction in the Philosophy of Edmund Husserl," in *Husserl: Expositions and Appraisals*, ed. Frederick Ellison and Peter McCormack (Notre Dame, IN: Notre Dame University Press, 1977), 126–49.

29. Cairns, *Conversations with Husserl and Fink*, 39.

30. See Husserl, *Cartesian Meditations*, § 15.

31. Fink prefers the word *Weltbefangenheit* to *natural attitude* for the very good reason that it captures the sense of being fascinated by the world, entangled in it and apparently unable to escape from it. See Fink, *Sixth Cartesian Meditation*, 74.

32. See Husserl, *Ideas . . . : Second Book*, § 49 e. Also see Thomas Nagel, *The View from Nowhere* (Oxford: Oxford University Press, 1986).

33. See Husserl, *Ideas . . . : Second Book*, §§ 2–5.

34. See, in particular, Rudolf Bultmann, "The New Testament and Mythology," in *The New Testament and Mythology and Other Basic Writings*, ed. and trans. Schubert M. Ogden (Philadelphia: Fortress, 1984), 1–44.

35. On generative phenomenology, see Anthony J. Steinbock, *Home and Beyond: Generative Phenomenology after Husserl* (Evanston, IL: Northwestern University Press, 1995), and "Generativity and the Scope of Generative Phenomenology," in Welton, ed., *The New Husserl*, 289–325.

36. See Husserl, *First Philosophy*, 304. The notion of a "spontaneous reduction" is explored in Jean-Yves Lacoste, "Appearance without Reduction," in *The Appearing of God*, trans. Oliver O'Donovan (Oxford: Oxford University Press, 2018), chap. 3.

37. See Husserl, *Ideas . . . : Second Book*, § 4.

38. Husserl's naming of the reduction changes considerably over his writing life. At times he writes as though transcendental reduction is distinct from phenomenological reduction. At other times he writes of the phenomenological-transcendental reduction. I shall not engage in narrow discussion of Husserl's nomenclature or offer a taxonomy of reduction. On "the awful tremor" of reduction, see Fink, *Sixth Cartesian Meditation*, 144.

39. Husserl, *Ideas . . . : First Book*, §§ 50, 88, and *The Crisis of European Sciences*, § 40.

40. See Husserl, *The Crisis of European Sciences*, § 35.

41. Husserl, *The Crisis of European Sciences*, § 55. More generally, see Iso Kern, *Husserl und Kant: Eine Untersuchung über Husserls Verhältnis zu Kant und zum Neukantianismus* (Dordrecht: Springer, 1964); and Tom Rockmore, *Kant and Phenomenology* (Chicago: University of Chicago Press, 2011).

42. See Husserl, *Cartesian Meditations*, § 12.

43. Roman Ingarden, *On the Motives Which Led Husserl to Transcendental Idealism*, trans. Arnór Hannibalsson (The Hague: Martinus Nijhoff, 1975), 28.

44. Fink, *Sixth Cartesian Meditation*, 36. For Husserl's riposte to this objection, see Cairns, *Conversations with Husserl and Fink*, 39. Also see Husserl, *Ideas . . . : First Book*, § 65. Fink continued in the direction of the sixth meditation and in the end came up with what we might consider a Gnostic phenomenology. See Eugen Fink, "Phänomenologische Werkstatt 2," in *Gesamtausgabe*, vol. 3, pt. 2 (Freiburg and Munich: Karl Aber, 2008).

45. Cairns, *Conversations with Husserl and Fink*, 83. Husserl made the remark on June 8, 1932.

46. See Husserl, "The Amsterdam Lectures," 247; and Edmund Husserl, "Alleged Difficulty That One, Remaining within the *Epoché*, 'Never Returns to the World,'" in *First Philosophy*, 599–603.

47. See William Wordsworth, "Preface to the Edition of 1814," in *The Excursion*, in *Poetical Works*, ed. Thomas Hutchinson, rev. Ernest de Selincourt (London: Oxford University Press, 1936), 590.

48. William Blake, "Annotations to Wordsworth's Preface to *The Excursion*, Being a Portion of *The Recluse: A Poem*," in *The Complete Poetry and Prose of William Blake*, ed. David V. Erdman, with commentary by Harold Bloom, new and rev. ed. (Berkeley and Los Angeles: University of California Press, 1982), 666.

49. See Plato, *Republic*, 516c.

50. This transformation is very clearly brought out in Jean-Luc Marion, *Questions Cartésiennes III: Descartes sous le masque du cartésianisme* (Paris: Presses Universitaires de France, 2021), 188.

51. Curiously enough, Hegel and Heidegger also choose trees as important examples in their writings. See Georg Wilhelm Friedrich Hegel, *The Phenomenology of Mind*, trans. and with introductions by J. B. Baillie and George Lichtheim (New York: Harper & Row, 1967), 68; and Martin Heidegger, *What Is Called Thinking?*, trans. and with an introduction by J. Glenn Gray (New York: Harper & Row, 1968), 41. Husserl returns to the tree as an example in *Ideas . . . : Third Book*, 27.

52. Husserl, *Ideas . . . : First Book*, §§ 89, 97.

53. I leave aside the perplexing question of the status of the noema. See Robert C. Solomon, "Husserl's Concept of the Noema," in *Husserl: Expositions and Appraisals*, ed. Frederick Elliston and Peter McCormick (Notre Dame, IN: Notre Dame University Press, 1977), 168–81.

54. See the strong language about phenomenology as idealism in Husserl, *Cartesian Meditations*, § 42. Husserl plainly felt close in some respects to the tradition of German idealism. See, e.g., the three lectures Edmund Husserl, "Fichtes Menschheitsideal," in *Aufsätz und Vorträge*, 267–93.

55. I attempt to refute this view, especially in the form that Paul Ricoeur gives to it, in my "Phenomenology as Hermeneutics," in *Hermeneutics and Phenomenology: Figures and Themes*, ed. Saulius Geniusas and Paul Fairfield (London: Bloomsbury, 2018), 31–47. I will not rehearse the detailed argument of that essay here.

56. See Martin Heidegger, *Being and Time*, trans. John Macquarrie and Edward Robinson (Oxford: Basil Blackwell, 1962), § 4.

57. Husserl, *Logical Investigations*, vol. 2, investigation 6, § 26. Natorp's charge of there being Platonic metaphysics in the *Logical Investigations* has been addressed earlier when discussing Husserl's understanding of universals. Charges of idealism are usually directed against *Ideas . . . : First Book*. Such charges have less force if *Ideas . . . : Second Book* is also considered.

58. See Husserl, *Ideas . . . : Third Book*, 11.

59. See Husserl, *Logical Investigations*, vol. 1, "Introduction," § 7.

60. Marion supplies a number of helpful formulations of how being gives itself in different regional ontologies. See Jean-Luc Marion, *Being Given: Towards a Phenomenology of Givenness*, trans. Jeffrey L. Kosky (Stanford, CA: Stanford University Press, 2002), esp. bk. 4.

61. Husserl, *Ideas . . . : First Book*, § 55.

62. See Husserl, "Philosophy as Rigorous Science," 122–47. For the world always being one, see Husserl, *The Crisis of European Sciences*, 317 (app. 3). The sense of passing from the world as pregiven to the world as given involves a movement from assuming that the world is absolute to a recognition that it is relative to one's noetic engagement with it. Yet this relativity is only a matter of passing from being to phenomenon: the world itself does not change during reduction.

63. Husserl, *The Crisis of European Sciences*, § 41.

64. See Husserl, *Ideas . . . : First Book*, § 55, and *Ideas . . . : Second Book*, 417–20 (epilogue).

65. Edmund Husserl, *Thing and Space: Lectures of 1907*, trans. and ed. Richard Rojcewicz (Dordrecht: Kluwer, 1997), 251. Husserl claims later that the objective world relies on the subjectivity of the other person, which resists one's own probing. See Husserl, *First Philosophy*, 619 n. 2. Given Husserl's insight, one might go a little further and say that it is the nonhuman animal that gives us greater assurance of the reality of the objective world.

66. See Husserl, *First Philosophy*, 332. Also see Edmund Husserl, *The Basic Problems of Phenomenology: From the Lectures, Winter Semester, 1910–1911*, trans. Ingo Farin and James G. Hart (Dordrecht: Springer, 2006), 41.

67. See Husserl, *Ideas . . . : First Book*, § 49. There is no phenomenology of intersubjectivity in *Ideas . . . : First Book*, only a very brief evocation of other ego subjects at § 29. This absence exposes Husserl to criticisms from Levinas, for whom the other person always disrupts contemplation. See, e.g., Emmanuel Levinas, *God, Death, and Time*, trans. Bettina Bergo (Stanford, CA: Stanford University Press, 2000), 198. Levinas does not, however, distinguish between the transcendental observer and the natural observer, in part because he does not accept the reduction. Besides, one need not assume that contemplation takes all one's time.

68. See Husserl, *Ideas . . . : First Book*, § 49. Sokolowski points out that *absolute* is used in two ways by Husserl, once in contrast with *presumption*, and again in contrast with *relative*. It is the former distinction that I have in mind here. See Robert Sokolowski, *The Formation of Husserl's Concept of Constitution* (The Hague: Martinus Nijhoff, 1964), 129.

69. See Husserl, *Ideas . . . : Second Book*, § 40.

70. See Husserl, *Ideas . . . : Second Book*, §§ 35–42. Also see Husserl, *Ideas . . . : Third Book*, § 3.

71. Husserl, *Logical Investigations*, 2:338 (investigation 2, "Introduction").

72. See Husserl, *Logical Investigations*, 1:78–80 ("Prolegomena").

73. See Husserl, *Logical Investigations*, vol. 1, investigation 1, § 11. *Objecte* are species of *Gegenstände*, which is the most general word for anything that can be intended.

74. See Husserl, *Logical Investigations*, investigation 5, § 37.

75. On this theme, see Jacques Derrida, *Speech and Phenomena: And Other Essays on Husserl's Theory of Signs* (1973), trans. and with an introduction by David B. Allison and a preface by Newton Garver (Evanston, IL: Northwestern University Press, 1973), esp. chap. 2.

76. For further detail on Husserl's treatment of the imagination, see Brian Elliott, *Phenomenology and Imagination in Husserl and Heidegger* (New York: Routledge, 2005), pt. 1. Elliot is especially adept at seeing Husserl's "wavering" between aligning imagination and signification on the one hand and with perception, on the other. For a discussion of Husserl's treatment of presence, see my *Kingdoms of God*, chap. 10.

77. See Husserl, *Phantasy, Image Consciousness, and Memory*.

78. Husserl, *Ideas . . . : First Book*, § 70.

79. See Husserl, *Logical Investigations*, 2:592. For a theory of the imagination as distinct from perception, see Jean-Paul Sartre, *The Imaginary: A Phenomenological Psychology of the Imagination*, rev. and with a historical introduction by Arlette Elkaïm-Sartre, trans. and with a philosophical introduction by Jonathan Webber (London: Routledge, 2004).

80. "Husserl an von Hofmannsthal (12. 1. 1907)," in *Briefwechsel*, vol. 7, *Wissenschaftlerkorrespondenz*, ed. Elisabeth Schuhmann and Karl Schuhmann (Boston: Kluwer, 1994), 135. I quote from the translation that prefaces Sven-Olov Wallenstein, "Phenomenology and the Possiblity of a Pure Art," *Site* 26-27 (2009), https://issuu.com/site magazine/docs/26-27/2. Also see Wolfgang Huemer, "Phenomenological Reduction and Aesthetic Experience: Husserl meets Hofmannsthal," in *Writing the Austrian Traditions: Relations between Philosophy and Literature*, ed. Wolfgang Huemer and Marc-Oliver Schustrer (Edmonton, AB: Wirth-Institute for Austrian and Central European Studies, 2003), 121-30. Husserl's first lectures referring to the phenomenological (or epistemological) reduction were given April 26–May 2, 1907. See Edmund Husserl, *The Idea of Phenomenology*, trans. William P. Alston and George Nakhnikian, with an introduction by George Nakhnikian (The Hague: Martinus Nijhoff, 1973), esp. 4, 31, 38, 44, 48.

81. On founding, see Husserl, *Logical Investigations*, investigation 3, § 14.

82. Cairns, *Conversations with Husserl and Fink*, 59. Husserl made the remark on December 23, 1931.

83. See Husserl, *First Philosophy*, 621.

84. On a sense in which phenomenology can be nonfoundational, see John J. Drummond, *Husserlian Intentionality and Non-Foundational Realism: Noema and Object* (Dordrecht: Kluwer, 1990), esp. chap. 9.

85. Such is Derrida's position as elaborated in *Speech and Phenomena*, *Of Grammatology* (1967), and *Writing and Difference* (1967). Derrida's diagnosis of Husserl's reliance on full or pure presence, which exposes a vulnerability in the German thinker, needs to be distinguished from Husserl's treatment of rendering phenomena present and absent, which is one of his most valuable contributions to philosophy.

86. See Robert Frost, "Stopping by Woods on a Snowy Evening," in *Collected Poems, Prose, and Plays*, ed. Richard Poirier and Mark Richardson (New York: Library of America, 1995), 207.

87. Husserl gave four lectures at the Sorbonne in February 1929; he expanded them, with the assistance of Fink, and they were translated into French and published as *Méditations cartésiennes* in 1931. Husserl added appendices that did not appear in the French edition. I quote from app. 12 of the German text, "Sprache, Urteilswahrheit, Umwelt (Heimwelt): Die Funktion der Sprachlichen Mitteilung für die Konstitution der Umwelt," which can be found in Edmund Husserl, *Zur Phänomenologie der Intersubjektivität: Texte aus dem Nachlass: Dritter Teil: 1929–1935*, ed. Iso Kern, Husserliana, vol. 15 (The Hague: Martinus Nijhoff, 1973). Also see Husserl's remarks on natural language in Ulrich Melle, ed., *Logische Untersuchungen. Ergänzungband: Erster Teil: Entwürfe zur Umarbeitung der VI. Untersuchung der "Logischen Untersuchungen,"* Husserliana, vol. 20, no. 1 (Dordrecht: Kluwer, 2002), and *Logische Untersuchungen. Ergänzungband: Zweiter Teil: Texte für die Neufassung VI. Untersuchung Zur Phänomenologie des Ausdrucks und der Erkenntnis (1893–94–1921)*, Husserliana, vol. 20, no. 2 (Dordrecht: Springer, 2005).

88. Husserl, *Zur Phänomenologie der Intersubjektivität*, 224–25. On home world and alien world, also see Husserl, *The Crisis of European Sciences*, 139. For commentary, see

Suzanne Cunningham's *Language and the Phenomenological Reductions of Edmund Husserl* (The Hague: Martinus Nijhoff, 1976), which does not take account of Husserl's *Nachlass* work on intersubjectivity, and Horst Ruthrof's *Husserl's Phenomenology of Natural Language: Intersubjectivity and Communality in the Nachlass* (London: Bloomsbury, 2021), which does. Ruthrof's volume is valuable especially for its attention to communal language and imaginability (*Vorstellbarkeit*).

89. I leave aside here any possible relation between Husserl's generative phenomenology and concepts of *Gemeinschaft*. These would require a long, differentiated analysis.

90. See Kant, *Critique of Judgement*, 14–18.

91. Wallace Stevens, "The Snow Man," in *CPP*, 8.

92. A. R. Ammons, "Visit," in *The Complete Poems* (hereafter *CP*), ed. Robert M. West, with an introduction by Helen Vendler, 2 vols. (New York: W. W. Norton, 2017), 1:89–90.

93. Geoffrey Hill, "Annunciations," in *Broken Hierarchies: Poems, 1952–2012* (hereafter *BH*), ed. Kenneth Haynes (Oxford: Oxford University Press, 2013), 40.

94. Philip Larkin, "Mr. Bleaney," in *Collected Poems*, ed. and with an introduction by Anthony Thwaite (London: Marvell Press/Faber and Faber, 1988), 102–3.

95. Attridge, "'This Strange Institution Called Literature,'" 46.

96. With respect to the other, I draw from Levinas's and Lacoste's appeals to him. See Emmanuel Levinas, "Phenomenon and Enigma," in *Collected Philosophical Papers*, trans. Alphonso Lingis (The Hague: Martinus Nijhoff, 1987), chap. 5; and Lacoste, "Appearance without Reduction," 58.

97. On sentences and propositions, see Robert Sokolowski, *Presence and Absence: A Philosophical Investigation of Language and Being* (Bloomington: Indiana University Press, 1978), chap. 8. *Registration*, as Sokolowski uses the word, denotes making statements when something is present and can be intuited, *reporting* is speech made when something is absent, and *opinion* denotes accepting a view merely as proposed. See ibid., chap. 13.

98. See Husserl, *Ideas . . . : First Book*, §§ 51 Remark and 58. For further elaboration, see my "'Children of the World': A Note on Jean-Yves Lacoste," in *God and Phenomenology: Thinking with Jean-Yves Lacoste*, ed. Joeri Schrivers and Martin Koči (Eugene, OR: Wipf & Stock, 2023).

99. See Husserl, *Ideas . . . : First Book*, § 51 Remark. For absolute consciousness, also see Edmund Husserl, *On the Phenomenology of the Consciousness of Internal Time (1893–1917)*, trans. John Barnett Brough (Dordrecht: Kluwer, 1991), app. 9.

Chapter Four

1. Richard of St. Victor, *AM*, 1.5. In the prologue to his *De trinitate*, Richard associates the eagle with contemplation. Achard of St. Victor does the same. See the sermon Richard of St. Victor, "On Quadragesima," in *Works*, 324. Godfrey of St. Victor follows suit while also adding that Christ is an eagle. See Godfrey of St. Victor, *Microcosmus*, ed. Philippe Delhaye (Lille: Facultés catholique, 1951), §§ 204, 223.

2. The first translation of the works of the Pseudo-Dionysius was accomplished by Hilduin of St. Denys ca. 838. A new translation undertaken by John Scotus Eriugena was completed by 862.

3. Pseudo-Dionysius the Areopagite, *The Divine Names*, 4.9, in *The Complete Works*,

78. Also see the commentary on this passage in Denis the Carthusian, *Contemplation*, 2.1.

4. See G. M. Hopkins, "Nondum," in *Poems of Gerard Manley Hopkins*, 138.

5. The translation of the work from Greek to Latin was undertaken by William of Moerbeke in the thirteenth century. Here I quote from Proclus, *Elements of Theology*, in *The Six Books of Proclus*, trans. Thomas Taylor (London: Law, 1816), proposition 35.

6. See, e.g., James McEvoy, ed., *Mystical Theology: The Glosses by Thomas Gallus and the Commentary of Robert Grosseteste on "De mystica theologia"* (Leuven: Peeters, 2003).

7. See Aristotle, *Physics*, trans. P. H. Wickstead and F. M. Cornford, Loeb Classical Library (Cambridge, MA: Harvard University Press, 1934), 8.7.260a26.

8. See, specifically, Aquinas, *ST*, 2a2ae q. 180 art. 4 ad 3.

9. Aquinas, *ST*, 2a2ae q. 180 art. 7 ad 3. Also see Aquinas, *Treatise on Separate Substances*, trans. Francis J. Lescoe (West Hartford, CT: Saint Joseph College, 1963), 149.

10. Aquinas, *ST*, 2a2ae q. 180 art. 6 ad 2. It would follow that human beings would usually be visited by angels, not by seraphs, e.g. Yet see Isa. 6:2 and 6:6. For Richard on angels and hovering on wings, see Richard of St. Victor, *AM*, 4.2.

11. On the "degrees of being," see Richard of St. Victor, *On the Trinity*, in *Trinity and Creation*, ed. Boyd Taylor Coolman and Dale M. Coulter, Victorine Texts in Translation, vol. 1 (Turnhout: Brepols, 2010), 1.11.

12. Richard of St. Victor, *AM*, 1.5.

13. See Dante, *Purgatorio*, 2.38.

14. St. Bernard of Clairvaux, *Five Books on Consideration: Advice to a Pope*, trans. John D. Anderson and Elizabeth T. Kennan (Kalamazoo, MI: Cistercian, 1976), 142. More detail is offered in chapter 5.

15. See Gilson, *The Mystical Theology of St. Bernard*, 241.

16. Tertullian, *De oratione liber: Tract on the Prayer*, trans. Ernest Evans (London: Society for Promoting Christian Knowledge, 1953), chap. 29.

17. Evagrius Ponticus, "On the Eight Thoughts," in *The Greek Ascetic Corpus*, ed. Robert E. Sinkewicz (Oxford: Oxford University Press, 2003), 7.11. Pliny the Elder says rather a lot about bees, though nothing about the height of their flight. Nonetheless, his remarks make the bee suitable as a model for the monk. See Pliny the Elder, *Natural History*, 11.4–23.

18. See Pseudo-Dionysius the Areopagite, *The Celestial Hierarchy*, in *The Complete Works*, 15.8. The power of the eagle's vision is traditional. See Pliny the Elder, *Natural History*, 10.3–6. Drawing on the traditional metaphor of St. John the Evangelist as an eagle, Eriugena goes a step further than others in the tradition and claims in his *Homilia in Johannem* that the eagle transcends all contemplation. See Christopher Bamford, *The Voice of the Eagle: John Scotus Eriugena's Homily on the Prologue to the Gospel of St. John* (Hundson, NY: Lindisfarne, 2000).

19. Gregory the Great, *MJ*, 9.32.48. Also see ibid., 31.51.104.

20. Gregory the Great, *MJ*, 19.1.2, 26.17.30.

21. Gregory the Great, *MJ*, 19.1.2.

22. Willene B. Clark, ed., trans., and commentary, *The Medieval Book of Birds: Hugh of Fouilloy's "Aviarium,"* Medieval and Renaissance Texts and Studies, 80 (Binghamton, NY: Medieval and Renaissance Texts and Studies, 1992), 137.

23. See, e.g., the *Gart der Gesundheit* of Johannes de Cuba (ca. 1430–ca. 1503), which details not only herbs but also birds.

24. See Pliny the Elder, *Natural History*, 10.9–10.

25. Clark, ed. and trans., *The Medieval Book of Birds*, chap. 11.

26. See Clark, ed. and trans., *The Medieval Book of Birds*, chap. 16. The whole of chap. 16 is taken from Gregory's commentary on Job 39:26. See Gregory the Great, *MJ*, 31.46.92–93.

27. Clark, ed. and trans., *The Medieval Book of Birds*, 144–45.

28. An account of Hopkins's training as a Jesuit is given in Alfred Thomas, *Hopkins the Jesuit: The Years of Training* (London: Oxford University Press, 1969). For a list of the refectory reading over his period of training, see ibid., app. 2.

29. See Thomas, *Hopkins the Jesuit*, 157.

30. See G. M. Hopkins, *Sermons and Spiritual Writings*, ed. Jude V. Nixon and Noel Barber, vol. 5 of *The Collected Works of Gerard Manley Hopkins* (hereafter *CW*) (Oxford: Oxford University Press, 2018), 292 (for Athanasius), 341, 367, and 521 (for Cassian), 229, 313, and 556 (for Clement of Alexandria), 579–83 (for Augustine), 267 (for Anselm), 124 and 555 (for Bonaventure), 80, 267, and 280 (for Lombard), and passim (for Augustine and Aquinas).

31. See John Henry Newman, "Mental Prayer," in *A Newman Reader*, ed. Francis X. Connolly (New York: Doubleday, 1964), 418–25. Also see Hopkins, *Sermons and Spiritual Writings*, esp. 470–76. Finally, see the remarks on Hopkins on contemplation in my *Poetry and Revelation*, chap. 2.

32. G. M. Hopkins, "Let me be to Thee as the circling bird," in *Poems of Gerard Manley Hopkins*, 37. Also see G. M. Hopkins, "The Caged Skylark" (1877), in *Poems of Gerard Manley Hopkins*, 75. In this later lyric, the soul is seen as a caged bird.

33. For Hopkins's view of Tennyson's "St. Simon Stylites," see G. M. Hopkins to Ernest Hartley Coleridge, September 3, 1862, in *Correspondence*, ed. R. K. R. Thornton and Catherine Phillips, vols. 1–2 of *CW* (Oxford: Oxford University Press, 2013), 1:18.

34. The extent of Hopkins's knowledge of Roman history and culture is indicated in G. M. Hopkins, "Notes for Roman Literature and Antiquities," in *Sketches and Scholarly Studies: Academic, Classical, and Lectures on Poetry*, ed. R. K. R. Thornton, vol. 6, pt. 1, of *CW* (Oxford: Oxford University Press, 2021), 349–424, and *The Dublin Notebook*, ed. Lesley Higgins and Michael F. Suarez, vol. 7 of *CW* (Oxford: Oxford University Press, 2014).

35. My intention is not to propose a possible influence on Hopkins's composition, such as has been suggested with respect to Robert Southwell's description of a hawk, but to follow a thread of contemplation with which Hopkins may or may not have been familiar but that is tied to an original natural theology. For the possible influence of Southwell on Hopkins, see Mary Eleanor, "Hopkins' 'Windhover' and Southwell's Hawk," *Renascence* 15, no. 1 (1962): 21–22, 27; and Gary M. Bouchard, "The Curious Case of Robert Southwell, Gerard Hopkins and a Princely Spanish Hawk," *Renascence* 51, no. 3 (1999): 181–91.

36. The falcon is named in Lev. 11:14 (RSV), but the Hebrew *'ayâh* is broader than just *falcon* and includes hawks.

37. G. M. Hopkins, "The Windhover," in *Poems of Gerard Manley Hopkins*, 29.

38. A list of analyses of the poem is given in Tom Dunne, ed., *Gerard Manley Hopkins: A Comprehensive Bibliography* (Oxford: Clarendon, 1976). Since then, the number of essays and chapters centered on the poem has multiplied. As an index only, see Joaquin Kuhn, "Being There to Catch the Kestrel," *Hopkins Quarterly* 43, nos. 1–4 (2016): 1–142, which gathers a number of texts with a view to recontextualize the poem around the figure of Jeanne d'Arc. Kuhn observes: "My notes and files on this 17-line composition take up ten times the space that this volume occupies." Ibid., iii. Further thoughts on Jeanne d'Arc are given in Joaquin Kuhn, "More on That Welsh 'Windhover,'" *Hopkins*

Quarterly 44, nos. 3–4 (2017): 91–94. Also see Juhani Rudanko, "Gerard Manley Hopkins 'The Windhover,'" *Neuphilologische Mitteilungen* 81, no. 2 (1980): 174–86. Rudanko reprises a good deal of the earlier commentary. For the textual genesis of the poem over the period 1877–84, see Thomas Owen, "Hopkins's Kestrel: 'The Windhover,' 1877–1884," *Victorian Poetry* 57, no. 1 (2019): 43–72. More generally, see Thomas P. Harrison, "The Birds of Gerard Manley Hopkins," *Studies in Philology* 54, no. 3 (1957): 448–63. Other essays on the poem are referenced in these notes.

39. For quite different approaches to the issue, see Maria R. Lichtmann, *The Contemplative Poetry of Gerard Manley Hopkins* (Princeton, NJ: Princeton University Press, 1989); Virginia Ridley Ellis, *Gerard Manley Hopkins and the Language of Mystery* (Columbia: University of Missouri Press, 1991); and Aakanksha Virkar Yates, *The Philosophical Mysticism of Gerard Manley Hopkins* (New York: Routledge, 2018).

40. G. M. Hopkins, "Lecture Notes on Poetry, II," in *Sketches and Scholarly Studies*, 307.

41. G. M. Hopkins, "Notes on Greek Philosophy," in *Oxford Essays and Notes*, ed. Lesley Higgins, vol. 4 of *CW* (Oxford: Oxford University Press, 2006), 307.

42. W. B. Yeats, "The Symbolism of Poetry," in *Early Essays*, ed. George Bornstein and Richard J. Finneran, vol. 4 of *The Collected Works of W. B. Yeats* (New York: Scribner, 2007), 117. Also see W. B. Yeats, "*Samhain*: 1905," in *The Irish Dramatic Movement*, ed. Mary FitzGerald and Richard J. Finneran, vol. 8 of *The Collected Works of W. B. Yeats* (New York: Scribner, 2003), 91.

43. Hopkins, "Lecture Notes on Poetry, II," 307.

44. On expression and indication, see Edmund Husserl, *Logical Investigations*, vol. 1, investigation 1, chap. 1.

45. For information about the kestrel, see Leslie Brown and Dean Amadon, *Eagles, Hawks and Falcons of the World*, 2 vols. (London: Country Life Books, 1968).

46. The older forms are *windcuffer* and *windfucker* (in which the verb means "to beat" or "to strike") and the seventeenth-century form *windsucker*. There is also the old dialectal name *standgale*.

47. The dedication was added to Robert Bridges's copy of the poem seven years after its initial composition.

48. See Augustine, *Expositions of the Psalms*, 1–32, trans. John E. Rotelle, vol. 3/15 of *WSA* (Hyde Park, NY: New City, 2000), 11.1. Also see St. Gregory Nazianzen, "Oration on Holy Baptism," in *Nicene and Post-Nicene Fathers*, ed. Philip Schaff and Henry Wace, 2nd ser., 14 vols., vol. 7 (1894; reprint, Peabody, MA: Hendrikson, 1994), sec. 19.

49. G. M. Hopkins, *Diaries, Journals, and Notebooks*, ed. Lesley Higgins, vol. 3 of *CW* (Oxford: Oxford University Press, 2015), 549 (emphasis added).

50. Hopkins, *Diaries, Journals, and Notebooks*, 603 (emphasis added).

51. Hopkins, *Diaries, Journals, and Notebooks*, 531–32.

52. An identification of *haecceitas* and inscape was proposed in W. H. Gardner, *Gerard Manley Hopkins: A Study of Poetic Idiosyncrasy in Relation to Poetic Tradition*, 2 vols. (London: Oxford University Press, 1944), 1:26. It was based on W. H. Gardner, "A Note on Hopkins and Duns Scotus," *Scrutiny* 5, no. 1 (1936): 61–70, which responded to Christopher Devlin, "Gerard Manley Hopkins and Duns Scotus," *New Verse* 14 (1935): 12–17. Many readers of Hopkins have followed Gardner. At the start of his commentary on Lombard's *Sentences*, however, Scotus writes on formal nonidentity. I refer to the *Ordinatio*, which is the version of the *Opus oxoniense* that Hopkins would have consulted. See Duns Scotus, *Ordinatio*, 1. d. 2 p. 2, qq. 1–4, nos. 388–410.

53. See Bernadette Waterman Ward, "Philosophy and Inscape: Hopkins and the

Formalitas of Duns Scotus," *Texas Studies in Literature and Language* 32, no. 2 (1990): 214–39, which was revised in Bernadette Waterman Ward, *World as Word: Philosophical Theology in Gerard Manley Hopkins* (Washington, DC: Catholic University of America Press, 2002), chap. 7. A clear and concise account of the formal distinction is given in Allan B. Wolter, "The Formal Distinction," in *The Philosophical Theology of John Duns Scotus*, ed. Marilyn McCord Adams (Ithaca, NY: Cornell University Press, 1990), 27–41.

54. John Buridan, *Quaestiones de anima*, in John Alexander Zupko, "John Buridan's Philosophy of Mind: An Edition and Translation of Book III of His 'Questions on Aristotle's *De anima*' (Third Redaction), with Commentary and Critical and Interpretative Essays" (PhD diss., Cornell University, 1989).

55. It has commonly been claimed that Scotus modified his realism with respect to the formal distinction in his later Parisian question on the subject. The claim is ably dismantled in Stephen Dumont, "Duns Scotus's Parisian Question on the Formal Distinction," *Vivarium* 43, no. 1 (2005): 7–62.

56. Leonardo Tarán, ed., *Parmenides: A Text with Translation, Commentary, and Critical Essays* (Princeton, NJ: Princeton University Press, 1965), 85.

57. On the transcendentals in this regard, see Allan B. Wolter, *The Transcendentals and Their Function in the Metaphysics of Duns Scotus* (St. Bonaventure: Franciscan Institute, 1946). Wolter points out that the number of transcendentals was extended before the time of Scotus and that Scotus regards Being as the first of the transcendentals. Ibid., 8 and 8 n. 34. It should be noted that Aquinas did not regard beauty as a transcendental.

58. See Wolter, *The Transcendentals and Their Function*, 184.

59. Hopkins writes of swelling buds carrying the spraying of trees to a high pitch. See Hopkins, *Diaries, Journals, and Notebooks*, 506.

60. Hopkins, *Diaries, Journals, and Notebooks*, 489. In his notes on Parmenides, Hopkins writes: "The inscape will be the proportion of the mixture." G. M. Hopkins, "Parmenides," in *Oxford Essays and Notes*, 316. It might be noted that, in speaking of beauty here, Hopkins is in the third level of contemplation that Richard specifies.

61. G. M. Hopkins, "Hurrahing in Harvest," in *Poems of Gerard Manley Hopkins*, 27.

62. Hopkins, "Parmenides," 311. On instress, see Leonard Cochran, "Instress and Its Place in the Poetics of Gerard Manley Hopkins," *Hopkins Quarterly* 6 (1979–80): 143–82.

63. Hopkins, "Parmenides," 311. For Hopkins's exposure to idealism, see Daniel Brown, *Hopkins' Idealism: Philosophy, Physics, Poetry* (Oxford: Clarendon, 1997).

64. Hopkins, "Parmenides," 311.

65. Hopkins observes: "We say that any two things however unlike are in something like." G. M. Hopkins, "First Principle and Foundation," in *Sermons and Spiritual Writings*, 349. The quest for inscape is also a quest for a land of likeness.

66. See Martin Heidegger, *The Fundamental Concepts of Metaphysics: World, Finitude, Solitude*, trans. William McNeill and Nicholas Walker (Bloomington: Indiana University Press, 1995), §§ 16–38. Heidegger also attends to fright (*Erschrecken*), restraint (*Verhaltenheit*), foreboding (*Ahnung*), and timidity (*Scheu*). See Martin Heidegger, *Contributions to Philosophy (of the Event)*, trans. Richard Rojcewicz and Daniela Vallega-Neu (Bloomington: Indiana University Presss, 2012), § 5.

67. Hopkins, *Diaries, Journals, and Notebooks*, 504. Counterintentionality is examined in Husserl, *Ideas . . . : Second Book*, 104. Also see Geoffrey Hill, "What You Look Hard at Seems to Look Hard at You," May 6, 2014, https://www.english.ox.ac.uk/professor-sir -geoffrey-hill-lectures.

68. Hopkins, *Diaries, Journals, and Notebooks*, 504.

69. Leonardo Tarán, ed. and trans., *Parmenides: A Text with Translation, Commentary, and Critical Essays* (Princeton, NJ: Princeton University Press, 1965), 32.

70. Hopkins, "Parmenides," 313. See Tarán, ed., *Parmenides*, 45.

71. Hopkins, "Parmenides," 314. See Tarán, ed., *Parmenides*, 86.

72. Hopkins, "Parmenides," 315.

73. Hopkins, "Parmenides," 311.

74. Hopkins, *Diaries, Journals, and Notebooks*, 544.

75. Hopkins, "Parmenides," 313.

76. Hopkins to Robert Bridges, February 15, 1879, in *Correspondence*, 1:334.

77. John Ruskin, *Elements of Drawing*, in *The Works of John Ruskin*, ed. E. T. Cook and Alexander Wedderburn, 39 vols. (London: George Allen, 1903–12), 15:116 (letter 3). For the influence of Ruskin on Hopkins, see Alison Sulloway, *Hopkins and the Victorian Temper* (New York: Columbia University Press, 1972). Hopkins's admiration for Ruskin's theories had started to dissipate before he converted to Roman Catholicism.

78. Ruskin, *Elements of Drawing*, 116.

79. On this understanding of idiom, see Jacques Derrida, *The Ear of the Other: Otobiography, Transference, Translation*, ed. Christie V. McDonald (New York: Schocken, 1985), 106–7, and "Che cos'è la poesia?," in *A Derrida Reader: Between the Blinds*, ed. Peggy Kamuf (New York: Columbia University Press, 1991), 229.

80. Alfred Lord Tennyson, "The Eagle," in *The Major Works*, ed. and with an introduction by Adam Roberts, The World's Classics (Oxford: Oxford University Press, 2009), 116. See Hopkins's remarks on the poem in his letter to Ernest Hartley Coleridge, September 3, 1862, in *Correspondence*, 1:23.

81. On this topic, see Walter J. Ong, *Hopkins, the Self, and God* (Toronto: University of Toronto Press, 1986), 14.

82. Glance and gaze are distinguished in G. M. Hopkins, "To What Serves Mortal Beauty?," in *Poems*, 103.

83. Shakespeare uses the word in its French sense when Henry IV says to Westmoreland: "A son who is the theme of honour's tongue, / Amongst a grove the very straightest plant, / Who is sweet Fortune's minion and her pride." *Henry IV Part 1*, in *The Arden Shakespeare*, ed. A. R. Humphreys (London: Methuen, 1960), 1.1.80–83. More generally, the reference in the poem to France — especially late medieval and early modern France — generates questions of how much weight to place on it. Should we recall the French *crécerelle* as the root of *kestrel*? Is it important that France, a Catholic country for the most part, is evoked, even in a Welsh landscape? The questions have no clear answers yet press nonetheless on any reading of the poem. Concerted effort has been made to link the French vocabulary with Jeanne d'Arc, who was burned at the stake on May 30, 1431, 446 years before the poem was composed. See Kuhn, "Being There to Catch the Kestrel." Yet there is no connection between Jeanne and birds. Above all, the reference is to a *chevalier*, not to a *chevalière*.

84. The Feast of Christ the King was instituted by Pius XI only in 1925. Yet Hopkins had a particular reverence for Christ as King, the title being biblical and patristic. See, e.g., "The Wreck of the Deutschland," stanza 35. The image of Christ as the sun is patristic. See, e.g., Augustine's interpretation of Ps. 18:7 in his *Expositions of the Psalms*.

85. On the crossing of gazes, see Jean-Luc Marion, "The Intentionality of Love," in *Prolegomena to Charity*, trans. Stephen E. Lewis (New York: Fordham University Press, 2002), 86–90.

86. Nicholas of Cusa, "On the Vision of God," in *Selected Spiritual Writings*, trans.

and with an introduction by H. Lawrence Bond and a preface by Morimichi Watanabe, Classics of Western Spirituality (New York: Paulist, 1977), 4.10.

87. On this point, see Thomas Pfau, *Incomprehensible Certainty: Metaphysics and Hermeneutics of the Image* (Notre Dame, IN: Notre Dame University Press, 2022), 560–61.

88. I should stress that intentionality does not begin with Husserl. He took the idea from Franz Brentano and developed it, Brentano learned of the idea from medieval logicians, especially, perhaps, Scotus, and classical philosophers were also aware of the notion to some extent. As already noticed, Parmenides tells us that it is impossible to think about that which is not.

89. Similar arguments could be made with respect to Hopkins's "The Starlight Night" and "Peace."

90. See Prudentius, *Peristephanon*, 3.161–65. Also see Michael Roberts, *Poetry and the Cult of the Martyrs: The "Liber Peristephanon" of Prudentius* (Ann Arbor: University of Michigan Press, 1993), 96; and Peter Dronke, *Imagination in the Late Pagan and Early Christian World: The First Nine Centuries AD* (Florence: Edizioni del Galluzzo, 2003), chap. 5.

91. For the basilaic attitude, see my *Kingdoms of God*, esp. 148–49. For Hopkins's later views on the kingdom, see the sermons delivered at St. Xavier's, Liverpool, in January 1880. G. M. Hopkins, *Sermons and Spiritual Writings*, sermons 19–22.

92. See Augustine, *Sermons on the New Testament*, sermon 144; and Aquinas, *ST*, 2a2ae q. 2 art. 2 *resp*. On this and other sorts of faith, see Henri de Lubac, *The Christian Faith: An Essay on the Structure of the Apostles' Creed*, trans. Richard Arnandez (San Francisco: Ignatius, 1986), chap. 8.

93. A canonical instance is given in Augustine, *Confessions*, 7.10.16.

94. See Augustine, *Confessions*, 13.9.10.

95. That flying birds appear like crosses has been noted before in English poetry. See, e.g., John Donne, "The Crosse," in *The Divine Poems*, ed. with an introduction and commentary by Helen Gardner (1952; Oxford: Clarendon, 1978), 26: "Looke downe, thou spiest out Crosses in small things; / Looke up, thou seest birds rais'd on crossed wings."

96. For mystery as an "incomprehensible certainty," see Hopkins to Bridges, October 24–25, 1883, in *Correspondence*, 2:619.

97. Richard Lovelace, "The Falcon," in *The Poems of Richard Lovelace*, ed. C. H. Wilkinson (Oxford: Clarendon, 1930), 141–45. Also see Richard Lovelace, "A Lady with a Falcon on Her Fist," in ibid., 103–4.

98. On this theme, see Jean-Louis Chrétien, "Saint Gregory the Great: Amplitude within a Narrow Confinement," in *Spacious Joy: An Essay in Phenomenology and Literature*, trans. Anne Ashley Davenport (London: Rowman & Littlefield, 2019), 45. The theme is lucidly explored in Jean-Louis Chrétien, "Retrospection," in *The Unforgettable and the Unhoped For*, trans. Jeffrey Bloechl (New York: Fordham University Press, 2002), 119–29.

99. See, e.g., Aquinas, *ST*, 1a q. 27 art. 3 ad 3. The position goes back to Augustine, *De trinitate*, 8.3.6 and 9.1.3.

100. See Bernard J. F. Lonergan, "Christology Today: Methodological Reflections," in *A Third Collection*, ed. Frederick E. Crowe (New York: Paulist, 1985), 77. Also see the note on Augustine and Pascal on this very point in Heidegger, *Being and Time*, § 29n.

101. M. H. Abrams points out that Hopkins takes Walter Pater's emphasis on the moment of intense sensation at the end of *The Renaissance* (1873) and reascribes it to God as giving us an epiphanic moment of illumination. See Abrams, *Natural Supernaturalism*, 419.

102. Gregory the Great, *MJ*, 31, 42; and *Ancrene Wisse*, in *Anchoritic Spirituality: "Ancrene Wisse" and Associated Works*, trans. and with an introduction by Anne Savage and Nicholas Watson and a preface by Benedicta Ward (New York: Paulist, 1991), 191. We will recall the dauphin lauding his horse in the French camp, near Agincourt, in Shakespeare's *Henry V* (in *The Arden Shakespeare*, ed. T. W. Craig [London: Methuen, 1995], 3.7):

> What a long night is this! I will not change my
> horse with any that treads but on four pasterns. Ch'ha!
> He bounds from the earth as if his entrails were
> hairs—*le cheval volant*, the Pegasus, *qui a les narines
> de feu*! When I bestride him, I soar, I am a hawk. He
> trots the air. The earth sings when he touches it; the
> basest horn of his hoof is more musical than the pipe of Hermes.

103. Stephen R. Reimer, ed., *The Works of William Herebert, OFM* (Toronto: Pontifical Institute of Medieval Studies, 1987). Reimer notes that Herebert found Isa. 63:1–5, 7, in the *lectio* for Wednesday of Holy Week. The connection between Christ and Isa. 63:1 goes by way of John 19:5. The figure of Christ as knight is also found in *The Dream of the Rood*, a tenth-century poem, and passuses 18 and 19 of *Piers Plowman*, which belongs to the fourteenth century. Also, in the fifteenth century, Robert Henryson (fl. 1460–1500) represents Christ as a knight in his allegorical poem "The Bludy Serk."

104. The *Flos sanctorum* is a paraphrase of the *Legenda aurea sanctorum*.

105. Certainly, Ignatius would have absorbed St. Paul's military metaphors in Phil. 2:25 and Philem. 1:2. Another well-known source is Erasmus's *Enchiridion militis Christiani* (1501). Also see the apostolic letter *Exposcit debitum* (1550). The idea of the Christian as knight gained impetus in Bernard of Clairvaux's *Liber ad milites templi de laude novae militiae* (composed ca. 1120–ca. 36).

106. For a quite different reading of "Buckle!," one based on construing the word as an imperative for Hopkins himself to perform the buckling, see Helen Vendler, "Catching Fire: 'The Windhover,'" *Victorian Poetry* 56, no. 2 (2018): 111–27.

107. Hopkins, "Hurrahing in Harvest," 27.

108. See the discussion of the poem in my *Poetry and Revelation*, chap. 2.

109. See, in particular, St. John Chrysostom, *The Homilies on the Gospel of Matthew*, trans. George Prevost, 2 vols. (1885; reprint, North Charleston, SC: Createspace, 2017), homily 56. St. Gregory Palamas defends the view that Christ's light on Mt. Tabor was uncreated and that the disciples were granted the mercy of seeing him as he really is. See St. Gregory Palamas, "The Declaration of the Holy Mountain," in *The Philokalia*, 4:422.

110. See Plato, *Ion*, 533d–536d; and D. J. Moores, ed., *Wild Poets of Ecstasy: An Anthology of Ecstatic Verse* (Nevada City, CA: Pelican Pond, 2011). In the West, consider the Rimbaud of *Les illuminations* (1886), e.g., and, in the East, Hafiz (1315–90), Kabir (1398–1448), and Mirabai (1498–1546). An account of Rimbaud *le voyant* as a sort of mystic poet is in Wallace Fowlie, *Rimbaud's Illuminations: A Study of Angelism* (New York: Grove, 1953). As a caveat, it should be kept in mind that even the most apparently ecstatic verse can be written with calm deliberation.

111. George Herbert, "Love" (III), in *The Works of George Herbert*, ed. F. E. Hutchinson (Oxford: Clarendon, 1941), 188–89.

112. See Hopkins to Bridges, June 22, 1879, in *Correspondence*, 1:362.

113. George Herbert, "The 23rd Psalm," in Hutchinson, ed., *The Works of George Herbert*, 172.

114. See Paul Ricoeur, *Freud and Philosophy: An Essay on Interpretation*, trans. Denis Savage (New Haven, CT: Yale University Press, 1970), 32–36.

115. See Coleridge, *Marginalia*, pt. 5, pp. 795–99; and Schopenhauer, *WWR*, vol. 1, § 34. Plainly, the style of criticism developed here also draws on earlier modes of literary criticism devoted to close reading.

116. See, e.g., Heidegger, *The Fundamental Concepts of Metaphysics*, §§ 16–38.

117. On reading with feeling, see McNamer, *Affective Meditation and the Invention of Medieval Compassion*, 131.

118. Also see in this regard "Spring" with its evocations of an Edenic kingdom.

Chapter Five

1. Walter Pater, *Gaston de Latour*, vol. 4 of *The Collected Works of Walter Pater*, ed. Gerald Monsman (Oxford: Oxford University Press, 2019), 91. Pater often evokes fascination. See, e.g., ibid., 103, 129, 147, 158. Also see Pater's *Imaginary Portraits* and other writings.

2. Meister Eckhart argues in "On Detachment" that love presumes inner detachment. See Maurice O'C. Walshe, ed., *The Complete Mystical Works of Meister Eckhart*, rev. and with a foreword by Bernard McGinn (New York: Crossroad, 2009), 566.

3. One prominent church father who was concerned with vision—corporeal, intellectual, and spiritual—and the sins that spring from the first named in particular is Augustine. For his remarks on what can happen when one gazes at the games, see Augustine, *Confessions*, chap. 6. More generally, see Augustine, *Sermons on the New Testament*, 277.10.

4. See Carlin A. Barton, *The Sorrows of the Ancient Romans: The Gladiator and the Monster* (Princeton, NJ: Princeton University Press, 1993), 95–96. Also see the discussion of *probaskania*. Ibid., 168–71. Children and cattle were alike subject to the influence of an evil gaze. For the latter, see Virgil, *Eclogues*, 3.103.

5. See Pliny the Elder, *Natural History*, trans. H. Rackham et al., 10 vols., Loeb Classical Library (Cambridge, MA: Harvard University Press, 1938–62), 28.7. Also see *Natural History*, 7.2.

6. On brooding, especially with respect to Walter Benjamin, see David Michael Levin, *The Philosopher's Gaze: Modernity in the Shadows of Enlightenment* (Berkeley and Los Angeles: University of California Press, 1999), 361.

7. I should stress that my concern is with the *phenomenon* of fascination, in one or another of its modes, not with the colloquial sense of the word *fascination*, which is often used loosely, without regard to phenomenological distinctions, to suggest interest, wonder, or another intentional state.

8. The effects of fascination on the human body have long interested some psychologists. See, e.g., John B. Newman, *Fascination; or, The Philosophy of Charming, Illustrating the Principles of Life in Connection with Spirit and Matter* (New York: Fowlers & Wells, 1856).

9. Romano's earlier work is deeply invested in phenomenology. Thereafter, he seeks to engage analytic philosophy and convene a conversation between the two approaches. See, in particular, Claude Romano, *At the Heart of Reason*, trans. Michael B. Smith and Claude Romano (Evanston, IL: Northwestern University Press, 2015).

10. See Ricoeur, *Freud and Philosophy*, 32–36.

11. See, e.g., Adolf Harnack, *The History of Dogma*, trans. Neil Buchanan, 7 vols. (1961; reprint, Eugene, OR: Wipf & Stock, 1997), vol. 7:272–73 (also see 1:21).

12. Only slightly different is the Marxist procedure of "demystification," which is threefold. What are presented as eternal truths are shown to have roots in history; ideas and commitments that seem inevitable are exposed as subject to change; and what is upheld as natural is unmasked as cultural.

13. See Kant, *Critique of Pure Reason*, A12.

14. For a table of the categories, see Kant, *Critique of Pure Reason*, B106.

15. See Kant, *Prolegomenon to Any Future Metaphysics That Will Be Able to Come Forward as a Science*, trans. Paul Carus, rev. James W. Ellington (Indianapolis: Hackett, 1977).

16. See Kant, *Religion within the Limits of Reason Alone*, esp. bk. 3.

17. See Joseph Breuer and Sigmund Freud, *Studies on Hysteria*, trans. James and Alix Strachey, ed. James and Alix Strachey assisted by Angela Richards, Pelican Freud Library, vol. 3 (Harmondsworth: Penguin, 1974), 393.

18. See Heidegger, *Being and Time*, § 29, and *The Fundamental Concepts of Metaphysics*, §§ 16–38. It is worth recalling what was observed in chapter 3, namely, that Fink preferred to speak of the natural attitude as *Weltbefangenheit*, which suggests the constraint of fascination.

19. For Husserl's response to Shestov's claim that philosophy is a struggle, see Leon Shestov, "In Memory of a Great Philosopher: Edmund Husserl," trans. George L. Kline, in *Speculation and Revelation*, trans. Bernard Martin (Athens: Ohio University Press, 1982), 272.

20. See Martin Heidegger, *Phenomenological Interpretations of Aristotle: Initiation into Phenomenological Research*, trans. Richard Rojcewicz (Bloomington: Indiana University Press, 2001), 113–14, and *Being and Time*, 177. A longer analysis would distinguish Heidegger's view in *Being and Time* from his later commending of *besinnliches Denken* (meditative thinking) as contrasted with *rechnendes Denken* (calculative thought). See, e.g., his claim in lectures of 1928–29 that the contemplative *Dasein* is not doing science, which requires practical experimentation, *Einleitung in die Philosophie*, ed. Otto Saame and Ina Saame-Speidel (Franfurt: Vittorio Klostermann, 1996), 178, and his much later formulation in *Discourse on Thinking*, trans. John M. Anderson and E. Hans Freund, intro. John M. Anderson (New York: Harper and Row, 1966), 46.

21. See Edmund Husserl, *Wahrnehmung und Aufmerksamkeit: Texte aus dem Nachlass (1893–1912)*, ed. Thomas Vongehr and Regula Giulani, Husserliana, vol. 38 (Dordrecht: Springer, 2004), 108, and *Zur phänomenologischen Reduktion*, no. 14.

22. See Basil of Caesarea, "Concerning Envy," in *Ascetical Works*, trans. M. Monica Wagner, Fathers of the Church, vol. 9 (Washington, DC: Catholic University of America Press, 1950), 463–74. Also see Frederick Thomas Elworthy, *The Evil Eye: The Origins and Practices of Superstition*, with an introduction by Louis S. Barron (New York: Collier, 1958); and John H. Elliott, *Beware the Evil Eye*, 4 vols. (Eugene, OR: Cascade, 2017).

23. See Sinkewicz, ed., *The Greek Ascetic Corpus*, chap. 3 (on Evagrius of Pontus). Also see Gregory the Great, *MJ*, 5.6; and Aquinas, *ST*, 2a2ae q. 36 art. 3 *resp*. Finally, see Angela Tilby, *The Seven Deadly Sins: Their Origin in the Spiritual Teaching of Evagrius the Hermit* (London: Society for Promoting Christian Knowledge, 2009), esp. chap. 8.

24. See Aquinas, *ST*, 1a q. 117 art. 3 ad 2. Aquinas's commitment to the activity of the human eye allows him to continue the view that old women (i.e., witches) can influence

people, especially children, simply by looking at them. Also, he agrees with Aristotle that women can tarnish mirrors by gazing into them when they are having menstrual periods. Yet he makes no mention of the evil eye in his article on envy. See Aquinas, *ST*, 2a2ae q. 36. Also see Aristotle, *On Dreams*, in *On the Soul, Parva Naturalia, On Breath*, trans. W. S. Hett, Loeb Classical Library (Cambridge, MA: Harvard University Press, 1936), 459b 27–32. For a woman's eyes having a troubling effect on a man, see Molière, *École des femmes*, 2.5.519–24.

25. See Andreas Degan, "Concepts of Fascination, from Democritus to Kant," *Journal of the History of Ideas* 73, no. 3 (2012): 371–93. For a remarkably concise instance of the persistence of the idea that "love and envy" are the two affections that "fascinate or bewitch," see Francis Bacon, *Essays*, with an introduction by Michael J. Hawkins (1906; reprint, London: J. M. Dent, 1972), 24–28.

26. Immanuel Kant, *Anthropology from a Pragmatic Point of View*, trans. with an introduction and notes by Mary J. Gregor (The Hague: Martinus Nijhoff, 1974), 29.

27. Richard of St. Victor, *AM*, 1.5. See, with respect to this example, Pierre Hadot, "Le mythe de Narcisse et son interprétation par Plotin," *Nouvelle revue de psychanalyse* 13 (1970): 81–108, esp. 99.

28. Ovid, *Metamorphoses*, trans. Frank Justus Miller, 2 vols., Loeb Classical Library (Cambridge, MA: Harvard University Press, 1977), 3.430–32, 437–40.

29. Kant, *Anthropology from a Pragmatic Point of View*, 29–30. Kant discusses the evil eye, an earlier conception of fascination, in his *Lectures on Anthropology*, ed. Allen W. Wood and Robert B. Louden, trans. Robert R. Clewis et al. (Cambridge: Cambridge University Press, 2012), 372.

30. This is not to say that all phenomenologists explore fascination. It is not a theme in the work of Eugen Fink, Michel Henry, Emmanuel Levinas (with the exception of his comments on Blanchot), Paul Ricoeur, or Jean-Luc Marion (save a passing remark about the idol to which I refer beneath). One reason is that it is not asterisked as an issue by Husserl, who, however, investigates fantasy very thoroughly indeed. See Husserl, *Phantasy, Image Consciousness, and Memory*.

31. Rudolf Otto's Habilitation dissertation is on Kant. See Rudolf Otto, *Naturaltische und religiöse Weltansicht* (Tübingen: J. C. B. Mohr [Paul Siebeck], 1904). The book that will interest us here is important in part for its insistence that the holy is an a priori category. See Rudolf Otto, *The Idea of the Holy: An Inquiry into the Non-Rational Factor in the Idea of the Divine and Its Relation to the Rational*, trans. John W. Harvey (Oxford: Oxford University Press, 1923), chap. 14, 17.

32. Otto, *The Idea of the Holy*, 31, 36.

33. See Otto, *The Idea of the Holy*, 26 n. 1 and 158.

34. Otto's treatment of contemplation is limited to his discussion of Schleiermacher. See Otto, *The Idea of the Holy*, 146–49.

35. See Otto, *The Idea of the Holy*, 35. He considers contemplation later on. See ibid., 146–49.

36. Otto, *The Idea of the Holy*, 52.

37. Otto, *The Idea of the Holy*, 146, 140.

38. Otto, *The Idea of the Holy*, 149.

39. See Otto, *The Idea of the Holy*, 155.

40. Heidegger, *Being and Time*, 316. Christopher Fynsk brings out the importance of fascination in Heidegger. See Christopher Fynsk, *Heidegger: Thought and Historicity*, expanded ed. (Ithaca, NY: Cornell University Press, 1993). Heidegger speaks almost entirely of *Benommenheit* rather than *Faszination*.

41. For "average everydayness," see Heidegger, *Being and Time*, 149, 394.

42. Heidegger, *Being and Time*, 394. After *Being and Time*, Heidegger shifts from focusing on *Dasein* as dazed or captivated by beings, especially when overcome by *Angst*. Rather, he attributes that state to animals. See Heidegger, *The Fundamental Concepts of Metaphysics*, § 59.

43. Jean-Paul Sartre, *Nausea*, trans. Robert Baldick (Harmondsworth: Penguin, 1965), 183. Relevant here is Sartre's view of the imagination. See Sartre, *The Imaginary*.

44. Sartre, *Nausea*, 188.

45. See Jean-Paul Sartre, *Being and Nothingness: An Essay on Phenomenological Ontology*, trans. and with an introduction by Hazel E. Barnes (New York: Philosophical Library, 1956), 177. In the original, Sartre writes: "Car la condition pour qu'il y ait fascination, c'est que l'objet s'enlève avec un relief absolu sur un fond de vide." Jean-Paul Sartre, *L'être et le néant: Essai d'ontologie phénoménologique* (Paris: Gallimard, 1949), 226. Immediately before this remark, he observes: "Dans la fascination il n'y a plus rien qu'un objet géant dans un monde désert." The emphasis on *objet* will be questioned by Blanchot in his attention to the image.

46. Sartre, *Nausea*, 188.

47. Maurice Blanchot, *The Space of Literature*, trans. and with an introduction by Ann Smock (Lincoln: University of Nebraska Press, 1982), 33, 32. Also see the opening passage of the fourth chapter of Maurice Blanchot, *Thomas l'Obscur*, nouvelle version (Paris: Gallimard, 1950). For reflection on the fascination of the moving image, see Calum Watt, *Blanchot and the Moving Image: Fascination and Spectatorship* (Oxford: Legenda, 2017). It should be noted that Blanchot approaches the question of fascination and writing several years earlier in a review essay on Jean Pouillon's *Temps et roman* (1946) that appeared in *Les temps modernes*, no. 19 (April 1947): 1304–17.

48. Blanchot, *The Space of Literature*, 32. Earlier, Blanchot argues that Mallarmé's poetry is not to be contemplated but that it contemplates the reader. See Maurice Blanchot, "Is Mallarmé's Poetry Obscure?," in *Faux pas*, trans. Charlotte Mandell (Stanford, CA: Stanford University Press, 2001), 111.

49. Ezra Pound, "A Few Don'ts by an Imagiste," *Poetry* 1, no. 6 (1913): 200.

50. See Ezra Pound, "In a Station of the Metro," in *Selected Poems*, with an introduction by T. S. Eliot (London: Faber and Faber, 1948), 113.

51. Blanchot, *The Space of Literature*, 32, 33. Maurice Merleau-Ponty remarks: "The painter lives in fascination [*Le peintre vit dans la fascination*]." Maurice Merleau-Ponty, "Eye and Mind," in *The Primacy of Perception and Other Essays on Phenomenological Psychology, the Philosophy of Art, History and Politics*, trans. and with an introduction by James M. Edie (Evanston, IL: Northwestern University Press, 1964), 167. For an analysis of Merleau-Ponty in this regard, see Glen Mazis, "The Artist's Gestures of Fascination in 'Eye and Mind,'" in *Understanding Merleau-Ponty, Understanding Modernism*, ed. Ariane Mildenberg (London: Bloomsbury, 2019), 73–85. Finally, for a somewhat different view on fascination and the artist, see Henry Maldiney, "L'équivoque de l'image dans la peinture," in *Regard Parole Espace*, ed. Christian Chaput, Philippe Grosos, and Maria Villela-Petit, with an introduction by Jean-Louis Chrétien, Oeuvres philosophiques (Paris: Cerf, 2013), 290. It is possible that Baudelaire stands behind all these authors: "Manier savamment une langue, c'est pratiquer une espèce de sorcellerie évocatoire [*To handle a language skillfully is to practice a kind of evocative witchcraft*]." Charles Baudelaire, "Théophile Gautier" (1859), in *Oeuvres complètes*, ed. Claude Pichois, 2 vols. (Paris: Gallimard, 1976), 2:118.

52. See Blanchot, "Literature and the Right to Death," 327.

53. See Husserl, *Phenomenological Psychology: Lectures, Summer Semester, 1925,* trans. John Scanlon (The Hague: Martinus Nijhoff, 1977), 80–83.

54. See Blanchot, *The Space of Literature,* 241.

55. See Heidegger, *Being and Time,* § 53; and Levinas, *Totality and Infinity,* 235.

56. Maurice Blanchot, *The Infinite Conversation,* trans. and with a foreword by Susan Hanson (Minneapolis: University of Minnesota Press, 1993), 240.

57. See Maurice Blanchot, *The Writing of the Disaster,* trans. Ann Smock (Lincoln: University of Nebraska Press, 1986), 50–51. On Blanchot's analysis, one cannot affirm atheism, rigorously formulated, for there is no substantial *I* with which that can be done.

58. Jacques Derrida, *Parages,* ed. John P. Leavey, trans. Tom Conley et al. (Stanford, CA: Stanford University Press, 2011), 80. The "*X* without *X*" syntax is also traditional in Christian theology of God. See, e.g., Augustine, *The Literal Meaning of Genesis,* in *On Genesis,* 4.8. For Augustine, God is transcendent, beyond phenomena, and so the *X* without *X* syntax elicits contemplation. For Blanchot, however, the Outside is anterior to phenomena, and the same syntax elicits fascination.

59. See Jacques Derrida, *The Death Penalty,* ed. Geoffrey Bennington, Marc Crépon, and Thomas Dutuit, trans. Peggy Kamuf, 2 vols. (Chicago: University of Chicago Press, 2014), 1:29, 58.

60. Jacques Derrida, "Plato's Pharmacy," in *Dissemination,* trans. with an introduction and notes by Barbara Johnson (London: Athlone, 1981), 70.

61. Yet these structures certainly appear in the region of signification, so it would be more accurate to refer to them as *limit phenomena.*

62. See Jacques Derrida, *Glas* (Paris: Éditions Galilée, 1974), 183. I should note that, where Blanchot and Derrida often figure fascination with reference to phenomena (and to what is anterior to phenomena), Jean-Luc Marion speaks of something similar, bedazzlement, in terms of an excess of quality (in Kant's sense) that cannot be borne. See Marion, *Being Given,* 202–6. He evokes fascination in Jean-Luc Marion, *In Excess: Studies in Saturated Phenomena,* trans. Robyn Horner and Vincent Berraud (New York: Fordham University Press, 2002), 60.

63. Claude Romano, *Event and World,* trans. Shane Mackinlay (New York: Fordham University Press, 2009).

64. I refer here to Claude Romano, *Event and Time,* trans. Stephen E. Lewis (New York: Fordham University Press, 2014), 109. *L'advenant* is also discussed throughout Romano, *Event and World.*

65. One possibility is torture before death. Another possibility is the thought of damnation after death. The dark theme of damnation surfaces with ever greater sureness in Cowper's letters, especially in his last years. See *The Correspondence of William Cowper: Arranged in Chronological Order: With Annotations by Thomas Wright,* 4 vols. (New York: Haskell House, 1969). The theme is presented with an almost unbearable intensity in his "Lines Written during a Period of Insanity" (ca. 1774):

Hatred and vengeance, my eternal portion
Scarce can endure delay of execution,
Wait with impatient readiness to seize my
    Soul in a moment.

Damned below Judas; more abhorred than he was,
Who for a few pence sold his holy Master!

Twice betrayed, Jesus me, the last delinquent,
Deems the profanest.

Man disavows, and Deity disowns me:
Hell might afford my miseries a shelter;
Therefore Hell keeps her ever-hungry mouths all
Bolted against me.

Hard lot! encompassed with a thousand dangers;
Weary, faint, trembling with a thousand terrors,
I'm called, if vanquished, to receive a sentence
Worse than Abiram's.

Him the vindictive rod of angry Justice
Sent quick and howling to the centre headlong;
I, fed with judgment, in a fleshy tomb am
Buried above ground.

William Cowper, *Poetical Works*, ed. H. S. Milford (London: Oxford University Press, 1967), 289–90.

66. See *Breviarium ad usum insignis ecclesiae Sarum*, 3 vols. (Cambridge: Cambridge University Press, 1879–86), 2:278. The passage runs: "Peccantem me quotidie et non poenitentem timor mortis conturbat me."

67. Among these heirs, of course, are those who inherit in the mode of refusal. See, e.g., Emmanuel Levinas, *God, Death, and Time*, 7–117 ("Death and Time"). To be distinguished from this group is Vladimir Jankélévitch, for whom life triumphs over death precisely because not even death can obliterate the very fact of someone's having lived, his or her quoddity. See Vladimir Jankélévitch, *La mort* (Paris: Flammarion, 1966), and *Penser la mort?*, ed. and with a foreword by Françoise Schwab (Paris: Éditions Liana Levi, 1994).

68. Romano, *Event and World*, 111.

69. See Schopenhauer, *WWR*, vol. 1, § 34.

70. Romano, *Event and World*, 112.

71. It should be noted that, at the time of the first version of the poem, Coleridge was a Unitarian. By the time of the glossed version of the poem, he was an orthodox Christian.

72. Coleridge read and annotated Kant's *Anthropologie* sometime over the period 1800–1804, after the composition of "The Rime." He does not comment there on Kant's sense of fascination. See Coleridge, *Marginalia*, pt. 3, pp. 236–40.

73. See Thomas Burnet, *The Sacred Theory of the Earth* (1719), with an introduction by Basil Willey, 2 vols. (reprint, London: Centaur, 1965), 1:109. Burnet does not use the word *sublime*. John Dennis first uses it in *Miscellanies in Verse and Prose* (London: James Knapton, 1693), 84. And Joseph Addison writes: "There may, indeed, be something so terrible or offensive, that the Horrour or Loathsomeness of an Object may over-bear the Pleasure which results from its *Greatness, Novelty* or *Beauty*; but still there will be such a Mixture of Delight in the very Disgust it gives us, as any of these three Qualifications are most conspicuous and prevailing." *The Spectator*, no. 412 (June 23, 1712), in Joseph Addison et al., *The Spectator*, ed. Gregory Smith, with an introduction by Peter Smithers, 2nd ed., 4 vols. (London: Dent, 1945), 3:279. Finally, see George Keate, *The Alps:*

A Poem (London: R. and J. Dodsley, 1763). On negative pleasure, see Kant, *Critique of Judgement*, 91.

74. Thomas Burnet, *Doctrina antiqua de rerum originibus; or, An Inquiry into the Doctrine of the Philosophers of All Nations, concerning the Original of the World*, trans. Mr. Mead and Mr. Foxton (London: E. Curll, 1736), 86–88 (emphasis added).

75. In the gloss to lines 131–34, Coleridge points us to Josephus (37–100) and Michael Psellos (1018–78) as writers who countenance the presence of invisible spirits on the planet, spirits who are neither souls nor angels. See the remarks on *phantasmata* in Josephus, *Jewish Antiquities*, 6.211. Also see Michael Psellos, *De operatione daemonum*, with the notes of Gilbert Gaulmini, ed. Jean-François Boissonade (Norimbergae: Apud Fr. Nap. Campe, 1838).

76. Samuel Taylor Coleridge, "The Rime of the Ancient Mariner," in *Poetical Works*, ed. J. C. C. Mays, vol. 16, pt. 1, of CC (Princeton, NJ: Princeton University Press, 2001), 504–39, 504.

77. Coleridge, "The Rime of the Ancient Mariner," 523 (emphasis added). In the original gloss to line 13, Coleridge writes: "The wedding guest is spell-bound by the eye of the old sea-faring man, and constrained to hear his tale." Ibid., 510.

78. Coleridge observes that the "Fascinati" are people who have lost their "Reason." Coleridge, *Marginalia*, pt. 1, pp. 621–22.

79. Coleridge, *Poetical Works*, 512.

80. Impressed by the evidence that Coleridge mined ships' captains' reports for lines of the poem, William Empson goes further and suggests that the mariner shoots the bird for food, albatross making "a tolerable soup which would help to keep off scurvy." William Empson, "'The Ancient Mariner,'" in *Argufying: Essays on Literature and Culture*, ed. and with an introduction by John Haffenden (London: Hogarth, 1988), 300. He refers to John Livingston Lowes, *The Road to Xanadu: A Study in the Ways of the Imagination* (London: Constable, 1927). More tellingly, Dorothy Bilk has suggested that Coleridge might have been thinking of the story of Mosollamus as related by Josephus in *Against Apion*. See Dorothy Bilk, "Josephus, Mosollamus, and the Ancient Mariner," *Studies in Philology* 86, no. 1 (1989): 87–95. According to the story, a bird was being watched with a view to supplying auspices while Alexander the Great marched to the Red Sea: "The Jew, without saying a word, drew this bow, shot and struck the bird and killed it. The seer and some others were indignant, and heaped curses upon him. 'Why so mad, you poor wretches' he retorted; and then, taking the bird in his hands, continued, 'Pray, how could any sound information about our march be given by this creature, which could not provide for its own safety? Had it been gifted with divination, it would not have come to this spot, for fear of being killed by an arrow of Mosollamus the Jew.'" Josephus, *The Life*, in *Against Apion*, trans. H. St. John Thackeray, Loeb Classical Library (Cambridge, Mass.: Harvard University Press, 1961), 244–47.

81. The albatross became an omen of bad luck after Coleridge's poem appeared. See Mary Shelley, *Frankenstein* (1823), letter 2; and Charles Baudelaire, "L'Albatross" (*Les fleurs du mal* [1857]), in *Oeuvres complètes*, 1:9. Herman Melville observes: "Think thee of the albatross, whence come those clouds of spiritual wonderment and pale dread, in which that white phantom sails in all imaginations?" Herman Melville, *Moby-Dick* (1851), in *Redburn, White-Jacket, Moby-Dick*, ed. G. Thomas Tanselle (New York: Library of America, 1983), 995. Melville's recollections of his first sight of an albatross, given as a note to this passage, are highly relevant. He refers to the albatross as having "vast archangel wings" and being "a mystic thing."

82. Philip Larkin, "Next, Please," in *Collected Poems*, 52.

83. See John Keats, "La Belle Dame sans Merci," in *John Keats*, ed. Elizabeth Cook (Oxford: Oxford University Press, 1994), 166–67.

84. The claim is not obvious. James Booth, e.g., regards "Aubade" as one of Larkin's "ten contemplative elegies." James Booth, *Philip Larkin: Life, Art and Love* (London: Bloomsbury, 2014), 281.

85. Philip Larkin, "Aubade," in *Collected Poems*, 208–9. For readers' fascination with the poem, see Richard Bradford, *The Importance of Elsewhere: Philip Larkin's Photographs*, with a foreword by Mark Hayworth-Booth (London: Frances Lincoln, 2017), 241.

86. See Plato, *Phaedo*, 118a; and Clement of Alexandria, *Stromata*, 5.11.67.1.

87. See Plato, *Apology*, 29a–b; Epicurus, "Letter to Menoecus," in *Letters, Principal Doctrines and Vatican Sayings*, trans. Russel M. Geer (Indianapolis: Bobbs-Merill, 1964), 124b–127a; Seneca, *Letters on Ethics: To Lucilius*, trans. Margaret Graver and A. A. Long (Chicago: University of Chicago Press, 2017), letter 24; and Baruch Spinoza, *Ethics*, in *Ethics Preceded by On the Improvement of the Understanding*, ed. and with an introduction by James Gutmann (New York: Hafner, 1949), proposition 67.

88. See Marguerite Yourcenar, *Memoirs of Hadrian*, trans. Grace Frick in collaboration with the author (1951; New York: Modern Library, 1984), 5.

89. William Dunbar's "Lament for the Makars," in *William Dunbar: The Complete Works*, ed. John Conlee (Kalamazoo: Medieval Institute Publications, 2004), 48–51.

90. "Fearful Death," in *Medieval English Lyrics: A Critical Anthology*, ed. and with an introduction by R. T. Davies (London: Faber and Faber, 1963), 279.

91. See, e.g., John Audelay, "Dread of Death," in *Poems and Carols: Oxford Bodleian MS Douce 302*, ed. Susanna Fein (Kalamazoo: Medieval Institute Publications, 2009), 1–14.

92. I am indebted to DeVan Ard's "Opus Lyricus: Liturgical and Lyric Forms in Late Medieval British Poetry" (PhD diss., University of Virginia, 2020) for insight into what Dunbar inherited from earlier poetry. The carol with the bird can be found in Bodleian MS Eng. Poet. e. 1.

93. The theme has recently attracted psychoanalytic interest. See, e.g., Michel Thys, "On Fascination and Fear of Annihilation," *International Journal of Psychoanalysis* 98 (2017): 633–55.

94. Robin Robbins, ed., *The Complete Poems of John Donne* (London: Routledge, 2013), 522. See the reflections on these lines in Jacques Derrida, *The Beast and the Sovereign*, ed. Michel Lisse, Marie-Louise Mallet, and Ginette Michaud, trans. Geoffrey Bennington, 2 vols. (Chicago: University of Chicago Press, 2009), 2:50–54.

95. See Horace, *Odes*, 3.30; and Ovid, *Metamorphoses*, 15.871–79.

96. John Keats, "Ode on a Nightingale," in *John Keats*, 174–77.

97. There is a tradition of contemplating death, as in Nicholas Ferrar's incomplete *Contemplations on Death*, but there is no pressing reason to take the word *contemplation* here to be distinct from *thoughts* or *meditations*.

98. See J. H. Newman, *An Essay in Aid of a Grammar of Assent*, with an introduction by Nicholas Lash (Notre Dame, IN: University of Notre Dame Press, 1979), chap. 4.

99. The sentence is quoted in Jankélévitch, *Penser la mort?*, 29. No page reference to Jacques Madaule's *Considération de la mort* (Paris: Éditions R.-A. Corrêa, 1934) is given. Various authors, mainly French, have quoted the line and also have not given a page reference. I have been unable to find the sentence in Madaule's book.

100. See Richard Ellmann, *Oscar Wilde* (London: Penguin, 1987), 546.

101. Philip Larkin, "Toads," in *Collected Poems*, 89, and "Toads Revisited," in ibid., 147–48.

102. See Jean Wahl, *Human Existence and Transcendence*, trans. William C. Hackett, with a foreword by Kevin Hart (Notre Dame, IN: Notre Dame University Press, 2016), 28.

103. D. H. Lawrence, *The Plumed Serpent (Quetzalcoatl)*, ed. L. D. Clark, The Works of D. H. Lawrence (Cambridge: Cambridge University Press, 1979), 183. Later in the novel, we are told by Kate that "Mexico *has* no soul," and the narrator evokes the "unknowable God-mystery" that lives and moves in Ramón. Ibid., 234, 337. We also hear in the "First Song of Huitzilopochtli": "Deeper than the roots of the mango tree / Down in the centre of the earth / Is the yellow, serpent-yellow shining of my sun." Ibid., 373.

104. Lawrence, *The Plumed Serpent*, 122, 123, 156.

105. See Wahl, *Human Existence and Transcendence*, 28.

106. On this last point, see Seamus Heaney, "Joy or Night: Last Things in the Poetry of W. B. Yeats and Philip Larkin," in *The Redress of Poetry* (New York: Farrar, Straus & Giroux, 1995), 146–63. Heaney responds here to the reservations about Larkin's "Aubade" in Czelaw Milosz, "The Real and the Paradigms," *Poetry Australia* 72 (1979): 59–63. Also see Milosz's comments on Larkin's poem in Cynthia L. Haven, *Czeslaw Milosz: Conversations* (Jackson: University Press of Mississippi, 2006), 64–65, 169. For Milosz, we learn in one conversation, poetry is "an act of struggle against . . . nothingness." Ibid., 35. Finally, see the short poem "Against the Poetry of Philip Larkin" in Czelaw Milosz, *New and Collected Poems, 1931–2001*, trans. Robert Hass (New York: Ecco, 2003), 718; and the remarks in Andrzej Frnaszek, *Milosz: A Biography*, ed. and trans. Aleksandra and Michael Parker (Cambridge, MA: Belknap Press of Harvard University Press, 2017), 392–93.

107. Melanie Klein, "Notes on Some Schizoid Mechanisms" (1946), in *Envy and Gratitude and Other Works, 1946–1963* (London: Hogarth, 1980), 4.

108. William of St. Thierry's *De natura et dignitate amoris* was known at the time as the *Anti-Nasonem*. For further discussion, see Gilson, *The Mystical Theology of St. Bernard*, apps. 4 and 5.

Chapter Six

1. Dante, *Paradiso*, 10. 131–32, Digital Dante, https://digitaldante.columbia.edu /dante/divine-comedy. Dante most likely has Cicerco, *Tusculanae disputationes*, 5.3, in mind when he writes of Richard being "più che viro."

2. Dante, *Paradiso*, 22.46–48.

3. See Martz, *The Poetry of Meditation*, 13–14.

4. Cicero, *De finibus*, 5.21.58, *Brutus*, 265, and *Tusculanae disputationes*, 5.3. Other instances of Cicero's use of *consideratio* appear in *Academica*, 35, 127, *De re publica*, 1.19, *In Verrem*, 2.22, *Pro rege Deiotaro oratio*, 16, and *De inuentione*, 2.33.103.

5. I take it that Milton draws from Cicero in his sonnet 16 (19), "On His Blindness" ("When I consider how my light is spent"). See John Milton, *The Complete Works of John Milton*, vol. 3, *The Shorter Poems*, ed. and with an introduction, notes, and commentary by Barbara Kiefer Lewalski and Estelle Haan (Oxford: Oxford University Press, 2012), 245.

6. Boethius writes: "rhetoricae einem vel poeticae convenientior consideratio est." Carolus Meiser, ed., *In librum Aristotelis Περὶ Ἑρμηνείας*, 2 vols. (Leipzig, Teubneri, 1877), 1:71. Also: "id est unde ipse tractaturus est, de postrema generis significatione quam dixit, id est de illo genere quod sub se species habet, disputatio consideratioque

uertitur. At uero de superioribus generibus id est de cognatione et loco ir quo quis ge-
nitus est, aut historicorum aut poetarum spectatio est." Samuel Brandt, ed., *In Isagogen
Porphyrii Commenta* (Leipzig: G. Freytag, 1896), 39.

7. Augustine, *De doctrina christiana*, 1.23.22. St. Bernard distinguishes *te, sub te, circa
te,* and *supra te* in *De consideratione*, 2.3.6.

8. See, e.g., the Platonic dialogue *Alcidiades* 1, 129a–b, where the concern is to know
the self and the forms. Relevant also is Cicero, *Tusculanae disputationes*, 1.52, and deeper
in the background there is the directive of the oracle at Delphi: "Know yourself" (γνῶθι
σεαυτόν). Cicero had rephrased Apollo's words so that *Nosce te,* as he prefers to state it,
is oriented more surely inward, *Nosce animum tuum* (Know your soul). *Tusculanae disputationes,* 1.52. Basil of Caesarea explores the exhortation "Give heed to thyself" in a
homily of that title. See *Ascetical Works,* 431–56. Ephraim the Syrian tells us that we
cannot hear scripture until we know ourselves. Ephraim the Syrian, "On Admonition
and Repentance," in *Hymns and Homilies,* with an introduction by John Gwynn (Scotts
Valley, CA: Create Space, 2012), 365–76. Augustine says, with Cicero in mind, "Deum
et animam scire cupio" (I desire to know God and the soul). *Soliloquia,* 1.2.7. More generally, for the classical sources, see Eliza Gregory Wilkins, *"Know Thyself" in Greek and
Latin Literature* (Chicago: University of Chicago Libraries, 1917).

9. St. Bernard of Clairvaux, *Five Books on Consideration,* 2.4.7.

10. St. Bernard of Clairvaux, *Five Books on Consideration,* 2.2.5.

11. St. Bernard of Clairvaux, *Five Books on Consideration,* 1.7.8. Also see St. Bernard
of Clairvaux, *The Steps of Humility and Pride,* trans. M. Ambrose Conway and with an
introduction by M. Basil Pennington, The Works of Bernard of Clairvaux, vol. 5, treatise
2 (Washington, DC: Cistercian, 1974), 1.2.

12. St. Bernard of Clairvaux, *Five Books on Consideration,* 5.2.4.

13. St. Bernard of Clairvaux, *Five Books on Consideration,* 5.2.3. On ascent and *raptus,*
see Gilson, *The Mystical Theology of St. Bernard,* 106.

14. St. Bernard of Clairvaux, *Five Books on Consideration,* 5.14.32.

15. St. Bernard of Clairvaux, *Five Books on Consideration,* 2.2.5.

16. Elizabeth Bishop, "Time's Andromedas," in *Poems, Prose, and Letters,* ed. Robert
Giroux and Lloyd Schwartz (New York: Library of America, 2008), 642.

17. Bishop, "Time's Andromedas," 642–43.

18. Bishop, "Time's Andromedas," 657.

19. Elizabeth Bishop, "Gerard Manley Hopkins," in *Poems, Prose, and Letters,* 663, 666.

20. Croll quotes Sir Henry Wotton's commonplace book, specifically, a quotation
from Sir Robert Cotton. See "Table Talk," in *The Life and Letters of Sir Henry Wotton,*
ed. Logan Pearsall Smith, 2 vols. (Oxford: Clarendon, 1907), 2:500. In fact, the original sentence in Cotton is much longer: "Publicke motion depends on the Conduct of
Fortune; private on our own carriage, we must beware of running down steep hill, with
weighty bodies, they once in motion *Suo feruntur pondere,* stoppes are not then voluntary; but Leicester at that instant, with the King, and out of the storm might have escaped, if his courage and hope had not made him more resolute by misfortune, so that
hee could neyther forske his followers, nor his ambition; thus making adversity the exercise of his virtue, hee came, and fell." Sir Robert Cotton, *A Short View of the Long Life
and Raigne of Henry III, King of England* (1627; London: William Bentley, 1651), 23.

21. Morris W. Croll, "The Baroque Style in Prose," ed. John M. Wallace, in *Style,
Rhetoric, and Rhythm: Essays by Morris W. Croll,* ed. J. Max Patrick and Robert O. Evans
with John M. Wallace and R. J. Schoeck (Princeton, NJ: Princeton University Press,
1966), 207–34. Croll goes on to reflect on Cotton's use of the word *deliberately.*

22. Bishop, "Gerard Manley Hopkins," 666. The emphasis in the quotation is Croll's. Bishop wrote about Croll's essay to Donald Stanford on November 20 1933, drawing attention to the discussion in "The Baroque Style in Prose" of the "curt period," and observing of the passage she quotes in "Time's Andromedas" that it "perfectly describes the sort of poetic convention I should like to make for myself." Elizabeth Bishop, *One Art: Letters*, ed. Robert Giroux (New York: Farrar, Straus, Giroux, 1994), 12.

23. I hew closely here to Sokolowski, *Introduction to Phenomenology*, 117–18.

24. See Herbert J. C. Grierson, ed., *Metaphysical Lyrics and Poems of the Seventeenth Century* (Oxford: Clarendon, 1921); and T. S. Eliot, "The Metaphysical Poets," in *CPE*, 2:375–85. Eliot's essay was originally a review of Grierson's anthology. See T. S. Eliot, "The Metaphysical Poets," *Times Literary Supplement*, no. 1031 (October 20, 1921): 669–70.

25. Bishop, "Gerard Manley Hopkins," 665.

26. Marianne Moore, "Archaically New," in *The Complete Prose of Marianne Moore*, ed. and with an introduction by Patricia C. Willis (New York: Viking, 1986), 327–28. Also see Moore's remark on Elizabeth Gaskell: "With poetry as with homiletics, tentativeness can be more positive than positiveness; and in *North & South*, a much instructed persuasiveness is emphasized by uninsistence." Marianne Moore, "A Modest Expert" (1946), in ibid., 408.

27. See John Koethe, "The Romance of Realism," in *Thought and Poetry: Essays on Romanticism, Subjectivity, and Truth* (London: Bloomsbury, 2022), 58.

28. Elizabeth Bishop, "Under the Window: Ouro Preto," in *Poems, Prose, and Letters*, 145.

29. Elizabeth Bishop, "Under the Window: Ouro Preto," in *Poems, Prose, and Letters*, 145.

30. Saintsbury observes in a discussion of Tennyson: "The greatest part, if not the whole of pleasure-giving appeal of poetry, lies in its sound rather than in its sense." George Saintsbury, *Collected Essays and Papers of George Saintsbury, 1875–1920*, 2 vols. (London: J. M. Dent, 1923), 2:199. Bunting remarks: "Poetry, like music, is to be heard. It deals in sound—long sounds and short sounds, heavy beats and light beats, the tone relations of vowels, the relation of consonants to one another which are like instrumental colour in music. Poetry lies dead on the page, until some voice brings it to life. . . . Poetry must be read aloud." Jonathan Williams, *Descant on Rawthey's Madrigal: Conversations with Basil Bunting* (Lexington, KY: Gnomon, 1968), n.p.

31. Elizabeth Bishop, "As We Like It," in *Poems, Prose, and Letters*, 682. Grace Schulman follows Martz in seeing "attentive contemplation" not only in Moore but also in D. H. Lawrence, Hopkins, Yeats, and Stevens. See Grace Schulman, *Marianne Moore: The Poetry of Engagement* (1986; New York: Paragon House, 1989), 75. Also see her remarks on composition of place. Ibid., 58–59.

32. See Richard Baxter, *The Saints' Everlasting Rest; or, A Treatise of the Blessed State of the Saints in Their Enjoyment of God in Glory* (London: Rob. White, 1649), 720–22.

33. Marianne Moore, "An Octopus," in *The Complete Poems of Marianne Moore* (London: Faber and Faber, 1968), 75. Baxter actually writes: "What the nature of this spiritual life is, is a Question exceedingly difficult: Whether, as some think (but (as I judg) erroneously) it be Christ himself in Person, or Essence? or the holy Ghost personally? (Or as some will distinguish (with what sense I know not) is it the person of the holy Ghost, but not personally;) Whether it be an Accident, or Quality? Or whether it be a spiritual substance, as the soul it felt? Whether it be only an Act? or a disposition? or a habit? (as its generally taken). Whether a habit infused? Or acquired by frequent Acts, to which the soul have been morally persuaded, viz. *potentia prexima intelligendi, credenda, volendi,*

&c in spiritualibus? Which some think, the most probable, and that it was such a power that Adam lost, and that the natural man (as experience tells us) is still devoid of." Baxter, *The Saints' Everlasting Rest*, 14–15.

34. Moore, "An Octopus," 76.

35. The expression *low modernist* was coined by Walter Jost. See Walter Jost, *Rhetorical Investigations: Studies in Ordinary Language Criticism* (Charlottesville: University of Virginia Press, 2004), chap. 2.

36. *Nearly Baroque* is Stephanie Burt's expression in a piece on contemporary poetry in *Boston Review* (April 21, 2014). See https://www.bostonreview.net/articles /stephen-burt-nearly-baroque.

37. Moore, "An Octopus," 71–72.

38. I draw here and throughout on Croll's analysis of the anti-Ciceronian loose period. See Croll, "The Baroque Style in Prose."

39. On quotation, see Robert Sokolowski, *Pictures, Quotations, and Distinctions: Fourteen Essays in Phenomenology* (Notre Dame, IN: University of Notre Dame Press, 1992), chap. 2.

40. Moore, "An Octopus," 76.

41. One also finds monstrous ants—mermecoleons or "ant lions." They are depicted by Jacob Meydenbach in his *Hortus sanitatis* (1481) as well as in other places.

42. In his various treatises on animals, Aristotle does not mention anything about fierce snails, nor does Albertus Magnus in his *De animalibus* or his *Quaestiones super De animalibus* (although he says there that snails are poisonous [4 q. 4]). The tradition of the fierce snail seems to flourish in the margins of medieval manuscripts. For discussion of this peculiar feature of snails in the medieval monk's imagination, see Lilian M. C. Randall, "The Snail in Gothic Marginal Warfare," *Speculum* 37, no. 3 (1962): 358–67; and Michael Camille, *Image on the Edge: The Margins of Medieval Art* (London: Reaktion, 1992), 31–36. Camille sensibly argues that the snail motif works "in different ways and mean[s] different things" in different medieval manuscripts. Ibid., 36. I would suggest that the snail represents the scribe who, doing very slow work, is actually more powerful than warriors since he copies the Word of God.

43. See Auguste de Bastard, "Rapport," *Bulletin des comités historiques* 2 (1850): 173. Yet see the skepticism over the claim registered in Jules Champfleury, *Histoire de la caricature du moyen âge et sous la renaissance*, 2nd ed. (Paris: E. Dentu, 1875), 40.

44. William writes: "Tepide enim amantes ad modum limacis obuiam Deum uadunt." Guillelmus Alvernus, *Opera homiletica*, vol. 1, *Sermones de tempore*, sermon 41 (*in uigilia natiutatis Domini*), Corpus Christianorum Continuatio Mediaevalis, 230 (Turnhout: Brepols, 2010), 158.

45. See, e.g., Richard Lovelace, "The Ant," in *The Poems of Richard Lovelace*, 134–35; and John Clare, "The Ants," in *Poems, Chiefly from Manuscript* (London: Richard Cobden-Sanderson, 1920), 85. For a poem that provides a midrash to Prov. 6:6, see David Curzon, "The Ant," in *Modern Poems on the Bible*, ed. and with an introduction by David Curzon (Philadelphia: Jewish Publication Society, 1994), 299.

46. See Christopher Smart, "Jubilate Agno," in *The Poetical Works of Christopher Smart*, ed. and with an introduction by Karina Williamson, 6 vols. (Oxford: Clarendon, 1980–96), 1:87–90.

47. Marianne Moore, "To a Snail," in *Complete Poems*, 85.

48. I refer to the second stanza of Cowper's "The Snail" (translated from the Latin of Vincent Bourne):

Within that house secure he hides,
When danger imminent betides
Of storm, or other harm besides
    Of weather.

See William Cowper, *Poetical Works* (London: Frederick Warne, 1872), 565.

49. Like Walter Pater, Moore thinks that style is a matter of impersonality. Pater writes: "If style be the man, it will be in a real sense 'impersonal.'" Walter Pater, "Style," in *Appreciations, with an Essay on Style* (London: Macmillan, 1889), 35. As it happens, both Pater and Moore were admirers of Browne's anti-Ciceronian prose style.

50. See Duns Scotus, *Ordinatio*, prologue p. 3 q. 1–3, no. 204.

51. See Henry Osborne Taylor, *The Mediaeval Mind: A History of the Development of Thought and Emotion in the Middle Ages*, 2 vols. (New York: Macmillan, 1911), 2:546.

52. See Aquinas, *ST*, 1a q. 1 art. 4 *resp.*

53. See the discussion of "To a Snail" in Natalie Cecire, "Marianne Moore's Precision," *Arizona Quarterly* 67, no. 4 (2011): 86–91. Cecire points out that the occipital horn is a tentacle. Most snails have their eyes in the long upper tentacles, although some species have them at the base of their tentacles.

54. At first, Moore mistook Democritus for Demetrius. Reference to the philosopher was dropped after the first publication of *Observations* in 1924.

55. *Consideratio* is commended by Luis de Granada in his *Of Prayer and Meditation* (1554) with respect to faith (1.1), hope (1.2), charity (1.3), and devotion (1.4). The book was widely read in England in the early seventeenth century. Also see Francis de Sales, *Introduction to the Devout Life* (1609), which details five aspects of *consideratio*: the excellence of the soul, the excellence of the virtues, the example of the saints, Christ's love for us, and God's eternal love for us. Also see the highly influential *The Spiritual Combat* (1589) of Lorenzo Scupoli (for whom the first phase of *consideratio* is self-distrust) and the various redactions (by Robert Parsons and Edmund Bunny) of Gaspar Loarte's *Booke of Christian Exercise* (1579), in which *consideratio* is commended in the second chapter. By the time we get to Juan de Valdés's unorthodox *One Hundred and Ten Considerations* (1638) as translated by Nicholas Ferrar and annotated by George Herbert, however, we are among the last embers of the religious practice of *consideratio* in the works of a major English poet. They flare to life again, from time to time, in Coleridge's prose writings on religious topics. In general, however, even in the Catholic world the language of *consideratio* is slowly absorbed into that of *meditatio*. The process begins in Aquinas (*ST*, 2a2ae q. 180 art. 3 ad 1) and becomes centered on reflection on the infused virtues with a view to making practical resolutions. It gains momentum thereafter. The change is precipitated by Ignatius of Loyola's *Spiritual Exercises* (approved by Pope Paul III in 1548), which is followed by the institutionalization of meditation in religious practices, most notably among female religious, very often to the detriment of the cultivation of *contemplatio*.

56. Thom Gunn's knowledge of seventeenth-century English poetry is attested in his edition of Fulke Greville's *Selected Poems* (London: Faber and Faber, 1968), but consideration appears broadly in the period. Recall the Archbishop of Canterbury's speech in Shakespeare's *Henry V* (1599?): "at that very moment, / Consideration like an angel came / And whipped th' offending Adam out of him" (Craig, ed., *The Arden Shakespeare*, 1.1.64–67). George Herbert (1593–1633) uses *consideration*, in one or another of its verbal forms, many times in *The Temple* (1633), as does John Donne (1572–1631) in

his devotional works. Of divines other than Donne, the word is used now and then by Lancelot Andrewes (1555–1626) and more frequently by Richard Hooker (1554–1600) and Robert Leighton (1611–84). Inevitably, the sense is often stretched beyond the spiritual meaning that one finds in St. Bernard. By the time of Johnson's *Dictionary* (1755), the first two senses of *consideration* are given as follows: (1) "the act of considering; mental view; regard; notice" and (2) "mature thought; prudence; serious deliberation."

57. For possible influences on "Considering the Snail," see the freewheeling essay by Paul Muldoon, "Considering 'Considering the Snail,'" in *At the Barriers: On the Poetry of Thom Gunn*, ed. Joshua Weiner (Chicago: University of Chicago Press, 2009), 269–76. To these one should add the example of Moore, not only in the syllabic meter, but also in writing poems about animals.

58. Thom Gunn, "Considering the Snail," in *Collected Poems* (London: Faber and Faber, 1993), 117.

59. Gunn's poem appears to have been prompted by Paul Klee's watercolor *Snail* (1924), but there is no trace of ekphrasis in it. See Thom Gunn to Douglas Chambers, July 2, 1984, in *The Letters of Thom Gunn*, ed. Michael Nott, August Kleinzahler, and Clive Wilmer (London: Faber and Faber, 2021), 400–401.

60. See Shakespeare, *As You Like It*, 4.1.55–66; and Cowper, "The Snail."

61. See Thom Gunn, "Carnal Knowledge," in *Collected Poems*, 15–16, "The Unsettled Motorcyclist's Vision of His Death," in ibid., 54–55, "Elvis Presley," in ibid., 57, and "Black Jackets," in ibid., 108–9.

62. The original French text is taken from Francis Ponge, "Escargots," in *Oeuvres complètes*, ed. Bernard Beugnot et al., 2 vols., Bibliothèque de la Pléiade (Paris: Gallimard, 1999), 1:24–28.

63. The association of snails with saints was made earlier by Richard Lovelace. See his "The Snayl," in *The Poems of Richard Lovelace*, 136–37.

64. Geoffrey Hill, "Merlin," in *BH*, 7.

65. Although Hill distances himself from Eliot's *Four Quartets*, his lines recall the end of pt. 3 of "Little Gidding." See Geoffrey Hill, "Dividing Legacies," in *Collected Critical Writings* (hereafter *CCW*), ed. Kenneth Haynes (Oxford: Oxford University Press, 2009), 377–78.

66. See the discussion of the problem in my *Poetry and Revelation*, chaps. 5, 7. In an interview, Hill compares himself to a snail, tracing "the track left by human beings, which is full of false directions and self-pity and nostalgia as well as lust, wrath, greed and pride." John Haffenden, "Geoffrey Hill," in *Viewpoints: Poets in Conversation with John Haffenden* (London: Faber and Faber, 1981), 89.

67. A. R. Ammons, "The City Limits," in *CP*, 1:498. Ammons uses *consideratio* elsewhere, though in more muted ways. See, e.g., A. R. Ammons, "Birthday Poem to My Wife," in *CP*, 2:874.

68. It is worth remembering that Richard of St. Victor forbids the contemplation or consideration of anything disgusting, and here Ammons includes such items.

69. See Ralph Waldo Emerson, "Nature," in *Essays and Lectures*, ed. Joel Porte (New York: Library of America, 1984), 10.

70. Yet see Aquinas, *ST*, 1a q. 38 art. 8 *resp*. Here, *claritas* or radiance is one of the three conditions of beauty. For Aquinas, something is radiant to the extent that it participates in the divine splendor. Even though Ammons has quite other aims in mind than those of Aquinas, whose text he probably did not know, there is nonetheless a hidden justification for the link between radiance and praise.

71. Sir Walter Scott, "Marmion: A Tale of Flodden Field," in *Poetical Works* (New York: Belford, Clarke, 1880), 100.

72. See Sherman Paul, *Emerson's Angle of Vision: Man and Nature in American Experience* (Cambridge, MA: Harvard University Press, 1952), 73–75. Harold Bloom told me, in a personal communication, that he proposed the title of the lyric to Ammons after the (untitled) poem had been written, that Ammons accepted it, and that *limits* was intended to be a substantive, not a verb.

73. George Fox, *A Journal or Historical Account of the Life, Travels, Sufferings, Christian Experiences and Labour of Love in the Work of the Ministry, Etc.,* 2 vols. (London: J. Sowle, 1709), 1:380.

74. Dante, *Divine Comedy,* 1.1–3, Digital Dante, https://digitaldante.columbia.edu /dante/divine-comedy.

Chapter Seven

1. Delmore Schwartz, "In the Orchards of the Imagination," *New Republic,* November 1, 1954, 17. Earlier, Schwartz had written twice on Stevens. See Delmore Schwartz, "New Verse," *Partisan Review* 4, no. 3 (1938): 49–52, and "The Ultimate Plato with Picasso's Guitar," *Harvard Advocate* 127, no. 3 (1940): 11. Before Schwartz, the only associations seen between Stevens and contemplation were made in passing. See, e.g., Frank Jones, "The Sorcerer as Elegist," *The Nation,* November 7, 1942, 488; and Richard Eberhart, "Notes to a Class in Adult Education," *Accent* 7, no. 4 (1947): 251–53. However, Louis Martz attended to the meditative element in Stevens's poetry in his important essay "Wallace Stevens: The World as Meditation," *Yale Review* 47, no. 4 (1958): 517–36. Martz had earlier written on Stevens. See Louis L. Martz, "Wallace Stevens: The Romance of the Precise," *Yale Poetry Review* 2 (1946): 13–20, and "Recent Poetry," *Yale Review* 37, no. 2 (1947): 339–41. He is also the author of the major study *The Poetry of Meditation.* As noted in chap. 5, he notes there that in the seventeenth century it can be difficult to distinguish between consideration, meditation, and contemplation and that the same is true about Stevens's practice. Later commentary on Stevens and meditation, in one or another sense, includes William W. Bevis, *Mind of Winter: Wallace Stevens, Meditation, and Literature* (Pittsburgh: University of Pittsburgh Press, 1988); and William Franke, "The Negative Theology of Wallace Stevens's 'Notes toward a Supreme Fiction,'" *Religions* 8, no. 4 (2017): n.p.

2. See Charles Baudelaire, "Le peintre de la vie moderne," in *Oeuvres complètes,* 2:691 (esp. sec. 9). Baudelaire suggests that the figure of the dandy has classical roots in Alcibiades, Caesar, and Catiline. For Baudelaire himself as dandy, see Théophile Gautier, *Baudelaire,* ed. Claude-Marie Senninger, with an introduction by Lois Cassandra Hamrick (Paris: Klincksieck, 1986).

3. See Louis Untermeyer, "Five American Poets," *Yale Review* 14, no. 1 (October 1924): 156–61; and Gorham Munson, "The Dandyism of Wallace Stevens," *The Dial* 79 (November 1925): n.p. Munson alludes to Baudelaire in his review and notes that dandyism "resolves itself into two elements: correctness and elegance," both of which he takes to apply to Stevens. Stevens himself might have added gaudiness. See Wallace Stevens, "On 'The Emperor of Ice Cream,'" in *CPP,* 905. Ivor Winters went one step further, considering Stevens a hedonist. See Ivor Winters, "Wallace Stevens; or, The Hedonist's Progress," in *The Anatomy of Nonsense* (New York: New Directions, 1943), 431–59. It should be noted that as early as 1926 Untermeyer nonetheless solicited poetry from

Stevens for his annual poetry anthology. See *Letters of Wallace Stevens*, ed. Holly Stevens (New York: Alfred A. Knopf, 1972), 247.

4. See Stevens, *Adagia*, 905. Also see the remarks on the dandy and money in Baudelaire, "Le peintre de la vie moderne," 710. The remarks on Stevens's air of contentment are taken from Munson, "The Dandyism of Wallace Stevens."

5. See the comments on the dandy in Charles Baudelaire, *Journaux intimes*, in *Oeuvres complètes*, 1:682, 697.

6. Schwartz, "In the Orchards of the Imagination," 17.

7. See Untermeyer, "Five American Poets," 160. Along with ten other poems, "Thirteen Ways of Looking at a Blackbird" appeared in *Others: An Anthology of the New Verse*, ed. Alfred Kreymborg (New York: Knopf, 1917). "Peter Quince at the Clavier" appeared in *Anthology of Magazine Verse for 1915*, ed. William Stanley Braithwaite (New York: Gomme & Marshall, 1915). Marianne Moore refers to Stevens's mastery of "the flambeaued manner" in her review of *Harmonium*. See Marianne Moore, "Well Moused, Lion" (1924), in *The Complete Prose of Marianne Moore*, 93.

8. Schwartz, "In the Orchards of the Imagination," 18.

9. Wallace Stevens, "An Old High-Toned Christian Woman," in *CPP*, 47.

10. The impact of books by Jean-Paul Sartre translated from the French supplies one index. The popularity of a book by Stevens's friend Jean Wahl yields another. See, e.g., Jean Wahl, *A Short History of Existentialism*, trans. Forrest Williams and Stanley Maron (New York: Philosophical Library, 1949). More generally, see Walter Kaufmann, "The Reception of Existentialism in the United States," *Salmagundi* 10/11 (1969–70): 69–86.

11. See Allen Tate, "American Poetry since 1920," *Bookman* 68 (January 1929): n.p.; and Winters, "Wallace Stevens; or, The Hedonist's Progress."

12. Stevens had a high opinion of Henri Focillon's *La vie des formes* (Paris: Presses Universitaires de France, 1934), which has been rendered in English as *The Life of Forms in Art*, trans. Charles B. Hogan and George Kubler (Cambridge, MA: Zone, 1989). See Wallace Stevens, "The Figure of the Youth as Virile Poet," in *CPP*, 671.

13. In a letter to Peter H. Lee of April 1, 1955, Stevens testifies to his love of Blanchot's writings. See Stevens, *Letters*, 879. He owned and annotated a copy of Benedetto Croce's *The Defence of Poetry: Variations on the Theme of Shelley* (Oxford: Clarendon, 1933), and the same is true of Charles Mauron's *Aesthetics and Psychology*, trans. Roger Fry and Katherine John (London: Hogarth, 1935). He praises Focillon's *La vie des formes* in "The Figure of the Youth as Virile Poet," 671. He corresponded with Jean Wahl and mentioned him in other letters, and he referred to Paulhan frequently and favorably in his correspondence. He also kept in touch with literary criticism and art criticism in its more theoretical ventures. He owned and annotated a copy of, e.g., I. A. Richards's *Coleridge on Imagination* (New York: Harcourt Brace, 1935).

14. In a letter to Henry Church of March 1941, Stevens says that he has been reading "two or three dozen books" in preparation for "The Noble Rider and the Sound of Words." Stevens, *Letters*, 388.

15. I allude to George Santayana's *Three Philosophical Poets: Lucretius, Dante, and Goethe* (Cambridge, MA: Harvard University Press, 1935). So far as I know, Stevens's poetry has been considered by only one academic philosopher in a professional journal. See Victor Tejera, review of *Transport to Summer* by Wallace Stevens, *Journal of Philosophy* 45, no. 5 (1948): 137–39. For the work of a poet who is also a philosopher and whose verse is marked by encounters with Stevens, see John Koethe's *Thought and Poetry*.

16. See T. S. Eliot, "Le dilemme poétique [Charybde et Scylla]," in *CPE*, 7:687. In

the original publication, the text bore the subtitle "Lourdeur et frivolité." See *Annales du Centre universitaire meditérranéan* 5 (1951–52): 71–82. The distinction is anticipated in T. S. Eliot, "Dante," in *CPE*, 3:717.

17. Such would be one burden of the uncollected essay Wallace Stevens, "A Collect of Philosophy," in *CPP*, 850–66. For an early, sympathetic view of Stevens's engagement with philosophical thought, see Frank Doggett, *Stevens' Poetry of Thought* (Baltimore: Johns Hopkins University Press, 1966).

18. Eliot, "'The Metaphysical Poets," 380.

19. Wallace Stevens, "Notes toward a Supreme Fiction," in *CPP*, 329–52, 344 (2.10.10–14).

20. For Coleridge on reflection, see Coleridge, *Notebooks*, vol. 4, § 5209 (May 1825).

21. Stevens, "The Figure of the Youth as Virile Poet," 667. The influence of Coleridge is perhaps apparent. See, e.g., Coleridge, *The Statesman's Manual*, 28–29. Also see B. J. Leggett, *Wallace Stevens and Poetic Theory: Conceiving the Supreme Fiction* (Chapel Hill: University of North Carolina Press, 1987), chap. 2.

22. See Ludwig Wittgenstein, *Culture and Value*, trans. Peter Winch (Oxford: Basil Blackwell, 1970), 5e. Also see Stevens, *Letters*, 364.

23. For both insights, see Munson, "The Dandyism of Wallace Stevens."

24. Wallace Stevens, "On the Road Home," in *CPP*, 186.

25. Wallace Stevens, "The Noble Rider and the Sound of Words," in *CPP*, 663. Also see Stevens, "The Figure of the Youth as Virile Poet," 679. Also recall Stevens's adage "In the long run the truth does not matter." See Wallace Stevens, *Sur Plusieurs Beaux Sujets*, in *CPP*, 915.

26. On Stevens and James, see Jonathan Levin, *Poetics of Transition: Emerson, Pragmatism, and American Literary Modernism* (Durham, NC: Duke University Press, 1999), chap. 7.

27. See George Rostrevor Hamilton, *Poetry and Contemplation: A New Preface to Poetics* (Cambridge: Cambridge University Press, 1937), 81. The lines are quoted in Stevens, "The Noble Rider and the Sound of Words," 652.

28. Quoted in Stevens, "The Noble Rider and the Sound of Words," 652. The most relevant of Croce's sentences runs: "It is the triumph of contemplation, but a triumph still shaken by past battle, with its foot upon a living though vanquished foe." Croce, *The Defence of Poetry*, 26. I should add that Stevens might have been encouraged also by remarks on contemplation made by Focillon in his *La vie des formes* and by comments in Charles Mauron's *Aesthetics and Psychology*. On the influence of Mauron on Stevens, see Leggett, *Wallace Stevens and Poetic Theory*, chap. 4. For Stevens and Croce, see T. J. Morris, "Stevens and Croce: Varieties of Lyrical Intuition," *Wallace Stevens Journal* 25, no. 2 (2001): 233–53.

29. Toward the end of his book, Hamilton distinguishes aesthetic contemplation and religious contemplation in clear terms, but Stevens says nothing at all about this aspect of Hamilton's thought in his essay. See Hamilton, *Poetry and Contemplation*, chap. 16.

30. Munson observed early on that Stevens's "imaginative order" is not based on religion, "for the religious man strives for a knowledge of the absolute." Munson, "The Dandyism of Wallace Stevens." Stevens's lack of a religious sensibility is apparent from his earliest letters. On March 10, 1907, he writes to Elsie, "I am not in the least religious," although he wishes Elsie to attend church. See J. Donald Blount, ed., *The Contemplated Spouse: The Letters of Wallace Stevens to Elsie* (Columbia: University of South Carolina Press, 2006), 68. On April 19, 1907, he tells her that he has thrown away his Bible,

along with "a pile of useless stuff," adding: "I hate the look of a Bible." Ibid., 86. Yet one should not jump to conclusions about the steadiness of his views. See, e.g., his letter to Elsie of May 2, 1909, in which he expresses a lack of understanding of people who deny God. Ibid., 186. In the same letter, however, he gives us reason to doubt that, at the time, he has anything like an informed sense of Christianity: "Before to-day I do not think I have ever realized that God was distinct from Jesus." Ibid., 185. A little later, on May 14, 1909. he opines: "It may be that Christianity is a feminine religion." Ibid., 197.

31. Wallace Stevens, "Sunday Morning," in *CPP*, 55–56.

32. Wallace Stevens, "Imagination as Value," in *CPP*, 731. On the question of belief in general in Stevens's poetry, see Adelaide Kirby Morris, *Wallace Stevens: Imagination and Faith* (Princeton, NJ: Princeton University Press, 1974); and David R. Jarraway, *Wallace Stevens and the Question of Belief: Metaphysician in the Dark* (Baton Rouge: Louisiana State University Press, 1993).

33. Wallace Stevens, "Of Modern Poetry," in *CPP*, 218.

34. Stevens, "Imagination as Value," 731.

35. My reservations about the expression *biblical imagination* are developed in my "Imagination and Kingdom: On the Theology of Christian Imagination," in *The Phenomenology of Christian Imagination*, ed. Javier Carreno and Katarzyna Dudek (London: Bloomsbury, forthcoming).

36. Wallace Stevens, "The Relations between Poetry and Painting," in *CPP*, 748. See Matthew Arnold, "The Study of Poetry."

37. Stevens, "Imagination as Value," 726.

38. Stevens, "The Relations between Poetry and Painting," 748. It is worth keeping in mind Santayana's words about poetry offering "religion without practical efficacy and without metaphysical illusion." George Santayana, *Interpretations of Poetry and Religion* (New York: Scribner, 1900), 289.

39. Stevens refers to "Notes" as "three notes" in *Letters*, 406.

40. See Wallace Stevens, "Esthétique du Mal," in *CPP*, 286. The allusion is to Victor Serge's encounter with Konstantinov, a Soviet official of the Cheka, in 1920. Stevens read about Serge's meeting with Konstantinov in "The Revolution at Dead-End (1926–28)," trans. Ethel Libson, *Politics* 1 (June 1944): 150.

41. Stevens, *Letters*, 369–70. Also see ibid., 377–78.

42. Yet see Santayana, *Interpretations of Poetry and Religion*, v.

43. In a letter to Elsie of August 16, 1911, Stevens writes of the effect of a candle in a room: "You would be surprised to find how pleasant a candle on this table makes the room. It gives such a quiet, uncertain light—very favorable to meditation and the likes o'that." Blount, ed., *The Contemplated Spouse*, 302.

44. Earlier, Stevens had written in similar terms about transparence as the fulfillment of contemplation, evoking how "the mind / Acquired transparence and beheld itself / And beheld the source from which transparence came." Wallace Stevens, "Owl's Clover," in *CPP*, 158. Also see Wallace Stevens, "Asides on the Oboe," in *CPP*, 227 (pt. 2).

45. It seems to me that Harold Bloom, Helen Vendler, and Charles Altieri, to name only a handful of Stevens's best and most eminent critics, are committed in one way or another to a form of naturalism and constantly repeat, in varied keys, the division that animates much of Stevens's verse. Stevens is open to regarding his poetry as contemplative, whereas his critics tend to eschew the philosophical or theological vocabularies needed to attend to this dimension of his work. I am indebted to Walter Jost for

conversations that have clarified my view of this topic. See, in particular, Harold Bloom, *Wallace Stevens: The Poems of Our Climate* (Ithaca, NY: Cornell University Press, 1977); Helen Vendler, *On Extended Wings: Wallace Stevens' Longer Poems* (Cambridge, MA: Harvard University Press, 1969), and *Words Chosen Out of Desire* (1984; reprint, Cambridge, MA: Harvard University Press, 1986) (along with later essays); and Charles Altieri, *Wallace Stevens and the Demands of Modernity: Toward a Phenomenology of Value* (Ithaca, NY: Cornell University Press, 2013).

46. For Augustine, reason spurs one from faith to understanding in a world of symbolic meanings. For Anselm, that world is in retreat, and reason is already a dialectical means of reaching the truth. Leibniz is responsible for an early and powerful formulation of the principle of sufficient reason. See G. M. Leibniz, *Monadology*, in *Philosophical Papers and Letters: A Selection*, ed., trans., and with an introduction by Leroy E. Loemker, 2nd ed. (Dordrecht: Reidel, 1976), 646. For Coleridge's view of reason as spiritual light, see *Marginalia*, pt. 3, p. 746.

47. Stevens, "The Figure of the Youth as Virile Poet," 668.

48. Stevens, "The Noble Rider and the Sound of Words," 665. Also see Wallace Stevens, "The Irrational Element in Poetry," in *CPP*, 786. It is worth noting that Hamilton speaks of ecstasy "in the strictest sense of the word" with respect to contemplation. See Hamilton, *Poetry and Contemplation*, 82.

49. *Libertas* is more than *liberum arbitrium*, freedom of choice; it is the freedom that comes in moving toward the good or love.

50. Stevens entertained the idea of adding a section—"It must be human"—to the poem. See Stevens, *Letters*, 863–64.

51. On abstraction and the imagination, see Stevens, "The Noble Rider and the Sound of Words," 657.

52. Percy Bysshe Shelley, *A Defence of Poetry*, bound with Thomas Love Peacock, *The Four Ages of Poetry*, ed. with an introduction and notes by John E. Jordan (Indianapolis: Bobbs-Merrill, 1965), 80.

53. With regard to the *Collected Poems* and its possible relation with a Supreme Fiction, see Wallace Stevens, "On Receiving the National Book Award for Poetry," in *CPP*, 878. Hamilton doubts that a long poem, or perhaps a very long poem, could be purely contemplative. See Hamilton, *Poetry and Contemplation*, 75.

54. Coleridge, *Notebooks*, vol. 4, § 4524.

55. See Stevens, *Letters*, 430. Also see Stevens, *Adagia*, 908.

56. An English translation is supplied in Smith Palmer Bovie, *The Satires and Epistles of Horace* (Chicago: University of Chicago Press, 1959), 271–91.

57. Stevens, *Letters*, 426–27.

58. The opening stanza recalls the third stanza of Wallace Stevens, "Another Weeping Woman," in *CPP*, 19.

59. The motif of learned ignorance goes back to Augustine's letter ca. 411 to the widow Proba: "There is in us, therefore, a certain learned ignorance, so to speak, but an ignorance learned [*docta ignorantia*] from the Spirit of God, who helps our weakness." Augustine, *Letters, 100–155*, trans. and with notes by Roland Teske, ed. Boniface Ramsey (Hyde Park, NY: New City, 2003), letter 130.14.28.

60. David Hume, *A Treatise of Human Nature*, ed. L. A. Selby-Bigge, 2nd ed., rev. P. H. Nidditch (Oxford: Clarendon, 1978), 1.1.1.

61. See Coleridge, *Marginalia*, pt. 1, p. 815, and *Notebooks*, vol. 4, § 4524.

62. See Peter Brazeau, ed., *Parts of a World: Wallace Stevens Remembered: An Oral*

Biography (San Francisco: North Point, 1985), 25, 68. Stevens also consulted *Webster's Dictionary*.

63. For "rotted names," see Wallace Stevens, "The Man with the Blue Guitar," in *CPP*, 150 (canto 32).

64. See John Keats, "The Fall of Hyperion: A Dream," in *John Keats*, 140 (pt. 3, line 13).

65. Stevens, "Imagination as Value," 730.

66. In the final line of the first canto — "but be / In the difficulty of what it is to be" — we might hear a faint echo of the closing lines of Archibald MacLeish's "Ars Poetica" (1926): "A poem should not mean / But be." See Archibald MacLeish, "Ars Poetica," in *Collected Poems, 1917–1982* (Boston: Houghton Mifflin, 1985), 107. Also see Wallace Stevens, "A Comment on Meaning in Poetry," in *CPP*, 826, "The Irrational Element in Poetry," 786, and *Adagia*, 910 (the *bon mot* "Poetry should resist the intelligence almost successfully"). W. H. Auden alludes to the end of this canto, rather reductively, as follows: "The poet / Admired for his earnest habit of calling / The sun the sun." W. H. Auden, "In Praise of Limestone," in *Collected Poems*, 415. See John Fuller, *W. H. Auden: A Commentary* (Princeton, NJ: Princeton University Press, 1998), 408.

67. Stevens, "Sunday Morning," 54.

68. Wallace Stevens, "First Warmth," in *CPP*, 597.

69. Relevant here is Angus Fletcher's idea of the "environment poem" in which "the poet neither writes *about* the surrounding world, thematizing it, nor analytically represents that world, but actually shapes the poem to be an Emersonian or esemplastic circle." Angus Fletcher, *A New Theory for American Poetry: Democracy, the Environment, and the Future of the Imagination* (Cambridge, MA: Harvard University Press, 2004), 9. Fletcher, however, is not invested in Stevens as someone who composes environmental poems, nor is contemplation one of his concerns.

70. The best discussion of parts and wholes that I know is given in Husserl, *Logical Investigations*, vol. 2, investigation 3. One might wish that Stevens had not included the final canto of "Notes," e.g., but it cannot be detached from the whole.

71. Stevens, "Man Carrying Thing," 306. Also see Stevens, *Adagia*, 910.

72. See Stevens, "The Irrational Element in Poetry," 788.

73. See Wallace Stevens, "The Whole Man," in *CPP*, 874.

74. See Wallace Stevens, "Two or Three Ideas," in *CPP*, 842.

75. See Shakespeare, *As You Like It*, 2.6.138.

76. Stevens's observation, "Weather is a sense of nature. Poetry is a sense," is relevant here. See Stevens, *Adagia*, 902.

77. Stevens, *Adagia*, 905.

78. See Wallace Stevens, "Of the Manner of Addressing Clouds," in *CPP*, 44.

79. See Wallace Stevens, "The Plot against the Giant," in *CPP*, 5.

80. See, e.g., Walt Whitman, "Facing West from California's Shore," "As I Ebb'd with the Ocean of Life," "On the Beach at Night," and "By Blue Ontario's Shore," in *Complete Poetry and Collected Prose*, ed. Justin Kaplan (New York: Library of America, 1982), 266, 394–96, 398, 468.

81. Stevens, "Asides on the Oboe," 226, 227.

82. Whitman, "Song of the Exposition" (*Leaves of Grass* [1891–92]), in *Complete Poetry and Collected Prose*, 342.

83. Whitman, "Song of Myself" (*Leaves of Grass* [1855]), in *Complete Poetry and Collected Prose*, 82. Also recall the remark: "The old poet is a tramp." Stevens, *Adagia*, 911.

Chapter Eight

1. See Stevens, "Owl's Clover," 160.

2. In the Christian tradition, it is the cherubim who are associated with the contemplation of God. See Pseudo-Dionysius, *The Celestial Hierarchy*, 7.1.31–37. The seraph in "Notes" is worn and contemplates, in melancholy fashion, the created order and its sorrows. The motif of birds is investigated in Morris, *Wallace Stevens*, 119–21; and Cary Wolf, *Ecological Poetics; or, Wallace Stevens's Birds* (Chicago: University of Chicago Press, 2020), esp. 98. Wolf concentrates mostly on the early "Thirteen Ways of Looking at a Blackbird" and, when he turns to Stevens's long poems, attends not to "Notes" but to "An Ordinary Evening in New Haven."

3. P. B. Shelley, "To a Skylark," in *Poetical Works*, 602.

4. Patristic readings of Isa. 14:12 take Lucifer to be Satan, the leader of the fallen angels, although the reference is to the fall of the King of Babylon.

5. It is possible that Stevens was thinking of Andrea del Verrocchio's *Equestrian Statue of Bartolomeo Colleoni* in Venice. He refers to it in "The Noble Rider and the Sound of Words," 646.

6. See Heraclitus, *Fragments*, § 53.

7. Stevens, "The Irrational Element in Poetry," 788–89.

8. P. B. Shelley, "Ode to the West Wind," in *Poetical Works*, 579.

9. That Paul Klee was important to Stevens is well attested in Brazeau, ed., *Parts of a World*, 119, 157, 117. Also see Sascha Feinstein, "Stanzas of Color: Wallace Stevens and Paul Klee," *Wallace Stevens Journal* 16, no. 1 (1992): 64–81.

10. P. B. Shelley, "Ozymandias," in *Poetical Works*, 550.

11. For the poet's view of Aquinas, see Wallace Stevens, "A Note on 'Les Plus Belles Pages,'" in *CPP*, 867.

12. Wallace Stevens to William Rose Benét, January 6, 1933, in *Letters*, 263.

13. Stevens, *Letters*, 446,

14. Stevens, "Imagination as Value," 731.

15. See Stevens, *Adagia*, 902.

16. See Wallace Stevens, *Adagia*, 903, and "Esthétique du Mal," 283.

17. Stevens, *Adagia*, 900.

18. Augustine, *Expositions of the Psalms*, trans. Maria Boulding, ed. Boniface Ramsey, 6 vols. (Hyde Park, NY: New City, 2004), 1:32.8.

19. See Vincent of Beauvais, *Speculum historiale*, 16.12.

20. See Aquinas, *ST*, 1a q. 1 art. 3 *resp.*

21. See Stevens, "The Irrational Element in Poetry," 783.

22. The point is well made in Morris, *Wallace Stevens*, 174–75.

23. "Bridal mysticism" speaks of mystic marriages with Christ that were undertaken by Catherine of Alexandria (ca. 287–ca. 305), Catherine of Siena (1347–80), and Teresa of Ávila (1515–82). Yet also see Richard of St. Victor, *AM*, 4.13.

24. Wallace Stevens, "Tattoo," in *CPP*, 64. Also see the line "the buxom eye brings merely its element / To the total thing." Wallace Stevens, "Poem Written at Morning," in *CPP*, 198.

25. See Joseph Bingham, *Origines ecclesiasticae; or, The Antiquities of the Christian Church and Other Works*, 9 vols. (London: William Straker, 1834), 7:23.20.

26. John Milton, *Paradise Lost*, ed. Alastair Fowler (London: Longman, 1971), 2.146–51.

27. Stevens, "The Man with the Blue Guitar," 137 (canto 5).

28. Wallace Stevens, "Flyer's Fall," in *CPP*, 295.

29. Stevens, *Adagia*, 903.

30. See Friedrich Nietzsche, "How the 'Real World' at Last Became a Myth," in *Twilight of the Idols; or, How to Philosophize with a Hammer*, bound with *The Anti-Christ*, trans. R. J. Hollingdale (Harmondsworth: Penguin, 1968), 40–41. Also see B. J. Leggett, *Early Stevens: The Nietzschean Intertext* (Durham, NC: Duke University Press, 1992).

31. See Kant, *Critique of Pure Reason*, 450.

32. See Kant, *Religion within the Limits of Reason Alone*, esp. bk. 2.

33. Stevens's thinking about the issue outside his poems seems to be less than clear. In a letter to Henry Church of December 8, 1941, he recounts a conversation with a student in which the student denies the possibility of believing in something one knows to be untrue. Stevens explains to Church: "There are fictions that are extensions of reality. There are plenty of people who believe in Heaven as definitely as your New England ancestors and my Dutch ancestors believe in it. But Heaven is an extension of reality." Stevens, *Letters*, 430. Of course, Stevens's contemporaries who believe in heaven do so because they think the teaching is true, not despite their conviction that it is a fiction.

34. See Wallace Stevens, "Description without Place," in *CPP*, 301. Stevens airs his views about the poem to Henry Church in a letter of April 4, 1945. See Stevens, *Letters*, 494. In a later poem, Stevens writes of "the nicer knowledge of / Belief, that what it believes in is not true." Wallace Stevens, "The Pure Good of Theory," in *CPP*, 291. Morris notes that in time Stevens's theory of poetry "became a mystical theology." Morris, *Wallace Stevens*, 82. That formulation pitches things quite high. It might be better said that it became a theory of contemplation in a modern sense.

35. See Aquinas, *ST*, 2a2ae q. 180 art. 6 ad 2.

36. Stevens, *Adagia*, 901. Also see ibid., 903, and Stevens, *Letters*, 369, 378, 402.

37. Stevens, *Adagia*, 907.

38. Wallace Stevens, "Final Soliloquy of the Interior Paramour," in *CPP*, 444.

39. Stevens, "The Figure of the Youth as Virile Poet," 681.

40. See Samuel Taylor Coleridge, *Biographia Literaria*, vol. 7 (in 2 pts.) of *CC* (Princeton, NJ: Princeton University Press, 1985), pt. 1, p. 275. Also see, however, 1 Cor. 15:10.

41. See Horace, *Odes*, 3.30.

42. This is of course a familiar theory of the celestial spheres, as propounded by Plato and continued by Ptolemy and others, up to Copernicus and even beyond him for a while. Yet the planets were not held to be in these spheres, and the earth was held to be at the center.

43. One should recall the suites of war poems. See Wallace Stevens, "Phases," *Poetry* 5, no. 11 (1914): 70–71, and "Lettres d'un Soldat," *Poetry* 12, no. 2 (1918): 59–65.

44. See Horace, *Odes*, 3.2.

45. Hamilton, *Poetry and Contemplation*, 81, 77, 81.

46. On the modern, largely Protestant sense of faith as having become an impediment to understanding rather than a system of symbols that leads to it, see Henri de Lubac, *Corpus Mysticum: The Eucharist and the Church in the Middle Ages*, trans. Gemma Simmonds with Richard Price and Christopher Stephens, ed. Laurence Paul Hemming and Susan Frank Parsons (Notre Dame, IN: University of Notre Dame Press, 2006), 240.

47. Hamilton, *Poetry and Contemplation*, 157. The view was given earlier—and somewhat more sharply—by Coleridge when he writes of "that barren contemplation

that rests satisfied with itself where the thoughts . . . ought to be embodied in action."
Coleridge, *The Friend*, pt. 1, pp. 399–400.

48. See Coleridge, *The Friend*, pt. 2, pp. 173.

49. Stevens, *Adagia*, 913.

Chapter Nine

1. A. R. Ammons, *Sphere: The Form of a Motion*, in *The Complete Poems of A. R. Ammons* (hereafter *CP*), ed. Robert M. West, with an introduction by Helen Vendler, 2 vols. (New York: W. W. Norton, 2018), 1:645–723. I will refer to lines from *Sphere* by section and line. Ammons is the author of several other long poems, beginning with *Tape for the Turn of the Year* (1965) and including "Essay on Poetics" (1969), "Hibernaculum" (1970–71), *The Snow Poems* (1977), *Garbage* (1993), and *Glare* (1997). A. R. Ammons, *Selected Longer Poems* (New York: W. W. Norton, 1980), includes "Pray without Ceasing," "Summer Session," "Essay on Poetics," "Extremes and Moderations," and "Hibernaculum." I will limit myself to *Sphere*. For a consideration of the longer poems in particular, see Steven P. Schneider, *A. R. Ammons and the Poetics of Widening Scope* (Rutherford, NJ: Farleigh Dickinson University Press, 1994); and Steven P. Schneider, ed., *Complexities of Motion: New Essays on A. R. Ammons's Long Poems* (Rutherford, NJ: Farleigh Dickinson University Press, 1999).

2. See Denis Cosgrove, *Apollo's Eye: A Cartographic Genealogy of the Earth in the Western Imagination* (Baltimore: Johns Hopkins University Press, 2001).

3. See David Lehman, "The *Paris Review* Interview," in *A. R. Ammons: Set in Motion: Essays, Interviews, and Dialogues*, ed. Zofia Burr (Ann Arbor: University of Michigan Press, 1996), 103. Also see William Walsh, "An Interview," in ibid., 65.

4. See Husserl, *Logical Investigations*, vol. 2, investigation 3.

5. Aquinas, *Commentary on the Gospel of John*, 1:3–4.

6. Marianne Moore, "The Sacred Wood," in *The Complete Prose of Marianne Moore*, 53.

7. A. R. Ammons, "Three Travelogues," in *CP*, 1:748.

8. Aquinas distinguishes *contemplatio*, which is reserved for God, from *speculatio*, which is appropriate to creatures. See Aquinas, 3 *Sententiae* d. 35 q. 1 a. 2 q. 3.

9. For Ammons's admiration of Coleridge and of his insight into the reconciliation of opposites in particular, see A. R. Ammons, "A Poem Is a Walk," in Burr, ed., *A. R. Ammons*, 13.

10. See Richard Howard, "A. R. Ammons," in *Alone with America: The Art of Poetry in the United States since 1950* (London: Thames & Hudson, 1970), 1–17. Howard links Ammons to Lucretius in his endorsement of *Sphere*.

11. On *Sphere* as didactic, see Willard Spiegelman, *The Didactic Muse: Scenes of Instruction in Contemporary American Poetry* (Princeton, NJ: Princeton University Press, 1989), chap. 4. John Sitter suggests that *Sphere* is more thoroughly a philosophical poem than I feel justified in asserting. See John E. Sitter, "About Ammons' *Sphere*," *Massachusetts Review* 19, no. 1 (1978): 203.

12. For instance: "The angle of your vision, O God, is not quantum but infinite. It is also a circle, or rather, an infinite sphere because your sight is an eye of sphericity and of infinite perfection." Nicholas of Cusa, "On the Vision of God," 249. Also see Nicholas of Cusa, "On Learned Ignorance," in *Selected Spiritual Writings*, 1.23.

13. Ralph Waldo Emerson, "Circles," in Porte, ed., *Essays and Lectures*, 401.

14. See Thomas Carlyle, *Sartor Resartus: The Life and Opinions of Herr Teufels-dröckh*, ed. Charles Frederick Harrold (New York: Odyssey, 1937), 194, 254. In addition, see the book that Ammons's colleague at Cornell published a year after *Sphere* appeared: Abrams, *Natural Supernaturalism*, 68.

15. On Ammons's interest in structures, see Patricia A. Parker, "Configurations of Shape and Flow," *Diacritics* 3, no. 4 (1973): 25–33.

16. See Xenophanes of Colophon, *Fragments: A Text and Translation with a Commentary*, ed. J. H. Lesher (Toronto: University of Toronto Press, 1992), 89.

17. On Theagenes, see Jean-Pierre Vernant, *Mythe et societé en Grèce ancienne* (Paris: Maspero, 1974), 212.

18. I take this conception from Walter Wilson, *The Architectonics of Meaning: Foundations of the New Pluralism* (1985; new ed., Chicago: University of Chicago Press, 1993), 71.

19. See Aristotle, *Nicomachean Ethics*, chap. 10.

20. See Aristotle, *Metaphysics*, 1013b; and Aquinas, "On the Principles of Nature," in *Basic Writings*, trans. Eleonore Stump and Stephen Chanderbhan (Indianapolis: Hackett, 2014), chap. 4. Francis Bacon observes: "The final cause rather corrupts than advances the sciences, except as have to do with human action." Francis Bacon, *The New Organon and Related Writings*, ed. and with an introduction by Fulton H. Anderson (Indianapolis: Bobbs-Merrill, 1960), 121. More generally, see Stephen Gaukroger, "Knowledge, Evidence, and Method," in *The Cambridge Companion to Early Modern Philosophy*, ed. Donald Rutherford (Cambridge: Cambridge University Press, 2006), 39–66.

21. I take the distinction from Gabriel Marcel, *Being and Having*, trans. Katherine Farrer (Westminster: Dacre, 1949), 117. Rudolf Otto drew the same distinction in passing. See Otto, *The Idea of the Holy*, 28. *Das Heilige* was first published in 1917.

22. See Walt Whitman, "When I Heard the Learn'd Astronomer," in *Complete Poetry and Collected Prose*, 409–10.

23. On this delicate issue of believing or partly believing in scientific theories, see Bradley Armour-Garb and Frederick Kroon, eds., *Fictionalism in Philosophy* (Oxford: Oxford University Press, 2019).

24. See Karl Rahner, "The Concept of Mystery in Catholic Theology," in *Theological Investigations*, vol. 4, *More Recent Writings*, trans. Kevin Smyth (London: Darton, Longman & Todd, 1974), 41–43.

25. On this theme, see Kevin Hart, "Poetry as Spiritual Exercise: On A. R. Ammons," *New Centennial Review* 21, no. 2 (2022): 7–40.

26. See Ammons, "Hymn" (1), in *CP*, 1:37. The large and the tiny, often in recursive relations, continue as a theme throughout *Sphere*. See, e.g., *Sphere*, 75.10–76.7.

27. See Plotinus, *Enneads*, vol. 7, 6.9.50. I cite the phrasing in Andrew Louth, *The Origins of the Christian Mystical Tradition from Plato to Denys* (Oxford: Clarendon, 1992), 51.

28. Claims have been made for Ammons as religious in his poetry by virtue of the senses of awe and humility that are apparent there. See, e.g., Josephine Jacobsen, "The Talk of Giants," in *Considering the Radiance: Essays on the Poetry of A. R. Ammons*, ed. David Burak and Roger Gilbert (New York: W. W. Norton, 2005), 120. Also see Ammons's self-description as a mystic in his letter of February 20, 1955, to Chris Knoeller. *An Image for Longing: Selected Letters and Journals of A. R. Ammons, 1951–1974*, ed. Kevin McGuirk (Victoria, BC: ELS, 2013), 76. Later that year, in a letter of September 12, 1955, to Josephine Mills, Ammons again refers to himself as a mystic but with an odd qualification: "I am a mystic—but by memory only." Ibid., 89. Ammons also testifies that he is religious, albeit in a naturalistic way. See Shelby Stephenson, "An Interview

with A. R. Ammons," *Pembroke Magazine* 18 (1986): 200. Again, one thinks of the Romantic project of natural supernaturalism. Ammons observes: "when I say // 'you' in my poems and appear to the addressing / the lord above, I'm personifying the contours // of the onhigh, the ways by which the world / works, however hard to see." A. R. Ammons, "Aubade," in *CP*, 2:686. There is no reason to doubt this, yet it does not quite account for the emotion in play in the address in *Sphere*.

29. See Lucretius, *De rerum natura*, 1.1–2.

30. See Lucretius, *De rerum natura*, 2.646–51.

31. Yeats stated the opposition in a polemical way, more to do with achieving sanctity than anything else, as "Perfection of the life, or of the work." See W. B. Yeats, "The Choice," in *The Poems*, 2nd ed., ed. Richard J. Finneran, vol. 1 of *The Collected Works of W. B. Yeats* (New York: Scribner, 1989), 251.

32. William Wordsworth, "Lines Composed a Few Miles above Tintern Abbey," in *Lyrical Ballads and Other Poems, 1797–1800*, ed. James Butler and Karen Green, Cornell Wordsworth (Ithaca, NY: Cornell University Press, 1992), 118–19 (emphasis added).

33. Of course, the relation of motion and spirit is traditional. For Nicholas of Cusa, e.g., motion is the bond of all things that have a spiritual love for one another. See Nicholas of Cusa, "On Learned Ignorance," 2.10.

34. See Iamblichus, *On the Pythagorean Way of Life*, chap. 12. Also see C. P. Bigger, *Participation: A Platonic Inquiry* (Baton Rouge: Louisiana State University Press, 1968), 7.

35. See Robinson Jeffers, "Pelicans," in *The Selected Poetry of Robinson Jeffers*, ed. Tim Hunt (Stanford, CA: Stanford University Press, 2001), 140.

36. The shift from *He* to *he* in line 1112 appears to be an error that Ammons did not correct.

37. Augustine, *Confessions*, 10.6.9.

38. See W. B. Yeats, "Byzantium," in *The Poems*, 252.

39. A. R. Ammons, "For Harold Bloom," in *CP*, 1:655.

40. Wallace Stevens, "Anecdote of the Jar," in *CPP*, 60.

41. The whole poem, Ammons observes in a letter of January 3, 1974, to Harold Bloom, is "a concrete, contemplatable sphere." *An Image for Longing*, 422.

42. The flight of the two eagles at the end of "Easter Morning" (1977) is another instance of a *templum* in Ammons's work, though one that is put in an unusual configuration: it points to the ongoing patterns and routes of natural life, even after loss. After mourning his brother and people from his childhood, Ammons looks into the sky and view two eagles circling: "it was a sight of bountiful / majesty and integrity: the having / patterns and routes, breaking / from them to explore other patterns or / better ways to routes, and then the / return: a dance sacred as the sap in / the trees." A. R. Ammons, "Easter Morning," in *CP*, 2:16.

43. See T. S. Eliot, "Tradition and the Individual Talent," in *CPE*, 2:105–14; and W. H. Auden, "In Memory of W. B. Yeats," in *Collected Poems*, 197–98.

44. *Form* is, however, a very difficult word to pin down in Ammons's work. See Stephen Cushman, "Stanzas, Organic Myth, and the Metaformalism of A. R. Ammons," *American Literature* 59, no. 4 (1987): 513–27.

45. See Guido II, *A Ladder for Monks and Twelve Meditations*, trans. Edmund Colledge and James Walsh (Kalamazoo, MI: Cistercian, 1981), 1–2. *Lectio divina* was made more methodical, however, under the influence of the techniques associated with *Devotio moderna* in late medieval and early modern Europe.

46. See A. R. Ammons, "Hibernaculum," in *CP*, 1:616–17 (§§ 49, 50).

47. The distinction in German between *Erfahrung* (the general course of experience) and *Erlebnis* (a decisive experience) is relevant here. Commonly, but not always, what we call *spiritual experience* tends to *Erfahrung*, while *aesthetic experience* includes more opportunities for *Erlebnis*.

48. In "Brot und Wein," Hölderlin asks, "Wozu Dichter in dürftiger Zeit?" See Friedrich Hölderlin, *Poems and Fragments*, trans. Michael Hamburger (London: Anvil, 1994), 271.

49. See Mike Erwin and Jed Rasula, "Interview with A. R. Ammons," *Chicago Review* 57, no. 1–2 (2012): 150.

50. See Plato, *Symposium*, 201–12; and Guido II, *A Ladder for Monks and Twelve Meditations*. Of course, there is another thread in the tradition, such as in Augustine, in which one goes inward to locate God; but this does not figure for Ammons. I discuss the inward movement in my *L'image vulnérable*.

51. Matthew Walker offers a well-conducted defense of the view that Aristotle thought that θεωρία had some uses. See Matthew D. Walker, *Aristotle and the Uses of Contemplation* (Cambridge: Cambridge University Press, 2018).

52. See Erwin and Rasula, "Interview with A. R. Ammons," 152.

53. A. R. Ammons, "Day," in *CP*, 1:594.

54. Stéphane Mallarmé, "Sainte," in *Oeuvres complètes*, ed. Bertrand Marchal, 2 vols. (Paris: Gallimard, 1998), 1:26–27.

55. See A. R. Ammons, *The Really Short Poems of A. R. Ammons* (New York: Norton, 1992).

56. See Lacoste, *Être en danger*.

57. See W. B. Yeats, "Long-Legged Fly," in *The Poems*, 347.

58. See Coleridge, *Notebooks*, vol. 4, § 4524. Ammons quotes Coleridge's *Biographia Literaria* in "A Poem Is a Walk," 13.

59. See Catherine Malabou, *The Future of Hegel: Plasticity, Temporality and Dialectic*, with a preface by Jacques Derrida, trans. Lisabeth During (London: Routledge, 2005), 8.

60. See Frank Kermode, *The Sense of an Ending* (Oxford: Oxford University Press, 1967).

61. See esp. the offhand ending of "Hibernaculum": "I'm reading Xenophon's *Oeconomicus* 'with / considerable pleasure and enlightenment' and with / appreciation that saying so fills this stanza nicely." *CP*, 1:640.

62. See Catherine Malabou, *Plasticité* (Paris: Éditions Leo Scheer, 2000).

63. Ammons, "A Poem Is a Walk," 20, 19, 13.

64. Richard Rolle, *The Fire of Love*, trans. Clifton Wolters (Harmondsworth: Penguin, 1972), 49.

65. It should be added that a sense of burning is associated with contemplative practice. See Rolle's *The Fire of Love*; and Giles of Assisi, "The *Dicta* or Golden Words," in *The Earliest Franciscans*, ed. Paul Lachance and Pierre Brunette, trans. Kathryn Krug (New York: Paulist, 2015), chap. 13.

66. Ammons, "A Poem Is a Walk," 15.

67. See Jean-Jacques Rousseau, *The Confessions*, trans. and with an introduction by J. M. Cohen (Harmondsworth: Penguin, 1953), 382; and Walt Whitman, "As I Walk, Solitary, Unattended," revised as "As I Walk These Broad Majestic Days," in *Complete Poetry and Collected Prose*, 595.

68. It would be remiss not to mention the brief fashion for walking and meditating that followed the example described in A. N. Cooper, *The Tramps of "The Walking*

Parson" (London: Walter Scott, 1902). Walking has recently become the subject of several scholarly works. See, e.g., Rebecca Solnit, *Wanderlust: A History of Walking* (Harmondsworth: Penguin, 2001); Joseph A. Amato, *On Foot: A History of Walking* (New York: New York University Press, 2004); and Matthew Beaumont, *The Walker: On Losing and Finding Yourself in the Modern City* (London: Verso, 2020).

69. A. R. Ammons, "Corsons Inlet," in *CP*, 1:91–92.

70. I should add that in "Saliences" (1962) Ammons observes that "where not a single thing endures, / the overall reassures," thereby according a value to the overall with respect to the particular. A. R. Ammons, "Saliences," in *CP*, 1:362.

71. See Roland Barthes, "To Write: An Intransitive Verb?," in *The Rustle of Language*, trans. Richard Howard (New York: Hill & Wang, 1986), 11–21.

72. Ammons, "Corsons Inlet," 91.

Chapter Ten

1. Ammons, "Corsons Inlet," 93–94 (emphasis added).

2. A. R. Ammons, "Cut the Grass," in *CP*, 1:490, and "Tape for the Turn of the Year," in ibid., 1:145.

3. The three most important writers in this regard are Maurice Blanchot, Jacques Derrida, and Jean-Louis Chrétien, and in what follows I shall mostly limit myself to references to their comments. American critics have before us the prime example of Whitman—especially his catalogues raisonnés—among other writers.

4. See Louis René des Forêts, "Le bavard," in *The Children's Room*, trans. Jean Stewart (London: John Calder, 1963); Henri-Frédéric Amiel, *Journal intime*, éd. Bernard Gagnebin and Philippe M. Monnier, 12 vols. (Lausanne: Éditions L'Âge d'homme, 1976–94); Marcel Proust, *À la recherche du temps perdu*, Bibliothèque de la Pléiade (Paris: Gallimard, 2019); Donatien Alphonse François, Marquis de Sade, *Les 120 journées de Sodome; ou, L'école du libertinage* (Paris: Gallimard, 2019); and Georges Perec, *Tentative d'épuisement d'un lieu parisien* (Paris: Christian Bourgois, 1975).

5. See Attridge, "'This Strange Institution Called Literature,'" 38.

6. That Ammons can be worse than boorish is apparent in other poems. See, e.g., the leering lines on female undergraduate students in A. R. Ammons, "Summer Place," in *CP*, 2:431.

7. I condense here several highly suggestive comments by Derrida. See, e.g., Jacques Derrida, *Sovereignties in Question: The Poetics of Paul Celan*, ed. Thomas Dutoit and Outi Pasanen (New York: Fordham University Press, 2005), and *Edmund Husserl's "Origin of Geometry": An Introduction*, trans. and with a preface by John P. Leavey Jr. (Stony Brook, NY: Nicolas Hays, 1978), 102–4. Also see Attridge, "'This Strange Institution Called Literature,'" 39.

8. See Maurice Blanchot, "Rousseau," in *The Book to Come*, trans. Charlotte Mandell (Stanford, CA: Stanford University Press, 2003), 45.

9. Maurice Blanchot, "Sade's Reason," in *Lautréamont and Sade*, 9.

10. See Michel Foucault, *Death and the Labyrinth: The World of Raymond Roussel*, trans. Charles Ruas, with an introduction by John Ashbery (Garden City, NY: Doubleday, 1986).

11. See Chrétien, *Spacious Joy*.

12. I refer to Fletcher's notion of "surrounding voice." See Fletcher, *A New Theory for American Poetry*, 119–22.

13. Maurice Blanchot, "Idle Speech," in *Friendship*, trans. Elizabeth Rottenberg (Stanford, CA: Stanford University Press, 1971), 126, 123.

14. des Forêts, "Le bavard," 11–12.

15. When the speaker alludes to the sorcerer's apprentice, however, and we think of the origin of the story in Lucian's "Lovers of the Lie or the Skeptic," we will soon think also of "A True History," also by Lucian (ca. 120–ca. 180) and see the point of the reference and no longer trust what we are being told. See Lucian, "Lovers of Lies; or, The Sceptic," in *Selected Dialogues*, trans. C. D. N. Costa (Oxford: Oxford University Press, 2005), 178. The image seems to be original to Lucian. "A True Story" is Lucian's incomparable narrative of complete falsity.

16. Maurice Blanchot, "The Narrative Voice (the 'He,' the Neutral)," in *The Infinite Conversation*, trans. and with a foreword by Susan Hanson (Minneapolis: Minnesota University Press, 1993), 384.

17. See Blanchot, *The Infinite Conversation*, xii.

18. Kant, *Critique of Judgement*, § 5. A reader might wonder whether Ammons's casual injunction to "dip in anywhere" expresses disinterest in his own poem.

19. For Blanchot's glossing of *mysticism* and *fusion*, see Maurice Blanchot, "The Relation of the Third Kind: *Man without Horizon*," in *The Infinite Conversation*, 66. For a more detailed exploration of Blanchot's views, see Hart, *The Dark Gaze*, and *Maurice Blanchot on Poetry and Narrative*, chap. 10. Suffice it to say here that mystical experience need not imply a strong sense of fusion with the divine. It may presume the bringing of the human will into accord with the divine will and not a fusion of being, e.g.

20. Blanchot, "The Narrative Voice," 384.

21. Blanchot, "Literature and the Right to Death," 332.

22. Blanchot, "The Narrative Voice," 384.

23. Samuel Beckett, *The Unnamable* (New York: Grove, 1958), 114, 116, 102. On the narrative voice in Beckett, see Maurice Blanchot, "'Where Now? Who Now?,'" in *The Book to Come*, 210–17.

24. See James Schuyler, "The Morning of the Poem," in *The Morning of the Poem* (New York: Farrar, Straus & Giroux, 1980), 57–117; and Frank O'Hara, "A Step away from Them" and "The Day Lady Died," in *The Selected Poems of Frank O'Hara*, ed. Donald Allen (New York: Random House, 1974), 110–11, 146. A signal volume of Frank O'Hara's verse is entitled *Meditations in an Emergency* (1957; reprint, New York: Grove, 1966). The title alludes ironically to Donne's *Devotions upon Emergent Occasions* (1624).

25. See Heidegger, *Being and Time*, § 35.

26. See John Koethe, "The Metaphysical Subject of John Ashbery's Poetry," in *Poetry and Thought*, 9–19. Bloom has recourse to kabbalah to affirm a deep self beneath the empirical personality that one finds in, e.g., Robert Lowell. To my knowledge from conversations with the poet, Ashbery knew neither Kant nor kabbalah. His attitude to the subject in his poetry is more likely to have come from his own reading of French modernism and surrealism, in the visual arts as much as in poetry. Yet Koethe's lucid explanation is convincing at the level of the philosophy of the subject and more helpful than reference to kabbalah.

27. For "Soonest Mended," see John Ashbery, *Collected Poems, 1956–1987*, ed. Mark Ford (New York: Library of America, 2008), 184–86. In the later poetry, *Flow Chart* has some "autobiographical" moments, especially, perhaps, the double sestina about Ashbery's mother. See John Ashbery, *Flow Chart*, in *Collected Poems, 1991–2000*, ed. Mark Ford (New York: Library of America, 2017), 196–203. The scare quotes around *autobiographical* are justified insofar as a sestina, let alone a double sestina, is a particularly

intractable form and Ashbery's very loose double sestina is, in any case, one that uses the terminal words of Swinburne's "The Complaint of Lisa," which itself retells a story in the *Decameron*, 10.7.

28. See Roland Barthes, "The Reality Effect," in *The Rustle of Language*, 141–48.

29. See Husserl, *Ideas . . . : Second Book*, § 53.

30. Ammons would sometimes devote a snowy winter in Ithaca, NY, to writing a long poem.

31. On the miscellany, see Michael Suarez, "The Production and Consumption of the Eighteenth-Century Poetic Miscellany," in *Books and Their Readers in Eighteenth-Century England*, ed. Isabel Rivers, 2 vols. (London: Continuum, 2001), 2:217–51. Ammons refers to anthologies in secs. 15 and 16 of *Sphere*. Anthologies go back to Meleager of Gadara (fl. first century BCE), whose *Garland* is testified, although it does not survive.

32. Edward Bullough is responsible for the drift from disinterest to distance. See Edward Bullough, "'Psychical Distance' as a Factor in Art and an Aesthetic Principle," in *A Modern Book of Esthetics: An Anthology*, ed. Melvin M. Rader (New York: Henry Holt, 1952), 87–118. It should be recalled that for Schopenhauer there is a fusion of subject and object in aesthetic contemplation.

33. Consider the terms in which Pius IX rejects theological modernism in his encyclical *Quanta cura* (1864): "The prophecies and miracles set forth and recorded in the Sacred Scriptures are the fiction of poets, and the mysteries of the Christian faith the result of philosophical investigations. In the books of the Old and the New Testament there are contained mythical inventions, and Jesus Christ is Himself a myth." § 7.

34. Nor Ovid, perhaps, though his claim is less bold: "di quoque carminibus, si fas est dicerre, fiunt, / taantaque maiestas ore canetis eget" (Even the gods, if 'tis right to say this, are created by verse; their mighty majesty needs the bard's voice). *Ex Ponto*, 4.8.55–56, in *Ovid*, vol. 6, *Tristia, Ex Ponto*, trans. Arthur Leslie Wheeler, Loeb Classical Library (Cambridge, MA: Harvard University Press, 1924).

35. See Stevens to Henry Church, December 8, 1942, in *Letters*, 430.

36. Dylan Thomas, "Replies to an Enquiry," in *Quite Early One Morning* (New York: New Directions, 1968), 119 (emphasis added).

37. For the visionary as seeing the world as it is, not as involving philosophy or religion, see Hyatt H. Waggoner, *American Visionary Poetry* (Baton Rouge: Louisiana State University Press, 1982).

38. On this issue, see Harold Bloom, "The Breaking of the Vessels," in *Figures of Capable Imagination* (New York: Seabury, 1976), 219.

39. Homer, *The Iliad*, trans. Richard Lattimore (Chicago: University of Chicago Press, 1951), 3.396–98. See Daniel Turkeltaub, "Perceiving Illiadic Gods," *Harvard Studies in Classical Philology* 103 (2007): 51–81. It should be noted that the Romans imitated the Greeks in this regard. See, e.g., Ovid, *Metamorphoses*, 3.609–10.

40. Ludwig Wittgenstein, *Tractatus Logico-Philosophicus*, trans. C. K. Ogden, with an introduction by Bertrand Russell (London: Kegan Paul, Trench, Trubner, 1922), 6.44.

41. Walt Whitman, "Salut au Monde!," in *Complete Poetry and Collected Prose*, 289.

42. See Edith Wharton, "A Backward Glance," in *Novellas and Other Writings*, ed. Cynthia Griffin Wolff (New York: Library of America, 1990), 923.

43. See Walt Whitman, preface to *Leaves of Grass*, in *Complete Poetry and Collected Prose*, 5.

44. See Lucian, "Icaromenippus or High above the Clouds," in *Selected Dialogues*,

45–60. For further discussion of Ammons's use of Stoic spiritual exercises, see my "Poetry as Spiritual Exercise."

45. The final section of the published version of *Sphere* was not the final version in draft form. See Susannah L. Hollister, "The Planet on the Screen: Scales of Belonging in A. R. Ammons's *Sphere*," *Contemporary Literature* 50, no. 4 (2009): 666–67. Ammons showed a draft of the poem to Harold Bloom, who annotated it. See Ammons's journal for August 22, 1973, in *An Image for Longing*, 414.

46. See Plato, *Laws*, 990a.

47. See Plato, *Phaedrus*, 247b–c.

48. See Hyginus, *Poeticon astronomicon*, 2.43. Ovid mentions the Milky Way in *Metamorphoses*, 1.169.

Chapter Eleven

1. Carl Phillips, "Geoffrey Hill: The Art of Poetry, No. 80," *Paris Review* 154 (spring 2000): 289–90.

2. Simone Weil, *The Need for Roots: Prelude to a Declaration of Duties towards Mankind*, trans. Arthur Wills, with a preface by T. S. Eliot (1952; reprint, London: Routledge, 2002), 214. See Geoffrey Hill, "A Postscript on Modernist Poetics," in *CCW*, 573.

3. See Chase, *Angelic Wisdom*, 61.

4. See Geoffrey Hill, "Poetry and Value," in *CCW*, 488.

5. In the Vulgate, ἀγάπη is variously translated by *caritas*, *amor*, and *dilectio*, with overwhelming preference given to *caritas*. On the lack of nuance between the Latin words with respect to the original Greek, see Augustine, *The City of God*, in *CWA*, 14.7.

6. See Aquinas, *ST*, 1a2ae q. 26 art. 3.

7. The King James Bible answers in principle to the *Textus Receptus*, rather than the Vulgate, but it often reproduces inconsistencies of translation with respect to ἀγάπη that are in the Vulgate.

8. The poem first appeared in the *Times Literary Supplement*, February 4, 1983, 101–3, with the epigraph immediately below the title. In *Broken Hierarchies*, the epigraph appears not on a page by itself but on the title page, coming directly after a dedication.

9. Charles Péguy, "Notre jeunesse," in *Oeuvres en prose complètes* (hereafter *OPC*), éd. Robert Burac, Bibliothèque de la Pléiade, 3 vols. (Paris: Gallimard, 1987–92), 3:10.

10. However, Péguy's tone sharpens when he touches on the lack of enthusiasm among Catholics for his long poem. See Péguy, "Notre jeunesse," 102.

11. For Péguy's long-standing wish to publish *le journal vrai*, see Yvonne Servais, *Charles Péguy: The Pursuit of Salvation* (Oxford: Blackwell, 1953), 17, 25. On the importance of publishing what is just, not merely what is agreeable, see Charles Péguy, "Personnalités" (1902), in *OPC*, 1:936.

12. In a letter dated December 21, 1899, Péguy writes: "Les journaux ont pour fonction de donner à leurs lecteurs les nouvelles du jour, comme on dit. Les journaux doivent donner les nouvelles vraies, toutes les nouvelles vraies qu'ils peuvent, rien que des nouvelles vraies." (The function of newspapers is to give their readers the news of the day, as one says. Newspapers have to give the real news, all the real news, all the real news they can, nothing but real news.) Charles Péguy, "Lettre du provincial," in *OPC*, 1:292.

13. Péguy observes: "Nous fussions morts pour Dreyfus. Dreyfus n'est point mort pour Dreyfus." (We were dead for Dreyfus. Dreyfus is not dead for Dreyfus.) Péguy,

"Notre jeunesse," 46. Dreyfus's defenders seem to have prized what the cause of his conviction represented for the Republic more than the suffering that the man and his family had to endure.

14. Péguy, "Notre jeunesse," 10. Also see Charles Péguy, "L'argent suite," in *OPC*, 3:944.

15. Péguy maintains that even a single injustice perforates the social body. See Péguy, "Notre jeunesse," 146. Halévy observed later that his difference with Péguy over Dreyfusardism was that of a historian and a poet. See Daniel Halévy, *Péguy et les Cahiers de la quinzaine* (Paris: Grasset, 1947), 110.

16. Péguy, "Notre jeunesse," 84. Shortly after, he adds: "On pourrait même dire que l'affaire Dreyfus fut un beau cas de la religion, de mouvement religieux, de commencement, d'origine de religion, un cas rare, peut-être un cas unique." (One could even say that the Dreyfus Affair was a fine case of religion, of a religious movement, of the beginning, of the origin of religion, a rare case, perhaps a unique case.) Ibid., 85. Elsewhere he observes: "Le *dreyfusisme* qui était un système de liberté absolu, de verité absolue, de justice absolue, et d'un ordre spirituel profonde." (Dreyfusism which was a system of absolute freedom, absolute truth, absolute justice, and a deep spiritual order.) Péguy, "L'argent suite," 3:943.

17. Péguy, "Notre jeunesse," 84. For the reference to Lazare as a prophet, see Péguy, "Notre jeunesse," 55.

18. Péguy, "Notre jeunesse," 84. Péguy had told his friend Joseph Lotte in September 1908 that he had regained his Catholic faith. See Pierre Pacary, *Un compagnon du Péguy: Joseph Lotte, 1875-1914*, with a preface by Pierre Batiffol, 2nd ed. (Paris: Victor Lecoffre, 1917), 29.

19. See "Une apologie de Dreyfus," *La petite république*, November 10, 1896, 1, a review of Bernard Lazare's pamphlet *Une erreur judiciare: La verité sur l'affaire Dreyfus* (Brussels: Imprimerie Veuve Monnom, 1896). *Une erreur judiciare* ends with "J'accuse," an expression taken up by Émile Zola in his famous open letter to M. Félix Faure, president of the Republic, on the front page of *L'aurore* for January 13, 1898. From Brussels, Lazare sent thirty-five hundred copies of the pamphlet to journalists, politicians, writers, and other interested parties in France.

20. Péguy, "Notre jeunesse," 20. This line is alluded to in the "Argument" to Geoffrey Hill, "Hymns to Our Lady of Chartres," in *BH*, 155. Also see Péguy, "Lettre du provincial," 296; and Charles Péguy, *Cahiers de la quinzaine*, June 16, 1903.

21. *Mystique*, used as an adjective, can certainly mean "mystical." When used as a noun, however, it resists easy translation, especially since it can be used in secular as well as sacred contexts.

22. Geoffrey Hill, *The Mystery of the Charity of Charles Péguy* (New York: Oxford University Press, 1983), 35 ("Charles Péguy").

23. See Péguy, "L'argent suite," 821. For Péguy's own sense of modernity, see Hans Urs von Balthasar, "Péguy," in *The Glory of the Lord: A Theological Aesthetics*, vol. 3, *Studies in Theological Style: Lay Styles*, trans. Andrew Louth et al., ed. John Riches (San Francisco: Ignatius, 1986), 455.

24. Perhaps needless to say, this erosion is not recent. For an example in England around the time when Péguy flourished, see G. K. Chesterton, "The Modern Martyr," in *All Things Considered* (London: Methuen, 1908), 85–90.

25. See Cecil Driver, *Tory Radical: The Life of Richard Oastler* (Oxford: Oxford University Press, 1946). Hill refers to Oestler in "Redeeming the Time," in *CCW*, 89. He speaks of his self-identification with radical Toryism in Haffenden, "Geoffrey Hill,"

85–86. Matthew Sperling quotes an unpublished letter from Hill to Geoffrey Trease, written on May 8, 1993, in which the poet describes himself as "an old-fashioned agrarian Tory Radical." Matthew Sperling, *Visionary Philology: Geoffrey Hill and the Study of Words* (Oxford: Oxford University Press, 2014), 99.

26. I take *committed individual*, one of the expressions of the day, from the title of Jon Silkin's anthology *Poetry of the Committed Individual: A "Stand" Anthology* (Harmondsworth: Penguin, 1973). Silkin includes five of Hill's poems in the anthology.

27. Hill, "Charles Péguy," 35. See the remarks on regarding Péguy as a "contradictory spirit" in von Balthasar, "Péguy," 404.

28. On Hill's lack of commitment to "balance," especially with regard to William Empson, see Martin Dodsworth, "Geoffrey Hill's Difficulties," in *Strangeness and Power: Essays on the Poetry of Geoffrey Hill*, ed. Andrew Michael Roberts (Swindon: Shearsman, 2020), 183–84.

29. The first *Jeanne d'Arc* is tilted toward socialism, while the second is oriented toward Catholicism. In *Oeuvres poétiques et dramatiques* (hereafter *OPD*), éd. Claire Daudin in collaboration with Pauline Bruley, Jérôme Roger, and Romain Vaisermann, Bibliothèque de la Pléiade (Paris: Gallimard, 2014), the blank spaces are not reproduced. Péguy also interlaces a portrait of Jeanne d'Arc in his defense of his use of Jeanne in *Le mystère de la charité de Jeanne d'Arc*. See Charles Péguy, "Un nouveau théologien, M. Fernand Laudet" (1911), in *OPC*, 3:392–591. It is worth noting that Péguy's treatments of Jeanne predate the publication of such different evocations of the maid as in Voltaire's posthumously published poem *La pucelle d'Orléans* (1899), which was composed and abandoned in 1730, and in Anatole France's biography *Vie de Jeanne d'Arc* (1908).

30. It is important to realize that, while Hill seeks to present Péguy as a whole in his poem, he does not seek to represent the totality of the man, a task that would be impossible in any case. For instance, we hear nothing of Péguy's hostility to the doctrine of hell or his admiration for Corneille, especially his *Polyeucte*, and nothing of his late dedication to prayer. Also, it should be noted that voices are used to interrupt the lines in the earlier poem Geoffrey Hill, "Funeral Music," in *BH*, esp. 49, 53. Hill plays low modernism to Eliot's high modernism.

31. In French, *la politique* refers to politics or, at times, government or party policy, while *le politique* (when used without an adjective) denotes the political.

32. Contemplation, however, will take in the intertwining of the intellectual and the emotional, as Hill points out. See Phillips, "Geoffrey Hill: The Art of Poetry," 283.

33. It is worth keeping in mind that Hill recognizes himself as a follower of Schopenhauer's aesthetics in their common prizing of music, including the music of poetry. See Haffenden, "Geoffrey Hill," 91.

34. See William Blake, "Jerusalem," in *The Complete Poetry and Prose of William Blake*, 146.

35. Henrik Ibsen, *Brand*, trans. Geoffrey Hill (Harmondsworth: Penguin, 1996), 59. A little later, Brand adds, in words that again remind one of Péguy: "This entire age is devoid / of grace or merit; / it's ruled by creeping pride, / dull frivolity, / meanness of spirit. / Say to the 'man-of-the-hour', / whether of peace or war, / 'Enough; be satisfied / with the true victory, / with the triumph of good.'" Ibid., 66.

36. Ibsen, *Brand*, 68.

37. See Charles Péguy, "Marcel, premier dialogue de la cité harmonieuse," in *OPC*, 1:55–117, and *De la cité socialiste*, in *OPC*, 1:34–39. Also see Servais, *Charles Péguy*, chap. 3.

The City of God and the kingdom are distinguished in the posthumous Charles Péguy, "Dialogue de l'histoire et de l'âme charnelle" (1909?), in *OPC*, 3:640.

38. The earliest known French farce is most likely the twelfth-century play *Le garçon et l'aveugle*. Others include *Pathelin: La farce du pâté et de la tarte, Le chaudronnier, La poulier,* and *Le cuvier*.

39. Nonetheless: "Péguy retrouve un trait traditionnel de l'écriture mystique: l'impossibilité de se formuler autrement que dans la contradiction." (Péguy rediscovers a traditional feature of mystical writing: the impossibility of expressing oneself other than in contradiction.) Alexandre de Vitry, "Mystique," in *Dictionnaire Charles Péguy*, ed. Salomon Malka (Paris: Albin Michel, 2018), 276.

40. See Péguy, *Le mystère de la charité de Jeanne d'Arc*, 411–12.

41. This was the time of Péguy's break with Jaurès. See Péguy, "Notre jeunesse," 109–10; and Charles Péguy, "Courrier de Russie" (1905), in *OPC*, 2:77. Also see the earlier strictures against leaguing socialism and atheism, which Péguy regarded as a metaphysics and a theology, in Charles Péguy, "Casse-cou" (1901), in *OPC*, 1:702–4.

42. For Jaurès views, see Martin Auclair, *La vie de Jean Jaurès* (Paris: Seuil, 1954), 535. For Péguy's view of Jaurès on the Alsace-Lorraine question, see Charles Péguy, "Le préparation du congrès socialiste national" (1900), in *OPC*, 1:362–63, and "L'argent suite," 923.

43. See, e.g., the remarks on Jaurès in Péguy, "L'argent suite," 798.

44. Jean and Jérome Tharaud maintain that Péguy's socialism was always closer to St. Francis of Assisi than to Karl Marx. See Jean Tharaud and Jérome Tharaud, *Notre cher Péguy*, 2 vols. (Paris: Plon, 1926), 1:19. Péguy writes (with "Notre jeunesse" in mind): "Notre socialisme était un socialisme mystique et un socialisme profond, profondément apparenté au christianisme, un tronc sorti de la vielle souche, littéralement déjà, (ou encore), une religion de la pauvreté." (Our socialism was a mystical socialism and a deep socialism, deeply related to Christianity, a trunk coming from the old stump, literally already (or again) a religion of poverty.) Péguy, "Un nouveau théologien," 528.

45. After his death, Péguy was claimed by the French Resistance (e.g., Edmond Michelet) and by the anti-Semitic right (e.g., Robert Brasillach). Henry Weinfield observes that Péguy did not extend much charity to Jaurès once he was no longer a pure Dreyfusard and wonders whether this is not registered in Hill's poem. Charity, for Péguy, seems to have been limited to those who did not abandon *la mystique*. See Henry Weinfield, "The Mystery of the Charity of Geoffrey Hill," *Religion and the Arts* 16 (2012): 5.

46. This is a theme of Hill's lectures as professor of poetry at the University of Oxford, 2011–15.

47. See Geoffrey Hill, *The Enemy's Country*, in *CCW*, 173–74.

48. Hill remarks in an interview that "every fine and moving poem bears witness" to the "lost kingdom of innocence and original justice," an expression he quotes from Christopher Devlin on Hopkins. See Haffenden, "Geoffrey Hill," 88. Devlin's remark occurs in *The Sermons and Devotional Writings of Gerard Manley Hopkins*, ed. Christopher Devlin (London: Oxford University Press, 1959), 6.

49. Péguy was no admirer of historical positivism, as exemplified by Ernest Renan (1823–92) and Hyppolite Taine (1828–93) and their disciples in the Sorbonne. It should be noted that there are poems that are murder mysteries. See, e.g., Robert Browning, *The Ring and the Book* (1868–69); and James Cummins, *The Whole Truth: A Poem* (San Francisco: North Point, 1986).

50. Péguy conceives History to be a somewhat incompetent general reviewing his troops, a figure in tension with Hill's here. See Péguy, "Dialogue de l'histoire," 1177.

51. See Barbara W. Tuchman, *The Guns of August: The Proud Power*, ed. Margaret MacMillan (New York: Library of America, 2012), 1096.

52. See G. W. F. Hegel, *The Philosophy of History*, trans. J. Sibree, with a preface by Charles Hegel, J. Sibree, and C. J. Friedrich (New York: Dover, 1956), 33. Hegel also refers to the idea in *The Science of Logic*, trans. and ed. George di Giovanni (Cambridge: Cambridge University Press, 2010), 663.

53. Plutarch, "Caesar," in *Fall of the Roman Republic*, trans. Rex Warner (Harmondsworth: Penguin, 1958), 241–42.

54. Péguy, "L'argent suite," 924.

55. In his note "Charles Péguy," Hill telescopes the two events: "A young madman . . . almost immediately shot Jaurès through the head." Hill, *The Mystery of the Charity of Charles Péguy*, 35. The note is not included in *Broken Hierarchies*.

56. See Geoffrey Hill, "Our Word Is Our Bond," in *CCW*, 146–69.

57. In "Notre jeunesse," 120, Péguy lays claim to the title of hero: "Nous fûmes des héros. Il faut le dire très simplement, car je crois bien qu'on ne le dira pas pour nous." (We were heroes. It must be said very simply, for I think that no one will say it for us.)

58. It is a tragic irony that the Gatling gun was invented so as to limit the number of deaths in war. Péguy seems to have set the lower bound for *la monde moderne*, in its negative sense, as 1881, just before Boulangisme, the Wilson Affair, the Dreyfus Affair, and so on. See Péguy, "Notre jeunesse," 22, and "L'argent suite," 804, 815. Also see Daniel Halvéy, *Péguy et les Cahiers de la quinzaine* (Paris: Gallimard, 1947), 112–13. Also see D. H. Lawrence, "Triumph of the Machine," in *The Complete Poems of D. H. Lawrence*, ed. and with an introduction and notes by Vivian de Sola Pinto and Warren Roberts (New York: Viking, 1971), 623–25.

59. Marx writes: "Hegel observes somewhere that all the great events and characters of world history occur twice, so to speak. He forgot to add: the first time as high tragedy, the second time as low farce." Karl Marx, *The Eighteenth Brumaire of Louis Bonaparte*, in *Marx: Later Political Writings*, ed. Terrell Carver (Cambridge: Cambridge University Press, 2012), 31. Marx is presumably thinking of the remarks on the Roman state and the Bourbons in G. W. F. Hegel, *Philosophy of History*, trans. J. Sibree, with a preface by Charles Hegel and an introduction by C. J. Friedrich (New York: Dover, 1956), 313.

60. The British poetic tradition is scarcely rich in poems on Jeanne d'Arc. However, see Robert Southey's early *Joan of Arc: An Epic Poem* (Boston: J. Nancrede, 1798). Also see the strictures on the poem in Coleridge, *Marginalia*, pt. 5, pp. 108–19.

61. For the view that there are analogies between Rome and France, see Péguy, "Dialogue de l'histoire," 700. There were *tribuni plebis* and *tribuni militum*, some of whom, over the period 444–367 BCE, had consular authority (*tribune militum consular potestate*). The metaphor of Péguy as one of the *tribuni militum* is apt in some ways since military tributes fulfilled both active and administrative roles, so Péguy's role with the *Cahiers* is quietly acknowledged in the metaphor. Yet the *tribuni militum* were drawn from the ranks of the *equites*, which would be rather above Péguy's social position. For the inauguration of the office of the tribune, as elected by the plebs, see Livy, *Ab urbe condita*, 2.33. For military tribunes, see ibid., 7.5. More generally, see Plutarch, *Coriolanus*, 7, and *Tiberius Gracchus*, 15.

62. Marjorie Villiers begins her life of Péguy with him acknowledging "the

Republican and the reactionary which are within me" and his desire to set them in harmony. See Marjorie Villiers, *Charles Péguy: A Study in Integrity* (London: Collins, 1965), 13.

63. See Charles Péguy, *Le mystère des saints innocents*, in *OPD*, 779.

64. Péguy had a lowly view of his editorial work. See Péguy, "Personnalités," 920. He believed that in the modern age, after 1880, work had deteriorated as a value. See Péguy, "Notre jeunesse," 7–8, and "L'argent suite," 790–93. Tharaud observes of Péguy: "On ne pouvait pas quitter les Cahiers [*sic*], mais on pouvait quitter la vie." (We couldn't leave the Cahiers but we could leave life.) Tharaud and Tharaud, *Notre cher Péguy*, 238. It should be made plain, however, that prominent writers—contemporaries of Péguy and later admirers—have prized some of his writings. Von Balthasar names André Gide, Jacques Copeau, and Romain Rolland, and soon I will mention Maurice Blanchot. See von Balthasar, "Péguy," 403.

65. Péguy was recommended to be made *chevalier* of the Légion d'honneur, but the awards were limited at the time to the fallen in the Battle of the Marne. He was posthumously granted the honor in 1920.

66. See the gloss on *genius* in Geoffrey Hill, "Unhappy Circumstances," in *CCW*, 184–85.

67. André Gide, "Journal sans dates," *Nouvelle revue française*, March 1910, 399–410 (discussion of *Le mystère de la charité de Jeanne d'Arc*). Maurice Blanchot praises Péguy's style in his review of Daniel Halévy's *Charles Péguy et les Cahiers de la quinzaine*. See *Faux pas*, 282.

68. See Péguy, *Le mystère des saints innocents*, 927.

69. For Jeanne's first vision, see W. S. Scott, ed. and trans., *The Trial of Joan of Arc: Being the Verbatim Report of the Proceedings from the Orleans Manuscript* (London: Folio Society, 1956), 74. It is worth noting that Jean Gerson, discussed in chap. 2, published a defense of Jeanne's life and actions. See Jean Gerson, *Super facto puellae et credulitate sibi praestanda* (1429), trans. Sean L. Fields as "A New English Translation of Jean Gerson's Authentic Tract on Jean of Arc: *About the Feat of the Maid and the Faith That Should Be Placed in Her*," *Magistra* 18, no. 2 (2012): 46–54.

70. Yet Hill has already translated and adapted part of it: "Happy are they who, under the gaze of God, / die for the 'terre charnelle'" (5.29–30). Péguy's lines can be found in Charles Péguy, *Ève*, in *OPD*, 1263.

71. See, e.g., Caesar, *The Gallic War*, trans. Carolyn Hammond (Oxford: Oxford University Press, 1996), 5.32–37.

72. Similar verbal tensions are common in Hill's verse and are found elsewhere in the poem. See, e.g., "risen / above all that . . . fallen flat on your face" (4.31–32), "an old faith devoted to new wars" (6.44), "a simple lesion of the complex brain," "his great work, his small body" (10.12).

73. It is worth recalling Allen Tate's comment to T. S. Eliot on July 13, 1926, about his own early verse: "a strained implication of meaning in telescoped images." Eliot and Haffenden, eds., *The Letters of T. S. Eliot*, 2:192 n. 2. A reader may well get the sense that Hill's poetry is written with the New Criticism as a template. The impression is not wholly mistaken, but Hill's concern is oriented less toward "fruitful ambiguity" than to "thornful ambiguity." See my review of *Broken Hierarchies*: Kevin Hart, "A Contemporary Master," *Notre Dame Review* 40 (2015): 256–70.

74. The sentence is taken from a conversation of September 20, 1910, that Joseph Lotte recorded: "Ah, mon vieux, les mots! Les mots! Il n'y a rien de comparable: ni la

musique ni la peinture ne valent. Avec les mots, il n'est pas un sentiment que l'on n'exprime." Charles Péguy, *Lettres et entretiens* (Paris: Éditions de Paris, 1954), 82.

75. We need to remember, however, that, for Péguy, *mystique* can resist being utterly devoured by *politique*. See Péguy, "Notre jeunesse," 20.

76. Patrick McCarthy writes of Péguy: "When the 1914 war broke out, he joined up eagerly: better the Marne than the *Cahiers*." Patrick McCarthy, "The Voice of the Consensus," *Times Literary Supplement*, June 16, 1978, 67. Also see Halévy, *Péguy et les Cahiers de la quinzaine*, 236.

77. For Péguy's view of life as fated and, in a way, of one becoming perfect when dead, see Péguy, "Dialogue de l'histoire," 1166.

78. For an exception, see *The Cloud of Unknowing*, chap. 4.

79. As a comparison, T. S. Eliot's "The Waste Land" runs to 433 lines, Wallace Stevens's "Notes toward a Supreme Fiction" is 643 lines, A. R. Ammons's *Sphere* is 1,860 lines, John Ashbery's "Self-Portrait in a Convex Mirror" (1975) is 552 lines (his *Flow Chart* is 216 pages), and James Merrill's *The Changing Light at Sandover* (1982) is 560 pages. Robinson Jeffers's "Cawdor" (1928) runs to 114 pages. Louis Zukofsky's A is 846 pages. Ezra Pound's *The Cantos* is in 116 sections, some quite long in themselves.

80. See Péguy's remark on the back cover of the March 1, 1904, issue of *Cahiers de la quinzaine*.

81. See Péguy, "Dialogue de l'histoire," 1191 and 1178, respectively.

82. See Péguy, "Personnalités," 921. Péguy countenances the thought that there is a disaster in *mystique* in "Dialogue de l'histoire," 647, 651.

83. See the remarks on George Eliot's *Middlemarch* in Geoffrey Hill, "Rhetorics of Value and Intrinsic Value," in *CCW*, 472. The essay appears for the first time in the volume.

84. Haffenden, "Geoffrey Hill," 86.

85. It should be stressed that Péguy was never in league with Action française, e.g.

86. See Charles Péguy, "De la situation faite à l'histoire et la sociologie dans les temps modernes" (1906), in *OPC*, 2:513.

87. Péguy's military experience goes back long before the First World War. His year of compulsory military service started on November 11, 1892. He joined the Second Company of the Third Battalion of the 131st Regiment in Orléans, and he was discharged with the rank of corporal on September 28, 1893, whereupon he was posted to the reserve. As a member of the reserve, he was required to undertake periods of military training each year.

88. See Villiers, *Charles Péguy*, 378.

89. Tuchman, *The Guns of August*, 45.

90. See Henri Bergson, *L'evolution créatrice* (Paris: Alcan, 1913), 5.

91. See Péguy, "De la situation faite à l'histoire et à la sociologie," 481–519. Péguy discusses Michelet, Renan, and Taine and also would have had professors such as Lavisse, Lauson, and Durkheim in his sights. For his remarks on method, see ibid., 515. Interestingly, Hill alludes to both W. H. Auden ("The Watchers") and Dylan Thomas ("Do Not Go Gentle into That Good Night") in this stanza. See Auden, *Collected Poems*, 63; and Thomas, *Collected Poems, 1934–1952* (London: J. M. Dent, 1952), 159.

92. Charles Péguy, "Note sur M. Bergson et la philosophie bergsonienne" (1913), in *OPC*, 3:1274.

93. It should be added that Péguy seems to have prophesied war on at least two occasions. See Charles Péguy, "Notre patrie," in *OPC*, 2:56–57, and "Les suppliants

parallèles" (1905), in *OPC*, 2:361. Péguy observes that he had seen "la menace alle-
mande" since 1905. Péguy, "L'argent suite," 991.

94. See Stevens, "Description without Place," 301, and my remarks on the poem in
chap. 7.

95. See Péguy, "L'argent suite," 1103–6.

96. See Alain Corbin, *Village Bells: Sound and Meaning in the Nineteenth-Century
French Countryside*, trans. Martin Thom (New York: Columbia University Press, 1998),
esp. xx and 290.

97. With regard to the image of sheaves as spires we are sent back to reread "Merlin,"
considered in chap. 6.

98. See Tuchman, *The Guns of August*, 44.

99. Hill's depiction of Gordon recalls the relevant scene played by Charlton Heston
in the film *Khartoum* (1966).

100. For the association of crystal with fine art, see Geoffrey Hill, "Of Commerce
and Society," in *BH*, 30.

101. Hill adapts a story related by Henri Roi in *Feuillets de l'amitié Charles Péguy*, November 1951, 4.

102. Péguy, "Notre jeunesse," 121.

Chapter Twelve

1. See, e.g., Jules Verne's posthumous novel, written in 1863, *Paris au XXe siècle*
(Paris: Hachette, 1994).

2. See Holger Schott Syme, "The Look of Speech," *Textual Cultures* 2, no. 2 (2007):
34–60.

3. Intriguingly, in the very month and year in which Dreyfus was disgraced there appeared Fred C. Conybeare, "On the Apocalypse of Moses," *Jewish Quarterly Review* 7, 2
(1895): 216–35.

4. Hill's sequences "The Pentecost Castle" and "Lachrimae" in *Tenebrae* (1978) multiply paradoxes such as this one.

5. Not all theologies of contemplation would countenance contemplating a human
being. Even Jesus, as God-Man, is not usually an example proffered for contemplation.
Yet contemplation of the man Jesus is commended in Love, *The Mirror of the Blessed
Life of Jesus Christ*, 10. Hill's contemplation of a "radical soul" looks back, very indirectly, to this shift of emphasis.

6. What is true of Péguy the man is true also of Péguy the writer. Blanchot observes
that he is inimitable: "It is doubtful whether Péguy is a good model for a novelist. It is
even far from certain whether that peerless writer should ever be an example for any
writer. He is a master and a model of greatness. His work is inaccessible to anyone who
seeks to borrow from it an art of his own." Maurice Blanchot, "Chronicle of Intellectual
Life," in *Into Disaster: Chronicles of Intellectual Life, 1941*, trans. Michael Holland (New
York: Fordham University Press, 2014), 20.

7. W. H. Auden, "Musée des Beaux Arts," in *Collected Poems*, 146.

8. See Thomas à Kempis, *The Imitation of Christ* (Harmondsworth: Penguin, 2013).

9. That soldiers saw ghosts of comrades and relations while fighting in the First
World War has been commonly reported. See, e.g., Will R. Bird, *Ghosts Have Warm
Hands: A Memoir of the Great War, 1916–1919* (Ottawa: CEF, 1997).

10. Hill puns wickedly on the ejaculations in the third section of "Funeral Music." See *BH*, 49.

11. See Suetonius, *The Twelve Caesars*, trans. Robert Graves, with a foreword by Michael Grant (Harmondsworth: Penguin, 2006). Also see Tacitus, *Annals*, 12.56.

12. See Péguy, *OPC*, 3:260–61.

13. See Husserl, *The Crisis of European Sciences*, 303.

14. See Péguy, "Un nouveau théologien," 399.

15. Péguy, "L'argent suite," 955.

16. See Péguy, "L'argent suite," 957.

17. See Arthur Rimbaud, *Oeuvres complètes*, ed. André Guyaux in collaboration with Aurélia Cervoni, Bibliothèque de la Pléiade (Paris: Gallimard, 2009), 340. In the *Times Literary Supplement* (February 4, 1983) and the original book publication, Hill writes "Je est un autre."

18. See Robert Tombs, *France, 1814–1924* (London: Longman, 1996), 196.

19. See Péguy, "L'argent suite," 787.

20. Sassoon's poem begins: "Why do you lie with your legs ungainly huddled, / And one arm bent across your sullen, cold / Exhausted face?" Siegfried Sassoon, "The Dug-Out," in *Collected Poems, 1908–1956* (London: Faber and Faber, 1984), 102. It needs to be kept in mind while reading Hill's poem that the poet had devoted critical attention to British poetry of the First World War, especially the writings of Ivor Gurney, Isaac Rosenberg, and Charles Sorley. See, in particular, Geoffrey Hill, "Gurney's 'Hobby'" and "Isaac Rosenberg, 1890–1918," in *CCW*, chaps. 25 and 26, respectively.

21. For Péguy's remarks on *comme si*, see "L'argent suite," 992.

22. Geoffrey Hill, *Liber Illustrium Virorum*, in *BH*, 719 (sec. 35).

23. Hill, *Liber Illustrium Virorum*, 738 (sec. 54). Also see Geoffrey Hill, "Mightier and Darker," *Times Literary Supplement*, March 23, 2016, 3–5.

24. Shakespeare, *Troilus and Cressida*, in *The Arden Shakespeare*, ed. David Bevington (London: Bloomsbury, 1998), 1.3.109–10.

25. Compare Péguy's claim that the Socialist Party is wholly composed of bourgeois intellectuals. See Péguy, "L'argent suite," 795.

26. Weil, *The Need for Roots*, 19.

27. For Hill on the debauching of language, see Haffenden, "Geoffrey Hill," 86.

28. Geoffrey Hill, "Civil Polity and the Confessing State," *Warwick Review* 2, no. 2 (2008): 19. The cadence recalls Milton's view in *Of Education* (1644), quoted by Hill in "Poetry as 'Menace' and 'Atonement'" and in interviews, that poetry is "simple, sensuous, passionate." Oliver Morley Ainsworth, ed., *Milton on Education: The Tractate "Of Education" with Supplementary Extracts from Other Writings of Milton* (New Haven, CT: Yale University Press, 1928), 60. Hill refers to egalitarianism and meanness as alienating democracy from "its proper majesty." See Geoffrey Hill, "Alienated Majesty: Gerard M. Hopkins" (2000), in *CCW*, 531.

29. The anonymous fifth–sixth-century Syrian writer known as Pseudo-Dionysius the Areopagite is the author of, among other works, *The Ecclesiastical Hierarchy* and *The Celestial Hierarchy*.

30. Hill, *Liber Illustrium Virorum*, 738 (sec. 54).

31. See Rufus M. Jones, *Mysticism and Democracy in the English Commonwealth: Being the William Beldon Noble Lectures Delivered in Harvard University, 1930–1931* (1932; reprint, Whitefish, MT: Kessinger, 2010), 12. To start the apophatic tradition with Gregory of Nyssa is conservative, for one can find it in the Hebrew scriptures as well as in Plato. William Franke grants a generous scope to the apophatic in his

On What Cannot Be Said: Apophatic Discourses in Philosophy, Religion, Literature and the Arts, 2 vols. (Notre Dame, IN: Notre Dame University Press, 2007). For a diagnosis of the possible dissolution of mysticism, see McGinn, *The Crisis of Mysticism*.

32. Jones, *Mysticism and Democracy*, 13.

33. See, in particular, Jones, *Mysticism and Democracy*, 4, 143, 147.

34. See John Milton, *Areopagitica*, in *Areopagitica and Other Prose Works of John Milton* (London: J. M. Dent, 1927), 1–41.

35. Jones is clear that the link between *mysticism* and democracy is more a matter of the Reformation than the views of individual Reformers. He notes his complete agreement with G. P. Gooch, *English Democratic Ideas in the Seventeenth Century*, 2nd ed., with supplementary notes and appendices by H. J. Laski (Cambridge: Cambridge University Press, 1927), 7. Another approach to mysticism in seventeenth-century Britain, one in which *mysticism* is characterized by mutual charity, is presented in Nicholas Lossky, *Lancelot Andrews, the Preacher (1555–1626): The Mystical Theology of the Church of England*, trans. Andrew Louth (Oxford: Oxford University Press, 1991).

36. The collection of short lyrics "Hymns to Our Lady of Chartres" is somewhat mixed in aims and quality. Its "Argument" is skepticism toward the Immaculate Conception of the Virgin Mary. Confusingly, Hill refers to the Virginal Conception of Jesus as another Immaculate Conception. The "Argument" ends by paraphrasing Péguy, "all begins in *mystique* and ends in *politique*." Geoffrey Hill, "Hymns to Our Lady of Chartres," in *BH*, 155. There is little about Péguy in the collection, and what is there is puzzling. In the ninth poem, Hill evokes David Jones as "Dai Greatcoat" and imagines Péguy subject to Jehovah's time, not ours, and therefore knowing of the Dead Sea Scrolls, discovered only in 1956: "We might have given / the temple scroll for Péguy to repair, / indomitable, as an unsold *Cahier*, / *mystique* and *politique* there intershriven." Ibid., 161. The Temple Scroll mostly concerns purity laws and the construction of the Temple of Jerusalem, and of course *pur* and *purité* are words that resonate throughout Péguy's writings.

37. Geoffrey Hill, "Mysticism and Democracy ('Ill-conceived, ill-ordained')," in *BH*, 220. It is worth noting that Hill does not place scare quotes here around the *we* as he does in *The Mystery of the Charity of Charles Péguy*.

38. Geoffrey Hill, "Mysticism and Democracy ('To the Evangelicals')," in *BH*, 210. As Jones sees, Bunyan is not a *mystic* in his sense of the word but rather a Puritan and hence more forensic than *mystical* in his religious sensibility. See Jones, *Mysticism and Democracy*, 114.

39. On allegory as a symbolic mode, see Fletcher, *Allegory*.

40. See Geoffrey Hill, *Speech! Speech!*, in *BH*, 318 (§ 60).

41. The corporeal works of Mercy stem from recognizing one's neighbor as *alter Christus*. They consist of feeding the hungry, offering drink to the thirsty, clothing the naked, giving shelter to those who need it, visiting the sick, ransoming captives, and burying the dead. The spiritual works of Mercy are teaching the ignorant, counseling the doubtful, rebuking sinners, bearing wrongs with patience, forgiving faults willingly, comforting the afflicted, and praying for the living and the dead.

42. Geoffrey Hill, "Mysticism and Democracy ('Great gifts foreclosed on')," in *BH*, 234.

43. Hill, "Mysticism and Democracy," in *BH*, 234.

44. Hill, "Mysticism and Democracy ('Great gifts foreclosed on')." It is not clear why the first Latin expression is not set in italics. Also, it is possible that Hill is alluding to Ezra Pound, "The Constant Preaching of the Mob," *Poetry* 8 (1916): 144–45.

45. Tacitus, *Annals*, 1.7.

46. The difference between *mystical* or religious democracy and liberal democracy should not be ascribed to Jones, who mentions Locke in the same breath as Algernon Sidney and William Penn as well as "the creative statesmen of the English revolution." Jones, *Mysticism and Democracy*, 161.

47. On de-Christianization, see Péguy, "Dialogue de l'histoire," esp. 644–46.

48. Péguy, "Notre jeunesse," 10.

49. See Roberta Florence Brinkley, ed., *Coleridge on the Seventeenth Century*, with an introduction by Louis I. Bredvold (Durham: Duke University Press, 1955), 125–379.

50. See von Balthasar, "Péguy," 400.

CREDITS

INDEX